E8·08
DAV

D0120333

# CHAMBERS

# GUIDE TO
# GRAMMAR
# AND USAGE

# CHAMBERS

---

# GUIDE TO
# GRAMMAR
# AND USAGE

---

*Compiled by*
George Davidson

**CHAMBERS**

CHAMBERS
An imprint of Chambers Harrap Publishers Ltd
7 Hopetoun Crescent, Edinburgh EH7 4AY

First published by Chambers 1996
Reprinted 1998

Copyright © Chambers Harrap Publishers Ltd 1997

A CIP catalogue record for this book is available
from the British Library.

We have made every effort to mark as such all words
which we believe to be trademarks.
We should also like to make it clear that the presence of a
word in this book, whether marked or unmarked, in
no way affects its legal status as a trademark.

ISBN 0550 18051 6 (Hardback)
ISBN 0550 18052 4 (Paperback)

The British National Corpus is a collaborative initiative
carried out by Oxford University Press, Longman,
Chambers Harrap, Oxford University Computing Services,
Lancaster University's Unit for Computer Research
in the English Language, and the British Library. The
project received funding from the UK Department of
Trade and Industry and the Science and Engineering
Research Council and was supported by additional
research grants from the British Academy and the British Library.

Typeset by Tradespools Ltd, Frome, Somerset
Printed in England by Clays Ltd, St Ives plc

# CONTENTS

# PREFACE

The aim of *Chambers Guide to Grammar and Usage* is to help you to write and speak English correctly and effectively. It is designed to enable you to do justice to your ideas and opinions by ensuring that they are expressed competently and convincingly and that what you have to say is not marred or obscured by errors of language or by poor style or presentation.

In its eight main chapters, the *Chambers Guide to Grammar and Usage* provides guidance on grammar, spelling, punctuation and the meaning and use of words, while the appendices give advice on how to set about writing reports, essays, letters and minutes from the first steps in planning what to say through to the final stages of polishing up what you have said.

If you are a student at school or college, and you want to improve the quality of your essays and dissertations, then this book can help you. If you are a secretary, and you want to be sure that the letters you write, the agendas you prepare and the minutes you take are properly composed and in good English, then this book can help you. But the *Chambers Guide to Grammar and Usage* is not intended solely for students, secretaries and business people — it is for anyone who at any time might need to write a formal letter (such as a letter of complaint or a letter to an MP or local councillor), submit a report or make a speech. It is, in short, a book for everyone who wants to speak and write correct, accurate and effective English.

For the most part, the *Chambers Guide to Grammar and Usage* is concerned with British English usage, but throughout the book there are many comparisons between British and American usage where these differ. (A summary of the main differences between British and American English can be found in Appendix H.) A particular feature of the book is the many real-life examples of usage, taken from a wide variety of sources including the British National Corpus (a 100-million-word database of contemporary written and spoken English) and Wordtrack, Larousse's own citation database.

No prior understanding of any linguistic terminology is assumed in this book, and all the technical terms used in it (and a few others that you might come across in other contexts such as modern dictionaries) are fully explained in the chapter on *How Language is Described*.

Finally, I would like to thank Robert Allen and Bill Henderson for their advice and support in the compilation of this book.

George Davidson

# HOW TO USE THIS BOOK

The *Chambers Guide to Grammar and Usage* is a book both for dipping into and for browsing through, a book to use both for finding quick answers to particular problems and equally well for a more leisurely and systematic read-through in order to find errors that you are unaware of making (you cannot, after all, correct an error in your speech or writing until you are aware that is an error).

Each chapter of the *Guide* deals with a separate topic (linguistic terminology, grammar, vocabulary, spelling, pronunciation, etc). Within most chapters, the entries are in straight-forward alphabetical order; two chapters — those dealing with common spelling errors (chapter 6) and pronunciation (chapter 8) — are divided into separate sections, within which again the entries are entered alphabetically.

The advantage of the chapter approach is that it allows you to home in very quickly on whatever topic you want information on: if you need an answer to a question on pronunciation, you go directly to the pronunciation chapter; if you have a question about a point of grammar, you look in the chapter on grammar; and similarly for spelling queries, punctuation problems, and so on. This approach is particularly helpful in the many cases where you might not know what heading or title to look under for a particular subject (some topics, especially in grammar, are known by a number of different names): even if you are not exactly sure what you are looking for, it is easier to find it by flicking through just one chapter of a book than to have to search through a whole book in which all the topics are entered in one single A—Z list.

To provide extra help, there is an index of words and topics at the end of the book (page 510), many of the topics being listed under several different titles to make it easier for you to find what you are looking for.

Two features of this *Guide* are the tinted notes and the information boxes. In many entries in the book, tinted notes are used to draw attention to the most important rules and instructions. The boxes contain warnings (indicated by a ⚠ symbol) and additional points of interest (indicated by a 🚩 symbol).

Other symbols used in the *Guide* are ✓, ✗ and ? , indicating respectively examples of correct, incorrect and doubtful usage.

# WHAT IS GOOD ENGLISH?

Is *data* singular or plural?
Should *controversy* and *formidable* be stressed on the first or the second syllable?
Is it wrong to spell *all right* as 'alright', or is 'alright' now all right too?
Is it correct to use *hopefully* in the sense of 'I hope'?
Is there a difference between *inferring* and *implying*, and between *refuting* and *denying*?
Should a letter be closed with *Yours sincerely* or *Yours faithfully*, or does it not matter which?

Most of us have occasion to ask questions like these at some time or another. While we may give little thought to our use of English in informal, everyday situations, there are nevertheless times when we want to be absolutely sure that what we are saying is 'good English'.

But what is good English? For many people, there is an obvious answer: good English is the form of English that we read in quality literature and high-class newspapers and that we hear in certain types of radio and television programme. Good English is what is described in grammar books and taught in schools. Any other form of English is 'bad English', and always to be avoided.

But in fact the situation is not as clear-cut as that. What is often called 'good English' is more correctly known as 'Standard English'. Standard English is just one of many forms (or dialects) of English, the one which is by tradition generally used, and generally expected to be used, in formal speaking and writing. It is not, however, the only correct or 'good' form of English. Other, non-standard, dialects are every bit as correct as Standard English, and colloquial language is just as correct as formal language. Where they differ is in appropriateness and acceptability. Just as swimwear is entirely acceptable on a beach but would be considered inappropriate for wearing in an office, non-standard and colloquial forms of English differ from formal Standard English in not being appropriate for use in certain types of speech and writing (eg in a report to a conference or an article in a learned journal) but are perfectly appropriate and acceptable in other contexts (eg chatting to friends in a pub or at home with one's family).

There is, therefore, no reason why anyone should try to avoid ever using non-standard forms of English if that is what comes naturally to them, so long as they do so only in appropriate contexts. But it is necessary for everyone to be able to speak and write formal Standard English correctly also, and to use it in situations where they would be expected to do so. Although there are occasional references to non-standard forms of English in the *Chambers Guide to Grammar and Usage*, it is in the main Standard English (particularly Standard British English) that is described in this book.

Armed with this *Guide*, you need never have doubts about the correctness of your English again.

# GUIDE TO PRONUNCIATION

The phonetic system used in this book has been designed to represent as wide a range of English accents as possible. It follows, therefore, that some of the symbols used are to be interpreted in slightly different ways by different speakers of English, according to their own accents and pronunciations. This can be illustrated by the following examples:

i)   In some accents of English, there are two 'a' sounds, represented in this book by /a/ and /ah/ respectively, as in *gas* (/**gas**/) and *pass* (/**pahs**/). In other accents, however, there is only one 'a' sound, and speakers of such accents will have to interpret the two symbols /a/ and /ah/ as both indicating the same sound in their pronunciation.

Similarly, *fool* and *full* have different vowel sounds in some accents, represented in this book by /uu/ and /oo/ respectively; but in other accents these two words rhyme, in which case the two vowel symbols must be treated as representing the same sound, not two different sounds.

ii)  The vowel-sounds of words such as *fir* and *fur* are the same in some accents, whereas in others they are different. Here again, therefore, the respellings must be interpreted according to one's own normal pronunciation.

iii) In some accents of English, a final *r* is pronounced in words such as *far* and *poor*, whereas in other accents it is not. In the transcriptions given in the *Guide*, the *r*'s are transcribed (eg /**kahr**/ for *car*) and must be ignored by those who do not normally pronounce them.

Phonetics are printed between slashes, thus /**book**/. Stressed syllables in transcriptions are indicated by boldface type, weak syllables by italic type, thus /**fo**-*ne*-tiks/. Where stress has to be indicated in written words (eg in examples), it is shown by a stress mark ( ' ) preceding the stressed syllable: *pho'netics*.

The following symbols have been used:

Consonants

| | | | | | | |
|---|---|---|---|---|---|---|
| /ch/ | as in | *church* | /sh/ | as in | *ship* |
| /dh/ | as in | *then* | /th/ | as in | *thing* |
| /kh/ | as in | *loch* | /zh/ | as in | *pleasure* |
| /ng/ | as in | *sing* | | | |

Other consonants are pronounced as in normal, everyday English.

## Vowels

| | | | | | | |
|---|---|---|---|---|---|---|
| /a/ | as in | *cat* | /aw/ | as in | *caught* |
| /ah/ | as in | *car* | /u/ | as in | *cup* |
| /e/ | as in | *egg* | /uu/ | as in | *boot* |
| /ee/ | as in | *deep* | /oo/ | as in | *book* |
| /ay/ | as in | *hay* | /uh/ | as in | *chauffeur* |
| /i/ | as in | *hit* | /a$^{ng}$/ | as in | French *vin* |
| /iy/ | as in | *fight* | /o$^{ng}$/ | as in | French *dans* |
| /o/ | as in | *pot* | /oh$^{ng}$/ | as in | French *bon* |
| /oh/ | as in | *coat* | /uh$^{ng}$/ | as in | French *un* |

# 1

# How Language is Described

In this chapter are explained and exemplified many of the words commonly used in the description of language. The list includes both the terminology of traditional grammar (such as *adjective* and *main clause*) and terms that have been introduced in modern grammars of English (such as *determiner* and *count noun*).

## abbreviation

*Abbreviations* are shortened forms of words and phrases. There are several different kinds:

i) *Abbreviations* in a narrower sense are parts of words written instead of the whole words (eg *approx.* for *approximately*, *neut.* for *neuter*, *Tues.* for *Tuesday*).

ii) *Contractions* are shortened forms of words that include (at least) the first and last letter of the shortened word (eg *Mr* for *Mister*, *Rd* for *Road*, *St* for *Street* and *Saint*).

Contractions may also be shortened forms of phrases which include (at least) the first letter of the first word and the last letter of the last word (eg *I'll* for *I will*, *isn't* for *is not*, *it's* for *it is*).

iii) *Initialisms* are abbreviations consisting of the first letters of a group of words, and which are pronounced as separate letters (eg *BBC*, *MA*, *PhD*).

 The everyday names of many institutions are formed in this way. For example, *BBC* is the name generally used, and *British Broadcasting Corporation* is found only in more formal contexts such as the headings of letters and documents.

iv) *Acronyms* are abbreviations formed from the initial letters, or in some cases the initial syllables, of the abbreviated words and which are themselves pronounced as whole words (eg *NATO*, pronounced /nay-toh/, from *North Atlantic Treaty Organization*; *SHAPE*, pronounced /shayp/, from *Supreme Headquarters Allied Powers Europe*; *Benelux*, pronounced /be-ni-luks/, from *Belgium*, *Netherlands* and *Luxembourg*).

 A number of common words were in origin acronyms, eg *radar*, from *radio detection and ranging*.

v)   ***Clipped forms*** are shortened forms of words which look like abbreviations but which are are now treated as full words in their own right (eg *exam* from *examination, deli* from *delicatessen, flu* from *influenza, bus* from *omnibus*).

> ◪ The same form may in some cases be an abbreviation and in others a clipped form:
>
> > *I'm seeing the* **prof** *this afternoon.* (= informal clipped form, written without a full stop, and pronounced /prof/)
> > **Prof.** *J McBean* (= abbreviation, eg on a letter, written with a full stop, and said as '*professor*')

vi)   ***Symbols*** are letters which are substitutes for words rather than shortenings of words, such as those used in chemistry (eg *Cu* for *copper, Fe* for *iron*) or in measurements (eg *lb* for *pound*).

## absolute

• An ***absolute*** construction is one which is not linked grammatically to the rest of the sentence it stands in. For example, in *Time permitting, we'll visit the museum tomorrow*, the words *time permitting* form an absolute clause, in that neither the subject of the clause (*time*) nor the verb (*permitting*) is directly linked to any element of the main clause (*we'll visit the museum tomorrow*).

Absolute clauses usually provide information about the circumstances or conditions concerning the action of the main clause. They are generally equivalent in meaning to a clause beginning with a conjunction and containing a finite verb instead of a participle:

> *If time permits, we'll visit the museum tomorrow.*

> ⚠ Absolute clauses containing a subject noun and a participle must be distinguished from similar constructions in which there is no expressed subject of the participle:
>
> > *Having at last received permission to go, we decided to visit the museum the next day.*
>
> In constructions of this latter kind, the subject of the main clause (in this case *we*) is also to be understood as the subject of the participle (ie, it is 'we' who 'received permission to go').
>
> The distinction between these two similar constructions is important for an understanding of the construction known as the DANGLING PARTICIPLE (see page 85).

• A transitive verb (ie, one which can be followed by an object, as in *Foxes have killed all my hens* and *He smokes a pipe*) is said to be ***absolute*** when it occurs with its object implied rather than expressed: *Soldiers are trained to <u>kill</u>* □ *Does she <u>smoke</u>?*

In some grammar books and dictionaries, absolute uses of transitive verbs are classified as *intransitive*, because in both cases the verb stands without an object. However, the difference between absolute uses of transitive verbs and true intransitive verbs is that the former have <u>implied</u> objects, usually understandable from the context (*Does she smoke?* = *Does she smoke cigarettes?*) whereas intransitive verbs have no object at all (*He looked back at the huge factory chimneys <u>smoking</u> in the distance*).

- An *absolute* adjective is one which is used as a noun, as in *the <u>living</u> and the <u>dead</u>* or *Help the <u>Aged</u>*. Absolute adjectives are sometimes called *adjectival nouns*.

## abstract noun see NOUN.

## accent

- An *accent* is a mark written or printed above a vowel, generally to indicate either that the vowel is to be pronounced in a particular way or that the vowel is to be stressed. Apart from their occurrence in borrowings from foreign languages such as French (eg *blasé*) or Spanish (eg *adiòs*), accents are not used in English.

In French, accents indicate how a vowel is to be sounded. The three accents of French are the *acute accent* (as in *née*), the *grave accent* (as in *à la*), and the *circumflex accent* (as in *raison d'être*).

In Spanish, on the other hand, accents indicate stress. They are used to show that a particular vowel in a word bears the main stress wherever this is contrary to the normal stress patterns of the language, as in *difícil* and *útil*.

 There are a number of other symbols written or printed above or below letters, such as the *diaeresis* (as in *naïve*) and the French *cedilla* (as in *façade*). These are not classed as accents, but as *diacritics* (see DIACRITIC).

- In a second sense, *accent* is another word for stress (see STRESS). In the discussion of Spanish in the paragraph above, it could equally have been said that the accent (= 'written symbol') in *útil* shows that the accent (= 'stress') is on the initial syllable.

- In a third sense of the word, a person's *accent* is the way in which he or she pronounces words. People may, for example, speak English with a Scottish accent, an American accent, a posh accent, a working-class accent, and so on.

Accent in this sense must be distinguished from *dialect* (see DIALECT): accents are a matter of pronunciation only, whereas differences in dialect involve vocabulary and grammar rather than pronunciation.

**accusative case** see CASE.

**acronym** see ABBREVIATION.

## active

A verb is said to be in the ***active*** voice when the subject of the verb is performing the action or is in the state described by the verb. ('Voice' is simply the technical word for that aspect of the grammar of verbs that is covered by the terms 'active' and 'passive'.) For example, in *The boy stroked the cat, the boy* is the subject of the verb *stroked* and it is the boy who is performing the action of stroking; *stroked* is therefore in the active voice. Other examples of active verbs are:

> She <u>doesn't like</u> my hat.
> We <u>were expecting</u> you.
> She <u>told</u> Denis that she <u>would marry</u> him.

The opposite of an active verb is a ***passive*** verb, as in *The cat was stroked by the boy* (see PASSIVE).

**acute accent** see ACCENT.

## adjectival clause

***Adjectival clauses*** perform the same describing and defining functions as adjectives:

> The reason <u>why she came at all</u> is not clear to me.
> The fellow <u>who was here yesterday</u> is actually her brother.

**adjectival noun** see ABSOLUTE (adjective).

## adjectival phrase

An ***adjectival phrase*** consists of an adjective and any adverbs that qualify it: *a <u>very big</u> lorry*.

## adjective

An ***adjective*** is a word which does one of two things:

   i)   It describes or refers to the shape, colour, size or any other quality of a noun or pronoun: *a <u>big</u> book* □ *Grass is <u>green</u>*. Such an adjective is called a ***descriptive adjective***.

   ii)   It picks out or identifies a noun or pronoun: <u>*This*</u> *book is cheaper than* <u>*that other*</u> *one*. An adjective of this type is called a ***limiting adjective***.

In traditional grammar, an adjective is said to ***qualify*** a noun or a pronoun.

**✦ Descriptive adjectives**

Most descriptive adjectives can

   i)   stand in ***attributive*** position, ie preceding a noun: *an <u>enormous</u> debt*;

ii)    stand in **predicative** position, ie following a verb: *That book looks good* □ *He found the speech rather tedious;*

iii)    be qualified by words such as *very* and *rather;*

iv)    form **comparatives** *(taller, more beautiful)* and **superlatives** *(tallest, most beautiful).*

---

 Not all words which are classified as descriptive adjectives possess all four of the above characteristics. For example:

✓    *an infinite number*
✓    *The possibilities are infinite.*
✗    *a very infinite number*
✗    *a more infinite number*

✓    *a mere boy* □ *an utter fool.*
✗    *The boy is mere/merer/very mere* □ *The fool is utter/more utter/very utter.*

✓    *The boy is asleep.*
?    *Maybe we were both asleep, but you were more asleep than me.*
✗    *the asleep boy*
✗    *You must have been very asleep when we called, if you didn't hear us.*

Some nouns that name materials behave like descriptive adjectives: *a stone wall* □ *an iron bridge* □ *a paper cup* □ *milk products.* These are not adjectives, but attributive uses of the nouns.

---

## ✦   Limiting adjectives

There are several categories of limiting adjective. These are grouped and classified in different ways by different authorities. One possible classification is as follows:

i)    **demonstrative adjectives**: *this* book □ *those* flowers

ii)    **interrogative adjectives**: *which* books? □ *what* flowers?

iii)    **possessive adjectives**: *my* books □ *her* flowers

iv)    **indefinite adjectives**: *any* books □ *some* flowers

v)    **distributive adjectives**: *each* book □ *every* flower

vi)    **relative adjectives**: *They were at sea for nineteen hours, during which time he simply slept.*

vii)    the **definite article** *the* and the **indefinite article** *a/an*

viii)    **numerals**: *two* books □ *the second* book

---

In some modern grammars of English, the words which are classed here, and in traditional grammar, as limiting adjectives are called **determiners**.

> Some of the words in the above categories can also function as pro-nouns, ie without a related noun:
>
> *Which do you want?*
> *Any will do.*
> *There were three of them, each holding a candle.*

### ✦ Adjectival nouns

Adjectives used as nouns, eg *help for the deaf and the blind*, are often referred to as **adjectival nouns**. (See also ABSOLUTE.)

### ✦ Comparatives and superlatives

For comparative and superlative adjectives, see COMPARISON OF ADJEC-TIVES AND ADVERBS.

## adverb

### ✦ Adverbs and their uses

As their name implies, adverbs have long been considered in traditional grammar to be especially closely related to verbs, and in many sentences the adverb does indeed impart information about the action described by the verb:

*She dances beautifully.*
*They arrived yesterday.*
*He jumped in.*

However, adverbs do not just **qualify**, or **modify**, verbs, they also modify adjectives (*a very big house* □ *a completely irrelevant suggestion*), prepositions (*The dog ran right in front of a car*), conjunctions (*I'll show you exactly how she did it*), and other adverbs (*I type very slowly* □ *She was standing right there*).

### ✦ Classification of adverbs

Traditionally, adverbs have been classified by their meaning or their function. The main categories are:

  i) **adverbs of place**: *We are here* □ *They went out.*

 ii) **adverbs of manner**: *They ran quickly* □ *She sang well.*

iii) **adverbs of time**: *Do it now* □ *I'll come tomorrow.*

 iv) **adverbs of degree**: *This is a very serious matter* □ *Their behaviour was completely unacceptable.*

  v) **adverbs of negation**: *She's not coming.*

 vi) **interrogative adverbs**: *When are you coming?* □ *How did you do that?*

vii) **conjunctive adverbs** (ie adverbs that act as conjunctions): *I don't know why I did that* □ *Have you any idea when she'll be coming?* (These are actually the same words as the interrogative adverbs, but they are classed as a different type of adverb because of the difference in function.)

> ◪  In some modern grammars of English, a number of other terms are used to give a different, and in some cases very detailed, description of adverbs and their uses. Among these are:
>
>     i)  ***intensifiers***, which can be subdivided into ***emphasizers*** (*Did he <u>actually</u> say that?* □ *I'm <u>definitely</u> not going*), ***amplifiers*** (*She <u>completely</u> ignored me* □ *I <u>utterly</u> reject that suggestion*), and ***downtoners*** (*I <u>hardly</u> know her* □ *She <u>almost</u> fell off*), with even smaller subdivisions of these subclasses, the description of which is beyond the scope of this book.
>
>     ii)  ***sentence adverbs***, which indicate, for example, the speaker's or writer's attitude to what is being said in the rest of the sentence:
>
>         <u>*Personally*</u>, *I couldn't care less.*
>
> (See SENTENCE ADVERB for fuller details.)
>
>     iii)  ***sentence substitutes***, words such as *yes* and *no* which can be used in place of a full sentence containing a finite verb:
>
>         *'Are you coming?'* *'<u>Yes</u>.'* (= 'I am coming').

### ✦  Phrasal verbs

For the role of adverbs in phrasal verbs (eg *run <u>away</u>, come <u>in</u>, put <u>up</u> with*), see PHRASAL VERB.

### ✦  Comparatives and superlatives

For comparative and superlative adverbs, see COMPARISON OF ADJECTIVES AND ADVERBS.

### adverbial clause

An ***adverbial clause*** is one which functions in the same way as adverbs, eg providing information about the time, place, manner, purpose, etc of an action, etc:

    *I'll come <u>when I'm ready</u>.* (adverbial clause of time)
    *I'll come <u>if I feel like it</u>.* (adverbial clause of condition)

### adverbial phrase

An ***adverbial phrase*** consists of a 'main' adverb plus any other adverbs that qualify it: *We had to work <u>very quickly</u>.*

### affirmative

A verb or sentence is in the ***affirmative*** when it states that something is so: *Cats are animals.* □ *I nearly fainted.* The opposite of affirmative is NEGATIVE.

### affix

An ***affix*** is a word-forming element that is
    i)  added to a word-root (the 'core' of a word) to form a word (eg the affix

*-ible* is added to the word-root *cred-* to form *credible*), or

ii)     added to an existing word to form a new word (eg the affix *-er* is added to the word *sing* to form *singer*) or another form of the same word (eg the affix *-s* is added to the word *sing* to form *sings*).

In English, there are only two types of affix:

>   ***prefixes*** are added to the beginnings of words (eg <u>un</u>*known*, <u>ir</u>*regular*, <u>re</u>*name*, <u>pre</u>*recorded*), and

>   ***suffixes*** are added to the ends of words or word-roots (eg *fool<u>ish</u>, foolish<u>ness</u>, sing<u>er</u>, sing<u>ing</u>, quick<u>ly</u>, repeat<u>able</u>, imper<u>ceptible</u>, accura<u>cy</u>*).

See also COMBINING FORM.

## agent

An ***agent*** is the noun or pronoun that denotes the person or thing performing the action expressed by the verb.

In an active sentence, the agent is the subject of the verb: <u>*Fred*</u> *kicked the ball through the window*. In a passive sentence, the agent is preceded by the preposition *by*: *He was killed by* <u>*his own men*</u>.

## agreement

In grammar, a word is said to ***agree*** with another word when it appears in a particular form under the grammatical influence of that other word.

In English, a verb has to agree with its subject in terms of ***number*** (singular *I* <u>*am*</u> versus plural *we* <u>*are*</u>) and ***person*** (first person *I* <u>*am*</u> versus second person *you* <u>*are*</u> versus third person *she* <u>*is*</u>). Similarly with regular verbs: *you* <u>*walk*</u> versus *the boy* <u>*walks*</u> versus *the boys* <u>*walk*</u>.

With regard to nouns and adjectives, the only examples of agreement in English involve agreement in ***number*** between the demonstrative adjectives *this, that, these* and *those* and the nouns they are attached to: *this* and *that* must be used with singular nouns (*this book* □ *that man*), *these* and *those* with plural nouns (*these books* □ *those men*).

There is also agreement in terms of ***gender*** between the relative pronouns *who* and *which* and the nouns they relate to, *who* being used to refer to people and *which* with all other nouns:

>   *The man* <u>*who*</u> *called by yesterday was back again today.*
>   *This is a question* <u>*which*</u> *I find on many people's lips.*
>   *The dog,* <u>*which*</u> *had obviously been hit by a car, was lying at the side of the road.*

These are the only examples of agreement in English. In languages with a large number of inflections (or 'word-endings'), such as Latin, French, Spanish, German and Russian, agreement has an even greater role in grammar. On the other hand, in some languages, such as Chinese, there is no grammatical agreement at all.

Agreement is also known as *concord*.

## ambiguity

*Ambiguity* is the possibility of a grammatical structure having more than one meaning. There are many kinds of ambiguity. Two common types are *ambiguity of reference* and *ambiguity arising from negatives*:

i)  In *ambiguity of reference*, the extent of a word's reference to other words in the construction is unclear, as in *large potatoes and cabbages* (= 'large potatoes + large cabbages' or else 'large potatoes + cabbages of any size') and *We laughed and sang loudly* (= 'we laughed, and we also sang loudly' or 'we laughed loudly and we sang loudly').

ii)  In *ambiguity arising from negatives*, it is unclear what part of the structure is being negated, as in *We didn't go because it was raining* (= 'we didn't go, and the reason for not going is that it was raining' or 'we did go, but not because it was raining'). Punctuation may help to resolve the ambiguity: *We didn't go, because it was raining.*

## anacoluthon

*Anacoluthon* is the breaking off of a grammatical construction before its end and continuing with an unconnected construction: *To think that she'd — well, there's no point in fretting about it now, I suppose.*

## analogy

*Analogy* is the process whereby a word or grammatical structure is altered in some way to match some other word or grammatical structure in form. For example, many plural nouns and past tenses of verbs that were formerly irregular (and sometimes still are in dialects) have become regular in Standard English by analogy with other regular forms:

i)  Among the nouns, the plurals *een/eyne*, *shoon* and *kye* or *kine*, for example, have been replaced by *eyes*, *shoes* and *cows*.

ii)  Among the verbs, the past tense of *reap*, formerly *rope*, is now *reaped*; the past tense of *laugh*, formerly *logh* or *lewgh* (and still *leuch* in Scots), is now *laughed*; and the past tense of *bow*, formerly *bey* or *bugh*, is now *bowed*.

## analysis

*Analysis* is the process of dividing a grammatical structure, usually a sentence, into its component parts (eg clauses and phrases), and describing the nature and function of each part. Along with PARSING, this gives a complete grammatical description of the structure.

## antecedent

An *antecedent* is the word, phrase or clause which a relative pronoun refers back to and is related to grammatically:

9

> *Anyone who did that must be crazy.* ('Anyone' is the antecedent of *who*.)
> *He played the bagpipes, which made him rather unpopular with the neighbours.*
>   ('He played the bagpipes' is the antecedent of *which*.)

**Antecedent** is sometimes also used to denote the word, phrase or clause to which a personal pronoun refers and is related:

> *When John arrives, tell him to come straight to my office.* ('John' is the antecedent of *him*.)
> *I found a stray dog and took it home with me.* ('A stray dog' is the antecedent of *it*.)
> *He plays the bagpipes, and it drives the neightbours crazy.* ('He plays the bagpipes' is the antecedent of *it*.)

## antonym

**Antonyms** are words that are opposite in meaning, eg *big* and *small*, or *buy* and *sell*.

## apposition

Two or more words phrases are said to be in **apposition** when they both (or all) refer to the same person, object, etc, and both (or all) have the same grammatical role in the sentence.

In *The Prime Minister, John Major, will be visiting three factories near Coventry this afternoon*, the two phrases *the Prime Minister* and *John Major* refer to the same individual and both function as the subject of the following verb; they are therefore in apposition.

Nouns and noun phrases in apposition are usually juxtaposed, but need not be, as in *He got a wonderful present for Christmas, a new car*, in which the two highlighted phrases are in apposition.

The second of the apposed elements is sometimes introduced by a word or phrase such as *namely, in other words, that is,* or *that is to say*:

> *He was accused of possessing an offensive weapon, namely a golf club.*

## appropriacy

**Appropriacy** is the use of a word or style of language appropriate to a particular context. It is largely a matter of social convention, and is not based on grammatical or lexical correctness. For example, it is appropriate to use *edifice* only in formal or technical contexts, *building* or *house* being more appropriate in other contexts. Slang and colloquialisms are generally inappropriate in formal writing, and formal language is often inappropriate in informal conversation. Inadvertent use of inappropriate words and structures may give rise to censure, while the deliberate use of them may serve as a form of humour.

See also REGISTER.

## article

The *definite article* is the word *the*, and the *indefinite article* is *a* (or *an*). In traditional grammar, these are usually classed as adjectives, but are sometimes treated as a separate part of speech on their own. In some modern grammars, they are classed as DETERMINERS.

## aspect

*Aspect* is a feature of verbs. It is closely connected with tense, and sometimes confused with it. While tense relates to the time of the action or state described by the verb relative to the time of speaking (ie, past, present or future, as in *He goes to school* versus *He went to school*), aspect is concerned with the manner in which the action or state described by the verb is performed or perceived (eg as a simple action, a repeated action, an ongoing or uncompleted action, etc). Differences in aspect can be seen in the following pairs of sentences:

> He *lived* in London for about five years.
> He *has lived* in London for about five years.
>
> I *read* a really interesting book last night.
> I *was reading* a book when she phoned me.
>
> She *sings* well.
> She *is singing* better than ever this evening.

See also PROGRESSIVE and PERFECT.

## assimilation

*Assimilation* is a change in a sound under the influence of another sound. For example, in rapid speech, *ten cups* is often said as /teng kups/, *ten minutes* as /tem min-its/, the /n/ of *ten* being assimilated to the following /k/ and /m/ sounds.

Sometimes the assimilation causes changes in spelling also: the prefix *in-* becomes *im-* before *p* and *b* (as in *impossible* and *imbalance*) and *ir-* before *r* (as in *irregular*).

## attributive

An *attributive* adjective precedes the noun it relates to: *a black cat □ a big house □ a mere boy*.

Nouns can also be used attributively, eg *a stone wall □ a denim shirt □ a table lamp*.

The opposite of attributive is PREDICATIVE.

## auxiliary verb

*Auxiliary verbs*, or simply *auxiliaries*, are verbs that serve a number of purposes, but mainly to indicate TENSE, ASPECT and MOOD.

The *primary auxiliaries* are *be*, *have* and *do*, as in *I am going □ I have gone □ I did go □ I have been working*.

11

Other auxiliaries are *may, might, can, could, will, would, shall, should* and *must*. These are known as ***modal auxiliaries***, and generally indicate notions such as possibility (*He might come* □ *He could have come*) and necessity (*You must come*). Also included among the modal auxiliaries are *ought to* and *used to*. See also DARE (page 78) and NEED (page 91).

>  Notice that some of the auxiliaries can also function as full lexical verbs: compare the use of *have* as an auxiliary verb in *I've bought a gun* and as a lexical verb in *I have a gun*.

## back-formation

***Back-formation*** is the formation of a new word from an already existing word that is wrongly thought to be a derivative of the new word, usually by the removal of an affix.

For example, just as *liar* is formed from the verb *to lie*, so the existence of the noun *burglar* would lead one to expect the existence of a verb *to burgle*. In fact, the nouns *burglar* and *burglary* are the earlier forms (used in the 16th century) and the verb *burgle* was created much later (in the 19th century) by back-formation. Similarly, *donate* is a back-formation from *donation, laze* from *lazy, grovel* from an old adverb *groveling* (meaning 'prone, face down') mistakenly taken to be a present participle, *sidle* similarly from an old adverb *sideling* (= 'sidelong'), and *upholster* from *upholstery*.

The same process has given rise to compound verbs such as *dressmake, panic-buy, stage-manage* and *ratecap*.

## bare infinitive see INFINITIVE.

## base

In word-formation, a ***base*** is a word or a part of a word to which one or more affixes may be or have been added, eg *fool* in *foolish, quick* in *quickly, friend* in *friendly, ed-* in *edible*, and *intellig-* in *intelligible* and *intelligence*.

There are two types of base: ***roots*** and ***stems***. In *friendliness* and *unfriendly*, both *friend* and *friendly* are bases, *friend* being the 'root' and *friendly* the 'stem' — see ROOT and STEM for a more detailed discussion of these terms.

## case

Case refers to the existence of nouns and pronouns (and adjectives which agree with them) in more than one form, the particular form a word appears in being selected according to the role or function the word has in a sentence. In Latin and German, for example, nouns, pronouns and adjectives all show case, whereas in English only pronouns show such variation:

*I saw <u>him</u>* versus *<u>He</u> saw <u>me</u>*

*Who are you?* versus *To whom should I send this?*

and so also with *she* and *her*, *we* and *us*, *they* and *them*, *thou* and *thee*.

There are, therefore, two cases (two different forms of each pronoun) in the English pronoun system. These can be called the ***subjective*** case (for the pronouns that are subjects of verbs — *I*, *she*, *we*, etc) and the ***objective*** case for the forms that are objects of verbs or pronouns — *me*, *her*, *us*, etc).

In modern English nouns, there are no examples of case, since nouns do not change in form according to their function in a sentence:

*The boy looked at the girl, and the girl looked at the boy.*

---

Any particular case may have more than one function in a language: in English, for example, the objective case acts as the direct object of the verb (as in *I saw him*) and as the indirect object (as in *I gave him the book*).

Some grammatical descriptions of English, taking Latin as their model, refer to the subjective case as being the ***nominative*** case, the objective case of the direct object as the ***accusative*** case and the objective case of the indirect object as the ***dative*** case.

*His, her, mine, whose*, etc are often referred to as being in the ***genitive*** case (another term taken from Latin grammar), but in modern English grammar, they are best treated as possessive adjectives and possessive pronouns.

Similarly, some grammar books refer to forms like *John's bike* and *the boy's bike* as being in the genitive case, but this is again only to apply the terminology of Latin grammar to equivalent possessive constructions in English. *John's* and *boy's* are not forms of the nouns *John* and *boy*, as -*'s* is an independent element in the sentence, not necessarily attached to a noun at all: *Is that the girl you came in with's bag?*

---

**cedilla** see DIACRITIC.

**circumflex** see ACCENT.

## clause

A ***clause*** is a string of words that act together as a unit of structure and meaning in a sentence:

*I could explain it all day / and you still wouldn't understand.*
*He says / he has papers to deliver to you / and that he will wait for an
    answer.*

Clauses are often linked by conjunctions (*and*, *but*, *because*, *since*, *although*, *if*, *while*, and so on):

> *Wait/till I get you home!*
> *We don't give an inch/until we get/what we want.*

but there may be no linking word:

> *I think/I'll have to go now.*

## ✦ Clauses and phrases

Traditionally, a clause is distinguished from a phrase by having a subject and a finite verb:

> *Jane arrived in the early afternoon* is a sentence comprising a single clause
> *I wonder/whether Jane has arrived yet* is a sentence comprising two clauses.

A phrase has no subject–verb structure (eg *in the early afternoon, has arrived, will be wearing* and *for Christmas* are phrases).

However, in many modern English grammars, the notion of clause has been expanded to take in not only *finite clauses* (ie, clauses which contain a finite verb) like those above, but also to what can be called *non-finite clauses* in which

i)   the verb is not finite (being eg a participle):

> *Time permitting, we will visit the museum tomorrow.*

ii)   the subject is implied rather than stated (and the verb is non-finite):

> *While running for the bus, John tripped and fell.*

and to *verbless clauses* in which both the subject and the verb are implied rather than stated:

> *If possible, come sometime next week.*

---

 Non-finite clauses can generally be expanded into or paraphrased as full finite clauses:

> *If time permits, we will visit the museum tomorrow.*
> *If it is possible, come sometime next week.*

Phrases cannot be expanded in this way.

---

## ✦ Co-ordinate clauses, main clauses and subordinate clauses

Clauses can be divided into three types according to their relationship to each other. If the clauses are of equal rank in a sentence, they are known as *co-ordinate clauses*. Alternatively, one clause may be considered the

**main clause** or **principal clause** and the other (or others) the **subordinate clause(s)** or **dependent clause(s)**.

• **Co-ordinate clauses** may be joined by words like *and, but, or, nor, so* and *yet*:

> *It was a warm, Mediterranean night, and there was a lovely cool breeze.*
> *It was a lovely, starry night, but there was a cool breeze blowing.*
> *We can leave now, or we can a stay a little longer.*

Co-ordinate clauses may simply be juxtaposed, as in the famous quotation from Julius Caesar:

> *I came, I saw, I conquered.*

Sentences consisting solely of co-ordinate clauses are called **compound sentences**.

• **Subordinate clauses** are not equal partners in a sentence, but are dependent on (or subordinate to) the **main clause** or another subordinate clause. Subordinate clauses begin with words such as *because, since, that, which, when* and *though*:

> *We'll have to see <u>if we like it</u>.*
> *I'll come <u>when I'm ready</u>.*
> *<u>When the train started</u>, the suitcases fell off the luggage rack.*

There may sometimes be no linking word:

> *I told you <u>she wouldn't come</u>.*

Sentences which consist of a main clause and one or more subordinate clauses are known as **complex sentences**. Sentences which consist of two or more main clauses and one or more subordinate clauses are known as **compound-complex sentences**.

Subordinate clauses can be divided into three categories according to their function in the sentences they occur in: **noun clauses**, **adverbial clauses** and **adjectival clauses**.

  i) **Noun clauses** have the same functions as nouns do in a sentence, acting for example as the subject or object of a verb or the object of a preposition:

> *<u>Why he did that</u> is far from clear.*
> *He wants to know <u>where you are going</u>.*
> *They were terrified by <u>what they had seen</u>.*

  ii) **Adverbial clauses** function in the same way as adverbs, eg providing information about the time, place, manner, purpose, etc of an action, etc:

> *I'll come <u>when I'm ready</u>. (adverbial clause of time)*
> *I'll dress <u>as I please</u>. (adverbial clause of manner)*

*I'll come <u>if I choose</u>.* (adverbial clause of condition)

  iii) ***Adjectival clauses*** function in the same way as adjectives do, eg

> *The reason <u>why she came at all</u> is not clear to me.*
> *The woman <u>who was here yesterday</u> called back again this morning.*

## clipped form see ABBREVIATION.

## collective noun see NOUN.

## collocation

A ***collocation*** is an expression consisting of two or more words that are frequently or usually spoken together. Examples of common collocations are *black coffee, white wine, maiden speech* and *hammer and tongs.*

Some collocations, such as *hammer and tongs,* are idioms; others, such as *vast majority,* are clichés.

## combining form

***Combining forms*** are word-forming elements such as *photo-, electro-, cardio-, -graphy, -lysis* and *-logy* that combine with each other to form words (as *electrolysis* and *photography*) or are attached to existing words to form new words (as *electromagnetic* and *photosensitive*). Most combining forms are derived from Latin and Greek.

---

  The ability of combining forms to join together to form words is what distinguishes them from suffixes and prefixes (like *-ly, -ness, -ion, in-* and *un-* which cannot form words by combining with each other but must be added to already existing words or to word-roots such as *-cede* or *-ceive:*

  **✗**   *unly, reness*
  **✓**   *unknown, quickly, reappear, goodness, receive*

---

## common noun see NOUN.

## comparative see COMPARISON OF ADJECTIVES AND ADVERBS.

## comparison of adjectives and adverbs

Traditionally, adjectives and adverbs are said to have three ***degrees*** of comparison: ***positive, comparative*** and ***superlative***.

  i) The ***positive degree*** is the basic form of the adjective or adverb:

*a strong man*  *a wonderful idea*  *a good book*
*He ran quickly*  *She sings well.*

ii) The **comparative degree** of an adjective is the form used to compare two individuals, things, groups, etc:

*a stronger man*  *an even more wonderful*  *a better book*
*idea*

The comparative degree of an adverb is the form used to compare two actions or states:

*You will need to work even more methodically than before.*
*She ran faster than she had ever thought she could.*
*He sings better than he dances.*

iii) The **superlative degree** of an adjective is that form which is used for comparisons between three or more individuals, things, etc:

*the strongest man of all*  *the most wonderful idea*  *the best book*

Similarly, the superlative degree of adverbs is seen in:

*Least said, soonest mended.*
*I work best under pressure.*
*The wind seems to blow most violently just before the calm.*

## complement

A **complement** is, as the name implies, a word or phrase that is needed to 'complete' the sense of a sentence. Complements say something about the subject or object of the sentence, as for example in

*He is very kind.*
*She is a teacher.*
*They considered him a bit of a fool.*
*They've proved you wrong.*

## complex sentence see CLAUSE and SENTENCE.

## compound

A **compound** is a word which is made up of two or more other words, eg *blackbird, textbook, dining-room, blood-red, long-lasting, bad-tempered, panic-buy, stage-manage.*

## compound-complex sentence see CLAUSE and SENTENCE.

## compound sentence see CLAUSE and SENTENCE.

## concord see AGREEMENT.

**concrete noun** see NOUN.

## conditional

- A *conditional clause* is a subordinate clause which expresses a condition affecting the action expressed in the main clause. Conditional clauses often begin with *if* or *unless*:

  *If you don't do as I tell you, you'll hurt yourself.*
  *You'll make a mess of it unless you follow the instructions carefully.*
  *So long as you do as I tell you, you won't come to any harm.*

- A *conditional verb*, or the *conditional tense* of a verb, is the form of a verb which is used to express the consequence in a conditional sentence. It is formed with *would* and *should*:

  *If you came with us, you would see him too.*
  *If you had been there, you would have seen him too.*

>  Notice that the conditional verb is <u>not</u> the verb in the conditional clause, but the verb in the main clause.

- A *conditional sentence* is one containing a conditional clause and/or a conditional verb.

## conjunction

A *conjunction* is a word that links words in a phrase or clauses in a sentence:

*He sings and dances.*
*I'm here because I want to be.*
*If you're coming tonight, bring that record with you.*

There are two types of conjunction: *co-ordinating conjunctions* and *subordinating conjunctions*.

i)   *Co-ordinating conjunctions* link words, phrases or clauses that are equal in rank or importance or which have the same function:

*My aunt and uncle are arriving tomorrow.*
*She neither sings well nor dances well.*
*I'm going, but you're not.*

See also CO-ORDINATION.

ii)   *Subordinating conjunctions* introduce subordinate clauses:

*She isn't coming because she doesn't feel very well.*
*It was a stupid thing to do, though it seemed a good idea at the time.*

**conjunctive adverb** see ADVERB.

## consonant

A *consonant* is a speech sound or a letter representing a speech sound.

i) As a speech sound, a consonant is distinguished from a vowel in that in the formation of a consonant, the breath from the lungs is blocked in some way (either completely or partially) as it passes through the pharynx and the mouth, whereas in the formation of a vowel, the passage of air is not blocked. For example, in the formation of the sounds /p/ and /b/, the passage of air is blocked at the lips and then released; in the formation of /m/, the air is blocked at the lips, but passes through the nose; in the formation of /f/ and /v/, the air passes through the mouth, but the close proximity of the upper teeth and the lower lip causes audible friction. These sounds are all consonants.

ii) As letters of the alphabet, consonants are those which represent consonant sounds, ie *b* represents the sound /b/, *p* represents /p/, *f* represents /f/, and so on.

Some consonants are used in the representation of vowel sounds also. For example, *w* represents a consonant sound in *win* and *wool*, but in *cow* it is part of the representation of the sound of a vowel, and similarly *y* represents a consonant sound in *yes* and *you*, but a vowel sound in *my* and *cry*. In the English alphabet, all the letters are considered to be consonants except *a*, *e*, *i*, *o* and *u*.

## continuous see PROGRESSIVE.

## contraction see ABBREVIATION.

## co-ordination

*Co-ordination* is the linking of two words or two parts of a sentence that are equal in rank or importance, by means of a word (a *co-ordinating conjunction*) or pair of words:

> You and I *will have to go.*
> Either you or I *will have to go.*
> *I* neither agree nor disagree *with what you say.*

See also CO-ORDINATE CLAUSE under CLAUSE.

## copula see LINKING VERB under VERB.

## count noun see NOUN.

## dangling participle see INCORRECT ATTACHMENTS, page 85.

## dative see CASE.

**defining** see RESTRICTIVE.

**definite article**
The word *the*.

**degree** see COMPARISON OF ADJECTIVES AND ADVERBS.

**demonstrative adjective** see LINKING ADJECTIVE under ADJECTIVE.

**demonstrative pronoun** see PRONOUN.

**dependent clause** see CLAUSE.

## derivation

• **Derivation** is the grammatical process by which words are altered by the addition of prefixes or suffixes to form new words (**derivatives**). Thus we have *goodness* formed from *good* by the addition of the suffix *-ness*, *quickly* formed from *quick* by the addition of *-ly*, *singer* formed from *sing* by the addition of *-er*, etc.

Derivation differs from the formation of compound words in that derivation involves the addition of a suffix or prefix to an existing word, whereas **compounding** involves the joining together of two or more words to form a new word (eg *black* + *bird* → *blackbird*).

Derivation should also be distinguished from **inflection**, which, like derivation, involves the addition of a suffix to a word, but which results not in a new word but in another form of the same word: compare *walking* and *walked*, which are inflections of the verb *to walk* (*I walk, I was walking, I walked*), and *walker*, which is a derivative of *walk* and which can itself take an inflection to form the plural *walkers*.

• In a second sense, **derivation** is the process by which a word develops from a word in a foreign language or from a word in an earlier stage of the same language. Thus we can say that modern English *rain* is derived from Old English *regn*, and that modern English *rail* is derived from Old French *reille*, which is itself a derivative of Latin *regula*.

**descriptive adjective** see ADJECTIVE.

## determiner

**Determiner** is one of the new grammatical terms brought in to replace or supplement the traditional ones where they have been found to be not totally adequate. It is now used in many dictionaries. Determiners are words which precede nouns (and also precede any adjectives which precede the nouns).

Among the determiners in English are *a*, *the*, *some*, *every*, *this*, *no*: *the black car* □ *a big, red bus* □ *some bread* □ *no milk* □ *every blue car* □ *this little boy.*

In traditional grammar, the determiners are classified as **limiting adjectives** (see ADJECTIVE).

## diacritic

A **diacritic** is a mark put above or below (or, in some languages, through) a letter to indicate that it is to be pronounced in a particular way. Examples of diacritics are the **accents** written or printed above vowels in French, Spanish and Italian (eg *bête noire*, *cliché*, *olé*), the French **cedilla** (as in *garçon*), the Spanish **tilde** (as in *mañana*), and the **diaeresis** (as in *naïve*).

## diaeresis see DIACRITIC.

## dialect

A **dialect** is a particular form of a language used by a particular group of people in a region or social class, and that is distinguished from other forms of the same language by its vocabulary and grammar (unlike **accents** which involve differences in pronunciation only).

Dialects are often contrasted to the standard form of a language (eg Scottish English as opposed to Standard British English, 'the Queen's English') but in fact the standard form is itself just one dialect of the language, the dialect that has acquired a certain prestige and which is generally used in the more formal media, etc.

The difference between a language and a dialect is often political rather than linguistic: although almost identical in grammar and vocabulary, Danish and Norwegian are considered separate languages because they are spoken in separate countries, whereas the so-called dialects of Chinese are mutually unintelligible and are as different as English, Dutch and German.

## digraph

A **digraph** is a combination of two letters that together represent a single sound. Examples from English are *ph* (as in *graph* and *photo*), *th*, *ee* and *oo* (as in *teeth* and *tooth*), *ch*, *sh*, *ng*, *ea*, *ow* and *ay*.

## diphthong

Two vowel sounds that act as one single sound, forming a single syllable, are called a **diphthong**. Examples of diphthongs in English are the sounds represented by the *y* of *my* and the *ow* of *cow*. If you say these sounds slowly, it is clear that they are made up of a sequence of two sounds, /a/ + /ee/ and /ah/ + /oo/ respectively.

**direct object** see OBJECT.

**direct speech** see INDIRECT SPEECH.

## double negative

A *double negative* is a construction containing two negative words (and sometimes more than two) which together have the force of a single negative:

> *I didn't do nothing.*

Double negatives are not considered correct in Standard English but are common in English dialects, and are standard in many other languages.

## elision

*Elision* is the omission of a vowel or a syllable in speech, eg in *he's* (for *he is*) and *she'll* (for *she will*).

See also CONTRACTION under ABBREVIATION.

## ellipsis

*Ellipsis* is the omission from a sentence of words which are needed to make the meaning complete but which the reader or listener can supply from the context. One kind of ellipsis involves the omission of elements of clauses which repeat some element of a previous clause, such as the bracketed phrases in *I'm going to Glasgow tomorrow,* [I'm going to] *Dundee the next day, and* [I'm going to] *Aberdeen the day after that.*

Some kinds of ellipsis, involving the omission of elements of the sentence which are not repeats of some element already stated are common and acceptable in colloquial speech, eg *Pity you can't come* for *It's a pity you can't come.* Still other forms of ellipsis are typical of newspaper headlines and notices: *MP snubs local council shock.*

## etymology

The *etymology* of a word is the statement of its origin and derivation (see the examples at DERIVATION, part 2. Etymologies are often included in dictionary entries.

## exclamation see INTERJECTION.

## feminine see GENDER.

## finite

Finite verbs are verbs that agree with their subject (see AGREEMENT), ie they are verbs in which the form of the verb is determined by its subject:

*He writes short stories.*
*They both write short stories.*

(They are called 'finite' because they are limited or restricted by their subjects, in that they have to agree with them with regard to **person** (first person *I → write*, third person *he → writes*) and **number** (singular *he → writes*, plural *they → write*).

However, in some cases, the form of the verb is not determined by a subject:

*He doesn't write poetry.*
*She wants to write poetry.*
*He started writing in his early twenties.*
*He was writing a letter.*
*He has written several short stories.*
*Writing poetry is a waste of time.*

In these examples, the forms of the verb *write* (*write, writing, written*) are not determined by agreement with a subject, but by the grammatical rules about what form of verb must follow another verb or, as in the last example, what form of a verb can function as a noun. Verb-forms that are not determined by agreement with a subject are called **non-finite** or sometimes **infinite**. The non-finite parts of a verb are the **infinitive** (*write* in the first two examples), the **participles** (*writing* and *written* in the next three examples), and the **verbal noun** or **gerund** (*writing* in the last example).

## future tense

According to traditional grammar, the future tense in English is formed with *will* or *shall* plus an infinitive: *he will leave □ we shall leave.*

In many modern grammars of English, it is argued that this construction is not strictly speaking a tense at all and that there is no future tense in English (although there are, of course, various ways of referring to future events, actions, etc, of which the *shall/will* construction is one).

• The **future perfect tense** is formed with *shall/will* plus *have* and a past participle:

*By the time she arrives, I will have been here for six hours.*

See also TENSE.

## gender

**Gender** exists in a language when nouns and pronouns are grouped into two or more classes according to their grammatical behaviour, such as imposing particular forms on adjectives that agree with them. There are, for example, two genders in French nouns, which can be exemplified by *le petit livre* ('the little book') and *la petite table* ('the little table'), and three genders in German, as can be seen from *der Bleistift* ('the pencil'), *die Tinte* ('the ink') and *das Buch* ('the book').

Notice that the grouping of nouns in this way is largely independent of sex, as can be seen from the above examples: all five nouns would be classified as 'things', but are split between two genders in French and three in German.

> ◪ Gender is not <u>completely</u> independent of sex. Most nouns referring to males are found in the '*le*' gender in French (eg *le garçon* 'the boy', *le vieillard* 'the old man') and in the '*der*' gender in German (eg *der Knabe* 'the boy', *der Mann* 'the man'), and most nouns referring to females are in the '*la*' gender in French (eg *la femme* 'the woman', *la fille* 'the girl') and the '*die*' gender in German (eg *die Tochter* 'the daughter', *die Mutter* 'the mother'). For this reason, the '*le*' gender in French and the '*der*' gender in German are referred to as the **masculine** gender, and the '*la*' gender in French and the '*die*' gender in German as the **feminine** gender.
>
> The third gender in German is referred to as **neuter** which means 'neither masculine nor feminine' (*neuter* means 'neither' in Latin), but note that in German some nouns that refer to people (eg *Mädchen* 'girl' and *Weib* 'woman') are in this 'neuter' gender, which again shows that sex and grammatical gender are largely unconnected.

There is no grammatical gender in English nouns. What are referred to traditionally as 'masculine nouns' eg *man*, *boy*), 'feminine nouns' (eg *woman*, *girl*) and 'neuter nouns' (eg *table*, *book*) are simply nouns which, classified on the basis of their sex, refer to males, females and things respectively (that is, they are classified according to their meaning, not according to their grammatical behaviour).

## genitive see CASE.

## gerund

A **gerund** is a noun ending in *-ing*, derived from a verb and, like a verb, describing an action, activity, etc:

> <u>Leaving</u> was a mistake.
> <u>Seeing</u> is <u>believing</u>.

> She cannot see an institution without <u>hitting</u> it with her handbag.
> — Julian Critchley, on Margaret Thatcher

Grammatically, a gerund behaves both like an ordinary verb and like a noun (and is therefore sometimes known as a **verbal noun**):

i) Like other forms of verbs, a gerund can govern an object and may be qualified by an adverb:

> <u>Leaving her</u> was a mistake.
> <u>Singing tunelessly</u> at the top of his voice is one of his most irritating habits.

ii) As a noun, a gerund may be the subject or object of a verb:

> <u>Running</u> gives me a stitch.

*I don't like <u>dancing</u>.*

it may be qualified by an adjective or a possessive:

<u>*Loud, tuneless singing*</u> *rent the air.*
*<u>His leaving</u> so abruptly was a mistake.*

or it may be the object of a preposition:

*<u>By leaving</u> her so suddenly, he finally showed his true feelings.*
*He is keen <u>on hunting</u>.*

• A gerund may behave like an adjective in compound nouns, describing, for example, what someone does or what something is used for:

*a hunting-horn* (= 'a horn used in hunting')
*a dining-room* (= 'a room for dining in')
*a singing-teacher* (= 'a person who teaches singing')

---

⚠ Gerunds should not be confused with present participles. Although identical in form, they are grammatically quite different. A participle never functions as a noun, only as a verb. Compare:

*<u>Leaving</u> was a mistake.* (gerund)
*We are <u>leaving</u> tomorrow.* (participle)

*He is keen on <u>hunting</u>.* (gerund)
*He was <u>hunting</u> for his keys.* (participle)

Like a gerund, a participle may serve as an adjective, but differs from a gerund-adjective in that it describes what the following noun is <u>doing</u> rather than what it is used for:

*a <u>hunting</u> lion stalking its prey* (participle; = 'a lion which is hunting')
*a <u>hunting</u>-dog* (gerund; = 'a dog used in hunting')

---

## govern

A verb or preposition is said to **govern** a noun or pronoun in two different senses of the word 'govern':

i) Firstly, it can be said that any verb or preposition which has an object **governs** that object: in *I saw you, saw* governs *you,* and in *I came with you, with* governs *you.*

ii) Secondly, a verb or preposition can be said to **govern** a particular <u>case</u> of a noun or pronoun, ie to require the object noun or pronoun to be in a particular case (see CASE). Only pronouns have more than one case in English (eg *I/me, we/us,* etc). Verbs and prepositions require pronoun objects to be in the *objective* case:

✓ *I saw <u>him</u>.*
✓ *She came with <u>us</u>.*

✗　*I saw <u>he</u>.*
✗　*She came with <u>we</u>.*

and so can be said to govern the objective case.

## grammatical word see WORD.

## grave accent see ACCENT.

## group possessive

*Group possessive* is the name given to the construction formed when the posessive element *-s* is attached not to a noun but to a whole noun phrase: <u>*the man we were talking to*</u>*'s car*.

## hard

The letters *c* and *g* are said to be **hard** when they are pronounced with the sounds /k/, as in *kick*, and /g/, as in *get*, respectively. The opposite of hard in this sense is **soft**.

## homonym, homograph, homophone

*Homonyms* are words that are identical in spelling and pronunciation but which have different meanings, eg *light* (= 'not heavy') and *light* (= 'not dark'), *mean* (= 'selfish, unkind') and *mean* (= 'to intend').

*Homographs* are words that are spelt the same but pronounced differently, eg the metal *lead* and a dog's *lead*, or a *tear* in a dress and a *tear* in someone's eye.

And *homophones* are words that are pronounced the same but written differently, eg *brooch* and *broach*, *bred* and *bread*.

## hypercorrection

---

'Whom are you?' he said, for he had been to night school.

— George Ade

---

*Hypercorrection* occurs when someone, in a effort to speak correctly, mistakenly applies a rule of pronunciation or grammar where it does not correctly apply. This may happen, for example, when someone is learning a language, or when a person who speaks a non-standard dialect of a language or who speaks with a non-standard accent attempts to produce the standard form of the language.

In the above facetious example, the speaker, attempting to avoid using *who* where *whom* is correct in Standard English, has used *whom* where *who* is quite correct, and has thus produced a hypercorrect form.

## idiom

An *idiom* is a compound word or a phrase whose meaning is not deducible from the meaning of the words of which it is composed, eg *to go at something* <u>*hammer and tongs*</u> □ *to* <u>*kick the bucket*</u> □ *to* <u>*put up with*</u> *someone*.

## imperative

An *imperative* is the form of a verb used in commands:

> <u>*Come*</u> *here!*
> <u>*Leave*</u> *that alone!*

Such a verb can be said to be in the *imperative mood* (see MOOD).

## indefinite adjective see LIMITING ADJECTIVE under ADJECTIVE.

## indefinite article

The word *a* or *an*.

## indefinite pronoun see PRONOUN.

## indicative

The *indicative* mood of a verb (see MOOD) is used to make statements or ask questions:

> *He'* <u>*ll be*</u> *here tomorrow.*
> <u>*Is*</u> *that your car?*

## indirect object see OBJECT.

## indirect speech

The form of speech as it is reported, as opposed to *direct speech*, which is the form of words actually spoken or written:

> *'* <u>*What are you doing?*</u> *' she asked.* (direct speech)
> *She asked* <u>*what he was doing*</u>*.* (indirect speech)

Indirect speech is also called *reported speech*.

## infinite see FINITE.

## infinitive

*Infinitive* is the name given to the form of a verb that is used, for example, after words such as *can, will, might* or *should*:

> *I will* <u>*come*</u> *tomorrow.*

> *He can't leave now.*
> *Let her speak.*

In other constructions, the infinitive may be preceded by *to*:

> *It's unnecessary for me to tell you.*
> *I want to do what is right.*
> *To leave now would be foolish.*

but does occur without a preceding *to*:

> *She watched him disappear into the crowd.*

Although in Old English, the *to* was simply a preposition (as it is in modern English) which just happened to precede the infinitive in certain grammatical constructions, it gradually came to be so closely attached to the following infinitive as to be felt to be part of it, so we can speak, for example, of '*to tell*' as being the infinitive of the verb *tell*. We can, in fact, call both forms the infinitive, the infinitive without *to* being known as the ***bare infinitive***, and the infinitive preceded by *to* the ***'to'-infinitive***. The bare infinitive is the form under which a word is listed in a dictionary, but the *to*-infinitive is often used to translate infinitives from foreign languages:

> '*Dormir*' *is French for* '*to sleep*'.

Infinitives can be subclassified as either ***simple infinitives***, in which the verb-form is a single word (eg *I want to go* □ *She can sing*) or ***complex infinitives***, in which the verb consists of more than one word (eg *She must have left by now* □ *They were thought to have been seen the day before*).

---

 **Infinitives and infinity**
Infinitives are 'infinite' in a special grammatical sense: they are one of the 'non-finite' parts of a verb, in that they do not have a subject with which they must agree in person or number (see FINITE).

---

## inflection

***Inflection*** is the process of adding a suffix to a word or changing the form of a word in order to indicate grammatical categories such as *number, person, tense* and *case*. For example, in order to show the past tense, English verbs may either add the suffix *-ed* (*walk* → *walked, collect* → *collected*) or alter the form of the verb (*write* → *wrote, swim* → *swam*). Similarly, plural nouns are formed from the singular either by the addition of an affix (*book* → *books, box* → *boxes*) or by changing the form of the noun (*man* → *men, foot* → *feet*). The forms created in this way can be called ***inflections*** of the base word (the 'base word' being the form in which the word would be listed in a dictionary, for example).

Inflection should be distinguished from the similar process of ***derivation***. In derivation, new words are created, while inflection creates different forms of the same word: *sings*, *singing*, *sang* and *sung* are all forms ('inflections') of the word '*sing*', whereas *singer* is a different word altogether, formed (or 'derived') from *sing* by the addition of the suffix *-er* and able itself to be inflected to form a plural, *singers*.

**initialism** see ABBREVIATION.

**intensifier** see ADVERB.

## interjection

An *interjection* is a word or phrase, such as *Ouch!*, *Yippee!*, *Oh!*, *Good heavens!* or *Oh dear!*, which expresses strong emotion such as surprise or pain or pleasure, but has otherwise no meaning (*Good heavens!* expresses surprise, but is not intended to convey any information about heaven). It is this lack of information content that distinguishes interjections from **exclamations** such as *What a pity!* or *What a nuisance!*

Some interjections are sounds rather than words, as for example the sounds represented by *Mmhmm* (indicating agreement), *Tsk-tsk!* (indicating disapproval) or *Phew!* (indicating relief).

## interrogative

*Interrogative* means 'asking a question'. An interrogative sentence is therefore one which asks a question (eg *Why are you here?* □ *Where are you going?* □ *Are you coming too?*). Many interrogative sentences contain interrogative words such as *why?*, *which?* and *where?* We can divide these interrogative words into three types:

    i)    *interrogative pronouns*, such as <u>Who</u>'s that? □ <u>Which</u> of the two do you prefer?

    ii)    *interrogative adjectives*, such as <u>What</u> rubbish has he sent us this time? □ <u>Which</u> picture do you prefer?

    iii)    *interrogative adverbs*, such as <u>Where</u> is it? □ <u>Why</u> did you come at all? □ <u>When</u> did you arrive?

## intransitive

A verb is said to be *intransitive* when it has no object:

> *I <u>came</u> as soon as I could.*
> *He <u>was lying</u> on the settee.*
> *She <u>fell</u> to the ground.*
> *We <u>drank</u> all night.*
> *Bombs <u>kill</u>.*

Some grammarians make a finer distinction, limiting the term ***intransitive*** to verbs which <u>never</u> take an object (eg *come, lie, fall*) and separating from these the verbs (such as *drink* and *kill*) which <u>could</u> be followed by an object (eg *We <u>drank beer</u> all night* □ *Bombs <u>kill people</u>*) but which in particular instances appear in sentences without an object (as in the examples above). Such instances of transitive verbs (ie, verbs that could take an object) without an expressed object are said to be ***absolute*** uses of the verbs.

## irregular

A word is said to be ***irregular*** if it does not obey the general rules of a language. For example, plurals are generally formed in English by adding *-s* to the singular form of the noun (eg *cat* → *cats*; *train* → *trains*). Plurals formed in other ways, such as with a change of vowel, are irregular, eg *man* → *men* and *mouse* → *mice*. Similarly, since the normal way of forming the past tense of a verb in English is by adding *-ed* to the base form, past tenses such as *ran*, *brought* and *wrote* are irregular.

## lexeme see WORD.

## lexical verb see VERB.

## linking verb see VERB.

## living see PRODUCTIVE.

## loan word

A ***loan word*** is a word taken into a language from another language. Examples of loan words in English are *blitzkrieg* (from German), *nom de plume* and *blasé* (from French), and *mañana* (from Spanish).

A ***loan translation*** is a word or phrase which consists of elements which are literal translations of the corresponding elements in a word or phrase in another language, such as *superman* for German *Übermensch*.

## main clause see CLAUSE.

## masculine see GENDER.

## mass noun see NOUN.

## modal auxiliary

Any of the words such as *can, could, may, might, would, should*. For more details see AUXILIARY VERB.

## modifier

A *modifier* is a word or phrase that precedes a noun in a noun phrase and gives some information about it. Adjectives and attributive nouns are modifiers: *a green bus* □ *a brick wall*.

Modifiers are also known as *qualifiers*.

## modify

An adverb is said in traditional grammar to *modify* the verb, adjective, adverb, etc it refers to, by specifying 'to what extent', 'in what way', etc. Thus, in *He sings well*, *well* can be said to modify the verb *sings* in that it gives information about how he sings; and in *He runs very quickly*, the adverb *very* can be said to modify the adverb *quickly* in that it gives information about how quickly he runs.

 Some grammarians make a distinction in terminology between *modify* and *qualify*, maintaining that adjectives 'qualify' while adverbs 'modify'; others use 'qualify' and 'modify' of both adjectives and adverbs. It is this latter, wider sense of 'modify' that is reflected in the term *modifier* as defined in the entry above.

## mood

*Mood* is one of the categories by which verbs are described and classified. A verb can be said to be in one mood or another according to what it indicates of the attitude of the speaker or writer to the action or state described by the verb (the word *mood* comes from Latin *modus*, meaning 'way' or 'manner'), eg whether the verb is being used in a statement, as a command or to express a doubt or possibility. There are three moods of the verb in English: the *indicative*, the *imperative* and the *subjunctive*.

   i)   The *indicative* mood is used to express matters of fact in statements, and also to ask about matters of fact in questions:

   *He eats a lot.*
   *Does he eat a lot?*

   ii)  The *imperative* mood is used to express commands:

   *Leave that alone!*

   iii) The *subjunctive* mood is used to express doubts, wishes, etc:

   *if that be the case* (compare the equivalent indicative form *if that is the case*)
   *God save the Queen.*

## negative

- A **negative** is a word such as *no, not, never, nowhere* and *nobody*.

- A **negative sentence** is a sentence containing any of these words: *I didn't do it* □ *He never came.*

See also DOUBLE NEGATIVE.

## neuter see GENDER.

## nominal

**Nominal** is the adjective relating to nouns: a *nominal compound*, for example, is a compound noun.

## non-defining see RESTRICTIVE.

## non-finite

**Non-finite** verbs are those verbs that are not directly linked to a subject, eg the **infinitive**, the **participles** and the **gerund**. For more discussion on finite and non-finite verbs, see FINITE.

## non-restrictive see RESTRICTIVE.

## non-standard see STANDARD ENGLISH.

## noun

A **noun** may be defined as a word used as the name of a person, animal, place, thing, quality or action. (The word 'noun' itself comes, via French, from Latin *nomen* 'a name').

Nouns can be classified into various types:

   i)   An **abstract noun** is a noun which names something that has no physical form or existence, ie something that exists only as a mental concept, a state or quality, or an action. Examples of abstract nouns are *anger, courage, courtesy, beauty, mercy, health, justice, honour, dancing.*

---

The most frequent abstract-noun suffix is *-ness* which is added freely to adjectives (*sadness, helpfulness, boyishness, cold-bloodedness, self-assertiveness*) and to phrases (*up-to-dateness, state-of-the-artness*), often with great freedom for eg comic effect:

> *The aunts raised their eyebrows with a good deal of To-what-are-we-indebted-for-the-honour-of-this-visitness.*
>
> — P G Wodehouse

---

Nouns that are not abstract are **concrete** nouns. Concrete nouns are the names of things which have a physical form and existence, such as *bird*, *house*, *London*, *Peter*.

 Some nouns may be both abstract and concrete: for example, *entrance* is an abstract noun in *She made a dramatic entrance*, but is a concrete noun in *She was standing near the entrance to the building*.

ii)   A **proper noun** is one which names an individual person, place, etc, eg *George*, *Paris*, *Australia*, *the Himalayas*. All other nouns are **common nouns**.

Proper nouns are generally spelt with an initial capital letter in English.

iii)   **Count nouns** are nouns which may have a plural form, ie nouns that denote things of which there may be more than one. Examples of count nouns are *woman*, *book*, *cat*, *cake* and *train*. **Mass nouns**, on the other hand, are only found in the singular: *furniture*, for example, never appears in the plural in Standard English, nor does *information*.

Count nouns can co-occur with numbers (*one car*, *two cars*, *fifty cars*), mass nouns with words indicating quantity such as *some* (*some furniture*, *some information*, but not *two furnitures*).

 Some words function as both count nouns and mass nouns:

>*a cake* (count noun) or *some cake* (mass noun)
>*some wine* (mass noun) but *the wines of France* (count noun)
>
>*Beauty is truth, truth beauty.* (mass nouns)
>*We hold these truths to be self-evident, . . .* (count noun)

iv)   **Collective nouns** are singular nouns which denote groups consisting of a number of individuals acting together, eg *committee*, *orchestra*, *team*, or else nouns which denote groups of items, such as *luggage* and *furniture*.

## noun clause

A **noun clause** is a clause which functions grammatically in the same way as a noun, eg as the subject of a verb or the object of a preposition:

>*What you think about it is completely irrelevant.*
>*Thanks to how you behaved the last time, you haven't been invited.*

## noun phrase

A **noun phrase** is a phrase comprising a noun plus any words grammatically dependent on it, such as adjectives and articles, eg *a girl*, *a good girl*, *a very good girl*.

## number

- *Number* is the technical term used to describe whether a noun, pronoun or verb refers to one individual (in which case it is *singular*) or to more than one (in which case it is *plural*).

 Note that number is a matter of grammar, not meaning: although a *team* or a *committee* generally comprises several people, they are both singular nouns (which of course can be pluralized: *teams, committees*).

- In another sense, familiar from everyday language, a *number* is a word that indicates how many individuals or items you are referring to (eg *two, fourteen, twenty*) or the order in which they occur (eg *first, second, thirtieth*). The first type of number is called a *cardinal number*, the second type an *ordinal number*.

Another word for number in this sense is *numeral*. See also LIMITING ADJECTIVE at ADJECTIVE.

 *Ord*inal numbers state the *order* in which things stand or occur.

## object

i) The *object* of a verb is the word or phrase denoting whoever or whatever is receiving the action of the verb (as against the *subject*, which performs the action):

> *The boy read the book.*
> *You dropped something.*
> *Keep the change.*

In some sentences, there are two objects, a *direct object* and an *indirect object*. In *He gave me a book*, *the book* is the *direct object* (ie, what is given) and *me* is the *indirect object* (ie, the person to whom the book is given). Other examples of indirect objects are:

> *He gave the dog a bone.*
> *He gave the robot a recharge.*
> *He gave the door a lick of paint.*

 An indirect object can often be replaced by a phrase beginning with *to* or *for*:
> *He gave his mother a present.* → *He gave a present to his mother.*
> *He bought his mother some flowers.* → *He bought some flowers for his mother.*

ii) *Object* is also used of the word or phrase governed by a preposition:

> *beside the river*     *under my pillow*     *near London*

## objective

*Objective* is the name sometimes given to the case English pronouns are in when they are the object of a verb or a preposition, eg *I saw <u>him</u>* □ *She saw <u>me</u>* □ *They came with <u>her</u>, or rather she came with <u>them</u>*. See CASE.

## orthographic word see WORD.

## parsing

*Parsing* is the grammatical description of the words in a sentence, stating what part of speech (in Latin, *pars orationis*, whence 'parsing') the word belongs to and describing certain other features of it (eg, for a pronoun, stating whether it is singular or plural; masculine, feminine or neuter; first person, second person or third person; and so on).

Analysis (see ANALYSIS) and parsing together give a complete statement of the grammatical structure of a construction.

## participle

*Participle* is the name given to certain forms of verbs. There are two types of participle in English:

   i)   *present participles* end in *-ing*: *coming, running, singing, laughing*;

   ii)  *past participles* generally end in *-ed*, *-t* or *-en*: *walked, cried, played, slept, dreamt, taught, broken, written, eaten*; some are formed by changing the vowel of the present tense of the verb rather than by adding an ending: *begun, sung, dug, sat, found, won*.

- The main use of the participles in English is in the formation of compound tenses with the verbs *to be* and *to have*:

  *Are you <u>coming</u> tonight?*
  *She'll be <u>arriving</u> on Friday.*
  *I was <u>getting</u> worried.*

  *We had <u>arrived</u> too late.*
  *His apology was <u>received</u> in stony silence.*
  *The Conservatives were <u>re-elected</u>, but with a reduced majority.*

Both present and past participles can occur without *to be* and *to have*:

  *<u>Laughing</u> uncontrollably, he walked off towards the beach.*
  *<u>Said</u> like that, it sounds rather rude.*

- Participles not only function as verbs, but also take on some of the functions of adjectives. (It is for this reason that participles are so called: they 'participate' in the grammatical behaviour of both verbs and adjectives.) The following are examples of present and past participles used as adjectives:

*the spoken word*
*frozen peas*
*The little boy was very frightened of dogs.*
*The au pair's stories were very amusing.*

---

 A present participle should not be confused with a gerund, although they are the same in form (see GERUND). Compare:

> *Leaving was a mistake* (gerund) and *We are leaving tomorrow* (participle)
> *He is keen on hunting* (gerund) and *He was hunting for his keys* (participle).

A participle acting as an adjective describes what the following noun <u>is doing</u>, whereas a gerund describes what it <u>generally does or is used for</u>:

> *a hunting lion* (participle; = 'a lion which is hunting')
> *a hunting-knife* (gerund; = 'a knife used in hunting')

---

For words such as *barring* and *regarding*, see PREPOSITION.

## particle

*Particle* is the name sometimes applied collectively to prepositions, conjunctions, interjections and adverbs.

## part of speech

Words that make up sentences can be grouped into different classes according to their function or role. For example: words such as *dog, car, book, sister, Thomas, Garfield* and *Liverpool* name things or people or places; words such as *walk, run, sing, think* and *hunt* describe actions; words like *big, black* and *angry* describe people and things; words like *sadly, angrily* and *furiously* describe how actions are performed; words like *for, with, to, by* and *beside* indicate relationships between things; and so on. In the simple sentence *The car is blue*, a number (a very large number) of words could be substituted for *car*, eg *book, sky, sea, coat, cup, door, carpet*, and so on. Similarly, *green, red, old, big, wet*, etc for *blue*; *a* or *her* for *the*; and *seems, looks, became*, etc for *is*. All the words that have the same function in a sentence, which could be substituted for one another and still make grammatically correct sentences, belong to the same word-class or *part of speech*.

Traditionally, English is said to have eight, or sometimes nine, parts of speech:

> **noun** (eg *book, car, bread*)
> **verb** (eg *walk, runs, sang*)
> **adjective** (eg *green, big, sad*)
> **adverb** (eg *quickly, soon, very*)
> **pronoun** (eg *I, us, you*)
> **preposition** (eg *in, from, with*)
> **conjunction** (eg *although, because, while*)

*interjection* (eg *ouch, oh, alas*)

and sometimes *article* (ie *the* and *a*, which are sometimes included in the adjectives, sometimes treated as a separate part of speech).

Some of these parts of speech have subcategories: *nouns*, for example, can be subclassified as *mass nouns* and *count nouns*; *verbs* as *lexical verbs, auxiliary verbs* and *linking verbs* (see NOUN and VERB).

In some modern grammars and dictionaries of English, several of the traditional parts of speech have been replaced or supplemented by others such as *determiner, intensifier* and *sentence substitute* (see DETERMINER and ADVERB).

 Many words belong to more than one part of speech. For example, *can* is a noun in *a can of worms*, an auxiliary verb in *I can come*, and a lexical verb in *They can tomatoes*. Similarly, *which* is a pronoun in *Which do you like best?* and an adjective in *Which book do you like best?*

## passive

The meaning of *passive* is most easily explained by comparison with its opposite, *active*. A verb is said to be in the active voice ('voice' is simply the technical word for that aspect of the grammar of verbs described by the terms 'active' and 'passive') when the subject of the verb performs the action described by the verb:

*The boy stroked the cat.*

The passive equivalent of the above sentence is *The cat was stroked by the boy*.

Passive constructions are generally formed in English with some part of the verb *to be* plus a past participle:

*You were seen outside the pub.*
*Was anyone hurt in the accident?*

Passives may also be formed with the verb *get*:

*If you do that, you'll get hurt.*

Passives formed with *to get* are generally more informal than those formed with *to be*: compare *We were beaten three – nil last week* and *We got beaten three – nil last week.*

 'Activeness' and 'passiveness' depend solely on the grammatical relationship between the subject and the verb of the sentence, and not on who performs the action implied in the event described: *He received a present from his mother* is an active sentence, and *He was given a present by his mother* is a passive sentence, although in both cases, as far as the meaning of the sentences is concerned, 'he' is receiving something and 'his mother' is giving it.

## past tense

The **past tense** (sometimes called the **simple past**) is the tense of the English verb that generally refers to events in the past, eg *came, went, saw*, etc.

The simple past tense is not the only way of referring to the past in English, however. Compare:

> *He <u>went</u> to London.*
> *He <u>has gone</u> to London.*
> *He <u>did go</u> to London.*
> *He <u>was going</u> to London.*

(In a more general sense, all these can be referred to as past tenses.) Nor does the simple past tense always refer to events in the past:

> *If only I <u>knew</u> what was going on* expresses a wish;
> *It would be a disaster if he <u>turned</u> up* expresses a possible event in the future.

## perfect tense

A **perfect tense** is a compound tense formed from the auxiliary verb *to have* and a past participle:

> *He <u>has arrived</u>.* (present perfect)
> *They <u>had</u> already <u>left</u>.* (past perfect)
> *They <u>will have left</u> by now.* (future perfect)

See also ASPECT.

## person

*Person* is a grammatical feature of verbs, personal pronouns, and possessive adjectives and pronouns.

The **first-person** personal pronouns are *I* and *we*, the **second-person** pronouns are *you* and the archaic *thou*, and the **third-person** pronouns are *he, she, it* and *they*. Similarly, *my* and *mine* are in the first person, *your, yours, thy* and *thine* the second person, and *his, her, hers, theirs*, etc the third person.

Verbs are in the same person as the words with which they agree: *come* is in the first person in *I come* and *we come*, in the second person in *you come* (and *thou comest*), and in the third person in *they come; comes* is in the third person in *she/he/it comes* and in *John comes*.

## personal pronoun

A **personal pronoun** is a pronoun that stands for or refers to a person or thing, eg *I, me, you*, etc.

See also PRONOUN.

## phonological word see WORD.

## phrasal verb

A *phrasal verb* is a phrase consisting of a verb followed by an adverb (such as *out, in, away*), a preposition (such as *for* or *of* ) or both:

> *She has just <u>come in</u>.*
> *Let's <u>talk</u> it <u>over</u> first.*
> *I don't think this <u>calls for</u> any urgent action on our part.*
> *I don't know how she <u>puts up with</u> it.*

 Some grammarians limit the term *phrasal verb* to those phrases comprising a verb and an adverb (eg *come in, talk over*), calling those which consist of a verb and a preposition (like *call for*) *prepositional verbs* and those with both an adverb and a preposition (like *put up with*) *phrasal-prepositional verbs*.

In some cases the meaning of the phrasal verb is deducible from the meanings of its parts (*come in = come + in*), but in others it is not (*put up with = 'tolerate'*, not deducible from the meanings of *put + up + with*). Some grammarians limit the term *phrasal verb* to this second category, treating the '*come in*' type as simply a sequence of a verb plus an adverb.

## phrase

A *phrase* is a group of words that functions as a unit of meaning in a sentence:

> *<u>More whales</u> / <u>had appeared</u> / <u>on the port side</u>.*
> *<u>Let's have</u> / <u>a midnight swim</u>.*

 The exact definition of a phrase depends to some extent on the definition of a clause, since any group of words forming a grammatical unit in a sentence must be one or the other, and certain groups of words that are treated as clauses in some grammars are dealt with as phrases in others:

i) If a clause is defined, as it is in traditional grammar, as a word-group containing a subject and a finite verb (see CLAUSE), then a phrase is any word-group that does <u>not</u> include both a subject and a finite verb. The following would be clauses, therefore:

> *<u>If time permits</u>, we will visit the museum tomorrow.*
> *<u>If it is possible</u>, come sometime next week.*

while the following would be phrases:

> *<u>Time permitting</u>, we will visit the museum tomorrow.* (the verb is not finite)
> *<u>While running for the bus</u>, John tripped and fell.* (the subject is not expressed)
> *<u>If possible</u>, come sometime next week.* (there is no subject or verb)

ii)  If a clause is given a rather wider definition, as in many modern English grammars, and in this book (see CLAUSE), and is taken to include word-groups with no subject or with no finite verb or with neither of these (as in the last three examples above), then the defining feature of a clause must be that it contains an actual or implied subject–verb structure, and a phrase is any group of words with no subject–verb structure, actual or implied.

- Phrases can be classified into a number of different types:

i)  A **noun phrase** consists of a noun plus any other words directly dependent on it, which together function in a sentence as a single unit:

*A big, black car pulled up outside his mother's house.*
*Some people are never satisfied.*

ii)  A **verb phrase** consists of all the verbs and parts of verbs that together function as a unit in a sentence:

*He must have left before us.*

iii)  An **adjectival phrase** consists of an adjective and any adverbs that qualify it:

*a very big lorry.*

iv)  An **adverbial phrase** consists of a 'main' adverb plus any other adverbs that qualify it:

*She ran very quickly but not quickly enough.*

v)  A **prepositional phrase** is one that is introduced by a preposition:

*She ran into the garden.*

## pluperfect tense

The **pluperfect tense** is formed from the past tense of the auxiliary *to have* plus a past participle: *he had gone □ they had been crying.*

## plural

- A noun is **plural** if it is in a form which indicates that it refers to more than one individual or item: *dogs, boxes, women, mice.*

 Note that plurality is a matter of grammar, not meaning: although a *team* or a *committee* comprises two or more people, they are both singular nouns.

• A plural verb is one which agrees with a plural noun. In English, which has lost all its verb endings except the -*s* of the third person singular of the present tense (*walks*, *swims*) and the archaic verb-ending that goes with the pronoun *thou* (*goest*, *dost*), there is no verb-form that specifically indicates a plural verb.

## positive

• The *positive* form of an adjective or adverb is the basic form, as opposed to the comparative and superlative forms. See COMPARISON OF ADJECTIVES AND ADVERBS.

• A *positive* statement is an affirmative statement, ie one that states that something is so.

## possessive

A noun is said to be *possessive* when it is in a form which indicates that it is the possessor of something else. Nouns in English have no specific possessive form, as possession is shown by *of* and *'s* (or, in the case of most plural nouns, by *'* alone):

> *the door of the house*
> *the boy's dog*
> *the boys' dogs*
> *the man we saw yesterday's picture* (an example of a GROUP POSSESSIVE)

In some languages, such as Latin and Greek, there are specific forms that nouns and pronouns take to indicate that they are possessive. These are usually called the *genitive* case (see CASE). For example, in the Latin phrase *anno Domini*, commonly used in dates in English in the abbreviated form *AD*, and which means 'in the year of our Lord', *Domini* is the genitive case of the Latin noun *dominus*, meaning 'lord'.

There are, however, in English *possessive adjectives* (*my*, *your*, *her*, *their*, etc) and *possessive pronouns* (*mine*, *yours*, *hers*, *theirs*, etc).

 Notice that 'possessive' constructions are used in English to denote relationships other than possession:

> *a month's leave*     *a moment's thought*     *a summer's day*

## post-positive

An adjective is in *post-positive* position when it immediately follows the noun to which it refers:

> *president elect*
> *a love of France and all things French*

## predicate

The *predicate* is the part of a sentence that gives information about the subject of the sentence, and which includes a verb which agrees with the subject with regard to person, number, etc:

> Hot air *rises*.
> Jack and Jill *went up the hill*.
> John *arrived early the next morning*.
> Pompeii *is now no more than an interesting archaeological site*.

## predicative

A *predicative adjective* is one which stands in the predicate of a sentence, ie after a verb such as *to be*:

> Grass is *green*.
> That looks *good*.

For further details, see ADJECTIVE.

## prefix

A *prefix* is a word-forming element that is added to the beginning of a word-root to form a word or to the beginning of a word to form another word:

> *con-* in *conflagration*     *un-* in *unimportant*     *re-* in *reappear*

## preposition

A *preposition* is a linking word that serves to show the relationship between nouns or noun phrases:

> a man *with* a gun     the bank *of* the river     the man *on* the seat over there

or to show the relationship of a noun or noun phrase to other words, such as adjectives and verbs:

> spoke *to* her   went out *into* the garden   absolutely crazy *about* horses   dressed *in* white

and in many idioms:

> *on* the contrary     *in* the meantime     *by* the way

• Some prepositions are closely attached to the verb they occur with, and form a single unit of meaning with it: *put up with*, *get up to*, *plump for*. Such word-groups are called ***phrasal verbs*** (see PHRASAL VERB).

• A number of common prepositions are like participles in form:

> *Barring* accidents, we should be finished by this time tomorrow.
> I am writing to you *regarding* your recent grant application.

• Some prepositions are not single words but short phrases, such as *along with, by means of, in return for, with regard to, in spite of, instead of, because of*. These are known as ***complex prepositions***.

## prepositional phrase

A *prepositional phrase* is one consisting of a preposition and its object:

> *a day <u>at the seaside</u>*
> *<u>In spite of all my precautions</u>, I've still mislaid the tickets.*

---

◁ Prepositional phrases usually have the same role in sentences as adjectives and adverbs, ie giving information about nouns (*their trip <u>to France</u>* □ *the man <u>in the moon</u>*) like adjectives do, or the action of a verb (*they went <u>to France</u> last year* □ *They went <u>by ferry</u>*) as adverbs do.

In some grammars, phrases of this type are classified as adjective phrases or adverb phrases respectively according to their function in a sentence.

---

## prepositional verb see PHRASAL VERB.

## present tense

The *present tense* of a verb is the tense which refers, among other things, to actions going on or states existing at the present time or in general:

> *She always <u>leaves</u> at five o'clock.*
> *Children usually <u>go</u> to school at the age of five.*
> *Roses <u>are</u> red, violets <u>are</u> blue, sugar <u>is</u> sweet and so <u>are</u> you.*

This form of the verb is usually called the *simple present*. This tense can also be used to refer to the future:

> *My train <u>leaves</u> in half an hour.*

• The *present progressive tense* or *present continuous tense* consists of the *-ing* form of the verb in combination with the auxiliary verb *to be*:

> *I <u>am working</u> on a new idea at the moment.*

## principal clause see CLAUSE.

## productive

A grammatical process is said to be *productive* if it can be freely employed by a speaker of a language to create new forms in that languge. For example, the formation of plural nouns by the addition of *-s* or *-es* is productive, in that if a new noun is created, its plural will generally be formed in this way. On the other hand, pluralization by vowel change (eg *man* → *men, foot* → *feet, mouse* → *mice*) or by the addition of *-en* (*ox* → *oxen*) is not productive: only a few words use these processes, and other words (and any new words) of a similar form use the productive process (*pans, cans, boots, roots, boxes, foxes*).

Similarly, word-forming elements, such as affixes, may be said to be productive if they can be freely used in grammatical processes. For example, the suffix *-ness* is productive in English in that it can be added freely to adjectives and phrases to form nouns, whereas *-th* is not productive in that it forms nouns from only a very small and fixed number of adjectives (*warm* →

*warmth, deep → depth, strong → strength*, etc). Productive elements are also said to be *living*.

## progressive

A *progressive tense* is one which consists of part of the verb *to be* plus a present participle:

> *they <u>are going</u>* (present progressive)
> *we <u>were going</u>* (past progressive)

Progressive tenses are also known as *continuous* tenses.

## pronoun

As the name suggests, in traditional grammar pronouns were considered to be words that were substitutes for nouns. In many cases, this is quite correct. Consider the following example:

> *I've just seen John. <u>He</u> asked me to tell you to wait for <u>him</u>.*

In the second sentence, *he* and *him* clearly refer back to the noun *John*, and could be considered to be substitutes for *John*. (The sentence would be rather bizarre if you were to say *I've just seen John. John asked me to tell you to wait for John.*) In many sentences, however, pronouns do not replace nouns. Sometimes the pronoun replaces a phrase:

> *I was really surprised at <u>his boorish behaviour</u>. In fact, <u>it</u> appalled me.*

And there are pronouns that are clearly not substitutes for anything at all. There are no nouns that the *I* and the *you* in the first example could be said to be replacing — they simply denote the speaker and the person being spoken to. The pronoun *it* in particular often simply fills a slot in the sentence because in English, unlike in some other languages, there cannot be a finite verb in a statement without an accompanying subject, and where there is no subject a dummy one (*it*) has to be inserted:

> *It's raining.*
> *It would be silly to go out in the rain.*

* Pronouns can be classified into a number of different types:

   i) *personal pronouns*: *I, me, you, he, him, she, her, it, we, us, they, them.*

   ii) *possessive pronouns*: *mine, yours, his, hers,* etc.

   iii) *reflexive pronouns*: *myself, herself, themselves,* etc.

   iv) *interrogative pronouns*, as in *<u>Whose</u> is that?* □ *<u>What</u> do you want?* □ *<u>Which</u> is yours?*

   v) *relative pronouns*, as in *That's the man <u>who</u> drives the school bus* □ *I just joined the wires together, <u>which</u> is, I admit, a daft thing to do* □ *He's the fellow <u>that</u> I was talking about.*

and also *whoever, whatever,* etc.

vi) **demonstrative pronouns**, as in *That is just the thing we need* □ *These are the best biscuits I've tasted in a long time.*

vii) **indefinite pronouns**: *somebody, anybody, everybody, some, none,* etc.

viii) **distributive pronouns**: *Each of them will get £1000* □ *neither of them*

ix) **reciprocal pronouns**: *each other, one another.*

## proper noun see NOUN.

## qualifier

*Qualifier* is another name for **modifier**.

## qualify

An adjective is said to **qualify** the noun it gives information about.

## quantifier

*Quantifier* is one of the terms that have been introduced into some modern grammars of English. Quantifiers are pronouns and determiners that indicate quantities, eg *all, every, many, much, no, none* and *some*.

## reflexive pronoun see PRONOUN.

## register

Differences in formality and style of language, such as slang, poetic language, formal language, etc, are differences in **register**.

See also APPROPRIACY.

## regular

A word or construction is said to be **regular** if it conforms to the general rules of a language. For example, the plural nouns *cats, days, trains, biscuits, boxes* are regular, as they are all formed by the general rule of adding *-s* or *-es* to the singular form of the noun, whereas *women, feet, mice, brethren* and so on are *irregular*.

## relative adjective see LIMITING ADJECTIVE under ADJECTIVE.

## relative clause

A **relative clause** is a clause which refers or relates to an antecedent (see ANTECEDENT), and which usually, but not always, begins with a word such as *who, which* or *that*:

*He slid it into the hole which had been drilled for that purpose.*

*The book you want is over there.*
*a man who is at peace with himself.*

## relative pronoun see PRONOUN.

## reported speech see INDIRECT SPEECH.

## restrictive

A *restrictive* relative clause is used to limit or restrict the import of its antecedent. For example, in

*The man we saw yesterday turned out to be the thief*

the relative clause *we saw yesterday* serves to define which man is being referred to. A *non-restrictive* relative clause simply adds information:

*The man, whom we happened to see again yesterday, turned out to be a thief.*

>  Notice the difference in punctuation: a non-restrictive clause is separated off from the rest of the sentence by commas, whereas a restrictive clause is not.

Restrictive and non-restrictive clauses are also called *defining* and *non-defining* clauses.

## root

- A *root* is what remains when all the prefixes and suffixes have been removed from a word. For example, *friend* is the root of *friendly*, *unfriendly* and *unfriendliness*, and *ed-* is the root of *edible*, *inedible* and *inedibility*.

See also BASE and STEM.

- In another sense, the *root* of a word is its source, the word from which it is derived. For example, the root of English *liberate* is Latin *liber* 'free'.

## semi-vowel

A *semi-vowel* is a speech sound that is vowel-like in sound but which functions as a consonant. The two semi-vowels in English are *w* and *y*, as in *will* and *you*.

## sentence

A *sentence* is sometimes defined as the complete expression of a thought. This unfortunately leaves open to question what a 'thought' is and what a 'complete expression' of it might be. A sentence is better defined as a unit of language which can stand alone and which contains at least one clause which has both a subject and a finite verb in it. Sentences in written English generally begin with a capital letter and end with a full stop, a question mark or an exclamation mark:

> *It'll be cooler outside.*
> *If I was as fit as that, I wouldn't waste my time doing press-ups.*
> *I shouldn't cross your bridges before you get to them if I were you!*

## ✦ Sentences and utterances

It is quite normal for people not to address each other in complete sentences; in fact, it would be very unnatural to do so:

> *'Where are you going?' 'I'm going into town.' 'Why are you going into town?'*
> *'I'm going into town to buy some shoes.'*

In ordinary conversation, parts of sentences are omitted if they can be taken as understood:

> *'Where are you going?' 'Into town.' 'Why?' 'To buy some shoes.'*

These part-sentences are called ***utterances*** or ***sentence fragments***. Utterances do not have a subject and a finite verb, although in writing they will, like sentences, begin with a capital letter and end with a full stop, question mark or exclamation mark. Other examples of utterances are exclamations, such as *What a pity!* or *Surely not!*

---

 In some grammatical descriptions of English, what are here called utterances or sentence fragments <u>are</u> considered to be sentences, because they are complete in context and can stand alone although they do not have a full subject–verb structure.

Note also that commands are traditionally considered to be complete sentences even though they do not have the usual subject–verb structure:

> *Go away!*
> *Hang on a minute!*

---

## ✦ Sentence types

Sentences can be classified according to the number and type of clauses they contain.

   i)   Many sentences consist of only a single clause:

> *Jane arrived yesterday.*
> *What time is it?*
> *He's coming back!*

Such sentences are known as ***simple sentences***.

   ii)   If two or more such clauses are joined into a larger unit on an equal footing, they form ***compound sentences***:

*I came, I saw, I conquered.*
*He unpacked; he showered; he dressed for dinner.*
*He arrived, and checked into his hotel.*
*He shut his eyes; however, he did not sleep.*

iii)   Sentences that consist of one main clause and one or more subordinate clauses are known as ***complex sentences***:

*We were delighted/when he told us/that you were coming.*
*When the news broke,/we wanted to know/what the consequences would be.*

iv)   Sentences with more than one main clause and one or more subordinate clauses are called ***compound-complex sentences***:

*He was waiting for us/when we arrived/and came out to greet us/although*
*    it was raining heavily.*

## sentence adverb

A ***sentence adverb*** is a word or phrase that qualifies a whole clause or sentence rather than a particular word in it. Sentence adverbs generally express the attitude of the speaker or writer to what is being said, rather than contributing to the meaning of the statement itself, and therefore usually stand to some extent outside the structure of the clause or sentence, often at the beginning of it. Typical examples are *amazingly, annoyingly, assuredly, certainly, fortunately, frankly, hopefully, obviously, personally, seriously* and *thankfully*:

*Fortunately, all four were wearing parachutes.*
*Thankfully, at weekends Clare felt almost normal again.*
*Clearly, getting a good training and working hard are important.*
*The company, amazingly, have offered to pay for your partner to go with you*
*    to the conference.*
*Both of them, tragically, died young.*

 Words that are sentence adverbs in some sentences may belong to other parts of speech in other sentences:

*Certainly, we could as a last resort borrow the money.* (sentence adverb, commenting on the whole of the following remark)
*We certainly aren't going to do that!* (intensifier, relating specifically to the following *aren't*)

## sentence substitute see ADVERB.

## silent letter

A ***silent letter*** is one which is written but not pronounced, eg the *w* of *wrong*, the *k* of *knot*, the *gh* of *caught*, and the *l* of *walk* and *would*.

Silent letters are usually leftovers from earlier forms of speech in which they were pronounced, and in some English dialects and in Scots (a 'sister' language of Standard English) they still are: compare *bright* and *night* with the Scots equivalents *bricht* and *nicht*, in which the *ch* is pronounced /kh/ (as in *loch*). Some silent letters are found in English words borrowed from other languages or derived from words in other languages in which the letters are pronounced: one example of this is the *p* in *pneumonia* and *psychology*, words which are derived from ancient Greek.

---

 Occasionally, silent letters appear in words that they do not belong to at all. This may be for either of two reasons:

i)   because of confusion and false analogy. *Could*, which in earlier English was written *coude*, gained an *l* under the influence of *should* and *would* in which the *l* had once been pronounced (compare the equivalent German words *konnte*, *sollte* and *wollte*);

ii)   because of scholarly pedantry. *Debt* and *doubt* came into English from Old French *dette* and *doute*, but because these words are ultimately derived from Latin *debitum* and *dubitum*, scholars in the 17th century 'improved' the spellings by adding in the Latin *b*'s, although they were never pronounced.

---

## simple sentence see SENTENCE.

## singular

• A noun is *singular* if it is in a form which indicates that it refers to one individual or item as opposed to more than one, ie *dog, box, man, mouse*, as opposed to *dogs, boxes, men, mice*.

---

 Note that whether a noun is singular or plural is a matter of grammar, not meaning: although a *team* or a *committee* comprise two or more people, they are both singular nouns.

---

• A singular verb is one which agrees with a singular noun. In modern English, which has lost almost all the verb-endings used in older forms of the language, the only verb-forms that specifically indicate a singular verb are those ending in *-s* (*walks, swims*) and the almost obsolete verb-ending *-st* that goes with the pronoun *thou* (*goest, dost, didst*), and irregular forms such as *am*, *is* and *has*.

## soft

The letters *c* and *g* are said to be *soft* when they are pronounced with the sounds /s/, as in *cent*, and /j/, as in *gem*, respectively. The opposite of soft in this sense is *hard*.

## split infinitive

A *split infinitive* is a '*to*-infinitive' (see INFINITIVE) in which there is a word or phrase between the *to* and the following verb:

> *It may be impossible <u>to properly clean</u> all the stones.*
> *I'd like <u>to utterly and completely refute</u> that suggestion.*

## Standard English

*Standard English* is the form of English generally used throughout the English-speaking world in education, the law-courts and government bodies, the media, and in all other formal speech and writing. It exists with very little variation from one English-speaking country to another. Indeed, some linguists describe it as the 'common core' of English, what would remain if all regional- or class-based variants were removed.

> All the varieties or dialects of English that are not Standard English are *non-standard*. This is <u>not</u> to say that they are 'substandard'. Standard English is just one variety or dialect of English among many, one which is used (as has been said above) for particular purposes and in particular situations. Non-standard varieties of English are not inferior to Standard English, they simply differ from it in their rules of grammar and in their vocabulary; nor are they 'bad English' simply because they are not Standard English. There is no difference in 'goodness' or 'correctness' between *I ain't done nothing* and *I seen it* on the one hand and *I haven't done anything* and *I saw it* on the other; they simply belong to two different dialects of English, the former pair of sentences to a non-standard variety of English and the latter pair to the standard variety. Where they do differ is in 'appropriacy': non-standard varieties of English are inappropriate in contexts where Standard English would be expected, and their use in such contexts may lead to criticism.

Unlike some languages, Standard English has never been standardized by any authority or committee. It has simply evolved over the centuries from the form of English spoken in London in the 15th century, and it continues to evolve at the present time. It is not something that is fixed for all time, although some attempts have been made in the past to give it a definitive and fixed form, but is constantly, albeit very slowly, changing in small ways. It is therefore not ever possible to give an absolute ruling on what is or is not 'standard': the central core of Standard English is clear, but the edges are inevitably fuzzy, and what one person will accept as standard, another may not.

Although there is a central core of English that may be taken as 'standard' throughout the English-speaking world, there is in fact no existing single variety of English anywhere that could be described simply as 'Standard English'. What actually exists is a number of national or regional variant forms of Standard English that are taken as standard within their specific regions. The two main ones are **Standard British English** (often called **BBC English** or **the Queen's English**) and **Standard American English**, very similar to each other but differing slightly in grammar and vocabulary (see Appendix H on page 504).

## stem

In word-formation, a **stem** is a word or part of a word to which an affix may be or has been added to form a new word. For example, the stem of *foolish* is *fool*; the stem of *foolishly* and *foolishness* is *foolish*; the stem of *friendly* is *friend*; the stem of *unfriendly* is *friendly*; and the stem of *unfriendliness* is *unfriendly*.

> Stems should be distinguished from **roots** (see ROOT). A stem is what remains when the last-added suffix or prefix is removed, a root is what remains when all the suffixes and prefixes have been removed: *fool* is the root of *foolishly* and *foolishness*, and *friend* the root of *unfriendly* and *unfriendliness*.
>
> Both stems and roots are **bases** (see BASE).

## stress

A vowel or a syllable in a word is said to be **stressed** when it is said with more force, loudness or emphasis than the other vowels or syllables in that word. For example, in *photograph* the stress is on the first syllable *pho-*, in *photography* the stress is on the second syllable *-to-*, and in *photographic* the stress is on the third syllable *-graph-*.

Stress position in English words is for the most part unpredictable, whereas in some other languages the stress is always on a particular syllable of a word — the first syllable in Finnish and Czech, the second-last syllable in Polish and Welsh.

## strong verb

**Strong verbs** are irregular verbs whose simple past tense is constructed by altering the vowel of the infinitive or present tense form of the verb, and whose past participle is constructed usually by altering the vowel and sometimes by the addition of *-en* or *-n*:

| | | |
|---|---|---|
| *begin* : *began* : *begun* | *fly* : *flew* : *flown* | *stand* : *stood* : *stood* |
| *bite* : *bit* : *bitten* | *see* : *saw* : *seen* | *steal* : *stole* : *stolen* |
| *fight* : *fought* : *fought* | *sing* : *sang* : *sung* | |

All other verbs are **weak verbs**. Weak verbs therefore include both regular verbs such as

| | |
|---|---|
| *end* : *ended* : *ended* | *walk* : *walked* : *walked* |

and also irregular ones such as whose past tense and past participle end in *-d* or *-t*, such as

51

| | | |
|---|---|---|
| *bend : bent : bent* | *dream : dreamt : dreamt* | *tell : told : told* |
| *buy : bought : bought* | *lose : lost : lost* | |

> ⚠ Some verbs are weak in their simple past tense but strong in their past
> participle form:
>
> *sew : sewed : sewn*     *show : showed : shown*

## subject

The *subject* of a sentence is often defined as the word or words about which
something is said in the sentence (what is said about the subject being the
*predicate*). For example, in *John is coming tomorrow*, it could be said that the
predicate '*is coming tomorrow*' is information being given about *John* the subject
of the sentence.

However, this is not always a helpful criterion, and the subject of a sentence is
better defined in <u>grammatical</u> terms, as the noun, pronoun, phrase or clause
that determines the form of the verb (ie, if the subject is plural, the verb will
be plural; if it is in the third person, the verb will be in the third person). The
subject generally precedes the verb in English, except in questions:

> <u>She</u>'s a trained singer.
> <u>To err</u> is human.
> <u>It</u> was a bright, frosty morning in February.
> Aren't <u>you</u> coming with us?
> <u>Whether you want to go or not</u> is of no consequence.

## subjective

Subject pronouns (*I, he, they*, etc) may be said to be in the *subjective* case, as
opposed to the *objective* case of the object pronouns (*me, him, us*, etc). See
CASE.

## subjunctive

The *subjunctive* is one of the three moods (see MOOD) of the English verbs,
used to express commands, necessity, wishes or doubts. It differs from the
indicative in the form of the third person singular of the present tense (there is
no *-s* ending for the subjunctive in regular verbs), and in forms of the verbs *to
be* and *to have*:

> If that <u>be</u> the case, we'll have to alter our plans.
> God <u>save</u> the Queen.
> There has been an anonymous suggestion that you <u>be</u> replaced as soon as
> possible.

## subordinate clause see CLAUSE.

## subordinating conjunction see CONJUNCTION.

## substantive

*Substantive* is another name for a noun.

## suffix

A *suffix* is an affix that is attached to the end of a word or root: *singing, singer, quickly, boxes, normality.*

## superlative see COMPARISON OF ADJECTIVES AND ADVERBS.

## syllable

A *syllable* is a segment of a spoken word (or sometimes a whole short word by itself). Although several definitions of the term have been proposed, it is easier to demonstrate what it is than to define it. Broadly speaking, a syllable usually consists of a vowel on its own or a vowel plus any consonants that are pronounced with it. If you say a sentence very slowly, you will tend to split the words into small parts: thus

> *if - you - say - a - sen - tence - ve - ri - slow - ly - you - will - tend - to - split - the - words - in - to - sy - la - bles.*

Each of these 'small parts' is a syllable.

 Not all syllables have a vowel in them; some have a consonant that provides the main 'body' of the syllable. Such a consonant is called a **syllabic consonant**. One example of this is the final syllable of the word *syllable* itself, which is pronounced /-bl/; other examples are in *little* /li-tl/ and *example* /ig-**zahm**-pl/.

## symbol see ABBREVIATION.

## synonym

*Synonyms* are words which have the same meaning, eg *big* and *large*.

## tag question

*Tag questions* are questions added at the end of statements:

> You are coming, <u>aren't you</u>?
> She isn't coming with us, <u>is she</u>?
> You already knew, <u>did you</u>?

Normally, positive statements are followed by negative tags, and negative statements by positive tags, as in the first two examples. A positive statement followed by a positive tag generally implies surprise, disbelief, anger, sarcasm, etc as in the third example.

## tautology

*Tautologies* are instances of the use of two or more words or phrases in a sentence which say the same thing:

> *Finally*, I would like to say *in conclusion* that ...
> *Everyone* was *unanimous* in their praise.

## tense

**Tense** comes, via Old French, from Latin *tempus* meaning 'time'. A verb tense is a particular form (or set of forms) of the verb that shows what time, relative to the time of talking, the action of the verb takes place:

> I *know* what to do. (present tense)
> I *knew* what to do. (past tense)
>
> She *sings* well. (present tense)
> She *sang* well. (past tense)

In English there are two basic tenses, the **simple present** (*come/comes, am/is/ are, have/has, run/runs*, etc) and the **simple past** (*came, was/were, had, ran*, etc). There are in addition a number of complex tenses, formed with the auxiliary verbs *to be* and *to have* (eg *is coming, has come, had been crying*).

 What in traditional English grammar is referred to as the **future tense** (eg *He will leave tomorrow* □ *I shall write as soon as I arrive*) is often not treated as a tense at all in modern grammars of English. Likewise forms such as *He would leave if he could*, traditionally referred to as the **conditional tense**.

## tilde see DIACRITIC.

## transitive

A **transitive** verb is one which has an object:

> I *saw* you yesterday.
> She quietly *left* the room whenever he *raised* the subject.

For transitive verbs without objects, see ABSOLUTE.

## uncountable noun

**Uncountable noun** is another name for a **mass noun**; see NOUN.

## utterance see SENTENCE.

## verb

A **verb** may be defined as the word in a sentence that describes an action or a state:

*He promised to come.*
*She wanted to help him cook the dinner.*

Verbs in English generally change form to indicate tense (*they come, they came*) and agree with their subject in terms of person (*I come, she comes*) and number (*he comes, they come*).

### ✦ Types of verb

i) Most verbs in any language are *lexical verbs*. Lexical verbs are those which convey information about actions, states, events, and so on:

*He was seventy-one years old, nudging old age.*
*I think he was beginning to recognize his failings.*
*I really resent his insinuations.*

ii) Other verbs act as links between the subject and the complement:

*He was seventy-one years old.*
*That looks good.*
*That doesn't taste quite right.*

These are called *linking verbs* or *copulas*. Other linking verbs are *appear, become, feel, get, go, grow, seem, smell* and *sound*.

iii) Some verbs serve to form tenses:

*John has come.*
*John is working.*
*John has been working.*

or to indicate attitudes or possibilities:

*John may come.*
*John can come.*
*John could come.*
*John must come.*

These verbs are called *auxiliaries* (see AUXILIARY VERB).

**verbal noun** see GERUND.

## verb phrase

A *verb phrase* consists of all the verbs and parts of verbs that together function as a unit in a sentence:

*He will be leaving soon.*
*He must have left by now.*

## voice

Transitive verbs can be in either of two *voices* in English: *active* and *passive*. An active verb is one whose subject performs the action of the verb (eg *The boy patted the dog*), whereas the subject of a passive verb is on the receiving end of the action described by the verb (eg *The dog was patted by the boy*).

## vowel

A *vowel* can be thought of in two ways: either as a speech sound, or as a letter representing a speech sound.

i)  As a speech sound, a vowel is distinguished from a consonant by the way that it is produced. In the formation of a consonant, the breath from the lungs is blocked in some way (either completely or partially) as it passes through the pharynx and the mouth, whereas in the formation of a vowel, the passage of air is not blocked. For example, if you say *oath* very slowly, you can feel the air moving freely out of the mouth for the *oa* part of the word, but when it comes to the *th* part, the tongue and the teeth come into close proximity, so causing audible friction. The first part of the word *oath* is a vowel, the second part is a consonant.

ii)  As letters of the alphabet, the vowels are those which normally represent vowel sounds. There is, however, not a complete match between speech and writing, and *y*, which in some words represents a vowel sound (eg in *cry* and *my*, and in *friendly* and *quickly*), is usually included among the consonants because it functions as a consonant in words such as *yes* and *you*. In the English alphabet, all the letters are considered to be consonants except *a*, *e*, *i*, *o* and *u*.

See also SEMI-VOWEL.

## weak verb see STRONG VERB.

## word

What a *word* is seems fairly clear at first sight. On a written page, words are separated from each other by spaces. The first sentence of this entry has, therefore, ten words in it. But if there are three words in the sentence *He will go*, how many words are there in *He'll go*? Two or three? In one sense, in terms of writing, there are two words: *He'll* and *go*, with a space between them. But in terms of meaning, it is clear that there are still three words: *He*, *'ll* (a short form of *will*), and *go*. There is clearly a distinction to be made between different senses of the word 'word'. Words considered in terms of writing are called *orthographic words*, and words considered in terms of meaning are known as *lexemes*. *He*, *will*, *go* and *he'll* are all orthographic words, and the first sentence therefore consists of three orthographic words and the second sentence of two; and on the other hand both sentences comprise three lexemes: *he*, *will/'ll* and *go*.

The same distinction can be made with regard to speech: /heel goh/ still represents three lexemes but comprises only two words of speech. Word units in spoken language are called *phonological words*.

There is one further type of word that needs to be distinguished. Consider *put* in the following conversation:

> 'Where have you <u>put</u> the butter?' 'I <u>put</u> it in the fridge this morning. I always <u>put</u> it in the fridge, every morning.'

Here there are three instances of the orthographic word *put*. In terms of meaning, there are three instances of the lexeme *put*. But nonetheless, there is a sense in which these three instances of *put* can be said not to be 'the same word'. This becomes clearer if we substitute forms of the lexeme *hide* for the three instances of *put*:

> 'Where have you <u>hidden</u> the butter?' 'I <u>hid</u> it in the fridge this morning. I always <u>hide</u> it in the fridge, every morning.'

The first *put* is, like *hidden*, a past participle; the second one is, like *hid*, a simple past tense form; and the third one is, like *hide*, a present tense form of the word. What we have, then, in the three *put*'s are three different **grammatical words** (a past participle *put*, a past tense *put*, and a present tense *put*) which are all forms of the lexeme *put*, and which are all represented in writing by the same orthographic word *put* and in speech by the same phonological word /poot/.

# 2

# Coping with Grammar

Grammar is concerned with the rules governing the formation of words and the construction of sentences.

The grammatical rules of a language are determined by an analysis of the language itself. In principle, grammarians do not impose rules of grammar on a language, but rather identify them and set them out in an orderly fashion. However, grammarians in the past have unfortunately not hesitated to impose on the grammar of English artificial and completely unnecessary rules of 'good' usage, particularly by taking Latin grammar as the norm of correctness and then forcing the English language into the mould so created. Among the rules of grammar imposed on English in this way are the two which condemn as incorrect the 'split infinitive' and 'ending a sentence with a preposition', both very common and entirely natural usages in English although neither possible in Latin.

Few people today would make the mistake of trying to fit English into a Latin mould, but some of these 'non-rules' are nevertheless still influential, and failure to comply with them can give rise to censure: in a list of twenty linguistic 'errors' that people complained about to the BBC, compiled by Professor David Crystal in 1981, the split infinitive ranked fourth and ending sentences with prepositions thirteenth.

The entries in this chapter deal with the main areas of uncertainty and error in English grammar. Since there is no clear dividing-line between grammar and style — for example, the 'split infinitive' might be condemned by some people as ungrammatical but by others as grammatical but stylistically undesirable — a number of matters that might be considered stylistic rather than grammatical are also dealt with here.

The technical terms used in the descriptions and explanations are themselves explained and illustrated in chapter 1.

## a, an

✦ *A* or *an*?

*A* before a consonant sound; *an* before a vowel sound.

Examples:

*a book* □ *a road* □ *a hand* □ *a woman* □ *a yellow dress*
*a one-way street* (*one* begins with the sound *w*)
*a union* (*union* begins with the sound *y*)

*an axe* □ *an egg* □ *an orange skirt*
*an hour* (the *h* is silent, so *hour* begins with a vowel sound)

---

⚠  ***A hotel* or *an hotel*?**

For a few words beginning with *h* and an unstressed initial syllable, usage varies. In *hotel*, *historian*, *historic*, *horizon* and *habitual*, for example, the first syllable is unstressed and, while most speakers of English pronounce the initial *h* as a full /h/, it is pronounced by some people either only very weakly or not at all. The *h*-less (or virtually *h*-less) pronunciation, while not common and now rather old-fashioned, is not wrong, and in such cases it is quite correct to precede the *h*-word by ***an*** rather than ***a***, both in speech and in writing:

> *After an obscure beginning at an hotel in Brigue, he arrived in Paris in 1867.*

> *There is an historical expectation in academia that university presses will publish whatever academics want to write.*

The simple rule is to make the choice between ***a*** and ***an*** match your own pronunciation of such *h*-words: ***if you give a full pronunciation to the initial letter* h, *precede it by* a; *if you do not, precede it by* an.**

***a MP* or *an MP*?**

In exactly the same way as for initial *h*, the choice between ***a*** and ***an*** before an abbreviation depends on the <u>pronunciation</u> of the abbreviation rather than on its spelling:

***if the abbreviation begins with a consonant sound, it is preceded by* a:** *a BA* □ *a UN peace-keeping force;*

***if the abbreviation begins with a vowel sound, it is preceded by* an:** *an MA* □ *an SOS* □ *an IOU.*

Some abbreviations may be correctly preceded by either ***a*** or ***an***, depending on how they are expected to be pronounced. For example, in

> *Ten years or so ago the only woman who ever appeared in a s-f story was usually the mad scientist's daughter*

the ***a*** before *s-f* implies that the writer intended *s-f* to be said as 'science fiction'. It would not, however, be wrong to pronounce the abbreviation /es ef/, in which case it would be preceded by ***an***.

---

◆  **Omission of *a* and *an***

For some rules governing the omission of ***a*** and ***an***, see OMISSION OF *A* AND *THE* IN APPOSITIONS under ARTICLES.

## adjectives and adverbs

### ✦ Position of adjectives

There are three positions in a sentence in which adjectives may stand:

**attributive** (ie before the noun), as in *a black car* and *the big house*;

**predicative** (ie following a verb in the predicate), as in *The car is black* □ *The house is big* □ *She made him happy*;

**post-positive** (ie immediately following a noun), as in *president elect*.

Some adjectives are restricted to only certain of these positions:

i)   Common adjectives found only in **attributive** position are *chief, elder, former, latter, lone, main, mere, only, out-and-out, outright, principal, sole, utter* and *very*:

✓   *the very thing I was looking for*
✓   *an utter fool*
✓   *restored to its former glory*
✗   *Its glory is former.*

ii)   Only found in **predicative** position are many adjectives beginning with **a-**, such as *ablaze, afloat, afraid, aghast, agog, akin, alight, alike, alive, alone, amiss, asleep, averse, awake, aware* and *awash*.

These adjectives may sometimes be used attributively when they are modified by an adverb:

*The <u>half-asleep</u> children and their <u>not fully awake</u> teachers got down wearily from the train.*

iii)   There are few adjectives that must always stand in **post-positive** position. One is *galore* (as in *books galore*).

Some adjectives are post-positive in certain senses only: compare

*Through a proper* (= 'correct') *understanding of this condition, human beings can break the chain of karma.*
*Autobiography proper* (= 'in the strict sense of the term') *implies a self-creation as well as self-criticism on the part of the author.*

---

| ¶ | In many cases, the noun and following adjective together form what is tantamount to a compound noun: *attorney general, court martial, heir apparent, heir presumptive, postmaster general, president elect, professor emeritus.* |
|---|---|

---

### ✦ Position of adverbs

What is perhaps the most controversial point with regard to the position of adverbs in a sentence is covered in the entry on the SPLIT INFINITIVE. Other important points are dealt with in the entries for EVEN and ONLY.

As a general stylistic point, care should be taken to avoid ambiguities arising from the positioning of an adverb between a preceding verb and a following adjective. It may not be clear whether it is the verb or the adjective that the adverb is modifying: in *I dislike intensely competitive sports*, for example, it is not clear whether what is being spoken of is an intense dislike of competitive sports or a dislike of intensely competitive sports.

### ✦ Formation of adverbs

Adverbs are regularly formed from adjectives by the addition of the suffix *-ly*:

| | | | | |
|---|---|---|---|---|
| *evident* | : | *evidently* | *quick* | : *quickly* |

In some cases, the *-ly* ending is not simply added to the adjectival base, but causes some alteration to the base as well:

| | | | | | |
|---|---|---|---|---|---|
| *dull* | : | *dully* (✗ *dullly*) | *simple* | : | *simply* (✗ *simplely*) |
| *greedy* | : | *greedily* | *whole* | : | *wholly* (✗ *wholely*) |

The rules governing these changes are covered fully in the chapter on *Spelling and Word-formation*, under -LY, page 270.

#### ● Adverbs ending in *-lily*

Opinions vary as to the acceptability of adverbs ending in *-lily* (*oilily*, *friendlily*, etc) which are formed by adding *-ly* to adjectives which themselves end in *-ly* (eg *oily*, *jolly*, *friendly*, *heavenly*).

   i)   If the final *-ly* of the adjective is not itself a suffix, the corresponding adverb is generally considered acceptable, eg *holily*, *jollily*, *oilily*, *sillily*, etc.

   ii)   If the final *-ly* of the adjective is a suffix (eg *friendly* = *friend* + *-ly*), many people feel that the corresponding adverbs sound rather clumsy (although they are not ungrammatical), and are therefore best avoided (eg by using a phrase such as *in a … manner*). Adverbs of three syllables (eg *friendlily*, *lovelily*) are generally more acceptable than those of four or more syllables (*heavenlily*, *ungodlily*).

### ✦ Adjective or adverb — which to use?

> **In general, where there are separate forms for the adjective and the adverb, use the adjective when what is described is the subject of the verb and the adverb when what is described is the action of the verb.**

Examples:

*He looked hungry.*
*He looked hungrily at the food on the table.*

Occasionally in informal speech and writing, the adjective form is used in place of the adverb form: *Come quick!* In formal contexts, always use the adverb form. Take particular care with comparatives and superlatives:

✓    *The ship was travelling more quickly than we had thought possible.*
✗    *The ship was travelling quicker than we had thought possible.*

---

📖    Adjectives may, however, be correctly used to describe the <u>result</u> of an action as opposed to the way an action is performed: *We piled the plates high □ He pulled the rope tight.*

A number of adjectives have two related adverbial forms, one identical to the adjective and the other ending in *-ly*:

*Which is the <u>deep</u> end of the pool?* (adjective)
*Don't go too <u>deep</u> into the wood or you might get lost.* (adverb)
*I'm <u>deeply</u> disappointed in you.* (adverb)

Where such pairs of adverbs exist, the one without the *-ly* ending is often more closely related to the adjective in meaning, while the *-ly* form may have a more figurative meaning:

*an eagle soaring <u>high</u> in the sky*
*We value your contributions very <u>highly</u>.*

---

## ✦  Comparatives and superlatives of adjectives and adverbs

The comparative and superlative forms of adjectives and adverbs are generally formed either by adding *-er* or *-est* to the simple form of the word (*fast* : *faster* : *fastest*) or by preceding the word by **more** or **most** (*beautiful* : *more beautiful* : *most beautiful*; *quickly* : *more quickly* : *most quickly*). Sometimes there are minor changes to the spelling of the base word (*big* : *bigger* : *biggest*; *dry* : *drier* : *driest*); see the entry COMPARATIVES AND SUPERLATIVES, in the chapter on the *Spelling and Word-formation*, page 229.

### •  Formation of comparative and superlative adjectives

#### One-syllable adjectives

> **As a rule, the comparatives and superlatives of one-syllable adjectives are formed by adding the inflections *-er* and *-est*.**

Examples:

*small* : *smaller* : *smallest*      *new* : *newer* : *newest*

---

⚠    *Mere* has a superlative form *merest* but no comparative form *merer*.

---

Monosyllabic past participles are an exception:

*bored* : *more bored* : *most bored*      *worn* : *more worn* : *most worn*

*Tired* has inflected forms: *tireder* and *tiredest*.

Note also *do one's <u>damnedest</u>*.

## Two-syllable adjectives

**Two-syllable adjectives ending in *-y* (but not the suffix *-ly*, as in *friendly*), *-ow* and *-er* generally form inflected comparatives and superlatives.**

Examples:

    *silly* : *sillier* : *silliest*            *clever* : *cleverer* : *cleverest*
    *shallow* : *shallower* : *shallowest*

 *Eager* and *proper* form comparatives and superlatives with *more* and *most*.

**Words ending in *-le* and *-ure*, and the *-ly* suffix, may have either type of comparative and superlative.**

Examples:

    *simple* : *simpler/more simple* : *simplest/most simple*
    *obscure* : *obscurer/more obscure* : *obscurest/most obscure*
    *lonely* : *lonelier/more lonely* : *loneliest/most lonely*

A number of other two-syllable adjectives also have both options: *common, cruel, extreme, handsome, honest, pleasant, polite, quiet, remote, sincere, solemn, solid, stupid* and *tranquil*.

**All other two-syllable adjectives take only the *more/most* form of comparative and superlative.**

 Comparatives formed with ***more*** are used in place of inflected forms in certain contexts:

    i)   when what is being compared is two adjectives in a sentence rather than two people, etc; compare

        *She is shyer than her sister.* (comparing 'she' and 'her sister')

and

        *She is more shy than unsociable.* (stating that 'shy' is a more apt
           description of her than 'unsociable')

    ii)  when the appropriateness of a particular adjective is being questioned:

63

> *She's no sillier than her sister.* (comparing 'she' and 'her sister')

and

> *She's no more silly than her sister.* (ie, it is not correct to say that 'she' is silly — the sister is not silly, nor is 'she')

iii) optionally, when two or more normally inflected comparatives are used together:

> *She is taller and slimmer than her sister.*
> *She is more tall and slim than her sister.*

## Adjectives of three or more syllables

**Adjectives of more than two syllables almost always form comparatives and superlatives with *more* and *most*.**

Example:

> *beautiful : more beautiful : most beautiful*

 The only exceptions are those three-syllable adjectives that are formed by the addition of ***un-*** to two-syllable words which have inflected comparatives and superlatives:

> *happy : happier : happiest → unhappy : unhappier : unhappiest*

Up until the end of the last century, it was possible to make inflected forms of comparatives and superlatives for two- and three-syllable words which nowadays can only have ***more*** and ***most*** forms. Thomas Carlyle wrote

> *People ought to be modester*

and in a magazine of 1788, there is a reference to a bird being '*one of the beautifullest of the whole parrot kind*'.

Such forms are not correct in 20th-century English.

## Compound adjectives

**Most compound adjectives form comparatives and superlatives with *more* and *most*, even if the first element of the compound form has an inflected comparative and superlative.**

Examples:

> *big : bigger : biggest* but *big-headed : more big-headed : most big-headed*
> *short : shorter : shortest* but *short-sighted : more short-sighted : most short-sighted*
> *bad : worse : worst* but *bad-tempered : more bad-tempered : most bad-tempered*

A few, however, do alter the first element of the compound:

> *good-looking : better-looking : best-looking*

Compound adjectives the first element of which is *well* or *ill* usually inflect this first part:

> *well-known* : *better-known* : *best-known*

although forms with **more** and **most** are not incorrect. Most other compound adjectives show the same variation:

> *hard-wearing* : *harder-wearing/more hard-wearing* : *hardest-wearing/most hard-wearing*
>
> *hard-working* : *harder-working/more hard-working* : *hardest-working/most hard-working*
>
> *long-lasting* : *longer-lasting/more long-lasting* : *longest-lasting/most long-lasting*

- **Double comparatives and superlatives**

Avoid double comparatives and superlatives, like Shakespeare's *This was the most unkindest cut of all* and Mr Bumble's remark to Oliver in Dickens's *Oliver Twist* that '*of all the the artful and designing orphans*' that he had ever seen, Oliver was '*one of the most barefacedest*'.

- **Words that cannot form comparatives and superlatives**

Some adjectives have an element of comparison already implied in their meanings, and so should not be used in a comparative form:

> ✗ *I think it would be more preferable to stay here.*
> ✓ *I think it would be preferable to stay here.*

Some words are not open to comparative or superlative forms because of their meaning:

*Unique*, for example, means 'the only one of its kind' and therefore something cannot, strictly speaking, be 'more unique' than something else. In casual speech, *unique* has taken on a looser meaning 'novel', 'scarce' or 'rare', but this should be avoided in formal contexts.

Similarly, people or things are either *equal* or not equal, they cannot be more equal or less equal. It is this that gives the ironic force to the famous dictum from George Orwell's *Animal Farm*:

> *All animals are equal, but some are more equal than others.*

- **Formation of comparative and superlative adverbs**

**Adverbs that are the same in form as adjectives**

> **Adverbs that are identical in form to adjectives have inflected forms of comparative and superlative.**

Example:

> *fast* : *faster* : *fastest*     *early* : *earlier* : *earliest*

**Adverbs formed by the addition of -*ly***

> **Adverbs formed by adding -*ly* to adjectives form comparatives and superlatives with *more* and *most*.**

Example:

*beautifully : more beautifully : most beautifully*

---

 *Badly* is an exception; it has the irregular comparative *worse* and the superlative *worst*.

---

- **Use of comparative and superlative adjectives and adverbs**

In general, the comparative form of the adjective or adverb is used when comparing two things, individuals, groups, etc and the superlative when comparing three or more:

*He is a better swimmer than his brother.*
*He is the best swimmer in the school.*
*He swims better than his brother.*

---

 **Superlatives in comparisons between two**

Although condemned by most traditional grammarians over the past two centuries, the use of the superlative in comparing two individuals, options, etc (eg *Which of the two do you like best?*) is nevertheless well established, and to be found in the works of some of the best writers of English. Opinions vary among authorities as to how acceptable this usage is in present-day English. It is certainly acceptable in informal contexts, but probably better avoided in more formal speech and writing, except in set phrases such as *may the best man win* and *put one's best foot forward.*

It is also quite correct, however, to use a superlative rather than a comparative when strongly recommending one option over another rather than simply saying that one is better than the other:

*I really do think it would be best to go.*

---

- It is sometimes recommended that a comparative adjective should not be used in comparative measurements after ***twice*** and ***times***, eg:

**?** *His garden must be three or four times larger than ours.*

However, this is a fairly common and acceptable construction, and need only be avoided in strictly formal English, in which ***as . . . as*** is to be preferred:

✓ *His garden must be three or four times as large as ours.*

## agreement of nouns, verbs and pronouns

✦ **The basic rules of agreement**

> **Verbs must agree with their subjects with regard to** *person* **(*I* *run*, *she* *runs*) and** *number* **(*She* *runs*, *they* *run*).**
>
> **Similarly, pronouns and possessive adjectives must agree with the nouns they refer to (*The boy told* *his* *mother* but *The boys told* *their* *mothers*).**

---

 When a noun phrase denoting a single item or individual ends in a plural noun, it is not uncommon for the phrase to be mistakenly followed by a plural verb, especially when the singular noun or noun phrase denotes something which consists of a number of items or individuals:

✗ *One set of books* *are* *missing.*
✓ *One set of books* *is* *missing.* (ie, one set is missing.)

Similarly:

✗ *One in two of the inhabitants of this town* *own* *a car.*
✓ *One in two of the inhabitants of this town* *owns* *a car.* ('Owns' has to agree with 'one'.)

---

● There are a number of words that are either exceptions to the general rule or with which usage varies:

### *number*
A noun phrase consisting of *a number of* followed by a plural noun is correctly followed by a plural verb:

> *A number of children* *were* *playing in the street.*

This use of *number* must be distinguished from the very similar construction *the number of* followed by a plural noun, which must be followed by a singular verb:

> *The number of children in the town* *is* *rising.*

### *rest*
If a phrase including *rest of* refers to a number of individuals, it is followed by a plural verb:

> *Three people in the bus died in the accident. The rest of the passengers* *were* *fortunate to receive only minor injuries.*

### *average*, *majority*, *maximum*, *minimum*, *minority* and *total*
Phrases including these words are generally followed by a plural verb when

they refer to a number of items or individuals, although it is not incorrect to use a singular verb (and perhaps more usual to do so with *total* ):

> *This is what a majority of women desire.*
> *The majority of Bosch's works are in the Prado in Madrid.*
> *A total of five research fellowships is/are available.*

**dozen**

Although *a dozen* is singular, it is regularly accompanied by a plural verb:

> *In the back of the car were a dozen boxes of chocolates.*

**more than**

Although *more than one* implies 'two or more' and is therefore plural, it is treated grammatically as singular:

> *If more than one syndicate collapses, the financial implications are immense.*

**measurements or quantities**

Similarly, **plurals denoting measurements or quantities** are correctly treated as singular nouns:

> *Three tons of sand seems far too much to me.*

### ✦ Agreement with linking verbs

When the subject and the complement of a linking verb (such as *seem* or *be*) differ with regard to number (ie, one is singular and the other plural), there is sometimes uncertainty about whether the verb should be singular or plural. The simple rule is that, *in this case as in all others, the verb agrees with its subject*:

> *Our main problem is our word-processors.*
> *Our word-processors are our main problem.*
>
> *What we need is more powerful word-processors.*
> *More powerful word-processors are what we need.*

 In informal, especially spoken, English, a word such as *what* is often followed by a plural verb (*What we need are more powerful word-processors*), thereby treating *what* as equivalent to a plural phrase 'the things which' rather than the strictly more correct singular 'that which'. For comments on this, see page 115.

**here is/are, there is/are**

With *here* or *there*, the verb should agree with the following noun or pronoun:

> *Here is John now.*
> *Here are John and Mary.*
> *There they are.*

In informal English, *is* is often used before a plural complement, especially in the reduced form *'s*: *There's several ways we could do this*. While acceptable in informal contexts, this usage is not acceptable in formal speech and writing. However, when a plural noun is thought of as denoting a single amount or unit, or a plural noun phrase consists of a series of singular nouns considered separately and successively, a singular verb is correct:

> *There is fifty pence in that bag.* (Compare *There are fifty 1p coins in that bag.*)
> *Who could we invite? Well, there's John and Peter and Mike and Sam for a start.* (= 'There's John and there's Peter and there's Mike and there's Sam ...')

## ✦ Agreement with linked subjects

When two or more singular noun subjects linked by *and* refer to different individuals or objects, the following verb, and any related pronouns, etc, should be in the plural:

> *Tea and coffee are very popular drinks.*

On the other hand, when two or more singular nouns or noun phrases linked by *and* refer to one and the same individual or object, the related verb, pronouns, etc should be in the singular:

> *Here lies an officer and a gentleman.*

Similarly, when linked nouns refer to different individuals or things which are nevertheless considered to form or function as one item, the verb, etc should be singular:

> *Bubble and squeak consists of fried potatoes and cabbage.*

In some cases, the linked phrase may be equally correctly viewed as either singular or plural:

> *Tea and toast is/are what I normally have for breakfast.*
> *Law and order is/are very important in a democracy.*
> *Two and two make/makes four.*

---

**◀** *Along with*, *as well as*, *together with* and similar prepositions must be followed by a singular verb. Compare:

> *My daughter and the little girl next door are both in the Junior Choir.*
> *My daughter, along with the little girl next door, is in the Junior Choir.*
> *My daughter, as well as the little girl next door, is in the Junior Choir.*

Similarly with other prepositions which link nouns or noun phrases (eg *as much as* and *more than*), the verb, etc must be in the singular:

> *It's his lying to me, more than his disobedience, that makes me angry.*

For subjects joined by *either ... or*, see the entry EITHER.

---

## ✦ Agreement with collective nouns

There is often uncertainty as to whether nouns such as *committee* should be followed by a singular or plural verb, pronoun, etc: *The committee was* (?)/*were* (?) *unable to make up* <u>*its*</u> (?)/<u>*their*</u> (?) <u>*mind*</u> (?)/<u>*minds*</u> (?). Collective nouns can be divided into two main categories, which behave differently grammatically:

i)    One type of collective noun is that which denotes a number of articles collected together as a group or considered as a class, eg *furniture, luggage, baggage, cutlery.* Such nouns are always singular and must be followed by a singular verb, etc:

   *Your luggage <u>is</u> in the luggage-rack above you. Where did you think <u>it was</u>?*

---

 **Cattle** is a plural noun, and must therefore be followed by a plural, not a singular, verb, etc:

   *The cattle <u>were</u> taken to market.*

---

ii)    The second category of collective nouns comprises nouns (mostly referring to people) which in the singular denote a group which may be thought of either as a number of separate individuals or as a single unit, eg

| | | | |
|---|---|---|---|
| air force | clergy | fleet | nobility |
| aristocracy | club | flock | orchestra |
| army | committee | gang | party |
| audience | company | gentry | press |
| band | congregation | government | proletariat |
| board | crew | group | public |
| bourgeoisie | crowd | herd | staff |
| cast | élite | intelligentsia | team |
| choir | enemy | jury | tribe |
| clan | family | laity | troop |
| class | firm | navy | |

In British English, such nouns may be treated as either singular or plural with regard to agreement with verbs, possessive adjectives, etc, normally being treated as singular nouns when the emphasis is on the group acting as a single body (*The committee <u>meets</u> every Tuesday*), and plural when the emphasis is on the group as a number of individuals (*The committee <u>were</u> all thoroughly confused by the report*). However, these words may be treated as plurals even when denoting a group acting as a single body:

   *Well, fancy giving money to the Government!*
   *Might as well have put it down the drain!*
   *... Well, <u>they've</u> no idea what money's for —*
   *Ten to one <u>they'll</u> start another war.*

                                        — A P Herbert

In some cases, the choice between singular and plural agreement conveys important information: compare

   *The staff was huge.* (= 'It was a very large staff.')
   *The staff were huge.* (= 'It was a staff of very large people.')

Notice that whatever choice is made regarding the singularity or plurality of a collective noun, the choice should be adhered to consistently:

✓ *The committee <u>has</u> considered your request and <u>it has</u> decided to accede to it.*

✓ *The committee <u>have</u> considered your request and <u>they have</u> decided to accede to it.*

✗ *The committee <u>have</u> considered your request and <u>it has</u> decided to accede to it.*

✓ *The audience <u>are</u> asked to remain in <u>their</u> seats.*

✗ *The audience <u>is</u> asked to remain in <u>their</u> seats.*

A collective noun must be treated as singular if it is qualified by an explicitly singular adjective such as *this, that, every,* etc:

✓ *<u>This</u> committee <u>has</u> considered your request ...*

✗ *<u>This</u> committee <u>have</u> considered ...*

• Also to be included in this second category of collective noun are ***names of public bodies, institutions, business companies, teams,*** and so on: *Celtic, Labour, Larousse, Parliament, the Vatican, the White House,* etc. Again, both singular and plural agreement can be found:

> *Larousse PLC <u>is</u> the UK arm of the giant French publishing corporation, Groupe de la Cité.*
> *Larousse <u>have</u> introduced a new breed of bilingual dictionaries this summer.*

 In American English, collective nouns are almost always treated as singular.

## ✦ Agreement in relative clauses

The verb in a relative clause must agree with the antecedent (ie, the word or phrase the relative clause relates to) with regard to ***number*** and ***person***:

> *The recommended best fish buy is witch, a kind of flounder which <u>is</u> an excellent substitute for plaice, sole and brill.*
> *Beverly Hills is now often sunless, in the perpetual shade of high-rises which <u>are</u> Manhattanising L.A.*

 Care must be taken to make the verb agree with its true antecedent, which may not be the noun immediately preceding the clause:

> *She is one of the most famous singers who <u>have</u> ever lived.* ('Have', not 'has', because the antecedent is 'singers'.)
> *One of the singers, who <u>has</u> lived in the same village all her life, is the vicar's wife.* ('Has', not 'have', because the antecedent is 'one'.)

If a *collective noun* is followed by a relative clause, the choice of relative pronoun, like the choice between singular and plural verb, depends on whether the noun is looked on as denoting a single body (in which case use *which*) or a number of individuals (in which case use *who*):

> The committee, <u>which meets</u> every second Friday, will consider your request at <u>its</u> next meeting.
> The committee, <u>who meet</u> together every second Friday, will consider your request as soon as <u>they can</u>.

## all, all of

● *All* is followed by the preposition *of* if it relates to a following pronoun, as in *All of us want to go*, unless the pronoun is in apposition to a noun, in which case the *of* is optional: *All of us lexicographers are a little mad* or *All we lexicographers are a little mad*.

*Of* is again optional when *all* relates to a demonstrative pronoun such as *this* or *that* or to a noun preceded by a definite article (*the*), a demonstrative adjective (*this*, *that*, etc), or a possessive adjective (*my*, *her*, etc):

> All the boys came or All of the boys came
> He ate all my cheese or He ate all of my cheese
> All these are mine or All of these are mine

● When the noun or pronoun modified by *all* is the subject of the sentence, *all* may follow the subject (*We all really want to go* □ *The boys all arrived yesterday*), unless the sentence contains a modal verb (such as *can, will, may, must*, etc), in which case *all* follows the modal verb (*We can't all go* □ *The boys must all come with me*).

● For possible ambiguities with *all . . . not*, see NEGATION.

**an** see A.

## and

✦ *And* **at the beginning of a sentence**
Contrary to what is sometimes recommended by purists, there is no reason not to begin a sentence with *and*. Doing so is often a good way of emphasizing the information contained in the sentence. Moreover, when the sentence beginning with *and* is the last of a series of sentences relating to one topic, it would often be clumsy and inappropriate to attach it as a co-ordinate clause to the end of the preceding sentence. The following example demonstrates an entirely appropriate use of a sentence beginning with *and*:

> The New People ... are the children of the industrialists and executives who built Japan Inc. They are as familiar with hamburgers as onigiri (rice

*balls), Guns N'Roses as ikebana (flower arranging), and folding a paper packet of cocaine or heroin as folding an origami crane. They belong to gangs, cliques, tribes and trends. And they are Japan's future.*

— *The Face*

## ✦ *And* or *to*?

The use of ***and*** after words such as ***try*** or ***sure*** (eg *I'll try and finish it by next week* □ *Be sure and come tomorrow night*) is acceptable only in informal English. In more formal contexts, use ***to*** (*I'll try to finish it by next week*).

## ✦ Agreement with compound subjects linked by *and*

For discussion of the rules governing verb agreement with phrases containing a linking ***and*** (eg *Tea and toast is/are*(?) *what I normally have for breakfast*), see AGREEMENT WITH LINKED SUBJECTS, page 69.

## articles

There are two 'articles' in English: the ***definite article*** '*the*' and the ***indefinite article*** '*a*' or '*an*'.

## ✦ Omission of *a* and *the* in appositions

When a phrase is put in apposition to a name in order to give further information about the person or thing named, it is normal for it to begin with a word such as a possessive adjective or an article:

> *Even John, his best friend, disapproves of what he has done.*
> *Sheila Jones, an unmarried mother-of-two, has won the first prize, a trip to the United States.*
> *Britain's veto of Jean-Luc Dehaene, the Belgian Prime Minister, at Corfu*

In ***journalism***, it is a common, and acceptable, practice to omit *a* and *the* (but not other words) from such phrases:

> *Jimmy Knapp, leader of the striking signalworkers*

**Outside journalism, however, this style of writing is not acceptable.**

**Another feature of journalese which is to be avoided** in other forms of writing is the conversion of phrases of the above type into pseudo-titles:

> *Belgian Prime Minister Jean-Luc Dehaene said today that . . .*

It is better to write, for example,

> *The Belgian Prime Minister, Jean-Luc Dehaene, said today that . . .*

with an article at the beginning of the descriptive phrase and commas round the name.

It is of course perfectly acceptable to use genuine titles without articles, eg <u>*President*</u> *Clinton* or <u>*Chancellor*</u> *Kohl*. There is thus a difference between

> <u>*The German Chancellor, Helmut Kohl,*</u> *said last night that ...* (apposition)

and

> <u>*Chancellor Kohl*</u> *said last night that ...* (title)

## ✦ Omission of *a* and *the* after *as*

**A, and less commonly *the*, may be omitted after *as* when the noun or noun phrase following the *as* is used as a generic term designating a type of person, thing, activity, etc, especially in comparisons.**

Examples:

✓ *While as sociologist she is unsurpassed, as teacher she is somewhat of a disappointment.*
✓ *While as a sociologist she is unsurpassed, as a teacher she is somewhat of a disappointment.*

The article will most often be omitted in 'noun *as* noun' constructions:

> *What we are concerned with in this programme is language as social tool.*

In other contexts following *as*, the article may or may not be present:

> *He was installed as (the) rector of Old St Paul's in 1947.*

 The more formal word **qua** (used in the same sense as *as* in 'noun *as* noun' constructions) is never followed by an article:

> *What we are concerned with in this programme is language qua social tool.*

## ✦ Omission of *a* and *the* in titles of jobs, etc

**When a noun or noun phrase designating a unique position or a position filled by one particular person at a given time follows a linking verb, such as *be* or *become*, the article may optionally be omitted.**

Examples:

> *He was (the) chairman of the company for nine years.*

> *He is also host to his own theme park in France, Parc Asterix.*
> — *The Bookseller*, on Asterix the Gaul

> Following a verb denoting a process of appointment, such as *elect* or *name*, the article is almost always omitted when the noun or noun phrase designates a unique position or a position filled by one person at a particular time.

Examples:

> *Elected MP for Leeds South in 1945, he became Parliamentary Secretary to the Ministry of Fuel and Power in 1946 and Minister in 1947. Appointed Minister of State for Economic Affairs in 1950 ... in December 1955 he was elected Leader of the Opposition by a large majority over Bevan.*

> *[Benny Hill] was named TV Personality of the Year in 1954.*

• When the following noun does not designate a unique position, it is usual to include the article:

> *He was elected an MP in 1945, and became a parliamentery secretary in 1946.*

although there are a few nouns with which the article is omissible even when the designated position is not unique: you could say, for example, *He was elected MP in 1945*, and similarly *He was named cardinal in 1875.*

*It is, however, always safer to include the article in such cases, as it is never wrong to do so and usually wrong not to do so.*

✦ **Omission of *a* and *the* in quoted titles of books, etc**

> When the first word of the title of a book, play, film, etc is *the* or *a/an*, the article may be omitted when the title is being quoted and when it is part of a phrase which itself includes an article or a possessive word or phrase.

Examples:

> *Her greatest triumph was as Katharina in The Taming of the Shrew.*
> *Her greatest triumph was as Katharina in Shakespeare's Taming of the Shrew.*
> *The local dramatic society put on a first-rate Taming of the Shrew last month.*

## as if, as though

> When referring to states or events that are true, seem true, or are likely to be true, *as if* and *as though* are followed by a verb in the present or the past indicative, whichever is appropriate.

Examples:

> *By the end of the film we feel as if he <u>is splashing</u> about in a bath and <u>can't</u> bear to get out.*
> *Have you tasted her cooking? It's as if her mother never <u>taught</u> her anything at all.*

> **When doubt is being expressed about what is being said or when what <u>seems</u> to be the case is being denied, the verb following *as if* and *as though* will normally be in the past-tense form.**

Example:

> *As if we went there every day!*

With the verb *to be*, the past subjunctive (ie *I/he/she were*, as opposed to *I/he/she was*) is common, but the indicative form *was* is also used:

> *We also want to give a platform to the Royal Opera Orchestra, which often appears as if it <u>were</u> the backing band for a handful of star singers.*
> —BBC Music

> **After a negative expressing denial of something supposedly ongoing at the present time, there is little if any difference in meaning between using a present tense and using a past tense.**

Examples:

> *It's not as though he buys a book every week.*
> *It's not as though he bought a book every week.*

## but

### ✦ *But* at the beginning of a sentence

It is often given as a rule of grammar that neither *and* nor *but* should begin a sentence. This is, in fact, one of the all-too-common 'non-rules' of English that have been passed down to generation after generation of school pupils, but which actually have no basis in grammar, style or logic.

There is no reason not to begin a sentence with ***but***, and often a good reason for doing so, such as the need to emphasize what follows or to mark a break or contrast with what has gone before. Other words with much the same meaning as ***but*** are available, such as *however* or *nevertheless*, but sometimes ***but*** is the only appropriately forceful word, no matter what the purists say, and the beginning of a new sentence, or even of a new paragraph, the correct place to put it. Consider, for example, the following, taken from Sir Bruce Fraser's foreword to F L Lucas's book on *Style*:

> *To flick over the pages of the book is to get an impression of immense erudition. Erudite it certainly is. But Lucas wears his learning lightly.*
>
> *Just what readership Lucas himself had in mind may be doubtful. A few passages seem to be addressed to undergraduates who serve up silly essays (for the book is founded on a course of lectures); some to his fellow-teachers; some (such as the last two chapters) to seriously aspiring authors; a great deal to a more general readership.*
> *But my own firm conclusion is that Lucas wrote it specially for me ...*

Lucas himself, a master of good style, begins many sentences in his book, and not a few paragraphs, with **but**.

To sum up, then, if you have a good reason for wanting to begin a sentence with **but**, then it is quite correct to do so. ***But make sure you have a good reason.***

✦ *No one but me* or *no one but I?*

See PRONOUN CASE AFTER PREPOSITIONS AND CONJUNCTIONS under PRONOUNS.

✦ *But ... though,* etc

***But*** is often used incorrectly along with another word carrying the same meaning and performing the same linking and contrasting function in the sentence, such as *though* or *however*.

> ✗ *A water birth usually calls for advance planning as not many hospitals have their own pools. But you may be able to hire your own birthing tub to use in hospital or at home though.*

> ✗ *A water birth ... their own pools. But you may, however, be able to hire your own birthing tub to use in hospital or at home.*

Be careful to avoid tautologies like these. Note, however, that ***but nevertheless*** (or ***nonetheless***) is acceptable:

> ✓ *But nevertheless you may be able to hire your own birthing tub ...*

## conjunctions that come in pairs

There are a number of conjunctions, or 'linking words', that frequently function in pairs in English. Among the common ones are ***both ... and***, ***either ... or***, ***neither ... nor***, and ***not only ... but also*** (or ***not just ... but also***). Such pairs are used to create, point out or emphasize contrasts or similarities between two parallel elements of a sentence:

> *We saw both John and Harry.*
> *We both saw John and heard him.*
> *There were piles of old newspapers both in the hall and on the stairs.*

To create or preserve the correct balance or contrast, therefore, it is necessary to be careful to construct sentences in such a way that whatever follows the first member of any of these pairs parallels in structure whatever follows the second member. Failure to make this balance is very common, both in speech and in writing:

✗    *You may either send John or his brother.*
✓    *You may send either John or his brother.*

✗    *We are not only interested in your book but also in you as a person.*
✓    *We are interested not only in your book but also in you as a person.*
✓    *We are not only interested in your book but also interested in you as a person.*

✗    *Not only does he fight and threaten them but also fails to pay his dues and rings their door bells at odd hours.*
✓    *He not only fights and threatens them but also fails to pay his dues and rings their door bells at odd hours.*
✓    *Not only does he fight and threaten them but he also fails to pay his dues and rings their door bells at odd hours.*

In informal contexts, this is not something to worry about, since the structural imbalance usually causes no confusion or ambiguity in what is being said; indeed, it is quite normal for **either** and **neither** to precede the verb in informal English, even where this causes an unbalanced sentence:

>    *I shall either read my magazine or a newspaper.*

Care should, however, be taken to avoid such imbalances in more formal contexts, especially in formal writing.

**dangling participle** see INCORRECT ATTACHMENTS.


## dare

●    When the verb **dare** means 'to challenge (someone to do something)', it is followed by **to** and an infinitive: *I dare you to say that to her* □ *Even if he dares you to do it, don't do it.*

●    When **dare** means 'to be brave enough to', it may be used with any of three constructions:

i)    It may be followed by **to** and an infinitive, with the forms of the verb being the same as those of any ordinary verb:

>    *If he dares to do that, I'll just walk out.*
>    *I do not dare to criticize him.*
>    *Would he dare to come?*

and similarly

>    *if I dare to go*
>    *do I dare to go?*
>    *he did not dare to go*

*didn't she <u>dare</u> to go?*
*he wouldn't <u>dare</u> to go*

ii) **Dare** may be followed by an infinitive without **to**, again with 'ordinary' word-endings:

*I <u>do</u> not <u>dare</u> criticize him.*
*Would he <u>dare</u> come?*
*If he <u>dares</u> do that, I'll just walk out.*

>  Some authorities deprecate this construction, preferring those indicated in either (i) or (iii).

iii) **Dare** may behave like an auxiliary verb (ie, like *can*, *will* or *must*), in which case it is again followed by an infinitive without **to**, but in this case, the constructions and forms of the verb are the same as for other modal auxiliaries:

*I <u>dare</u> not criticize him.*
*<u>Daren't</u> he come?*
*If he <u>dare</u> do that, I'll just walk out.*

Similarly:

*<u>dare</u> I go?*
*<u>dared</u> she go?*
*she <u>dared</u> not go*

Notice in particular that in this third type of construction, the third person singular is **dare**, not **dares**, as in the third example above.

>  As an auxiliary, **dare** also functions in informal speech as a past-tense form when combined with **not**: *I was so frightened that I daren't leave the room* (= 'I did not dare leave the room').

- **dare say**

The phrase **dare say** (= 'to expect, suppose, agree') is used only with the pronoun **I** and in the present tense:

*I dare say you're right.*

It is now normally written as two words, but it may also be written as a single word:

*I daresay you're right.*

## do

**Do** is often used in English to avoid the repetition of a verb or verb-phrase, as in *He enjoys that as much as I do* (= 'as much as I enjoy it'). There are, however, certain constructions in which this use of *do* is not correct, and care must be taken to avoid these:

i)   *Do* should not be used as a substitute for a verb which has not actually been used already but has only been implied:

✗   *No reply was forthcoming although they had promised <u>they would do</u>.*
(*Do* replaces an implied verb *reply* which does not in fact appear in the sentence; *reply* in the example is a noun).

✓   *No reply was forthcoming although they had promised <u>to send one</u>.*

ii)   Particular care must be taken to ensure that *do* and the previous occurrence of the verb it replaces agree with regard to active or passive voice:

✗   *John <u>was laughed at</u> by the girls this morning <u>just as we did</u> last night.*
(*Was laughed at* is passive but *did* is an active verb.)

✓   *The girls <u>laughed at John</u> this morning <u>just as we did</u> last night.*

iii)   *Do* should not be used as a substitute for the verb *to be*:

✗   *He told me to <u>be</u> careful but I <u>didn't</u>.*
✓   *He told me to <u>be</u> careful but I <u>wasn't</u>.*

iv)   In informal English, *do* may be used as a substitute for the verb *to have* or for a verb in a tense formed with *have*:

*I <u>have</u> more difficulty with English grammar than you <u>do</u>.*
*I <u>have read</u> more books than he <u>has done</u>.*

Such constructions are not approved of by some people and are therefore perhaps better avoided in formal speech and writing:

*I <u>have</u> more difficulty with English grammar than you <u>have</u>.*
*I <u>have read</u> more books than he <u>has</u>.*

## double negative

A construction with two negative words (such as *not, never, nothing*) which together are equivalent in meaning to a single negative is called a 'double negative'. For example, there is a double negative in *I **never** did **nothing***, if what is meant is 'I never did anything'. Such double negatives are common in non-standard and dialectal English:

*Well, I <u>couldn't see no advantage</u> in going where she was going, so I made up my mind I wouldn't try for it. But I never said so, because it would only make trouble, and <u>wouldn't do no good</u>.*

— Mark Twain, *Huckleberry Finn*

The Standard English equivalents of the underlined phrases would be '*couldn't see any advantage*' and '*wouldn't do any good*'.

Such double negatives are not acceptable in modern Standard English and must therefore be avoided in all formal speech and writing.

⚠️  It has often been asserted by traditional grammarians of English that the double negative is to be condemned as illogical, because two negatives cancel each other out and are therefore equivalent to an affirmative (eg '*I didn't see nobody*' = '*I saw somebody*'). However, double negatives are found, not only in non-standard English, but also in the standard educated forms of many modern European languages (such as Spanish and Russian), and were perfectly acceptable in educated English also up until the 18th century.

Of course, if *I never did nothing* means 'There was never a time when I did nothing', the use of the two negatives is quite correct even in Standard English, as here both words carry their full negative meaning. Compare:

> <u>Not</u> one of them did <u>not</u> walk with a limp or drag a distorted limb. (= 'Every one of them did walk with either a limp or a distorted limb.')
>
> — Michael Moorcock

Similarly, two negative words may be used together in a sentence as a stylistic device, eg to make a less forceful statement than the corresponding positive word would: *I was <u>not disinclined</u> to go* means 'I was quite inclined to go'.

• Particular attention must be paid to sentences including words such as **hardly**, **scarcely** and **without**, which are negative in force but not in form. These words also occur inadvertently in a sort of double-negative construction which is less easy to spot than the type discussed above:

> He <u>hadn't scarcely</u> a penny in the bank. (= 'He had scarcely a penny in the bank.')
> I <u>don't believe hardly anything</u> he tells me. (= 'I believe hardly anything he tells me.')

• Yet another type of double-negative construction is sometimes heard in statements of surprise or wonder:

> I <u>wouldn't</u> be surprised if it <u>didn't</u> rain this afternoon. (meaning 'I expect it will rain')

Double-negative constructions like these arise from a confusion between two similar constructions, each containing a single negative word:

> I wouldn't be surprised if it rained this afternoon.
> I would be surprised if it didn't rain this afternoon.

Opinions as to the acceptability of such constructions vary: with words such as *wonder* and *surprised*, they are accepted by some authorities as correct. Like other double negatives, however, they are best avoided in formal English, especially in writing, and replaced by one or other of the single-negative forms.

Similar mistakes may occur after other words, eg *doubt*:

*I don't doubt that a solution may not be found soon.*

(where the second *not* is superfluous if what is meant is that the speaker expects a solution to be found soon).

These are less acceptable than the examples with *surprise* and *wonder*.

• In general, care should be taken not to include so many negative words or words of negative force (like *doubt* and *deny*) in a sentence that its meaning becomes obscured, even if not actually distorted. If the negatives start to pile up, rephrase the sentence.

## each

• When *each* is the subject of the sentence, it should be followed by a singular verb and, if appropriate, singular pronouns, possessive adjectives, etc:

*The rule is that each looks after his own tools.*

(For the use of *they, their*, etc with singular reference, rather than *he, his, she, her, his or her*, etc, see THEY, THEM, THEIR, ETC.)

When *each* precedes the word to which it refers, it should be followed by a singular verb, etc, no matter whether the word it refers to is singular or plural:

*Each child has six pencils.*
*Each of the children has six pencils.*

When *each* follows the word it refers to (which will be in the plural), it should be followed by a plural verb:

*The children each have six pencils.*

• When *each* precedes the main describing word (verb or adjective) of the sentence, the possessive adjectives, pronouns, etc occurring later in the sentence agree with the subject of the sentence:

*We are each responsible for our own children.*

When *each* follows the main descriptive word, subsequent pronouns, etc are singular, agreeing with *each*:

*We are responsible each for his or her own children.*

## either

As a pronoun, *either* must be used to refer to only two people, things, etc:

*I have examined both machines. Either of them would be suitable for our purpose.*

If the reference is to more than two individuals, use *any*, not *either*.

Since *either* refers to one or other of two, it is singular in reference and should be followed by a singular verb:

✓    *I don't think that either of them <u>is</u> capable of doing it.*
✗    *I don't know whether either of them <u>are</u> suitable.*

As any other part of speech, *either* may correctly be used when referring to more than two options:

*You may either come with us, go with John, or stay here on your own.*

### ✦  *Either . . . or*

i)  If *either . . . or* links two singular noun or noun-phrase subjects of a verb, the verb is singular:

*Either John or Mary <u>is</u> wrong.*

If one of the linked subjects is plural, so must the verb be (and the plural word or phrase should be placed nearest the verb):

*Either John or his friends <u>are</u> wrong.*

If both the linked subjects are singular, but differ with regard to person (eg *you or I, you or she*), the verb should agree with the subject closest to it: *Either you or I <u>am</u> wrong* □ *Either you or she <u>is</u> wrong*; but although correct, such constructions usually sound a little uncomfortable, and it is generally better to rephrase them to avoid the difficulty, eg *Either you are wrong or I am.*

ii)  Since *either . . . or* is used to compare or contrast two individuals, items, phrases, etc, care must be taken to ensure that the words or phrases which follow *either* and *or* parallel each other in construction:

✓    *You may send <u>either</u> John <u>or</u> his brother.*
✗    *You may <u>either</u> send John <u>or</u> his brother.*

(For further discussion of this, see CONJUNCTIONS THAT COME IN PAIRS.)

### *even*

Careful attention must be paid to the placing of the adverb *even* in a sentence, as its position affects the meaning of the whole sentence. *Even* should, at least in formal, written English, stand immediately before the word or words in a sentence which it is meant to emphasize, as in the following sentences:

*Even John helped me.* (= 'Of all people, I did not expect John to help me, but he did.')
*John even helped me.* (= 'He didn't just watch or offer advice.')
*John helped even me.* (= 'He didn't just help other people, but me as well.')

In spoken English, stress and intonation patterns help to convey the meaning intended, and *even* is frequently placed before the verb even when it is modifying some other word or phrase in the sentence. In *John even helped me* (with stress on '*me*'), it is clear that *even* is modifying *me* even though it is standing before *helped*. Similarly, in *John even helped me* (with stress on '*John*'), it is clear that *even* is modifying *John*. Informal written English tends to follow the pattern of spoken English, and this is acceptable.

## every

A noun phrase which includes *every* is followed by a singular verb:

> *Every room is painted white.*
> *Not every family has a car.*

---

 *A televison in every room* or *televisions in every room*?
When you are saying that there is one of something in, beside, for, belonging to, etc every X (whatever X might be), then refer to that 'something' in the singular: *There is a present for every child.*

*There are presents for every child* would suggest that there is more than one present for each child.

---

- For possible ambiguities with *every* . . . *not*, see NEGATION.

## fused participle see -*ING* WORDS.

## have

An error often heard in speech and not unknown in writing is the insertion of an extra *have* after *had* in conditional constructions:

> ✗ *If he had have done it, I would have been very angry.*

The extra *have* is particularly common when either it or the preceding *had* is in an abbreviated form:

> ✗ *If he'd have done it, . . .*
> ✗ *If he had've done it, . . .*

Such constructions are ungrammatical, and must be avoided; *had* on its own is all that is needed:

> *If he had done it, . . .*

## here is/are, there is/are see AGREEMENT WITH LINKING VERBS under AGREEMENT.

## -ics see NOUNS ENDING IN -*S*: SINGULAR OR PLURAL?

## incorrect attachments

When a subordinate clause which has no subject of its own precedes the main clause to which it relates, it is a general rule of English that the subject of the main clause is equally the subject of the subordinate clause:

> *While running for a bus, she fell and broke her arm.* ('She' was doing the running.)
> *Changing the subject for a minute, I'd like to turn your attention to the financial aspects of the scheme.* ('I' am changing the subject.)
> *Propped up against the wall like that, those poles are a danger to everyone who passes.* ('The poles' are propped against the wall.)

A common error is to construct a sentence in such a way that the subject of the main clause is not the word the subordinate clause is meant to modify. In the following examples, the highlighted clauses do not modify the subject of the main clause but some other element in it:

> *While driving through the farm, a cow ran into his car.*
> *Propped up against the wall like that, anyone could trip over those poles.*
> *Badly damaged by fire last year, I am in the process of rebuilding the house.*

Such constructions are often known as ***dangling participles*** or ***misrelated participles***, but similar constructions occur in which there is no participle at all:

> *I hope to visit China soon. As the biggest nation in the world, I want to learn as much about it as possible.*

Opinions vary as to the gravity of this error. As can be seen from some of the examples, the effect of this misrelating of the subordinate clause is sometimes rather comical or ludicrous, and that is often grounds enough for avoiding it. Also, since such constructions are considered incorrect by many people, they are best always avoided in formal speech and writing, by rephrasing the sentence to make the implied subject of the subordinate clause and the subject of the main clause match (eg *Propped up against the wall like that, these poles could cause someone to trip*) or by supplying an explicit subject for the subordinate clause (eg *While he was driving through the farm, a cow ran into his car*).

Sometimes there is no word in the main clause that could be taken to be the implied subject of the verb in the subordinate clause :

> *Sitting in a hot and stuffy office, it seemed as if five o'clock would never come.*

Such constructions are generally felt to be more acceptable than those in which there is a word in the main clause to which the subordinate clause could be wrongly related, but they should still be avoided in formal contexts by rephrasing the sentence.

- **Exceptions to the general rule**
   i)   Clauses which indicate the speaker's or writer's attitude to what is said in the rest of the sentence are not required to follow the rules explained above:

> *Strictly speaking, a whale is not a fish at all.*

ii)   The rule is often broken when the subject of the subordinate clause is to be understood as a vaguely and broadly inclusive 'one', 'we', 'they' or 'people in general':

> *Looking ahead to the weekend's sport now, Arsenal should have an easy win against Manchester United.*
> *To be a successful bird-watcher, what is needed is a notebook and pencil, a guidebook and a pair of binoculars.*

This is particularly common in scientific literature:

> *To avoid this difficulty, the acid should be added 1cc at a time.*

iii)   The rule is quite acceptably broken in the case of words in present-day English which are in origin participles but which are now treated as prepositions and conjunctions:

| | | | |
|---|---|---|---|
| *assuming* | *following* | *provided* | *talking* (*of*) |
| *barring* | *given* | *providing* | *seeing* |
| *concerning* | *granted* | *regarding* | |
| *considering* | *including* | *speaking* (*of*) | |
| *excepting* | *pending* | *supposing* | |

> *Regarding your recent inquiry, I am writing to inform you that we are now able to supply the type of paper you require.*
> *Considering the dangers involved, he was very lucky to get out alive.*
> *Talking of John, here he comes now.*
> *Seeing that you only have three days to complete the job, you had better get started now.*

## infinitives

When a sentence including a main verb and a dependent infinitive refers in some way to the past, there is often uncertainty about whether it is the finite verb or the infinitive (or both) that should be in the past tense: is it, for example, correct to say *He would like to have been there* or *He would have liked to be there* or *He would have liked to have been there*?

The correct rules are fairly straightforward:

i)   When the finite verb refers back to a time in the past and the attached infinitive describes a state or action existing, occurring, beginning, etc at that same time in the past, the finite verb should be in the past tense and accompanied by the simple infinitive:

> *We wanted to come.*
> *We meant to change a nation, and instead, we changed a world.*
> — Ronald Reagan
> *They tell me that you have had to kill a man in the course of an assignment.*

The same applies to possible, rather than actual, past states or actions:

> *We would have wanted to come if we had known about it.*

ii)   In all other cases, if the state or action described by the infinitive is in any way prior to the (actual or possible) state or action described by the finite verb, the finite verb should be in whatever tense is appropriate and it should be followed by a past infinitive:

> *Before you could even think of being Prime Minister, you<u>'d need to have done</u> a*
> *good deal more jobs than that.*

— Margaret (later Lady) Thatcher

A double past tense (ie, a past tense of the finite verb and a past infinitive) is therefore correct when the finite verb refers to a past time and the infinitive refers to a time prior to that:

> *I <u>would have liked to have discussed</u> this with you before yesterday's meeting.*
> *They <u>needed to have left</u> before then if they were to have any hope of catching the*
> *last train.*

---

   The same rules apply when what precedes the infinitive is not a full verb but a linking verb plus an adjective:

> *It <u>would be better to leave</u> at once.*
> *It <u>would have been better to have discussed</u> this before the meeting.*

---

## *-ing* words: problems with present participles and gerunds

***Present participles*** and ***gerunds*** are forms of verbs which end in *-ing*: *running, screaming, growing*, etc.

A present participle is the form of the verb that is used to form a continuous tense such as *he <u>is coming</u>* and *they <u>were singing</u>*, and is also used as an adjective, as in *a <u>growing</u> boy*.

A gerund is a noun — it is sometimes called a 'verbal noun' — which describes an action, as in *<u>Seeing</u> is <u>believing</u>* and *<u>Going</u> there was a big mistake*.

There are two main problems with regard to the use of present participles and gerunds, usually referred to as the ***dangling participle*** and the ***fused participle***.

### ✦   Dangling participles

It is a rule of English grammar that if a participle in a subordinate clause has no explicitly stated subject, the subject of the main clause is to be taken as being the subject of the participle also:

> *<u>Walking</u> in the hills the other day, <u>I</u> saw a large flock of geese.* (= 'While I was
> walking . . . I saw . . .')

When this rule is broken, the result is often referred to as a ***dangling participle*** or ***misrelated participle***, eg:

> *<u>Driving</u> in the hills the other day, <u>a tree</u> fell on our car.*

For further discussion of these and similar constructions, see INCORRECT ATTACHMENTS.

### ✦ Gerund or participle — which to use?

Since a gerund is a noun, a noun or pronoun governing a gerund should in theory be in the possessive form:

> *The main feature of her acting is her obvious sincerity.*
> *The leading man's poor acting could hardly be compensated for by the efforts of the rest of the cast.*

When the focus of the statement is on the action described by the gerund, this is the construction generally used. However, in some cases the focus is not simply on the action described by the gerund but on both the action and the individual(s) performing the action. In such cases, a different but similar construction is often used, involving a noun in its basic form or a pronoun in its objective case followed by a present participle. Compare

> *John's acting like that really upset her.* (= possessive noun + gerund)

and

> *John acting like that really upset her.* (= noun + present participle)

In traditional grammar, this participial construction, which is known as a *fused participle*, is condemned as ungrammatical, but notwithstanding these objections, there is no reason at all to avoid using it in informal language, nor in formal speech or writing either unless you want to steer clear of the criticisms of those who do not approve of the construction.

There are even a number of cases where the only possible idiomatic construction is the non-possessive form. *The fused-participle construction must be used* with

i)   nouns and pronouns linked together by a preposition or a conjunction:

> *I don't mind some of the children going, but not all of them.*
> *I don't mind some of them going.*
> *I don't mind John and you going.*

ii)  abstract nouns:

> *It was foolish to have bought the picture without its authenticity being checked first.*

iii) most inanimate concrete nouns:

> *It isn't my luggage getting lost that I mind, it's the courier's couldn't-care-less attitude I object to.*

iv)  indefinite pronouns such as *something* or *anything*:

> *There is no hope of anything being done about it now.*

- There is a similar choice between a gerund and a participle in constructions following words such as *difficulty*, *point* and *trouble*:

*You shouldn't have any difficulty finding a room for the night* (= participle)
*You shouldn't have any difficulty in finding a room for the night.* (= gerund, object of the preposition *in*)

In informal English, either construction is acceptable, but in formal English the construction with a preposition and a gerund is preferred.

## inversion of subject and verb

In English, the subject of a verb normally precedes the verb in statements: *John arrived yesterday evening.* There are, however, certain contexts in which the subject of a verb follows the verb in a statement:

i) Inversion is frequently used **when the subject of the sentence is longer than the predicate**:

*Across the road stood a little thatched cottage with tiny windows and with ivy and hollyhocks growing up its walls.*

Inversion of this sort should not be used if the relative lengths of the subject and predicate do not justify it:

✓ *Attending the fête this afternoon will be the mayor, the mayoress, and several members of the borough council.*
✗ *Attending the fête this afternoon will be the mayor.*

ii) In story-telling, inversion may be used for a dramatic effect, or to emphasize the subject or some element of the predicate by moving them out of their normal positions in the sentence:

*Came the day of the fête, and the children were all excited.*

This literary device should not be used in formal writing such as reports, but is useful in narratives if not overused. It should not be used when there is nothing being emphasized in the sentence.

Some inversions of this type are virtually set phrases: *Down came the rain.*

There is no inversion with a pronoun subject: *Off he went, whistling happily.*

iii) When reporting direct speech and naming the person speaking, the subject and verb may be inverted:

*'You could inquire for him,' said Mr Fredericks benignly, 'at an address I'll give you in Islington.'*

— Ellis Peters

*'Rats!' murmured Winston. 'In this room!'*

— George Orwell

It is equally correct not to invert the subject and object:

> *'Murders are committed so easily on paper,' Gerard said sceptically, 'but in real life they seem to me to provide a lot of practical difficulties.'*
>
> — Ellis Peters

It is generally recommended that inversions of this sort should only be used with verbs denoting straightforward notions of saying, writing, thinking, answering, laughing and so on, and should be avoided with verbs less commonly used along with direct speech such as *admonish, rejoin, remember*, etc. This principle is correct, but it is unfortunately impossible to draw a line between the verbs that can readily be inverted and those that should not be: the most that can be said as a rule of thumb is that ***the less frequently a verb is generally to be found in conjunction with direct speech, the less desirable is the inversion of subject and verb***.

When the verb of speaking, etc precedes the direct speech, inversion is generally deprecated:

> **?** *Murmured Winston: 'Rats! In this room!'*

---

 There is nowadays generally **no inversion when the subject is a pronoun**. Inversion with a pronoun subject is rather old-fashioned:

> *'It is fine,' said she. . . .*
> *'I believe you,' said I.*

but is also found in a very informal modern style of story-telling:

> *'Well,' says she, 'if that's the case, I don't see much point in going at all.'*

---

## measurements and numbers

Why is a pole that is *six feet* long a *six-foot* pole? What are the rules governing the choice of singular and plural forms in measurements?

i) ***Nouns denoting measurements are always in the singular when they occur in combination with a numeral in a compound adjective used attributively*** (ie before another noun): *three-inch nails □ a ten-mile hike □ a ten-pound note*.

ii) In non-attributive expressions of measurement, ***metric measurements are always used in the plural***: *twenty metres of wire □ three litres of milk*.

***Most non-metric measurements are likewise used in the plural***: *three tons of sand □ thirty yards of rope*. However, **stone** may be used in either the singular (*She only weighs four stone*) or the plural (*I'll need two stones/stone of potatoes*) and **hundredweight** always is singular (*two hundredweight of sand*).

**Foot** is used in the singular when following a number (*He's over six foot now*) but in the plural when there is a following adjective (*He is over six feet tall*). When a number expressing a number of inches is added, ***foot*** is again used in the singular (*He's six foot four now*) unless the word ***inches*** itself is present, in which case ***foot*** is in the plural (*He's at least six feet four inches by now*).

Other singular uses of nouns of measurement are acceptable only in informal speech and writing: *I've only got three pound forty on me. Will that be enough?*

iii) Preceded by a numeral, words such as *hundred, thousand* and *million* are used in the singular: *three million people* □ *two hundred pounds*.

With more indefinite expressions without a numeral, they are plural: *millions of people* □ *Many hundreds of pounds have been lost in this way*.

**misrelated participle** see INCORRECT ATTACHMENTS.

## *need*

The verb ***need***, when followed by an infinitive, may be constructed in two ways:

i) It may be followed by ***to*** and an infinitive, and have the verb-endings of any ordinary verb:

> *I do not need to go.*
> *Would he need to go?*
> *If he needs to go, I'll go with him.*

Similarly:

> *I need to go.*
> *Did she need to go?*
> *Didn't he need to go?*
> *He wouldn't need to go.*

ii) ***Need*** may be followed by an infinitive without ***to***, in which case the forms of the verb are the same as for verbs such as *can, must* and *shall* (differing from the 'ordinary' verb forms in that the *he/she/it* form of the verb does not end in *-s*):

> *You need not tell him.*
> *He need not leave.*
> *Needn't he come?*

This second construction with ***need*** is possible only in the present tense and only in questions or negative statements. In all other cases, the first type of construction is obligatory.

## negation

When a negative word such as ***not*** or ***no*** is used in a sentence, care must be taken to avoid ambiguities or errors with regard to what the negative word is negating.

- **not all** and **all not**

There may be ambiguity in a sentence which includes both **not** and **all** or **every**. If you say, for example, *All the members of the union have not signed the new contract*, it is not clear whether some members have signed (but not all of them) or no members at all have signed. Take care to phrase such sentences in such a way that no ambiguity is possible: eg *Some members have not signed . . .* or *None of the members have signed . . .* or *Not every member has signed . . .*

- **not, no**, etc in linked clauses

When there is a negative word in the first of two (or more) linked clauses, make sure that the negation does, or does not (according to what is intended), carry over into the later clause (or clauses). Errors in this respect are common:

i) A negative word in the first clause should apply to the following clause also, but the sentence is structured in such a way as to prevent this interpretation:

> *I prefer to work with people <u>who have not studied drama and have any experience of acting</u>*.

(It is clear that what is wanted is people who have <u>no</u> experience of acting, but the negative **not** does not extend its influence to the second *have*. The final clause should read . . . *and have no experience of acting* or . . . *nor have any experience of acting*.)

ii) A negative word in the first clause should apply to the following clause but not to a later one, but the sentence is structured in such a way that it actually applies to both:

> *I don't think <u>that sentence is very clear and needs to be rewritten</u>*.

(The negation strictly applies to both subordinate clauses (ie 'I think that sentence is not very clear and does not need to be rewritten') when what is intended is clearly 'I think that sentence is not very clear and needs to be rewritten', with the negation in the main clause applying only to the first of the linked subordinate clauses but not to the second. The sentence needs to be rephrased, eg *I don't think that sentence is very clear; it needs to be rewritten*.)

## neither

- As a pronoun, **neither** should only be used when referring to one of two individuals, things, etc: *I've tried both pens but neither of them works*; with larger numbers, use **none** or **no**: *I've tried all my pens but none of them works* □ *No pen works as well as the one I lost last week*. However, as any other part of speech, **neither** may correctly be used when referring to more than two alternatives: *I'm afraid I can't manage a meeting this week, neither this afternoon, nor tomorrow, nor Friday*.

- **Neither** may be followed by a singular verb: *Neither of them <u>is</u> free to go*. However, a plural construction is common and generally accepted (and has been for several hundred years): *Neither of us <u>like</u> tomatoes*. There is no reason to avoid this plural construction in informal English, whatever purists say, but it is better to keep to the singular construction in more formal contexts, unless the singular would sound awkward for some reason. For example, while of two males it could be said *Neither of them has brought his music*, and of two females *Neither of them has brought her music*, if speaking of one male and one female, the possessive must be *their* (neither *his* nor *her* would do) and the tendency is therefore to make the verb plural also, ie *Neither of them have brought their music*.

**✦   neither ... nor**

i)   Always follow **neither** by **nor**, not **or**:

   ✓    *Neither Richard nor David is coming.*
   ✗    *Neither Richard or David is coming.*

ii)   In formal speech and writing, always place the **neither** and the **nor** next to the words or phrases that are being contrasted, and make sure that the balance of the sentence and the implied contrast between its parts are correctly stated:

   ✓    *I can think of neither a better method nor a cheaper one.*
   ✗    *I can neither think of a better method nor a cheaper one.*

(In informal speech and writing, it is common, and quite acceptable, for **neither** to be placed before the verb, as in the second example, in cases where the contrast is actually between the objects of the verb — indeed, the strictly correct form could sound rather over-precise and pompous — but care should be taken not to do this in formal writing such as reports.)

iii)   When there is a double subject linked by **neither ... nor**, the verb should agree with the noun or pronoun closest to it, ie the one following **nor**, but strict adherence to this rule does cause problems and it is therefore subject to certain exceptions:

(a) When both of the linked subjects are singular and in the third person, the verb should strictly speaking be in the third person singular: *Neither the chairman nor the secretary is able to attend the meeting.* This rule should be adhered to in formal English, but in informal contexts a plural verb is quite acceptable: *Neither the chairman nor the secretary are able to attend the meeting.*

(b) When one of the subjects is singular and the other is plural, the verb should be plural: *Neither John's brothers nor his sister are going.* Some authorities recommend that in such cases the plural subject should be placed after **nor** in order that it be beside the plural verb: *Neither John's sister nor his brothers are going.*

(c) When the linked subjects are not both in the third person, the verb should be made to agree with the subject closer to it: *Neither you nor I am going* ▫ *Neither you nor John is going.* However, this often sounds awkward, a plural verb being preferred and quite acceptable: *Neither you nor I are going* ▫ *Neither you nor John are going.*

## none

*None* may be followed by either a singular or a plural verb, whichever is logically appropriate.

When denoting a quantity or amount, *none* should be followed by a singular verb: *None of the milk was spilt.*

When referring to a plural noun, *none* is followed by a singular verb if the emphasis is on each individual person or thing within the group, but by a plural verb if the emphasis is on all or part of the group as a whole:

> *We all had to sing a song or recite a poem — none of us was allowed to say no.*
> *None of us have been to France.*
> *None of them speak French.*

## nouns ending in -s: singular or plural?

- **clothes**

The names of various items of clothing look like and function as plural nouns, although there is no corresponding singular form or the corresponding singular is very restricted in use. Among these are *clothes, drawers, jeans, knickers, pants* and *trousers*.

The singular form of some of these words may be used attributively, eg *knicker elastic* and *trouser suit*. (*Trouser* may occasionally be heard in the singular in clothes shops: *This is a particularly fine trouser, sir*; otherwise the correct singular form is *a pair of trousers*, etc. In the case of *clothes*, the singular is *an item of clothing*.)

- **diseases**

The names of diseases which end in *-s* (eg *measles, mumps, rabies, shingles*) are treated as singular nouns:

> *Rickets occurs in infancy and early childhood.*

*Measles* and *rickets* may also be treated as plural nouns.

- **games**

The names of games ending in *-s* (eg *billiards, bowls, darts, dominoes, skittles, snakes and ladders*) are treated as singular nouns:

> *Draughts is thought to have been played in ancient Egypt.*

Of course, when the noun refers to the counters, pieces or other items used in these games, it is correctly treated as plural: *If you hit the skittles, they fall over.*

- **-ics**

Nouns ending in *-ics*, when denoting subjects of study, academic disciplines or fields of activity are singular:

> *Politics is perhaps the only profession for which no preparation is thought necessary.*
>
> — Robert Louis Stevenson

> *Metaphysics is the finding of bad reasons for what we believe upon instinct.*
>
> — F H Bradley

> *Mathematics, rightly viewed, possesses not only truth, but supreme beauty — a beauty cold and austere, like that of sculpture.*
>
> — Bertrand Russell

However, when such words denote data, ideas, actions, etc, they are treated as plural nouns, as again shown by the verb-forms in the following examples:

> *Their politics at that time were much more left-wing than they are now.*

Note the two following examples, in which *Olympics* is treated first as a collective singular noun and second as a plural. Both are acceptable:

> *It's not like home, but I think the Olympics is about sportsmen being together.*
>
> — Ed Moses

> *The Olympics are about performance, doing the best you can do.*
>
> — Carl Lewis

- **parts of the body**

Names of muscles such as *biceps* and *triceps* are singular: *His right biceps seems to be more fully developed than his left biceps.* These nouns have the same form in the plural as in the singular.

*Genitals* and *entrails* are plural nouns.

- **tools and instruments**

The names of many tools and instruments are plural in form and use: *Where are the pliers?* □ *a pair of scissors.* Among the other words that come into this category are *binoculars, calipers, compasses, dividers, glasses, pincers, scales, shears, spectacles, tongs* and *tweezers.*

*Forceps*, on the other hand, is strictly speaking a singular noun forceps), with a plural also *forceps* (*two forceps*) but due to its form and meaning is now often treated as a plural in the same way as the words listed above (*Where are the forceps?* □ *a pair of forceps*), and although some purists may object to this, it is a well-established usage and should not now be considered incorrect.

*Bellows* is equally correctly a singular or a plural noun.

- **towns and countries**

Most names of towns and countries which end in *-s* are singular nouns:

> *Athens is the capital of Greece.*
> *The Netherlands is among the most densely populated countries in the world.*

However, 'the Bahamas' and 'the Philippines' denote not only countries but also groups of islands. For this reason, they may sometimes be treated as plural nouns, and are always so in the sense of groups of islands rather than states. Compare the following quotations from *Chambers World Gazetteer*:

> *The Philippines is divided into 72 provinces.* (= 'The Philippines' as a state, treated as a singular noun)
> *The Bahamas comprise the following 17 islands and island groups.* (= 'The Bahamas' as a state, but treated as a plural noun)
> *The Bahamas were visited by Christopher Columbus in 1492.* (= 'The Bahamas' as a group of islands, therefore treated as a plural noun)

- **Other potentially problematic words ending in -*s***

There remain a number of other words of this type that cannot easily be grouped into categories like those given above. Some are plural in use as well as in form, others are plural in form but function grammatically as singulars, and some can be either singular or plural.

i)   The following words are plural nouns, although there is no commonly used corresponding singular form for most of them: *alms, banns, contents, dregs, goods, minutes* (of a meeting), *premises, proceedings, proceeds, remains, takings* and *victuals*.

ii)   *Mews* is in origin the plural of *mew*, a place where hawks were kept while moulting, but it is now generally treated as a singular noun with the plurals *mews* or *mewses*.

Similarly *innings* is in origin the plural of *inning*; it still is in the vocabulary of baseball, but in the terminology of cricket it functions as both singular and plural (the plural form *inningses* is not correct).

*News* is now only used as a singular noun, although until the end of the last century it could be treated as either singular or plural.

iii)   A number of words may be treated as either singular or plural: *barracks, headquarters, whereabouts, works* (and so also *gasworks, ironworks, waterworks*, etc).

*Gallows* may likewise be treated as a singular or a plural noun, but unlike the other words in this category, it also has another plural form *gallowses*.

In the sense of 'method or way of achieving', *means* may be either singular or plural: *This is just a means to an end, not the end in itself* □ *There are various means of achieving what we want.* In the sense of 'financial resources', it is always plural: *Our means are insufficient for our needs.*

## *of* and *'s*

### ✦   *of* or *'s*?

It is impossible to give a concise rule governing the choice between *of* and *'s* in the formation of possessives and similar constructions. Indeed, with many nouns both *of* and *'s* are possible: *this car's engine* or *the engine of this car, a bee's wings* or *the wings of a bee*. As a general rule, the more animate and personal a noun is, the more likely it is to form a possessive with *'s*; the more inanimate and non-personal a noun is, the more likely it is to co-occur with *of*. The following guidelines illustrate the tendencies:

i)     *'s* is very much more common than *of* with nouns denoting or naming people, animals and places: *John's dog* □ *the boy's dog* □ *the dog's tail* □ *Scotland's oil*.

With short proper nouns, *'s* is virtually obligatory in a genuine possessive sense: *John's book*, not *the book of John; of* is acceptable in the sense of 'depicting' (*a statue of John*) or 'directed towards' (*for the love of John*).

ii)    *'s* is often used with nouns denoting regions, institutions, etc: *the country's economic development* □ *the town's ratepayers* □ *the earth's core* □ *the school's playing-fields* □ *our party's policies. Of* is also possible: *the economic development of the country*.

iii)   *'s* is usually used with nouns denoting time: *a day's holiday* □ *today's task* □ *a year's leave of absence*.

iv)    *'s* is more commonly used than *of* with a number of other nouns denoting parts of the body, means of transport, certain activities and qualities, etc: *the car's tyres* □ *life's disappointments* □ *the brain's functions* □ *the play's first scene. Of* is also possible: *the function of the brain*.

v)     With most other nouns, *of* rather than *'s* is normal, if not obligatory: *the roof of the house* □ *the width of the road*.

## ✦ Linked *of*, *'s*, and possessive adjectives

When two or more possessive words are linked to the same noun, there may be some ambiguity with regard to the meaning of the linked construction or a certain awkwardness in the form of the construction.

i)     If a linked plural possessive modifies a plural noun, some ambiguity may arise. For example, it is not clear in *The Committee would have to take account of the Smiths' and the Browns' objections* whether the Smiths and the Browns are raising the same objections or different ones. It may not, of course, be ambiguous in context, but if there is any possibility of ambiguity, especially in reports and minutes of meetings, then the sentence should be rephrased and clarified (eg . . . *take account of the objections raised by the Smiths and of those raised by the Browns*).

There is less ambiguity when the possessives are in the singular: *Smith and Brown's objections* would be objections raised jointly by Smith and Brown, *Smith's and Brown's objections* objections raised separately by them.

ii)    If the linked possessive phrase includes one or more possessive adjectives (eg *my* or *your*), it may sound rather clumsy, even though it is perfectly grammatical:

**?**    *Will the committee take your and his objection into account, do you think?*

If it sounds awkward, rephrase the sentence.

If the linked possessives would include both a possessive adjective and the possessive form of a noun, the sentence almost always has to be rephrased:

**✗**    *John and I's car*
**✗**    *my and John's car*
**✗**    *me and John's car*
**✓**    *the car that John and I own*

Slightly more acceptable is '*X's and my* ...':

**?**    *It's John's and my anniversary*

but this is still best confined to informal speech and writing.

## omission of words

The omission of words which readers or listeners can supply for themselves in order to make the meaning of a sentence complete is called *ellipsis*. Examples of ellipsis are very common, both in speech and in writing:

*I don't want to go, but I have to.* (= '... I have to go.')
*Delighted to make your acquaintance.* (= 'I'm delighted to make your acquaintance.')
*You better go now.* (= 'You'd better go now.')
*Told you I'd do it, didn't I?* (= 'I told you I'd do it'.)

Some ellipses are, however, unacceptable, either because they create ambiguities or because the resulting sentences are ungrammatical.

i)    To avoid ambiguities, always check that there can be no doubt as to what has been omitted. In *She admitted that she had seen one of the stolen cars outside a hotel, but she would not say which*, for example, it is not clear whether it is 'which car' or 'which hotel' that is meant.

ii)    To avoid grammatically incorrect ellipses, check that what remains forms a grammatically correct construction. The following examples illustrate ways in which this rule is often broken.

(a) *Incorrect ellipsis with verbs*:

**✗**    *The alternatives, everyone knows, <u>have not and will not work</u>.*
**✗**    *He stressed that the company <u>had not and would not meet</u> any ransom demands.*
**✗**    *Some of the natives make excellent sheep-men ... but I'm not certain how many of them <u>either wish to or would be capable of running</u> a small flock for themselves.*

— Quoted by David Attenborough, *Quest in Paradise*

For ellipsis to be acceptable, ***the deleted word must be identical in form to the word that remains***. In the above examples, the deleted words are *worked, met* and *run* (*have not worked, had not met, wish to run*) while the corresponding words that remain are *work, meet* and *running*. Ellipsis is therefore not possible in any of these cases.

Notice, however, that where the two verb forms are not identical, ellipsis is often acceptable if it is the second rather the first occurrence of the verb that is omitted:

✓ *The alternatives have not worked and never will.* (ie ... *never will work*)

Note also that for ellipsis to be acceptable the omitted word need not be grammatically identical to the one which remains so long as the two words would be identical in form:

✓ *This is something that I never have and never will put up with.* (ie ... *never have put up with* and *never will put up with*, in which case *put* would be a past participle after *have* but an infinitive after *will*)

(b) *Incorrect ellipsis of prepositions*:
Many adjectives and verbs have to be followed by particular prepositions (eg *happy with, approve of*). If two or more such adjective or verb constructions occur together, it is acceptable to omit the first preposition only if it is the same as the second one:

✓ *I was dreaming of and hoping for a puppy for Christmas.*
✓ *I was praying and hoping for a puppy for Christmas.*
✗ *I was dreaming and hoping for a puppy for Christmas.*

(c) *Incorrect ellipsis in comparisons*:
A very common error is illustrated by the following example:

✗ *People the world over thought of her as being as great, if not better, than her father.*
✓ *People the world over thought of her as being as great as, if not better than, her father.*

The *as* after 'great' cannot be omitted, as can be seen if 'if not better' is deleted, leaving the quite ungrammatical '... *as great than her father*'.

Another common error in comparisons in which some element is deleted is for the deletion to leave behind a comparison between two things that are not in fact the things really being compared:

✗ *Unlike George, Tom's pictures are much admired.*
✓ *Unlike George's, Tom's pictures are much admired.*

## one

In British English, if the pronoun *one* has been used in a sentence, all subsequent pronouns with the same reference must be *one, one's*, etc: *One must look after oneself and one's own property*. In American English, *one* is normally followed by *he, him*, etc: *One must look after himself and his own property*.

Take care not to mix examples of *one* with examples of *you*:

✓    *One can easily correct <u>one's</u> mistakes when <u>one</u> checks the final draft of the text.*

✗    *One can easily correct <u>your</u> mistakes when <u>you</u> check* . . .

## ✦ One of those who . . .

Another common mistake in sentences with *one* is failure to make the verb agree with its true subject because the structure or meaning of the sentence wrongly encourages agreement with some other word or words. In

✗    *He is one of those people who enjoys gardening*

*enjoys* has been made singular to agree with *he* or *one*, whereas it should actually be the plural form *enjoy* to agree with *those people who*. On the other hand

✓    *I am one who really enjoys gardening*

is correct as the verb here must be singular to agree with *one who*. A similar mistake can be seen in

✗    *One in two of the citizens of this town own a car*

in which the verb has been made plural in agreement with the notional plural subject (ie 'one in two of the citizens' = 'half the citizens'), whereas the true subject of the verb is *one*, and the verb must therefore be singular (as can more easily be seen if the sentence is rephrased slightly: *Of the citizens of this town, one in two owns a car*).

## only

Like *even*, *only* must be positioned carefully in a sentence. In formal, written English at least, *only* should stand immediately before the word or words which it is meant to refer to, as in the following examples.

*<u>Only John</u> wrote to me.* (= 'John and no one else')
*John <u>only wrote</u> to me.* (= 'He did nothing more than write')
*John wrote <u>only to me</u>.* (= 'To me and to no one else')

In spoken English, intonation and stress usually help to convey the intended meaning, and there is therefore greater freedom in the positioning of *only*:

*John only <u>wrote</u> to me* (with the stress on *wrote*) means 'He did nothing more than write'.
*John only wrote to <u>me</u>* (with stress on *me*) means 'He wrote to me and to no one else'.

Informal written English tends to follow the pattern of spoken English, and this is entirely acceptable.

## ought

The correct negative form of *ought* in Standard English is *ought not*, which may correctly be shortened to *oughtn't*. *Didn't ought* is not correct in

Standard English, but it may be heard in non-standard dialects. The same holds true for negative 'tag questions': *We ought to leave now, oughtn't we?* is correct (in Standard English), and *We ought to leave now, didn't we?* is incorrect.

## passive

Many authorities on good style recommend that an active sentence is generally to be preferred to a passive one. In *Politics and the English Language*, the writer George Orwell goes so far as to say 'Never use the passive where you can use the active', but this is far too strong a recommendation: even where an active construction would be <u>possible</u>, there are often good reasons for preferring the passive.

The passive is, for example, appropriate when the agent ('doer') of the action is unknown or irrelevant to what is being said, or when you do not for some reason want to identify the agent. Use of the passive rather than the active allows a different focus or emphasis to be put on the various elements of the sentence: compare *A car ran over the dog* and *The dog was run over by a car*. And using a passive construction instead of an active one often gives what is said a more impersonal and objective tone, for which reason the passive is often used in scientific and technical writing — it allows the writer to avoid the necessity of repeatedly saying 'I did this, then I did this, then I did this, . . .' and so on.

### • double passives

It is possible to have two passive constructions functioning together in a sentence:

> *She <u>is expected to be elected</u> leader of the Labour group on the council.*
> *This play <u>was never intended to be produced</u> on stage.*
> *This construction <u>is shown</u> by our evidence <u>not to be</u> very much used nowadays.*

This is entirely acceptable. However, some superficially similar double-passive constructions are not correct:

> ✗   *The play <u>was attempted to be produced</u> on stage.*
> ✗   *This privilege <u>was threatened to be withdrawn</u> if it was abused.*

For the double passive to be acceptable, the 'passiveness' must apply to each of the verbs separately and independently. This can be used as a test for acceptability of a double-passive construction: if the double passive is acceptable, it will be possible to convert the first verb into an active verb and still leave a grammatical sentence. For example, taking the first two sentences from the 'acceptable' group above, we could make the first verb active and equally correctly say

> ✓   <u>We expect her to be elected</u> leader of the Labour group.
> ✓   *The author never <u>intended</u> the play <u>to be produced</u> on stage.*

The active equivalents of the unacceptable double passives would require <u>both</u> verbs to be made active:

✓    They <u>*attempted to perform*</u> *the play on stage.*
✓    They <u>*threatened to withdraw*</u> *the privilege if it was abused.*

✗    They <u>*attempted*</u> *the play* <u>*to be performed*</u> *on stage.*
✗    They <u>*threatened*</u> *the privilege* <u>*to be withdrawn*</u> *if it was abused.*

In addition to *attempt* and *threaten*, other verbs that often occur in these faulty double passives are *begin, hope, omit, propose* and *seek*.

---

 Double passives are acceptable with verbs of thinking and saying even though what results from making the first verb active is not a grammatical sentence:

   ✓    *This species* <u>*is thought to be found*</u> *only on this one island.*
   ✗    *I think this species* <u>*to be found*</u> *only on this one island.*

and similarly

   ✓    *This play* <u>*is said to have been performed*</u> *only once on stage.*

---

## prepositions

### ✦ Ending sentences with a preposition

**The best rule for prepositions is to put them where they sound most natural. There is no reason to artificially distort word order to avoid ending a sentence with a preposition.**

In the past, authorities on good style frequently insisted that a sentence or clause should not end with a preposition, ie that it is incorrect to say *He can never go into a supermarket without buying something he has absolutely no need <u>for</u>* and that the sentence should be rephrased as *He can never go into a supermarket without buying something <u>for</u> which he has absolutely no need*.

Many people, having been taught this rule in school, try to adhere to it religiously, at least in formal speech and writing, and expect others to do so also (this 'error' was still in a 'top twenty' of complaints about incorrect language use made to the BBC in 1981), but in fact, like the so-called split infinitive, this is a 'non-rule' of English imposed in the past by grammarians on the basis of Latin grammar (in which it <u>is</u> impossible to end a sentence with a preposition). There is no need, and there never has been any need, for such a rule in English. Putting prepositions at the end of sentences is entirely natural and quite correct in English, and is to be found in the works of many good writers.

There are indeed some constructions in English in which it is impossible to have the preposition in any position other than at the end of the clause or sentence, eg with a passive form of a phrasal verb: *It doesn't bear <u>thinking about</u>*, or with certain types of questions: *What did you do that <u>for</u>?*

Be careful not to repeat prepositions. This sometimes happens when someone has tried to avoid putting a preposition at the end of a clause by putting at it at the beginning, but has then without thinking put the same preposition at the end as well:

> <u>In</u> what sort of conditions were they living <u>in</u> at that time?

### ✦ Case after prepositions

For ***between you and I/me***, see PRONOUNS IN LINKED SUBJECTS AND OBJECTS in the entry on PRONOUNS below.

## pronouns

Pronouns in English exhibit what is known as 'case'; that is to say, they change their form according to the role they play in a sentence: compare *I saw <u>her</u>* and *<u>She</u> saw <u>me</u>*. Normally this causes no problems, but there are a number of areas of uncertainty that need clarification. (*Who* and *whom* present similar problems, which are dealt with at the entry WHO, WHOM, WHICH, THAT.)

### ✦ Pronoun complements after *to be*

**After the verb *to be*, it is correct to use the objective form of pronouns.**

Expressions such as *It's <u>me</u>* and *It was <u>him</u>* are entirely acceptable in modern English. The use of *I* or *he* in such expressions would sound over-formal or pompous. However, if the pronoun is linked to a following clause, *I, he*, etc rather than *me, him*, etc should be used in formal English: *It was <u>I</u> who broke the window*; *It was me who broke the window* would be acceptable only in informal speech.

### ✦ Pronouns standing alone

**A pronoun on its own should be in the objective form.**

In formal English, a pronoun standing alone should strictly speaking be in the same case as it would be in a full sentence:

> *'Who did that?' 'I.'* (= 'I did')
> *'Who did you see?' 'Him.'* (= 'I saw him')

However, in all but the most formal situations, this sounds over-precise and pedantic, and the objective case-form is generally to be preferred whatever

103

the actual role of the pronoun:

> *'Who did that?' 'Me.'*

## ✦ Pronoun case after prepositions and conjunctions

**After a preposition, a pronoun should be in the objective case.**

Examples:

> *Come with me.*
> *I did it for her.*
> *They can share the sweets between them.*
> *Like me, John is very much an optimist.*

This causes few problems except where the pronoun is linked with some other word (see the next section).

- The only preposition that does not behave like this is **but**, which traditionally is followed by whichever form of pronoun (subjective or objective) is required by the implied relationship of the pronoun to the verb in the sentence or to a verb which is understood:

> *No one but I will be there.'* (= 'I will be there.')
> *There is no one I can turn to for help but him.* (= 'I can turn to him for help.')

However, the objective case is now increasingly accepted as correct after **but** in all contexts. The present position is to allow both the subjective and objective case forms for pronouns standing before the verb in the sentence (*No one but me/I will be there*), and to use the objective form in other positions (*No one will be there but me □ There is no one I can turn to for help but him*).

- There are some other words with which it is not always immediately obvious which case should be used. Among such words are **as** and **than**, which are not prepositions but conjunctions, which behave grammatically rather differently from prepositions. In formal English, the case of a pronoun following these words should be the same as it would be if there were also a verb present, ie the pronoun takes the case that is appropriate to express its relationship to the verb that is understood:

> *He is as good at it as I.* (= 'He is as good as I am.')
> *John is taller than I.* (= 'John is taller than I am.')
> *We paid more than they.* (= 'We paid more than they paid.')
> *I like her more than him.* (= 'I like her more than I like him.')

In informal English, such forms sound pedantic and over-precise, and it is normal to use the objective forms in all cases:

*She is as good as <u>me</u>.*
*John is taller than <u>me</u>.*

Many people would accept the use of objective forms of pronouns after ***than*** and ***as*** in formal English also nowadays: *He seems taller than me* □ *He runs faster than me.*

 Notice that constructions such as *You love him more than me* are ambiguous. This sentence could mean either 'You love him more than I love him' or 'You love him more than you love me'. In order to make such sentences completely unambiguous, it is often better to add a verb to what follows: *You love him more than I do* or *You love him more than you do me.*

## ✦ Pronouns in linked subjects and objects

There are few mistakes made with regard to case when a single pronoun follows a preposition or a verb. However, when the pronoun is linked in some way to a noun, another pronoun or a following clause, mistakes over the choice of case are not infrequent:

✗ *Between <u>you and I</u>, I don't think she's got what it takes.*
✗ *She's going to meet <u>John and I</u> for a drink tomorrow.*
✗ *For <u>we parents</u>, bringing up teenagers nowadays is not easy.*
✗ *For <u>we</u> who have to bring up children on our own, life is far from easy.*

In all these cases, the pronouns should have been in the objective case, since they are the objects of prepositions:

✓ *Between <u>you and me</u>, I don't think she's got what it takes.*
✓ *She's going to meet <u>John and me</u> for a drink tomorrow.*
✓ *For <u>us parents</u>, bringing up teenagers nowadays is not easy.*
✓ *For <u>us</u> who have to bring up children on our own, life is far from easy.*

 Check for such mistakes by mentally removing the element linked to the pronoun and checking that the pronoun that is left is the in the correct form:

✗ *She's going to meet [ John and] I for a drink tomorrow.*
✗ *For we [parents], bringing up teenagers is not easy.*

With the bracketed parts removed, what remains is '*She's going to meet I*' and '*for we*', which are clearly ungrammatical.

• The above examples are all of linked pronoun objects, but the same sort of mistake can arise with linked pronoun subjects:

✗ *<u>John and them</u> are going to a party tonight.*

Here again, the error is clearly seen if the linked element is removed:

✗    *[John and ] Them are going to a party tonight.*

Only in very informal English, especially in speech, is the use of objective case pronouns as subjects when linked to something else generally accepted:

?    *Me and Tom are going too.*

## ✦  *He, she* or *they?*

For discussion of the use of *they* as a singular pronoun, see THEY, THEM, THEIR, ETC.

## ✦  Reflexive pronouns

Reflexive pronouns (ie *myself, yourself, themselves,* etc) generally refer back to the subject of the clause in which they stand:

*I promised myself I wouldn't cry.*
*You're not going all by yourself, are you?*

In such cases, the use of the reflexive pronoun is obligatory. However, **when the pronoun refers to a noun or pronoun that is not the subject of the clause, there is a choice between the reflexive pronouns and the equivalent non-reflexive forms** (*me, you, them,* etc):

*So vivid is the narrative that you almost feel that what is happening to them is happening to you/ yourself as well.*

Both forms of pronoun are grammatical in such constructions.

• With some constructions, there is often uncertainty about which case of a non-reflexive pronoun to use, eg *There is no one sorrier than me(?)/than I(?) that this has happened* (see the discussion of this problem above). In such cases, some people prefer to avoid the problem of case altogether by using a reflexive pronoun instead: *There is no one sorrier than myself that this has happened.*

The reflexive pronouns are particularly common after *as* (and *as for*), *but* (and *but for*), *except* (and *except for*), *like* and *than*. Deprecated by many people, they are now accepted as correct by most authorities, as also in linked constructions such as *on behalf of my wife and myself,* where again the reflexive pronoun obviates the necessity of choosing between the subjective and objective case of a non-reflexive pronoun (*on behalf of my wife and me* and the common but incorrect *on behalf of my wife and I*).

## reported speech

When converting direct speech to reported speech or indirect speech, a number of changes have to be made:

i)  *Changes to the tenses of verbs*:

If the verb of reporting is in the past tense (eg *he said*), then present tenses in what is reported become past tenses (eg *goes* becomes *went, is* becomes *was, can* becomes *could*); simple past tenses either remain the same or change to pluperfect tenses (eg *went* stays as *went* or changes to *had gone*), and compound past tenses become pluperfect tenses (eg *has gone* and *had gone* are both realized as *had gone*).

 The only exception to these tense changes is that if something said in the past is still valid in the present, the present tense need not change to a past tense.

If the verb of reporting is in the present tense, the tenses do not change.

ii) **Changes to pronouns**:

Pronouns may be changed with regard to person (eg *I* becomes *he/she*) according to the meaning of what is said.

iii) **Changes to punctuation**:

Question marks and exclamation marks are not used in reported speech. The reported forms of questions are statements that begin with *whether* or *if*.

These guidelines can be seen exemplified in the following:

| | | |
|---|---|---|
| '*I want to come,*' she said. | → | *She said that she wanted to come.* |
| *She says, 'I'll get round to it soon'.* | → | *She says that she will get round to it soon.* |
| *She said, 'I'll get round to it soon'.* | → | *She said that she would get round to it soon.* |
| '*Are you coming with us?*' I asked. | → | *I asked whether she/he was coming with us* (or possibly *I asked whether they were coming with us*) |
| '*Have they arrived yet?*' she asked. | → | *She asked if they had arrived yet* (or possibly *She asked if we had arrived yet*) |
| '*I lived there for years,*' she said. | → | *She said that she lived there for years* or *She said she had lived there for years* |
| '*They want to come too,*' she said. | → | *She said that they want to come too* or *She said that they wanted to come too* |
| '*I have often heard that,*' he said. | → | *He said that he had often heard that* or *He said that he has often heard that* |

## shall, will

In its simplest form, the traditional rule governing the use of **shall** and **will** is as follows:

> **To express an action or state in the future, use *shall/will* with the bare infinitive of a verb (ie the infinitive without *to*), using *shall* with *I* and *we*, and *will* with *you, he, they*, etc; to express permission, obligation, determination, compulsion, etc, use *will* with *I* and *we*, and *shall* elsewhere.**

Examples:

> *I shall be glad when this book is finished.*
> *Shall we see you again next week?*
> *They will be very angry.*
>
> *I will not do it!*
> *You shall go whether you want to or not.*
> *You shall have a bicycle if you pass your exams.*
> *I am determined that they shall never do that again.*

There are, however, many exceptions to this basic rule:

i) **Shall** is becoming less common as a means of referring to a simple future, and nowadays **will** is often used with *I* and *we*: *I will be glad when this book is finished.* This use of **will** is very widespread and generally acceptable, but is best still avoided in formal written British English. **Will** rather than **shall** is preferred among Scottish and Irish speakers of British English, whereas **shall** is still preferred by many of the speakers of British English living in England and Wales. In other parts of the world, **will** is standard.

 The distinction between **shall** and **will** is of course often lost in any case when the shortened form *'ll* is used:

> *They'll be very angry.*
> *We'll be back next week.*

ii) **Shall** is often used with *I* and *we* to express the speaker's firm intentions, or to ask for instructions:

> *We shall overcome.*
> *We shall fight them on the beaches.*
> *What shall we drink?*
> *Shall I tell him or shan't I?*

 A distinction can often be made between a **request for instructions** and a **request for information**: *Shall we go to the pictures this evening?* (instructions wanted = 'Do you want us to go?') and *Will we go to the pictures next week, then?* (information wanted = 'Is that what is going to happen?').

Another distinction that can be made by choosing between **shall** and *will*, this time with a second-person pronoun, is one between a ***request for information*** (with ***shall***) and a ***request or invitation*** (with ***will***): eg the request for information *Shall you come to the cinema with us?* as opposed to the invitation *Will you come to the cinema with us?* (or, with a negative, *Won't you come to the cinema with us?*).

***Shall*** is used to form tag questions after ***let's***: *Let's go to the cinema, shall we?*

## should, would

The rules governing the use of ***should*** and ***would*** are a little more complicated than those for ***shall*** and ***will***, but are nonetheless fairly straightforward:

i)   As past tense equivalents of ***shall*** and ***will***, ***should*** is generally used where ***shall*** would be used for a simple future and ***would*** where ***will*** would be used:

> *I said I should see him tomorrow.*
> *He said he would see me tomorrow.*

Those who would say *I/we will* for simple future reference would say *I/we would* rather than *I/we should*: *I said I would see him tomorrow.* ***Would*** is sometimes preferred to ***should*** even by those who would use ***shall*** rather than ***will***, in order to avoid ambiguities arising from the other senses of ***should*** listed below.

ii)   The same distribution of ***should*** and ***would*** is found in main clauses linked to conditional clauses:

> *If we had not caught the bus, we should not have got there on time.*
> *If he had missed the bus, he would have been late.*

In such cases also, ***would*** is often preferred to ***should***: *If we hadn't caught the bus, we wouldn't have got there on time.*

In formal English, ***should*** may also be used in *if*-clauses: *If he should happen to call, tell him I'm out.* In this case, ***would*** is not a possible alternative.

iii)   ***Would*** rather than ***should*** is used with ***rather*** and ***sooner***: *I would rather stay here.* On the other hand, with other words denoting likes and preferences, ***should*** is normal (for those who usually use this with first-person pronouns):

> *I should prefer you not to smoke.*
> *We should be glad if you would refrain from smoking.*

***Would*** is also used in this sense: *I would prefer it if you didn't smoke.*

iv)   ***Should*** is correctly used in the first, second and third persons in the sense of 'ought to':

*I know I should go but I don't want to.*
*He really should stop smoking.*
*They should be there by now.*

**Should** is also used to express doubtful or tentative conditions (as in *Let me know if he should happen to arrive*) and after expressions of surprise, sorrow or other emotions (as in *I am very sorry that this should have happened □ It is quite unthinkable that he should get off scot-free*).

v)   **Would** is used in the first, second and third persons when it denotes habitual actions or determination:

*We would always have bacon and eggs for breakfast when I was young.*
*He would insist on going out without a coat and hat.*
*It's my own fault — I would insist on going there alone.*

**Would** is also used with constructions such as *if only,* expressing desires or conditions necessary for something desirable:

*If only he would come.*
*If they would only stop arguing for a moment, they might realise that there is really nothing worth arguing about.*

**Should**, on the other hand, is used in *that*-clauses following words and phrases expressing intentions and desires or other reactions:

*It is essential that you should be there.*
*It is very sad that he should think that.*

vi)   **Should** is used (for those who usually use this with first-person pronouns) to express tentative opinions: *I should think that would be all right.* Here again, **would** is also used: *I would think that would be all right.*

---

   A common mistake found with **should** and **would** when referring to the past is the creation of a 'double past tense' construction when a single past tense is all that is required:

✗   *I should have liked to have been there.*
✓   *I should like to have been there.*
✓   *I should have liked to be there.*

See INFINITIVE.

---

## split infinitive

An infinitive is a form of a verb which is often, though not always, preceded by the word *to*: *I came to watch the parade.* A *'split' infinitive* is one in which there is an adverb between the *to* and the following verb:

*The economic climate for graduates was good, though many of those new jobs were destined to simply disappear in the face of hard times.*

*It may be impossible <u>to properly clean</u> all the stones.*

and the by now classic example from the television series *Star Trek*:

... *<u>to boldly go</u> where no man has gone before.*

Although there have been split infinitives in English since at least the 14th century and they are to be found in the works of some of the best writers in the English language, the split infinitive gives rise to more criticism than any other supposed grammatical error. (It ranked sixth in a 'Top Twenty' of language 'errors' about which the BBC received complaints in 1981, and publishers still receive letters about it in the mid-nineties.)

Condemnation of the split infinitive is, however, fairly recent, and is based on the principles of Latin grammar, in which there is no comparable construction. Grammarians who took Latin as a model of good grammar and style condemned in English a hitherto perfectly acceptable and well-established grammatical usage simply because it was not possible in Latin. This ruling unfortunately came to be generally accepted and was passed down from grammarian to grammarian and from teacher to class, and in spite of the efforts of a number of 20th-century grammarians to demonstrate the illogicality, false origins and sheer unnecessariness of the rule, it remains firmly rooted to this day in the minds of many people.

Nevertheless, the rule for positioning adverbs in sentences is quite simple:

> **If the most logical, most natural and most unambiguous position for an adverb in a sentence is between *to* and a following infinitive, then that is where the adverb should be put.**

If we look at the split infinitive purely from the point of view of English grammar, it is clear that it is a perfectly grammatical form of expression, and that there is no reason to avoid it at all costs, as some teachers would advise. Indeed, *avoidance of the split infinitive has produced more bad writing than the use of it*, and there are often good stylistic reasons for splitting infinitives:

i) *rhythm*:
It has been noted that split infinitives are often rhythmically preferable to the 'non-split' alternatives. *To boldly go*, for example, has a rhythmic pattern ◡–◡–, which may sound more pleasant than *boldly to go* (–◡◡–) or *to go boldly* (◡––◡).

ii) *clarity*:
Sometimes the only way of indicating clearly and unambiguously that an adverb is to be understood as modifying infinitive in a sentence as opposed to some other word standing before or after the infinitive is to place the adverb between the infinitive and the preceding *to*. The following example

> *Part of a personnel officer's job <u>is really to get to know</u> all the staff*

has two possible interpretations depending on whether the *really* is felt to be attached to what precedes it or to what follows it, but with a split infinitive, the meaning is unambiguous:

> *Part of a personnel officer's job <u>is to really get to know</u> all the staff.*

iii) **necessity**:

There are some constructions in English which absolutely require a split infinitive. One such is *more than*, which must immediately precede the verb it relates to and therefore necessarily splits the infinitive: *You've done enough <u>to more than make up</u> for the damage you originally caused.*

---

 There are, however, <u>some</u> restrictions on splitting infinitives. It is preferable not to split an infinitive with negative words such as *not* or *never*.

---

## subjunctive

Apart from its obligatory use in certain set expressions, such as *as it <u>were</u>, <u>be</u> that as it may, long <u>live</u> the Queen, so <u>be</u> it* and *<u>suffice</u> it to say*, the subjunctive mood of verbs is not very common in present-day English. In most cases, the subjunctive form of a verb is identical to the indicative form (the form used in ordinary statements), and therefore most people are aware of subjunctives only in the cases where subjunctive forms (as in *if I <u>were</u> you, if he <u>were</u> here, if that <u>be</u> the case*) differ from the corresponding indicative forms (ie *I <u>was</u>, he <u>was</u>, that <u>is</u> the case*) — and sometimes not even then.

There are two main uses of the subjunctive in English, both more or less restricted to formal language and replaced by other constructions in less formal contexts:

i) After verbs and other constructions denoting **commands, requests or wishes**:

> *It is imperative that he <u>resign</u> now.* (not '*resigns*', therefore subjunctive, not indicative)
> *I insist that he <u>do</u> it at once.* (not '*does*')

---

 Where the subjunctive and indicative forms are identical (eg in the third person plural), this construction can lead to ambiguities: in *He suggests that children <u>learn</u> how language works by studying grammar*, it is not clear whether '*learn*' is an indicative, in which case he is suggesting that this is how children <u>do</u> learn language, or a subjunctive, in which case he is suggesting that this is how they <u>should</u> learn language.

If the second meaning is intended '*learn*' would be better replaced by '*should learn*', which is unambiguous.

---

In non-formal contexts, *should* or an indicative verb is commonly substituted for a subjunctive, especially in British English.

ii)   Especially in formal language, a subjunctive verb may be used after *if* and certain other conjunctions (eg *as if, as though, supposing*) in **expressions involving hypotheses, unreal situations** (ie, things that might have been the case but in fact are not), **suggestions and concessions**, nearly always with the verb *to be* in the form '*were*':

> *Even if he <u>were</u> here, we wouldn't recognize him.*
> *Whatever <u>be</u> the reason for his disappearance, I'm sure he hasn't been murdered.*

Similarly, the subjunctive *were* is often found instead of *was* after the verb *to wish*:

> *I wish I <u>were</u> going with you.*

In less formal language, an indicative verb is often used instead of a subjunctive:

> *Even if he <u>was</u> here, we wouldn't recognize him.*

---

 Note that when what follows *if* refers to a <u>possible</u> event rather than to a purely <u>hypothetical</u> one, the verb should be in the indicative: *If he <u>was</u> here yesterday, there is no sign of it now.* (In general, if the following clause contains *would* or *should*, the verb of the *if*-clause will be, or at least may be, in the subjunctive; otherwise, it will be in the indicative.)

---

iii)   *Were* rather than *was* may be, but need not be, used in subordinate clauses expressing indirect questions following words or phrases denoting asking or wondering:

> *Her behaviour was becoming so irrational, I began to wonder whether she <u>were/was</u> pregnant.*

## *that* (omission of)

Both as a conjunction and as a relative pronoun, ***that*** may often be omitted, and frequently is in informal speech and writing. There are some restrictions on this, however:

i)   As a relative pronoun, ***that*** may be omitted when it is the object of the verb in its clause, but must not be omitted when it is the subject of the verb:

> *A car <u>that keeps breaking down</u> is no use to me at all.*
> *The car <u>that you sold me</u> keeps breaking down.*
> *The car <u>you sold me</u> keeps breaking down.*

This is acceptable in formal as well as informal language.

ii)   As a conjunction, ***that*** introducing a noun clause which is the object of a verb of saying, thinking, etc, should be omitted only in informal English, and then only if there is nothing other than an indirect object between it and the verb governing it:

✓  *I told the man I would be coming today.*
✓  *I told the man, and I told his wife too, that I would be coming today.*
✗  *I told the man, and I told his wife too, I would be coming today.*

iii)  As a conjunction, when **that** is the second part of a pair of words which function together (such as *so that*), it may be omitted <u>but only in informal language</u>:

*Anne walks <u>so</u> fast I have to run to keep up with her* (in formal language, . . . *so fast <u>that</u> I have to run . . .*)

*<u>Now</u> you are here, we can make a start* (in formal language, *<u>Now that</u> you are here, . . .*)

**there is/are**  see AGREEMENT WITH LINKING VERBS under AGREEMENT.

## they, them, their, etc

One annoying gap in English vocabulary is that created by the lack of a third-person singular pronoun that does not state explicitly the sex of the person or persons referred to, as *he, him, she, her*, etc do. The lack of such a pronoun leads to some uncertainty about the correct pronoun to choose to refer back to words such as *anyone, each, every, everyone, no one, some* or *someone*, or *person, teacher, doctor, driver*, etc, which may refer to an individual whose sex is not known or stated or which denotes something such as a profession which includes both males and females. In the past, grammarians have recommended the use of *his, him*, etc. in such contexts, and this must still be considered correct today:

*<u>Anyone</u> can come if <u>he</u> pays <u>his</u> share.*
*<u>A teacher</u> should always get to know <u>his</u> pupils as individuals.*

However, quite naturally many people today dislike the use of an otherwise masculine pronoun to refer to males and females alike, but equally regard the more explicit *him and her, him/her*, etc as very awkward and cumbersome:

*<u>Anyone</u> can come if <u>he or she</u> pays <u>his or her</u> share.*
*<u>A teacher</u> should always get to know <u>his or her</u> pupils as individuals.*

The choice of pronoun is even more of a problem in the case of a male and female noun linked together:

*Neither John nor Mary has finished <u>his</u> (???)/<u>his or her</u> (?)/<u>their</u> (?) work yet.*
*The teacher told the boys and girls that each of them must finish <u>his</u> (???)/<u>his or her</u> (?)/<u>their</u> (?) work by the end of the week.*

For this reason, *them, their*, etc are often used in such contexts instead of the *him, his*, etc recommended by traditional grammarians:

*Has <u>anyone</u> lost <u>their</u> pencil?*
*Has <u>everyone</u> finished <u>their</u> work?*

This is now acceptable to almost all speakers of English in informal contexts, and is increasingly common in formal speech and writing as well, though still disapproved of by some purists.

- **themself**

A recent innovation in the language is the introduction of **themself** as a singular form of *themselves*, when it refers to a single individual:

> *Each one would have had an attendant to stop them doing themself harm.*

This is not yet acceptable outside very informal contexts.

## used to

There is often uncertainty about the correct negative forms of this phrase. The following are all acceptable:

| | |
|---|---|
| *He used not to do it* | *He didn't use to do it* |
| *He usedn't to do it* | *He didn't used to do it* |
| *He usen't to do it* | |

Similarly, the following question forms are all unexceptionable:

| | |
|---|---|
| *Did he use to do it?* | *Didn't he used to do it?* |
| *Did he used to do it?* | *Used he not to do it?* |
| *Used he to do it?* | *Usedn't he to do it?* |
| *Didn't he use to do it?* | |

The form *Used he not to do it?* is appropriate only in very formal contexts, and *Used he to do it?* is relatively rare. The other forms may be used informally, and in formal speech and writing the best forms to use are *He used not to do it, Used he to do it?* and *Did he not use to do it?*

- The tag questions for **used to** are formed with *did*:

> *She used to live near here, <u>didn't</u> she?*
> *She didn't use to live near here, <u>did</u> she?*

## what

### ✦ *What* — singular or plural?

There is sometimes some uncertainty about whether to follow **what** with a singular verb or a plural verb. The rule is, however, very simple:

> **When *what* means 'that which', it is singular and must be followed by a singular verb; when it means 'those which' or 'the things which', it is plural and must be followed by a plural verb.**

Examples:

*What I need is a cup of tea.*
*They looked through all their books and what they didn't need were sold at a jumble sale.*

**What** should be considered plural only when it refers <u>back</u> to a previously stated plural noun or pronoun. Sometimes, when a linking verb (such as *to be*) following **what** is followed by a plural noun, the verb is made plural to agree with the plural noun:

✗   *What we need <u>are</u> a few sticks and some string.*
✓   *What we need <u>is</u> a few sticks and some string.*

This is acceptable only in informal speech or writing.

> ⚠   However, there <u>are</u> occasions when, regardless of this last rule, a plural verb sounds more natural than a singular verb:
>
> > *What <u>were</u> formerly semi-ruined farmworkers' cottages <u>have</u> been converted into holiday homes for executives from suburbia.*
>
> The use of singular verbs (*what <u>was</u> formerly semi-ruined farmworkers' cottages <u>has</u> been converted . . .*) would also be possible and correct, but would be more appropriate if the cottages were formed into, for example, a terrace and were being thought of as a single entity, whereas the plural verbs are better if the cottages are being thought of as a number of separate units.

## ✦ *What* versus *who*, *which* and *that*

### • *What* as a relative pronoun
**What** must never be substituted for **who**, **which** or **that** in relative clauses:

✗   the man <u>what I saw yesterday</u>
✗   the chairs <u>what were in the shop</u>

### • Interrogative *what* and *which*
**Which** and **what** may both be used as interrogative adjectives (ie to ask questions about a choice or selection): <u>What/ Which is the best way to cook rice?</u> They are not, however, interchangeable: **which** generally implies choice from a limited number of options, whereas **what** is used when the choice is unlimited or from an unspecified number of options.

## ✦ *Than what*

In some non-standard varieties of English, **what** is sometimes added after **than** in comparative constructions:

✗   *You can do that better <u>than what</u> I can.*

Such an expression is not correct in Standard English. Only if **what** means 'that which' or 'the thing(s) which' can it correctly follow **than**:

✓    *Those are better <u>than what</u> we saw in the shops yesterday.*
(**what** = 'the things which')

## who, whom, which, that

### ✦ *Who* or *whom*?

Strictly speaking, **who** is a subject pronoun, **whom** the objective form, comparable to **he** and **him**, **they** and **them**, etc:

> <u>Who</u> *told you that?* (Compare *<u>He</u> told you that.*)
> <u>Whom</u> *should we send?* (Compare *We should send <u>him</u>.*)
> *To <u>whom</u> is the letter addressed?* (Compare *The letter is addressed to <u>him</u>.*)

However, in modern English, **whom** is generally replaced by **who** when it stands at the beginning of a sentence or clause, regardless of its role in the sentence:

> <u>Who</u> *should we send?*
> <u>Who</u> *is the letter addressed to?*
> *I don't know <u>who</u> it is addressed to.*

Although still deprecated by some people, this is entirely acceptable now in anything but the most formal speech and writing.

In normal, informal speech and writing, the pronoun is often omitted in any case when it is not the subject of a verb:

> *The man you are looking for is not here.*
> *The man he gave the letter to is a spy.*

---

    Care must be taken not to substitute **whom** for **who** when **who** is the subject of a following verb but appears to be the object of an intervening phrase, such as '*I said*':

> ✗    *He was the man <u>whom I said would be waiting for us</u>.*
> ✗    *That is the man <u>whom I believe was in charge of the investigation</u>.*
> ✗    *The little girl <u>whom they say is going to win the prize</u> is my neighbour's daughter.*

In all three examples, **whom** should in fact be **who**, as is clear if, as a test, the words *I said*, *I believe* and *they say* are removed:

> ✗    *He was the man <u>whom would be waiting for us</u>.*
> ✗    *That is the man <u>whom was in charge of the investigation</u>.*
> ✗    *The little girl <u>whom is going to win the prize</u> is my neighbour's daughter.*

The correct forms of these sentences clearly require **who**, eg:

> ✓    *He was the man <u>who would be waiting for us</u>.*

So also do those with the inserted *I said*, etc:

> ✓    *He was the man <u>who I said would be waiting for us</u>.*

---

> Note that if the verb that follows is an <u>infinitive</u>, not an indicative, the objective form of the pronoun is correct, because in this case the pronoun <u>is</u> the object of the verb of hearing, saying, believing, etc:
>
> *That is the man <u>whom I believe to have been</u> in charge of the investigation.*
> (Compare *<u>I believe him to have been</u> in charge of the investigation.*)

**Whom** rather than **who** should always be used after **than**:

*Their choice fell on Dr Jones, <u>than whom</u> there was no one better qualified to be the editor of the book.*

• The rules outlined above mostly apply equally to **whoever** and **whomever**, but regardless of its role in the sentence, **whoever** generally replaces **whomever** in all but the most formal English:

*<u>Whoever</u> said that must have been crazy.*
*Give it <u>to whoever</u> you please* or, very formally, *Give it <u>to whomever</u> you please.*
*<u>Whoever they tell to do it</u> will just have to do it.*

✦ **who, which** or **that**?

In deciding whether to use **who, which** or **that** to introduce a relative clause, two factors have to be taken into account:

i)  whether the clause is restrictive or non-restrictive, and

ii)  whether the antecedent is a person or not.

A restrictive clause is one which defines and limits what the antecedent refers to: eg in *The man <u>who was here last night</u> is her father*, the underlined clause tells us which man is being referred to, and thus 'restricts' the reference of '*the man*' to one particular man. On the other hand, in *The man, <u>who was here last night</u>, is her father*, it is assumed that we already know which man is being referred to, and the words '*who was here last night*' simply gives us more information about him. This is a non-restrictive relative clause.

The basic rule regarding the choice of relative pronoun is:

> **In non-restrictive clauses, the relative pronoun must be *who(m)* when the antecedent is a person, and *which* when it is anything else.**
>
> **In restrictive clauses, the pronoun may be *who(m)* or *that* when the antecedent is personal, and *which* or *that* if it is not personal.**

Examples:

*The man, <u>who</u> was here again last night, claimed to be your uncle.*

*The car, <u>which</u> was later found abandoned, was identified as the one which had*
    *been used in the robbery.*

*The man <u>who</u>/<u>that</u> was here last night claimed to be your uncle.*
*A car <u>which</u>/<u>that</u> keeps breaking down is no use to anyone.*

Notice that one of the benefits of using **that** is that it applies to both people and things, and so can be used when you are not sure whether **who** or **which** would be appropriate, or when the antecedent includes both personal and non-personal nouns:

*The man and the dog <u>that</u> you saw yesterday . . .*

However, when referring to personal antecedents alone, **that** is best confined to informal contexts; in formal speech and writing it is better to use **who(m)**.

**That** as a relative pronoun can be omitted altogether when it is the object of the verb in its own clause (just as it can when functioning as a conjunction):

*The car he sold me keeps on breaking down.*

---

⚠ **Refinements to the general rule**

    i)  **That** is sometimes used instead of **which** in non-restrictive clauses. This is acceptable in informal language, but should be avoided in formal speech. In written English in particular, the distinction between **which** and **that** is a useful distinguishing mark to differentiate restrictive from non-restrictive clauses (although the distinction should be adequately shown by the presence or absence of a comma in any case):

*I never watch westerns, <u>which</u> gratify the public's thirst for violence.*
    (non-restrictive)
*I never watch westerns <u>which</u> gratify the public's thirst for violence.*
    (restrictive, but it is only the comma that shows the difference between this and the sentence above)
*I never watch westerns <u>that</u> gratify the public's thirst for violence.*
    (restrictive)

    ii)  When the antecedent is an indefinite pronoun such as *anything, nothing, something,* **that** is generally used rather than **which**. This is also the case when the antecedent is a noun phrase containing a superlative adjective:

*That must be the <u>biggest</u> ship <u>that</u> they have ever built here.*

---

- **Who** or **which** after a collective noun

If a collective noun, such as *committee* or *band*, is followed by a relative clause, the choice of relative pronoun, like the choice between singular and plural verb, possessive adjectives, etc, depends on whether the collective noun is looked on as denoting a single body (in which case use *which*) or a number of individuals (in which case use *who*):

*The committee, <u>which meets</u> every second Friday, will consider your request at*
    *<u>its</u> next meeting.*

*The committee, <u>who meet</u> together every second Friday, will consider your request as soon as <u>they</u> can.*

## ✦ *whose* and *of which*

**Whose** is correctly used to mean both 'of whom' and 'of which':

*the boy <u>whose</u> father is a policeman*
*the book <u>whose</u> pages are torn*

**Of which** may also be used of things, as in *the book, the pages <u>of which</u> are torn*, but **whose** is now generally preferred.

 Note the correct spelling of **whose**. **Who's** does not mean 'of whom', but is short for 'who is' or 'who has'.

- When **who** is linked with **else**, **who else's** is more usual than **whose else**.

# 3

# Confused and Misused Words

Many of the entries in the following chapter distinguish through explanation and example words that are commonly confused because of similarity of meaning or similarity of sound (or both). In some cases, not all possible meanings of the words are discussed, but only those that give rise to confusion.

Other entries provide guidance on individual words, such as the correct prepositions to use with particular nouns, verbs or adjectives (eg *affinity for/to/with*).

## ability, capability, capacity

*Ability* is a fairly general term, denoting the simple fact of something being possible: *This demonstrated our ability to work together in spite of our cultural differences.* *Ability* also denotes the possession of a particular aptitude or of necessary skills, knowledge, powers, resources, etc: *Teaching and managerial ability are no less important* □ *his ability to write a catchy tune* □ *He showed exceptional ability in mechanics.*

*Capability* also may denote the possession of an aptitude, especially one deriving from a person's character and which enables them to cope with whatever situation they find themselves in: *I never cease to be amazed at my mother's organizational capabilities.* *Capability* also denotes the existence of the potential to do something, especially in the shape of the required resources, or the opportunity to do something: *'Strategic capability' is the capability of countries with long-range missiles or aircraft to make war or carry out reprisals* □ *a lack of research capability at the Institute.* Someone who has the *ability* to do something may need particular resources in order to have the *capability* of doing it.

*Capacity* denotes physical or mental power which gives a person the potential to do something: *He had an immense capacity for rows, and fell out with everybody sooner or later* □ *their capacity to manage resources effectively* □ *her innate capacity for organization* □ *A first-strike capability' is a country's capacity to launch an initial attack on an enemy.* Someone who has the *capacity* to do something may, however, lack the knowledge or training that would give them the *ability* to do it, and may also not be in a position where they would have the *capability* of doing it.

## abuse, misuse

*Abuse* and *misuse* both mean 'the use (of something) in the wrong way', but the two words do differ slightly in meaning and use.

*Misuse* refers mostly to the use of substances or objects in an incorrect way, eg in a way contrary to manufacturers' instructions:

> *Bacteria may acquire resistance to a particular antibiotic by its overuse or misuse*

or in a way that will damage the thing being used:

> *Large parts of the physical environment are suffering from misuse and overexploitation.*

The wrong use may not be deliberate, but rather caused by ignorance. The results are usually, but not always, harmful or undesirable.

*Misuse* also describes the deliberate use of something for the wrong ends rather than in the wrong way: *the misuse of nuclear materials for military purposes □ misuse of foreign financial aid □ the misuse of power.*

However, when what is meant is the use of something for the wrong purposes rather than in the wrong way, *abuse* is more common: *substance abuse* (eg glue-sniffing) □ *facing trial on charges of treason, corruption and abuse of power.*

The difference between *misuse* and *abuse* can be further illustrated as follows: if a drug is incorrectly administered to a patient although for valid medical reasons, that is *misuse*, whereas drug *abuse* is the use of drugs for reasons society as a whole considers unacceptable or immoral.

- The above distinctions apply equally to the verbs *abuse* and *misuse*:

  > *Hoover was later criticized for abusing his position by engaging in vendettas against liberal activists.*

  > *Some renewable resources are sustainable in the long term only through careful management, so that they are not overexploited or misused in the short term.*

## accord, account

Be careful not to confuse *of one's own accord* and *on one's own account*. If you do something *of your own accord*, you do it on your own initiative, without being told to do it or forced to do it, and if something happens *of its own accord*, it happens without anyone or anything acting to cause it:

> *She had undertaken of her own accord not to tell anyone else.*
> *The condition will clear up of its own accord eventually.*

If, on the other hand, you do something *on your own account*, you do it for your own benefit:

> *After five years, he was ready to set up in business on his own account.*

***On your own account*** may also mean 'by yourself' as opposed to 'from other sources':

> *A feature of an actuary's work is that you never stop learning — both on your own account and from your colleagues.*

## acquiesce

***Acquiesce*** may be used on its own, meaning 'to agree': *After much persuasion, he finally acquiesced.* When it is followed by a preposition, the preposition is usually ***in***: *They were by no means inclined to acquiesce in the proposed arrangements.*

***Acquiesce to*** has in the past been considered incorrect, but probably should no longer be. What was originally an error has now become standard usage, even if some people still object to it: *They accepted that they would have to acquiesce to some kind of compromise.*

***Acquiesce*** is sometimes seen followed by ***with***, but this is not common, and should probably be considered incorrect at this time, and certainly avoided in formal English.

## adherence, adhesion

Both these words mean 'sticking to' something, but they differ slightly in use.

***Adhesion*** is used most often when what is being described is one thing literally sticking to another: *Its strong adhesion to most surfaces means it is extremely durable and flexible.*

***Adherence***, on the other hand, is generally used to refer to a person's 'sticking to' something in a more figurative sense, eg remaining faithful to an ideal, principle, agreement, policy, etc (*his strict adherence to a low-fat diet* □ *rigid adherence to middle-class morality*) or, less commonly, belonging to a group or organization (*his nominal adherence to the Government* □ *Britain's adherence to the sterling area*).

***Adherence*** may, like ***adhesion***, be used of a literal sticking to something, especially in technical contexts: *rapid drug adherence to the cell wall*. ***Adhesion*** is rarely, but still correctly, used, like ***adherence***, of agreement to a treaty, etc: *Adhesion is accepted as a way in which a party can become bound to certain parts of a treaty, but not to its entirety.*

## adjacent, adjoining, contiguous

***Adjacent*** means 'close to, next to, beside': *the house adjacent to mine* □ *adjacent fields*. Although beside each other, things which are adjacent are not necessarily in contact with each other: *adjacent rooms* in a building may only be separated by the wall between them, but *adjacent houses* may be separated by gardens, garages, etc.

***Adjoining*** means 'next to and touching'. *Adjacent houses* may have gardens between them, but *adjoining houses* will be separated by nothing more than the wall between them. ***Adjoining*** very often carries the further implication of there being direct access from one to the other: *adjoining rooms* may have a door between them, *adjoining fields* a gate through which you can pass from one field to the other.

***Contiguous***, like ***adjoining***, means 'next to and touching, having an edge or boundary in common'. It is generally found in formal or technical contexts. ***Contiguous*** may be followed by ***with*** or, much less commonly, ***to***: *a wide ring of water contiguous with the southern Atlantic*. ***Contiguous*** may also be used figuratively: *We need to ensure that any diversification is into areas contiguous to our own existing areas of expertise.*

## admission, admittance

***Admission*** means 'the act of entering' or 'permission to enter'. It is generally used when what is being referred to is either entry into a public place such as a theatre or cinema, or the price or conditions of entry: *Admission £1 □ Admission by ticket only □ No admission after 10 o'clock*. ***Admission*** is also used for entry into membership of a club or society, or into a school (as a pupil) or hospital (as a patient).

***Admittance*** also means 'the act of entering', 'the right to enter' or 'permission to enter' a place, used especially when referring to a place not generally open to the public, such as a house or factory. The word is rather formal, and occurs most frequently in such phrases as *to gain admittance* but may be used in more general contexts instead of ***admission*** when a certain formality in the situation is implied: *those who are denied admittance to Paradise □ restricted admittance to handicapped persons.*

***Admission*** also means 'a confession or acknowledgement': *an admission of guilt*. ***Admittance*** is rarely, and perhaps incorrectly, used in this sense.

## adopted, adoptive

***Adoptive*** is generally used of people who adopt a child: *adoptive father/mother/parents/family*. The adjective applied to the child is usually ***adopted***, but ***adoptive***, although much less common in this sense, is also correct: *an adoptive son/sister.*

## adverse, averse

***Adverse*** means 'unfavourable, hostile, harmful'. It is most often applied to abstract nouns, such as *condition, reaction, comment, circumstances, publicity*: *adverse weather conditions □ adverse criticism*. It may be followed by the preposition ***to***: *It is our duty to listen to those affected before coming to any decision adverse to their interests.*

***Averse*** means 'having a dislike', 'disinclined', and almost always applies to people. It is generally followed by the preposition ***to*** or, formerly but now very infrequently, ***from***: *She's not averse to walking over people to get what she wants.*

## aeroplane, airplane, aircraft

*Aeroplane* is the correct form of the word in British English, *airplane* the normal form in American English, although it is sometimes found in British English also.

*Aircraft* is a more technical word than *aeroplane*, and is wider in meaning, including not only aeroplanes, but also helicopters, gliders, airships, etc.

## affect, effect

*Effect* can be used both as a noun and as a verb. As a noun, it means 'result, consequence, impression', as in *He has recovered from the effects of his illness □ Your action will have little effect on him*. As a verb, *effect* is rather formal, and means 'to cause, bring about': *He tried to effect a reconciliation between his parents*.

*Affect* is always a verb. It generally means 'to have an influence on, cause a change in, alter the circumstances, prospects, etc, of': *Your answer will not affect my decision □ The accident has affected his eyesight □ These changes to the law will affect farmers throughout Europe □ I was worried that this conviction would affect my career prospects*.

 Note therefore that to *affect* something is to have some *effect* on it: *Your answer will have no effect on my decision □ The accident has had a bad effect on his eyesight*.

The effect may be on a person's mind or emotions: *Your remarks affected me deeply*. As can be seen from the second and fourth examples in the paragraph above, *affect* often means specifically 'to have a <u>bad</u> effect on' something.

Another sense of *affect*, generally used only in more formal speech and writing, is 'to pretend to have, feel, etc' (*She began to affect an interest in the Soviet Union □ Later Greeks affected to despise the Persians as soft barbarians*).

Two other senses of *affect*, rarer but still correct, are 'to wear, especially habitually' (*I hate these gaudy hats she always affects*), often implying criticism or disapproval of what is being worn, and 'to behave, think, etc habitually in a particular way' (*He affects little sympathy with the plight of the unemployed □ She affects not to care about the unemployed*). In this latter context, *affect* is ambiguous, as it could be taken to mean 'to pretend to have, etc', as in the paragraph above.

## affinity

When used with the meaning 'liking, attraction, close feeling', *affinity* is often followed by *for*: *a long-standing affinity for the music of Berlioz □ his enthusiasm and affinity for young people* and by *with* (*his affection for and affinity with Henrietta □ She had little affinity with Dublin*). *For* is sometimes criticized by authorities, but it is certainly acceptable in informal English, and probably should be accepted as standard in formal contexts now too. *Affinity* may also in this sense be followed by *between* (*the affinity that exists between friends* □ *Women's predominantly domestic work experiences create an affinity between women and conservatism*), and is occasionally found with *to*.

When *affinity* is used in the sense of 'closeness in relationship, form or origin', *affinity* is followed by *between* and *to*: *the deep-rooted affinity between nationalism and socialism* □ *This bird shows a certain affinity to the duck family.*

In scientific writing, *affinity* is followed by *for* in describing chemical attraction and bonding: *differences in affinity for DNA.*

## afflict, inflict

*Afflict* means 'to cause pain or distress to': *Pre-fight nerves afflict almost everyone.* Rarely, but correctly, it may be followed by the preposition *with*: *They believed that it was their god who had afflicted them with a plague of rats.*

*Afflicted* may be followed by *with* or *by*: *He is afflicted with/by headaches.* When referring to an action, an event, or the onset of a condition rather than to a continuing state, use *by* rather than *with*: *He was deeply afflicted by the news of his wife's death.*

*Inflict* means 'to impose (something unpleasant or unwanted)' on someone. Confusion between *afflict* and *inflict* arises from their similarity in sound and meaning, but the constructions following these two verbs are quite different: you *afflict* someone *with* something, but *inflict* something *on* someone, as in *They inflicted heavy casualties on the enemy.*

## aggravate

The original meaning of the word *aggravate* is 'to make worse': *An unexpected reduction in tourism aggravated the country's economic problems*; but *aggravate* is also used with the meaning 'to annoy, irritate': *Loud music always aggravates her.* This latter use of *aggravate* is very common, and although still regarded as incorrect by some people, it is well established in the language (*aggravate* having been used in this sense for over 300 years), especially in the adjective form *aggravating*, and cannot now justifiably be condemned even in the most formal or literary English.

## ago, since

*Ago* is sometimes wrongly used in combination with *since*:

    ✗   *It is months ago since I last saw her.*

The correct construction is with either *since* or *ago* alone:

    ✓   *I last saw her months ago.*
    ✓   *It is months since I last saw her.*

Alternatively, follow *ago* with *that*:

    ✓   *It was months ago that I last saw her.*

## aircraft, airplane see AEROPLANE.

## alibi, alias

*Alibi* is a Latin word meaning 'somewhere else'. It is correctly used in English to refer to one form of defence against a criminal charge, the defence being that the accused person was 'somewhere else' (ie not at the scene of the crime) when the crime was committed: *I have an alibi for at least two of the previous murders.*

In present-day English, however, *alibi* is often used simply to mean 'an excuse':

> *a marvellous catch-all alibi for failure and inadequacy*
> *a not unconvincing alibi for their political conformism*

This broader use of *alibi*, while fairly common in informal speech, is not yet accepted as correct by many people, and should still be avoided in formal English.

*Alibi* should not be confused with *alias*. An *alias* is a false name a person uses to hide their identity:

> *'Leon Trotsky' was the alias of the Russian revolutionary Lev Davidovich Bronstein.*

## allegory, analogy, allusion

An *allegory* is a story, painting or other work of art which is intended to be understood symbolically. That is to say, what is read or seen is meant to symbolize or be representative of something else. For example, a story or a painting depicting a battle between a knight in armour and a dragon might be intended as an *allegory* on the battle between good and evil.

In an *analogy*, one thing is taken not to represent another thing but rather to serve as an illustration, explanation or justification of another thing. For example, one of the arguments for the existence of God is based on the supposed *analogy* between the universe and a watch, the argument being that just as a watch is a complicated mechanism that manifestly needs to have been put together by a watchmaker, so the universe is a complicated mechanism that must similarly have been put together by a 'universe-maker', ie God.

In language, *analogy* is the use of a word, grammatical rule, etc as a pattern on the basis of which another word is created or altered: *ageism*, for example, was coined by analogy with *sexism*, and the past tense form *digged* was replaced by *dug* by analogy with *sung, swum*, etc.

An *allusion* is an indirect reference to something made in passing while talking of something else:

> *His writings contain frequent allusions to the incidents of his private life*

or a reference to someone or something that is felt to be in some way similar to whoever or whatever is being spoken about:

*The founders of the Social Democratic Party were known as the 'gang of four'
— an allusion to the four politicians who held power in China during the
Cultural Revolution of the 1960s.*

Sometimes an **allusion** is visual rather than verbal:

*his latest reflections on symbolism and allusion in contemporary architecture.*

- To **allude** to something is to speak of it indirectly:

*He did not allude to the previous speaker's remarks.*
*In speaking of 'She-who-must-be-obeyed', he was understood to be alluding to
his wife.*

**Allude** should not be used as a synonym of 'mention' or 'refer to':

✗ *He alluded to his wife by name at least ten times in as many minutes.*

## alternate, alternative

The adjective **alternate** refers either to something happening, coming, etc
in turns, one after the other, as in *The water came in alternate bursts of hot and cold*
(ie, first hot, then cold, then hot, then cold, and so on), or to something which
happens, comes, etc every second day, week, year, etc, as in *He visits us on
alternate Tuesdays*. **Alternative** refers to the offering of a choice between two
possibilities (or sometimes more than two — see below): *If that doesn't work,
we'll have to think up an alternative plan.*

- The same distinctions in meaning apply to **alternately** and **alternatively**:

*The water ran alternately hot and cold.*
*They could go by bus, or alternatively they could take the train.*

---

 **Alternative**, as a noun or adjective, originally referred to one of <u>two</u>
choices:

*If this plan doesn't suit you, we can always find an alternative.*

It is frequently used in present-day English to refer to one of more than
two choices:

*We are using this method because all the alternatives (or all the alternative
methods) have failed.*
*We have only three alternatives: fight them, pay up or move on.*

Although some people still regard this as incorrect, it is well established and
unexceptionable. If, however, you wish to avoid this use of **alternative**, you
may use an adjective such as **other** and nouns such as **choice** or **option**: *We
are using this method because all other methods have failed □ We have only three options.*
Note that the use of **choice** or **option** is in some cases less ambiguous than
**alternative**: if you speak of there being 'three alternatives', it may not always
be clear whether you mean there are <u>three</u> options or whether you mean that
there are <u>four</u> options (ie a preferred option and three alternatives to it).

---

## ambiguous, ambivalent

*Ambiguous* means 'having more than one possible meaning':

> *After the cat caught the mouse, it died is ambiguous because it is not clear whether the 'it' refers to the cat or to the mouse.*

*Ambivalent* means 'having mixed feelings or emotions about something'; when accompanied by a preposition, the preposition is generally *about*, but *towards* is also found:

> *Marxists tended to be ambivalent about parliamentary socialism.*
> *Women are more likely than men to feel ambivalent about their own bodies.*
> *Living in Normandy made him ambivalent towards his old enemy.*

## amend, emend

To *amend* something is to alter it or add to it in order to improve or correct it: *The powers of the House of Lords to amend legislation are limited.* Things that are typically amended are budgets, laws, proposals, regulations, schemes and statutes.

*Emend* means 'to correct errors in', and applies specifically to the correction of a piece of writing by removing or altering minor errors such as mistakes in spelling or incorrect punctuation: *We will emend your manuscript where necessary.*

To *emend* a text is therefore to remove errors that make it different from what was intended or different from its original form. However, if changes are made to a piece of writing that make it better than it originally was, it is being *amended*.

• The noun from *amend* is *amendment*: *amendments to the constitution.* The noun from *emend* is *emendation*: *The text had been so corrupted over the centuries that many emendations had to be made before it could be published.*

## America, American

When it was originally coined in the 16th century, the name *America* was applied to the whole of the landmass from Alaska in the north to Tierra del Fuego in the south. This sense is now obsolete. Sometimes this area of land may be referred to as *the Americas*, but this is now rare and it would be more usual to refer to 'North and South America'.

*South America* denotes all the countries from the northern border of Colombia southwards, sometimes including that part of Panama south of the Panama Canal. *North America*, however, is ambiguous in three ways: it may denote (a) all the countries to the north of South America, or (b) Mexico, the United States and Canada (in which case the countries between Mexico and South America are referred to as *Central America*), or, more usually, (c) Canada and the United States alone (in which case Mexico is by implication in Central America).

*Latin America* denotes all the countries from Mexico southwards, in which the official language is Spanish, Portuguese or French, and is usually taken to include the Spanish-speaking islands of the Caribbean also. Strictly speaking, *Latin America* does not include the countries of Central and South America in which English or Dutch is the official language, but these are often included on geographical grounds.

On its own, *America* is usually understood nowadays as denoting 'the United States of America'.

- The adjectives *American*, *North American*, *South American* and *Latin American* are used in senses corresponding to the different meanings of *America* outlined above.

## amiable, amicable

*Amiable* means 'friendly, pleasant, good-natured' and is normally used of people, facial expressions, moods, personalities, etc: *an amiable enough young man □ an amiable disposition*. When applied to other things, it means 'congenial, pleasant, agreeable, not causing offence, etc': *He began his speech with a few amiable anecdotes □ an amiable chat □ amiable delusions about the reformation of criminals.*

*Amicable* is generally used when referring to arrangements, agreements or discussions, and means 'done in a friendly way, showing goodwill'. When, rarely, it is applied to people, *amicable* refers to their friendly behaviour or attitude: *While their marriage may have had its ups and downs, they were now amicable companions pursuing separate interests but united by a common duty.*

## among see BETWEEN.

## amoral see IMMORAL.

## analogy see ALLEGORY.

## annual, perennial

*Annual* means 'happening once every year', as in *The flower-show is an annual event*, or 'of one year', as in *What is her annual salary?* When applied to plants, *annual* means 'lasting for only one year' or, as a noun, 'a plant which lives for only one year'.

*Perennial* originally meant 'lasting or continuing through the year', but is now used, mostly in formal or facetious contexts, in the sense of 'perpetual', 'continual' or 'recurrent': *I'm tired of listening to her perennial complaints □ This is a perennial problem for us.* When used of plants, *perennial* means '(a plant) which lasts for more than two years'.

See also the article BIENNIAL, BIANNUAL.

## anticipate

The verb *anticipate* is often used with the meaning 'to foresee (something) and take action to prevent it, counter it, meet its requirements, etc':

*She's an excellent chess-player — she anticipated every move I made.*
*A good businessman must try to anticipate his customers' requirements.*

Some people still consider this to be the only correct meaning of ***anticipate***, but for most speakers of English this verb has another meaning, equivalent simply to 'foresee' or 'expect': *The police said that they were not anticipating any trouble from the strikers.*

Although it is perhaps unfortunate that ***anticipate*** has taken on this wider meaning — in some contexts, it may not be clear whether someone is merely expecting something or both expecting it and taking some action with regard to it — this use of the verb is well established and widely accepted and should not now be condemned as incorrect. However, care should be taken, especially in writing, to avoid any confusion that might possibly arise from the use of this now ambiguous verb.

## antiquated, antique

An ***antique*** is any old object such as a piece of furniture or an ornament which is considered valuable because of its age. By some definitions, an ***antique*** is required to be over 100 years old, but the word is generally used in a looser sense, and antique shops will usually display, and antique collectors buy, objects that are not as old as that.

***Antiquated*** also means 'old', but has a more derogatory connotation than ***antique***, nearly always implying scorn or derision: *a kitchen full of antiquated gadgets.* While something that is ***antique*** is generally valued because of its age, ***antiquated*** implies that whatever it applies to is not to be valued. In a colloquial, non-technical sense, ***antique*** too may imply scorn or mockery: *Their furniture's positively antique!*

## antisocial see UNSOCIABLE.

## appraise, apprise

To ***appraise*** someone or something is to form an opinion about their value, quality, competence, etc: *Her vivid blue eyes appraised him kindly but keenly* □ *General managers are appraised by area managers* □ *His entire worldly goods were appraised at a mere £53.*

To ***apprise*** someone (usually ***of*** something) is to inform them: *They will need to be apprised in advance of your intentions.*

## apprehend see COMPREHEND.

## apt see LIABLE.

## Arab, Arabian, Arabic

*Arab*, *Arabian* and *Arabic* apply to race, geographical region and language respectively.

An *Arab* is a member of one of the Semitic peoples found in North Africa and the Middle East, and the *Arab* countries are those countries in which Arabs form the largest part of the population.

*Arabian* means 'belonging to or connected with Arabia': *the Arabian Desert* □ *stepped out of the plane into the Arabian summer heat.* Formerly, it was used in the same sense as *Arab*, but this is uncommon nowadays.

*Arabic* is the Semitic language spoken by Arabs, and other people, in many countries of North Africa and the Middle East. *Arabic numerals* are the ones we use in everyday life: *1, 2, 3*, etc.

An *Arab*, or *Arab horse*, is a horse of a particular breed which originated in Arabia. It is also known as an *Arabian* or *Arabian horse*.

## arbiter, arbitrator

The word *arbiter* is used to denote a person who has the power or influence to control or make decisions about something: *the great arbiter of fashion, Beau Brummel* □ *He was the supreme arbiter of protocol and courtly behaviour.*

An *arbitrator* is a person chosen by people involved in a dispute to decide between them in order to settle the dispute: *The decisions of the arbitrator are subject to the right of appeal.* The word *arbiter* may quite correctly be used in this sense also: *He was called upon to act as arbiter in the dispute.*

## arouse see ROUSE.

## artist, artiste

An *artist* is a person who paints pictures or one who is skilled in another of the fine arts such as sculpture or music: *a stained-glass artist.* In a more general sense, *artist* may be applied to anyone who shows great skill in what they do: *He is a real artist with a fishing-rod.*

An *artiste* (pronounced /ahr-**teest**/) is a performer in a theatre or circus or on television, eg a singer, dancer, juggler, comedian or, rather less frequently, an actor: *a celebrated mime artiste.* *Artist* is also used in this sense, and is now more common than *artiste*.

## as see LIKE.

## as . . . as, so . . . as

In making comparisons, you should use the form *as . . . as*: *He is as tall as his brother* □ *I will come as soon as I can.* After a negative word such as *not*, the first *as* may be replaced by *so*:

  ✓  *It's not as difficult as you think.*
  ✓  *It's not so difficult as you think.*

When the second *as* is followed by *to* and an infinitive, the correct construction is *so . . . as*: *Do you think he would be so foolish as to come?*

See also LIKE, AS.

## assent, consent

Both these verbs convey the notion of 'agreeing to' or 'complying with' something, but there is usually a slight difference in implication between the two words.

To *assent* to something (normally an opinion or proposal) is to indicate agreement with it, without any doubts, objections or persuasion:

> *He readily assented to their suggestions.*
> *They assented to the proposal to widen the road.*

*Consent*, on the other hand, indicates not just agreement but approval and/or willingness, and often implies that a certain amount of thought or persuasion has been involved in the decision-making process:

> *An adult patient has the absolute right to choose whether to consent to medical treatment.*
> *She would never consent to such a proposal.*

It may also indicate that the person consenting is giving in to or agreeing to comply with a request or proposal in spite of doubts or objections which he or she had and perhaps still has:

> *I felt he was too young to go into town alone, but in the end I consented.*

• The same distinctions hold for the nouns *assent* and *consent*:

> *He nodded assent and didn't ask for a reason.*
> *There was general assent about his achievement.*

> *In spite of their doubts, they finally gave their consent to the marriage.*

## assignation, assignment

An *assignment* is a task, duty or post given to someone: *She knew she should refuse the assignment, and even resign if necessary.* An *assignation* is a meeting, especially one arranged in secret for some romantic or illicit purpose: *He was being teased about his 'assignation' with an older woman.*

*Assignment* is also the usual word for the act of assigning (eg a task to someone, something to a group or category, etc): *This would permit the assignment of the lease to you.* *Assignation* may also be used in this sense, but its use with this meaning is rare.

**assure, assurance** see INSURE.

**aural** see ORAL.

## auspicious, propitious

Both these words mean 'favourable to future success'. Circumstances are *auspicious* when they give hope of success (ie because they are considered to be a good omen), whereas they are *propitious* when they are directly conducive to success (ie by providing favourable conditions for whatever is being done):

> *The first meeting was less than auspicious.*
> *It was not an auspicious time for the new play to open.*
>
> *This didn't seem a propitious time to launch into an explanation.*
> *Franco considered the moment propitious to pressing the Spanish claims to Gibraltar.*

*Propitious* may be followed by *to* or *for*.

Because of its frequent occurrence in phrases such as *on this auspicious occasion*, *auspicious* has now taken on the meaning of 'important', without any notion of implied future success.

## authoritarian, authoritative

*Authoritarian* means 'demanding obedience, considering obedience to authority more important than personal freedom': *authoritarian parents* □ *an authoritarian government*.

*Authoritative* usually means 'having authority, said or done with authority', as in *an authoritative statement/opinion* (= one which can be relied on because the person making it has the necessary authority, status or expertise).

## avenge, revenge, vengeance

The verbs *avenge* and *revenge* are almost identical in meaning, and indeed many people treat them as synonyms. However, these words do differ slightly in both meaning and use, and the differences are worth observing and preserving.

*Revenge* is rarely used as a verb, but it should be used when the subject of the verb is acting in retaliation for harm (real or imagined) or suffering, in order to satisfy his or her feeling of anger or resentment: *He vowed to revenge himself on his enemies for what they had done to him*. Usually the subject of the verb *revenge* is the person who suffered the original offence, and it is only very rarely used with an object other than a reflexive pronoun: *Ghosts often go haunting to revenge their horrible murders.*

*Avenge* is the correct verb to use when the subject of the verb is acting in retaliation for a wrong suffered (usually by someone else) in order to achieve justice of a sort by inflicting harm or suffering more or less equivalent to the original offence: *He vowed to avenge his father's death.*

- The distinctions in meaning and use that exist between *avenge* and *revenge* should similarly apply to the nouns *vengeance* and *revenge*:

*You cannot really blame him for seeking revenge for the wrong done to him.*
*He was desperate to wreak his personal vengeance on her killer.*

In practice, however, the two words are used interchangeably:

*I was wielding the sword of justice, the son seeking revenge on behalf of the*
   *father.*
*He would have his vengeance on this meaningless universe.*

**averse** see ADVERSE.

## avoid, evade

To **avoid** someone or something is to keep away from them/it, to take action in order not to come into contact with them/it: *He walked through the back-streets to avoid the crowds.* To **avoid** something happening is to do something to prevent it happening: *They agreed on the need to avoid a public row over the plan.* To **evade** someone, on the other hand, is to use trickery or cunning to escape from them or to prevent yourself being caught by them: *He managed to evade his captors by climbing through the toilet window.*

In some cases, **avoid** and **evade** are virtually interchangeable. There is little difference between **avoiding** a question and **evading** it, though **evade** generally implies the use of verbal trickery more than **avoid**, which usually has a more neutral sense: *He was so tentative that she wondered if she could avoid the question, but then he persisted.* And again, **evade** implies something illegitimate, underhanded or illegal, whereas **avoid** does not:

*I'm not going to be there because I want to avoid all responsibility for it if*
   *everything goes wrong.*
*Although he was the organizer of the march, he managed to evade all*
   *responsibility for the ensuing riot.*

● **Tax avoidance** involves legal ways of reducing the amount of tax you have to pay, whereas **tax evasion** involves illegal ways of doing so.

**await** see WAIT.

**awake, awaken** see WAKE.

## award, reward

An *award* is something given or received for excellence, merit or bravery: *He has received many awards for his dress designs.* **Award** also applies to something given or received as a result of a decision by a judge or arbitrator: *The accident victims each received an award of £2000.*

A *reward* is given or received in return for good work, a service rendered, etc: *A reward was offered for capturing the bandits* □ *The children were very well-behaved, and were given 10p each as a reward.*

- The same distinction applies to the related verbs:

  *They were awarded £2000 by the court.*
  *Bring them back alive and you will be well rewarded.*

## bacterium, bacillus, virus

*Bacteria, bacilli* and *viruses* may all be spoken of informally as *germs.* *Bacteria* are microscopic plants which can cause disease and putrefaction. *Bacillus* is correctly used to refer to any member of a particular group of rod-shaped bacteria, but the word is often loosely applied to any disease-causing bacterium. *Viruses* are much smaller than *bacteria,* and are complex substances, consisting of proteins, etc, which behave in some ways like living organisms. They can reproduce themselves only inside the living cells of plants or animal bodies, by doing which they usually cause disease.

Note that *bacteria* is a plural noun. It is sometimes used incorrectly as a singular, but the correct form of the singular noun is *bacterium.*

## bail, bale

*Bail* is money given to a court of law to gain the release of an untried prisoner until the time of his or her trial. To *bail out* a person is to get the person released from prison by providing bail.

To *bale out* means either 'to remove water from a boat' or 'to parachute from an aircraft in an emergency'. The spelling *bail* is also possible with these meanings, but is much less common than *bale.*

*Bale* is also the correct spelling for a bundle of hay.

## baited, bated

Note the difference between *a baited trap* (ie, a trap with some bait in it) and *with bated breath* (= 'while holding your breath'; *bated* is related to the word *abate,* ' to lessen').

## baneful, baleful

*Baneful* means 'harmful, destructive': *the supposed baneful effects of television violence on the young people of today. Baleful* can also be used in this sense, but more often means 'menacing', in other words 'threatening harm' rather than 'causing harm'. Less commonly, *baleful* may mean 'sad, dismal': *We left them to their baleful conjecturing. A baleful look* may therefore be either actively hostile or simply doleful. Be aware of this ambiguity.

## barbarian, barbaric, barbarous

A *barbarian* is a person belonging to a relatively uncivilized, but not primitive, society. Used figuratively, it denotes a person whose behaviour is crude, rude or uncultured. The adjective *barbarian* means 'of, or typical of, barbarians': *barbarian tribes □ barbarian splendour.*

*Barbaric* also means 'typical of a barbarian'. It can be used of something tolerated or even admired, or on the other hand of something considered excessively or tastelessly showy: *The notion of a barbaric wisdom gained acceptance among the Greeks □ the barbaric splendour of the Abyssinian Empire.* **Barbaric** is most frequently used in the sense 'typical of, or as bad as, the worst or cruellest side of barbarian behaviour': *barbaric crimes.*

This last sense of *barbaric* is also conveyed by *barbarous*: *barbarous crimes.* **Barbarous** is also used of language, and means 'ungrammatical, not idiomatic, offensive to scholarly knowledge and good taste'.

● Among the related nouns, **barbarity** means 'cruelty, inhumanity', **barbarism** denotes a barbarous use of or form of language, and **barbarism** and **barbarousness** together relate to the other senses of the three adjectives.

**bated** see BAITED.

## bath, bathe

As a verb, **bath** means 'to wash (usually the whole body) in a bath': *I'll bath the baby □ She had aways wanted to bath in warm milk.* **Bath** may be used as a verb only in British English; American English uses the phrases 'give a bath to' and 'take a bath'.

To **bathe** means 'to wash (a part of your body) in order to make it clean or to lessen pain': *He should bathe his feet in hot water.* In American English, **bathe** is also used in the sense of 'take a bath'. The verb **bathe** also means 'to go swimming': *The children went bathing in the sea every day.*

## bathos, pathos

**Bathos** is a term used in literary criticism. It denotes a sudden change in speech or writing from a serious and elevated topic to a trivial or common-place one, a deliberate or unintentional anticlimax which creates a some-what ludicrous effect: eg *Cast up alone on the island, abandoned (as he thought) by both God and man, he found himself without companionship, without solace, without hope, and with no clean underwear.*

**Pathos** is a quality of something that arouses pity or compassion. There may be *pathos* in a situation or in the telling of a story, for example, or in a piece of music or a work of art.

## because

● **Because** should not be used to introduce a subordinate clause referring back to *reason* or *reason why* in a main clause:

✗ *The reason (why) he stole the money is because he wanted to buy food.*

The *because* in such a construction simply duplicates the information already conveyed by *reason* or *reason why*. The correct construction is with *that*, not *because*:

✓     *The reason (why) he stole the money is that he wanted to buy food.*

● **because of, due to, owing to**
*Because of* and *owing to* are used to introduce adverbial phrases explaining the reason for something described by the <u>verb</u> of the sentence:

*The match was cancelled because of the heavy rain.*
*Owing to the bad weather, half the guests failed to turn up.*

*Due to* is often also used in this way: *The match was cancelled due to the heavy rain.* Formerly, this was considered to be incorrect, and traditional grammars insisted that, *due* being an adjective, *due to* must follow or refer back to a <u>noun</u>: *His success was due to hard work* □ *The cancellation of the match was due to the heavy rain.* Although there are still some people who consider the use of *due to* to refer back to the action of a verb as incorrect, it is now very common and quite acceptable to most people. There is no good reason now to adhere to the traditional rule.

## behalf, part

Do not confuse *on behalf of* and *on the part of*. *On behalf of* means 'for' or 'as a representative of', *on the part of* means 'by' or 'of':

✗     *This is surely an error on behalf of your accountants.*
✓     *This is surely an error on the part of your accountants.*

✓     *I am writing on behalf of the local Community Council.*

## benign, benignant, malign, malignant

In medical contexts, *benign* means 'not fatal or harmful to health', as in *a benign tumour.* The opposite of *benign* in this sense is *malignant*: *a malignant growth.*

In other contexts, *benign* and *malign* should generally be used when it is the impact, influence or effect of a person, action or thing that is being referred to, and *benignant* and *malignant* when it is intentions, attitudes, feelings or personalities that are being spoken of: *He had a benign/malign influence on the course of events* but *He is benignant/malignant by nature.* However, these distinctions are by no means consistently observed by all English-speakers: in particular, *benign* is frequently used in the sense given here for *benignant*, as in *a benign smile,* and this use is so well established that it must now be accepted as correct.

## beside, besides

The preposition *beside* means 'next to, at the side of', as in *He was standing beside me.*

**Besides** means 'as well as, in addition to, except', as in *Is anyone coming besides John?* **Beside** may also be used in this sense, but it is generally considered better to keep the distinction between the two words.

## between, among

i)   Where there is a sense of sharing out or dividing up, it is correct to use **between** for two people or things and **among** for larger numbers: *The sweets were shared between the two children* □ *The sweets were shared out among all the children in the class.* **Between** is used when two groups of individuals are involved: *The sweets were shared out equally between the boys and the girls.* Where the exact number of the participants in the sharing is stated, both **between** and **among** are correct, regardless of the number involved: *The sweets were shared out equally between/among the seven children.*

Where the reference is to discussions, agreements, relationships, position, etc, **between** is quite correctly used to relate three or more people, groups or things: *Switzerland is situated between France, Germany, Austria and Italy* or *discussions between shareholders, employers and trade unionists.* (Note that in this last example, **between** conveys the notion that all three groups are involved in the same discussion, whereas **among** would suggest that each group is holding a separate discussion.) Shared knowledge, opinions, etc also require **between**, as for example in the idiomatic expression *between you, me and the bedpost.*

When a co-operative group activity is involved, **between** is again correct regardless of the number involved: *Several of my neighbours came round to lend a hand, and between us we shifted the whole pile of bricks in just over an hour.*

ii)   The second or last of the words being linked by **between** should correctly be preceded by **and**, not **or**:

✓   *a choice between whisky and brandy*
✗   *a choice between whisky or brandy*

When two quantities or amounts are being referred to, use **between ... and** or *from ... to*:

✓   *pay rises of between £3000 and £10 000*
✓   *pay rises of anything from £3000 to £10 000*
✗   *pay rises of anything between £3000 to £10 000*

iii)   **Between** should not be followed by a singular noun or noun phrase on its own. This is a common error with phrases containing *each* or *every*:

✗   *He paused between each sentence.*
✓   *He paused between sentences.*
✓   *He paused after each sentence.*

## biennial, biannual

*Biennial* means 'happening, etc every two years', *biannual* 'happening, etc twice a year'. When applied to plants, *biennial* means '(a plant) that lives for two years'.

## billion see MILLION.

## biweekly, bimonthly, etc

Notice that these words are ambiguous, meaning that something happens, etc 'twice a week, month, etc' or 'once every two weeks, months, etc'. If the context does not make the meaning clear, serious confusion could arise: in such cases, these terms should be replaced by unambiguous words such as *two-monthly, fortnightly, half-yearly, twice-weekly,* etc.

## blanch, blench

Both *blanch* and *blench* mean 'to (cause to) turn pale or white'. Fear or some awful sight or thought may cause a person to *blench* or *blanch*. However, there is another unrelated word *blench* which means 'to flinch or shrink back', so if it is said that someone *blenched*, it may not be clear whether they turned pale or shrank back: *He blenched, and hurriedly made his exit.*

When you immerse fruit or vegetables briefly in boiling water, you are *blanching* them.

## blatant see FLAGRANT.

## blench see BLANCH.

## bloc, block

A *bloc* is a group of nations, etc who have an interest or purpose in common: *the European trade bloc* □ *the former Communist bloc.* In all other senses the correct spelling is *block*: *a block of wood* □ *a block of flats* □ *a road block* □ *a chopping block.*

## blond, blonde

*Blond* is masculine, *blonde* feminine: *He is blond* □ *She is blonde* □ *He has blond hair* □ *She has blonde hair.* Some authorities would allow *She has blond hair* since here the *blond* refers not to *she* but to *hair,* but *She has blonde hair* is more common.

When used as a noun in speaking, /blond/ is generally taken to mean *blonde,* not *blond,* that is, to refer to a female rather than a male person.

## boil see BROIL.

## born, borne

*Borne* is the usual past participle of the verb *to bear,* both in the senses of 'to carry' and 'to give birth to': *He was borne shoulder-high after his victory* □ *She has borne him seven children* □ *English monarchs since Henry VIII have borne the title 'Defender of the Faith'.*

**Born** may only be used, and must be used, in passive constructions when the verb is not followed by the preposition *by*: *She was born in London* □ *She was born of Indian parents*, but *Of the seven children borne by her* (or *born to her*), *none survived to adulthood.*

## both

**Both** should be followed by **and**, not **as well as**:

✓  *He is both rich and handsome.*
✗  *He is both rich as well as handsome.*

## bravery, bravado, bravura

**Bravery** is simply courage. **Bravado** is a boastful or defiant act of bravery intended to impress or intimidate or a boastful pretence of bravery aimed at concealing cowardice: *She felt her defiant bravado disintegrate like shattered glass.*

**Bravura**, often confused with **bravado**, has nothing to do with courage; it denotes a particularly brilliant or skilful performance, especially in music but also in other forms of the arts: *the bravura and individualism of his painting of birds and animals.*

## Britain, Great Britain, British Isles, United Kingdom

**Great Britain** is the island consisting of England, Scotland and Wales. Also included are the numerous small islands around the coast, but not the Isle of Man or the Channel Islands.

The **United Kingdom** is a political term, denoting 'the United Kingdom of Great Britain and Northern Ireland', again excluding the Isle of Man and the Channel Islands.

**British Isles** is a geographical term. The **British Isles** consist of the United Kingdom, the Republic of Ireland, the Isle of Man and the Channel Islands.

**Britain** is a term with no official status. It is generally used as a synonym of Great Britain and of the United Kingdom. Similarly, the adjective **British** relates to both Great Britain and the United Kingdom, and the noun **Briton** to a native of Great Britain or to a citizen of the United Kingdom.

## broil, boil

To **boil** food is to cook it in hot liquid, especially water. **Broiling** is cooking by direct heat, especially grilling.

## broad, wide

The adjectives **broad** and **wide** can often be used interchangeably to describe a noun: *a wide road/river/lawn* is essentially the same as *a broad*

*road/river/lawn*. However, these two words are not absolutely synonymous and in some contexts only the one or the other is appropriate.

One difference between these words is that **broad** refers to the extent across something and often has the connotation of spaciousness or ampleness, whereas **wide** refers to the distance separating, or gap between, its sides, edges or tips. Hence one speaks, for example, of a person's *broad back* or *broad shoulders* but of a jacket's *wide sleeves*. Openings and passages are in general **wide** rather than **broad**: *a wide doorway*. The same object may thus be looked at and described in two different ways: to talk of a *broad staircase* is to consider the distance across it, whereas to talk of a *wide staircase* is to emphasize its adequate size as a passageway.

Another difference is that **wide** rather than **broad** is used with measurements: a *broad* river might be 200 metres *wide*.

**Broad**, rather than **wide**, is used to describe categories, concepts, criteria, goals, guidelines, etc that are not narrowly defined or limited. **Wide** in this sort of context denotes great extent: *a wide choice of sports facilities* □ *a wide variety of foods*. *Broad agreement* is very general agreement, while *wide agreement* is extensive agreement; similarly *broad powers* are very general powers, while *wide powers* are extensive.

## can, could, may, might

- **can not** versus **cannot**

In British English, the form **cannot** must be used unless the word **not** is linked to the following word or words in a way that requires it to have particular emphasis. Compare for example *He cannot sing* and *You cannot just walk into the room without knocking on the door first* with *The study of pottery can not only provide information about trade but also enlighten us about the economy of the Roman empire.*

In American English **can not** may be used, and is generally preferred, where British English requires **cannot**.

- **can** versus **may**

According to the traditional rule, **may** should be used when the idea of 'giving permission, allowing something' is intended: *You may go to the party if you wish* (= 'I am giving you permission to go'). **Can** should only be used to convey the idea of 'ability, possibility': *I can speak Chinese* □ *You can walk to the party if you miss the bus*. However, this rule simply does not hold any longer, and in general **can** is used instead of **may** in all but the most formal contexts: *You can go to the party if you want to.*

**May** is in any case sometimes ambiguous, as it is not always clear whether it is being used to give permission or to state a possibility. Is the notice *In emergency cases, cars may be parked at the front entrance* giving permission or simply information? Similarly, is *The authorities may not release the names of the dead and injured until their next of kin have been contacted* stating what might happen or stating what must happen? In many cases, the ambiguity does not matter much, but in others it might be important. **Can** unambiguously indicates permission: *The authorities cannot release the names of the dead . . .*

- **could** versus **might**
The same ambiguity as exists between the **may** of permission and the **may** of possibility exists equally with **might**, but **might** is more likely to be interpreted as stating a possibility than as giving permission. Where permssion is intended, it is better to use **could**: compare *She said we might go* and *She said we could go*.

- **may** versus **might**
In many cases referring to something that could happen in the future, there is often little difference between **may** and **might**: *If I don't get a move on, I may/might miss the last bus*. Sometimes **may** suggests a more likely possibility than **might**: compare *I may well miss the last bus, so don't worry if I'm not back tonight* and *I suppose I might miss the last bus, but it's not likely*.

In questions or suggestions, **might** is often more tentative or deferential than **may**: compare *May I suggest that we leave this matter aside for the time being?* and *Might I suggest that we leave this matter aside for the time being?* Sometimes the supposed deference is ironic rather than real, in which case **might** comes across as more forceful than **may**: *Might I suggest, young man, that you leave such matters to those who are better able to decide on them?*

After a verb in the past tense in a main clause, **might** rather than **may** should be used in a subordinate clause:

   ✓   *I told you you might miss the train.*
   ✗   *I told you you may miss the train.*

- **may have** versus **might have**
**May have** and **might have** both refer to past possibilities. Generally **may have**, and less commonly **might have**, are used to signify that there is still uncertainty at the time of speaking as to whether the possible event has occurred, and **might have** when it is clear that it has not:

   *She may/might have survived the crash; we don't know yet.*
   *She might have survived the crash if the ambulance had got there sooner.*

Nowadays, **may have** is increasingly used instead of **might have** to refer to possibilities that definitely did not happen:

   *She may have survived the crash if the ambulance had got there sooner, but as it was, she didn't.*
   *It was a modest stage for a competitor whose talents may have yielded an Olympic medal.*

Although increasingly common, especially in journalism, this is still deprecated by many people, not just linguistic purists. It is still better to maintain the distinction outlined above.

## cannon, canon

With two *n*'s in the middle, a **cannon** is a large gun. A **canon**, with a single *n*, is a churchman, and also 'a generally accepted principle' (*the canons of good taste*), 'a church law' (*the canons of the Roman Catholic Church*), 'the accepted books of the Bible', or 'the set of recognized genuine works of a particular author'.

## canvas, canvass

**Canvas** is a material: *a canvas tent* □ *a canvas for painting on*. To **canvass** is to ask for votes or support: *canvassing on behalf of the Labour Party*.

## capability, capacity see ABILITY.

## catastrophe, cataclysm

A **catastrophe** is a sudden disaster or misfortune. A **cataclysm** is more of an upheaval than a disaster, especially a major social or political change affecting the whole of society.

## Celsius see CENTIGRADE.

## cement, concrete, mortar

A **cement** is any substance that makes other substances or objects stick together (*a tile cement*), or which serves as a building material (*They masticate earth and saliva to produce a cement that sets as hard as rock*). The best-known type of cement is the grey powder made by burning a mixture of clay and limestone. This cement is mixed with sand and water to form **mortar** or with sand, water and small stones to form **concrete**.

Both **mortar** and **concrete** are loosely known as 'cement' also, both informally and in some technical expressions: a 'cement mixer', for example, actually mixes concrete or mortar.

## censor, censure

A **censor** is an official who examines books, films, letters, etc and who has the power to delete parts of the material or to forbid publication, showing, etc. **Censure** is criticism or blame.

• Both words may be used as verbs, and it is here that most of the errors and confusions occur. Note the correct uses: *His letters home were censored* □ *The Home Secretary was severely censured for abusing his powers.*

144

• The related adjectives are even more likely to be confused: the adjective meaning 'pertaining to censors and censorship' is ***censorial***, and the adjective meaning 'pertaining to censure' is ***censorious***.

## centigrade, Celsius

***Centigrade*** means 'having one hundred degrees'. A ***centigrade*** temperature scale is one which has 100 degrees between the freezing-point of water and the boiling-point of water (as opposed, for example, to the Fahrenheit scale, which has 180 degrees between the freezing-point and boiling-point of water, and the Réaumur scale, which has 80 degrees). The Fahrenheit and Réaumur scales were in use by the early 18th century, but in 1742 the Swedish astronomer Anders Celsius outlined the advantages of using a thermometer scale of 100 degrees, the ***centigrade*** scale. Although ***centigrade*** could in theory apply to any temperature scale which has 100 degrees between the freezing-point of water and the boiling-point of water, the term has usually been applied to a scale based on Celsius's proposals, on which the freezing-point of water is 0° and the boiling-point 100°. (Celsius himself actually proposed the opposite, with water freezing at 100° and boiling at 0°!)

The ***centigrade scale*** was officially renamed the ***Celsius scale*** in 1948, to avoid possible confusion with another technical sense of *centigrade* (= 'one-hundredth of a *grade*', a unit of measurement of angles). Although ***centigrade*** continued to be used after that time, it has since then been increasingly replaced by ***Celsius***, and has now been almost completely superseded by it.

## centre

• ***centre* versus *middle***

There are slight differences between these two words in meaning and use. Firstly, ***centre*** has a connotation of exactness that is lacking in ***middle***: the ***centre*** of a room is at or near a point equally far from the walls of the room, whereas the ***middle*** of the room covers a much larger and more vaguely defined area. In referring to long things, ***middle*** rather than ***centre*** is normal: *the middle of the road*.

In a figurative sense, ***centre*** implies a degree of influence or agency, ***middle*** only involvement: *He is at the centre of a dispute* means the dispute is over him or something he has or has not done; *He is in the middle of a dispute* means only that he is involved in it, whatever its cause and subject.

• ***centre round***

The phrase ***centre round/around*** is frequently condemned as illogical (***centring*** implying a single point and ***round*** implying an inclusive area), but logical or otherwise — and it certainly would not be the first illogical idiom in English — it must now be considered correct, in informal speech at least. In formal contexts, however, it is perhaps better to avoid this construction, and use *centre on* or *be centred in/on* instead.

## ceremonial, ceremonious

*Ceremonial* means 'relating to or appropriate for a formal ceremony': *ceremonial dress* □ *a ceremonial occasion.* *Ceremonial* may also be used as a noun, meaning 'a ceremony, rite' or 'ceremonial rules or ritual': *the pomp and ceremonial of a coronation.*

*Ceremonious* is most often applied to a person or to someone's action or behaviour and means 'much concerned with ceremony, carefully formal or polite', usually with the implication of being excessively or inappropriately so: *With a ceremonious bow, he took his leave.*

## charge

*In charge of* means 'in control of, responsible for': *The policeman asked who had been in charge of the dog.* *In the charge of* means 'in the care of, being looked after by': *The children were in the charge of two teachers.*

Note that this distinction is valid only for British English. In American English, *in charge of* is ambiguous, meaning both 'in control of' and 'under the control of'.

## chary, wary

Both *chary* and *wary* imply cautiousness, but different types of cautiousness in differing circumstances. *Wary* implies a cautiousness that arises from an awareness of potential danger, difficulties or harm (the word is related to both *aware* and *beware*): *She kept a wary eye on the cows as she crossed the field* □ *Clutching her walking-stick like a club, she crept warily down the stairs.* *Wary* may also imply a cautiousness arising from being in a new and uncertain situation: *Faced for the first time with a female vicar, many parishioners seemed rather wary of her.*

*Chary* is similar in meaning to *wary*, but often implies a hesitation or reluctance in addition to the cautiousness: *I'm always chary of crossing a field of cows in case there's a bull in the field too* □ *She's chary of giving money to beggars in the street.*

## childish, childlike

*Childish* and *childlike* are generally applied to adults rather than to children, and mean 'of or like a child' in a bad sense and a good or neutral sense respectively. *Childish* is thus a term of disapproval, and *childlike* generally a term of approval. A person may be liked for their *childlike innocence*, but will be disliked if they make *childish remarks* or indulge in *childish tantrums*.

**chord** see CORD.

## chronic

The original sense of *chronic* is 'lasting a long time': *chronic heart disease*. Since many things (eg diseases) that are *chronic* are also very unpleasant, *chronic* has taken on a second sense of 'very bad, deplorable': *That film was absolutely chronic*. This use is slang, or at best informal; it should be avoided in formal speech and writing.

**clad** see CLOTHED.

## classic, classical

A *classic* is 'an established work of art or literature of high quality': *Dickens's novels are considered classics*. *Classic* also denotes an established sporting event, especially any of the five main annual horse races, the Two Thousand Guineas, the One Thousand Guineas, the Oaks, the Derby and the St Leger. The plural *classics* denotes 'Greek and Latin studies', as in *She is studying classics at university*.

The adjective related to *classic* in the above sense is also *classic*: *Dickens's novels are among the classic works of English literature*. However, the adjective denoting 'pertaining to the classics (= Greek and Latin studies), or to ancient Greece and Rome' is *classical*: *classical studies □ a classical education □ classical writers □ classical mythology*. *Classical* is also used to refer to the art, writing, etc of similar periods of history and civilization in other cultures: *classical Chinese poetry*.

Another sense of *classic* is 'typical': *a classic example of his stupidity □ the classic symptoms of heart disease*. It may also mean 'particularly excellent, outstanding': *a classic display of virtuoso drumming*. *Classic* also has the sense 'simple and elegant, balanced in form' (as in *classic clothes* or *a building of classic proportions*) generally, and especially with regard to clothes, implying that the thing so designated is not subject to or based on passing trends and fashions. A related sense of *classic* is 'pure, perfect', often accompanying nouns such as *purity* and *simplicity*. In this last sense, some authorities also accept *classical* as correct, but there is perhaps a useful, if subtle, distinction to be maintained between these two words in this context, *classic* emphasizing excellence and *classical* emphasizing simplicity of form or movement and lack of embellishment: *moving across the stage with a classical grace unexpected in one so young*.

In art and architecture, *classical* means 'following or imitating the style of ancient Greece and Rome', denoting a style that emphasizes restraint, simplicity, order and discipline as opposed to innovation, decoration and the expression of emotion.

*Classical*, applied to music, has a number of different but related senses. In its most general sense current today, *classical music* is music which is traditional and stately in form, following the style of the great composers of the past, and in this sense it stands in opposition to *pop music, folk music, dance music*, etc. In this sense, we can say that there are still **classical** composers writing **classical music** at the present time. Similarly, **classical ballet** is more formal and traditional in theme and style than modern ballet. **Classical**, in the sense of 'formal and traditional' may be applied to the music, dance, etc of other cultures also, not just those of European countries: *classical Japanese music.*

**Classical** may also mean 'standard, well-established, composed of standard works': *Chekhov's plays are firmly established in the classical repertoire of European theatre companies.* And in certain fields of activity, **classical** may be applied to a theory or style which was long established and is therefore worthy of respect but which is now superseded: *contrasting the classical cost-of-production theories of economics with those of the late 20th century □ Jack Hobbs is considered to be one of the great exponents of classical English batsmanship.*

## clean, cleanse

To **clean** something is to 'remove dirt, etc from' it: *I must clean the car this morning.* The verb **cleanse** is also used to mean 'to remove dirt, germs, etc from' something, especially as applied to a part of the body and with a further connotation of a very thorough cleaning: *This cream cleanses the skin more thoroughly than any of its rivals* or *She bathed and cleansed the wound carefully before bandaging it.* It is often used figuratively to mean 'to make pure, free from wickedness', as in *He asked God to cleanse him of his sins.*

Substances such as soaps or detergents used for household cleaning purposes are generally **cleaners**, but sometimes **cleansers**, especially scouring-powders. A **cleanser** is also a cosmetic for cleaning the skin when removing make-up.

Note that in many parts of Britain at least, it is the local authority's **Cleansing** Department which is responsible for cleaning the streets and removing household refuse.

## climatic, climactic

**Climatic** is related to 'climate': *Climatic changes were probably partly to blame for the disappearance of dinosaurs.* **Climactic** is related to 'climax': *In the light of history, we can see that the arrest of the priest was the climactic act of oppression that led eventually to the downfall of the regime.*

## clothed, clad

The current normal past tense and past participle of **clothe** is **clothed**: *Reacting against her own childhood poverty, she always clothed her children expensively and in accordance with the latest fashions.* **Clad** in this sense is archaic.

As an adjective, both *clothed* and *clad* are used. In the simple sense of 'wearing clothes', *clothed* is normal: *I knew I wasn't suitably clothed for going climbing in winter.* *Clad* is used when there is a connotation of protection (or lack of it) in what is being worn: *fishermen clad in oilskins □ The knights were clad in armour and their ladies clothed in silk.* Even without the connotation of protectiveness, *clad* is often preferred to *clothed* in compounds and with accompanying adverbs: *a rather dull and always sensibly clad schoolteacher □ Hearing the alarm, many of them dashed out of their rooms semi-clad and ran into the street.* The same holds true in figurative and poetic contexts: *a hillside clothed in yellow flowers □ snow-clad mountains.*

## coherence, cohesion

Both these words mean 'sticking together'. *Coherence* refers to the degree to which plans, thoughts, ideas, proposals, etc 'hang together' logically, intelligibly or consistently to form a sensible, workable or intelligible whole: *Until now, their policies have lacked consistency and coherence □ This has little to do with the conceptual coherence of her theory.* *Coherence* also refers to the degree to which an organization, etc functions effectively as a whole, or to the degree to which the component parts of a situation, state, lifestyle, etc form an observable or intelligible unity: *It is up to the chairman to maintain the overall integrity and coherence of the organization □ The inner coherence of Masai life was threatened by their actions.*

*Cohesion* refers to the literal sticking together of two things or, in a figurative sense, to the closeness of people in a group, etc: *the cohesion of the family unit.*

● Of the related adjectives, *coherent* refers to the state of coherence, while *cohesive* refers to what creates coherence or cohesion: *coherent policies □ an examination of the role of cohesive devices in creating coherence in a text.*

## comic, comical

The adjective *comic* means 'pertaining to comedy', 'intended to amuse': *a comic actor □ comic opera.* *Comical* means 'funny, amusing', and applies to anything which causes laughter whether intended to do so or not: *a comical sight.* *Comic* is increasingly often used in this sense also, but *comical* may not be used in the sense given for *comic*.

## commander, commandant, commodore

In the Royal Navy, *commodore* is the rank immediately above *captain*, *commander* the rank below *captain* (with *lieutenant commander* the rank below *commander*).

In the Royal Air Force, *air commodore* is the rank above *group captain*, and

149

***wing commander*** the rank below *group captain*.

In addition, regardless of rank, the officer in charge of a military establishment, such as an army barracks, may be referred to as a ***commandant***, and the commanding officer of a body of troops may be referred to as their ***commander***. The ***commander*** of certain types or sizes of ships in the navy may have the rank of *captain* on the one hand or *lieutenant commander* on the other. The senior captain in a fleet of merchant ships has the rank of ***commodore***, and ***commodore*** is also the title given to the president of a yacht club.

A ***commander*** is also a high-ranking police officer in charge of a district, and the highest-ranking officer in the RSPCA.

## commitment, committal, commission

The most common sense of ***commitment*** nowadays is that of 'being committed' to some cause or organization: *her commitment to socialism □ criticized for showing a lack of commitment*. ***Commitment*** is also used for 'obligation, something that a person has promised to do or has to do': *I have a number of family commitments to attend to first.*

***Committing*** would be the normal word to use of a crime (*the committing of a murder*), though in formal language ***commission*** is also correct, and both ***committing*** and ***commitment*** for committing eg facts to memory or paper.

***Committal*** is a rather formal or technical word which is normally used for the act of committing a person to prison, a mental hospital, etc, or a body to the grave.

## commodore see COMMANDER.

## common, mutual

***Common*** means 'belonging to, or shared by, two or more people, etc': *We share a common language □ our common love of classical music □ This knowledge is common to all of us.*

***Mutual,*** strictly speaking, means 'given by each to the other or others involved', and implies a two-way flow of feelings, etc, as in *mutual respect* and *Their dislike was mutual*. Some people disapprove of the use of ***mutual*** in the sense of 'common' given above, as in *our mutual friend/acquaintance* or *a matter of mutual interest*, but this use is well established and there is no reason to avoid it in phrases such as these, at least in informal English. In formal English it is better to keep to the distinction in meaning outlined above and speak of, for example, *a matter of common interest*, but *a mutual friend* and *a mutual acquaintance* are now set phrases acceptable in any style of speech.

Care should be taken not the use the word ***mutual*** superfluously in a sentence in which the notion of 'two-wayness' is already conveyed by some other word or words:

✗    *their <u>mutual</u> respect <u>for each other</u>*
('mutual' and 'for each other' convey the same information)
✓    *their mutual respect*
✓    *their respect for each other.*

However, some phrases, such as *mutual agreement*, are now well established and need not be avoided, even though they are strictly speaking tautological ('agreement' itself means that both parties are involved and 'mutual' is therefore superfluous — you could not come to an agreement unless it was mutual).

## compare, comparable, comparative, comparison

- *compare to* **versus** *compare with*

**Compare** should be followed by the preposition ***to*** when it means 'to point out or suggest similarities between things that are essentially different', as in *She compared her husband to a toad* (= 'She said he looked, behaved, etc like a toad') □ *He compared his girlfriend to a wind-tossed leaf.*

When **compare** means 'to examine two or more things in order to find similarities, differences and especially their relative merits, etc', it should be followed by the preposition ***with***: *If you compare this book with that one, you will find this one far more informative* □ *She compared him with a toad, and decided that the toad was better-looking* □ *His last two plays just don't compare with his earlier works* (= they are not as good as the earlier ones).

Like ***compare***, the adjective ***comparable*** may be followed by ***to*** or ***with*** depending on the sense in which it is used. However, ***comparable to*** has encroached on the territory of ***comparable with***: *His work is comparable to that of many contemporary artists.* In particular, ***comparable to*** is often used in the sense of 'similar to': *We need to work out a strategy comparable to the one that got him elected four years ago.*

With ***compared*** or ***as compared,*** both ***with*** and ***to*** are considered correct (and ***to*** is now the commoner of the two), but the meaning is always that of ***compare with***: *Compared to/with you, I'm an absolute genius* □ *His house is a palace as compared to/with mine.*

The phrase ***by/in comparison*** should be followed by ***with,*** not ***to,*** as the sense is always that of ***compare with*** given above: *This book may seem expensive, but it is cheap in comparison with some you see in the shops.* ***Comparison*** should, of course, be followed by ***to*** when the sense is that of ***compare to***: *I thought his comparison of the managing director to an ignorant baboon was quite uncalled-for.*

- *comparable* versus *comparative*

**Comparable** means 'of the same kind, on the same scale, to the same degree, etc': *The houses were comparable in size* □ *The engine designed by Diesel was twice as efficient as a comparable steam engine.*

**Comparative** means 'judged by comparing with something else': *When the children stopped playing express trains, we had a period of comparative quiet* (= it may not have been absolutely quiet, but it was quieter than it had been before).

## compel, impel

**Compel** means 'to force': *I was compelled to resign* □ *They compelled me to betray my country.* **Impel** means 'to urge or drive (someone) to do something': *Hunger impelled the boy to steal.* **Compel** should be used when there is a sense of irresistible force or pressure exerted on a person by some other person or thing, **impel** when the person is being driven to some action by his or her own feelings, needs, etc.

## complaisant, complacent, compliant

**Complaisant** and **compliant** both denote being willing to do what others want, and they are almost synonymous, but **complaisant** sometimes has a connotation of a cheerful and laid-back willingness to please, while **compliant** often implies rather a sense of giving in to someone.

Neither of these words should be confused with **complacent**, which means 'smugly pleased with yourself or confident of your own abilities, etc', especially if not sufficiently concerned about potential difficulties or dangers.

## complement, compliment, supplement

A **complement** is 'something that when taken with or added to something else makes the other thing better or together make something complete or perfect': *Good wine is a complement to good food* (= 'good wine makes good food taste even better' or 'good food and good wine together make a perfect meal'). A ship's **complement** is the full number of officers and crew that the ship has or ought to have.

A **compliment** is 'an expression of praise or flattery': *He is always paying her compliments.*

The difference between **complement** and **supplement** is that while a **complement** makes something perfect or complete, a **supplement** is seen as being added to something else which is already complete, eg as a bonus (*a newpaper's colour supplement*) or to make up for some deficiency in it (*Most vegans have to take vitamin supplements*).

- The same distinctions apply to the verbs **complement, compliment** and **supplement**:

*Good wine complements good food.*
*He complimented her on her work.*
*She supplements her diet with vitamin pills.*

The distinction between ***complement*** and ***supplement*** is often a fine one depending very much on the nuance to be conveyed: to say that *intuition complements reason* is to emphasize that the two functioning together are better than either on its own, without implying any inadequacy in either of them, whereas to say that *intuition supplements reason* is to focus more on the inadequacy of reason alone and the need to use intuition as well.

**compliant** see COMPLAISANT.

**compose** see COMPRISE.

## comprehend, apprehend

Among their various meanings, both ***comprehend*** and ***apprehend*** may be used in the sense of 'to understand'. They are not, however, synonymous. To ***comprehend*** is 'to understand (something) completely, to understand the reasons for (something)'; to ***apprehend*** means 'to grasp, to be or become aware of, to form an idea of', and does not imply full understanding: *I apprehend that what he is trying to do is bankrupt this firm, but I cannot comprehend such stupidity.*

• The same distinction applies to ***apprehension*** and ***comprehension***:

> *The theory of relativity is beyond the comprehension of many people* (ie, they do not understand what it means) *and beyond the apprehension of animals and insects* (ie, they are not even aware it exists).

## comprise, compose, consist, constitute, include

Being similar both in form and in meaning, ***comprise*** and ***compose*** are sometimes confused and misused. The difference between them is that while you can say that a whole ***comprises*** its parts and equally that the parts ***comprise*** the whole, you can only say that parts ***compose*** the whole, not vice versa: *Great Britain comprises Scotland, England and Wales* □ *The three countries which comprise/compose Great Britain are Scotland, England and Wales.*

---

 ***Comprise*** is often used in the passive:

**✗** *Great Britain is comprised of Scotland, England and Wales.*

While this passes without comment, and often unnoticed, in informal situations, it has not yet been fully accepted as standard and should still be avoided in formal English.

---

***Constitute*** is similar in meaning to ***compose*** (parts of something <u>constitute</u>

the whole), but *compose* often implies a greater degree of intermixing and the creation of a new substance than *constitute* does: you could say that *good food and exercise constitute a healthy lifestyle* but not that they *compose a healthy lifestyle.*

*Comprise* and *include* are sometimes confused, the one being used where the other would be correct. The difference can be seen clearly in the following examples: *The book includes chapters on Shakespeare and Milton* (ie, there are chapters on other people or topics as well) □ *The book comprises four chapters on Shakespeare and three on Milton* (ie, these seven chapters constitute the whole book).

• Distinguish *consist of* from *consist in*. *Consist in* means 'to lie in, be contained in, be based on, be defined as': *The beauty of her poetry consists in its very simplicity.*

## compulsive, impulsive
*Impulsive* means 'done without thought' or 'prone to doing things without thought'. *Compulsive* means 'unable to stop yourself doing something': *a compulsive liar.*

## concrete see CEMENT.

## consent see ASSENT.

## consequent, subsequent, consequential
*Consequent* usually means 'following as a result': *There were rumours of food shortages yesterday and consequent riots in many towns.* *Consequent* may in formal contexts be followed by *on* or *upon*, as in *riots consequent on the rumours of food shortages,* but expressions such as *caused by* or *resulting from* would be more natural in informal contexts.

*Consequential* is less common than *consequent.* Its most usual meaning is 'important' or, when applied to people, 'self-important' or 'pompous'. In certain formal or technical contexts, it has a meaning similar to that of *consequent*, but whereas *consequent* implies that one thing is a direct result of another, *consequential* implies a less direct link between the two, the one thing logically implying or requiring the other, or in practice giving rise to it, but not actually causing it: *After the riots, there were a number of consequential alterations to the law* (ie, the riots did not actually cause the changes to the law, but were nonetheless the reason for the changes being made).

*Subsequent* means 'following, coming after'. It may, but does not always, imply that one thing is a result of another: *his misbehaviour and subsequent dismissal from the firm* □ *At our first meeting, we simply discussed the outlines of the plan; only in subsequent meetings did we look at the details of the project.*

**consist** see COMPRISE.

## consistent, persistent

Both of these adjectives mean 'repeated', but **consistent** has a positive connotation and **persistent** a negative one: *consistent good work throughout the year □ persistent lateness.*

**constitute** see COMPRISE.

## constrain, restrain

The verb **constrain** means 'to force, compel'. It is usually used in the form of the past participle, as in *You mustn't feel constrained to go, but I would appreciate it if you did.*

**Restrain** means 'to prevent, control, hold back', as in *He had to be restrained from hitting the man □ He was so angry, he could hardly restrain himself.*

**contagious** see INFECTIOUS.

## contemptible, contemptuous

**Contemptible** means 'deserving contempt'; **contemptuous** means 'showing contempt'.

**contiguous** see ADJACENT.

## continual, continuous

These two adjectives are frequently confused. **Continual** means 'very frequent, happening again and again', as in *I've had continual interruptions all morning.* **Continuous** means 'without a pause or break', as in *continuous rain* or *The queue stretched in a continuous line right round the block. Continuous noise* is noise that never stops; *continual noise* comes in repeated bursts.

## cord, chord

**Cord** is the only correct spelling for the word which means 'string or cable' (*They tied his hands with a piece of cord*) or 'a ribbed fabric' (*a dress of brown cord*). Both **cord** and **chord** may be used for the parts of the body known as the *vocal cords* and the *spinal cord,* but **cord** is nowadays the preferred form. In the musical and geometrical senses, **chord** alone is correct: *A chord is a number of notes played together □ the chord of a circle.*

It is from the musical sense of the word that the idiom *strike the right chord* is derived, so **chord** alone is the correct spelling.

## correspond

The verb **correspond** may be followed by *to* or *with*. To **correspond to** means 'to be similar or equivalent to', as in *An associate professor in America* *generally corresponds to a reader or senior lecturer in British universities* □ *A bird's wing corresponds to the human arm.*

To *correspond with* means 'to match, be consistent with', as in *His treatment of his staff hardly corresponds with his political ideas.* *Correspond to* is also used in this sense. *Correspond with* is also a formal way of saying 'to communicate with by exchanging letters'.

## counsel, council

*Counsel* is a rather formal word for 'advice'. It is also the legal term for the lawyer or lawyers acting for a person in a law-court: *counsel for the defence.* A *council* is 'a body of people who organize, control, advise or take decisions': *a county council* □ *The king set up a council of wise men to advise him* □ *a member of the Central Council for Physical Recreation* □ *the Marriage Guidance Council* □ *the Privy Council.*

A *counsellor* is a person who gives advice. A member of a *council* may often be correctly referred to as a *councillor*, especially if the *council* is one of the various bodies of people elected to control the workings of local government in counties, regions, etc: *a local councillor.* However, if the function of a *council* is to give advice, its members will more correctly be referred to as *counsellors*: *the king's wise counsellors* □ *marriage guidance counsellors* □ *Privy Counsellor* (*Privy Councillor* is also correct). Often when a *council* is simply an executive or organizing committee, its members are referred to simply as 'members of the council' or 'council members'.

## credible, credulous, creditable

*Credible* means 'believable', even if untrue:

> *They had assumed that he was an out-of-work clerk, and so had unwittingly provided him with a credible cover story.*

*Credulous* means 'too easily convinced, too ready to believe, easily fooled', as in *Only someone as credulous as Peter could believe a story like that.*

*Creditable* means 'worthy of praise or respect', as in *Although he didn't win, he gave a very creditable performance in the competition.*

## cringe see FLINCH.

## cynic(al), sceptic(al)

A *cynic* is a person who has a low opinion of human nature, who thinks the worst about everyone and everything, and who believes that behind something apparently good there must be lurking something unpleasant or undesirable: *He's such a cynic, he thinks that people who work for a charity must be stealing half the money they collect.* *Cynical* means 'of, like, or showing oneself to be, a cynic': *I've a somewhat cynical attitude to politics.* *Cynical* may also be used to describe behaviour or attitudes that would suggest the opinions of cynics are correct: *The film portrays the redemption of a cynical asset-stripper and his metamorphosis into a successful and dynamic industrialist.*

A *sceptic* is a person who believes that nothing can be known with absolute certainty, or, more loosely, a person who is unwilling to believe some particular statement, theory, etc, especially religious belief: *Most people now accept this hypothesis, but there are still a few sceptics.* **Sceptical** means 'of, like, or showing that one is, a sceptic': *They do say that apples help to clean your teeth, but I'm a bit sceptical about that.*

## decimate

**Decimation** was a form of capital punishment used by the Roman army against units which had mutinied or deserted, in which one-tenth of the soldiers were chosen by lot and then executed. (The Latin word *decimatio* comes from the root *decimus* meaning 'tenth'.) **Decimate** and **decimation** may be used in English in the same sense as their Latin equivalents:

> *By decimation ... take thou the destin'd tenth.*
> — Shakespeare

However, the meaning of these words has now widened, and implies a more general sense of destruction:

> *During the 19th century, European settlers and prospectors fought with the Indians over land. In the ensuing wars, most groups were decimated, and the survivors forced into reservations.*
> *After the general election, he became Leader of the decimated Liberal Party in the House of Commons.*

Although use of this word in this sense of 'to kill a large number of or destroy a large part of' is still disapproved of by some people, it is so well established, and has been for so long, that it must be now be considered completely correct and acceptable in even the most formal speech and writing.

## deduction, induction

As methods of reasoning, these two processes operate in opposite directions. **Deduction** takes a general principle and applies it to particular cases: *All birds have two legs. An ostrich is a bird. Therefore an ostrich has two legs.* **Induction** argues from particular cases to a general rule: *All birds that I have seen or heard of have two legs. Therefore all birds have two legs.* Both words also apply to the result of the process of reasoning as well as to the process itself: thus, in the above examples, *An ostrich has two legs* is a **deduction** and *All birds have two legs* is an **induction**.

> ⚠ Even if you are clear about the difference between the two processes, it is sometimes hard to remember which is which. It may be helpful to think of the words in this way:

157

> General principles may be considered more important than particular instances, therefore the key element in both these processes of thought is the principle, not the individual cases. **Deduction** reasons <u>from</u> a general principle (Latin *de* 'from'), and **induction** reasons <u>towards</u> a general principle (Latin *in* 'towards, into').

## defective, deficient

The adjective **defective** means 'having a fault or flaw': *The crash was caused by defective wiring in the signalling system.* **Deficient** means 'inadequate, lacking in what is needed': *A vegan diet is generally found to be deficient in essential vitamins and minerals.*

## definite, definitive

These words are not synonymous. **Definite** means 'clear' or 'certain': *I'll give you a definite answer later.* **Definitive** means 'final, settling things once and for all': *He has written the definitive study of Ben Jonson.*

## delusion see ILLUSION.

## deny see REFUTE.

## deprecate, depreciate

**Deprecate** is a formal word meaning 'to disapprove of, express disapproval of', as in *The government issued a statement deprecating the soldiers' actions.*

To **depreciate**, means 'to fall in value' or, much less commonly nowadays, 'to reduce the value of': *Perishable goods depreciate faster than non-perishable goods □ Doubts about the state of the world market depreciated the shares significantly.* In a technical, financial sense, a currency **depreciates** when the rate of exchange between it and another currency falls: for example, if the rate of exchange of the pound sterling falls from \$1.50 to \$1.42, the pound has **depreciated** against the dollar (which has *appreciated* against the pound).

**Depreciate** also means 'to speak of as having little value or importance': *Modesty is all very well, but I wish you wouldn't persist in depreciating your achievements the way you do.* **Deprecate** should not be used in this sense. However, while this distinction still holds for the simple verbs, it is nonetheless true that **deprecate** is steadily encroaching on **depreciate**'s territory through its derived forms **deprecating**, **deprecatory** and **self-deprecation**:

> *Barry made deprecating remarks about the meal he had produced.*

⚠ In some cases, it may not be clear which meaning is intended:

> *Van Mechelren wagged his hands deprecatingly. 'There are maybe some diff'rent opinions on that.'*
>
> — Keith Roberts, *Synth*

> (Van Mechelren had just been complimented on his knowledge and expertise, but was he *deprecating* the compliment or *depreciating* his skill?)
>
> While less common, the forms *depreciating*, *depreciatory* and *self-depreciation* are not incorrect:
>
> > *On hearing herself praised by the headmaster, she blushed and laughed in self-depreciation.*

## derisive, derisory

Formerly, these words were synonymous, but they are no longer so: *derisive* means 'mocking, showing derision', as in *derisive laughter*; *derisory* means 'ridiculous, deserving derision or mockery', as in *a derisory offer □ a derisory amount.*

## differ

To *differ from* is 'to be different from', as in *Her house differs from mine in that it has the staircase at the side.* To *differ with* is 'to disagree with': *He differs with me over the value of nuclear weapons.*

## different

Contrary to what many people believe, both *different from* and *different to* are both correct English. *Different than* is less acceptable than *different from/to* in British English, permissible perhaps in informal speech but best avoided in formal speech and writing; it is entirely acceptable in American English.

## dilemma

Strictly speaking, a *dilemma* is not just any problem or difficulty, but a situation in which a person is faced with having to choose between two possible courses of action, both unpleasant, undesirable or unsatisfactory: *During his years at Oxford, he wrestled with the Vietnam dilemma, wishing to show himself a patriot but unconvinced of the justice of US involvement in the war.*

The word may be applied to situations in which there are more than two possible courses of action, but strictly speaking it should not be used when there is only one, and the possiblities should always be things you would wish to avoid. However, *dilemma* is now often used as a synonym of *problem*, and although not yet accepted by all authorities, this usage should be considered acceptable now in informal English at least, though perhaps still better avoided in formal contexts: *the traditional media dilemma about how far people know what they want until they have been shown choices beyond their current experience.*

In a looser sense sometimes encountered nowadays, *dilemma* is used to denote the unpleasant necessity of choosing between two or more attractive alternatives, but this is not yet accepted by many authorities, and for this reason should perhaps be avoided in formal speech and writing.

**disassociate** see DISSOCIATE.

## discomfit

*Discomfit* is not a common word, and for that reason is sometimes misused. It has nothing to do with a lack of *comfort*. It means 'to defeat', 'to thwart' or 'to disconcert': *He saw with satisfaction that his unexpected kindness had discomfited her* □ *Discomfited by the new security system, the thieves fled empty-handed when the police arrived.* The sense 'to defeat in battle' is now considered old-fashioned.

- The noun related to *discomfit* is *discomfiture*.

## discrete, discreet

*Discrete* and *discreet* derive from the same Latin word, but in English they are different words with separate meanings. *Discreet* means 'prudent, cautious, not saying or doing anything that might cause trouble': *My secretary won't ask awkward questions; she's very discreet. Discrete* means 'separate, not attached to others': *a suspension of discrete particles in a liquid.*

- Note that *discretion* means 'discreetness', not 'discreteness'.

**discrepancy** see DISPARITY.

## disinterested, uninterested

The adjective *disinterested* is often used where *uninterested* would be correct. *Uninterested* means 'not interested, not showing any interest'. *Disinterested* means 'not biased, not influenced by private feelings or selfish motives': *I think we need the opinions of a few disinterested observers.*

## disparity, discrepancy

Both these words denote the existence of a difference between two things, but *disparity* emphasizes the fact of the difference or the extent of the difference (eg that it is more than normal or more than expected), whereas *discrepancy* indicates that it is a difference that should not exist: *There was, unfortunately, a disparity between their expected takings at the auction and their actual takings* □ *They noted a serious discrepancy between the value of the goods sold and the amount of money in the till.*

## dissociate, disassociate

Both these verbs are correct and they mean the same thing: *I would like to dissociate/disassociate myself from the remarks made by some of my colleagues earlier.* The shorter verb is the commoner nowadays.

## distinct, distinctive

**Distinct** means 'definite', 'clearly or easily seen, heard, smelt, etc': *a distinct smell of alcohol* □ *There is a distinct Scottishness in her pronunciation.*

**Distinctive** means 'characteristic', 'distinguishing one person or thing from others': *She has a very distinctive walk* □ *the distinctive call of a barn owl.*

## distrust, mistrust

**Distrust** and **mistrust** are virtually synonymous, but **distrust** usually suggests a greater doubt, suspicion or lack of trust than **mistrust**.

## disturb see PERTURB.

## divers, diverse

**Divers** means 'several': *There are divers ways of looking at this problem.* It is considered a very formal or rather old-fashioned word now.

**Diverse** means 'various, different' or 'made up from a variety of different individuals or types': *Insects are the most diverse group of organisms on Earth* □ *Hinduism embraces diverse religious beliefs and doctrines* □ *He had a diverse career, being among other things a lifeguard, a teacher, a tax inspector and a pavement artist.*

## dominate, domineer

**Dominate** means 'to have power, control or a major influence over': *Although technically king, he was dominated by his uncles* □ *Her book is a study of marriage in male-dominated society.* In a more figurative sense, something may be said to **dominate** when it occupies a noticeable or commanding position (*The castle, perched on a rock above the gardens, dominates the whole city*) or occupies a large part of something (*Her reign was dominated by political intrigues*).

**Domineer** also has the sense of having power over someone, but in the more negative sense of power used arrogantly or overbearingly: *Only through marriage did she manage to escape the influence of her manipulative and domineering mother.* As in this example, it is most often found in the present-participle form used as an adjective, but may also be found in other forms: *Although small in stature, he used his wealth and status ruthlessly to domineer over his fellow councillors.*

## doubt, doubtful, dubious

● *doubtful* versus *dubious*

Although these words are virtually synonyms, there are certain differences between them. Firstly, **doubtful** expresses a simple, neutral state of uncertainty: *The outcome of the debate was doubtful right until the end.* Secondly, **doubtful** may express a milder or more tentative doubt than **dubious**: *I'm dubious about the wisdom of accepting her invitation* is expressing greater doubt than *I'm doubtful about the wisdom of accepting her invitation.* Thirdly, **dubious** rather

161

than **doubtful** is used when the doubtfulness lies more in the object of the uncertainty than in the mind of the doubter: *I am doubtful whether King Arthur ever lived, and I consider the evidence adduced for his existence very dubious.*

But the most common use of **dubious** now is not to express uncertainty at all but rather to express serious reservations about the existence, morality or worthiness of something or someone: *dubious musical talent* □ *dubious business transactions* □ *dubious friends and associates* □ *morally dubious behaviour.* **Doubtful** can also express this sense: *There are some doubtful/dubious characters hanging around outside,* but here again it may express a slightly milder reservation than **dubious**.

Even with **doubtful**, the degree of doubt expressed may vary according to the preposition which accompanies the adjective. Looking to the future, *I'm doubtful of the outcome* expresses greater expectation of and concern about possible failure than *I'm doubtful about the outcome* does.

- **Conjunctions with *doubt* and *doubtful***
There are two factors that influence the choice of conjunction: the construction of the sentence and the degree of doubt.

When **doubt** and **doubtful** are part of an affirmative statement (ie, one that is neither a question nor has a negative word like *not* or *never* in it), they may be followed by **whether**, **if** or **that**. **Whether** is more often used than **if** in formal speech and writing (*I doubt whether he is coming* □ *I am doubtful whether he is coming*). Combinations of prepositions and conjunctions are best kept to informal speech and writing: *I'm doubtful about whether to go or not.* **That** is perhaps slightly less formal than **whether**, but the main difference is that **whether** and **if** express simple uncertainty whereas **that** (which may be omitted) is felt by some people to imply greater certainty that what is being spoken of is unlikely: *I doubt whether/if he'll show up* (= 'I am not sure whether he will show up') □ *I doubt he'll show up* (= 'I am pretty certain that he will not show up').

In a negative statement or a question, **doubt** and **doubtful** should be followed by **that**: *I do not doubt that he is coming* □ *There is no doubt that he is coming.*

In a question, **doubt** and **doubtful** may be followed by **whether** or **that**. As with affirmative statements, **whether** asks a simple question about the existence of a doubt (*Do you doubt whether he can do it?*), whereas **that** in this case expresses a greater confidence on the part of the speaker that something is likely or possible: *Do you doubt that he can do it?* (= 'I think that you think he cannot do it, but I think he can').

## draft, draught

In British English, a **draft** is 'a rough sketch or outline' (*a rough draft of my speech*) or 'an order to a bank for the payment of money' (*a bank draft for £40*).

A **draught** is 'a current of air', 'a quantity of liquid drunk at one time' (*He took a long draught of beer*), 'the amount of water a boat requires to float' (*Fortunately* *the boat has a shallow draught*), 'beer taken from a barrel' (*draught beer*), and 'one of the pieces used in the game of *draughts*'.

In American English, ***draft*** is the normal spelling for all the above meanings, except for the game of draughts, which in American English is called *checkers*. It is also the spelling of the word meaning 'military conscription'.

**dubious** see DOUBT.

**due to** see BECAUSE.

## each other, one another

Some people prefer to use ***each other*** when referring to two people or things, and ***one another*** when more than two are involved, as in *The two children helped each other* and *The four children helped one another*. Although some authorities insist on this rule, this supposed difference between ***each other*** and ***one another*** is not, and never has been, a rule of English grammar, and there is no reason to abide by it. Treat the two phrases as grammatical equivalents.

## eatable, edible

In some contexts, these words are virtually synonymous: *I left the apple pie in the oven too long, but it's still edible/eatable*. However, there is a difference between the two, which in some cases is vitally important: if something is ***edible***, it is by nature safe or good to eat, whereas if it is ***eatable***, it is in a condition that makes it possible to eat it (whether or not it is safe to do so). As is sometimes proved by tragic accidents, poisonous mushrooms are ***eatable*** but they are not ***edible***, while on the other hand a bag of flour is perfectly ***edible*** but would scarcely be ***eatable***.

## economic, economical

***Economic*** means 'pertaining to economics' or 'pertaining to the economy of a country, etc': *economic history* □ *the country's economic future*. It also means 'giving an adequate profit or fair return', as in *We must charge an economic rent/price*.

***Economical*** means 'thrifty', 'not wasteful, expensive or extravagant': *This car is very economical on petrol* □ *the economical use of limited supplies*.

**edible** see EATABLE.

**effect** see AFFECT.

## effective, effectual, efficacious, efficient

These four words all have meanings relating to 'the producing of desired results'.

*Effective* and *effectual* are almost synonymous. *Effective* has a number of meanings:

i) 'producing, or likely to produce, the intended result': *Aspirin is effective against many types of pain and inflammation □ There is no effective treatment for motor neurone disease □ Sanctions eventually proved effective, and they sued for peace □ The government promised effective measures against crime.*

ii) 'impressive', 'powerful': *He's a very effective speaker □ I thought her speech was most effective.*

iii) 'in reality, even if not in theory': *Although not the king, he was the effective ruler of the country for twenty years □ Although the ceasefire did not begin until some days later, this battle marked the effective end of the war.* (In this sense, the adverbial form of the word is very common: *This battle was effectively the end of the war.*)

iv) 'in operation, in force': *The new regulations become effective at midnight tonight.*

*Effectual* puts more emphasis on the actual achievement of the desired result than *effective* does. If the police take *effective* measures to combat the rising crime rate, these measures either are having the desired effect, or are expected to, whereas if the police take *effectual* measures, there is no doubt that these measures are succeeding in reducing the crime rate.

The negative forms, *ineffective* and *ineffectual* are again close but not identical in meaning. *Ineffectual* is more likely to be applied to people than *ineffective*, and implies not only that a person does not achieve the desired results but that they are incapable of doing so because of some weakness or other fault in their character, whereas *ineffective* applied to people implies simply the inability to be effective: *He was an ineffective speaker and a completely ineffectual ruler.* When not applied to people, *ineffective* is probably commoner than *ineffectual*: *ineffective negotiations.*

*Efficacious* is nowadays applied only to medicines and medical treatment. It means 'producing the intended result (ie a cure)': *Jenner became convinced that cowpox was efficacious as a protection against smallpox.*

*Efficient* applies more to the way in which a result is achieved rather than to the result itself. It means 'producing results competently, without wasting time, effort, etc': *efficient methods of handling data in the office □ an efficient secretary.*

## egoist, egotist

Strictly speaking, an *egotist* is a person who is too preoccupied with himself or herself, who is self-important and vain, and who uses 'I' and 'me' too much in speaking, whereas *egoist* is a technical philosophical term for a person who believes that the only thing one can be certain of is one's own existence, or that self-interest is the correct basis of morality. People who are simply selfish are *egotists*; if their selfishness is based on the philosophical principle of self-interest, they are *egoists*.

*Egoist* is often used where *egotist* would correctly convey the intended meaning, but the distinction between these words is useful and worth maintaining.

## elder, older

The normal comparative and superlative forms of *old* are *older* and *oldest*. *Elder* and *eldest* can only apply to people, not things, and are now used only to describe relative seniority within a family: *He is my elder brother* □ *She is the elder of the two sisters* □ *Her eldest son is at university*. *Older* and *oldest* would be equally correct in these sentences.

When not immediately followed by a noun or immediately preceded by a determiner such as *the, my, his*, etc, *older* rather than *elder* must be used, even for family relationships: *My brother is older than me*.

 *Elder*, meaning 'senior', also occurs in a few idioms, such as *elder statesman*.

## electric, electrical, electronic

*Electric* should be used when referring to something which is powered by or caused by, or which produces, electricity: *an electric shock* □ *an electric light* □ *an electric eel*. *Electrical* means 'relating generally to electricity or things connected with electricity': *electrical engineering* □ *the electrical department of a shop*. *Electrical*, rather than *electric*, is used when referring to general classes of things powered by electricity rather than to specific types of thing: <u>*Electric kettles*</u> *and* <u>*electric*</u> *irons are examples of* <u>*electrical*</u> *goods*.

*Electronic* is used of sophisticated electrical apparatus, such as television sets or computers, in which the electric current is controlled by valves, transistors or the like. It is also applied to the use or production of such equipment: *electronic engineering*.

## emend see AMEND.

## enormity, enormousness

Of these two nouns, only *enormousness* should be used when referring to size. *Enormity* means 'great wickedness, seriousness (of a crime, etc)', as in *He came in time to realize the enormity of his actions*. *Enormity* is sometimes used as a synoym of *enormousness*, but this is not generally considered correct.

## enquire, inquire

To most people *enquire* and *inquire*, and *enquiry* and *inquiry*, are simply alternative spellings. There are some who maintain that *enquire* and *enquiry* are to be preferred when all that is meant is a simple asking and

165

*inquire/inquiry* when a more detailed investigation is meant, but this distinction is not recognized by many authorities on English and is not adhered to by many speakers of English, although in phrases such as *court of inquiry*, which imply a detailed investigation, *inquiry* is the form normally used, not *enquiry*.

## ensure see INSURE.

## envisage, visualize

To *visualize* something is to form a picture of it, especially a picture in the mind: *I have to work on the garden very slowly because I can't really visualize how it should look in the end.* *Envisage* can also be used in this sense, but more often means 'to foresee, expect': *I don't envisage any more problems now.*

## epoch, era

*Era* means 'a period of time marked out by some particular feature': *the Christian era □ the Elizabethan era.* *Epoch* is often also used to mean 'a period of time' (*This novel began a new epoch in Italian literature*) but it also has the meaning 'the point of time marking the beginning of a new era', especially in the compound adjective *epoch-making*: *an epoch-making discovery in medicine □ The Origin of Species is rightly considered an epoch-making work.*

## equable, equitable

*Equable* means 'not extreme and without great variation': *Britain has an equable climate.* It also means 'even-tempered': *That child would infuriate the most equable parent.*

*Equitable* means 'fair, just': *She attempted to organize a more equitable and efficient administration □ The staff demanded a more equitable distribution of profits.*

## era see EPOCH.

## especially, specially

These two words are often treated as synonyms, but they are not. *Especially* means 'particularly': *These insects are quite common, especially in hot countries □ I was especially pleased to meet him.* *Specially* means 'for a special purpose, for a particular person, etc': *I made this cake specially for your birthday.* Something that is done *especially* for someone is done mostly, but not solely, for that person; something that is done *specially* for a person is done solely for that person and for no one else.

## evade, evasion see AVOID.

## evoke, invoke

Both of these words mean 'to call up' in some sense. To *evoke* is to call up into the mind: *His pictures evoke atmospheres of terror and angst □ poems that evoke the time when his fellow citizens rose up against their oppressors.*

To *invoke* is to call on a god, spirit or spiritual power to appear or to assist: *In Byron's poem, Manfred invokes the Witch of the Alps to summon his dead sister □ During the seance, the spirit of Elvira is invoked*. Curses, blessings, assistance, etc may also be invoked: *The theft is discovered, and a great curse invoked on the thief □ Invoking the help of neighbouring tribes, they overran the city*. In a different sense, *invoke* may mean 'to use (a law, principle, etc) as justification or explanation' or 'to bring into operation': *Blasphemy is technically a crime in this country, but the law is rarely invoked □ Wear and tear is often invoked as a cause of osteoarthritis*.

## exceptional, exceptionable

*Exceptional* means 'out of the ordinary': *There's nothing exceptional about what he's done □ She shows exceptional ability in mechanics.*

*Exceptionable* means 'objectionable'. It is not a word in common use, and generally appears after a negative word: *There's nothing exceptionable about the poem that I can see.*

• The same distinctions as above apply to the related negatives **unexceptional** and **unexceptionable**: *His achievements are fairly unexceptional in my opinion, so I can't see what the fuss is about □ She made a few unexceptionable remarks and sat down again.*

## Far East, Middle East

Generally, the *Far East* denotes China, Korea, Japan, Mongolia and the eastern part of Siberia. In a broader sense, it may be taken to include also the Philippines, Vietnam, Laos, Kampuchea, Thailand, Burma, Malaysia, Singapore and Indonesia.

The *Middle East* was formerly used of the countries from Iran to Myanmar (Burma), but is now taken to denote an area including the Arabic-speaking countries around the eastern end of the Mediterranean Sea and in the Arabian Peninsula, together with Turkey, Cyprus, Iran and the greater part of North Africa, and sometimes even Greece.

## farther see FURTHER.

## fatal, fateful

*Fatal* means 'causing death or disaster': *a fatal accident □ She made the fatal mistake of telling him what she really thought*. *Fatal* can also mean 'chosen or appointed by fate': *He little knew that he was to meet his death on that fatal day.*

*Fateful* means 'of great importance, involving important decisions, having important consequences, etc', as in *At last the fateful day arrived, the day she was to be married.*

## female, feminine

The adjective *female* means 'of the sex that gives birth to children, produces eggs or seeds, etc' and may be applied to people, animals, plants, or anything that has sexual differences between members of the species: *A female pig is called a sow.*

*Feminine* can be applied only to people (men or women), and means 'characteristic of a woman, having the qualities or characteristics one would expect or wish for in a woman': *He has a rather feminine voice. Feminine* is also a technical term in grammar for the gender to which nouns denoting female people, animals, etc belong (see *How Language is Described*, page 24).

## ferment, foment

Both these words relate to the notion of stirring up trouble. *Foment* is used with an object denoting the sort of trouble that is being caused, and often implies that the stirring-up is deliberate and caused by a human agency:

> *He was arrested for fomenting anti-government riots.*

However, the cause of the trouble need not be human, and the trouble need not be caused deliberately:

> *A series of economic disasters fomented rebellion.*
> *Anti-government feelings fomented riots in some cities.*

Note that the object of the verb is always the word denoting the type of trouble caused, not the people who are aroused:

> ✗ *A series of economic disasters fomented the people to rebel.*

*Ferment* may also be used to denote the causing of trouble, but the implication of this word is that there is no deliberate intention to do so: *A series of economic disasters fermented rebellion.*

*Ferment* is more likely to be used without an object: *After three bad harvests, discontent was fermenting in many parts of the country.*

• *Ferment*, but not *foment*, may also be used as a noun, denoting disruption, agitation or disturbance: *Kropotkin contributed to the revolutionary ferment in Russia at the beginning of the century.*

## fervent, fervid

Both these adjectives mean 'showing ardour or zeal', but *fervent* is by far the more common of the two:

> *a fervent anti-communist*
> *a fervent follower of the tariff reform movement*
> *She was fervent in her Marxist beliefs.*
>
> *There was a sound of rattling chains, and the fervid snarling of the dogs increased.*

In some cases, *fervid* has a more negative, disapproving tone than *fervent*:

> *Your fervid imagination is running away with you again.*
> *With my fervid temper and my republican principles, I was soon persona non grata with the government.*

Note that *fervid* cannot be applied to people, although *fervent* can.

## fewer, less

*Fewer* and *less* are not interchangeable: *fewer* should be used when reference is being made to numbers of individuals, *less* when an amount or quantity is denoted. *Fewer* is followed by or linked to a plural noun: *I grew fewer leeks this year and more onions □ Fewer boys than girls want to become nurses.* *Less* is normally followed by a singular noun (*You need slightly less salt, I think, and a little more pepper*), but may be followed by a plural noun if that noun is thought of as denoting an amount rather than a number of individuals: *He earns less than £500 per month* (compare *There were fewer than 500 people at the match*).

## fictional, fictitious

Both *fictional* and *fictitious* mean 'invented, unreal', but the purpose of the invention is not the same in each case.

*Fictional* means unreal in the sense of 'occurring in or created for fiction': *fictional detectives such as Sherlock Holmes and Father Brown □ a fictional central-European country.*

*Fictitious* may simply mean 'unreal or invented, having no basis in reality or history': *Margaret of Anjou's appearance in <u>Richard III</u> is, from the point of view of history, wholly fictitious* (Margaret of Anjou is not a *fictional* character, as she did in fact exist, but she was not in England at the time the action of the play took place, so her appearance in the play is *fictitious*, a device Shakespeare used for dramatic purposes.) Sometimes, *fictitious* means 'invented in order to deceive': *He gave the police a fictitious name and address.*

## flagrant, blatant

Both words imply condemnation, but *flagrant* implies a greater degree of condemnation than *blatant*. *Blatant* means 'glaringly or shamelessly obvious': *a blatant lie/liar*. *Flagrant* means 'scandalous, very obvious and wicked': *a flagrant misuse of his powers*. It could be said that *blatant* focuses on the obviousness of the act, and *flagrant* on the offensiveness of it. Of the two, only *blatant* should be applied to people.

## flammable, inflammable

*Flammable* and *inflammable* mean the same thing, 'able or likely to burn' but accidents have been caused by people thinking that *inflammable* meant 'not flammable'. *Inflammable* is the form normally used in everyday situations, *flammable* the form preferred in technical contexts. The opposites of these words are *non-flammable* and *non-inflammable*.

## flaunt, flout

These two words are often confused, although their meanings are not at all similar. To *flaunt* something is 'to show (something) off, display (something) ostentatiously': *She was flaunting her new fur coat in front of her colleagues.* **Flout** means 'to treat (something) with contempt, to refuse to obey or comply with (something)': *He constantly flouts authority/the law/his mother's wishes.*

## flinch, wince, cringe

To *wince* is 'to jump or start because of pain (physical or mental)': *He winced as the dentist touched his broken tooth □ I wince every time I think of what I said to him that afternoon.*

**Flinch** may be used in the same way as *wince*, but it is also correct to use *flinch*, but not *wince*, when referring to someone reacting in fear or to <u>anticipated</u> pain: *He flinched as the dentist switched on her drill □ She flinched as he raised his hand as if to strike her.*

To *cringe* is to shrink back in fear: *The dog cringed when the man raised his hand to strike it. Cringe* also means 'to behave in an obsequious, fawning way towards someone': *He is portrayed in the book as a mean, cringing, selfish and dishonest youth.* More informally, *cringe* is often used with the same meaning as *wince* or *flinch*: *I cringe with embarrassment every time I think of what happened that afternoon.* This last sense of *cringe* is not accepted by some people yet, and it is therefore perhaps better avoided in formal English.

**flout** see FLAUNT.

**foment** see FERMENT.

## forcible, forceful

In one sense of the word, *forcible* means 'carried out by force': *The police made a forcible entry into the flat to search for drugs. Forcible* may also mean 'having a powerful effect': *It was one of the most forcible performances of <u>Macbeth</u> I have ever seen. Forceful* means 'performed with force or power': *It was one of his most forceful performances, and yet for some reason not entirely persuasive.*

## former, latter

**Former** should only be used to refer to the first, and *latter* to the second, of <u>two</u> people or things just mentioned. In referring to items or individuals in larger groups, use *first, second, last*, etc.

## fortunate, fortuitous

**Fortunate** means 'lucky', 'timely', 'convenient', 'opportune' or good in some other way.
**Fortuitous** does <u>not</u> mean lucky. It means 'accidental, occurring by chance': *The French Revolution is not to be taken as a purely fortuitous occurrence □ His first experience of linguistic research was a fortuitous consequence of the First World War.*

## Frankenstein

In Mary Shelley's book, Frankenstein is the name, not of the monster, but of the creator of the monster. Something monstrous, therefore, should strictly speaking be referred to as 'Frankenstein's monster', not **Frankenstein**. However, the wrong usage is so well established now that it is perhaps too much to expect that the more correct form could ever become fashionable, but there is no reason not to use the more correct form if you choose to.

## further, farther

*Further* is now commoner than *farther*. *Farther* should only be used when there is a real sense of 'distance' involved in the meaning: *I cannot walk any farther*. *Further* may equally be used in this sense, and must be used when the sense is 'more', 'additional', 'beyond this stage', etc: *I would like to make one further point □ further education □ closed until further notice.*

* *Further*, and not *farther*, is also used as a verb meaning 'to help to proceed towards success, completion, etc': *This will further his promotion prospects.*

## golden goose

Like *Frankenstein*, the *golden goose* is another error that has now become firmly established:

> *If direct taxation is too high, it weighs heavily on the wealth-producing section; it kills off the golden goose, as it were.*

The correct phrase is *the goose that lays the golden eggs*: in the original Greek fable, it was not the goose that was golden but the eggs that it laid. The goose's owner killed it, expecting thereby to get immediately all the eggs that the goose would have produced in the future, but there were of course no eggs in the goose. Seeking to get rich quickly, the man had destroyed a steady source of income.

## gourmand, gourmet

A *gourmand* is a person who enjoys eating large quantities of food, a glutton. A *gourmet* is a person who has an expert knowledge of, and a passion for, good food and wine. *Gourmand* is sometimes seen used in the sense of *gourmet*, but the distinction between the two words is best maintained.

* Only *gourmet* can be used as an adjective: *a gourmet Christmas hamper □ gourmet vegetarian cuisine.*

## Great Britain see BRITAIN.

## hanged, hung

The normal past tense and past participle of the verb *hang* is *hung*: *He hung his clothes in the wardrobe □ The pictures were hung on the wall.* When the verb refers

171

to suicide, capital punishment, etc, the correct past-tense and past-participle form is **hanged**: *He hanged himself in a fit of depression.* **Hung** is increasingly used in this sense also, but in formal English it is better to use **hanged**.

## historic, historical

These words are not synonyms. **Historic** means 'famous or important in history': *a historic battle* □ *On this historic spot, a battle was fought which changed the course of history.*

**Historical** means 'of or about history or people and events from history', as in *books on military and historical topics* □ *Before becoming emperor, Claudius devoted himself to historical studies*, or 'having actually happened or lived, as opposed to existing only in legend or fiction', as in *Is Macbeth a historical person?* □ *Is his murder a historical event/fact?*

## hoard, horde

A **hoard** is a store or hidden stock of something. A **horde** is a crowd or large number of people, etc: *Hordes of tourists come here every year.*

## hopefully

The use of **hopefully** to mean 'I hope, it is hoped' is sometimes condemned or deprecated, but there is no good reason why this use of the word should not be accepted, and it seems now to be generally acceptable to most speakers of English in informal contexts at least: *Hopefully we can go all the way to Wembley* □ *I'll hopefully get this finished by tomorrow afternoon.*

There is no reason not to use **hopefully** in this sense in formal contexts also, but be prepared for severe criticism from purists if you do so.

**horde** see HOARD.

**hung** see HANGED.

## illegal, illicit, illegitimate, unlawful

**Illegal** means 'not allowed by law, against the law': *In some countries, the Communist Party is an illegal organization* □ *After Watergate, illegal measures were taken to cover up the implication of those closest to the president.* **Illegal** may also mean 'not allowed by the rules of a game or sport': *an illegal move in chess.*

**Unlawful** also means 'not allowed by law, against the law'. It may, like **illegal**, be used to denote something that is against the laws of a particular state, especially in technical legal contexts: *Arson may be defined as the unlawful destruction of, or damage to, property by means of fire* □ *Such a policy amounts to unlawful sexual discrimination.* In other contexts, **unlawful** means 'not allowed by a religious law': *They were fully competent to advise Henry whether in the light of the Scriptures it was unlawful for a man to marry his deceased brother's wife.*

*Illegitimate* also means 'contrary to law, not recognized by the law', and its main use is in reference to childen born of parents who are not married to each other: *Charles II was the father of many illegitimate children but his marriage was childless*. This is by far the most common use of the word.

---

 Some people object to this use of *illegitimate*, preferring the term *natural*: *He believed his wife to be the duke's natural child □ He was only allowed to see his natural son twice a month*. This use of *natural* is gaining acceptance and is increasingly used by social work organizations that are involved with such children and their parents.

---

In other contexts, *illegitimate* means 'not correct or valid by the rules of logic' (*an illegitimate inference*) or 'unacceptable, unwarranted or unjustified' (*Feminists claim that marriage gives men illegitimate power over women*).

*Illicit* is used to describe something which, although not illegal or unlawful, is not allowed in the particular case referred to, and usually implies a certain amount of secrecy or deception: *an illicit love affair □ Many crofters had illicit stills which they kept hidden from the excise men*.

## illegible, unreadable

*Illegible* refers to the quality of writing or printing, and means 'impossible to decipher': *illegible handwriting*. *Unreadable* refers to the style, content, etc of the written or printed material, or to its legibility, and means 'too difficult or boring to read': *His article was so full of jargon, it was quite unreadable □ Although very neat, his handwriting was so faint, it was unreadable*.

## illegitimate, illicit see ILLEGAL.

## illusion, delusion

The basic difference between a *delusion* and an *illusion* is that the former is a false belief arising in one's own mind, whereas the latter is a false impression coming into one's mind from the world outside it. When a magician appears to saw a person in half, that is an *illusion*; for the magician to believe that he really is doing so would be for him to be suffering from a *delusion*.

## immoral, amoral

*Immoral* means 'wrong', 'wicked', 'not conforming to what are considered correct moral standards', whereas *amoral* means 'not concerned with questions of right and wrong', 'not accepting that there are any moral standards by which actions may be judged': *An amoral person may behave in a way other people consider immoral*.

## immunity, impunity

*Immunity* means 'freedom (from)' or 'resistance (to)': *immunity to measles □ Foreign diplomats enjoy diplomatic immunity, which means that they cannot be prosecuted for committing a crime.* **Impunity** refers specifically to 'freedom from punishment or other unpleasant consequences': *You can't expect to break the law with impunity.*

### impel see COMPEL.

### imperial, imperious
**Imperial** means 'of an empire or emperor': *the imperial crown.* **Imperious** means 'proud and overbearing', 'behaving as if expecting to be, or in the habit of being, obeyed': *She disliked his imperious manner.*

### imply see INFER.

### impracticable, impractical, unpractical
**Impracticable** means 'that cannot be carried out or put into practice': *The whole project has become completely impracticable.*

When referring to suggestions, plans, etc, **impractical** means 'possible to carry out but not sensible or convenient': *The complexities of a modern developed economy make barter totally impractical for most purposes*; when referring to people, it means 'not able to do or make things in a sensible and efficient way': *Paul was impractical and dreamy, with a head full of foolish notions.* Clothing also can be **impractical**: *She was wearing the sort of impractical outfit you would expect to see worn only by models in a fashion magazine.*

**Unpractical** is much less common than **impractical**, but means the same: *Such precautions are for many people too costly and sometimes unpractical.*

### impulsive see COMPULSIVE.

### impunity see IMMUNITY.

### include see COMPRISE.

### incredible, incredulous
**Incredible** means 'unbelievable'; **incredulous** means 'not believing, showing disbelief'. If you are told an **incredible** story, you may become **incredulous**, and show your **incredulity** at the **incredibility** of the tale.

### induction see DEDUCTION.

### infectious, contagious
An **infectious** disease is one which is spread through the air, etc by germs. A **contagious** disease is one which is spread by direct physical contact with a

person suffering from the disease or by contact with something which has itself been in direct contact with such a person. However, when *infectious* and *contagious* are used figuratively, there is no difference in meaning: laughter, for example, can be *contagious* or *infectious*.

## infer, imply

Traditionally, the difference between *infer* and *imply* is that *infer* means 'to form an opinion by reasoning from what one knows', and *imply* means 'to suggest or hint at (something) without actually stating it': *I inferred from your silence that you were angry □ Are you implying that I'm a liar?*

The use of *infer* in the sense of *imply* is common. It is often condemned as a modern error, but it has in fact been in common use for over four centuries, and is to be found in the works of many of the best writers:

> Lucy directly drew her work table near her and seated herself with an alacrity
> and cheerfulness which seemed to infer that she could taste no greater delight
> than in making a fillagree basket for a spoilt child.
>
> — Jane Austen, *Sense and Sensibility*

Nevertheless, because many people consider this use of *infer* an error and an indication of ignorance, it is possibly better avoided in formal contexts.

## inferior

The adjective *inferior* behaves like a comparative adjective (eg like *better* or *worse*) but must be followed by *to*, not *than*: *His short stories are generally considered inferior to his novels.*

## infinite, infinitesimal

*Infinitesimal* is not another way of saying *infinite*. These words are opposites. *Infinite* means 'without limits' or, loosely, 'extremely large or great': *If we follow that course of action, the dangers are infinite*; *infinitesimal* means 'infinitely small' or, loosely, 'extremely small': *Personally, I consider the dangers infinitesimal.*

## inflammable see FLAMMABLE.

## inflict see AFFLICT.

## informant, informer

An *informant* is in a quite neutral sense 'someone who provides information': *According to our informant, the council will not be supporting this motion at tomorrow's meeting.* *Informer* usually has connotations of giving incriminating information, eg to the police: *Casanova worked as a spy for Louis XV and as an informer for the Inquisition.*

## ingenious, ingenuous

*Ingenious* means 'clever, skilful' or 'cleverly made or thought out': *an ingenious plan*. *Ingenuous* means 'frank, trusting, not cunning or deceitful': *It was rather ingenuous of you to believe a compulsive liar like him.*

## inhuman, inhumane

When referring to cruel conditions, treatment, behaviour, etc, *inhuman* is stronger than *inhumane*. *Inhumane* means 'unkind, cruel, showing a lack of compassion', whereas *inhuman* means 'showing cruelty and lack of compassion to a degree almost unbelievable in a human being': *We oppose the use of torture and all other forms of inhuman and degrading treatment of prisoners.* *Inhuman* also means simply 'not human': *Something inhuman bellowed and roared in the stairwell.*

## inquire see ENQUIRE.

## institute, institution

There is virtually no difference between these two words. Both are used in the titles of organizations set up for scientific, cultural, educational, charitable, etc purposes, or for the buildings that house them or their headquarters: *the British Standards Institution* □ *the Royal Institution* □ *the Royal National Lifeboat Institution* □ *the Royal National Institute for the Blind* □ *the Scottish Women's Rural Institute* □ *the Institute of Horticulture* □ *the Educational Institute of Scotland* (a Scottish teachers' trade union). *Institution* is perhaps used more often when designating a broadly philanthropic organization or the building that houses it (*Perhaps a secure mental institution would be a better place for him*), and *institute* when designating an organization for advanced study or teaching (*the Massachusetts Institute of Technology*), but the distinction is certainly not clear-cut. *Institution* is the broader of the two terms, being correctly used to refer in a general way to any organization, whether an *institute* or an *institution*: *Among the institutions that benefited from her support were the Educational Institute of Scotland and the Institute of Horticulture.*

*Institution*, but not *institute*, also denotes someone or something well-known and well-established: *The poet Sir John Betjeman became a national institution.*

## insure, ensure, assure

To *insure* someone or something is to arrange for the payment of a sum of money in the event of loss, accident or injury: *He insured his life for £20 000.* To *ensure* is a rather formal word for 'to make sure': *You should ensure that your television set is switched off at night.* To *assure* means 'to state positively', as in *I assured him that the house was empty* or, in rather formal usage, 'to make (someone) sure' as in *You may wish first to assure yourself of his honest intentions.*

*Assure* is now only rarely used in the sense of *insure* given above. There is, however, a slight technical difference between *assurance* and *insurance*, in that *assurance* does not depend on some uncertain future possibility. With *assurance*, there is guaranteed payment of a fixed sum of money at a certain agreed time (*life assurance* paid on the death of the person insured, *endowment assurance* paid at a stated date), whereas with *insurance* a variable sum is payable and only in the event of certain circumstances occurring (eg a fire, a theft or an accident).

*Assurance* also means 'confidence', as in *I envy him his assurance* and *self-assurance*, or 'a promise' as in *He gave me his assurance that he would help.*

## intense, intensive

*Intense* means 'very great': *the intense heat from the furnace* □ *a feeling of intense bitterness*. *Intensive* means 'concentrated, thorough, taking great care': *an intensive search* □ *the intensive-care unit of a hospital*.

## internecine

Because of the word-forming element *inter-* at the beginning of this word, *internecine* is often taken to mean 'internal' or 'mutual', referring to fighting between members of a group. This is, however, to misunderstand the meaning of *inter-* in the Latin root of the word, which does not in this case mean 'between' but simply adds a sense of intensity: Latin *necare* means 'to kill', and *internecare* means 'to slaughter'. *Internecine* war, therefore, is strictly speaking not civil war (though it could be), but fierce and bloody war. However, the more recent 'mutual' sense of the word has now become firmly established, and can no longer be considered incorrect: *Newspapers gleefully reported the latest outburst of internecine bickering* □ *internecine rivalries*.

## intrusive, obtrusive

*Intrusive* means 'thrusting itself in', and *obtrusive* means 'thrusting itself forward'. Something that is *intrusive*, therefore, 'butts in', forces itself upon or into something else disruptively and uninvited: *the most stringent and intrusive verification procedures ever incorporated into an arms-control treaty*. Something that is *obtrusive*, on the other hand, 'sticks out' so that it cannot fail to be noticed: *The view is nice but that new factory is a bit obtrusive.*

## invoke see EVOKE.

## irony, sarcasm

*Sarcasm* is intended to be hurtful or scornful. One way of being *sarcastic* is through the use of *irony*, which involves the use of words to convey a meaning opposite to the literal meaning of the words used, eg saying something complimentary while obviously meaning to be critical. *That was a pretty stupid thing to do!* is *sarcastic*; *That was clever of you!* is both *ironic* and *sarcastic*. Something that is *ironic* need not be *sarcastic*, though: *Harriet took me in as a paying guest, although for her there must be something ironic about the paying part of it* (ie, the speaker was not actually able to pay).

## irregardless

There is no such word in English. *Irregardless* results from a confusion between *regardless* and *irrespective*.

## judicial, judicious

*Judicial* is a formal word meaning 'pertaining to judges and law-courts'. *Judicious* means 'showing wisdom and good sense': *a judicious choice of words.*

## junction, juncture

A *junction* is a point or place where things meet, such as roads or wires (eg in a *junction box*). A *juncture* is a point in time, strictly speaking a critical or important point but now generally used of any point, especially in the phrase *at this/that juncture*:

> *Purkiss at this juncture would have been more than he could have coped with.*
> — P G Wodehouse

In some technical senses and in old-fashioned or formal language, *juncture* may, like *junction*, mean 'a joining' or 'a point of joining'. In linguistics, for example, *juncture* is the name given to the features of pronunciation that indicate where word breaks are in speech, eg that indicate the difference between *a name* and *an aim*.

## kind of

In informal speech and writing, *kind of* is usually preceded by *these* or *those* rather than *this* or *that* when what follows is a plural noun: *those kind of people* □ *these kind of flowers*. Although strictly speaking ungrammatical, such constructions are quite acceptable in informal language, but they are perhaps better avoided in formal contexts. Constructions with the singular adjectives *this* and *that* followed by a plural noun (eg *this kind of flowers*) often sound awkward or pedantic, so in formal speech and writing the only thing to do is rephrase the expression, and say *this kind of flower* with a singular noun or *flowers of this kind* with the plural noun at the head of the phrase.

The same applies to *sort of*.

**Latin America** see AMERICA.

**latter** see FORMER.

**lawful** see LEGAL.

## lay, lie

These words are very frequently confused. *Lay* means 'to place in a flat, prone or horizontal position'. It is a transitive verb, ie it requires an object. The past tense form is *laid* and the past participle *laid*:

> *If you lay the pen down there, it will roll off the table.*
> *I'm sure I laid it here yesterday.*

*Lie* means 'to be or move into a flat, prone or horizontal position'. It is an intransitive verb, ie it does not have an object. The past tense is *lay*, the past participle *lain*:

> *She went into the bedroom and lay down on the bed.*

*Lay* is often incorrectly used in the sense of *lie*:

✗      *Tomorrow I intend to lay in bed all morning.*
✓      *Tomorrow I intend to lie in bed all morning.*

In the sense of 'to tell lies', the past tense and past participle of *lie* are *lied* and *lied*: *He lied to me yesterday* □ *He has often lied to me.*

## legal, lawful, legitimate

*Legal* means 'connected with the law' (*the legal profession*) or 'conforming to or allowed by law or rules' (*Are you quite sure it's legal to break into his flat like this?* □ *You can't put your pawn there — that isn't a legal move in chess*). *Lawful* also means 'conforming to or allowed by law', but is now rather old-fashioned and is used only in certain technical phrases, such as *lawful wedded wife*, or in connection with moral or religious laws as opposed to the ordinary laws of a country:

> *Your disciples are doing what is not lawful to do on the sabbath.*
>
>              — *Bible, Matthew 12:2*

*Legitimate*, like *legal*, can mean 'conforming to or allowed by law or rules', as in *After serving eight years for armed robbery, he set up a legitimate cash-and-carry business* and *You can't put your pawn there — that's not a legitimate move*. Derived from this sense, *legitimate* may mean 'born to parents who are married or who subsequently marry'. It also means 'correct according to the rules of logic' (*a legitimate conclusion*) and 'fair, reasonable, justified' (*By his high-handedness, he made himself a legitimate target for their scorn*).

See also ILLEGAL.

## lengthy see LONG.

## lend, loan

*Lend* is always a verb: *Can you lend me £5?* *Loan* may be used as a noun or a verb: *a loan of £5* □ *Can you loan me £5?* The use of *loan* as a verb is more common in American English than in British English, and many speakers still prefer to use *lend* rather than *loan* as the verb form, but both are accepted by the best authorities.

## less see FEWER.

## liable, apt, likely, prone

*Apt* should be used to convey the idea that a person or thing has a tendency to do something or is in the habit of doing something, as in *She is apt to ask silly questions* or *Nails as thin as that are apt to break*. **Liable**, on the other hand, conveys not only the idea that something will probably happen or generally happens, but moreover that what will or does happen has unpleasant or undesirable consequences, especially for the subject of the sentence, and usually, but not always, that it is a consequence of some previous action or event: *Children who play with pins are liable to prick themselves* □ *If she drinks too much wine, she is liable to say something silly*.

**Likely** is correctly used when referring to the probability of something happening at a particular time or place or in a particular set of circumstances: *If you don't hurry up, you are likely to miss the bus* □ *You had better take an umbrella, it's likely to rain this afternoon*.

**Prone** is close in meaning to **apt**, but should only be used of people or of nouns denoting things in which people are involved, such as *factory*, *industry*, etc. **Prone** is more appropriate than **apt** when referring to bad or unpleasant aspects of a person's disposition or personality, as in *She is prone to lose her temper* or *She is prone to tantrums*, or to the tendency for unpleasant or unfortunate things (such as illness or accidents) to happen to a person, as in *She is prone to catch colds* (or *She is prone to colds*).

---

**Apt to, liable to** and **likely to** should be followed by an infinitive: *apt to break* □ *liable to break* □ *likely to break*. **Prone to**, on the other hand, may equally correctly be followed by a noun, an infinitive or a verb ending in *-ing*: *She is prone to accidents* □ *He is prone to dream in school* □ *He is prone to dreaming in school*. **Prone** is also frequently used to form compound adjectives, such as *accident-prone*.

---

### libel, slander

In English law, the essential difference between these two terms is that **libel** is an untrue defamatory statement made in a permanent form such as print, writing or pictures or broadcast on radio or television, whereas **slander** is one made by means of the spoken word (not broadcast) or gesture. In Scots law, both are **slander**. The distinction in American law is essentially the same as in English law.

### **lie** see LAY.

### like, as

There are certain constructions in English involving the notion of comparison, in which **like** and **as** (or **as if**) are sometimes confused or misused. The following general rules apply in such cases:

  i)  When making comparisons of any sort, **like** should be used when what follows is a noun, noun phrase or pronoun: *He talks like his father* □ *It looks like a stone* □ *He talks like an expert on the subject, but in fact he knows nothing about it*.

ii)   When comparisons are made between actions, events, etc, and when what follows is a clause rather than a noun or pronoun, *like* is generally used and accepted in informal contexts: *I just can't sing like I used to* □ *Do like I do*. In formal speech and writing, many people prefer *as* to *like* in such constructions, eg *Do as I do*, but *like* is also widely accepted, and is found in the works of some of the best English writers.

If a rough generalization and distinction can be made, *like* is often preferred when a <u>real comparison</u> is being made between the way in which things are done, and *as* when someone is commenting on the fact of something being done again, giving an example to follow, or in other cases where <u>no actual comparison</u> is involved: compare, for example, *She sings just like her mother did* (= in the same way as her mother) and *She sings just as her mother did* (ie, her mother sang and she does too). However, this is not a hard-and-fast rule.

If the comparison is being made to some <u>hypothetical or possible event</u>, *like* is acceptable only in the most informal speech, and it is generally preferable to use *as if*: *It looks like we might win after all* (informal) □ *It looks as if we might win after all* □ *He was running as if all the devils in hell were after him*.

iii)   Like *like*, *as* may be followed in some constructions by a noun or noun-phrase: *I am speaking to you now as a friend*. The difference between *as* and *like* in such constructions is that *as* is used when the person, etc actually has the role or status defined by what follows the preposition, whereas *like* is used when they are simply behaving as if they had such a role or status: *He treats me like a child* (ie, I do not think I am a child but he treats me as if I were) □ *You are a child and I shall treat you as a child* □ *He treats me not just as a son but as a friend* (ie, I am his son and he also considers me to be his friend). However, *like* is not infrequently found where *as* would, according to the above rules, be expected: *You are a child and I shall treat you like a child*.

iv)   Notice that *like* and *as,* when used as prepositions, should be followed by *me*, *him*, etc rather than *I*, *he*, etc: *He sings like me*, not ✗ *He sings like I*.

---

   Care must be taken with *like* and *as* to ensure that the comparison that is made actually compares the things that were intended to be compared:

✗   *Like me, my brother's hatred of nuclear weapons is intense.*
✓   *Like me, my brother has an intense hatred of nuclear weapons.*
(What is actually linked by *like* in the first sentence is 'me' and 'hatred', although it is clearly 'me' and 'my brother' that are being compared.)

---

**likely** see LIABLE.

## literally

Do not use *literally* unless you literally mean 'literally', ie 'exactly what is meant by the following or preceding words'. A statement such as *I had had nothing to eat since lunchtime so I was literally starving* is clearly not meant to be taken literally at all. Use *literally* only if you wish to emphasize that what is being said is to be understood in a straightforward literal way (eg *Because of the drought, many people in Africa are literally starving*).

## loan see LEND.

## long, lengthy

*Long* is the normal adjective for describing things of great length. *Lengthy* is generally applied only to speaking or writing (*a lengthy speech □ a lengthy essay*) and often has an implication of something being too long or tediously long.

## luxuriant, luxurious

*Luxuriant* has nothing to do with luxury but means 'abundant, prolific, growing vigorously', as in *He was amazed at the luxuriant growth of the jungle plants □ a luxuriant moustache.*

*Luxurious* means 'pertaining to luxury and riches, expensive' as in *a luxurious house.*

## madam, madame

The normal form of this word in English is *madam*, pronounced /ma-*dam*/ and often written with a capital *M*. It is used as a polite term of respect, as in *I'll see if I can find the coat you are looking for, madam,* and is sometimes used before the title of a lady's official position when she is being addressed formally, as in *Madam Speaker.*

*Madame*, pronounced /ma-*dam*/ or /ma-dahm/, is the French equivalent of *Mrs*, and is correctly used instead of *Mrs* when referring to ladies from French-speaking countries.

The plural of *madame* is *mesdames* (pronouced /may-dahm/ or /may-dahm/). *Mesdames* is also sometimes used as the plural of *madam*, which has no plural of its own in the sense given above (in other senses, the plural is *madams*).

## magic, magical

The adjective *magic* generally means 'pertaining to magic': *a magic wand □ He took them for a ride on a magic carpet.*

*Magical* may be used in the same sense as *magic*: *No one knows which ingredients are responsible for these almost magical properties □ They were reputed to employ magical arts against their enemies. Magical*, on the other hand, may also mean 'as if caused by magic, enchanting', as in *It was a magical experience* or *a magical change of character.*

## male, masculine

The adjective *male* differs from *masculine* in the same way as *female* differs from *feminine*. *Male* means 'of the sex that normally fathers young or has similar sexual characteristics': *A male horse is called a stallion* □ *a male flower on a plant.*

*Masculine* may only be applied to people (men or women), and means 'characteristic of a man, having the qualities or characteristics one would expect or wish for in a man': *a woman with a rather masculine bearing.* *Masculine* is also a technical term in grammar, denoting the gender of nouns that refer to male people, animals, etc. See GENDER, page 23.

## malign, malignant see BENIGN.

## masculine see MALE.

## masterful, masterly

These two adjectives were once synonymous, but are no longer so. *Masterful* means 'showing power, authority or determination': *She loves his strong body and masterful ways.* *Masterly* means 'showing the skill of a master': *a masterly display of swordsmanship* □ *a masterly swordsman.*

*Masterful* is sometimes used in the sense of *masterly* given here (*his sustained and masterful display as a raconteur*), but the distinction between the two words is best adhered to.

## may see CAN.

## meet

In British English, you *meet* a person, but *meet with* approval, misfortune or opposition. In American English, it is correct to say *meet with* with people also: *They met with the representatives of various companies while they were in Britain.*

## meretricious

This word is not the same as 'meritorious', and has nothing at all to do with *merit*. *Meretricious* had originally to do with prostitution (Latin *meretrix*, a prostitute), and may still be used with this meaning: *While legally a marriage, their relationship was condemned by many as meretricious.* Nowadays, however, the word is more often used in the senses 'flashy, gaudy', 'superficially attractive' or 'insincere': *the meretricious attractions of a stage career* □ *wooing potential voters with meretricious promises of pay increases and tax cuts.*

**Middle East** see FAR EAST.

**might** see CAN.

**militate** see MITIGATE.

## millennium

A *millennium* is a period of a thousand years. Since the first *millennium* AD began at the beginning of the year 1 and closed a thousand years later at the end of the year 1000, the current millennium began at the beginning of the year 1001 (not 1000) and will close at the end of the year 2000, (not 1999). The next millennium begins in 2001.

## million, billion, etc

A *million* is 1 000 000, both in British and American English. In British English, a *billion* is a million millions, 1 000 000 000 000; in American English, it is a thousand millions, 1 000 000 000. Similarly, a *trillion* is a million billions (1 followed by eighteen zeros) in British English, but a thousand billions (1 followed by twelve zeros) in American English. For each number further up the scale, eg *quadrillion, quintillion, sextillion* (none of which are, admittedly, very common), British usage adds six zeros to the preceding number, while American usage adds three (eg, in British usage, a *sextillion* is $10^{36}$, in American usage $10^{21}$).

The situation is further confused by the fact that in scientific and economic contexts, most speakers of British English use *billion* in the American rather than the British sense. Be aware of the ambiguity.

**mistrust** see DISTRUST.

**misuse** see ABUSE.

## mitigate, militate

*Mitigate against* is a common error:

    ✗    *The time involved can in some contexts mitigate against home cookery.*

This should have read *militate against* (ie, 'to act against, to exert a strong influence against, to be a decisive factor against'):

    ✓    *The time involved can in some contexts militate against home cookery.*

*Mitigate* means 'to lessen the severity or evil of': *Counsel said her client admitted the crime, but argued that there were mitigating circumstances the court should take into account.*

**mortar** see CEMENT.

## Moslem, Muslim, Mohammedan

Both *Moslem* and *Muslim* are correct, but the second is now more common than the first. The term *Mohammedan* is not acceptable to many Muslims, and is therefore better avoided altogether lest it cause offence.

## *mutual* see COMMON.

## *natural* see ILLEGAL.

## *naught* see NOUGHT.

## nauseous

*Nauseous* originally meant 'nauseating' (*a nauseous smell*), but is now as commonly, if not more commonly, used in the sense of 'nauseated': *She felt awful, nauseous and light-headed and clammy.*

## non-flammable, non-inflammable see FLAMMABLE.

## North America see AMERICA.

## nought, naught

*Nought* and *naught* are in origin one and the same word. However, in present-day English, the two spellings are normally kept separate: a *nought* is a zero, the figure 0; *naught* is nothing, usually found in phrases such as *come to naught* and *set at naught.*

## O, oh

*Oh* is the normal form of this word in present-day English: *Oh, what a surprise!* □ *Oh, look at that big red balloon!* It is normally followed by a comma or an exclamation mark except in short exclamations like *Oh no!* or *Oh dear!* In phrases expressing wishes which begin *Oh for . . .* and *Oh to . . .*, there may, or equally correctly may not, be a comma: *Oh for a nice cup of tea!* □ *Oh, to be indoors out of this rain!*

*O* is now found almost only in poetry or in language that is, or is attempting to appear, archaic, especially when addressing someone or something or in exclamations. In poetic or archaic language, *O* may be used instead of *oh* in expressing wishes:

> *O, for a horse with wings!*
> — William Shakespeare

## oblivious

Originally, *oblivious* meant 'forgetting, no longer aware', and was followed by the preposition *of*. Now the meaning has widened to 'unaware,

185

unconscious (of)' and in this sense *oblivious* may correctly be followed by *of* or, albeit less acceptably to some people, by *to*:

> *The planet beneath them was almost perfectly oblivious of their presence.*
> *It was as though he had been oblivious to the row he and his staff had made.*

## observance, observation

*Observance* and *observation* each correspond to different meanings of the verb *observe*. To *observe* a law is to obey that law, to *observe* a tradition is to follow or comply with that tradition, and the noun corresponding to these senses of *observe* is *observance*: *the observance of the speed limit □ the observance of religious holidays.*

*Observe* also means 'to watch' and 'to remark', and to these meanings of the verb corresponds the noun *observation*, which means 'the act of watching or noticing', as in *The police kept the man under observation*, and which is also a rather formal word for 'a remark, comment', as in *He made a few polite observations about her new dress.*

## obtrusive see INTRUSIVE.

## off of

Although common in American English, *off of* is not correct in formal standard British English. *Off* alone should be used:

> ✗ *He took it down off of the top shelf.*
> ✓ *He took it down off the top shelf.*

## official, officious

*Official* means 'done by someone in authority', 'pertaining to authority', etc: *We think she has won, but we're still waiting for the official result of the race.*

*Officious* means 'too eager to meddle, offering unwanted advice or assistance' or, more often, 'holding too rigidly to rules and regulations': *free from the attentions of busybodies and officious bystanders □ Back in the street, I found that an officious traffic warden had decided to make my day.*

## oh see O.

## older, oldest see ELDER.

## one another see EACH OTHER.

## oppress see SUPPRESS.

## oral, aural, verbal

*Oral* means 'of the mouth', 'taken in by the mouth', 'spoken as opposed to written': *oral hygiene □ an oral contraceptive □ an oral exam. Aural* means 'pertaining to the ear': *an aural-comprehension test.*

The adjective *verbal* is ambiguous. It may mean either 'spoken as opposed to written' (*a verbal agreement*) or 'in spoken or written words as opposed to gestures, etc' (*Diagrams are often more helpful than verbal explanations*). In some contexts, the meaning of *verbal* will no doubt be quite clear; in others, it may be necessary to avoid a possible ambiguity either by replacing *verbal* with *oral* or by rephrasing the sentence altogether.

**owing to** see BECAUSE.

## paramount, tantamount

These two words are sometimes confused, with *tantamount* being used in place of *paramount*. Here is one example, from an educational report:

✗ *Indeed the concentration of educational and social disadvantage in areas of deprivation suggests that the need for Basic Education programmes in a community such as this is of tantamount importance.*

What the writer meant was that such education programmes were of *paramount* importance. *Paramount* means 'supreme, greater than any other', and, in a looser sense, is often taken simply to mean 'very great', as in the phrase (now almost a cliché) *of paramount importance*.

*Tantamount to* means 'in effect the same as, amounting to': *This action was considered tantamount to a declaration of war* □ *The new tsar treated Bulgaria as tantamount to a province of Russia.*

**part** see BEHALF.

## partly, partially

*Partly* and *partially* are not synonymous. *Partly* means 'in part or parts, concerning only a part', as in *The house is constructed partly of stone and partly of wood*. To say that someone is *partly* responsible for an accident means that someone or something else also bears some of the responsibility for it.

*Partially* means 'not to a state of completion', as in *The house is only partially built* (ie, it is not yet completely built).

**pathos** see BATHOS.

## peaceable, peaceful

*Peaceable* means 'not inclined to fight, not quarrelsome' or 'existing in peace', and is used mostly of people or their temperaments, or of places, etc: *I considered myself a peaceable man, a listener, an observer of life* □ *Later we reached a walled but obviously peaceable village.*

*Peaceful* means 'calm, without disturbance' or 'done in peace', and is normally applied to situations, scenes, periods of time and activities: *a peaceful*

187

*night's sleep* □ *a peaceful settlement of the dispute* □ *What was intended to be a peaceful demonstration against the Act turned into a riot in the late afternoon.* **Peaceable** is also used in the sense of 'calm, undisturbed': *It was a warm, peaceable silence.*

## peremptory see PERFUNCTORY.

## perennial see ANNUAL.

## perfunctory, peremptory

Something which is done **perfunctorily** is done hastily, superficially and without interest or enthusiasm, often for form's sake as a matter of routine or duty: *The customs officers gave the car a perfunctory once-over and then waved him through.*

**Peremptory** means 'allowing no refusal or denial' (*a peremptory demand/summons*), or 'abrupt, imperious' (*a peremptory manner/gesture*).

## perimeter, periphery

A **perimeter** is the boundary of a two-dimensional figure or of anything similar: *measured the perimeter of the triangle/field.* The **perimeter** of a circle is its circumference.

A **periphery** may be a **perimeter** but it may also be the outer surface of a three-dimensional object: *the periphery of the eyeball.* In a figurative sense, **periphery** denotes the outer regions of an area, group, etc: *He remained always on the periphery of the group, tolerated but never fully belonging.*

## persistent see CONSISTENT.

## persona non grata

**Persona non grata** is a Latin phrase meaning 'a person not liked by or acceptable to (some other person)'. In a formal, technical sense, it is applied to someone whose presence in a country is not acceptable to the government of that country (as in *He has been declared persona non grata by the British government*), but it is often used loosely and facetiously, as in *I'm persona non grata with the boss at the moment.*

 Although grammatically singular in form, this phrase may refer back to a plural noun or pronoun (*We're all persona non grata at the moment*), but a plural form **personae non gratae** may also be used.

The opposite of **persona non grata** is **persona grata**, but this is less common.

## perturb, disturb

**Perturb** means 'to cause anxiety or worry': *His threats did not perturb her in the least.* **Disturb** also has the meaning 'to upset or worry', as in *This news clearly* *disturbed him greatly*, but has the further meaning 'to irritate, interrupt the work, thoughts or rest of, etc', as in *His singing doesn't disturb me at all*. If the disruption or agitation is physical rather than mental, ***disturb*** must be used, not ***perturb***: *A violent storm disturbed the surface of the lake*.

## piteous, pitiable, pitiful

***Pitiful*** is the commonest of these three adjectives. It means 'very sad, arousing or deserving pity' (*She was a pitiful sight*) and also 'arousing or deserving contempt, very bad, very poor' (*He made a pitiful attempt at catching the ball*). ***Pitiable*** is synonymous with ***pitiful*** but is rather less common: *He was in a pitiable condition* □ *That was a pitiable attempt you made*. ***Pitiful*** is more likely to be used than ***pitiable*** when what is being referred to is an inanimate object.

***Piteous*** is a rather formal or literary word meaning 'arousing or deserving pity', as in *She gave a piteous cry*. ***Piteous*** should not be used to denote 'arousing or deserving contempt'.

## politic, political

***Political*** means 'pertaining to politics': *the political system of the USA* □ *party political broadcasts*. ***Politic*** is a rather formal word meaning 'wise, sensible', as in *a politic decision* □ *He considered it politic to leave before there was any further trouble*.

 The adverb formed from ***political*** is ***politically***; the adverb corresponding to ***politic*** is ***politicly***.

## portentous, pretentious

Both words can mean 'pompous, self-important', ***pretentious*** being the commoner: *A portentous/pretentious minor official informed us that our comments would be noted*. ***Portentous*** also means 'important, ominous': *He believed the dream contained portentous warnings about the future*.

## practicable, practical

***Practicable*** means 'able to be done, used, carried out, etc': *a practicable plan* □ *There's a practicable path to the house, if somewhat steep and muddy*.

***Practical***, when applied to things, suggestions, etc also means 'able to be done, used or carried out' but has the further connotation of 'efficient, sensible, useful': *Both these suggested courses of action are practicable, but John's is certainly the more practical of the two* □ *Book tokens are a very practical present* □ *High heels aren't very practical for hill-walking*. Applied to people, ***practical*** means 'able to do, make or deal with things well or efficiently': *He's not a very practical person — he has lots of ideas for redesigning the bathroom but he doesn't have a clue how to put up a shelf*.

See also IMPRACTICABLE.

## precipitate, precipitous

*Precipitate* means 'hasty', often 'too hasty': *a precipitate decision*. *Precipitous* means 'very steep, like a precipice': *The path through the mountains is narrow and precipitous.*

*Precipitous* is now frequently used in much the same sense as *precipitate*, but not all authorities accept this as correct:

**?** *Let's not be precipitous. We should stop and think for a minute.*

There may, moreover, be a slight difference in implication between the two: dashing *precipitately* towards the door may imply a lack of thought before acting, whereas dashing *precipitously* may emphasize the speed of the action.

## prefer, preferable

*Prefer* should be followed by *to*, not *than*:

**✓** *I prefer tea to coffee.*
**✗** *I prefer tea than coffee.*

The same rule applies to *preferable*:

**✓** *Tea is preferable to coffee.*
**✗** *Tea is preferable than coffee.*

## prescribe, proscribe

Confusion between these two verbs may lead to someone saying the exact opposite of what they intend. To *prescribe* is to advise or order; to *proscribe* is to ban, outlaw or forbid:

*The books prescribed for study on this course are all in the library.*
*This book was formerly proscribed by the church.*

*The law prescribes severe penalties for such offences.*
*Such actions are proscribed by law.*

**presume** see ASSUME.

**pretentious** see PORTENTOUS.

## prevaricate, procrastinate

To *prevaricate* is 'to talk evasively in order to avoid telling the truth, coming to the point or answering a question': *When faced with difficult questions, politicians usually prevaricate.* *Prevarication* always involves an attempt to deceive or to avoid admitting the truth.

*Procrastination* is putting off until later on things that should be done immediately.

**prone** see LIABLE.

**propitious** see AUSPICIOUS.

**proscribe** see PRESCRIBE.

## purposefully, purposely

*Purposefully* means 'obviously, or apparently, having some purpose': *She strode purposefully towards him, clearly intent on settling things once and for all.*

*Purposely* means 'intentionally, on purpose': *She didn't want to go to college so she purposely failed her exams.*

## racism, racialism

There is no difference in meaning between these words.

## rapport, repartee

These words are sometimes confused:

✗    *The authors of both books obviously have a natural repartee with their pupils.*

*Repartee* is a series of quick, witty remarks or replies, or a conversation which has many of these in it. What the writer should have said was that the authors had a natural *rapport* with their pupils, ie a close relationship with them based on a good understanding of their feelings, outlook, etc.

## rebound, redound

To *rebound* is 'to bounce back', in either a neutral, a good or a bad sense: *She was throwing the ball against the wall and catching it as it rebounded □ Profits were higher than average in the first half of the year, rebounding unexpectedly from an unprecedented low last year □ His overweening ambition rebounded on him, as, having ousted his father from the throne, he was in turn ousted by those who would not accept him as the legitimate ruler.*

To *redound* (now a rather old-fashioned or formal word) is 'to have advantageous or disadvantageous consequences': *His actions redounded to the credit of the regiment □ A child's bad behaviour in public inevitably redounds on the parents.*

## refute, deny

To *deny* means 'to declare (something) not to be true': *He denied that he had stolen the money.* Strictly speaking, *refute* means 'to prove or show (something) to be untrue': *You can easily refute his arguments.* Unfortunately, *refute* is now used by many people to mean 'to deny strongly'. This has rendered the word dangerously ambiguous, in writing at least, as it is often not obvious whether allegations, for example, that are said to have been refuted have been proved wrong or merely emphatically denied. To avoid ambiguity, especially in written material, it is necessary either to avoid the word *refute* altogether, or to make sure that there is sufficient information in the rest of the passage to make the intended meaning clear.

### regal, royal

*Regal* means 'like or suitable for a king or queen': *regal splendour* □ *regal bearing.* *Royal* means 'of a king or queen': *the Royal Family* □ *a royal decree.* Occasionally, *royal* is used in a sense close to that of *regal* given above, ie 'splendid, magnificent': *a royal feast.*

### regretful, regrettable

*Regretful* means 'full of regret, sad, sorry'; *regrettable* means 'causing regret, to be regretted': *It is regrettable that you have behaved so foolishly, and I feel regretful that I must now ask you to leave.*

### relation, relative

In the sense of 'a person to whom you are related', these two words are synonymous and interchangeable.

### remittance, remission

These two nouns correspond to different senses of the verb *remit*, and should not be confused. *Remittance* is a formal word for the sending of money in payment for something, or for the money itself: *We are grateful for your remittance of the correct sum of money* □ *Thank you for your remittance.*

*Remission* means 'a lessening in force or effect' (as in *Remissions in that form of cancer are not unknown*), 'the shortening of a prison sentence', 'the cancelling of a debt or punishment', and, in Christian theology, 'the forgiveness (of sins)'.

### repartee see RAPPORT.

### repetitive, repetitious

*Repetitious* is normally applied to speech or writing and always carries the connotation of excessive or tedious repetition: *I'm tired of listening to his repetitious speeches. Repetitive* may be applied to speech and writing or to actions, activities, etc. It may, like *repetitious*, have a connotation of tedium, but it may also be used in a more neutral sense, meaning simply 'characterized by repetition': *The work is of a very repetitive nature* □ *I realize that what I am saying is rather repetitive, but I do want to make sure that you grasp the point.*

### replace see SUBSTITUTE.

### repress see SUPPRESS.

**restrain** see CONSTRAIN.

**revenge** see AVENGE.

### review, revue

A *revue* is a type of amusing theatre show. A *review* is a report, study or critical consideration of something: *Have you seen the review of her latest novel in today's paper?* □ *We'll have a review of your progress at the end of the month.*

**reward** see AWARD.

### rouse, arouse

In the sense of 'to waken', *rouse* is commoner than *arouse*: *She had to shake him several times to rouse him. Arouse* is used in this sense also, but now not often: *You were unable to arouse Sir Thomas, so you asked the servants to break down the door?*

In the sense of awakening feelings or stirring to action, there is little difference in meaning between the two words, but a slight difference in use and connotation:

i)    Firstly, *rouse* rather than *arouse* is usually used when the object of the verb is a person rather than an emotion: *His poems were intended to rouse the people to action* □ *She was determined that he would not rouse her to anger.* Both *arouse* and *rouse* are used of feelings, etc: *This high-handedness aroused the anger of the mob* □ *state propaganda intended to rouse nationalistic pride.*

ii)    Secondly, some people feel that, when applied to feelings, *rouse* should be used with strong emotion, whereas *arouse* may be used of both mild and strong emotions: *Their actions roused the fury of the crowd* □ *Their activities aroused her interest/anger.*

In the sense of 'awaken sexual feelings in' a person, only *arouse* is correct: *Him kissing her with firmly closed lips did nothing to arouse her.*

**royal** see REGAL.

**sarcasm** see IRONY.

**sceptic(al)** see CYNIC(AL).

### scorn, spurn

In *scorn*, the main focus is on the feeling or expressing of contempt for someone or something: *Various literary vices were exposed and scorned by Pope in his Dunciad* □ *Courbet had little formal art training and scorned the rigid classical outlook of the time. Scorn* is generally accompanied by a rejection of whoever or whatever is scorned, but the emphasis is on the contempt rather than on the rejection.

In *spurning*, the emphasis is on the rejection rather than the contempt. Whoever or whatever is *spurned* is rejected, usually with contempt: *Spurned by her family, she moved to London* □ *He spurned their offer of help.*

## Scottish, Scotch, Scots

*Scottish* is the normal adjective meaning 'of or belonging to Scotland': *She's Scottish, not English* □ *an exhibition of Scottish books.* The form of English spoken in Scotland, differing from Standard English in both grammar and vocabulary is *Scottish English.*

*Scotch* was once correctly and acceptably used in the sense given above for *Scottish*, and still is by some non-Scots, but many Scottish people now find it unacceptable and it is best to limit its use to the names of certain products, animals, plants, etc from or associated with Scotland: *Scotch egg* □ *Scotch mist* □ *Scotch pine* □ *Scotch terrier* □ *Scotch thistle* □ *Scotch whisky.* Similarly, *Scotchman* and *Scotchwoman* are now to be avoided: use *Scotsman* and *Scotswoman*, or simply *Scot*, instead.

The adjective *Scots* is also more restricted in use than *Scottish*: it is used in *Scots law* (which is different from English law), *Scots pine* (= *Scotch pine*), the *Scots language* and in the names of certain army regiments such as the *Scots Guards.* Note that the *Scots language*, or simply, *Scots*, is not a dialect of English, but is a separate language which developed from Old English in parallel to English, just as French, Spanish and Italian all developed from Latin.

## sensual, sensuous

*Sensuous* means 'perceived by or affecting the senses, especially in a pleasant way', as in *I find his music very sensuous* □ *Her sculptures have a certain sensuous quality to them.* *Sensuous* pleasures are likely to appeal to the mind rather than to the body, eg art and music.

*Sensual* means 'of or concerning the physical senses and the body rather than the mind', and is used especially with a connotation of sexuality or sexual arousal: *a full, sensual mouth* □ *a strong desire for sensual pleasure* □ *He kissed her on the mouth with slow sensual desire* □ *The air was heavy with some exotic odour, dense and sensual.*

## series, serial

In literature and drama, a *serial* is a single story presented in separate parts, and a *series* is a set of separate stories.

## shrift, shift

Since *shrift* is now an archaic word, no longer in general use, it is sometimes mistakenly replaced by *shift* in the idiom *give (someone) short shrift.* Originally, to give someone *short shrift* was to allow them only a short time for confession and absolution (*shriving*) before they were executed; hence, it came to mean 'to give someone little time or consideration'.

### silicon, silicone

Those who are not aware that these words are the names of two different substances may be confused by the existence of two spellings. **Silicon** is an element, used especially in the computer industry in *silicon chips*. **Silicone** is a compound, which contains the element silicon as well as carbon and oxygen, and is used in lubricants and polishes, and in *silicone breast implants*.

**since** see AGO.

**slander** see LIBEL.

**so ... as** see AS ... AS.

### sociable, social

The adjective **sociable** is usually applied to people and means 'friendly, fond of the company of others': *Our new neighbours aren't very sociable □ He's a cheerful, sociable sort of bloke.* **Social** means 'of or concerning society', as in *Problems such as this are social rather than medical in origin* and *social class*, or 'concerning the gathering together or meeting of people for recreation and amusement' as in *a social club* and *His reasons for calling round were purely social.*

**sort of** see KIND OF.

### so therefore

The expression **so therefore** is heard more and more frequently nowadays, where **so** or **therefore** alone would be quite sufficient:

   ✗   *There was no one in the office, so therefore I just left a note on the desk and went out again.*
   ✓   *There was no one in the office, so I just left a note on the desk and went out again.*

Although **so therefore** often passes unnoticed in informal speech, it is certainly to be avoided as a tautology in formal contexts.

### South America see AMERICA.

**speciality** see SPECIALTY.

**specially** see ESPECIALLY.

### specialty, speciality

To all intents and purposes, these two words are synonymous. **Speciality** is the commoner form in British English, **specialty** in American English.

**spurn** see SCORN.

## stalactite, stalagmite

*Stalactites* hang down from the roof of a cave, *stalagmites* grow up from the floor. One way of remembering which is which is to reflect that it is the *stalactites* that have to hang on *tight* to the roof. It is also worth remembering that *stalactites* hang down from the <u>c</u>eiling and *stalagmites* grow up from the <u>g</u>round.

## stammer, stutter

In technical contexts, a distinction is sometimes drawn between these two words, *stuttering* being defined as a form of speech in which sounds in words, usually the initial sounds, are repeated, and *stammering* being defined as a hesitant form of speech in which either words or syllables are repeated or the flow of speech stops altogether while the speaker tries to produce the next word. However, this distinction is not observed nowadays by most authorities, and in general contexts the words can be taken as synonymous, with *stammer* being the commoner in British English.

## stanch, staunch

In the sense of 'to stop the flow of' (especially the flow of blood from a wound), either form is correct, but *staunch* is the commoner. Its use in a literal sense is seen in the following examples: *staunch a wound □ staunched the blood □ staunched the flow of blood from the wound*; and its figurative use is seen in *They acted too late to staunch the decline of royal authority □ This helped to staunch the Danish invasion.*

●  As an adjective, the form to use is *staunch*: *a staunch ally/Catholic/opponent □ staunch resistance.*

## stimulant, stimulus

Both these nouns refer to something which promotes or produces an increase in activity. *Stimulant* is normally used only of a drug or medicine which makes a person more alert or part of their body more active: *Tea and coffee contain stimulants □ a powerful heart stimulant. Stimulant* may also be used figuratively: *A visit to the art gallery is the best stimulant I know.*

A *stimulus* is something which causes a reaction in a living thing: *Light is the stimulus that causes a flower to open. Stimulus* is often used to mean 'something which causes or encourages a person to make greater efforts': *Many people think that children need the stimulus of competition to make them work well at school.*

## straight, strait

*Straight* is generally used as an adjective: *a straight line □ Your tie isn't straight □ It was so funny I could hardly keep my face straight when I was telling him □ I can never get a straight answer from him.* **Straight** may also be used as an adverb and as a noun: *Go straight home* □ *He walked straight across the garden* □ *The horses are in the final straight* (= 'the straight part of a racecourse'). **Straight** is also used in compounds and phrases such as *straightforward, straight away,* and *the straight and narrow.*

**Strait** is an old adjective meaning 'narrow', 'confined' or 'confining'. It is now found only in compound words such as *strait-jacket* and *strait-laced.* As a noun, **strait** is still in common use, especially in the plural. It means 'a narrow strip of sea between two pieces of land' as in *the Straits of Gibraltar* and *the Bering Strait,* or 'difficulty, need', as in *She had been in great straits financially since her husband died* and *in dire straits.*

## strategy, stratagem

A **stratagem** is a plan or trick, intended to deceive someone or gain an advantage over them: *He was a master of the cunning stratagem and the bare-faced lie.* **Strategy** is used more of a long-term plan of campaign: *adopted a strategy of civil disobedience* □ *Mao's guerrilla tactics were replaced by a strategy of conventional warfare.*

---

 In general usage, there is little difference between **strategy** and **tactics**. In military terms, however, **strategy** involves the <u>formation</u> of plans and **tactics** the <u>implementation</u> of those plans.

---

**stutter** see STAMMER.

**subsequent** see CONSEQUENT.

## substitute, replace

If X is put in the place of Y, X is **substituted for** or **replaces** Y and Y is **replaced by** or **with** X:

   ✗    *One day I found I had been substituted by a computer.*
   ✓    *One day I found I had been replaced by a computer.*

## superior

When **superior** means 'better' or 'more important', it behaves like a comparative adjective, but unlike true comparative adjectives, it should be followed by **to**, not **than**: *Is a captain superior to a commander in the navy?* □ *This carpet is far superior to that one* (compare *This carpet is much better than that one*).

In the sense of 'disdainful, showing that one considers oneself better than others', **superior** behaves as an ordinary adjective: *I can be more superior than her if I want to.*

**supplement** see COMPLEMENT.

## suppress, repress, oppress

To *suppress* is 'to put a stop to something, to stamp it out or prevent it being published or divulged': *The government attempted to suppress corruption/piracy/a rebellion/the story/indigenous culture* □ *His diaries were eventually published despite attempts to suppress them.*

To *repress* is much the same as to *suppress*, but may not involve complete abolition or stamping out, only a lessening or controlling of something: *Protestantism was severely repressed during his reign* □ *attempts to repress trade unionism/opposition/an insurrection.*

To *oppress* someone is to treat them with cruelty and injustice, or to burden them with heavy taxes, overwork, etc: *working for the rights of politically oppressed minority groups throughout the world* □ *oppressed peasants.*

## tactics see STRATEGY.

## tantamount see PARAMOUNT.

## testimonial, testimony

A *testimonial* is a letter describing a person's character and abilities. It is thus a kind of reference, but differs from it in that a reference is usually given to a person's potential employers in respect of an application for a particular post whereas a *testimonial* is given to the person concerned to be used as and when they like. Another sense of *testimonial* is 'something presented to someone, especially at a public ceremony, as a token of respect': *For inventing a miners' safety lamp, he received a public testimonial of £1000.*

A *testimony* is a statement of evidence, eg that of a witness at a trial: *He was convicted mainly by the testimony of his former partner* □ *Her book is a remarkable testimony to her vision for the future of her country.*

## till see UNTIL.

## transpire

*Transpire* is often used, especially in formal contexts, as a substitute for *happen* or *occur*. Some people deprecate this use of *transpire*, which originally meant 'to leak out, become known gradually', but it has become so widespread that it must now be accepted as correct: *It transpired that the snow went as quickly as it had come* □ *They continued as if nothing untoward had transpired.*

## treble, triple

In the sense of 'three times as much', *treble* and *triple* may both be used as verbs, adverbs and nouns. There is no difference in meaning between them, but *treble* is the commoner of the two: *It doesn't matter what he offers you, I'll offer you treble* □ *I'll offer you treble what he offers you* □ *He trebled his earnings in just six months.*

*Treble* and *triple* may both also be used as adjectives, but as adjectives they do differ slightly in use. *Treble* is commoner than *triple* in the sense of 'three times as much or as many': *I ordered a double Scotch and he ordered a treble.* *Triple* is more frequently used than *treble* in the sense of 'of three kinds, parts, units, etc', as in *They have the triple handicap of poverty, parental neglect and bad schooling □ Round the prison they built a triple wall □ the treble chance on the football pools.*

## truism

A *truism* is not just something which is true, but something that is so obviously true that it is hardly worth saying, a self-evident truth, eg *Every parent was once a child.* Another, now less common, sense of *truism* is 'a tautology', a statement part of which simply repeats what is said in or implied by another part, eg *Children are young people.*

## try and, try to

In all contexts, *try* may be followed by the preposition *to* and an infinitive: *He tried to catch the ball □ Will he try to talk to her? □ He has been trying to see her for days but she's always out.* *Try and* is sometimes substituted for *try to*, but is subject to two important restrictions: it should not be used in formal speech and writing, and it may only be used when *try* is not modified by a suffix such as *-ing* or *-es:*

   ✓   *Do try and come to the party.*
   ✓   *I will try and come.*
   ✓   *He did try and come.*
   ✗   *He tried and came to the party.*
   ✗   *He was trying and coming to the party.*

## unexceptional, unexceptionable see EXCEPTIONAL.

## uninterested see DISINTERESTED.

## unique

Strictly speaking, *unique* means 'being the only one of its kind, having no like or equal': *This vase is unique — there isn't another one like it in the world □ a comedian with a unique sense of timing.* It follows, therefore, that *unique* is a 'yes or no' term, not a 'more or less' term: either something is unique or it isn't, it cannot be 'more unique', 'very unique', 'fairly unique' or 'slightly unique'. In informal language, *unique* is quite frequently used to mean 'rare, remarkable, unusual', often modified by adverbs such as *more, fairly,* etc: *He's got a pretty unique job □ This is a rather unique picture.* This use of the word is not generally considered correct for formal speech and writing.

## United Kingdom see BRITAIN.

## unlawful see ILLEGAL.

**unpractical** see IMPRACTICABLE.

**unreadable** see ILLEGIBLE.

## unsociable, unsocial, antisocial
*Unsociable* is usually applied to people and means 'unfriendly, disliking the company of others, not willing to have a friendly chat', as in *I'm not really interested in parties and pub nights — I'm a bit unsociable really □ She never stops to talk when you meet her in the street — she's very unsociable.*

*Unsocial* may be used in much the same sense as *unsociable*, but is slightly stronger in meaning: an *unsocial* person does not simply dislike company, social gatherings, etc, but positively turns his or her back on society. Moreover, *unsociable* may denote a temporary attitude or feeling, whereas *unsocialness* will generally be a permanent characteristic. However, *unsocial* is more often used nowadays in phrases such as *unsocial* hours, ie hours of work that are outside the normal working day (and so prevent the person working them from taking part in normal social activities).

*Antisocial* may mean the same as either *unsociable* or *unsocial*, but often refers to behaviour that is considered harmful or upsetting to other people: *Many people now consider smoking an antisocial activity, on a par with spitting in buses.*

## urban, urbane
*Urban* means 'of a town': *urban development □ urban life □ urban violence*. *Urbane* means 'sophisticated, elegant, refined': *urbane wit*.

## use, usage
*Use* refers to the act of using something or the purpose for which it is used: *The use of force cannot be justified even in these circumstances □ That is an incorrect use of the word □ This little lamp has many uses.*

*Usage*, on the other hand, means 'the manner of using or being used', as in *These tools have been subjected to rough usage*, or 'custom or habit, especially with regard to the generally accepted rules of language': *We must be aware of ancient traditions and usages □ This book is a guide to modern English usage.*

**vengeance** see AVENGE.

**verbal** see ORAL.

**virus** see BACTERIUM.

**visualize** see ENVISAGE.

## wait, await

Apart from its use in certain fixed expressions such as *wait your turn* and *wait your chance*, **wait** is not usually followed by an object:

   ✗  *I'll wait your arrival.*
   ✓  *I'll wait until you arrive.*

Before an object, there are two options: either the verb must be followed by *for* (*I'll wait for you □ I'll wait for the train to arrive*) or else you must use the rather more formal word **await** (*I'm awaiting the arrival of the train □ We are awaiting your instructions*). The object of **await** is usually an abstract noun (*arrival, opportunity, breakthrough, trial, death, divorce,* etc) rather than a concrete noun (ie, one denoting an object or a person). *Await* cannot be used without an object:
✗ *I'll await until you come.*

**Await** also means 'to be in store for, be waiting for': *A warm welcome awaits you at this church on Sunday.* In this sense, it is usually followed by a person as object, and cannot be replaced by **wait for**.

## wake, waken, awake, awaken

These four verbs are virtually synonymous and are interchangeable in most contexts. **Wake** is the most commonly used of the four: *He woke to find that it was snowing □ He went upstairs and woke the others.*

**Waken** may also be used with or without an object: *Have you wakened the children yet? □ I wakened at seven o'clock.* It is often used figuratively, in the sense of 'to arouse' (*wakening them at last from their complacency and idleness*) or 'to make aware' (*wakening him to the problems and pitfalls of life*).

**Awake** and **awaken** can both be used in the literal sense of 'to rouse from sleep' or 'to arouse, cause': *I awoke to find her gone □ It was this that first awoke in me my lifelong love of art □ In spite of her cosseted upbringing, by the end of the play she has finally awakened to the realities of life.*

**Wake** may be followed by **up** (*I woke up at seven o'clock*) and **waken** sometimes is; **awake** and **awaken** are never followed by **up**.

**wary** see CHARY.

## wherefore

This word, no longer in general use in modern English, is most often to be heard nowadays in quotations of the famous line from Shakespeare's *Romeo and Juliet*:

   *O Romeo, Romeo! Wherefore art thou Romeo?*

Apart from in performances of the play itself, the line is now usually said with the stress on *art*, and the intended sense is always 'Where are you, Romeo?'. This is, however, incorrect. **Wherefore** does not mean 'where?', it means 'why?'. Juliet is not asking where Romeo is, but wishing that he was not Romeo at all, given the feud between their two families. **Wherefore** is related to *therefore* in the same way as *where* is related to *there*. Its meaning is shown in the idiomatic phrase ***the whys and wherefores*** (= 'the reasons for something'). One example of its use in rather old-fashioned and literary English is:

> *I am simply stating wherefore I did as I did.*
>
> — Dornford Yates

**wide** see BROAD.

**wince** see FLINCH.

### zero

**Zero** is sometimes used, especially in advertising and journalism, as an emphatic or stylistic substitute for *no*: pools winners are promised *zero* publicity, users of certain toothpastes are offered the hope of *zero* fillings. This is not yet acceptable in formal English, apart from its use instead of *no* or *naught* in technical contexts (*The distance between lines of longitude is zero at the North and South Poles* □ *zero electrical resistance* □ *zero rainfall*) or in business contexts (*zero growth/costs/benefits*).

# 4

# Spelling and Word-formation

English spelling and word-formation are notoriously unpredictable (eg *harass* and *embarrass*, *batted* and *budgeted*, *assistance* but *subsistence*), but there are nonetheless some clear spelling and word-formation rules of very general application which cover many of the areas of difficulty. These rules are highlighted in shaded boxes in the relevant entries of this chapter.

There are, however, many areas of English spelling where the rules become rather complicated (eg those governing the choice between *-tion* and *-sion*), and some where there are almost no discernible rules at all. These problem areas are also covered in detail in the entries in this chapter, in some cases by a simple listing of correct spellings.

---

**Sound and spelling**

English spelling would seem to have been designed chiefly as a disguise for pronunciation.

—Jerome K Jerome

---

Many of the explanations in this chapter make use of the '*word-family*' as an aid to correct spelling. If you are having difficulty remembering the correct spelling of a word because its pronunciation does not give sufficient guidance, and you cannot remember the appropriate rule (or there is no rule to apply), try to find a related word in which the spelling is clear from the pronunciation. For example, if you were uncertain whether to write *photograph* or *photagraph*, it would be useful to remember the related word *photography* in which the second *o* is clearly pronounced. Likewise, if you are not sure whether to write *vigilance* or *vigilence*, think of *vigilante*, in which the *a* is clearly sounded. There are many spelling difficulties that can be solved by using word-families in this way.

Another way to cope with spelling problems is the use of invented 'memory aids'. For example, to remember that there is only one *b* but two *t*'s in *abattoir*, you could think of the phrase *beef and mutton*. It does not matter how ridiculous your invented memory aids are, so long as they help you to remember the correct spellings of your problem words. For further examples, see the *Difficult Words* chapter on page 327.

> Note: *Where possible, information in this chapter has been entered under the particular word-element being described, eg -ance, -er, -ful, -ing, -o, -y. However, in some cases, information has, for convenience or of necessity, been entered under more general topic headings, eg past tense and past participle or doubling of final consonants. In all cases, full cross-references have been given so that information is easy to find, and sometimes, if it has been thought helpful to do so, the same information has been provided in more than one entry.*

**-a** see -AE, -AS.

**-a, -ons** see -ON.

**-a, -ums** see -UM.

## abbreviations

Abbreviations, in the broadest sense, are shortened forms of words, phrases, titles, etc. There are several different types: see page 1 for details.

The two main spelling problems with abbreviations are:

(a) when to insert full stops (see below), and

(b) when to insert apostrophes (see page 206).

Also covered in this entry are the use of capital letters in abbreviations (page 206) and the formation of plural abbreviations (page 207).

### ✦ Full stops in abbreviations

The modern trend in English is to have as little punctuation as possible in a text. This gives the written page a much cleaner and clearer look than a heavily punctuated page would have. This 'minimal punctuation' approach means that abbreviations should be written without full stops wherever possible. The question is: where are full stops obligatory, and where are they optional and omissible? The following rules apply:

> **Contractions are usually written without full stops in British English.**

Examples: *Mr, Dr, St* (= *Saint* or *Street*)

However, the full stops are not incorrect, and are still preferred in American English.

*Contractions formed with numbers are never written with full stops*: *1st, 2nd, 3rd, 4th, 4to* (= *quarto*).

**Abbreviations of the names of countries and organizations are usually written without full stops.**

Examples: *USA, USSR, UN, EU*

When such abbreviations are treated as **acronyms** — pronounced as single words rather than as strings of letters — they are now almost always written without full stops: *NATO, UNICEF, UNESCO, NALGO*. Sometimes such acronyms are written as if they were simple words, with only an initial capital (*Nato, Unesco*).

**Abbreviations of metric measurements, of the temperature scales, and symbols for chemical elements are written without full stops.**

**Symbols for non-metric measurements may be written with full stops, but in line with the current tendency to omit full stops where possible, they too are frequently written without.**

Examples:

*km, cm, kg*
*C* (= *Centigrade*), *F* (= *Fahrenheit*)
*Cu, Fe, Pb*
*hr* or *hr.* (= *hour*)

**Other abbreviations are generally written with full stops.**

Examples: *ibid., viz.*

Here again there is an increasing tendency to omit the full stops, especially in **strings of letters representing two or more words**: *e.g.* or *eg, i.e.* or *ie, a.m.* or *am, PLC, BSc* or *B.Sc., MBE* or *M.B.E.* Similarly with **initials in personal names**: *T. S. Eliot* or *T S Eliot*.

 There are no full stops when the letters of the abbreviation stand for parts of words rather than complete words: *TV* (= *television*), *MS* (= *manuscript*).

> **Clipped forms, being considered whole words, are never followed by a full stop.**

Examples: *demo, exam, bus*

## ✦ Apostrophes

> **Contractions of two or more words are generally spelt with apostrophes.**

Examples:

**pronouns + verbs** (*I've, they're*, etc)
**verb + not** (*can't, don't, won't, hasn't*, etc)

Sometimes, in representations of colloquial speech, more than one apostrophe may be necessary: *they'd've* for *they would have*. Note also the spelling of archaic forms like *'tis* and *'twas*.

---

 Take care where you put the apostrophe in the **negative contractions** formed with -*n't* — it replaces the deleted *o*: *do not* → *don't, have not* → *haven't*. Putting the apostrophe before rather than after the *n* of such words is a common error: ✗ *has'nt*, ✓ *hasn't*.

**Clipped forms** like *flu* and *bus* were once treated as abbreviations (*'flu, 'bus*), but should never be spelt with an apostrophe nowadays.

---

## ✦ Capital letters

> **Abbreviations consisting of the initial letters of two or more words are usually written completely in capitals.**

Examples:

*APR* (= *annual percentage rate*), *BBC, ESE* (= *east-south-east*), *MA, MOT, NUJ, USA*

A few abbreviations, not the names of countries or organizations, are written with lower-case letters: *agm* (also *AGM*), *aka* (= *also known as*), *asap* (= *as soon as possible*), *a.m., bcg* (also *BCG*), *e.g., fob* (= *free on board*), *gbh, i.e., plc* (also *PLC*), *p.m.*, and some abbreviations of measures: *g, l, m, p, mph*, etc.

*If more than the first letter of a word is taken into an abbreviation, only the first letter is capitalized*: *BSc* (= *Bachelor of Science*), *PhD* (= *Doctor of Philosophy*), *BMus* (= *Bachelor of Music*).

In the abbreviated forms of the names of some organizations with 'of' in their title, the 'of' may be shortened to either a capital *O* or a lower-case *o*: *DoE* (= *Department of the Environment*, also *DOE*), *FoE* (*Friends of the Earth*; also *FOE*). In some such abbreviations, either a capital or a lower-case letter is acceptable while in others only one or other is correct. In all cases, follow the practice of the organization concerned.

With **acronyms**, all but the first letter may be written in lower-case letters: *NATO* or *Nato*, *AIDS* or *Aids*; and some acronyms are now spelt entirely with lower-case letters, eg *radar* (from *radio detection and ranging*), *sonar* (from *sound navigation and ranging*), *scuba* (from *self-contained underwater breathing apparatus*).

## ✦ Plural abbreviations

- ### Adding *-s*

> **Abbreviations of metric measurements do not have an *-s* in the plural.**

Examples: *3 cm, 50 kg*

> **With non-metric measurements, *-s* is sometimes added and sometimes not.**

i) Some abbreviations <u>must</u> have an *-s* added in the plural: *hrs* (= *hours*), *yds* (= *yards*), *pts, qts, gals* (= *pints, quarts, gallons*), *qrs* (= *quarters*).

ii) In some cases, forms with or without an *-s* are both acceptable (*3 lb* or *3 lbs* for *3 pounds*, *6 oz* or *6 ozs* for *6 ounces*) but in modern practice the *s* tends to be omitted.

iii) The following <u>never</u> have an *-s* in the plural: *cwt* (= *hundredweight*), *in.* (= *inches*), *min.* (= *minutes*) and *sec.* (= *seconds*).

- ### Full stops

If the abbreviation has a full stop in the singular form, it will have one in the plural also; even though the *s* is the last letter of the abbreviated word (eg *volumes*), the plural abbreviations are not treated as contractions (*vols.*).

 If an abbreviation ending in a full stop stands at the end of a sentence, its full stop serves to mark the end of the sentence as well:

✓ *I'm going to write to my M.P.*

There should <u>never</u> be two full stops at the end of a sentence:

✗ *I'm going to write to my M.P..*

- **Doubled forms**

Some abbreviations have a special form in the plural, formed by doubling the singular form or a part of it:

> *p* or *p.* (= *page*), plural *pp* or *pp.*
> *ms* (= *manuscript*), plural *mss*
> *qv* (= Latin *quod vide* 'which see', ie *see this*), plural *qqv.*

Note also that the plural of *Mr* is *Messrs*, from French *Messieurs*, the plural of *Monsieur*.

- **Apostrophes**

Sometimes an apostrophe is inserted into the plural of an abbreviation. Although quite common and inoffensive to most people, this is not strictly correct. The recommended plural of *MP*, for example, is ✓ *MPs* rather than ✗ *MP's*. Similarly, with the optional full stops, the correct form is ✓ *M.P.s*, not ✗ *M.P.'s*.

However, if the abbreviation is written in lower-case letters, then an apostrophe may be inserted in the plural for the sake of clarity: *lbw*, plural *lbw's* □ *Dot your i's and cross your t's.*

## -*ability* see -ABLE.

## -*able*, -*ible*

The two main problems connected with these word-endings are

(a) which spelling to choose (see below), and

(b) what changes to make to the form of the 'core' words the endings are added to (see page 211).

Also covered by this chapter are the spellings of words in -***bly*** and -***bility*** (see page 212).

### ✦ Choosing -*ible* or -*able*

The endings -***able*** and -***ible*** have come down to us via French from Latin -*abilis* and -*ibilis*. By the rules of Latin grammar, certain words would predictably end in -*abilis* and others equally predictably in -*ibilis*, but unfortunately there is no equivalent rule in English, and the choice between -***able*** and -***ible*** is very much less predictable. Since both word-endings sound the same in modern English, you cannot judge by pronunciation which spelling to use. There are, however, a number of clues and rules of thumb which may help you to decide whether a particular word should be spelt with an *a* or an *i*.

> **If the core of the -*ble* word is itself a recognizable word, spell the ending -*able*; if the core is not a recognizable word, spell the ending -*ible*.**

The 'core' of a word is what remains when any prefixes or endings have been removed. For example, the core of *singing* is *sing*, the core of *lovely* is *love*, and the core of *unacceptable* is *accept*.

● **-able**

The following **-ble** words, for example, have cores that are recognizable English words; they end in **-able**:

| | | | | |
|---|---|---|---|---|
| break | : | breakable | lament | : | lamentable |
| detest | : | detestable | pay | : | payable |
| fashion | : | fashionable | | |

Certain minor and quite predictable changes (such as dropping a final silent *e* or doubling a final consonant — see page 211) are regularly made to the cores when the **-ble** ending is added. In such cases, the cores are still considered to be proper words and the ending is **-able**:

| | | | | | |
|---|---|---|---|---|---|
| love | : | lovable | bid | : | biddable |

Similarly, when the core of a **-ble** word is a recognizable phrase, the ending will be **-able**:

| | | | | | |
|---|---|---|---|---|---|
| get at | : | ungetatable | put down | : | unputdownable |
| a quite unthrowoffable cold | | | an easily put-on-able suit. | | |

● **-ible**

The following **-ble** words have cores that are not English words, and end in **-ible**: *audible, horrible, terrible, visible* (there are no related words *aud, horr, terr* or *vis*).

---

⚠️ Note that even if the core is a recognizable English word, if it is also the core of a word ending in **-ion** (not **-ation** or **-ition**, just **-ion**), then the ending will almost always be **-ible**:

| | | | | |
|---|---|---|---|---|
| corrupt | : | corruption | → | corruptible |
| depress | : | depression | → | depressible |
| exhaust | : | exhaustion | → | exhaustible |
| interrupt | : | interruption | → | interruptible |
| perfect | : | perfection | → | perfectible |

A few words allow both **-ible** and **-able** forms:

| | | | | |
|---|---|---|---|---|
| collect | : | collection | → | collectable or collectible |
| correct | : | correction | → | correctable or correctible |
| detect | : | detection | → | detectable or detectible |
| prevent | : | prevention | → | preventable or preventible |

Note, however,

| | | | | |
|---|---|---|---|---|
| predict | : | prediction | → | predictable alone. |

---

Using the word-family as a guide, you can guess that if a *-ble* word you want to spell is related to some other word which ends in *-acity*, *-ality*, *-ate* or *-ation*, then the correct spelling of the word-ending will be *-able*.

*Note that this rule applies even if the core is not a recognizable English word:*

| | | | | | |
|---|---|---|---|---|---|
| application | : | applicable | navigate | : | navigable |
| capacity | : | capable | placate | : | implacable |
| estimate | : | inestimable | separate | : | inseparable |
| hospitality | : | hospitable | tolerate | : | intolerable |
| inflammation | : | inflammable | | | |

Some of the connections may not at first sight be obvious, but once you know them, they may act as useful memory aids:

| | | | | | |
|---|---|---|---|---|---|
| satiate | : | insatiable | probation | : | probable |
| commemorate | : | memorable | transportation | : | portable |
| palpate | : | palpable | associate | : | sociable |

Using pronunciation as a guide: if the word-ending is preceded by a *c* pronounced /k/ or a *g* pronounced /g/, the ending must be *-able*.

The pronunciation of the core can be a clue to the spelling of the ending: if a *c* or a *g* at the end of the core word is pronounced /k/ or /g/ respectively, the following letter must be an *a* (because if it was an *i*, the *i* would 'soften' the pronunciation of the *c* and *g* and they would be pronounced /s/ and /j/ respectively):

| | | |
|---|---|---|
| amicable | despicable | irrevocable |
| communicable | implacable | navigable |

When all else fails, opt for *-able*.

There are many more *-able* words than *-ible* words in English, and most new words are formed with *-able*. While this is of little help if you want to be absolutely certain about the spelling of a particular word, it is nevertheless a useful fact to keep in mind if you are forced to rely on guesswork.

⚠ Some words are exceptions to the above rules, and others are difficult to classify under any rule. These must simply be noted and learned individually:

| | | | |
|---|---|---|---|
| affable | culpable | inevitable | pliable |
| amenable | equitable | inexorable | unconscionable |
| amiable | formidable | inscrutable | viable |
| arable | indomitable | malleable | vulnerable |

| | | | |
|---|---|---|---|
| *accessible* | *convincible* | *forcible* | *irresistible* |
| *collapsible* | *deducible* | *gullible* | *reducible* |
| *comprehensible* | *discernible* | *indestructible* | *reprehensible* |
| *contemptible* | *expressible* | *inflexible* | *responsible* |
| *convertible* | *flexible* | *insensible* | *sensible* |

## ✦ Changes to the spelling of the 'core' word

### • Final *e*

**If the core word ends in a single *e*, this *e* is normally dropped before -*able* or -*ible* is added.**

Examples:

| | | | | | |
|---|---|---|---|---|---|
| *advise* | : | *advisable* | *excuse* | : | *inexcusable* |
| *complete* | : | *completable* | *sense* | : | *sensible* |
| *deduce* | : | *deducible* | *use* | : | *usable* |

⚠ If the core word ends in **two *e*'s**, both are retained:

    *agree* : *agreeable*    *foresee* : *foreseeable*

If the core word ends in -*ce* or -*ge*, the *e* is retained before -*able* in order to preserve the soft /s/ and /j/ sounds of the *c* and *g*:

| | | |
|---|---|---|
| *changeable* | *peaceable* | *unchallengeable* |
| *noticeable* | *pronounceable* | |

If the core word ends in a consonant followed by -*le*, the *e* is retained: *handleable, settleable, whistleable*.

Some derivatives of one-syllable words retain the *e* before the ending, and in a number of cases the *e* may be either dropped or retained. In American English, the forms without the *e* are preferred, but in British English the preferred form is quite unpredictable. In the following list, the preferred forms are given first:

| | |
|---|---|
| *blameable* (also *blamable*) | *rateable* (also *ratable*) |
| *browseable* (also *browsable*) | *ropeable* |
| *dyeable* | *saleable* |
| *giveable* (but *forgivable*) | *shapable* (also *shapeable*) |
| *hireable* | *shareable* |
| *holeable* | *sizeable* (also *sizable*) |
| *likeable* (also *likable*) | *tameable* (also *tamable* |
| *livable* (also *liveable*) | *timeable* |
| *lovable* (also *loveable*) | *tuneable* (also *tunable*) |
| *movable* (also *moveable*) | *unshakeable* |
| *nameable* | |

- **Final _y_**

> **A final _-y_ becomes _i_ before _-able_.**

Examples:

| | | | | | |
|---|---|---|---|---|---|
| *classify* | : | *classifiable* | *rely* | : | *reliable* |
| *envy* | : | *enviable* | *vary* | : | *variable* |

> ⚠ *Flyable* is an exception.

- **Doubled consonants**

In the case of verbs whose final consonant is doubled in the formation of the present participle (for details on this, see DOUBLING OF FINAL CONSONANTS, page 236), the final consonant is similarly doubled in forming *-able* adjectives:

| | | | | |
|---|---|---|---|---|
| *bid* | : | *bidding* | : | *biddable* |
| *forget* | : | *forgetting* | : | *unforgettable* |
| *stop* | : | *stopping* | : | *unstoppable* |

> ⚠ Verbs ending in *-fer* generally do not double the *r* before *-able*:
>
> | | | | | |
> |---|---|---|---|---|
> | *prefer* | : | *preferring* | : | *preferable* |
> | *transfer* | : | *transferring* | : | *transferable* |
>
> but note the two *r*'s in *conferrable*.

✦ **-ability, -ibility, -ably, -ibly**

Nouns formed from *-able* and *-ible* adjectives end in *-ability* and *-ibility* respectively:

| | | | |
|---|---|---|---|
| *adaptable* | : | *adaptability* | *eligible* : *eligibilty* |

Adverbs formed from *-able* and *-ible* adjectives end in *-ably* and *-ibly* respectively:

| | | | |
|---|---|---|---|
| *presumable* | : | *presumably* | *responsible* : *responsibly* |

## accents on words of foreign origin

There are many words of foreign origin in general use in English which are spelt with an accent in the language from which the borrowing has come, especially French. Some of these words have become so well established in English that they are no longer considered foreign words at all and are never spelt with an accent (eg *hotel*, from French *hôtel*). Others, however, are not yet fully naturalized as English words, and in these the accent is generally kept, eg:

| | | |
|---|---|---|
| *à la carte* | *déjà vu* | *pièce de résistance* |
| *à la mode* | *Führer* | *précis* |
| *bête noire* | *idée fixe* | *raison d'être* |
| *cause célèbre* | *maître d'hôtel* | *señorita* |
| *détente* | *mañana* | *tête-à-tête* |

Some words fall into an intermediate category, formerly spelt with the accent but nowadays increasingly not. Among these are (with the currently preferred form given first):

| | |
|---|---|
| *après-ski* or *apres-ski* | *fiancée* or *fiancee* |
| *clientele* or *clientèle* | *Fräulein* or *fraulein* |
| *debris* or *débris* | *née* or *nee* |
| *debut* or *début* | *negligee* or *negligée* |
| *fête* or *fete* | *première* or *premiere* |
| *débutante* or *debutante* | *role* or *rôle* |
| *discotheque* or *discothèque* | *séance* or *seance* |
| *divorcee* (now rarely spelt with an accent) | *soirée* or *soiree* |

The trend towards dropping the foreign accents is unexceptionable, but it is best nevertheless to retain accents in words where they indicate a particular pronunciation of a letter which would in English be pronounced differently (or not at all) if there were no accent (particularly in words including the French *ç* or ending in the French *é*), eg:

| | | | |
|---|---|---|---|
| *attaché* | *cliché* | *fiancé* | *risqué* |
| *blasé* | *communiqué* | *manqué* | *soufflé* |
| *café* | *façade* | *passé* | *soupçon* |

## -acy, -asy

> **The 'best guess' when in doubt is *-acy*.**

Almost all nouns of this type are spelt with a *c*, eg *conspiracy, diplomacy, fallacy, pharmacy* and *supremacy*.

• There are in fact only eight common nouns that sound as if they might end in *-acy* but do not:

four end in *-asy* — *apostasy, ecstasy, fantasy, idiosyncrasy*;

two end in *-isy* — *hypocrisy* (think of the related adjective *hypocritical*, in which the *i* is clearly pronounced) and *pleurisy* (compare *pleuritic*);

two end in *-icy* — *policy* (think of the related words *police* and *political*) and *theodicy*.

213

As a further spelling hint, note that words ending in *-cracy* are related to words ending in *-crat*:

| | | | |
|---|---|---|---|
| *bureaucrat* | : | *bureaucracy* | *democrat* | : | *democracy* |

Many other words ending in *-acy* are related to words ending in *-ate*:

| | | | | | |
|---|---|---|---|---|---|
| *accurate* | : | *accuracy* | *intimate* | : | *intimacy* |
| *delicate* | : | *delicacy* | *private* | : | *privacy* |

## adjectives

For the formation of adjectives ending in *-ed* and *-d*, see -ED, -D.

For the formation of comparatives and superlatives (ie, the *-er* and *-est* forms) of adjectives, see COMPARATIVES AND SUPERLATIVES.

## adverbs

For the construction of adverbs, see -LY.

For the formation of comparatives and superlatives (ie, the *-er* and *-est* forms) of adverbs, see COMPARATIVES AND SUPERLATIVES.

## -ae, -as

**Most words ending in -*a* form a plural by adding -*s*.**

Examples:

*dilemmas, ideas, spatulas, umbrellas*

**Some words of Latin origin which end in -*a* form a plural by adding -*e*.**

Examples:

| | | |
|---|---|---|
| *alga* | : | *algae* |
| *alumna* | : | *alumnae* |
| *antenna* | : | *antennae* (also *antennas*) |
| *formula* | : | *formulae* (also *formulas*) |
| *larva* | : | *larvae* |
| *nebula* | : | *nebulae* (also *nebulas*) |
| *scapula* | : | *scapulae* (more commonly *scapulas*) |
| *verruca* | : | *verrucae*, pronounced /ve-ruu-see/ (but more commonly *verrucas*) |
| *vertebra* | : | *vertebrae* (also *vertebras*) |

Certain technical medical terms ending in **-a**, all of Greek origin, may form plurals in **-mata** (though plurals in **-s** are also possible): *carcinomata* or *carcinomas*, *melanomata* or *melanomas*, etc.

Note also *stigmata*, the plural of *stigma* in the sense of 'marks resembling Christ's wounds that appear on the bodies of certain holy people', as opposed to *stigmas*, the plural of *stigma* in the sense of 'disgrace'.

## -ae-, -e-

There are a number of words in English — *mediaeval, encyclopaedia, haemoglobin, aesthetic*, for example — in which the *a* is optional. In American English, the forms without the *a* — *medieval, encyclopedia*, etc — are standard; in British English, the *a* is generally retained, except in *medieval*, which is now far more common than *mediaeval*, and *encyclopedia*, which is now as common as *encyclopaedia*.

 Although the *a* and *e* were formerly often written as a ligature *æ*, they are now normally written as separate letters.

See also -OE-, -E-.

## all

In most compounds, **all** is spelt with a double *l*: *all-important, all-in*, etc. In a few words, the **all** is reduced to a prefix **al-**: *almighty, almost, already, altogether*.

 Notice the difference between the following:

> *He had already left when I arrived* (= 'before I arrived')
> *Are you all ready now?* (= 'all of you')
>
> *I'm not altogether satisfied with your work* (= 'completely')
> *Altogether, we've collected £500* (= 'in total')
> *Altogether, it's not been a bad day* (= 'all things considered')
> *I'll put these books all together on the shelf* (= 'all in a group in one place')

Note also that although *alright* is appearing with increasing frequency in present-day colloquial written English and will doubtless one day become fully accepted, it is not yet an acceptable variant of *all right* in formal writing.

## -ance, -ence

The two main problems connected with these word-endings are

(a) which spelling to choose (see below), and

215

(b) what changes to make to the form of the words the endings are added to (see page 218).

Also covered in this entry are the spellings of words ending in **-nt** and **-ncy** (see page 218).

### ✦ Choosing between *-ance* and *-ence*

As with some other difficult areas of English spelling, this problem has its origins in Latin grammar, where the choice between *a* and *e* was predictable. Unfortunately, there are no easy-to-learn general rules to assist you to make the correct choice in English. There are, however, a number of clues to the correct spelling, and the most helpful of them are given here.

> **Follow the sounds /k/ and /g/ with *-ance*; follow /s/ and /j/ with *-ence*.**

If the letter before the ending is a 'hard' *c* or 'hard' *g*, then **-ance** will be the correct ending (because if the ending was **-ence**, the *e* would 'soften' the *c* to an /s/ sound and the *g* to a /j/ sound): *arrogance, elegance, significance.*

It follows that if the letter is a 'soft' *c* or *g* (pronounced /s/ or /j/ respectively), the ending will almost always be **-ence**: *adolescence, effervescence, innocence, intelligence, negligence, reminiscence, reticence.*

>  There are only two common exceptions to the above rule, *allegiance* and *vengeance*.
>
> Notice also that the rule does not work for words where the ending is preceded by the letter *s*, which will of course be pronounced /s/ even before **-ance**. Fortunately, there are only four common words in this category: *nuisance, obeisance, reconnaissance* and *renaissance*.

> **Look for guidance from the word-families.**

Words related to verbs ending in **-ate** or to nouns ending in **-ation** will normally end in **-ance**:

|  |  |  |  |
|---|---|---|---|
| dominate | : | dominance | tolerate : tolerance |

Similarly, many words ending in **-ence** are related to adjectives which end in **-ential** or **-ental**:

| consequential | : | consequence | providential | : | providence |
|---|---|---|---|---|---|
| incidental | : | incidence | prudential | : | prudence |
| influential | : | influence |  |  |  |

or to verbs ending in a stressed **-ent**:

| absent | : | absence | present | : | presence |
|---|---|---|---|---|---|

216

Other words in a word family may equally give a clue to the correct spelling if the corresponding *a* or *e* they contain is clearly pronounced:

| | | | |
|---|---|---|---|
| *ignoramus* | : *ignorance* | *circumstantial* | : *circumstances* |
| *vigilante* | : *vigilance* | *intelligentsia* | : *intelligence* |

> ⚠ One exception is *violate* : *violence*.

> **The form of the 'core' word to which the ending has been added may sometimes give a clue to the correct ending to use.**

i)  Nouns formed from verbs ending in **-ear**, **-ure** and **-y** end in **-ance**:

| | | | |
|---|---|---|---|
| *ally* | : *alliance* | *endure* | : *endurance* |
| *appear* | : *appearance* | *forbear* | : *forbearance* |
| *assure* | : *assurance* | *insure* | : *insurance* |
| *clear* | : *clearance* | *vary* | : *variance* |
| *defy* | : *defiance* | | |

ii)  Nouns formed from verbs which end in **-ere** will end in **-ence**:

| | | | |
|---|---|---|---|
| *cohere* | : *coherence* | *revere* | : *reverence* |
| *interfere* | : *interference* | | |

> ⚠ Note *perseverance*.

iii)  Thanks to the rules of Latin grammar, you can nearly always be sure that words which have **-cid-**, **-sid-**, **-fid-**, **-vid-**, **-flu-**, **-qu-** or **-sist-** immediately before the ending will end in **-ence**:

| | | |
|---|---|---|
| *confidence* | *influence* | *sequence* |
| *eloquence* | *providence* | *subsistence* |

> ⚠ The only two common exceptions are *assistance* and *resistance*.

iv)  For verbs which end in *r* preceded by a single vowel, the general rule is that if the final syllable of the verb is stressed, the ending for the noun will be **-ence**; whereas if the stress is on any other syllable, the ending will be **-ance**:

| | | | |
|---|---|---|---|
| con'fer | : *conference* | o'ccur | : *occurrence* |
| de'ter | : *deterrence* | pre'fer | : *preference* |

but

| | | | |
|---|---|---|---|
| de'liver | : *deliverance* | 'hinder | : *hindrance* |
| 'further | : *furtherance* | 'utter | : *utterance* |

In spite of the stress pattern of the base verb *'differ*, notice that *difference* ends in *-ence*.

## ✦ Changes to the form of the 'core' word

### ● Final *e*

The final *e* of a verb is dropped before *-ance* and *-ence*:

| | | | | |
|---|---|---|---|---|
| assure | : | assurance | guide | : | guidance |
| cohere | : | coherence | persevere | : | perseverance |

### ● Doubling of final consonants

In general, with consonants other than *r*, it is safe to follow the spelling of the present participle (the *-ing* form of the verb). That is to say, when there is a doubled consonant in the present participle, there will be a doubled consonant in the *-ance/-ence* noun also:

| | | | | |
|---|---|---|---|---|
| admit | : | admitting | : | admittance |
| rid | : | ridding | : | riddance |
| excel | : | excelling | : | excellence |

For further details, see DOUBLING OF FINAL CONSONANTS.

⚠ The rule for a final *r* is more complicated. The doubling or non-doubling of the *r* depends on the stress pattern of the *-ence* noun (not of the core verb it is based on) in accordance with the following rule: *if the noun is stressed on the vowel immediately preceding the r, double the r; if it is not, leave a single r.* Thus we have *de'terrence* and *oc'currence* with a double *r*, and *'conference*, *'difference*, and *'preference* with a single *r*. (Note that this is <u>not</u> quite the same as the rule for doubling the *r* in the present and past participles – see DOUBLING OF FINAL CONSONANTS.)

### ● Loss of the *e* before the *r*

In a few words, the *e* before the *r* in the core verb is dropped in the noun: *encumbrance* (from *encumber*), *entrance* (from *enter*), *hindrance* (from *hinder*) and *remembrance* (from *remember*).

## ✦ *-ant, -ent, -ancy, -ency*

The guidance on words ending in *-ance* and *-ence* generally applies equally well to related words in *-ant/-ent* and *-ancy/-ency*.

There is a small group of words ending in ***-ant/-ent*** which present a particular problem, in that their spelling varies according to whether they are used as nouns or as adjectives:

> *dependant, descendant, pendant* and *propellant* are <u>nouns</u>;
>
> *dependent, descendent, pendent* and *propellent* are <u>adjectives</u>.

If in doubt, remember that just as the indefinite article *a* is used with nouns (eg *a dog, a book*, etc), so also the vowel *a* is the right one to use for the nouns in the above list. This also works for the noun *intendant*.

*Independent* is the only correct spelling for this word whether an adjective or a noun. Notice also the spelling of the noun *superint<u>e</u>ndent*.

## anti-

Words beginning with ***anti-*** are generally written without a hyphen before a consonant but usually with a hyphen before a following vowel (eg *anti-aircraft, anti-establishment*), and always before a following *i* (eg *anti-inflationary*) and before a capital letter (eg *anti-Semitic*). The following words are nevertheless usually hyphenated:

| | | |
|---|---|---|
| *anti-gravity* | *anti-marketeer* | *anti-personnel* |
| *anti-hero* | *anti-novel* | |

## apostrophe

### ✦ Use of the apostrophe to mark deletions

An ***apostrophe*** is often used to show that one or more letters or figures have been omitted from a word or number: *can't* is a shortened form of *cannot*, *it's* of *it is* (as is the archaic form *'tis*), *she'll* of *she will*, *I'd* of *I would* or *I had*, the *'30s* of the *1930s*.

Some words, known as ***clipped forms*** (see page 2), are in origin abbreviations of longer words and were formerly often spelt with an apostrophe (eg *'bus* for *omnibus*, *'plane* for *aeroplane*). This is no longer correct, and these and similar words should be written without apostrophes: *bus, flu, phone, plane*, and similarly *decaff* (= *decaffeinated coffee*), *exam, trad* (= *traditional*), *vac* (= *vacation*), etc.

Note that when *and* is abbreviated in informal writing to *'n'*, there should be <u>two</u> apostrophes, one for each letter omitted: *rock'n'roll* □ *cheese 'n' onion crisps*.

Apostrophes have in the past been regularly used in dialect writing to indicate where a consonant of Standard English did not appear in the equivalent dialect word: eg Scots *ba'* for *ball*, *wa'* for *wall*, etc. This often wrongly gives the impression that dialects are slovenly, substandard forms of English and that dialect speakers are carelessly dropping consonants, whereas in fact the consonants of the Standard English forms of the words simply do not belong in the dialect forms of the words at all. This use of apostrophes is now deprecated and, at least in Scots, increasingly abandoned.

### ✦ Use of apostrophes in possessive nouns

The general rules which apply to the use of apostrophes with possessives are quite straightforward, but there are a few important exceptions to the rules which must also be noted. The following are the basic rules —

> **The possessive form of a noun is shown in writing by the addition of *'s* to the noun.**

Examples:

| | |
|---|---|
| *the child's dog* | *James's dog* |
| *the children's dog* | *Robert Burns's dog* |

> **If the noun is plural and already ends in *s*, add an apostrophe alone.**

examples:

| | |
|---|---|
| *the boys' dog* | *in two months' time* |

Together, these two rules amount to a very simple rule:

> **Write what you hear or say.**

In all the examples above, the written form mirrors the spoken form: where an additional *s* is pronounced in a spoken possessive form (*child* → *child's*, *James* → *James's*), it is added in the written form, and where no *s* is added in the spoken form, none is added in the written form either (*boys* → *boys'*).

 In a few exceptional cases, a singular noun ending in *s* is followed by an apostrophe alone rather than by *'s*. The main exceptions are names whose pronunciation with an additional *s* would be difficult or clumsy: *If you compare the two cars, you'll find that the Mercedes' engine is the more powerful.* Biblical and ancient Greek and Roman names which end in *s* may also be treated in this way, as in *Moses' laws* and *Xerxes' army*, but although still correct, this practice is not as prevalent as it used to be. The existence of such exceptions to the general rule will not, however, cause you any problems if you remember that in all such cases, ***the written form should reflect the pronunciation of the spoken form***: if you pronounce an extra *s* in the possessive, write one; if you do not pronounce an extra *s*, do not write one.

In certain expressions with *sake*, nouns ending in *s* which by the nature of the construction ought to be spelt with a possessive *'s* are now usually written without even an apostrophe: compare *for heaven's sake* and *for goodness sake* (not *goodness's sake*, nor even *goodness' sake*).

Do not insert apostrophes into possessive pronouns: the correct spellings are *yours, hers, its* (*it's = it is*), *ours, theirs*. *One's*, however, <u>is</u> correct: *One must look after one's own family.*

Note also that the possessive form of *who* is *whose* (*who's = who is*): *Whose book is this?*

## ✦ Apostrophes in plural nouns

 Apostrophes should <u>not</u> normally be used in the formation of plural nouns. Plural forms such as *book's, bag's, lolly's* are very common but incorrect.

An apostrophe is permitted in plurals in certain specific cases, mainly for the sake of clarity:

i) An apostrophe is frequently written in ***the plurals of certain short words***:

*do's* (as in *do's and don'ts*)
*me's* (as in *I feel there are two me's at the moment*)
*set-to's* (eg *I've had a few set-to's with her recently*)
*he's* and *she's* (as in *Are the puppies he's or she's?*)

*Dos, set-tos, mes, hes* and *shes* are equally correct.

ii) When the word in the plural is ***the title of a book, play, etc***, *'s* is often used instead of *s* alone: *There have been three <u>Macbeth's</u> performed in Edinburgh in the past six months* (= three different versions of the play 'Macbeth'). Here again, *s* alone is equally correct.

iii) *'s*, rather than *s*, is normal for ***the plural form of a word quoted*** from something else: *There are too many <u>that's</u> in that sentence.*

iv) *'s* should be used to form ***the plural of single letters and figures***: *Dot your i's and cross your t's* □ *Write a row of 2's and then a row of 3's.*

With ***longer numbers***, eg in dates, both *'s* and *s* are permissible: *Were you around in the 1930s/1930's?* □ *How many 30s/30's are there in 240?*

v) An *s* alone should be used to form ***the plural of abbreviations*** made up of a sequence of initial letters: the correct plural of *MP*, for example, is *MPs*, not *MP's*. However, for the sake of clarity, an apostrophe may be used when the letters are all lower-case: *lbw's*.

**-ar** see -ER.

**-asy** see -ACY.

## -ary, -ery, -ory

Since these endings all sound the same in British English, many people have great difficulty in remembering, or deciding, which words to spell with *a*, which with *e* and which with *o*. Unfortunately, there are only a few very general hints that can be given as guidelines to the correct spelling of such words, but looking at both the word-family and certain grammar points may be of help.

> **Use the word-family to find a related word in which the corresponding vowel is clearly pronounced.**

Examples:

| | | | | |
|---|---|---|---|---|
| *arbitration* | : | *arbitrary* | *militate* | : | *military* |
| *categorical* | : | *category* | *parliamentarian* | : | *parliamentary* |
| *contemporaneous* | : | *contemporary* | *sanitation* | : | *insanitary* |
| *imagination* | : | *imaginary* | *secretarial* | : | *secretary* |
| *historic* | : | *history* | | | |

> **Even where pronunciation is of no help, look at the structure or vowels of related words.**

For example, many nouns which end in **-ery** are related either to 'doer' nouns which end in **-er**:

| | | | | | |
|---|---|---|---|---|---|
| *baker* | : | *bakery* | *distiller* | : | *distillery* |
| *brewer* | : | *brewery* | *milliner* | : | *millinery* |
| *confectioner* | : | *confectionery* | *stationer* | : | *stationery* |

or to verbs which end in **-er**:

| | | | | | |
|---|---|---|---|---|---|
| *deliver* | : | *delivery* | *embroider* | : | *embroidery* |
| *discover* | : | *discovery* | *upholster* | : | *upholstery* |

The same parallels usually hold true for **-ory** and **-ary** words also:

| | | | | | |
|---|---|---|---|---|---|
| *director* | : | *directory* | *burglar* | : | *burglary* |
| *predator* | : | *predatory* | | | |

In a similar way, adjectives which end in **-ery** are generally derived from nouns or verbs which end in **-er**:

| | | | | | |
|---|---|---|---|---|---|
| *flower* | : | *flowery* | *thunder* | : | *thundery* |

| rubber | : | rubbery | water | : | watery |
|--------|---|---------|-------|---|--------|
| splutter | : | spluttery | | | |

---

⚠ Notice that some words in the above categories drop the vowel before **-ry**:

| ancestry | idolatry | ministry |
|----------|----------|----------|
| forestry | laundry | |
| angry | hungry | wintry |

*Jewellery/jewelry* are both correct.

---

**If what precedes the *-ry* ending in a <u>noun</u> is recognizable as an English word, the ending is likely to be *-ery*.**

Examples:

| buffoon | : | buffoonery | green | : | greenery |
|---------|---|------------|-------|---|----------|
| debauch | : | debauchery | tomfool | : | tomfoolery |

Compare on the other hand *dignitary*, *laboratory* and *vocabulary* — there are no words *dignit*, *laborat* or *vocabul* in English.

This rule applies equally to words in which predictable spelling changes are made, such as the doubling of final consonants or the dropping of a final silent *e*. Such changes must be ignored when the status of the core word is considered:

| distil | : | distillery | pig | : | piggery |
|--------|---|-----------|-----|---|---------|
| machine | : | machinery | slave | : | slavery |

---

⚠ The following words do not fit into any predictable pattern:

| accessory | depository | functionary | missionary |
|-----------|-----------|-------------|------------|
| artillery | derisory | gallery | preparatory |
| boundary | dictionary | grocery | provisory |
| cemetery | directory | infirmary | satisfactory |
| commentary | dispensary | inventory | secretary |
| compulsory | dysentery | legionary | tributary |
| consistory | effrontery | migratory | visionary |

Note the difference between the noun *stationery* (= writing-paper, envelopes, etc) and the adjective *stationary* (= not moving).

---

**-as, -ae** see -AE.

## -c

> In order to preserve the hard /k/ sound of the letter *c*, words ending in a *c* add a *k* before word-endings which begin with *e, i* or *y*.

Examples:

| | | |
|---|---|---|
| *bivouac* | : | *bivouacking, bivouacked* |
| *colic* | : | *colicky* |
| *frolic* | : | *frolicking, frolicked, frolicker* |
| *garlic* | : | *garlicky* |
| *mimic* | : | *mimicking, mimicked* |
| *panic* | : | *panicking, panicked, panicker, panicky* |
| *picnic* | : | *picnicking, picnicked, picnicker* |
| *plastic* | : | *plasticky* |
| *rheumatics* | : | *rheumaticky* |
| *tarmac* | : | *tarmacking, tarmacked* |
| *traffic* | : | *trafficking, trafficked, trafficker* |

---

⚠️ *Arc, sync* (= *synchronize*), *talc* and *zinc* are exceptions to the rule:

| | | |
|---|---|---|
| *arc* | : | *arcing, arced* |
| *sync* | : | *syncing, synced* |
| *talc* | : | *talcing, talced* or *talcking, talcked,* and *talcky* |
| *zinc* | : | *zincing, zinced, zincy* or *zinking, zinked, zinky* or *zincking, zincked, zincky* |

---

## capital letters

✦ **The basic rules of capitalization**

> **The first word of a sentence must begin with a capital letter.**
>
> **Capitals are required for the first letter of the names of people, towns, countries, religions, etc, and of words derived from these.**

Examples:

*John □ Anne □ Bernard Smith □ Australia □ Ireland □ Jesus Christ □ South Africa □ Islam*

*Georgian furniture □ the Cromwellian army □ the Australian cricket team □ the Irish Republic □ the former Soviet Union □ a South African plant □ Christian □ Muslim □ Sikh □ Shakespearian □ Kafkaesque*

*Chestnut Avenue □ the Great North Road □ Waterloo Station □ the Bay of Biscay □ Mount Everest □ the Thames □ the River Clyde □ Loch Lomond*

Many words which are in origin proper names or are derived from proper names do not take a capital letter: *pasteurize* (from *Louis Pasteur*), *wellington* (from the *Duke of Wellington*), *sandwich* (from the *Earl of Sandwich*), *watt* (from *James Watt*), *ampere* (from *Louis Ampère*). The difference between these words and the words in the category above is that these exceptions denote things that are <u>named after</u> people or places rather referring directly to the people or places themselves.

Nevertheless, if an adjective is one which denotes or relates to a country or region, it will begin with a capital letter whether the relationship is still close or not: *Cornish pasty, Dutch courage, French leave, Turkish baths*. The two main exceptions to this rule are *arabic numbers* and *roman numerals*.

In some cases, forms with or without a capital are equally correct: *plaster of paris/Paris □ platonic/Platonic love*.

Names of **seasons** should not normally be capitalized, but if necessary write *Spring* instead of *spring* for the sake of clarity.

*Sir, Madam*, etc should always have a capital in the formal salutation at the beginning of a letter (ie *Dear Sir*), but not elsewhere (*Can I help you, sir?*).

---

**Capitals must be used for the first letter of all 'important' words in titles of books, plays, people, organizations, etc.**

(Words that are <u>not</u> 'important' in this sense are *a/an, the*, conjunctions such as *and, but, if, when*, and prepositions such as *at, in, of, off, on, with*).

Examples:

> *President Clinton □ Queen Elizabeth □ the Prince of Wales □ Sir Bernard Smith
> □ Admiral of the Fleet Lord Brown
> the Department of Social Services
> a book entitled 'Big Fish'*

(Note, however, that when one of the 'unimportant' words is the first word in the title of a book or play, it must have a capital: *This book is called 'The Biggest Fish in the World'*.)

---

 When a title is hyphenated, both parts take capitals: *Major-General Smith*.

 Words which require a capital in names and titles do not necessarily require one in other circumstances:

*the Republic of South Africa* but *South Africa is a republic*

> *South America* but *holidaying in the south of France* (*in the South* if 'south' is taken as a definable region, eg the southern part of the United States)
>
> *the President of the United States* (= a particular person, the current holder of that office) but *How many presidents of the United States have there been?*
>
> *a liberal host* (= 'generous') but *the Liberal Democrats* (= the title of a political party)
>
> On the other hand, words that are not usually capitalized should be if they are used as proper names:
>
>> *For I must go where lazy Peace*
>> *Will hide her drowsy head;*
>> *And, for the sport of kings, increase*
>> *The number of the dead.*
>>
>> — William Davenant
>
> When a book or periodical title begins with *The*, it is correct not to capitalize the *The* when referring to the book or periodical within a sentence:
>
>> *I saw that in the* Times *yesterday.*
>
> But it is also correct to write
>
>> *I saw that in* The Times *yesterday.*

## ✦ Capitals with proprietary names

Capitals are required for all brand names, even where the proprietary name has come to be used generically, although *hoover, xerox*, etc are often found. Companies generally deprecate their trademarks being used as generic terms and written without capital letters, as it threatens the trademark status of the proprietary name, so although it is acceptable not to use capitals in general, informal contexts, it is advisable to use a capital letter with any word that has trademark status in formal or technical writing. Check in a reliable dictionary or a trademark directory. No capital is required when such words are used as verbs, however: *He went off to xerox the report.*

## ✦ Capitals in abbreviations

For the use of capital letters in abbreviations, see ABBREVIATIONS, page 206.

## ✦ Capitals in German nouns

All nouns in German are written with initial capital letters, and it is normal practice to use capitals when writing such words in English: *Ostpolitik, Weltanschauung, Weltschmerz, Zeitgeist.*

However, some nouns of German origin are now so well established in English that they are no longer written with a capital: *blitzkrieg, festschrift, kitsch, lederhosen, lieder, realpolitik, schadenfreude.* A few words may be written with

## -ce, -se

**Words of this type which are pronounced with a /z/ sound are written with an s.**

Examples: *advise, devise, exercise, house* (verb), *refuse* (verb), *revise, treatise*, etc.

(But see also -ISE, -IZE.)

**Words which are pronounced with an /s/ sound immediately following a vowel are generally spelt with a c.**

Examples: *advice, deduce, device, justice, lice, mice, office, rejoice, voice*, etc.

 Among the exceptions are *house* (noun), *louse, mouse, obtuse, profuse, 'refuse* (noun).

Note also the spelling of the <u>noun</u> *prophecy* and the <u>verb</u> *prophesy*.

**Nouns related to adjectives ending in -ant or -ent are spelt with a c.**

Examples:

| | | | |
|---|---|---|---|
| *different* | : *difference* | *ignorant* | : *ignorance* |

The same holds for nouns ending in /-an-si/, and for all nouns related to verbs in the ways indicated in the article -ANCE, -ENCE:

| | | | |
|---|---|---|---|
| *accountant* | : *accountancy* | *guide* | : *guidance* |
| *expedient* | : *expediency* | *interfere* | : *interference* |

<u>**Adjectives**</u> **ending in /-ens/ are spelt with an s.**

Examples: *dense, immense, intense, tense*.

Other words which are pronounced with an /s/ following a consonant might have either *c* or *s* in writing, eg:

| | | | |
|---|---|---|---|
| *advance* | *endorse* | *pence* | *romance* |
| *commence* | *fence* | *pronounce* | *sense* |
| *commerce* | *finance* | *recompense* | *since* |
| *dance* | *hence* | *response* | *tense* (noun) |

227

**American English and British English**

In British English, *licence* and *practice* are nouns, *license* and *practise* the corresponding verbs. In American usage, the forms *license* and *practice* are used for both the noun and the verb. In British English, the nouns *defence*, *offence* and *pretence* are written with a *c*, but the corresponding forms in American English are written with *s*. Note that the related adjectives *defensive* and *offensive* are written with an *s* in both British and American English.

The noun *vice* in the sense of 'a fault or bad habit' is written with a *c* in both British and American English, but in the sense of 'a tool for holding things firmly' it is written with *c* in British English and *s* in American English.

## -cede, -ceed, -sede

**The best guess is always *-cede*.**

Examples: *concede, precede, recede*, etc.

 Only four words do not follow this rule: *exceed, proceed, succeed; supersede*.

*Supersede* comes from the same Latin root as *sedentary* and *sediment*.

For the other three, there is a little nonsense jingle that runs 'With *suc, ex* and *pro*, the *e*'s together go'.

## -ch, -tch

There is a *t* in *dispatch* but not in *detach*, and in *fetch* but not in *teach*. The general rules, which cover most cases, are as follows:

**If what precedes the /ch/ sound is a consonant, the /ch/ will be written *ch*.**

Examples:

| | | | |
|---|---|---|---|
| *branch* | *filch* | *squelch* | *zilch* |

and for those who pronounce *r*'s in this position:

| | | | |
|---|---|---|---|
| *arch* | *church* | *search* | *torch* |

**If what precedes the /ch/ sound is a vowel written with a single letter, /ch/ will be written *tch*.**

Examples:

| | | | |
|---|---|---|---|
| *catch* | *fetch* | *scratch* | *watch* |
| *dispatch* | *hutch* | *vetch* | *witch* |

**If what precedes the /ch/ sound is a vowel written with more than one letter, /ch/ will be written *ch*.**

Examples:

| | | | |
|---|---|---|---|
| *approach* | *couch* | *mooch* | *teach* |
| *brooch* | *debauch* | *screech* | *touch* |

and for those who do not sound an *r* in this position (therefore treating the *r* as part of the vowel):

| | | | |
|---|---|---|---|
| *arch* | *church* | *search* | *torch* |

> ⚠ A few common words have *ch* where *tch* would be expected by the above rule:
>
> | | | | |
> |---|---|---|---|
> | *attach* | *much* | *sandwich* | *such* |
> | *detach* | *ostrich* | *spinach* | *which* |
> | *enrich* | *rich* | | |
>
> Many ***place-names*** are similarly exceptions:
>
> *Bromwich, Greenwich, Harwich, Norwich, Sandwich, Woolwich*, etc, and *Sandbach* and *Wisbech*.
>
> One word, *aitch*, the name of the letter *h*, has *tch* where *ch* would be expected by the above rule.
>
> Note also that this rule does not in any case apply if the *ch* is not pronounced /ch/: *broch, Czech, Enoch, epoch, Harlech, loch, Munich, pibroch*.

**-*cion*** see -TION.

## comparatives and superlatives

The comparative and superlative forms of adjectives and adverbs are generally formed in one of two ways:

a) by adding **-*er*** or **-*est*** to the simple form of the 'core' word (*fast* : *faster, fastest*)

b) by preceding the word by ***more*** or ***most*** (*beautiful* : *more beautiful, most beautiful*; *quickly* : *more quickly, most quickly*).

Sometimes there are minor changes to the spelling of the 'core' word (*big* : *bigger, biggest*; *dry* : *drier, driest*).

## ✦ Comparatives and superlatives of adjectives

### • One-syllable adjectives

> **The comparatives and superlatives of one-syllable adjectives are generally formed by adding the inflections *-er* and *-est* to the simple form of the 'core' word.**

Examples:

| | | |
|---|---|---|
| *black* | : | *blacker, blackest* |
| *new* | : | *newer, newest* |
| *small* | : | *smaller, smallest* |

 ***One-syllable past participles*** are an exception:

| | | |
|---|---|---|
| *bored* | : | *more bored, most bored* |
| *worn* | : | *more worn, most worn* |

However, *tired* <u>has</u> inflected forms *tireder, tiredest*.

Note also *do one's damnedest*.

Also exceptions are *good* and *bad*:

| | | |
|---|---|---|
| *good* | : | *better, best* |
| *bad* | : | *worse, worst* |

*Mere* has a superlative form *merest* but no comparative form *merer*.

### • Two-syllable adjectives

> **Two-syllable adjectives ending in *-y*, *-ow* and *-er* generally form inflected comparatives and superlatives.**

Examples:

| | | |
|---|---|---|
| *silly* | : | *sillier, silliest* |
| *shallow* | : | *shallower, shallowest* |
| *clever* | : | *cleverer, cleverest* |

 *Eager* and *proper* form comparatives and superlatives with ***more*** and ***most***.

> **Words ending in *-le* and *-ure*, or which end in the *-ly* word-ending, may have either type of comparative and superlative.**

Examples:

>  *simple*   :   *simpler/more simple, simplest/most simple*
>  *obscure*  :   *obscurer/more obscure, obscurest/most obscure*
>  *lonely*   :   *lonelier/more lonely, loneliest/most lonely*

---

 A number of other two-syllable adjectives also have both options:

> *common*   :   *commoner/more common, commonest/most common*

and similarly *cruel, extreme, handsome, honest, pleasant, polite, quiet, remote, sincere, solemn, solid, stupid* and *tranquil*.

---

**All other two-syllable adjectives take only the *more/most* form of comparative and superlative.**

- **Adjectives of three or more syllables**

**Adjectives of more than two syllables almost always form comparatives and superlatives with *more* and *most*.**

Examples:

>  *beautiful*   :   *more beautiful, most beautiful.*

---

 The only exceptions are three-syllable adjectives that are formed by the addition of *un-* to two-syllable words. If the two-syllable words have inflected comparatives and superlatives, so also will the *un-* forms:

> *happy, happier, happiest* → *unhappy, unhappier, unhappiest*

Up until the end of the last century, it was possible to make *-er/-est* forms of comparatives and superlatives for two- and three-syllable words which nowadays can only take *more* and *most*. For example,

> *People ought to be modester*
> — Thomas Carlyle

and in a magazine of 1788, there is a reference to a bird being '*one of the beautifullest of the whole parrot kind*'.

Do not be surprised if you come across such forms in older writing but do not copy them: they are not correct in 20th-century English.

---

- **Compound adjectives**

> **Compound adjectives the 'core' of which is a noun form comparatives and superlatives with *more* and *most*.**

This is true even if the first element of the compound form has an inflected comparative and superlative:

| | | |
|---:|:---:|:---|
| *big* | : | *bigger, biggest* |
| *big-headed* | : | *more big-headed, most big-headed* |

(*head* is a noun)

| | | |
|---:|:---:|:---|
| *short* | : | *shorter, shortest* |
| *short-sighted* | : | *more short-sighted, most short-sighted* |

(*sight* is a noun)

| | | |
|---:|:---:|:---|
| *bad* | : | *worse, worst* |
| *bad-tempered* | : | *more bad-tempered, most bad-tempered* |

(*temper* is a noun)

> **Compound adjectives of which the 'core' is a verb form comparatives and superlatives either with *-er* and *-est* or with *more* and *most*.**

Examples:

| | | |
|---:|:---:|:---|
| *hard-wearing* | : | *harder-wearing/more hard-wearing, hardest-wearing/most hard-wearing* |

(*wear* is a verb)

| | | |
|---:|:---:|:---|
| *hard-working* | : | *harder-working/more hard-working, hardest-working/most hard-working* |

(*work* is a verb)

| | | |
|---:|:---:|:---|
| *long-lasting* | : | *longer-lasting/more long-lasting, longest-lasting/most long-lasting* |

(*last* is a verb)

> **Compound adjectives of which the first element is *good*, *well* or *ill* usually inflect this first part.**

Examples:

| | | |
|---:|:---:|:---|
| *well-known* | : | *better-known, best-known* |
| *good-looking* | : | *better-looking, best-looking* |

although forms with ***more*** and ***most*** are not incorrect.

## ✦ Adverbs

### • Adverbs that are the same in form as adjectives

> Adverbs that are the same in form as adjectives have inflected forms of comparative and superlative (ie, with the word-endings *-er* and *-est*).

Examples:

> *fast* : *faster, fastest*      *early* : *earlier, earliest*

### • Adverbs formed by the addition of *-ly*

> Adverbs formed by adding *-ly* to adjectives form comparatives and superlatives with *more* and *most*.

Example:

> *beautifully* : *more beautifully, most beautifully*

> ⚠ *Badly* is an exception; it has the irregular comparative *worse* and the superlative *worst*.
>
> Also exceptions are *well* and *ill*:
>
> > *well* : *better, best*      *ill* : *worse, worst*

## ✦ Spelling rules

> In general, *-er* and *-est* are added directly to the basic 'core' forms of the adjectives and adverbs.

Examples:

> *hard* : *harder, hardest*      *fast* : *faster, fastest*

### • Final *e*

When the adjective ends in *e*, the *e* is dropped before *-er* and *-est* are added:

> *white* : *whiter, whitest*      *simple* : *simpler, simplest*

> ⚠ If the word ends in two *e*'s, one *e* is dropped:
>
> > *free* : *freer, freest*

> **If the word ends in a single consonant, and if the vowel preceding that consonant is written with a single letter, and if the vowel and consonant are part of the stressed syllable of the word, then the consonant is doubled before the ending.**

Examples:

*red* : *redder, reddest*        *big* : *bigger, biggest*

 A final *l* is doubled regardless of the stress:
*cruel* : *crueller, cruellest*

### • Final *y*
A final *y* preceded by a consonant changes to *i*:

*funny* : *funnier, funniest*        *silly* : *sillier, silliest*

 In the case of certain one-syllable words in which the *y* is pronounced /iy/ as in *my*, both *y* and *i* are correct:

*shy* : *shyer* or *shier, shyest* or *shiest*
*sly* : *slyer* or *slier, slyest* or *sliest*
*wry* : *wryer* or *wrier, wryest* or *wriest*

In the case of *dry*, the preferred forms are *drier* and *driest*; with *spry*, *spryer* and *spryest*.

A final *y* preceded by a vowel remains as *y* (eg *grey* : *greyer, greyest*), unless it is part of an adjective ending in *-ey* which has been formed from a noun (eg *clayey* from *clay*, *matey* from *mate*), in which case the *ey* changes to *i*:

*funny* : *funnier, funniest*        *matey* : *matier, matiest*

## -ction, -xion

> **If in doubt, opt for *-ction*.**

Most nouns of this type are spelt **-ction**, eg:

| | | | |
|---|---|---|---|
| *action* | *conviction* | *genuflection* | *protection* |
| *collection* | *deflection* | *infection* | *reflection* |
| *conjunction* | *distinction* | *instruction* | *satisfaction* |
| *connection* | *extinction* | *production* | *section* |

In British English, but not American English, a number of words may be written either *-xion* or *-ction*, eg *connexion, deflexion, flexion, genuflexion, inflexion, reflexion, retroflexion*. The *-ction* forms are generally now commoner than the *-xion* forms, except for *flexion*, but some people still prefer *connexion, genuflexion* and *inflexion*. *Reflexion* is found mostly in scientific texts.

Two common words <u>must</u> be written with an *x*: *complexion* and *crucifixion*. Note these, and the not quite so common *fluxion* and *transfixion*.

**-cy** see -ACY and -CE.

**-d** see -ED.

## -dge

In most cases, the final *e* of words ending in *-dge* (such as *hedge, fridge, knowledge*) is dropped before suffixes beginning with *e*, *i* or *y*, but retained before all other suffixes:

| | | | | | |
|---|---|---|---|---|---|
| *judge* + *-ed* | : | *judged* | *judge* + *-s* | : | *judges* |
| *judge* + *-ing* | : | *judging* | *judge* + *-ship* | : | *judgeship* |
| *dodge* + *-er* | : | *dodger* | *dodge* + *-s* | : | *dodges* |
| *dodge* + *-y* | : | *dodgy* | | | |
| *bridge* + *-ed* | : | *bridged* | *bridge* + *-less* | : | *bridgeless* |
| *drudge* + *-ery* | : | *drudgery* | *drudge* + *-ism* | : | *drudgism* |
| *wedge* + *-ed* | : | *wedged* | *wedge* + *-like* | : | *wedgelike* |

 Words formed with the suffixes *-able*, *-ment* and *-ling* are exceptions to this rule:

i)  Before *-able*, the *e* may be dropped, but nowadays is usually retained:

  *bridge* + *-able*  :  *bridgeable* or *bridgable*
  *knowledge* + *-able*  :  *knowledgeable* or *knowledgable*

ii)  Before *-ment*, the *e* is again usually retained but may equally correctly be dropped:

  *judgement* or *judgment*
  *acknowledgement* or *acknowledgment*

iii)  Before the ending *-ling*, the *e* is usually dropped (eg *fledgling*), but, although less common, forms with *e* retained (*fledgeling*) are not incorrect.

- In most **compound words**, the *e* is retained (*bridgehead, edgeways, hedgehog, lodgepole, sledgehammer*).

However, many **place-names** and **family names** are exceptions: compare *Bridgeport, Bridgetown, Bridgewater* (name of various places in North America), *Edgecombe, Edgefield, Sedgefield* and *Sedgemoor*, all of which follow the rule and retain the *e*, and *Bridgford, Bridgnorth, Bridgwater* (in Somerset), *Edgware, Hodgkin, Sedgwick* and *Wedgwood*, which do not.

---

 Note some commonly misspelt words which do <u>not</u> end in **-dge**: *allege, college, privilege, sacrilege*. Similarly *pigeon* and *wigeon* (*widgeon* is also correct but not common).

---

## double consonants within words

A common error is the writing of a single instead of a double consonant in words such as *misspell, really, illegible* and *unnecessary*. If, however, you think for a moment how such words are made up, and consider the spelling of each part of the words separately, no such mistakes should occur:

| | | |
|---:|:---:|:---|
| *misspell* | = | *mis-* ('wrongly') + *spell* |
| *unnecessary* | = | *un-* ('not') + *necessary* |
| *illegible* | = | *il-* ('not') + *legible* |
| *immortal* | = | *im-* ('not') + *mortal* |
| *dissatisfaction* | = | *dis-* ('not') + *satisfaction* |
| *really* | = | *real* + *-ly* |
| *suddenness* | = | *sudden* + *-ness* |
| *drunkenness* | = | *drunken* + *-ness* |

## doubling of final consonants

The final consonant of many words is doubled when a suffix (or 'word-ending') is added:

| | | | | | |
|---:|:---:|:---|---:|:---:|:---|
| *drop* | : | *dropped, dropping* | *occur* | : | *occurrence* |
| *forget* | : | *unforgettable* | *leg* | : | *leggings* |
| *grit* | : | *gritty* | *god* | : | *goddess* |
| *big* | : | *bigger, biggest* | *red* | : | *redden, reddish* |
| *council* | : | *councillor* | | | |

but in many apparently similar words the final consonant is <u>not</u> doubled:

| | | | | | |
|---:|:---:|:---|---:|:---:|:---|
| *stoop* | : | *stooped, stooping* | *prefer* | : | *preference* |
| *beat* | : | *unbeatable* | *book* | : | *booking* |
| *gossip* | : | *gossipy* | *lion* | : | *lioness* |
| *common* | : | *commoner, commonest* | *cheap* | : | *cheapen, cheapie* |

and so on. The following are the main rules governing the doubling or non-doubling of the final consonant of the 'core' word in such circumstances:

> **If the suffix begins with a consonant, eg *f*, *l* or *m*, then the final consonant of the 'core' word is never doubled.**

Examples:

| | | | |
|---|---|---|---|
| *defer* | : | *deferment* | *chief* | : | *chiefly* |
| *sin* | : | *sinful* | *glad* | : | *gladness* |
| *spot* | : | *spotless* | | |

Problems arise only with word-endings that begin with the vowels *a, e, i, o, u* or *y*.

> **If the 'core' word ends in a single consonant which is preceded by a single stressed vowel-sound written with a single letter, then the final consonant of the base is doubled when a suffix is added. If any of these conditions is not met, then the consonant is not doubled.**

Examples:

*begin, beginning, beginner*
(*Begin* ends in a single consonant preceded by a single, stressed vowel.)

*plan, planned, planning, planner*
(*Plan* ends in a single consonant; since *plan* is only one syllable long, the vowel must be stressed.)

*visit, visited, visiting, visitor*
(Stress is not on the final syllable of *visit*, so the *t* is not doubled.)

*dream, dreamed, dreaming, dreamer, dreamy*
(*Dream* ends in a single consonant, but the vowel, although stressed, is written with two letters, therefore the *m* is not doubled.)

---

 Particular care must be taken not to confuse the spelling of suffixed forms of words that end in a single consonant and those derived from words ending in a silent *e*, eg:

| | | | | | | |
|---|---|---|---|---|---|---|
| *hop* | : | *hopping, hopped* | | *hope* | : | *hoping, hoped* |
| *cap* | : | *capped* | | *cape* | : | *caped* |
| *bar* | : | *barring, barred* | | *bare* | : | *baring, bared* |

---

• **Final *c***

When the hard /k/ sound of the letter *c* is to be preserved in a word in which the *c* comes before a word-ending beginning with *e, i* or *y*, the *c* becomes *ck*:

| | | |
|---|---|---|
| *frolic* | : | *frolicking, frolicked, frolicker* |
| *garlic* | : | *garlicky* |
| *panic* | : | *panicking, panicked, panicker, panicky* |

⚠️ Note, however,

> arc : *arcing, arced*

and other exceptions noted in the entry -C, page 224.

A *k* is, of course, <u>not</u> added when the /k/ sound is 'softened' to /s/ or /sh/:

> critic : *criticism, criticize*
> electric : *electrician*

- ### Final *h*

A silent *h* which is part of the written representation of a vowel sound does not count as a consonant for the purposes of this spelling rule and is not doubled:

> hoorah : *hoorahing, hoorahed*

- ### Final *l*

Words ending in *l* are a headache, as they neither obey the basic rules consistently, nor (unfortunately) consistently disobey them.

> **Regardless of the stress pattern of the word, a final *l* preceded by a single vowel sound written with a single letter is doubled before most of the common word-endings.**

The 'common' word-endings in this case are **-ing**, **-ed**, **-er/-or**, **-ery**, **-ance/-ence**, **-ation/-ion**, **-ious/-ous**, **-y**. Thus we have not only:

> appal : *appalling, appalled*
> rebel : *rebelling, rebelled, rebellion, rebellious*
> propel : *propelling, propelled, propellor, propellant*

which follow the second of the two basic rules explained above (page 237), but also

> signal : *signalling, signalled, signaller*
> counsel : *counselling, counselled, counsellor*
> jewel : *jeweller, jewellery*
> equal : *equalling, equalled*
> gravel : *gravelly*
> libel : *libellous*
> marvel : *marvelling, marvelled, marvellous*
> cancel : *cancelling, cancelled, cancellation*

in which the *l* is doubled even though the stress is not on the last syllable of the core word.

If the vowel before the *l* is written with a double letter, *l* is not doubled (which is to say that in this case *l* follows the first general rule given above, page 237):

> sail : *sailor*    fool : *fooling, fooled*
> appeal : *appealing*

⚠  There are a number of exceptions to these rules:

  i)   *Parallel*: the *l* does not double in *paralleling* and *paralleled*. Note also the spelling of *parallelogram*.

  ii)  *Woollen* and *woolly* (in American English usually *woolen*, but *woolly*).

  iii) Two adjectives which end in **-ous** have only a single *l* before the suffix: *perilous* and *scandalous*.

One *l* is also the rule for all adjectives which are not derived from a core word which ends in *l*: *anomalous* (from *anomaly* — there is no word *anomal*), *bilious* (from *bile*, not *bil*), *credulous, fabulous, garrulous, meticulous, miraculous, nebulous, populous, querulous, ridiculous, scrupulous, scurrilous, supercilious*.

  iv)  Before the suffixes **-ise/-ize**, **-ism, -ist** and **-ity**, the final *l* is usually not doubled:

|          |   |                                       |
|----------|---|---------------------------------------|
| equal    | : | equalize, equality                    |
| special  | : | specialize, specialist, speciality    |
| final    | : | finalize, finalist, finality          |
| civil    | : | civilize, civility                    |

Here again there are exceptions:

|          |   |                                       |
|----------|---|---------------------------------------|
| crystal  | : | crystallize (and also crystalline)    |
| tranquil | : | tranquillize, tranquillity            |
| panel    | : | panellist                             |

Note also the spelling of *tonsillitis*, much more common than *tonsilitis*, although both are correct.

## • Final *p*

In British English, three common verbs which end in *p* double this when according to the stress pattern (with stress on the initial syllable) you would not expect it:

|           |   |                                          |
|-----------|---|------------------------------------------|
| worship   | : | worshipping, worshipped, worshipper      |
| kidnap    | : | kidnapping, kidnapped, kidnapper         |
| handicap  | : | handicapping, handicapped                |

(In American English, a single *p* is preferred in the derivatives of *worship*, and is optional in the derivatives of *kidnap*, but a double *p* is obligatory in *handicapping* and *handicapped*.)

## • Final *r*

A final *r* which is not pronounced at the end of the core word (in accents which do not pronounce final *r*'s) <u>is</u> doubled when a suffix is added (if the other criteria listed above are met) and the *r* is then pronounced :

|         |   |                                       |
|---------|---|---------------------------------------|
| mar     | : | marring, marred                       |
| oc'cur  | : | occurring, occurred, occurrence       |

239

(But see the note below about words that end in *-fer*.)

- **Final *t***

In a few words, the final *t* is, or may be, doubled before a suffix even where the preceding vowel is not stressed, contrary to the second basic rule (page 237). Illustrated with a following *-ed*, these are (with the preferred form given first where there is a choice):

> *benefited* (or *benefitted*)
> *formatted*
> *leafleted* (or *leafletted*)
> *parqueted* (or *parquetted*)
> *photostatted*
> *ricocheted* (but *ricochetted* if pronounced /-'she-tid/)
> *riveted* (formerly also *rivetted*)

Other words of this type should always be spelt with a single *t*: *budgeted*, *targeted*, etc.

- **Final *x***

Although only a single consonant in writing, *x* is pronounced /ks/ and counts as two consonants rather than one. The *x* is therefore not doubled before a suffix:

> box : boxed, boxer, boxes, boxing
> relax : relaxed, relaxing
> sex : sexes, sexy

- **Final *y* or *w***

A *y* or *w* which is part of the written representation of a vowel sound does not count as a consonant for the purposes of this spelling rule and is not doubled:

> enjoy : enjoying, enjoyed, enjoyable
> allow : allowing, allowed, allowable

- **-fer**

Words ending in *-fer* (eg *confer*, *prefer*) for the most part follow the general rules. Notice that when such words are followed by *-able* and *-ence*, the stress moves away from the *-fer* onto the first syllable, and the *r* is therefore not preceded by a stressed vowel and so not doubled:

> pre'fer : pre'ferring but 'preferable, 'preference
> con'fer : con'ferred but 'conference

---

 Note that although the stress does not shift from *-fer* in *in'ferable* and *trans'ferable*, the *r* is still not usually doubled. (Forms with a doubled *r* are far less common, although correct.)

---

- **-gram**

Words ending in *-gram* double the final *m* regardless of the stress pattern:

> program : programmed, programming, programmer
> diagram : diagrammatic

## • *qu-*

A *u* following a *q* counts as part of the consonant group *qu*. Therefore in a word like *quit* the *t* is considered to be preceded by only one vowel, not two. The *t* is therefore correctly doubled in *quitting* and *quitter*.

## • Silent letters

A single silent consonant at the end of a word is never doubled, even if the final syllable is stressed, eg the *z* of *pince-nez* in *pince-'nezed* (pronounced /pans-**nayd**/).

However, if one consonant <u>within</u> a written consonant group is not pronounced, it still counts for the purposes of the rules being considered in this chapter. For example, the final *n* of *condemn* is not pronounced, nor is the *l* of *calm*, but even though there is only a single pronounced consonant at the ends of these words (eg /m/ not /mn/ or /lm/), in their written form the words end in two consonants and the final consonant is therefore not doubled before a suffix:

| | | |
|---|---|---|
| *condemn* | : | *condemning, condemned* |
| *calm* | : | *calmer, calmest, calming* |

## • Compound words

A compound word is a word which is composed of two or more shorter words, eg *blackboard* (= *black* + *board*) or *snowman* (= *snow* + *man*). No matter what the stress pattern of the word is, the final consonant of a compound is doubled if, in accordance with the two basic rules (see page 237), it <u>would</u> have been doubled when not in a compound. For example, in accordance with the rules, the final *p* of *whip* is doubled in *whipping* and *whipped*; it is, therefore, correctly doubled also in *horsewhipping* and *horsewhipped*, even though the stress is not on the final syllable of *horsewhip*. Similarly:

| | | |
|---|---|---|
| *leapfrog* | : | *leapfrogging, leapfrogged* |
| *quickstep* | : | *quickstepping, quickstepped* |
| *foxtrot* | : | *foxtrotting, foxtrotted* |

A few words of a similar form also double the final letter:

| | | |
|---|---|---|
| *humbug* | : | *humbugging, humbugged* |
| *zigzag* | : | *zigzagging, zigzagged* |
| *hobnob* | : | *hobnobbing, hobnobbed* |

> ⚠ Note that there is no doubling of consonants <u>within</u> compound words:
> eg *get, getting* but *getaway*; *stop, stopped* but *stopover*.

## • And finally ...

Some words allow both single and doubled consonants, eg *focusing* or *focussing*. In some cases the words behave differently in this respect according to whether they are nouns or verbs. Note the following:

| | | |
|---|---|---|
| *bias* | : | noun plural *biases* |
| | | verb has single or double *s* before *-ing*, *-ed*, etc |

| *bus* | : | noun plural usually *buses*, but *busses* is also correct although rare<br>verb parts usually with single *s*, but *ss* also correct |
| *focus* | : | noun plural *focuses*<br>verb parts with single or double *s* |
| *gas* | : | noun plural *gases*<br>verb *gasses, gassing, gassed* |
| *plus* | : | plural *pluses* or *plusses* |
| *yes* | : | plural *yeses* or *yesses* |

> ⚠️ If the above list looks too complicated to remember, then notice that you will never actually be wrong if you keep to a single letter in the noun plurals and always double the letter in the verb parts, and ignore the other variants even if they are the more common forms: **'Single in the noun, dou<u>b</u>le in the verb'.**

## -e

> When adding a word-ending which begins with a vowel to a word which ends in a silent *e*, drop the *e*; when adding a word-ending which begins with a consonant, do not drop the *e*.

Examples:

$$move + \text{-}ing \rightarrow moving \qquad grace + \text{-}ed \rightarrow graced$$
$$move + \text{-}ment \rightarrow movement \qquad grace + \text{-}ful \rightarrow graceful$$

and similarly

| *change* | : | *changing* |
| *guide* | : | *guidance* |
| *admire* | : | *admirable, admiration, admirer, admiring* |
| *culture* | : | *cultured, cultural* |
| *concise* | : | *concisely, conciseness* |
| *use* | : | *used, using* |
| *use* | : | *useless, useful* |
| *bone* | : | *bony* |
| *desire* | : | *desirous, desirable* |
| *awe* | : | *awesome* |
| *safe* | : | *safety* |

* **-able**

A number of words retain (or may retain) an *e* before the suffix **-able**, eg *likeable/likable, lovable/loveable*. For a list of these, see the entry for -ABLE.

- **-ce, -ge**

In order to preserve the 'soft' sound of *c* and *g* (ie /s/ and /j/ respectively), the *e* is not dropped before a suffix beginning with *a*, *o* or *u*:

| | | | | | |
|---|---|---|---|---|---|
| *change* | : | *changeable* | *peace* | : | *peaceable* |
| *courage* | : | *courageous* | | | |

- **-dge**

In derived words whose core ends in **-dge**, the *e* may be dropped before a consonant and also before a suffix beginning with *a*, *o* or *u*:

| | | |
|---|---|---|
| *knowledge* | : | *knowledgeable* or less commonly *knowledgable* |
| *judge* | : | *judgement* or less commonly *judgment* |
| *acknowledge* | : | *acknowledgement* or less commonly *acknowledgment* |
| *fledge* | : | *fledgling* or less commonly *fledgeling* |

- **-ee, -oe, -ye**

Verbs and nouns ending in **-ee**, **-oe** and **-ye** generally keep the final *e* before all suffixes except those beginning with an *e*:

| | | |
|---|---|---|
| *absentee* | : | *absenteeism* |
| *agree* | : | *agreeing, agreeable* (but *agree* + -ed → *agreed*) |
| *canoe* | : | *canoeing, canoeist* |
| *dye* | : | *dyeing* (but *dyed*; compare *dying*, from the verb *die*) |
| *eye* | : | *eyeing* (but *eying* is also correct) |
| *hoe* | : | *hoeing* |
| *shoe* | : | *shoeing* |

- **-ie**

Verbs which end in **-ie** change this to **-y** before **-ing**:

| | | | | | |
|---|---|---|---|---|---|
| *belie* | : | *belying* | *tie* | : | *tying* |
| *die* | : | *dying* | *vie* | : | *vying* |
| *lie* | : | *lying* | | | |

- **-le**

Adjectives which end in **-le** preceded by a vowel form adverbs in the regular way:

| | | | | | |
|---|---|---|---|---|---|
| *agile* | : | *agilely* | *pale* | : | *palely* |
| *docile* | : | *docilely* | | | |

However, if the **-le** is preceded by a consonant, the corresponding adverb is generally formed by replacing the *e* by *y*:

| | | | | | |
|---|---|---|---|---|---|
| *double* | : | *doubly* | *simple* | : | *simply* |
| *predictable* | : | *predictably* | *subtle* | : | *subtly* |
| *possible* | : | *possibly* | *supple* | : | *supply* |

(though *supplely* is also correct and in common use)

- *-y*

The final *e* is retained before an added *-y* in words which end in *-ue*:

> glue : gluey

and also unpredictably

|       |       |       |       |
|-------|-------|-------|-------|
| cage  | cagey | pace  | pacey |
| dice  | dicey | price | pricey |
| mate  | matey |       |       |

Both *nosy* and *nosey* are correct. Notice the difference between *holy* (= 'sacred') and *holey* (= 'full of holes').

- **singe, route**, *etc*

A final *e* is retained before **-ing** where it is needed to distinguish between words that would otherwise be indistinguishable. Compare *sing* : *singing* with *singe* : *singeing*. Similarly *routeing*, *swingeing* and *tingeing*.

Note also the difference in spelling between *probable* (= 'likely') and *probeable* (= 'able to be probed').

- **Compounds**

The *e* does <u>not</u> drop out in compound words: *hideout*, *giveaway*, *takeover*.

- **And finally ...**

There remains a mixed bag of exceptions which must simply be listed:

|                    |                    |         |
|--------------------|--------------------|---------|
| acreage            | duly               | ninth   |
| ageing or aging    | eerily             | truly   |
| ageism             | mileage or milage  | whilst  |
| awful              | mortgagor          | wholly  |
| cueing or cuing    |                    |         |

# *-e-/-ae-, -e-/-oe-* see -AE- and -OE-.

# *-ed, -d*

## ✦ Verbs

> **To form a past tense or past participle of most regular verbs, add *-ed* to the basic form of the 'core' word.**

Examples:

|       |         |       |         |
|-------|---------|-------|---------|
| claim | claimed | toast | toasted |
| link  | linked  | taxi  | taxied  |
| toss  | tossed  | veto  | vetoed  |

- **Final *c***

Words which end in *c* generally add a *k* before the **-ed**:

> *mimic* : *mimicked*    *panic* : *panicked*

> ⚠ Note the exceptions:
> >    *arc* : *arced*
> >    *sync* (= 'synchronize') : *synced*
> >    *talc* : *talced* or *talcked*
> >    *zinc* : *zinced, zinked* or *zincked*

- **Final *e***

If the core verb ends in *e*, the *e* is dropped before the **-ed** is added:

> *bake* : *baked*    *change* : *changed*    *agree* : *agreed*

- **Final *y***

Verbs that end in *y* change the *y* to *i* if it is preceded by a consonant but not if it is preceded by a vowel:

> *cry* : *cried*    *apply* : *applied*

but

> *stay* : *stayed*    *destroy* : *destroyed*

> ⚠ Note the spelling of *laid, paid* and *said*.

- **Words ending in a vowel other than *e* and *y***

After a final vowel, normally add **-ed**: *baaed, tangoed*, etc, though after a final *a*, **-'d** is also acceptable. (It is also preferable to use *ski'd* for the past tense of *ski* in order to avoid confusion with *skied*, the past tense of *sky*.)

If the verb ends in *-é*, as in many borrowings from French, the best practice is to add **-ed** (*clichéed, flambéed*), but **-d** alone and also **-'d** are accepted (eg *clichéd, cliché'd*).

- **Doubling of the final consonant**

For the rules about when to double the final consonant of the base verb (eg *fit* : *fitted, drop* : *dropped*) and when not to (eg *seat* : *seated, droop* : *drooped*), see DOUBLING OF FINAL CONSONANTS.

✦ **Adjectives**

Adjectives that end in **-ed** or **-d** follow the same rules as those given above for the past-tense and past-participle forms of verbs: that is to say, they are formed by, for example, simply adding **-ed** or **-'d** to the base form (*bearded, long-haired, hennaed/henna'd*), dropping the final silent *e* of the core word before adding the word-ending (*leisured, good-natured*), doubling the final consonant of the core word before the word-ending (*long-legged*) or not doing so (*long-tailed*).

Note that the adjective *moneyed* (= 'having money, rich') may also correctly be spelt *monied*.

See also PAST TENSE AND PAST PARTICIPLE.

## -efy see -IFY.

## -ei-, -ie-

**'*I* before *e* except after *c*'.**

This well-known and very useful rule applies only to words which are pronounced with an /ee/ sound: *believe, ceiling, chief, deceive, siege, receipt*.

 A few common words pronounced with an /ee/ sound have *ei* where *ie* would be expected:

| | | | |
|---|---|---|---|
| *caffeine* | *heinous* | *protein* | *skein* |
| *codeine* | *inveigle* | *seize* | *weir* |
| *counterfeit* | *neither* | *sheikh* | *weird* |
| *either* | | | |

Notice that some of these words (eg *heinous, either*) may be pronounced in more than one way (eg /**ee**-*dher*/ or /**iy**-*dher*/) and also appear in some of the lists below.

Some ***personal names*** and ***place-names*** do not obey the general rule either: *Keith, Neil, Sheila, Reid, Madeira*.

**When words of this type are pronounced with an /ay/ sound, *ei* is correct.**

Examples:

| | | | |
|---|---|---|---|
| *deign* | *heir* | *reign* | *veil* |
| *eight* | *inveigh* | *rein* | *vein* |
| *feign* | *inveigle* | *sheikh* | *weigh* |
| *freight* | *neigh* | *skein* | *weight* |
| *heinous* | *neighbour* | *sleigh* | |

and also the Chinese dish *chow mein*.

⚠ For this group of words, remember the spelling of *eight*, which most people spell correctly.

**Words pronounced /iy/ are usually written with *ei*.**

Examples:

| | | |
|---|---|---|
| *either* | *leitmotif* | *sleight of hand* |
| *Fahrenheit* | *neither* | |
| *height* | *seismograph* | |

However, before *r*, *ie* is correct:

| | | |
|---|---|---|
| *fiery* | *hierarchy* | *hieroglyphics* |

**Following a *c* or a *t* which is pronounced /sh/, *ie* is always correct.**

Examples:

| | | |
|---|---|---|
| *ancient* | *patient* | *species* |
| *conscience* | *quotient* | *sufficient* |
| *efficient* | | |

• There remain a number of words that do not fit neatly into any rule:

| | | |
|---|---|---|
| *counterfeit* | *handkerchief* | *mischievous* |
| *foreign* | *heifer* | *sieve* |
| *forfeit* | *leisure* | *sovereign* |
| *friend* | *mischief* | *surfeit* |

**-ence** see -ANCE.

**-eous** see -IOUS.

**-er, -est** see COMPARATIVES AND SUPERLATIVES.

**-er, -or, -ar**

✦ **Nouns**

• *-er*

The suffix **-er** can be added to verbs in English to form nouns meaning 'someone or something that —s': *builder, singer, mixer, worker, talker*, etc. There

247

is practically no limit to the number of nouns which can be formed in this way, as this is the ending generally added to form new words of this type.

In addition, there is a small group of *-er* nouns that are based on or related to other nouns or adjectives, rather than formed from core verbs:

| | | |
|---|---|---|
| *foreigner* | *lawyer* | *sorcerer* |
| *idolater* | *mariner* | *treasurer* |
| *jeweller* | *prisoner* | *usurer* |

- ## *-or*

There are a large number of 'doer' words which end in *-or*. The following are the ones most likely to be met with:

| | | | |
|---|---|---|---|
| *accelerator* | *councillor* | *incubator* | *perpetrator* |
| *actor* | *counsellor* | *indicator* | *professor* |
| *administrator* | *creator* | *inheritor* | *projector* |
| *arbitrator* | *decorator* | *inspector* | *prospector* |
| *auditor* | *depositor* | *inventor* | *protector* |
| *calculator* | *dictator* | *investigator* | *radiator* |
| *collaborator* | *director* | *investor* | *refrigerator* |
| *collector* | *distributor* | *legislator* | *sailor* |
| *commentator* | *duplicator* | *mediator* | *spectator* |
| *competitor* | *editor* | *microprocessor* | *supervisor* |
| *conductor* | *educator* | *narrator* | *surveyor* |
| *conqueror* | *elevator* | *navigator* | *survivor* |
| *conspirator* | *escalator* | *objector* | *translator* |
| *constructor* | *excavator* | *operator* | *vendor* |
| *contractor* | *executor* | *oppressor* | *ventilator* |
| *contributor* | *governor* | *orator* | *visitor* |

> As a possible clue to the -or spelling, notice that many of the words in the above list end in *-ator*, *-itor* or *-utor*, and that many are related to words that end in *-ion*, eg
>
> | | | | | |
> |---|---|---|---|---|
> | *collector* | : | *collection* | *oppressor* : *oppression* |
> | *objector* | : | *objection* | *supervisor* : *supervision* |

There are a few other words which end in *-or*:

| | | | |
|---|---|---|---|
| *ambassador* | *creditor* | *janitor* | *sponsor* |
| *ancestor* | *curator* | *major* | *successor* |
| *author* | *debtor* | *mayor* | *suitor* |
| *aviator* | *doctor* | *pastor* | *tailor* |
| *bachelor* | *emperor* | *predecessor* | *tenor* |
| *benefactor* | *equator* | *proprietor* | *tractor* |
| *captor* | *impostor* | *rector* | *traitor* |
| *censor* | *inquisitor* | *senator* | *victor* |
| *chancellor* | *jailor* | *solicitor* | |

Some words have both **-or** and **-er** forms, eg *carburettor/carburetter, conjuror/conjurer*. Both *caster* and *castor* are correct, but the **-or** form is the commoner.

In some cases, the two forms differ slightly in meaning, eg *adapter/adaptor, conveyer/conveyor, resister/resistor*. In such cases, the **-er** form has a more general meaning ('someone or something that —s'), while the **-or** form is more specialized or technical in meaning (*adaptor* and *resistor* are special pieces of electrical apparatus; *conveyor* = 'conveyor-belt').

## • *-ar*

Some common 'doer' words are spelt **-ar**:

| | | | |
|---|---|---|---|
| *beggar* | *burglar* | *liar* | *pedlar* |

Other common **-ar** nouns are:

| | | | |
|---|---|---|---|
| *altar* | *cellar* | *hangar* | *registrar* |
| *bursar* | *collar* | *mortar* | *scholar* |
| *calendar* | *dollar* | *nectar* | *vicar* |
| *caterpillar* | *grammar* | *pillar* | *vinegar* |
| *cedar* | *guitar* | | |

## ✦ Adjectives

Adjectives ending in /-ar/ are usually spelt **-ar**:

| | | | |
|---|---|---|---|
| *angular* | *molar* | *perpendicular* | *singular* |
| *circular* | *molecular* | *polar* | *spectacular* |
| *familiar* | *muscular* | *popular* | *stellar* |
| *insular* | *particular* | *regular* | *tubular* |
| *jocular* | *peculiar* | *similar* | *vulgar* |
| *lunar* | | | |

 Note that many of the words in the above list are related to nouns that end in **-arity**, in which the *a* is clearly pronounced:

| | | | | |
|---|---|---|---|---|
| *circular* | : | *circularity* | *vulgar* | : | *vulgarity* |

A small group of adjectives end in **-or**:

| | | | |
|---|---|---|---|
| *inferior* | *interior* | *anterior* | *major* |
| *superior* | *exterior* | *ulterior* | *minor* |
| | | *posterior* | |

and also *tenor*.

Many of the words in the above list are related to nouns that end in *-**ority*** in which the *o* is clearly pronounced:

> inferior : inferiority     minor : minority

## ✦ Changes to the basic word-form

There are some fairly predictable spelling rules (predictable in that the same rules apply to the formation of many types of English word) which must be observed in the formation of words that end in *-er*, *-or* and *-ar*:

### • Final *c*
A final *c* in the core word becomes *ck* before the ending:

> picnic : picnicker

### • Final *e*
The final *e* of a verb drops before the the ending:

| | | | | |
|---|---|---|---|---|
| bake | : | baker | lie : | liar |
| burgle | : | burglar | manage : | manager |
| contribute | : | manager | | |

### • Final *y*
A final *y* preceded by a consonant becomes *i*; a *y* preceded by a vowel remains *y*:

> carry : carrier     survey : surveyor

⚠ Both *flier* and *flyer*, and *drier* and *dryer*, are correct.

### • Doubling of final consonants
A final consonant which would be doubled in the formation of the *-ed* and *-ing* forms of the verb (see DOUBLING OF FINAL CONSONANTS ) also becomes a double consonant in the formation of *-er*, *-or* and *-ar* derivatives:

| | | | | |
|---|---|---|---|---|
| begin | : | beginning | : | beginner |
| beg | : | begging | : | beggar |
| counsel | : | counselling | : | counsellor |

Even where there is no corresponding verb form, the rules set out in DOUBLING OF FINAL CONSONANTS apply:

> council : councillor

See also the entry -OR, -OUR for the spelling of words such as *humour*, *colour* and *neighbour*.

**-ery** see -ARY.

## ever, -ever

When **ever** is used to emphasize words like *why, how, where*, etc, it is written as a separate word: *What ever shall I do?* □ *How ever did you manage that?* When **ever** means 'any — at all', it is joined to the word it modifies: *You may do whatever you please* □ *Go wherever he tells you to go.* Notice that **where ever, why ever,** etc are questions, while **wherever, whatever,** etc are parts of statements or commands.

In British English, **for ever** is more often written as two words than one, but **forever** is also correct. Some people make a distinction between **forever** meaning 'continually' and **for ever** meaning 'for all time' but, while such a distinction has much to recommend it, it is not recognized by most dictionaries or speakers of English. In American English, **forever** is the standard form.

## -fs/-fes, -ves

> **Many common words ending in -f and -fe alter the f to v in the plural.**

Examples:

    calf  :  calves          elf  :  elves

and so also *halves, knives, leaves, lives* (but still-life paintings are *still lifes*), *loaves, selves, sheaves, shelves, thieves, wives* and *wolves.*

- Some plurals may be spelt with either *f* or *v*:

      dwarfs/dwarves          scarfs/scarves
      handkerchiefs/handkerchieves    wharfs/wharves
      hoofs/hooves

> ⚠ The plural of *roof* is generally *roofs*. However, because *roofs* may be pronounced /ruuvz/ as well as /ruufs/, it is sometimes spelt *rooves*, but this spelling is not generally accepted as correct and should be avoided.

- Other words that end in **-f** or **-fe** make regular plurals, ie by adding **-s** alone, eg:

      aperitifs        chefs        proofs
      beliefs          chiefs       reliefs

## -ful

**Plurals of words ending in *-ful* end in *-fuls*.**

Examples:

| | | |
|---|---|---|
| *armfuls* | *cupfuls* | *spadefuls* |
| *bucketfuls* | *handfuls* | *spoonfuls* |
| *capfuls* | *mouthfuls* | |

---

 A few authorities allow *-sful* (eg *cupsful, spoonsful*) as an acceptable alternative plural form, but this is considered incorrect by most people and is therefore best avoided.

Be careful to distinguish between, for example, *three cupfuls of flour* (a cupful is a particular amount, regardless of whether it is held in a cup or not — you could measure out three cupfuls of flour with a spoon if you chose to) and *three cups full of flour* (= three cups filled with flour).

---

## hyphens

Hyphens add clarity to a text by helping to show in writing what stress and intonation would help to indicate in speech. Basically, ***hyphens are used to link words or parts of words in order to show that they are to be considered a single unit***. This they do in two contexts:

a)   where two or more words are to be understood as functioning as a single unit in a sentence, eg *a never-to-be-forgotten experience*, and

b)   where a word has to be split at the end of a line of writing or printing, with the second part being taken over to the beginning of the next line, as for example in a newspaper column:

> *We experienced an engine failure in Liverpool on a Satur-*
> *day morning and by 10.30 a.m. on the Sunday the stand-*
> *by was in operation.*

At first sight, there seem to be few, if any, consistent and easy-to-learn rules governing hyphenation in English. But although there <u>are</u> certain categories of words — in particular, compound nouns — in which hyphenation does not seem to follow any logical or consistent rule, for the most part hyphenation is really quite straightforward, and once you have grasped what hyphens are for and mastered one or two basic principles, almost everything else can be left to common sense.

## ✦ Hyphens used to link words

### • Hyphens linking three or more words

**Multi-word phrases describing a following noun require hyphens.**

Examples:

*an up-to-date report*
*a balance-of-payments problem*
*mouth-to-mouth resuscitation*
*her absurd caught-in-at-the-knees skirt*

 Phrases of this type should not be hyphenated in other positions in the sentence:

*The report is completely up to date.*
*a problem with the country's balance of payments*

**When a phrase is made to function as a single word by the addition of a suffix or word-forming element, all the elements of the phrase must be linked with hyphens to show that they are functioning as a single unit.**

Examples:

*The aunts raised their eyebrows with a good deal of To-what-are-we-indebted-for-the-honour-of-this-visitness ...*

— P G Wodehouse

*Esmond was being very Justice-of-the-Peace-y.*

— P G Wodehouse

*There aren't usually many vacancies for non-shouting and non-pushing-people-about officers, so I think I'd better stick to what I know.*

— Douglas Adams

**Multi-word phrases functioning as nouns are generally hyphenated.**

Examples:

*his mother-in-law*          *a man-about-town*
*a bunch of forget-me-nots*   *a jack-in-the-box*

> ⚠ However, if the phrase is of the form 'X of Y' or 'X of the Y', hyphens are generally omitted, as in
>
> | | |
> |---|---|
> | *a Justice of the Peace* | *a guard of honour* |
> | *a man of the world* | *a maid of all work* |
>
> but are inserted in compounds with figurative meanings, such as *man-of-war* (= a ship, or a jellyfish, but not literally a man).

- **Hyphens linking two words**

> **Numbers from 21 to 99 and fractions should be hyphenated.**

Examples:

  *twenty-three*                    *three-quarters*

> **Two-word compound adjectives are hyphenated when preceding a noun and often (but not always) in other positions (eg after the verb *be*).**

Examples:

  i)  Preceding a noun:

| | |
|---|---|
| *a pitch-dark night* | *those so-called friends of hers* |
| *sixteenth-century stained glass* | *a young red-faced officer* |
| *the average young middle-class male* | *home-made fruit cake* |
| *a repertoire of all-time favourites* | *a panic-stricken rush for the door* |
| *my next-door neighbour* | *a half-open door* |
| *a never-ending struggle* | *a self-inflicted wound* |

  ii)  In other positions, eg following a verb:

  (a)  *An adjective and a following past or present participle or word ending in -ed should be linked by a hyphen*:

   *We are dreadfully short-staffed here.*
   *Jams, chutneys and marmalade are home-made.*
   *The wound was self-inflicted.*
   *The toll of job losses seems never-ending.*

  (b)  *Combinations of adjective plus noun should be hyphenated*:

   *I thought the performance was pretty second-rate.*

  (c)  *Combinations of noun plus adjective are optionally hyphenated*:

   *The path was ankle-deep in weeds.*
   *Ankle deep in mud, we squelched across the meadow.*

> *It was pitch-black and still oppressively hot.*
> *The stage was pitch black.*

(d) ***Other word-groups should not be hyphenated****:*

> *married the girl <u>next door</u>.*
> *living in a house <u>near by</u>.*

- If the first word of a compound adjective is ***well***, ***better***, ***best***, ***ill***, ***worse*** or ***worst***, a hyphen is inserted only when the compound <u>precedes</u> a noun; in other positions in the sentence, there should be no hyphen:

> *His wife was a well-known writer.*
> *She began working in television in 1951 and became one of its best-loved characters.*
> *He is well known for his introductions to music on radio and television.*
> *He was professor of law at Oviedo, but better known as a literary figure.*

- An ***adverb ending in*** -ly should not normally be linked to a following word by a hyphen in any position in a sentence:

> *a beautifully illustrated book*
> *the problem of feeding the greatly expanded army*

Examples of hyphenation in this position are, however, not uncommon, especially where the ***-ly*** adverb and the following word are felt to be very closely bound together and functioning as a single unit of meaning:

> *the problems of mentally-handicapped children*
> *Jessie passed the closely-written sheet across to Stephen.*
> *The British Civil Service is a beautifully-designed and effective braking mechanism.*
>
> — Shirley Williams

But strictly speaking a hyphen should only be inserted if it is needed for the sake of clarity.

> **When two or more hyphenated words occur together and have one part in common, the part they have in common may be omitted in all but the last instance. In such cases, the hyphen must be retained where the second part of the compound has been deleted.**

Example:

> *fourteenth-century, fifteenth-century and sixteenth-century stained glass* could be shortened to *fourteenth-, fifteenth- and sixteenth-century stained glass.*

In some cases, the presence or absence of a hyphen in such positions conveys important information: note the difference between *his brother and sister-in-law* (= 'his brother and his sister-in-law') and *his brother- and sister-in-law* (= 'his brother-in-law and his sister-in-law').

**Nouns and adjectives formed from phrasal verbs are often hyphenated.**

Phrasal verbs are combinations of a simple verb like *give, pull, send* or *take* and an adverb such as *in, out* or *off* or a preposition such as *for* or *with*, eg *decide on, give back, hanker after, kill off, pick at, put up with, run away, send away for.*

- Examples of **nouns** formed from phrasal verbs are:

| | | | |
|---|---|---|---|
| *line-up* | *knock-on* | *fly-past* | *share-out* |
| *drive-in* | *shake-up* | *send-up* | *write-off* |

However, in some compounds the hyphen is optional (eg *takeaway* or *take-away, takeover* or *take-over, shutdown* or *shut-down*) and many well-established compounds are now written without a hyphen:

| | | | |
|---|---|---|---|
| *fallout* | *hangover* | *hideout* | *stowaway* |
| *getaway* | *layabout* | *knockout* | |
| *giveaway* | *layout* | *stopover* | |

There is no certain rule that can be followed here. In case of doubt, consult a reliable dictionary.

---

 If the verbal part of the compound noun has a word-ending added, the noun is always hyphenated: *going-over, passer-by, listener-in, grown-up.*

Notice the difference between *His going-over* (noun) *of the accounts was very thorough* and *His going over* (verb + preposition) *the accounts caused a lot of anxiety.*

---

- **Adjectives** formed from phrasal verbs are hyphenated before nouns (*a desperately hung-up young man* □ *an unhoped-for success* □ *knock-down prices*). In other positions, usage is less fixed, but the best rule is to hyphenate a sequence of verb plus preposition (eg *with* or *for* — *His success was quite unhoped-for*) but to leave unhyphenated sequences of verb plus adverb (eg *in, out, past, by, up* — *He was really hung up about the whole affair*).

---

 A hyphen should <u>not</u> be used to join the parts of a phrasal verb itself:

✗   *He says he is going to give-up his job next week.*
✗   *They cheer-up some of the patients, who otherwise would not get any visitors.*
✓   *He says he is going to give up his job next week.*
✓   *They cheer up some of the patients, who otherwise would not get any visitors.*

---

In general, a compound noun is written as two separate words if it is felt that the first word simply qualifies the second word like an adjective, but as a hyphenated word or as a single word with no hyphen if the compound is felt to be a single lexical item denoting a particular individual or thing or type of thing.

Examples: *a bus company, trade figures* but *bus-driver, trademark.*

A comparison of the entries in two or more dictionaries or spelling guides will quickly show that there are many nouns in which hyphenation usage is not clearly established: *diningroom, dining-room* or *dining room.* There are differences between British and American usage in this respect, hyphens being used more in British English than American English (though fewer now than formerly).

If the 'single lexical item' type of word is well established and frequently used, and if it is built up from one-syllable words, it is likely to be written without a hyphen: *bedroom, bloodbath, teacup.*

A hyphen is more likely in longer words, and also where the absence of a hyphen would cause an undesirable or potentially confusing juxtaposition of letters:

*heart-throb* rather than *heartthrob*
*time-exposure* rather than *timeexposure*

Compound words formed with *half* and *self* are usually hyphenated.

Examples:

*half-brother*          *half-term*
*self-induced*          *self-respect*

⚠ Note the spelling of *halfway, halfwit* and *halfpenny.*

- *Hyphens with word parts*

In general, hyphens are not used with prefixes and suffixes (*un-, dis-, re-,* etc; *-ly, -ness, -dom,* etc) nor with word-forming elements (*hydro-, electro-, photo-, -lysis, -itis, -logy,* etc).

Examples:

> *unhappy, dissatisfied, rewrite*
> *quickly, sadness*
> *electrolysis, enteritis, hydroelectric*

However, **a hyphen may be used**

i) **to avoid the juxtaposition of two identical letters**, eg *re-enter, re-elect, co-op*

ii) **to distinguish words that would otherwise be indistinguishable**, eg

> *re-cover* (= to 'cover again') but *recover* (= to 'become well again' or 'get back')
> *re-count* (= to 'count again') but *recount* (= to 'tell')

• There are certain refinements to these general rules that must be considered:

**Prefixes**

i) **un-**, **dis-**, **mis-**, **pre-** and **re-** are not normally followed by a hyphen: *unknown, disappear, recapture,* etc.

However, if the 'core' word begins with a capital letter, a hyphen is usually inserted after **un-** (*un-American, un-English*). Although there is an increasing tendency nowadays not to use a linking hyphen in this position (eg *unChristian*), the hyphenated forms are still preferable.

ii) **Anti-** is not normally followed by a hyphen: *anticlockwise, antifreeze* (but *anti-hero, anti-marketeer* — see the list at ANTI-, page 219).

iii) **Ex-** and **non-** are normally followed by a hyphen: *ex-wife; non-inflammable.*

iv) Words beginning with **co-** generally do not now have a hyphen. The tendency is more and more for words with this prefix not to be hyphenated, eg what used to be written *co-ordinate* is now more frequently written *coordinate*. As a rule, omit the hyphen unless it is needed for clarity: for example, *coordinate* and *cooperate* are fine without hyphens, but it is probably better to retain the hyphen in *co-opt* and certainly better in *co-op; coefficient* and *coed* are always written unhyphenated.

In all cases where the letter or letters following the prefix **co-** might at first glance be thought to form a sense unit with it, it is better to hyphenate to show the correct syllable split: *co-driver* is therefore preferable to *codriver* which could be interpreted at first glance as 'cod-river'.

In addition, most new coinages with **co-** as a living prefix meaning 'fellow' or 'joint' are hyphenated (but not obligatorily so): *co-agent, co-author, co-chair.*

Note the important difference between a *correspondent* 'someone with whom you correspond' or 'a person employed to send reports to eg a newspaper (*foreign correspondent, war correspondent*) and a *co-respondent* or *corespondent* in a divorce case.

**Suffixes**

Word-endings (eg *-ish*, *-ism*, *-ly*, *-most*, *-ness*) are not preceded by a hyphen:

| | | | |
|---|---|---|---|
| *singer* | *walking* | *quickly* | *kingship* |
| *tenfold* | *greenish* | *innermost* | *lengthwise* |
| *childhood* | *sexism* | *meanness* | *icy* |

unless they are attached to phrases to form words:

*pie-in-the-sky-ism*
*greeting him in a hail-fellow-well-met-ish sort of way*

- **And finally ...**

Note the position of the hyphen in the following idioms:

*go over something with a fine-tooth comb*
(a *fine-tooth comb* = a comb with fine teeth)
✗    *fine tooth-comb*

*send someone on a wild-goose chase*
✗    *wild goose-chase*

✦ **Word-splitting hyphens**

Hyphens are used to mark breaks in words not normally hyphenated, either when only part of the word is written, as in *four- or fivefold* where the *four-* is to be understood as meaning 'fourfold' (compare page 255), or at the end of a line of writing where part of the word has to be taken over to the next line. In the latter case, the following principles apply:

> If possible, split the word into logical parts in such a way that the former part suggests the whole word, or at least does not mislead the reader by suggesting the wrong word.

Examples:

*mis-/shapen* not *miss-/hapen*
*re-/install* not *rein-/stall*
*ther-/apist* not *the-/rapist*

In some cases it may not be possible to split a word at all without producing something ludicrous. In such cases, take the whole of the word over to the next line.

> **Do not split letters that together represent a single sound (eg
> *th, ch, sh, ea, ee*).**

Examples:

> *heat-/ing* not *he-/ating*
> *picnick-/ing* not *picnic-/king*

Similarly, a letter that influences the pronunciation of another letter should
not be separated from it at a line-break:

> *spe-/cial* not *spec-/ial*
> *ma-/gi-/cian* not *magic-/ian*

> **Do not split words of one syllable.**
>
> **Do not split personal names.**

Examples:

> ✗   *wash/-ed* (but ✓ *wash/-ing*)
> ✗   *thou-/ght*
> ✗   *Ri-/chard*


**-i, -os** see -O.


**-i, -uses** see -US.


**-ible, -ibility** see -ABLE.


**-icy** see -ACY.


**-ie** see -Y.


**-ie-** see -EI-.


**-ies**

> **Words ending in *-ies* (eg *congeries*, *series*, *species*) have the
> same form in the plural as in the singular.**

Example: *two species of crab*

# -ify, -efy

**The best guess is *-ify*. Most words that end in /fiy/ are spelt *-ify*.**

Examples:

| | | | |
|---|---|---|---|
| *classify* | *horrify* | *notify* | *simplify* |
| *falsify* | *identify* | *purify* | *solidify* |

Only four common verbs end in ***-efy***: *liquefy, putrefy, rarefy, stupefy*.

---

 As a spelling hint, notice that while many of the verbs that end in ***-ify*** are related to nouns that end in ***-fication*** (*classify, classification; identify, identification*), the four verbs that end in ***-efy*** are related to nouns that end in ***-faction*** (*putrefy, putrefaction; stupefy, stupefaction*).

But note that related to the verb *petrify* are both *petrifaction* and *petrification*.

---

# il-, im-, in-, ir-

The prefixes *il-, im-, in-, ir-* mostly occur in English words that are derived from Latin, with either the meaning 'not, opposite of', as in

| | | |
|---|---|---|
| *illegal* | = | 'not legal' |
| *impossible* | = | 'not possible' |
| *inaccurate* | = | 'not accurate' |
| *inseparable* | = | 'not separable' |
| *irrelevant* | = | 'not relevant' |

or the meaning 'in, into, on', as in

| | | |
|---|---|---|
| *illuminate* | = | 'to cast light (Latin *lumen*) on' |
| *immigration* | = | 'migration into (a country)' |
| *inflammable* | = | 'able to burst into flames' |
| *innate* | = | 'in-born' (Latin *natus* 'born') |
| *irradiate* | = | 'to put radiation into' (ie, to treat by exposure to radiation) |

## • ill-, imm-, irr-

Any word beginning with /il-/, /im-/ or /ir-/ and which has the meaning 'not something' or 'in/into/on something' will have a double *l*, *m* or *r*. This in fact covers the great majority of English words beginning /il-/, /im-/ or /ir-/, including the ones in which the 'not' or 'in/into/on' notion is not obvious, such as *illuminate* (mentioned above), *immense* (= 'so big as to be *not measurable*', Latin *mensus* 'measured'), *irrigate* (= 'to bring water into fields', Latin *rigare* 'to water').

- *inn-, in-*

Words beginning with /in-/ pose more of a problem. To be certain how many *n*'s to write, you have to know whether the *in-* has been added to a 'core' word that begins with a vowel or to one that begins with an *n*. Sometimes you would need a good knowledge of Latin to be sure of this, but there is a quick test to apply, based on word-families, which works most of the time:

> If what follows the /in-/ is recognizable as an English word which begins with a vowel, or is clearly related to such a word, only one *n* will be needed.

> If what follows the /in-/ is recognizable as an English word which begins with an *n*, or is clearly related to such a word, two *n*'s will be needed.

Examples:

| | | | | | |
|---|---|---|---|---|---|
| accurate | : | inaccurate | imitate | : | inimitable |
| audible | : | inaudible | offensive | : | inoffensive |
| exact | : | inexact | | | |

| | | |
|---|---|---|
| <u>nume</u>rate | : | in<u>nume</u>rable (= 'not countable') |
| <u>nov</u>elty | : | in<u>nov</u>ation (= 'something that is brought in as something new') |

Apart from these, there are a few words with a single *n*: *inimical, iniquity, initial, initiate, inoculate, inundate*. And with a double *n*: *innards, innate, inner, innings, innocent, innocuous* and *innuendo*.

---

**◱** *In-* and *un-*

There is often some uncertainty over the choice between *in-* and *un-* in the formation of negative words. There are some general rules which may go some way towards helping to select the correct prefix, but there are, unfortunately, many exceptions and many words where no rule seems to apply at all:

i)   The *in-* prefix is generally preferred to *un-* as the negative prefix in words of Latin or French origin, but the correct prefix to use is far from predictable: *illiterate* and *unliterary* both contain the same 'core' *liter-* from Latin *litera* 'letter'. However, words which begin with *ad-*, *con-* (and its variants *co-*, *col-*, *com-*, *cor-*), *de-*, *ex-* and *per-* (all of which are prefixes derived from Latin) tend to take *in-* as a negative prefix (eg *inconclusive, inexpressible, imperfect*), as do words which end in suffixes of Latin origin such as *-ible*, *-uble*, *-ence*, *-ent*, *-ity*, *-ice* and *-tude* (*inedible, insoluble, incoherence, indecent, insanity, injustice, ingratitude*).

ii)   Adjectives ending in *-ing* and *-ed* usually take *un-* (*unexciting, uncommitted*), unless they are formed from verbs which already have the *in-* prefix: *indisposed*. (Note also *incapacitated* and *inexperienced*.)

iii)   Some words may form negatives with either *in-* or *un-*. In these cases, words which begin with *in-* tend to have narrower and more specific meanings than those with **un**-: compare, for example, *irreligious* 'opposed to or lacking in respect for religion or generally accepted religious principles' and *unreligious* 'not religious (in a general sense)', 'having nothing to do with religion'.

## -im, -s

A few words of Hebrew origin have, or may have, irregular plurals:

*cherubs* or (especially in religious contexts) *cherubim*
*kibbutzim* (also *kibbutzes*)
*seraphs* or (especially in religious contexts) *seraphim*

## -ing

**The present participle of a verb is generally formed by adding -*ing* to the basic form of the verb.**

Examples:

| | | | | | |
|---|---|---|---|---|---|
| walk | : | *walking* | see | : | *seeing* |
| ring | : | *ringing* | stay | : | *staying* |

- **Final *c***

Verbs ending in *c* generally add a *k* before **-ing**:

| | | | | |
|---|---|---|---|---|
| mimic | : | *mimicking* | picnic | : | *picnicking* |

For exceptions such as *arcing*, see the entry for -C, page 224.

- **Final *e***

Verbs ending in a silent *e* drop the *e* before adding **-ing**:

| | | | | | |
|---|---|---|---|---|---|
| bake | : | *baking* | queue | : | *queuing* |
| dangle | : | *dangling* | refine | : | *refining* |

 Verbs ending in **-ee**, **-oe** and **-ye** do not drop the *e*:

| | | | | | | | | |
|---|---|---|---|---|---|---|---|---|
| agree | : | *agreeing* | hoe | : | *hoeing* | dye | : | *dyeing* |

Verbs ending in **-ie** alter this to *y* before **-ing**:

die : *dying* (compare *dye* : *dyeing*)

Certain words retain the *e* in order to be distinguishable from similar words with no *e*:

singe : *singeing* (as opposed to *sing* : *singing*)

and similarly *routeing*, *swingeing* and *tingeing*.

One or two words may correctly be written either with or without the *e*:

| | | | | | |
|---|---|---|---|---|---|
| age | : | *ageing* or *aging* | cue | : | *cueing* or *cuing* |

- **Final *i***

|          |   |            |          |   |                          |
|----------|---|------------|----------|---|--------------------------|
| *ski*    | : | *skiing*   | *taxi*   | : | *taxiing* or *taxying*   |

- **Doubling of final consonants**

Present participles in **-ing** obey the general rules for the doubling of final consonants outlined in the article DOUBLING OF FINAL CONSONANTS, eg:

i)   after a single stressed vowel:

|         |   |           |          |   |               |
|---------|---|-----------|----------|---|---------------|
| *run*   | : | *running* | *prefer* | : | *preferring*  |

ii)   after *l* regardless of stress

|          |   |             |
|----------|---|-------------|
| *signal* | : | *signalling* |

iii)   in certain other words as outlined in DOUBLING OF FINAL CONSONANTS:

|           |   |               |          |   |               |
|-----------|---|---------------|----------|---|---------------|
| *worship* | : | *worshipping* | *zigzag* | : | *zigzagging*  |

## **-ious, -eous**

> **Most words of this type are spelt *-ious*.**

Examples:

| | | |
|---|---|---|
| *abstemious* | *copious* | *oblivious* |
| *ambitious* | *dubious* | *obvious* |
| *anxious* | *glorious* | *religious* |
| *atrocious* | *gracious* | *scrumptious* |
| *cautious* | *ignominious* | *spurious* |
| *ceremonious* | *imperious* | *tedious* |
| *conscious* | *infectious* | *various* |
| *contagious* | *ingenious* | |

Words spelt **-eous** can be grouped into four categories:

i)   Words in which the *e* belongs to the 'core' word rather than to the word-ending:

|                  |   |                 |               |   |               |
|------------------|---|-----------------|---------------|---|---------------|
| *advantage*      | : | *advantageous*  | *homogeneity* | : | *homogeneous* |
| *courage*        | : | *courageous*    | *nausea*      | : | *nauseous*    |
| *outrage*        | : | *outrageous*    | *time*        | : | *timeous*     |
| *heterogeneity*  | : | *heterogeneous* |               |   |               |

ii)   Words that end in /-ay-*ni*-us/:

| | | | |
|---|---|---|---|
| *contemporaneous* | *instantaneous* | *momentaneous* | *spontaneous* |
| *extraneous* | *miscellaneous* | *simultaneous* | *subcutaneous* |

iii)   Technical and scientific terms that end in **-*aceous***, such as *cretaceous*, *herbaceous*, *orchidaceous*, *rosaceous*, *sebaceous*, to which can be added the non-technical words *curvaceous* and *predaceous*.

iv)   The rest, difficult to classify according to any rule:

| | | | |
|---|---|---|---|
| *aqueous* | *(dis)courteous* | *gorgeous* | *plenteous* |
| *beauteous* | *duteous* | *hideous* | *righteous* |
| *bounteous* | *erroneous* | *igneous* | *vitreous* |
| *consanguineous* | *gaseous* | *piteous* | |

**ir-** see IL-.

## -is

> **Almost all words ending in -*is* form plurals by changing the *i* to *e*.**

Examples:

| | | | | | |
|---|---|---|---|---|---|
| *analysis* | : | *analyses* | *hypothesis* | : | *hypotheses* |
| *basis* | : | *bases* | *oasis* | : | *oases* |
| *crisis* | : | *crises* | *thesis* | : | *theses* |

> *Metropolis* is an exception, with a plural *metropolises*. So also is *proboscis*, with two possible plural forms, *proboscises* and, in scientific and technical contexts, *proboscides*.
>
> *Pelvis* and *mantis* may have either form of plural, but *pelvises* and *mantises* are much more common than *pelves* and *mantes*.

## -ise, -ize

Many words in English may be spelt equally correctly with **-*ise*** or **-*ize***, eg *equalise/equalize*, *terrorise/terrorize*. Others may only be spelt with an *s*: *advertise*, *despise*, *televise*. A few words must be spelt with a *z*: *capsize*, *prize*, *size*. The problem is to remember which group a word belongs to.

The rules are easier to state if verbs are treated separately from nouns and adjectives.

### ✦   Verbs

The basic distinction is between verbs consisting of a 'core' plus a word-ending (eg *equalise* = *equal* + *-ise*), in which case the ending may be either **-*ise*** or **-*ize***, and those in which the **-*ise*** is part of the 'core' (eg *advise* and *despise*, not formed from *adv* or *desp* + a word-ending), in which case the spelling will usually be **-*ise***. The following guidelines may be of further help:

> **If the /-iyz/ is added to something that is recognizable as an English word, both *-ise* and *-ize* will be correct.**

Examples:

| | | | | | |
|---|---|---|---|---|---|
| *critic* | : | *criticise* or *criticize* | *modern* | : | *modernise* or *modernize* |
| *item* | : | *itemise* or *itemize* | *victim* | : | *victimise* or *victimize* |

In some cases, the core word is no longer in common use, which can cause problems, but these are few, eg *pulver* (= 'dust'): *pulverise* or *pulverize*.

The *-ize* spelling is now standard in American English, and is becoming more and more used in British English although the *-ise* form is still preferred by many users of British English.

⚠ When the core word ends in a silent *e*, this *e* is dropped before the ending is added (as you would expect from the general rule — see -E):

*fertile* : *fertilise* or *fertilize*     *oxide* : *oxidise* or *oxidize*

Words ending in *l* do not double this *l* before *-ise/-ize* is added: *equalise*, *specialize*, etc (see DOUBLING OF FINAL CONSONANTS.) But note that unpredictably *crystallise/-ize* and *tranquillise/-ize* have double *l*'s.

> **In words in which the /-iyz/ ending could be replaced by another word-ending to form a recognizable and related English word, both *-ise* and *-ize* will be correct.**

Examples:

| | | |
|---|---|---|
| *antagonist* | = | *antagon* + *-ist*, so *antagonise* and *antagonize* both correct |
| *ostracism* | = | *ostrac* + *-ism*, so *ostracise* and *ostracize* both correct |
| *harmonic* | = | *harmon(y)* + *-ic*, so *harmonise* and *harmonize* both correct |
| *maximal* | = | *maxim(um)* + *-al*, so *maximise* and *maximize* both correct |
| *recognition* | = | *recogn* + *-ition*, so *recognise* and *recognize* both correct |
| *sympathetic* | = | *sympath(y)* + *-etic*, so *sympathise* and *sympathize* both correct |

⚠ In a few cases, the word root changes slightly in form:

*synthetic* = *synthet* + *-ic*, so *synthesise* and *synthesize* both correct.

If what precedes the ending is **not** recognizable as an English word nor is related to any English word in the way outlined above, the ending will always be *-ise*.

Examples:

| | | | |
|---|---|---|---|
| *apprise* | *despise* | *improvise* | *supervise* |
| *arise* | *disguise* | *incise* | *surmise* |
| *circumcise* | *excise* | *revise* | *surprise* |
| *comprise* | *exercise* | *rise* | *televise* |
| *compromise* | *franchise* | | |

If the final syllable of the verb is **not** pronounced /-iyz/, the final *-ise* must be part of the core word and must not be written with a *z*.

Examples:

| | | | |
|---|---|---|---|
| *appraise* | *cruise* | *practise* | *promise* |
| *braise* | *liaise* | *praise* | *raise* |
| *bruise* | | | |

⚠ There are a few exceptions to the above guidelines, and a few words that do not easily fit into any general rule:

*advertise*, *advise*, *chastise* and *devise* must always be spelt with an *s*;

*apprise* and *misprise* may also be spelt with a *z*;

*merchandise*, when used as a verb, may also be spelt *merchandize*, but the *s* form is by far the commoner (as a noun, it is always spelt with an *s*);

in the sense of 'to force open with a lever', *prise* may also be spelt with a *z*, but the *s* form is much the commoner; in the sense of 'to value', only *prize* is correct;

*capsize*, *seize* and *size* must always be written with a *z*.

A few words are spelt with a *y*, not an *i*:

*analyse* (and any words based on it, such as *psychoanalyse* and *breathalyse*) and *paralyse*.

These words are always spelt with an *s* in British English, and always with a *z* in American English.

### ✦ Nouns and adjectives

**The best guess for a noun or an adjective is always -*ise*.**

Almost all the nouns and adjectives of this type end in **-*ise***, whatever their pronunciation: eg

| | | | |
|---|---|---|---|
| *bruise* | *guise* | *praise* | *rise* |
| *concise* | *malaise* | *precise* | *surprise* |
| *cruise* | *mortise* | *premise* | *tortoise* |
| *demise* | *noise* | *promise* | *treatise* |
| *disguise* | *paradise* | *raise* | *turquoise* |
| *expertise* | *porpoise* | *reprise* | *wise* |

> ⚠ *Assizes, baize, maize, prize* and *size* are exceptions.
>
> There are no nouns that may be equally correctly spelt with *s* or *z*. There is always only <u>one</u> correct form for each of the nouns of this type, <u>either</u> with *s* <u>or</u> with *z*.
>
> Be careful not to confuse the verbs *advise*, *devise* and *practise* with the nouns *advice*, *device* and *practice*.

See also -CE, -SE.

**-*isy*** see -ACY.

## -*l*, -*ll*

**If a word ending in /l/ is only one syllable long and the vowel in it is a single letter, the chances are that the word will end with a double *l*.**

Examples:

| | | | |
|---|---|---|---|
| *all* | *chill* | *full* | *thrall* |
| *bill* | *dull* | *ill* | *toll* |
| *call* | *fell* | *mill* | *will* |

> ⚠ The only common exceptions are *gel*, *nil* and *pal*, and also *gal* (= 'girl').

**In all other cases, the word will end in a single *l*.**

Examples:

| | | | |
|---|---|---|---|
| *appeal* | *initial* | *sandal* | *trail* |
| *appal* | *instil* | *soil* | *trial* |
| *distil* | *model* | *soul* | *wool* |
| *equal* | *prevail* | *symbol* | |

## ✦ Changes to the basic form

### ● *-l* becomes *-ll*

For the rules covering the doubling of a single final *l* before a suffix beginning with a vowel (as in *controlling*, *distillation*, and so on), see DOUBLING OF FINAL CONSONANTS.

### ● *-ll* becomes *-l*

The *ll* spelling is generally retained in compounds and derivatives based on any of the *-ll* words:

| | | | | | |
|---|---|---|---|---|---|
| *call* | : | *recall* | *fall* | : | *pitfall* |
| *fill* | : | *refill* | *mill* | : | *sawmill* |

and so on. In certain cases, however, the *-ll* becomes reduced to a single *-l*:

i)   A double *ll* drops one of the *l*'s before any suffix beginning with a consonant, except *-ness*:

| | | |
|---|---|---|
| *dull* + *-ly* | = | *dully* |
| *full* + *-ly* | = | *fully* |
| *full* + *-some* | = | *fulsome* |
| *install* + *-ment* | = | *instalment* |
| *skill* + *-ful* | = | *skilful* |
| *thrall* + *-dom* | = | *thraldom* |
| *will* + *-ful* | = | *wilful* |
| *smell, spell, spill* + *-t* | = | *smelt, spelt, spilt* |

but before *-ness*

| | | |
|---|---|---|
| *dull* + *-ness* | = | *dullness* |
| *ill* + *-ness* | = | *illness* |
| *full* + *-ness* | = | *fullness* (though an older spelling *fulness* is still sometimes seen and is still considered correct) |

A few other words show similar changes. The spelling of the following should be noted:

| | | |
|---|---|---|
| *all* | : | *almighty, almost, already, altogether* |
| *bell* | : | *belfry* |
| *chill* | : | *chilblain* |
| *full* + *fill* | : | *fulfil* |
| *thrall* | : | *enthral* |
| *well* | : | *welfare* |

⚠ Note the spelling of the word-ending *-ful* (as in *spoonful* and *cupful*), and also the spelling of *annul, enrol* and *install* (also *instal*).

Note also that, although common in informal English, *alright* is not yet accepted in formal English. Write *all right*.

## -ly

**Adverbs are generally formed by adding -ly to an adjective.**

Examples:

| | | | | |
|---|---|---|---|---|
| foolish | : foolishly | | surprising | : surprisingly |
| initial | : initially | | careful | : carefully |
| strange | : strangely | | free | : freely |

### • Final -le

Adjectives which end in *-le* preceded by a vowel form adverbs in the regular way:

|  |  |  |
|---|---|---|
| agile : agilely | docile : docilely | pale : palely |

⚠ Note *whole : wholly* (not ✗ *wholely*).

However, if the *-le* is preceded by a consonant, the corresponding adverb is generally formed by replacing the *e* by *y*:

| | | | |
|---|---|---|---|
| double | : doubly | simple | : simply |
| predictable | : predictably | subtle | : subtly |
| possible | : possibly | supple | : supply |

⚠ *Supplely* is also in common use and is correct.

### • Final *ll*

If an adjective ends in a double *l*, the corresponding adverb will end in *-lly*:

| | | |
|---|---|---|
| dull : dully | full : fully | shrill : shrilly |

### • Final *y*

If an adjective ends in *y* precede by a consonant, the corresponding adverb will generally end in *-ily*:

| | | | |
|---|---|---|---|
| funny | : funnily | silly | : sillily |
| hasty | : hastily | weary | : wearily |

⚠️ Certain short adjectives ending in a *y* which is pronounced /iy/ (as in *my*) retain, or may retain, the *y*:

| | | |
|---|---|---|
| *dry* | : | *drily* or *dryly* |
| *shy* | : | *shily* or *shyly* |
| *sly* | : | *slily* or *shyly* |

but only *spryly* and *wryly* are correct.

If the *y* is preceded by a vowel, it does not change to *i* before **-ly**:

| | | | | |
|---|---|---|---|---|
| *coy* | : | *coyly* | *grey* | : | *greyly* |

⚠️ Adjectives ending in **-ey** which are formed from nouns that end in *-e* change the **-ey** to **-i-**:

| | | | | |
|---|---|---|---|---|
| *mate* | : | *matey* | : | *matily* |
| *dice* | : | *dicey* | : | *dicily* |

Note that the adverb from *gay* is *gaily*; note also the spelling of *daily*.

## • Final *-ly*

If the 'core' adjective on which the adverb is based itself ends in **-ly**, (eg *oily*, *jolly*, *friendly*, *heavenly*), opinions vary as to the acceptability of the corresponding adverbs (*oilily*, *friendlily*, etc):

i)   If the final **-ly** of the adjective is not itself a word-ending added to a core noun, the corresponding adverb is generally considered acceptable, eg *holily*, *jollily*, *oilily*, *sillily*, etc.

ii)   If the final **-ly** of the adjective is itself a word-ending (eg *friendly* = *friend* + *-ly*), many people feel that the corresponding adverbs sound rather clumsy (although they are not ungrammatical), and are therefore best avoided (eg by using a phrase such as *in a ... manner*). Three-syllable adverbs (eg *friendlily*, *lovelily*) are generally considered more acceptable than those of four or more syllables (*heavenlily*, *ungodlily*). However, it is generally considered better to avoid such formations by refashioning the sentence and substituting a phrase such as *in a friendly way*.

⚠️ Note that some words function as both adjectives and adverbs, eg *slovenly*, *weekly*, *daily*, *yearly*:

*paid on a weekly basis* (adjective)
*Do you want to be paid weekly or monthly?* (adverb)

## • And finally ...

Three adverbs unpredictably drop the final *e* of the corresponding core adjectives: *duly*, *eerily*, *truly*.

**noun plurals** see PLURAL NOUNS.

## -o

### ✦ Plural nouns

- *-os* or *-i?*

> Most words of Italian, French or Spanish origin which end in
> *-o* have regular plurals in *-s*.

Examples:

| | | |
|---|---|---|
| *bronchos* | *gigolos* | *stilettos* |
| *casinos* | *risottos* | |

Some words of Italian origin have, or may have, a plural in *-i*:

i)   The *-i* plurals in the following list are generally confined to technical musical contexts only: *librettos* or *libretti*, and similarly *crescendos/crescendi*, *diminuendos/diminuendi*, *solos/soli*, *sopranos/soprani*, *tempos/tempi*, *virtuosos/virtuosi*.

> ⚠  Note that the only correct plural of *alto* is *altos*, never *alti*.

ii)   Only *graffiti* and *confetti* are correct.

iii)   Words that refer to people or things with strong associations with Italy usually have the Italian plural in *-i*, eg *mafiosi* rather than *mafiosos*.

- *-os* or *-oes?*

> Nouns that end in *oo* or in which the *o* is preceded by another
> vowel always add *-s* alone.

Examples:

| | | | |
|---|---|---|---|
| *cameos* | *igloos* | *radios* | *videos* |
| *embryos* | *kangaroos* | *studios* | *zoos* |
| *duos* | *patios* | | |

> Most nouns that end in *o* preceded by a consonant add *-s*
> alone.

Examples:

| | | | |
|---|---|---|---|
| *albinos* | *Eskimos* | *pianos* | *quangos* |
| *altos* | *kimonos* | *piccolos* | *rhinos* |
| *concertos* | *memos* | *placebos* | *torsos* |
| *discos* | *photos* | | |

272

⚠ Some exceptions must be noted:

1. A number of nouns may add either **-s** or **-es** in the plural:

| | | |
|---|---|---|
| *archipelago* | *grotto* | *peccadillo* |
| *banjo* | *halo* | *portico* |
| *dado* | *innuendo* | *proviso* |
| *desperado* | *lasso* | *salvo* |
| *fiasco* | *manifesto* | *tuxedo* |
| *flamingo* | *memento* | *virago* |
| *fresco* | *mosquito* | *zero* |
| *ghetto* | | |

2. The following words <u>must</u> have **-es** in the plural:

| | | |
|---|---|---|
| *buffalo* | *hero* | *potato* |
| *cargo* | *hobo* | *tomato* |
| *dingo* | *lingo* | *tornado* |
| *domino* | *mango* | *torpedo* |
| *echo* | *motto* | *veto* |
| *embargo* | *Negro* | *volcano* |
| *go* | *no* | |

3. The plural of *do* is *dos* or *do's* (as in *do's and don'ts*).

## ✦ Third person singular present tense of verbs

There are relatively few verbs (compared to the nouns) that end in *o*, most of them being words that can serve as nouns or verbs (eg *lasso, radio, shampoo, video*). As with the nouns, both **-s** and **-es** are possible (*She shampoos her hair □ He goes into town*), but the rules for verbs are not quite the same as those for nouns:

> **If the noun adds -es in the plural, add -es in the verb.**
> **If the noun plural allows both -s and -es forms, add -es in the verb.**
> **If the noun adds -s, or if there is no related noun, add -s.**

Examples:

| | | |
|---|---|---|
| *echoes* | *lassoes* | *vetoes* |
| *embargoes* | *torpedoes* | *zeroes* |
| *discos* | *radios* | *videos* |
| *memos* | *shampoos* | |

⚠ The only exception is *does*, which cannot be spelt *dos*.

## -oe, -e-

There are a number of words in English in which there is an *oe* which is pronounced /ee/ — *amoeba, diarrhoea, homoeopathic*, for example. In American

English, some of these words are generally written without the *o*, eg *diarrhea*, *homeopathic*, but in British English, the *o* is generally retained.

 Although the *o* and *e* were formerly often written as a 'ligature' *œ*, they are now normally written as separate letters.

See also -AE-, -E-.

## -oes, -os see -O.

## -on

A few words which end in **-on** form, or may form, their plurals in **-a**:

| | | |
|---|---|---|
| automaton | : | automata (also automatons) |
| criterion | : | criteria |
| ganglion | : | ganglia (also ganglions) |
| phenomenon | : | phenomena |

## -or, -our

**All agent nouns (ie 'doer' words) in this category end in -or, with the sole exception of *saviour*.**

**For other words, the best guess is -our.**

The commonest **-our** nouns in English are the following :

| | | | |
|---|---|---|---|
| ardour | favour | labour | savour |
| armour | fervour | misdemeanour | splendour |
| behaviour | flavour | neighbour | tumour |
| candour | glamour | odour | valour |
| clamour | harbour | parlour | vapour |
| colour | honour | rigour | vigour |
| endeavour | humour | rumour | |

Notice that many of these words are abstract nouns (eg refer to ideas and feelings rather than to objects and things).

 In American English all the words in the above list are spelt **-or**, not **-our**, with the exception of *glamour*, which is a commoner spelling than *glamor*.

Common words written **-or** in British English are:

| | | | |
|---|---|---|---|
| anchor | languor | pallor | tenor |
| error | liquor | squalor | torpor |
| horror | mirror | stupor | tremor |

See also -ER, -OR, -AR for the rules for choosing between *-or*, *-er* and *-ar* for agent (or 'doer') words like *swimmer* and *actor*.

● **Dropping the *u***
When certain word-endings are added to *-our* words, the *u* is dropped. These word-endings are *-ary*, *-ation*, *-ial*, *-iferous*, *-ific*, *-ious*, *-ise/-ize* and *-ous*:

| | | | | | |
|--------|---|-------------|----------|---|-------------|
| honour | : | honorary | honour | : | honorific |
| colour | : | coloration | labour | : | laborious |
| armour | : | armorial | glamour | : | glamorize |
| odour | : | odoriferous | humour | : | humorous |

Before most other word-endings the *u* is retained:

| | | | | | |
|--------|---|-------------|--------|---|-------------|
| honour | : | honourable | humour | : | humourless |
| labour | : | labourer | armour | : | armoury |
| colour | : | colourful | savour | : | savoury |
| favour | : | favourite | | | |

Words ending in *-ism* and *-ist* are inconsistent: *behaviourism* and *watercolourist*, but *rigorism* and *humorist*.

**-ory** see -ARY.

**-os, -i** see -O.

**-os, -oes** see -O.

**-our** see -OR.

**-ous, -us**

> *-ous* is an adjective ending, *-us* is a noun ending.

Examples:

| | | |
|-----------|-----------|-----------|
| anonymous | enormous | nervous |
| cancerous | famous | poisonous |
| covetous | impetuous | spacious |

| | | | |
|--------|---------|---------|-----------|
| abacus | foetus | lotus | thesaurus |
| cactus | impetus | octopus | virus |
| circus | | | |

⚠ Adjectives taken directly from Latin, in which many adjectives end in *-us,* do not follow this rule, eg *professor emeritus, regius professor.*

## past tenses and past participles

✦ **Formation**

**To form a past tense or past participle of most regular verbs, add *-ed* to the basic form of the 'core' word.**

Examples:

| | | | | | |
|---|---|---|---|---|---|
| *claim* | : | *claimed* | *toast* | : | *toasted* |
| *link* | : | *linked* | *taxi* | : | *taxied* |
| *toss* | : | *tossed* | *veto* | : | *vetoed* |

● **Irregular past forms**

Some English verbs are, however, irregular in formation, and there are a number of verbs which have more than one possible form for their past tense and past participle. In many cases, the choice of one variant or the other is a matter of personal preference, but in other cases, the variants differ with regard to meaning, use or modernness and the choice is therefore not entirely free.

*abide*: When used in the phrase *abide by* (= 'to act according to, be faithful to'), the past tense and past participle are *abided*: *He said he would abide by our decision and he has abided by it.* However, in the archaic or literary sense of 'to live', the past tense and past participle are *abode*: *She abode by a lake.*

*awake*: Past tense usually *awoke*, but *awaked* is not incorrect. Past participle usually *awoken*, but again *awaked* is not incorrect.

*begin*: Past tense *began*, past participle *begun*.

*bereave*: Past tense and past participle *bereaved*. The past participle may be used as an adjective meaning 'deprived by death' (*The bereaved parents refused to talk to reporters*) and as a noun (*They tried to comfort the bereaved*). *Bereft* is an adjective meaning 'deprived' in a more general sense: *Bereft of every reason to go on living, he tried to hang himself.*

*beseech*: Past tense and past participle both *beseeched* or *besought*.

*bet*: Past tense and past participle usually *bet*. *Betted* is very rare.

*bid*: In the sense 'to make an offer, make a bid', the past tense and past participle are both *bid*: *John bid £500 for the painting. Bidded* is not correct in Standard English. In the archaic, literary or formal sense of 'to ask, say or tell', the past tense is usually *bade*, the past participle usually *bidden* (*He bade me enter* □ *He bade me farewell*) but *bid* is sometimes used as the past tense and past participle in this sense also.

*bite*: Past tense *bit*, past participle *bitten*; *bit* as a past participle is archaic.

*bleed*: Past tense and past participle *bled*.

*blow*: Past tense *blew*, past participle *blown*.

*break*: Past tense *broke*, past participle *broken*.

*bring*: Past tense and past participle *brought*.

*burn*: When the verb has no object, *burned* is commoner than *burnt* in both British and American English. With an object present, the former is commoner in American English and the latter commoner in British English. In both American and British English, *burnt* is the form used as an adjective: *burnt toast*.

*cast*: Past tense and past participle *cast*. The past tense and past participle of *broadcast* are both *broadcast*, and similarly the past tense and past participle of *forecast* are *forecast*.

*catch*: Past tense and past participle *caught*.

*choose*: Past tense *chose*, past participle *chosen*.

*cleave*: In the sense 'to adhere', the past tense and past participle are *cleaved*. In the sense 'to split', the past tense forms used are *clove*, *cleft* and less commonly *cleaved*, the past participle forms *cloven*, *cleft* and less commonly *cleaved*. As adjectives, the past participle forms used are generally *cleft* and *cloven*, but they are not interchangeable: you speak of a *cleft stick* and a *cleft palate*, but a *cloven hoof* and *cloven-footed*.

*come*: Past tense *came*, past participle *come*.

*cost*: In the sense of 'to have as a price', the past tense and past participle are both *cost*; in the sense of 'to estimate the cost of', *costed*.

*creep*: Past tense and past participle *crept*.

*dig*: Past tense and past participle *dug*.

*dive*: In standard British English, the past tense is *dived*. In American English, both *dived* and *dove* are considered correct, although some authorities deprecate the use of *dove* in formal speech and writing. In both American and British English, the past participle is *dived*.

*do*: Past tense *did*, past participle *done*.

*draw*: Past tense *drew*, past participle *drawn*.

*dream*: Both *dreamed* and *dreamt* are correct for both past tense and past participle, the former being the commoner in American English, the latter in British English. Some British authorities suggest that the *-ed* form is more likely to be used than the *-t* form when the emphasis is on the duration of the dream (*She dreamed of him all night* but *She dreamt about him again last night*).

*drink*: Past tense *drank*, past participle *drunk*. *Drunken* is an adjective.

*drive*: Past tense *drove*, past participle *driven*.

*dwell*: Past tense and past participle *dwelled* and *dwelt*; *dwelt* is commoner than *dwelled* in both American and British English.

**earn**: Past tense and past participle **earned** only. **Earnt** is seen occasionally, but is not correct in standard formal English.

**eat**: Past tense **ate**, past participle **eaten**.

**fall**: Past tense **fell**, past participle **fallen**.

**fit**: In British English, the past tense and past participle are always **fitted**. In American English, usage varies between **fit** and **fitted**, but the latter is the more common in a passive construction and is the form used as an adjective (*a fitted jacket*).

**flee**: Past tense and past participle **fled**.

**fling**: Past tense and past participle **flung**.

**fly**: Past tense **flew**, past participle **flown**.

**forget**: Past tense **forgot**, past participle **forgotten**.

**forgive**: Past tense **forgave**, past participle **forgiven**.

**freeze**: Past tense **froze**, past participle **frozen**.

**give**: Past tense **gave**, past participle **given**.

**go**: Past tense **went**, past participle **gone**.

**grow**: Past tense **grew**, past participle **grown**.

**hang**: The normal past tense and past participle forms are **hung**. When the verb refers to suicide, capital punishment, etc, the correct past tense and past participle form is **hanged**, but **hung** is also used and acceptable in informal English.

**hear**: Past tense and past participle **heard**.

**hide**: Past tense **hid**, past participle **hidden**.

**hurt**: Past tense and past participle **hurt**.

**keep**: Past tense and past participle **kept**.

**kneel**: Past tense and past participle **kneeled** or **knelt**. The **-ed** form is usual in American English, the **-t** form generally preferred by speakers of British English, especially for the past participle.

**knit**: Past tense and past participle **knitted** or **knit**. **Knitted** is the normal form when the verb denotes the making of garments, etc with knitting-needles and wool: *She knitted a pair of socks □ a knitted hat*. **Knit** is generally used in metaphorical contexts: *Their dependence on one another knit them into a close group*; but when the verb is linked with the noun *brows*, **knitted** is also possible: *He knit/ knitted his brows as he read the letter*.

**know**: Past tense **knew**, past participle **known**.

**lay**: Past tense and past participle **laid**.

**lean**: Past tense and past participle **leaned** or **leant**. The **-ed** form is usual in American English, the **-t** form generally preferred by speakers of British English, especially for the past participle.

*leap*: Past tense and past participle *leaped* or *leapt*. (See note at LEAN.)

*learn*: Past tense and past participle *learned* or *learnt*. (See note at LEAN.)

*lie*: Past tense *lay*, past participle *lain*.

*light*: Both *lighted* and *lit* are possible for both the past tense and past participle, but *lit* is the more common except when the past participle is being used as an attributive adjective: *She lit the fire* □ *a lighted match*. Note, however, that when the attributive adjective is preceded by an adverb, the form *lit* is used: *a badly lit room*. The past tense and past participle of *high-light* and *spotlight* are both regularly formed with *-ed*.

*make*: Past tense and past participle *made*.

*mistake*: Past tense *mistook*, past participle *mistaken*.

*mow*: Past tense *mowed*, past participle *mowed* or *mown*.

*pass*: Past tense and past participle always *passed*, never *past*.

*pay*: Past tense and past participle *paid*.

*plead*: In standard British English, the past tense and past participle are both the regular form *pleaded*. *Pled* is a dialect form, acceptable in Scottish and American English.

*prove*: The past tense is *proved*. The preferred past participle form in British English is *proved*, although *proven* is also used. In American English, the opposite is the case. As an adjective, the past participle form used is usually *proven*: *a proven track record*.

*put*: Past tense and past participle *put*.

*quit*: The past tense and past participle may both be either *quit* or *quitted*, the former being preferred in American English and the latter in British English.

*rid*: Past tense and past participle usually *rid*, but *ridded* is also correct although rather old-fashioned.

*ring*: Past tense *rang*, past participle *rung*, except in the sense 'put a ring on', 'mark with a ring', 'form a ring around', for which the past tense and participle are regularly formed by the addition of *-ed*: *He identified the bird as having been ringed as a nestling in Norway*. *Rung* as a past tense form is not correct in Standard English in this sense.

*rise*: Past tense *rose*, past participle *risen*.

*saw*: Past tense *sawed*, past participle *sawed* or *sawn*. *Sawn* is used in British English when the participle is used as an adjective, but *sawed* in American English.

*say*: Past tense and past participle *said*.

*see*: Past tense *saw*, past participle *seen*.

*sell*: Past tense and past participle *sold*.

*sew*: Past tense *sewed*, past participle *sewed* or *sewn*. *Sewn* is preferred when the participle is used as an adjective.

*shake*: Past tense *shook*, past participle *shaken*.

*shave*: Past tense and past participle *shaved*. The old past participle *shaven* is now used only as an adjective or in compounds: *clean-shaven*.

*shear*: The past tense is *sheared*. The past participle is *shorn* in most senses, but *sheared* is also correct, and is the only form to be used when talking of the cutting or breaking of metal objects: *A piece of the girder had sheared off*.

*shine*: The past tense and past participle are both *shone*, except in the sense of 'to polish', in which case both are regular *-ed* forms.

*shit*: Correct past tense and participle forms are *shit*, *shat* and *shitted*. *Shat* is the commonest of the three.

*shoe*: Past tense and participle *shoed* or *shod*; as an adjective, *shod*.

*shoot*: Past tense and past participle *shot*.

*show*: Past tense *showed*; past participle *showed* or *shown*. In the passive, use *shown*: *He was shown no mercy*.

*shrink*: Past tense usually *shrank*; although some authorities accept *shrunk* also, others consider it now to be old-fashioned. Past participle *shrunk*. *Shrunken* is now rarely used except as an adjective.

*shut*: Past tense and past participle *shut*.

*sing*: Past tense *sang*, past participle *sung*.

*sink*: Past tense usually *sank*; *sunk* is acceptable, but rare. Past participle *sunk*. *Sunken* is now rarely used except as an adjective.

*sit*: Past tense and past participle *sat*.

*slay*: In the sense of 'to kill', the past tense is *slew* and the past participle *slain*. *Slayed* is the usual past tense and participle form in the sense of 'to impress or amuse greatly', but *slew* may be used as the past tense form in this sense also.

*sleep*: Past tense and past participle *slept*.

*sling*: Past tense and past participle *slung*.

*slink*: Past tense and past participle *slunk*.

*smell*: Past tense and past participle *smelled* or *smelt*. The *-ed* form is usual in American English, the *-t* form generally preferred by speakers of British English, especially for the past participle.

*sow*: Past tense *sowed*; past participle *sowed* or *sown*.

*speak*: Past tense *spoke*, past participle *spoken*.

*speed*: In the sense of 'to move or travel fast', the past tense and participle are both *sped*. In the sense of 'to travel faster than is permitted' or in combination with *up*, the correct form is *speeded*.

*spell*: In the sense of 'to name or write down the letters of a word', both *spelled* and *spelt* are correct, the former being the form almost always used in American English. In the sense of 'to relieve someone at work', the past tense and past participle are *spelled*.

*spill*: Past tense and past participle *spilled* or *spilt*. The *-ed* form is usual in American English, the *-t* form generally preferred by speakers of British English, especially for the past participle, and particularly when the past participles are used as adjectives: *spilt milk*.

*spin*: Past tense and past participle *spun*.

*spit*: In British English, the past tense and past participle are both *spat*. In American English, an alternative past tense is *spit*. In the sense of 'to impale', the past tense and participle are regular *-ed* forms.

*spoil*: Past tense and past participle *spoiled* or *spoilt*. The *-ed* form is usual in American English, the *-t* form generally preferred by speakers of British English, especially for the past participle, and particularly when the past participles are used as adjectives: *a spoilt child*.

*spring*: Past tense *sprang*, past participle *sprung*.

*stand*: Past tense and past participle *stood*.

*stave*: Past tense and past participle *staved* or *stove*; *staved* is the form to use in the sense of 'to delay or ward off'.

*steal*: Past tense *stole*, past participle *stolen*.

*stick*: Past tense and past participle *stuck*.

*sting*: Past tense and past participle *stung*.

*stink*: Past tense *stank* or *stunk*; past participle *stunk*.

*strew*: Past tense *strewed*, participle *strewed* or *strewn*.

*stride*: Past tense *strode*, past participle *stridden*.

*strike*: Past tense and past participle *struck*; the old past participle *stricken* is now used only in figurative senses : *grief-stricken* □ *stricken with remorse*.

*string*: Past tense and past participle *strung*, never *stringed*, which is derived from the <u>noun</u> *string*, as in *stringed instruments*.

*strive*: Past tense *strove*, past participle *striven*. In American English, *strived* is also acceptable for the past tense.

*swear*: Past tense *swore*, past participle *sworn*.

*sweat*: Past tense and participle usually the regular forms, both *sweated*, but *sweat*, though less common, is not incorrect.

*sweep*: Past tense and past participle *swept*.

*swell*: Past tense *swelled*. Past participle *swelled* or *swollen*, the former being the more common, *swollen* being used mostly in the passive: *Soon the citizen army is swollen by provincial troops*. As an adjective, the form to use is *swollen*; the only exception is in conjunction with the noun *head*, it being correct to speak of a *swollen head* or, much less commonly, a *swelled head*.

*swim*: Past tense *swam*, past participle *swum*.

*take*: Past tense *took*, past participle *taken*.

*teach*: Past tense and past participle *taught*.

*tear*: Past tense *tore*, past participle *torn*.

*tell*: Past tense and past participle *told*.

*think*: Past tense and past participle *thought*.

*thrive*: The regular past tense and past participle form *thrived* is probably as common as the irregular forms *throve* and *thriven*.

*throw*: Past tense *threw*, past participle *thrown*.

*tread*: Past tense *trod*, past participle *trod* or *trodden*.

*wake*: Past tense *woke*, rarely (but quite correctly) *waked*; past participle *woken*, also (but rarely) *waked*.

*wear*: Past tense *wore*, past participle *worn*.

*weave*: In the context of cloth, the past tense is *wove* and the past participle *woven*. Most people are unaware that in the sense of 'to move in a winding course', they are dealing with a totally different verb, whose past tense and past participle are *weaved*. When *weave* means 'to make up a story', it seems clear that it is the first verb that is being used in a figurative sense, and the past tense and past participle forms should be *wove* and *woven*, but some authorities accept *weaved* for this sense also.

*wed*: Past tense and participle *wedded*; *wed* is non-standard.

*weep*: Past tense and past participle *wept*.

*wet*: Both *wet* and *wetted* are correct, but the former is the commoner except in passive constructions where there could be confusion between the past participle *wet* and the adjective *wet* after the verb *to be*: compare *Her hair was slightly wet* (adjective) and *Her hair was slightly wetted* (verb).

*win*: Past tense and past participle *won*.

*wind*: Pronounced /wiynd/, past tense and past participle *wound*. Pronounced /wind/, past tense and past participle *winded*.

*write*: Past tense *wrote*, past participle *written*.

## ✦ Spelling

> **For the past tense and past participle of most regular verbs, add *-ed* to the basic form of the 'core' word.**

Examples:

| | | | | | |
|---|---|---|---|---|---|
| claim | : | claimed | toast | : | toasted |
| link | : | linked | taxi | : | taxied |
| toss | : | tossed | veto | : | vetoed |

For the rules governing certain changes to the 'core' word, such as altering a final *y* to *i* (eg *cry*, *cried*), see -ED.

## plural nouns

> To form a plural noun, it is generally sufficient to add -*s* to the singular form of the noun.

Examples:

*book* : *books*     *table* : *tables*     *alibi* : *alibis*

For the formation and spelling of the plurals of nouns ending in -*a*, -*f*/-*fe*, -*ful*, -*ies*, -*is*, -*o*, -*on*, -*um*, -*us* and -*y*, see -AE, -FS/-FES, -FUL, -IES, -IS, -O, -ON, -UM, -US and -Y. See also DOUBLING OF FINAL CONSONANTS, -IM and -X.

For apostrophes in plurals, see APOSTROPHE.

Other questions and problems are dealt with below.

- **Nouns ending in *s*, *z*, *x*, *sh* or *ch***

To a noun ending *s*, *z x*, *sh* or *ch* (pronounced /ch/), add -*es* to form the plural:

*kiss* : *kisses*     *box* : *boxes*     *church* : *churches*
*waltz* : *waltzes*     *bush* : *bushes*

> ⚠ If the final *ch* is not pronounced /ch/, add -*s* alone:
>
> *monarch* : *monarchs*     *loch* : *lochs*
> *stomach* : *stomachs*

A few one-syllable nouns ending in *s* and *z* double their final consonant when -*es* is added: *fezzes*, *quizzes*. (Compare the rules given in DOUBLING OF FINAL CONSONANTS.) Note that in some cases the plural is, or may be, spelt with a single letter where a doubled letter would be expected: *buses*, *gases*.

- **Irregular plurals**

A number of small groups of nouns have completely irregular plurals:

*foot* : *feet*     *tooth* : *teeth*
*goose* : *geese*
*louse* : *lice*     *mouse* : *mice*
*man* : *men*     *woman* : *women*
*child* : *children*     *ox* : *oxen*

(Also *brother*, which in the religious sense has the plural *brethren*.)

*penny* : *pence* (as an amount)
        *pennies* (as coins)

> ⚠ **Regular plurals which might be expected to be irregular**
>
> *Brahmans, caymans, Germans, ottomans, shamans, talismans, Walkmans*
> *mongooses*
> *tenderfoots* (but also *tenderfeet*)

A number of words have so-called '***zero plurals***', in which the plural form is the same as the singular: *one sheep, two sheep; one grouse, two grouse.* (See the section on ANIMAL AND BIRD NAMES below.)

## • Animal and bird names

Most animal and bird names have a plural form different from the singular form of the noun: *cats, dogs, mice, thrushes, cows, squirrels, tortoises, beetles,* etc. Some, however, have two possible plural forms, a regular one and a so-called 'zero plural' which is identical in both written and spoken form to the singular, the regular ***s***-plural generally being used when talking of individuals or species, the zero plural when considering animals collectively.

i)  Among the common animal and bird names that have only a zero plural are, in addition to *sheep* and *grouse* mentioned above, *bison, cod, deer, moose* and *swine.*

ii)  With some other animal names, the zero plural is used when a number of the animals are considered collectively (eg *fishing for mackerel □ keen on tropical fish*), but the marked plural form with *-s* may be equally used when considering the group as a number of individuals (eg *They caught half a dozen mackerel/mackerels*) and the marked form is always used when talking of separate species (eg *The Spanish mackerels are slender fishes with strong, knife-like teeth*). Among other words in this category are *antelope, elk, haddock, herring, pheasant, pike, quail, reindeer, salmon, trout* and *woodcock.* The zero plural is also used after words denoting quantities: *a brace of pheasant.*

iii)  A third category comprises those animal names that almost always occur with a regular plural, but which may occasionally occur with a zero plural when spoken of collectively and especially when considered as game or food animals: *duck* (only if wild duck — farmyard ducks never take a zero plural), *elephant, lion, tiger.*

## • Compound nouns

> **Most compound nouns form their plurals in the same way as simple nouns, ie by altering or adding *-s* to the final element.**

Examples: by adding *-s* to the end of the word (eg *blackbird : blackbirds*) or to the second word (eg *grass snakes*), or by making some change to the form of the singular word (eg *fireman : firemen*).

There are, however, a number of specific categories of compound words where the rules are not so straightforward:

i)  ***Compound nouns formed from phrasal verbs*** (eg *take-off* from *take off, let-down* from *let down*) form their plurals by adding *-s* to the end of the word, unless the first element of the compound ends in an affix such as *-er*, in which case the *-s* is added to the first element: *take-offs, close-ups, grown-ups, sit-ins,* etc, but *passers-by, hangers-on, listeners-in, goings-on,* etc.

ii) ***Compound nouns consisting of a noun followed by a preposi-tional phrase*** form plurals by pluralizing the first noun: *men-of-war, rights of way, commanders-in-chief, mothers-in-law.* (However, in informal speech and writing, 'in-laws' are often pluralized by the addition of an *-s* at the end of the compound: *mother-in-laws*, etc). Similarly with compound nouns of this type borrowed from other languages, eg *noms de plume, pièces de résistance.*

Compound nouns consisting of other types of phrases generally form plurals by adding *-s* to the end of the phrase: *gin-and-tonics, forget-me-nots, hors d'oeuvres.*

iii) ***Compounds consisting of a noun and a following adjective*** form plurals by pluralizing the noun (eg *notaries public, heirs presumptive, courts martial, attorneys general, poets laureate*), but many of these now have acceptable and often more common alternatives with the *-s* added to the adjective (*court martials, attorney generals, poet laureates*).

Compound nouns consisting of a noun and an adjective which have been borrowed from other languages are often pluralized according to the rules of the language concerned. Thus in borrowings from French, for example, both the noun and the adjective should be pluralized: *femmes fatales, faits accomplis, nouveaux riches, belles lettres.* However, there are many exceptions to this rule: in general the better established a compound is in English, the more likely it is to take an English plural form: eg the plural of *petit four* may be either *petits fours* or *petit fours*, and *prima donnas* is more common as the plural of *prima donna* than the Italian plural form *prime donne.*

iv) ***Compounds in which the first element is either* man or woman** form plurals by pluralizing both parts: *menservants, gentlemen farmers, women doctors.*

• **Peoples and tribes**
The names of many peoples and tribes have two possible plural forms, a regular one and the zero plural identical to the singular. The regular *s*-plural is generally used when talking of individuals, and either the regular plural or the zero plural when considering the people as a group collectively:

> *The Apache were basically hunters and gatherers.*
> *The Zulu are a Negroid people, a distinct tribe of the Nguni group.*
> *In 1879 the Zulus under Cetewayo were defeated by the British.*

## -s, -es

For the formation of plural nouns in *-s/-es*, see PLURAL NOUNS.

For the formation of third person singular forms of the present tense of verbs, see VERBS.

See also -OS, -OES.

## -se see -CE.

## -sede see -CEDE.

## -sion see -TION.

## -sy see -ACY.

## -tch see -CH.

## -tion, -sion , -cion

The rules for deciding between *-tion*, *-sion* and *-cion* are, unfortunately, quite complicated, and there are many words whose spellings simply have to be learned without the aid of a rule at all. But there are one or two helpful guidelines, using pronunciation or word-families as clues.

> **If the ending is pronounced /-zhon/ it will be written *-sion*.**

Examples:

| | | | |
|---|---|---|---|
| adhesion | decision | fusion | persuasion |
| confusion | division | incision | vision |

> **There are only two common words that end in *-cion*: *coercion*, *suspicion*.**

---

⚠  There are a large number of words that end in *-cian*:

| | | |
|---|---|---|
| magician | musician | politician |
| mathematician | optician | technician |

These are all words which describe a person's job or occupation, most of them related to words ending in *-ic*, *-ics* or *-ical*:

| | | | | |
|---|---|---|---|---|
| magic | : | magician | technical : | technician |
| politics | : | politician | | |

---

> **The best guess otherwise is *-tion* unless the word-family suggests *-sion*.**

If the ending is pronounced /-shon/ and follows a vowel, it will almost always be written *-tion* (eg *nation, position, ration*). The word-family may, however, give a clue that a spelling with *ss* is correct (eg *discuss : discussion; obsessed : obsession; possess : possession*). Similarly after a consonant, the word-family may give a useful clue to the correct spelling (eg *adopt : adoption; invent : invention; averse : aversion; tense : tension*).

In addition, there are certain predictable patterns in some word-families which are helpful to remember:

| | | | | |
|---|---|---|---|---|
| ab*stain* | : | abs*tention* | re*tain* | : | re*tention* |
| contra*vene* | : | contra*vention* | inter*vene* | : | inter*vention* |
| ad*mit* | : | ad*mission* | per*mit* | : | per*mission* |
| ac*cede* | : | ac*cession* | pro*ceed* | : | pro*cession* |

The following words are related to words which end in **-vert**:

| | | |
|---|---|---|
| a*version* | extro*version* | per*version* |
| con*version* | intro*version* | |
| di*version* | in*version* | |

And there is also the large group of words ending in **-ation** which are formed from words ending in **-ate**:

| | | | | |
|---|---|---|---|---|
| create | : | cre*ation* | meditate | : | medit*ation* |
| educate | : | educ*ation* | rotate | : | rot*ation* |

Beyond this, however, there are so many subrules and exceptions that it is simpler to list all the other common **-tion/-sion** words:

| | | | |
|---|---|---|---|
| abortion | deception | infection | prevention |
| action | digestion | intention | proportion |
| addition | disruption | mention | question |
| adoption | distortion | nation | ration |
| assertion | exemption | notion | solution |
| attention | exertion | option | station |
| caption | exhaustion | portion | suggestion |
| combustion | extortion | position | taxation |
| contention | fiction | | |
| ascension | emulsion | immersion | recursion |
| aspersion | expansion | mansion | scansion |
| comprehension | expulsion | pension | submersion |
| dimension | extension | propulsion | version |

⚠ A few words may end in **-xion**. See -CTION, -XION, page 234, for details.

## -um

Many of the words which end in **-um** form regular plurals by adding **-s**, eg *albums*, *museums*, *nasturtiums*, *pendulums*, *vademecums*.

A number of words have, or may have, plurals in **-a**:

| | | |
|---|---|---|
| addendum | : | addenda |
| aquarium | : | aquaria (but more often *aquariums*) |
| bacterium | : | bacteria |
| candelabrum | : | candelabra (*candelabra* also treated as a singular noun, plural *candelabras*) |

287

| | | |
|---|---|---|
| *corrigendum* | : | *corrigenda* |
| *curriculum* | : | *curricula* (also *curriculums*) |
| *datum* | : | *data* is in origin the plural of *datum*, but *datum* is rarely used; although it is not incorrect to treat *data* as a plural noun, referring for example to *these data* , it is now more usually treated as a collective singular noun (eg *this data*) |
| *desideratum* | : | *desiderata* |
| *dictum* | : | *dicta* |
| *erratum* | : | *errata* |
| *maximum* | : | *maxima* in technical contexts, otherwise *maximums* |
| *medium* | : | in the sense of 'a channel of mass communication such as radio or television', plural *media* |

⚠ Do not use *media* in this sense as a singular noun: television is one of the media, not 'a media'.

| | | |
|---|---|---|
| | | in the sense of 'a person through whom spirits are said to communicate with people in this world', plural *mediums* |
| | | in other senses, either plural is acceptable |
| *memorandum* | : | *memoranda* (also *memorandums*) |
| *millennium* | : | *millennia* (also *millenniums*) |
| *minimum* | : | *minima* in technical contexts, otherwise *minimums* |
| *moratorium* | : | *moratoria* (also *moratoriums*) |
| *ovum* | : | *ova* |
| *podium* | : | *podia* (also *podiums*) |
| *referendum* | : | *referenda* (also *referendums*) |
| *sanatorium* | : | *sanatoria* (more often *sanatoriums*) |
| *spectrum* | : | *spectra* (also *spectrums*) |
| *stadium* | : | *stadia* (but much more commonly *stadiums*) |
| *stratum* | : | *strata* |
| *symposium* | : | *symposia* (also *symposiums*) |
| *ultimatum* | : | *ultimata* (more often *ultimatums*) |
| *vacuum* | : | *vacua* (but more usually *vacuums*, and always so as the plural of the 'vacuum cleaner') |

## -*us*

- **-*us* and -*ous***

For **-*us*** versus **-*ous*** (as in *callus* and *callous*), see -OUS.

- **Nouns**

Many nouns ending in **-*us*** form their plurals regularly, ie by adding **-*es***, eg *bonuses, circuses, ignoramuses, viruses*.

Some words have, or may have, plurals in -*i*:

| | | |
|---:|:---:|:---|
| *alumnus* | : | *alumni* |
| *bacillus* | : | *bacilli* |
| *cactus* | : | *cacti* (also *cactuses*) |
| *focus* | : | *foci* in technical contexts, otherwise *focuses* |
| *fungus* | : | *fungi* (also *funguses*) |
| *hippopotamus* | : | *hippopotami* (but more commonly *hippopotamuses*) |
| *locus* | : | *loci* in technical contexts, otherwise *locuses* |
| *nucleus* | : | *nuclei* (also *nucleuses*) |
| *octopus* | : | *octopi* is acceptable only as a joke; the correct plural is *octopuses* |
| *radius* | : | *radii* (also *radiuses*) |
| *rhombus* | : | *rhombi* (but more commonly *rhombuses*) |
| *sarcophagus* | : | *sarcophagi* (also *sarcophaguses*) |
| *stimulus* | : | *stimuli* (also *stimuluses*) |
| *stylus* | : | *styli* (also *styluses*) |
| *syllabus* | : | *syllabi* (but more commonly *syllabuses*) |
| *terminus* | : | *termini* (more commonly *terminuses*) |

> ⚠ Note also the plurals of *corpus* and *genus*: *corpora* (*corpuses* is also possible) and *genera*.

## verbs

For the formation of the past tense and past participle of regular verbs, see -ED. For irregular verbs, see PAST TENSE AND PAST PARTICIPLE.

For the formation of the present participle, see -ING.

For the formation of the third person singular of the present tense (eg *he stays, she lies*), see the following section.

> **To form the third person singular form of the present tense of most verbs, add -*s* to the basic form of the verb.**

Examples:

| | | | |
|:---|:---|:---|:---|
| *bites* | *kicks* | *rows* | *walks* |
| *buys* | *runs* | *sings* | |

As with the -*ed* forms of the verb, a number of changes have sometimes be made to the base form. See -C; DOUBLING OF FINAL CONSONANTS; -E; -OS, -OES; and -Y.

- **Verbs ending in *s, z, x, sh* or *ch***

To a verb ending *s, z x, sh* or *ch* (pronounced /ch/), add -*es*:

| | | | | | | | |
|:---|:---|:---|:---|:---|:---|:---|:---|
| *kiss* | : | *kisses* | *box* | : | *boxes* | *lurch* | : | *lurches* |
| *waltz* | : | *waltzes* | *rush* | : | *rushes* | | | |

- ### Words ending in a silent *s*

In words of French origin which end in a silent *s* (eg *chassis*, pronounced /sha-si/), the plural is identical in form to the singular, but the final *s* is pronounced: *two chassis* (pronounced /sha-siz/), not *two chassises*; and so also with *chamois*, *corps*, *faux pas*, *fracas*, *patois*, *rendezvous*, etc.

---

⚠ One minor difference between plural noun formation in *-es* and verb forms in *-es* is in words of French origin which end in a silent *s*. Although nothing is added in the plural noun (see above), *-es* is added in the verb:

> *two rendezvous* but *he rendezvouses with them at 8 o'clock* (the two words being pronounced the same although spelt differently)

---

- ### Words ending in *i*

Note that although the plural of the noun *taxi* is *taxis*, the third-person singular of the present tense of the verb is *taxies* or *taxis*.

The third-person singular of *ski* is *skis*.

**-ves** see -FS.

## -x

Many nouns which end -*x* form regular plurals:

| | | |
|---|---|---|
| *boxes* | *hoaxes* | *taxes* |
| *equinoxes* | *jinxes* | |

A number of nouns which end in -*x* have irregular plural forms (some also having regular forms):

| | | |
|---|---|---|
| *apex* | : | *apices* (also *apexes*) |
| *appendix* | : | *appendices* in books; *appendixes* in anatomy |
| *codex* | : | *codices* |
| *index* | : | *indices* in mathematics and science; in other senses *indexes* |
| *larynx* | : | *larynges* (also *larynxes*) |
| *matrix* | : | *matrices* (also *matrixes*) |
| *phalanx* | : | *phalanges* in biology; in other senses *phalanxes* |
| *pharynx* | : | *pharynges* (also *pharynxes*) |
| *vertex* | : | *vertices* (also *vertexes*) |
| *vortex* | : | *vortices* (also *vortexes*) |

Added to these are the words ending in *-trix* which denote the female equivalents of nouns ending in **-tor** (eg *executor, executrix*). These are almost all obsolete, except for a few technical legal terms. All have plurals ending in **-trices**, though one or two (of which *executrix* is the only common example) also have plurals ending in **-trixes**.

## -x, -s

Nouns of French origin ending in **-eu** and **-eau**, which regularly add an **-x** in the plural in French, usually do so also in English, although in most cases the regular English plural ending **-s** is also correct:

| | | |
|---|---|---|
| adieu | : | adieux or adieus |
| beau | : | beaux |
| bureau | : | bureaux or bureaus |
| château | : | châteaux |
| gâteau | : | gâteaux or gâteaus |
| milieu | : | milieux or milieus |
| plateau | : | plateaux or plateaus |
| portmanteau | : | portmanteaux or portmanteaus |
| tableau | : | tableaux |
| trousseau | : | trousseaux or trousseaus |

## -xion see -CTION.

## -y

### ✦ Nouns

### • Plurals

> If the final *y* of a noun is preceded by a consonant, the plural will end in **-ies**.

Examples:

*cry* : *cries*    *lady* : *ladies*

> ⚠ 1. Proper names usually retain the *y*:
> *the two Germanys*        *the four Marys*
> But note that historians refer to *the Kingdom of the Two Sicilies*.
>
> 2. The plural of *poly* (= 'polytechnic') is *polys*.
>
> 3. If the *y* is part of an adverb or preposition which is part of a compound noun, the *y* remains: *stand-bys, lay-bys*.

> **If the final *y* is preceded by a vowel, *-s* alone is added to form the plural.**

Examples:

| | | | | |
|---|---|---|---|---|
| *day* | : | *days* | *buoy* | : | *buoys* |
| *monkey* | : | *monkeys* | *guy* | : | *guys* |

> ⚠ Note that the plural of *money* may be *moneys* or *monies*.
>
> A *u* following a *q* counts as a consonant, not as a vowel:
>
> *soliloquy* : *soliloquies*

## • Other word-endings

When some other ending is added to a noun, the *y* usually remains unchanged whether following a consonant or a vowel:

| | | | | | |
|---|---|---|---|---|---|
| *boy* | : | *boyhood, boyish* | *lady* | : | *ladyship* |
| *baby* | : | *babyhood, babyish* | *entry* | : | *entryism* |
| *Disney* | : | *Disneyesque, Disneyfy* | *belly* | : | *bellyful* |

> ⚠ The only exceptions to this are adjectives formed by the addition of *-ful*, in which the *y* changes to *i*, eg:
>
> *beauty* : *beautiful*     *duty* : *dutiful*     *pity* : *pitiful*

## ✦ Verbs

### • Word-endings indicating tenses

Verbs follow essentially the same pattern of construction as nouns:

> **If the final *y* of a verb is preceded by a consonant, the third person singular of the present tense will end in *-ies* and the past tense will end in *-ied*.**
>
> **If the *y* is preceded by a vowel, *-s* alone is added in the present tense and *-ed* in the past tense and participle.**

Examples:

| | |
|---|---|
| *cries, cried* | *denies, denied* |
| *conveys, conveyed* | *stays, stayed* |

> ⚠ *Laid*, *paid* and *said* are exceptions.

## • Other word-endings

The same rules apply when other word-endings are added:

| | | | | | |
|---|---|---|---|---|---|
| *vary* | : | *variable* | *enjoy* | : | *enjoyable* |
| *ally* | : | *alliance* | *annoy* | : | *annoyance* |

| | | | | | |
|---|---|---|---|---|---|
| *carry* | : | *carrier* | *employ* | : | *employer* |
| *try* | : | *trial* | *betray* | : | *betrayal* |

and so on, except that *y* does not change to *i* before another *i*:

| | | | | | |
|---|---|---|---|---|---|
| *vary* | : | *varying* | *copy* | : | *copyist* |
| *carry* | : | *carrying* | | | |

Some one-syllable words in which the *y* is pronounced /y/ as in *my* are exceptions to the general rule:

| | | |
|---|---|---|
| *dry* | : | *drier* or *dryer* |
| *fly* | : | *flier* or *flyer* |

(note also *flyable*)

| | | |
|---|---|---|
| *fry* | : | *frier* or *fryer* |

but only *trier* is correct.

## ✦ Adjectives

### • Comparative and superlative forms

> **To form the comparative and superlative of adjectives ending in *y* preceded by a consonant, change the *y* to *i* and add *-er* and *-est*.**

Examples:

| | | | | | |
|---|---|---|---|---|---|
| *silly* | : | *sillier, silliest* | *happy* | : | *happier, happiest* |

1. As with the verbs, certain one-syllable words are exceptions to the general rule:

| | | |
|---|---|---|
| *shy* | : | *shyer/shyest* or *shier/shiest* |
| *sly* | : | *slyer/slyest* or *slier/sliest* |
| *wry* | : | *wryer/wryest* or *wrier/wriest* |

but only *drier/driest* and *spryer/spryest* are correct.

2. Adjectives in which the *y* is preceded by a vowel usually retain the *y*:

| | | | | | |
|---|---|---|---|---|---|
| *coy* | : | *coyer, coyest* | *grey* | : | *greyer, greyest* |

With adjectives that end in *-ey* (eg *clayey, gooey, matey, pricey*), the *-ey* changes to *i*:

| | | |
|---|---|---|
| *pricey* | : | *pricier, priciest* |

### • Other suffixes

The same rules apply before other word-endings:

| | | |
|---|---|---|
| *happy* | : | *happily, happiness* |
| *coy* | : | *coyly, coyness* |

| | | |
|---|---|---|
| *merry* | : | *merrily, merriment* |
| *likely* | : | *likelihood* |
| *forty* | : | *fortieth* |

As with verb derivatives, the **y** remains before a following *i*: *prettyish, fortyish, voluntaryism.*

> ⚠ 1. Note the options in *drily/dryly, shyly/shily, slyly/slily*; but only *spryly* and *wryly*.
>
> In the nouns, only **y** forms are correct: *dryness, shyness, slyness, spryness, wryness.*
>
> 2. Note the forms of the adverbs *cagily, matily*, etc.
>
> The corresponding nouns are more of a problem, as according to most authorities some of the **-ey** adjectives change the *ey* to *i* before **-ness** while others do not, and there is no agreement as to which words belong to which category. Faced with this uncertainty, it seems simpler to adopt a straightforward rule and change the *ey* to *i* when it is preceded by a consonant (including *y* and *w*) and not when it is preceded by a vowel:
>
> | | | | | | |
> |---|---|---|---|---|---|
> | *matey* | : | *matiness* | *clayey* | : | *clayiness* |
> | *gluey* | : | *glueyness* | *gooey* | : | *gooeyness* |
>
> Nevertheless, write *sameyness.*
>
> 3. Note *gaily* and *daily.*
>
> 4. The noun from *busy* is *busyness*, to distinguish it from *business*, pronounced /'biz-nis/.

## ✦ Adjectives formed by the addition of *-y*

A number of common adjectives are formed from other words (mostly nouns) by the addition of **-y**:

| | | | | | |
|---|---|---|---|---|---|
| *flour* | : | *floury* | *meat* | : | *meaty* |
| *flower* | : | *flowery* | *shadow* | : | *shadowy* |

Such adjectives follow the general rules of English regarding doubling of consonants, dropping of final silent *e*'s, etc (see DOUBLING OF FINAL CONSONANTS; -E; -C):

| | | | | | |
|---|---|---|---|---|---|
| *grit* | : | *gritty* | *choose* | : | *choosy* |
| *pal* | : | *pally* | *ice* | : | *icy* |
| *sag* | : | *saggy* | *noise* | : | *noisy* |
| *bone* | : | *bony* | *panic* | : | *panicky* |

> ⚠ 1. The final *e* is always retained in certain words:
>
> | | | |
> |---|---|---|
> | *cagey* | *matey* | *pricey* |
> | *dicey* | *pacey* | *samey* |
> | *gluey* | | |

and optionally retained in others (the preferred form being given first):

| | |
|---|---|
| caky/cakey | horsy/horsey |
| chocolaty/chocolatey | nosy/nosey |
| cliquey/cliquy | ropy/ropey |
| dopey/dopy | winey/winy |

2.  When the 'core' noun ends in *y*, *-ey* rather than *-y* alone is added:

    clay  :  clayey

3.  Note also the spelling of *gooey* and *phoney*.

## -y, -ie

The majority of English words ending in /i/ are spelt with a *-y*, eg

| | | | | |
|---|---|---|---|---|
| nouns: | berry | dairy | library | poppy |
| verbs: | carry | dally | marry | scurry |
| adjectives: | angry | cheery | happy | silly |

Certain nouns, however, end in *-ie*. These include

i)   some shortened forms of words:

| | | |
|---|---|---|
| bookie | goalie | movie |
| budgie | mountie | nightie |

ii)   diminutives, especially those used in speaking to young children, and terms of endearment:

| | | | |
|---|---|---|---|
| birdie | dearie | fishie | laddie |
| chappie | doggie | horsie | lassie |

> ⚠ Notice the difference in spelling between these nouns and similar or related adjectives which end in *-y*: *a fishy smell* □ *a rather horsy face*.

iii)   certain other nouns:

| | | | |
|---|---|---|---|
| brownie | coolie | kiltie | quickie |
| cookie | genie | oldie | walkie-talkie |

iv)   some words may be spelt with either *-ie* or *-y*, in all cases the *-ie* forms being the commoner:

| | | |
|---|---|---|
| caddie/caddy (in golf; | girlie/girly | pixie/pixy |
| but only *tea-caddy*) | hippie/hippy | rookie/rooky |
| ghillie/gillie/gilly | junkie/junky | softie/softy |

> ⚠ Do not confuse these three words:
>
> *bogey* (= the score in golf fixed as a standard for a good player)
> *bogie* (= a low truck or undercarriage on a locomotive)
> *bogy* (= a goblin or bugbear; it may also be spelt *bogey*)

# 5

# Word-building: Beginnings, Middles and Endings

One way of learning to spell correctly or of checking your spelling is to split words up into their component parts and to check that each part is correctly spelt. Many words, particularly those of Latin and Greek origin, contain elements whose spelling is consistently the same in all the words in which they appear. Learning to recognize such 'word-building elements' at the beginning, in the middle or at the end of words is therefore a useful spelling aid.

Learning about these regular word-parts is also useful as an aid to increasing your understanding of technical, medical and scientific words. If, for example, you know that *-vorous* has to do with 'eating', then you will easily guess that an *insectivorous* animal is one which feeds on insects. Further, if *carni-* has to do with 'flesh' or 'meat' and *herbi-* is related to 'plants', a *carnivorous* animal must be one which eats meat and a *herbivorous* animal one which eats plants. Similarly, since *-cide* refers to something that kills or destroys, an *insecticide* must be something that kills insects and a *herbicide* something that kills plants, eg a weedkiller.

The following chapter lists some of the most frequently occurring of these word-building elements in English, along with a description of the meanings associated with them and examples of the words in which they are found.

## *a-*

This prefix of Greek origin means 'not' or 'without', as in *atheist* 'a person who believes that there is no God' (see THEO-) and *asymmetrical* 'not symmetrical'.

Before a vowel, *a-* is replaced by *an-*: *anarchy* 'the absence of law or government' (see -ARCH) and *anonymous* 'without the person's name being given' (see -ONYM). Other words that contain this element are *analgesic* 'a medicine that relieves pain' (see -ALGIA) and *anorexia* 'a loss of appetite' (Greek *orexis* 'desire, appetite').

In some cases, the force of the initial *a-* element may not be obvious. An *atom*, for example, is so called because it was formerly incorrectly thought to be the

296

smallest particle of matter, not divisible (see -TOMY) into smaller parts.

 There is generally a difference in sense between words beginning with *a-/an-* and similar words beginning with *in-*, *il-*, etc, which also mean 'not' or 'the opposite of'. For example, *amoral* means 'showing no interest in moral standards, not accepting any moral standards' whereas *immoral* means 'not acceptable according to generally agreed moral principles'.

### aero-, aer-

This word-building element denotes 'air' and 'aircraft', but note that it is spelt with an *e*: *aero-* (Greek and Latin *aer* 'air'). Among the common *aer(o)-* words are *aeroplane* 'a machine that flies in the air', *aerodrome*, *aeronautics* 'the science of air travel' (see NAUT-), *aerobics* 'rhythmic exercises to increase the body's intake of oxygen from the air', *aerial* 'an antenna for receiving or transmitting signals through the air', and *aerate* 'to put air, or some other gas, into something'.

 Notice that what in British English is an *aeroplane* is in American English an *airplane*.

### agri-, agro-, agr-

From Latin *ager* and Greek *agros* 'field' (which are related to the English word *acre*, which originally also meant a field). Words containing these elements have to do with farming (*agriculture*, *agribusiness*, *agrochemical*) or with land ownership and use (*agrarian* 'relating to the distribution or management of land', *agronomy* 'the science of land cultivation and crop production').

 Note the single *g* in these land-related words. Do not confuse this spelling with that of words that begin with *aggr-*, such as *aggravate*, *aggressive*, *aggregate* and *aggrieved*, none of which have anything to do with farming or land.

### -algia, -alg-

This is found in many medical terms which describe pain in some part of the body, such as *neuralgia* 'pain in a nerve' (see NEURO-) and *myalgia* 'pain in a muscle' (Greek *mys* 'muscle'). To relieve pain, you may take an *analgesic* such as aspirin (see A-).

*Nostalgia* may not be something you would think of as painful, but sometimes a longing for the past (Greek *nostos* 'return') may cause mental pain.

### ambi-

*Ambi-* means 'both' or 'on both sides' (Latin *ambo* 'both'), as in *ambidextrous* 'able to use both hands equally well' (ie, able to use the left hand as well as the right — Latin *dexter* 'right'), and *ambivalent* 'having opposing attitudes towards something at one time' (Latin *valens* 'being valued').

## an- see A-.

## ann-

From Latin *annus* 'year', a word used in the phrases *per annum* (= 'per year') and *anno Domini* (= 'in the year of our Lord'). Note the double *n*.

**Ann-** is the base of words such as *annual*, *anniversary* 'something that comes round once a year', *annals* 'records of events, originally listed under the years in which they occurred', *annuity* 'a guaranteed payment which falls due every year', and *superannuation*, money put aside towards a pension to be paid when a person is 'past the years' (Latin *super* 'above') for working.

Latin *annus* also underlies the form **-enn-**, as in *biennial* 'happening or appearing once every two years'(see BI-), *perennial* 'happening year after year', *centennial* 'happening every hundred years' (see CENTI-), *millennium* 'a period of a thousand years' (see MILLI-), and *bicentennial* 'happening every two hundred years'.

>  *Centenary* does not have the *annus* root in it and does not have a double *n*.

## ante-

From Latin *ante*, meaning 'before', 'in front of'. *Antenatal* means 'before birth' (Latin *natus* 'born'), as in *antenatal clinics* for pregnant women, and an *anteroom* is a room, such as a waiting-room, which leads into a larger room.

>  Do not confuse *ante-* and *anti-* (see below).

## anthropo-, anthrop-

This word-building element, from Greek *anthropos* 'human being', refers to 'people' or 'humans', as in the words *anthropoid* 'humanlike' (as applied, for example, to apes such as chimpanzees and gorillas — see -OID), *anthropology* 'the study of human beings and their way of life' (see -LOGY), and *philanthropy* 'love for people, especially as shown by acts of charity' (see PHILO-).

## anti-

**Anti-** means 'against' (Greek *anti* 'against'), as in *anti-aircraft*, *antifreeze*, *antisocial*, *antibiotic* 'a medicine that destroys bacteria', *anti-Nazi* and *anti-Semitic*.

Do not confuse this with **ante-** 'before' (see above). As a memory aid, notice that **anti-** has the same *a* and *i* vowels as 'against', whereas **ante-** has an *e*.

## aqua-

*Aqua* is Latin for 'water', and this root is found in many English words that relate to water in some way, such as *aquatic* 'living or taking place in water', *aqualung* 'an apparatus that allows you to breathe under water', *aquarium*, and *subaqua* 'swimming under water' (Latin *sub* 'under').

 Notice that there is no *c* in **aqua-**. Do not confuse the spelling of the 'water' words with that of words (not related to water) which begin with *acqu-*, such as *acquire*, *acquaint* and *acquit*.

## arch-

This comes originally from the Greek word *archos*, meaning 'chief'. When added to other words, it denotes a chief or leading example, as in *archbishop* 'a chief bishop', *arch-enemy* 'a great enemy', and *archangel* 'a chief angel'.

 **Arch-** is usually pronounced as in *March*, but in *archangel* it is pronounced as '*ark*'.

## -arch

This word-building element has to do with 'ruling' and 'rulers' (Greek *arche* 'rule'). A *monarch* is a person who does not share the power to rule with anyone else (see MONO-) and an *anarchist* is a person who believes that society does not need laws or government (see A-).

 Notice that this **-arch** is always pronounced '*ark*'.

## archaeo-

This word-building element is sometimes spelt **archeo-** in British English, and usually so in American English. It comes from the Greek word *arche*, meaning 'beginning', and is found in words relating to the distant past or to the study of the distant past, such as *archaeology* and *archaeopteryx* (which is a primitive species of bird found as fossils from the Jurassic period). This same Greek root is also found in *archaic* 'antiquated, old-fashioned, ancient'.

 The *ch* is always pronounced /k/.

## astro-, astr-

*Astronomy* is the study of the stars and planets (see -NOMY), *astrology* the study of the supposed influence of the stars and planets on our lives (see -LOGY). The **astro-** element found in both these words comes from Greek *astron* 'star'.

In some words, the **astro-** refers not so much to the stars and planets in particular as to outer space in general, as in *astronaut* (see NAUT-).

## audio-

From Latin *audire* 'to hear', **audio-** relates to 'sound' and 'hearing'. *Audiovisual* means 'concerned with or involving both sound and sight' (see VIS-) as in *audiovisual aids* to teaching (such as cassette-players and videos). An *audiotypist* is one who can type directly from a dictating machine. *Audiology* is the science of hearing, particularly the diagnosis and treatment of hearing disorders (see -LOGY).

The same Latin root is to be found also in *audible* 'able to be heard' and in *audience* 'people who listen to a performance or a speaker'.

## auto-, aut-

From Greek *autos*, meaning 'self'. An *autobiography* is a biography written by the subject himself or herself, an *autograph* is a signature (something that is 'written by the person himself or herself' — see -GRAPH) and an *automobile* is 'a machine that moves by itself, not requiring to be pulled by a horse', a 'horseless carriage'. *Autonomy* is the right to self-government or to determine your own actions (see -NOMY). *Autism* is the name in psychiatry for a mental condition in which a person is absorbed in his or her own mental activity with a loss of contact with reality and an inability to communicate with others.

Not all the examples of **auto-** in modern English are derived directly from the Greek word *autos*. In some words, the **auto-** stands for 'automobile' (as in *autocrime* 'theft of or from a car') or for 'automatic' (as in the *autofocus* in a camera and the *autopilot* in an aeroplane).

## bi-

Derived from Latin *bis* 'twice', **bi-** denotes 'two': a *bicycle* has two wheels (Greek *kyklos* 'wheel'), someone who is *bilingual* speaks two languages (Latin *lingua* 'tongue'), and *bifocals* are glasses with lenses that have been ground so as to allow clearly focused vision on objects both near and at a distance. *Bidirectional* means 'able to operate in two directions', and *bilateral* talks involve two participants or delegations, ie two sides (Latin *lateris* 'of a side').

Notice that in some words the meaning of the **bi-** may be 'twice' rather than 'two': *biannual* means 'happening twice a year', *biennial* means 'happening once every two years' (see ANN-).

See also DI-.

## biblio-

The word *Bible* comes via Latin from the Greek *biblion* 'a book', and it is from this Greek word that the modern English word-building element **biblio-**, denoting 'books', also comes. A *bibliography* is a list of books on a particular subject or by a particular author (see -GRAPH), and a *bibliophile* is a person who loves, and usually collects, books (see PHILO-). (If the urge to collect books gets out of hand, it may become a *bibliomania*!)

## bio-

**Bio-**, from the Greek *bios* 'life', has two main senses. It may denote the life of a person, as in *biography* 'a written account of someone's life' (see -GRAPH), or it may denote a reference to 'living things', as in *biology* 'the scientific study of animals and plants' (see -LOGY), *biochemistry* 'the chemistry of living things', *biodegradable* 'able to be broken down into harmless substances by bacteria'.

In many modern coinages, **bio-** stands for 'biology' or 'biological': *bioscience*, *bioengineering*, etc. *Biorhythms* are physiological, intellectual and emotional rhythms or cycles in a person's life which are thought to cause variations in that person's mood and behaviour. In other recently coined words, **bio-** stands for 'biographical': a *biopic* is a 'biographical picture', ie a film which tells the life-story of someone, usually a celebrity.

## broncho-, bronch-

Note the *ch* spelling of this, although it is pronounced /brongk-/. The *bronchial* tubes are the tubes of the windpipe leading from the throat to the lungs (Greek *bronchos* 'windpipe') and *bronchitis* is an inflammation of these tubes (see -ITIS). A *bronchodilator* is a drug which causes these tubes to expand.

## cardio-, cardi-

*Kardia* is the Greek word for 'heart'. From this is derived the modern English word-building element **cardi(o)-**, as in *cardiology* 'the branch of medicine dealing with the diagnosis and treatment of heart diseases' (see -LOGY).

Also from Greek *kardia* is *cardiac*, an adjective used mainly in medical terminology (*cardiac arrest* 'stopping of the beating of the heart', *cardiac failure* 'heart failure', *cardiac massage*).

## carni-

*Carnivorous* animals (and some plants) are ones which eat meat (Latin *carnis* 'of flesh'; see also -VORE).

The same Latin word is also at the root of English words such as *carnal* 'concerned with bodily, unspiritual matters' and, via Italian and French, *carnage* 'great slaughter'.

## centi-, cent-

From the Latin *centum* 'one hundred'. In measurements, **centi-** denotes a unit which is equal to one hundredth of some basic unit: a *centimetre* equals a hundredth of a metre, a *centilitre* one hundredth of a litre, and so on.

In other words, **centi-** and its shorter form **cent-** denote 'one hundred', as in *centigrade* 'denoting a scale divided into a hundred degrees' (such as the Celsius scale for measuring temperatures, which has 100 degrees between the freezing point and the boiling point of water), *centipede* (most species of which have far fewer than one hundred legs), and words relating to a period of a hundred years — *century, centenary, centennial* (see ANN-).

Latin *centum* is also the root of the names of several foreign units of currency which are equal to one hundredth of some other unit: *centime, céntimo, centavo,* and of course *cent.*

## chrono-, chron-

From the Greek word *chronos*, meaning 'time', this word-building element occurs in English words with meanings related to time, such as *chronometer* 'an instrument for measuring time' (see -METER), *chronological* 'according to time or in order of occurrence in time', as in *chronological order* (*chronology* was originally the science of measuring time — see -LOGY), *chronic* 'continuing a long time' (*a chronic disease*), and *chronicle* 'a record of events in the order in which they occur in time'. Also in *synchronize* 'to set to the same time, or cause to occur at the same time' (see SYN-) and *anachronism* 'something from the wrong period of time' (Greek *ana-* 'backwards').

## -cide

A word-building element that means 'murder' or 'killing', or a 'murderer' or 'killer', as in *suicide* (Latin *sui* 'of oneself'), *homicide* (see HOMI-), etc. From Latin *caedere*, meaning 'to kill'. Also used in the names of substances which kill or destroy, such as *insecticides* and *herbicides* (Latin *herba* 'grass, green plant').

## circum-

Note the *c* at the beginning of this word-building element, which comes from the Latin word *circum* 'around'. The *circumference* of a circle is the line around it, *circumlocution* is the expressing of an idea in more words than are necessary (ie talking about it in a roundabout way), to *circumnavigate* the world is to sail or fly right round it, and the *circumstances* surrounding an action are the facts or conditions 'around' it (Latin *stare* 'to stand').

## contra-

The word-building element **contra-**, from Latin *contra* 'against', is found both in long-established words of Latin origin such as *contradict* (to say something 'against' what someone else has said — Latin *dicere* 'to say') and in new coinages such as the *contraflow* system used on motorways when one carriageway is closed and traffic is therefore flowing in two directions on the other carriageway.

Latin *contra* also forms the basis of words such as *contrary* and *contrast*.

## -cracy

From Greek *kratos* 'power', as in *democracy* 'government by the people' (Greek *demos* 'people'), *aristocracy* 'government by, or the members of, a privileged group, eg the nobility' (Greek *aristos* 'best'), etc. A recent coinage is *quangocracy*, 'government by quangos'.

The word-building element **-crat** denotes a person who believes in, or is a member of, some '-cracy' or other, eg *democrat, aristocrat*.

## crypto-, crypt-

From Greek *kryptos* 'hidden'. A *crypto-Communist* is a person who keeps his or her allegiance to Communism secret, a *cryptogram* is anything written in code in order to keep its meaning secret (see -GRAM), and *cryptic* means 'mysterious, obscure, hard to solve or understand'.

## -cyte, cyto-

In Greek, *kytos* meant a container or hollow vessel. In modern medicine and science, the word-forming elements derived from *kytos* refer to cells (eg in the body). *Cytology* is the study of cells (see -LOGY), and many of the cells in the body have names which end in **-cyte**, eg *leucocyte, lymphocyte* and *phagocyte*.

 Note that *parasite* is not connected with *kytos*.

## deca-, dec-

**Deca-** comes from the Greek word *deka*, meaning 'ten'. It is common as a prefix in words denoting units of measurement that are ten times larger than the basic unit: a *decalitre* is equal to ten litres, a *decagram* equivalent to ten grams, and so on. In some words, **deca-** means simply 'ten': a *decathlon* is a ten-event contest (Greek *athlon* 'contest') involving tests of running, jumping, vaulting and throwing.

The same Greek word is at the root of the word *decade* 'a period of ten years'.

 Do not confuse **deca-** and **deci-**.

## deci-

**Deci-**, from Latin *decimus* 'tenth', is used as a prefix in measurements to denote a unit that is one tenth of the basic unit: a *decilitre* is equal to a tenth of a litre, a *decigram* equivalent to a tenth of a gram, and so on.

Also from this Latin root are derived words such as *decimal* 'using ten as a base number' (*decimal currency*), and *decimate*, which originally meant 'to kill or destroy one in every ten'.

> ⚠ Do not confuse **deci-** and **deca-**.

## demi- see SEMI-.

## dermato-, dermat-, -derm-

*Derma* is the Greek word for 'skin', and is the root of English **dermat(o)-** and **derm-**. A *dermatologist* is a specialist in the treatment of diseases of the skin (see -LOGY), *dermatitis* is a medical term for 'inflammation of the skin' (see -ITIS), and *dermabrasion* is a modern cosmetic treatment in which the skin of the face is scrubbed, peeled away and then allowed to heal again. A *hypodermic needle* is used in medicine to inject substances under the skin (Greek *hypo* 'under'; see HYPER-).

In the animal world, elephants, rhinoceroses and hippopotamuses are sometimes, now usually facetiously, referred to as *pachyderms*, which means 'animals with thick skins' (Greek *pachys* 'thick'), and a *taxidermist* is a person who prepares, stuffs and mounts the skins of animals and birds (Greek *taxis* 'arrangement').

## di-

From Greek *dis*, meaning 'two', 'twice' or 'double'. Used in a number of technical and scientific terms, as for example the names of chemicals such as *carbon dioxide*, which contains two oxygen atoms in its molecule.

See also BI-.

## -dox

In most words this word-building element has a meaning related to opinions or beliefs (Greek *doxa* 'opinion'): someone who is *orthodox* believes or agrees with the opinions or doctrines that are generally accepted by people belonging to the same group (see ORTHO-), whereas someone who does not agree with the opinions of those around him or her is considered to be *heterodox* (see HETERO-).

## dys-

**Dys-**, from a Greek prefix meaning 'badly', occurs in a few, mainly medical, terms, most of which denote disorders of some part of the body or of the mind. Among the common words with this element are *dyslexia* 'difficulty in learning to read and spell' (Greek *lexis* 'word'), *dysfunction* 'impaired functioning of an organ', *dyspepsia* 'indigestion' (Greek *pepsis* 'digestion') and *dysentery* (see ENTERO-).

Do not confuse **dys-** with **dis-** meaning 'not', as in, for example, *dissatisfied* or *disorder*.

## -ectomy see -TOMY.

## -enn- see ANN-.

## entero-, enter-

From Greek *enteron* 'gut', this is the base of the words *enteritis* 'inflammation of the intestine' (see -ITIS) and *dysentery* (see DYS-) 'a bacterial infection of the intestine'.

## equ-

This word-building element relates to horses (Latin *equus* 'horse'), as in *equine* 'relating to horses', *equestrian* and *equitation* 'horse-riding'.

 Note that there is no *c* before the *q*. (There are in fact no words in English that begin with *ecq-*).

## equi-

From Latin *aequus*, meaning 'equal'. Points that are *equidistant* from some other point stand at an equal distance from it, and in geometry an *equilateral triangle* has three sides of equal length (Latin *lateris* 'of a side').

 Note that, as with **equ-** above, there is no *c* before the *q*.

## -esc-, -sc-

In Latin words this implies a process of 'becoming' something, and this can be a useful memory aid for the correct spelling of many English words derived from Latin. For example, an *adolescent* is a young person who is becoming an adult, someone who is *convalescing* is becoming well again after an illness, something that is *obsolescent* is becoming obsolete, a *deliquescent* substance readily absorbs moisture from the air and becomes a liquid, and if two things *coalesce*, they become fused together.

The *-sc-* is also found with the same meaning in *irascible*, which means 'easily made angry, quick to become angry'.

In some English words derived from Latin, the 'becoming' sense no longer applies: *effervescent* comes from a Latin word meaning 'to begin to boil' but now just means 'bubbly' or 'fizzy', and *crescent*, which originally meant 'becoming bigger' (a crescent moon was one which was growing larger as it turned into a full moon, and only in the Middle Ages did *crescent* take on a

305

meaning denoting the shape of the moon rather than its state). The word *crescendo*, meaning 'an increase in loudness' comes from the same Latin root but via Italian. In this word the *-sc-* is pronounced /sh/. Another *-sc-* word is *reminiscent*.

And finally, this *-esc-* element is also to be found, again without a sense of 'becoming', in many scientific or technical terms relating to types of light, such as *fluorescent*, *iridescent* and *phosphorescent*.

## -ferous

Words with this ending have something to do with the notion of 'carrying' or 'containing' (Latin *ferre* 'to carry'). These are for the most part technical words of botany or geology: a *coniferous* tree produces cones, the *Carboniferous* rock system contains coal, and *metalliferous* ores yield metals.

 Do not confuse this ending with *-vorous*, meaning 'eating' (see -VORE).

## fore-, for-

These word-building elements are sometimes confused, but there is little difficulty in distinguishing them if you remember that *fore-* is connected with 'be<u>fore</u>', 'in front of' or 'be<u>fore</u>hand', and *for-* is not.

A *foregone conclusion* is an obvious or inevitable conclusion, ie one which, in a sense, you already know <u>before</u> the matter is discussed or concluded, and your *forebears* are your ancestors, those who have gone <u>before</u> you. Other common *fore-* words are *forearm*, *foreboding*, *forefather*, *foreground*, *forerunner*, *foresee*, *forestall* and *forewarn*, all of which include the notion 'before in time' or 'before in position'.

In many, but not all, words beginning with *for-*, there is a notion of 'loss' or of 'not having or not doing something', and this also can be a useful clue to spelling: to *forgo* something is to do without it, to *forbear* is to refrain from doing something. Other common *for-* words are *forbid*, *forfeit*, *forfend*, *forget*, *forgive* and *forlorn*.

There are few words that do not fit the general rule of thumb: note the spelling of *foreclose* and *forward*. There are also a few words for which both spellings are permitted: on the one hand, *forgo* may also be spelt *forego* (but do not confuse this with *foregone*), *forfend* also spelt *forefend*, and *forgather* also spelt *foregather*; on the other hand, *forebear* may also be spelt *forbear*.

## frater-, fratri-

*Fraternal* means much the same as 'brotherly', and the *frater-/fratri-* element is indeed derived from the Latin word *frater*, meaning 'brother'. To *fraternize* with someone was originally to be in close fellowship with them, just

like brothers, and a *fraternity* is much the same as a 'brotherhood'. *Fratricide* is the murder of a brother, or someone who murders his or her own brother (see -CIDE).

See also MATER- and PATER-.

## -gam(y)

*Monogamy* is the state or custom of being married to only one husband or wife at a time (see MONO-), *bigamy* the state of being married to two people at the one time (see BI-), and *polygamy* the custom of being married to several wives or husbands at the same time (see POLY-).

The *-gam-* part of this word is a word-building element that comes from the Greek word *gamos*, which means 'marriage'. Related adjectives end in *-gamous*: *polygamous*, etc.

## gastro-, gastr-

This word-building element forms part of a number of words relating to the stomach (Greek *gaster* 'stomach'). *Gastroenteritis* is an inflammation of the lining of the stomach and the intestines (see ENTERO- and -ITIS), and *gastronomy* is the art of eating well (ie, following the 'rules of the stomach' — see -NOMY).

## -gate

*-gate* is a very recent addition to the stock of English word-forming elements, and is one of the few discussed here that is not of Latin or Greek origin. From the time of the Watergate scandal in the United States in 1972 (involving an attempted break-in at the Democratic Party's headquarters in the Watergate building and leading eventually to the downfall of the then US President, Richard Nixon), *-gate* has been freely used as a word-building element added to the names of people, places or things to form new coinages denoting any public or political scandal, eg *Muldergate* (South Africa), *Stalkergate* (UK), *Irangate* (USA). Two more recent coinages, denoting scandals involving members of the British Royal Family in 1993, are *Squidgygate* and *Camillagate*.

Such *-gate* words are most often journalistic coinages. They remain current only as long as the particular scandal is in the news, but *-gate* itself seems now to be firmly established in the language, at least in the language of journalism.

## geo-

From Greek *ge* 'earth', this element is found in *geography* and *geology*, studies of two aspects of the Earth (see -GRAPH and -LOGY), and shows that originally *geometry* was concerned with measuring the Earth (see -METER).

*Geo-* can be freely added to other words to indicate that the denoted study or subject has to do with the Earth in particular: *geomagnetism*, *geochemistry*, *geophysics*, etc.

## -gon

**-gon** (from Greek *gonia* 'angle') is a common word-building element in mathematical terminology: a *polygon* is a figure with several angles and sides (see POLY-) and a *hexagon* is a polygon with six angles and six sides (see HEXA-). *Trigonometry* is the branch of mathematics that deals with the measurement of and the relationships between the size of the sides and angles of triangles (see TRI- and -METER).

## -gram, -gramme

From Greek *gramma* 'something drawn or written, a letter'.

>  Notice that although the Greek word has two *m*'s, almost all the English words in this category end in a single *m*.

The basic meaning of **-gram(me)** is 'something that is written or printed', but the basic notion has developed in several different directions over the years. There is, for example, the idea of a 'printed message', as in *cryptogram* 'a message written in code' (see CRYPTO-), *telegram* 'a message sent over a distance' (see TELE-), from which has developed *cablegram*, and more recently *kissagrams*, *strippagrams* and *gorillagrams*, from which the notion of <u>written</u> message is almost totally absent.

Medically, **-gram** is used to refer to photographic or printed information about the functioning or state of parts of the body, such as *cardiogram* (see CARDIO-), *electrocardiogram*, *mammogram* (Latin *mamma* 'breast'). Such **-grams** are often produced by equipment whose name ends in **-graph** (from Greek *graphein* 'to write') in a process or for a field of study the name of which ends in **-graphy** (eg *electrocardiograph* and *electrocardiography*).

Some of the **-grams** involve drawing rather than writing, eg a *diagram* and a *histogram* (= a type of graph in which quantities and frequencies are shown by rectangles of varying sizes).

Other **-gram** words are *anagram* (Greek *ana* 'backwards'), which is a word or phrase formed by writing the letters of another word or phrase in a different order (eg *evil*, *live* and *vile*), *epigram* 'a pointed saying or short witty poem about someone or something' (Greek *epi* 'on'), and *monogram* 'a design consisting of several letters interwoven to form a single symbol' (see MONO-). *Radiogram*, on the other hand, does not have this **-gram** element in it, being short for 'radio-gramophone'; but the initial part of *gramophone*, the former name for a record-player, comes from the same Greek root as **-gram**, indicating that records are a means of recording sound by 'writing' grooves on plastic (see -PHONE).

Of the words that may be spelt with a double *mm*, note *programme* (the usual spelling in British English except for computer programs, whereas *program* is standard in American English for all senses of the word), and also the weight *gramme/gram* (the latter now being the usual spelling). Note also the double *m* in derived words: *diagrammatic, epigrammatic,* etc.

Some **-gram** words may also be **-graphs**: *mammograms* are also known as *mammographs* and *cryptograms* as *cryptographs*, for example. Others must always be distinguished, eg *telegram* 'a message sent by telegraph' and *telegraph* 'the apparatus for sending telegrams', and *monogram* (described above) and *monograph* (see the entry for -GRAPH below).

## -graph, grapho-

The word-building element **-graph/grapho-** is found in many English words denoting 'writing', as for example *biography* 'writing about a person's life' (see BIO-), *autograph* 'a person's signature (ie something they write themselves — see AUTO-), *monograph* 'a book or dissertation written on one particular topic' (see MONO-), and *graphology* 'the study of hand-writing' (see -LOGY). In some other words, this word-building element denotes 'something printed' or 'a picture', as in *photograph* (see PHOTO-).

See also -GRAM above.

## gyno-, -gyn(y)

From Greek *gyne,* 'a woman'. A *misogynist* is someone who hates women (Greek *miseein* 'to hate'), and *gynophobia* is a fear or strong dislike of women (see -PHOBIA). An *androgynous* person shows both male (Greek *andros* 'of a man') and female characteristics. And while *monogamy* is marriage to one husband or one wife at a time (see -GAMY), a less common but more specific term for marriage to just one wife is *monogyny* (see MONO-).

This word-building element is also found in the related form **gynaeco-** (**gyneco-** in American English), as in *gynaecology* 'the branch of medicine that deals with diseases specific to women' (see -LOGY).

## haemo-

Also spelt **hemo-**, especially in American English. From Greek *haima* 'blood'. A *haemorrhage* is a 'flow of blood' (see -RRH-), *haemoglobin* is the oxygen-carrying protein in red blood cells, and *haemophilia* is a hereditory disease in which a person's blood does not readily form clots (the *-philia* in this case meaning 'having a tendency to produce' — see PHILO-). This word-building element is also the root of *haemorrhoids* or 'piles' (see -RRH-).

## hecto-, hect-

Via French, from Greek *hekaton* 'one hundred'. Used as a prefix in words of measurement such as *hectolitre* (= 100 litres) and, in the shortened form **hect-** before a vowel, *hectare* (= 100 ares, or 10 000 m$^2$).

## helio-

From Greek *helios,* 'the sun', this word-building element is found in English words pertaining in some way to the sun, such as *heliograph* 'an apparatus used for sending messages by using mirrors to flash the sun's rays' (see -GRAM and -GRAPH), *heliotrope* 'a plant that turns its flowers or leaves towards the sun' (Greek *tropos* 'a turn'), and *helioscope* 'a device that allows you to look at the sun without harming your eyesight' (see -SCOPE).

The same Greek word forms the root of *helium*, a chemical element first discovered in the atmosphere of the sun.

### hemi- see SEMI-.

### hemo- see HAEMO-.

### hepta-

A *heptagon* is a seven-sided geometrical figure (see -GON). The **hepta-** part of this word comes from Greek *hepta*, meaning 'seven'. The same element (in the shorter form **hept-**) is found in the word *heptathlon*, a seven-event contest (Greek *athlon* 'contest') at the Olympic Games comprising tests of jumping, running and throwing.

### herbi-, herb-

From Latin *herba* 'grass, green plant', **herbi-** denotes in English either 'plant', as in *herbicide* a 'weedkiller' (see -CIDE) and *herbivorous* 'meat-eating' (see -VORE), or 'herb' (in the technical sense of a plant whose stems are not woody and which die back every year), as in *herbaceous*.

### hetero-

**Hetero-**, from Greek *heteros* 'other', is the opposite of both **homo-** and **ortho-**: *heterosexual* 'sexually attracted to people of the opposite sex' is the opposite of *homosexual* (see HOMO-), and *heterodox* 'having views or opinions that differ from those generally held' is the opposite of *orthodox* (see ORTHO- and -DOX).

### hexa-

A *hexagon* is a six-sided geometrical figure (see -GON). The **hexa-** part of this word comes from Greek *hex*, meaning 'six'. The same word-building element is found in other fairly technical words such as *hexameter*, which is a line of poetry which can be divided into six feet (Greek *metron* 'measure' — see also -METER), and *hexagram*, a star-shaped hexagon (see -GRAM).

### homi-

The Latin word for 'man' is *homo*, as in the biological name for human beings, *Homo sapiens*. The Latin root occurs in only a few English words, such as *homicide* 'murder' or 'murderer' (see -CIDE).

 Note that this is not the same element as **homo-** (see below), which comes from Greek, not Latin.

## homo-, hom-

*Homo-*, from the Greek *homos*, means 'same': a *homosexual* is someone who is sexually attracted to people of the same sex. Other words formed with **hom(o)-** are *homonym* 'a word with the same sound and spelling as another word' (see -ONYM), *homogeneous* 'consisting of parts or elements that are the same throughout' (Greek *genos* 'type'), and *homograph* 'a word spelt the same as some other word but having a different sound and meaning' (see -GRAM and -GRAPH).

In some words, the **homo-** element denotes 'homosexual', as for example in *homophobia* 'a strong dislike of homosexuality' (see -PHOBE).

>  Note that this is not the same word-building element as **homi-**.

• Related to Greek *homos* is *homoios* 'similar', from which is derived the modern English **homoeo-** (American English **homeo-**) found, for example, in *homoeopathy* 'treatment of disease by means of a substance that induces the same symptoms as the disease does' (see -PATH(Y)).

>  **Homoeo-** is pronounced /hoh-mi-o-/ in *homoeopathy*, and /hoh-mi-oh-/ in *homoeopathic*.

## hydro-, hydr-

*Hydor* is the Greek word for 'water', and from it is derived the modern English word-building element **hydr(o)-**, seen in such words as *hydroelectricity* 'electricity produced by water power' and *hydrophobia* 'fear of water' (see -PHOBE) — really an inability to swallow water due to a contraction of the throat caused by rabies, and hence a name sometimes used for rabies itself.

Although based on the same Greek root, *hydraulic* no longer necessarily implies the presence or use of water: a hydraulic device (eg a *hydraulic brake*) operates by pressure transmitted through a pipe containing a liquid, but the liquid need not be water: it could, for example, be oil.

## hyper-, hypo-

These two word-building elements of Greek origin are very similar in shape and sound, but are opposite in meaning: **hyper-** means 'over' or 'too much', and **hypo-** means 'under' or 'too little'.

A *hyperactive* child is over-active or unusually active and *hypertension* is a medical term for higher-than-normal blood pressure. In some words, the word-building element **hyper-** has the sense 'very great' rather than 'too great': a *hypermarket* is simply a very large supermarket.

Two common words used in medicine which contain the **hypo-** element are *hypodermic*, as in a *hypodermic needle* which is used for injecting medicine, etc 'under the skin' (see DERMATO-), and *hypothermia* 'the condition of having an abnormally, and usually dangerously, low body temperature' (see THERMO-).

## iatro-, iatr-

*Iatros* is the word for a doctor in ancient Greek, and *iatrikos* means 'medical'. The word-building element ***iatr(o)-*** is found in several words that describe branches of medicine, such as *psychiatry* 'medical treatment of diseases of the mind' (see PSYCHO-), *geriatrics* 'medical care of old people' (Greek *geras* 'old age'), and *paediatrics* 'the medical care of children' (see PAEDO-).

## iso-

From Greek *isos* 'equal', this word-building element appears in a number of technical words, such as *isobar* 'a line on a map joining points of equal atmospheric pressure' (Greek *baros* 'weight'), *isotherm* 'a line joining points of equal temperature' (see THERMO-), *isotope* 'any of a set of two or more atoms of a chemical which have the same number of protons in their nucleus but different numbers of neutrons' (Greek *topos* 'place', indicating that isotopes of an element occupy the same place on the chart of chemical elements), and *isomer*, denoting any of two or more substances with the same elements (Greek *meros* 'part') in the same chemical formula but differing in the way the atoms of these elements are arranged.

• The Latin-based equivalent of ***iso-*** is ***equi-***: in geometry, an *isosceles triangle* is one which has two equal sides (Greek *skeles* 'leg'), whereas an *equilateral triangle* has all three sides (Latin *lateris* 'of a side') of equal length.

## -itis

***-itis*** (derived from Greek words ending in *-itis*, which mean 'belonging to —') is used in medicine to denote a disease which involves inflammation: *tonsillitis* is an inflammation of the tonsils, *bronchitis* an inflammation of the lining of the bronchial tubes (see BRONCHO-), *laryngitis* an inflammation of the larynx, and so on.

Notice the difference between an ***-itis*** and an ***-osis***: an ***-itis*** involves inflammation, whereas an ***-osis*** is a diseased condition. In a looser and more colloquial sense, *-itis* is in modern English freely attached to words and phrases to denote some sort of mania or obsession: *crosswordpuzzleitis*, *Nintendoitis*.

## kilo-

Added to units of measurement such as gram and metre, ***kilo-*** means 'a thousand' (Greek *chilioi* 'a thousand'): a *kilogram* equals 1000 grams, a *kilometre* 1000 metres, and so on.

In computing terminology **kilo-** does not mean exactly 1000, but 1024 ($= 2^{10}$), as in *kilobyte*.

Compare MILLI-.

## -logy

Although commonly thought of as '*-ology*', this word-building element is strictly speaking **-logy** (from Greek *logos* 'word', 'reason'). The preceding *o* usually belongs to the element the **-logy** is attached to (eg *biology = bio-* + *-logy*, not *bi-* + *-ology*; *psychology = psycho-* + *-logy*). However, in cases where the preceding element does not end in *o*, an *o* i̲s̲ added between the two parts of the word, eg *dialectology, Kremlinology, Egyptology*, which of course reinforces the notion that the second element is *-ology*.

Most words ending in **-logy** denote scientific or serious studies of something or another, eg *graphology* the 'study of hand-writing' (see -GRAM and -GRAPH), *psychology* the 'study of the mind' (see PSYCHO-) and *sociology* the 'study of human society'. Some **-logies**, however, denote not, or not only, the study of some subject but the subject of study itself, eg *mythology* (= myths collectively rather than the study of myths). Notice also that *astrology* has taken on a special sense and has been replaced by *astronomy* (see ASTRO- and -NOMY) in the sense of the strict scientific study of the stars and planets.

Some **-logies** are not studies but relate to the 'word' sense of Greek *logos*, eg *tautology* 'the unnecessary or mistaken use of two words or phrases that say the same thing' (such as *A̲l̲l̲ ̲a̲t̲ ̲o̲n̲c̲e̲ she s̲u̲d̲d̲e̲n̲l̲y̲ remembered where she should be*) from Greek *tauto* 'the same', and *trilogy* 'a set of three related books, plays, etc' (see TRI-).

## -lysis

From Greek *lysis* 'a loosening', this word-building element denotes a splitting-up or breaking-down into smaller or simpler parts, eg by means of electricity (*electrolysis*) or water (*hydrolysis* — see HYDRO-). Similarly, *analysis* (Greek *ana* 'up') involves splitting something up into its component parts.

## macro-

Words beginning with **macro-** denote things that are long, large or great (Greek *makros* 'long, great'). *Macrobiotics* is the art of prolonging life (see BIO-) by means of correct diet, *macroeconomics* is the study of the economics of large units, eg the study of national income or international trade, and *macrofauna* are animals large enough to be seen by the naked eye (compare *megafauna* at MEGA-).

See also MICRO-.

## mater-, matri-

From Latin *mater* 'mother'. Note the single *t*. *Maternal* means 'relating to a mother or to motherhood' (*maternity*). *Matricide* means 'the murder, or murderer, of one's own mother' (see -CIDE).

The Latin word *mater* is also the root of *matrimony*.

See also FRATER- and PATER-.

## mega-

In units of measurement, **mega-** (from Greek *megas* 'big') means 'a million', as in *megawatt* and *megaton*.

 In computing, **mega-** means $1\,048\,576$ (= $2^{100}$), as in *megabyte*.

In other words, **mega-** simply means 'large'. *Megafauna* is a technical name for animals that are large enough to be seen with the naked eye (compare *macrofauna* at MACRO-), and a *megaphone* is a device for making the voice louder (see -PHONE).

## -meter, -metre

A **meter** is an instrument for measuring something. As a word-building element, it occurs in many compound words denoting measuring devices: *speedometer, barometer, swingometer*, etc.

A **metre** is a measure of distance, and also occurs in compounds such as *kilometre* and *centimetre* (see KILO- and CENTI-).

Both words are derived from the Greek word *metron* 'measure'.

 Note that in American English, **meter** is the correct spelling for both words and both word-building elements, eg to British English *kilometre* corresponds American English *kilometer*.

## micro-

**Micro-**, from Greek *mikros* 'small', means in English 'very small'. It is a very common word-building element in modern technology, eg in computers, where the tendency is to make things as small as possible: *microchip, microprocessor, microcomputer*. A *microscope* is an instrument (see -SCOPE) for making tiny things visible, and a *microphone* is a device which can make small sounds louder (see -PHONE, and compare *megaphone* at MEGA-). *Microfauna* are very small animals, especially those that are invisible to the naked eye (compare *macrofauna* and *megafauna* at MACRO- and MEGA-).

In some words, **micro-** denotes 'using a microscope', as in *microsurgery*.

### milli-, mill-

In units of measurement, *milli-* means 'one thousandth', as in *millimetre*, a thousandth of a metre, and *milligram*. But this word-building element, derived from the Latin word *mille* 'thousand', also occurs in a number of English words in the sense of 'a thousand' rather than 'thousandth': a *millennium* is a period of a thousand years (see ANN-), and a *millipede* is an insect-like animal with many legs (Latin *pedis* 'of a leg'), although not as many as a thousand legs.

See also KILO-.

### mono-, mon-

The word-building element *mono-*, from the Greek *monos* 'single', 'alone', means in English words 'one', 'alone' or 'single'. A *monarch* is a person who is the sole ruler of a country (see -ARCH), a person who is *monogamous* has only one husband or wife at a time (see -GAM(Y)), and if you are *monolingual*, you speak only one language (Latin *lingua* 'tongue' or 'language'). A *monoplane* has only one set of wings, as opposed to a *biplane* which has two sets (see BI-), and a *monorail* is a railway which runs on a single rail as opposed to the normal two rails. In chemistry, a *monoxide* is a chemical with only one oxygen atom in its molecule, as opposed to a *dioxide*, for example, which has two (see DI-).

The same Greek root is seen in *monocle* (= a form of spectacles with a single lens).

See also UNI-.

### multi- see POLY-.

### naut-

Words with *naut-* in them have to do with ships and sailing, eg *nautical*, but in some cases the ships are spaceships whose crews are *astronauts* (see ASTRO-) or, especially from Russia and other countries of the former Soviet Union, *cosmonauts* (Greek *kosmos* 'the universe').

### neo-

*Neo-*, from Greek *neos* 'new', in English usually means 'new' in the sense of 'revived in a new and modern form' or 'appearing in a later, more developed form'. Many of the words to which *neo-* is attached are 'isms' or are related to 'isms': *neofascism*, *neo-Nazism* and *neo-Nazi*, *neopaganism*, *neocolonialism*, and so on.

A *neologism* is a new word or the use of an existing word in a new sense (Greek *logos* 'word'; see -LOGY).

A slightly different sense of *neo-* ('newly', 'recently') is to be seen in *neonatal*, 'relating to new-born babies' (Latin *natus* 'born'). *Neolithic* denotes the later, more advanced, part of the Stone Age (Greek *lithos* 'stone').

## neuro-, neur-

*Neuro-*, from Greek *neuron* 'nerve', denotes 'nerve', 'nerves' or the 'nervous system' in many medical and scientific words in modern English. A *neurologist* is a doctor who specializes in the diagnosis and treatment of diseases of the nervous system (see -LOGY), *neuralgia* is pain along a nerve (see -ALGIA), *neuromuscular* means 'relating to the nerves and muscles together'.

## -nomy

From Greek *nomos*, which means 'law', as in *astronomy* (see ASTRO-). *Gastronomy* is the art of eating well (ie, doing what is right according to the 'rules of the stomach' — see GASTRO-), and *autonomy* (see AUTO-) allows you to be a 'law unto yourself'. In the Bible, the book known as *Deuteronomy* is so called because it contains a second account of the Law given to Moses (Greek *deuteros* 'second'), the first account being found in the book of Exodus.

## -nym see -ONYM.

## octo-, oct-, octa-

From Latin and Greek *octo* 'eight', as in *octopus* 'a sea creature with eight legs' (Greek *pous* 'leg'), *octave* 'a set of eight notes in music', and *octagon* 'a geometrical figure with eight sides and eight angles' (see -GON).

*October* is so called because it was the eighth month in the Roman calendar, not the tenth month as it is for us. (In the Roman calendar, *December* was the tenth month — Latin *decem* 'ten'; see DECI-.)

## -oid

From Greek *eidos* 'form', this is the equivalent in technical terminology of '-like': *anthropoid* apes are the ones that are considered to be humanlike (eg chimpanzees and gorillas), and *androids* are humanlike robots (both the *anthrop-* and *andr-* parts of these words are derived from Greek words for 'man' — see ANTHROPO-). *Asteroids* (from a Greek word meaning 'starlike') are the minor planets in orbit between Mars and Jupiter, and *meteoroids* are meteors which have not reached the Earth's atmosphere (as opposed to *meteorites* which have reached the Earth's atmosphere and have fallen to Earth as lumps of stone or metal). In mathematics, a *cuboid* is a solid figure which is similar in certain respects to a cube: like a cube, it has six rectangular faces, but unlike a cube, in which all six faces are identical squares, in a cuboid only opposite sides need be identical in size and shape.

---

 **Tablets and tabloids**

Among the *-oid* words, *tabloid* has perhaps the most interesting history: originally a trademark for a medicine produced in tablet form, it came to be applied, often facetiously, to anything produced in concentrated form, and in particular to newspapers which provided news coverage in a condensed, easily digestible style, with large headlines, many photographs and pages smaller than those of the 'heavier' papers.

Since tabloid newspapers are considered to have a rather informal and sometimes sensationalistic style of presenting news, the term *tabloid* has now taken on this further meaning and can be applied to, for example, television programmes of a similar informal approach intended to have mass appeal.

## *-ology* see -LOGY.

## omni-

**Omni-** comes from the Latin word *omnis* 'all'. This word-building element is found in such English words as *omniscient* 'all-knowing' (see SCI-), *omnipotent* 'all-powerful' (compare the English word *potent*), *omnidirectional* 'able to act in all directions', and *omnivorous* 'feeding on both animal and vegetable food' (see -VORE).

 **Buses for all**

The Latin *omnis* is also the root of the word *bus*, a shortened form of *omnibus*, which in Latin means 'for everyone'. Public transport is transport for everybody!

## *-onym*

Note the spelling: *y*, not *i*. This word-building element, which comes from the Greek *onyma* 'a name', is found in words such as *antonyms* (= words that are opposite in meaning — see ANTI-), *synonyms* (= words that have the same meaning — see SYN-), *homonyms* (= words that are the same in sound and spelling, but different in meaning — see HOMO-).

A *pseudonym* is a false name (see PSEUDO-), used to conceal a person's true identity, and people who wish to remain *anonymous* do not want their name to become known at all (see A-).

## ortho-, orth-

**Ortho-** has much the same meanings as the Greek word *orthos* from which it is derived. In Greek, *orthos* means 'straight', 'upright', 'correct', and English words with this word-building element in them also contain the idea of 'straightness' and 'correctness'. Among these are *orthodox* 'agreeing with generally accepted opinions, especially in religion' (see -DOX), *orthography* 'spelling', (originally the art of spelling words correctly — see -GRAM and -GRAPH), *orthodontics* 'the straightening of teeth that are crooked or out of place' (Greek *odontos* 'of a tooth'). *Orthopaedics* is the correction of deformities arising from disease of or injury to the bones (see PAEDO-).

## *-osis*

English *-osis* comes from a Greek word-ending *-osis* used to form nouns from verbs (rather like *-ation* is in English, as in *starvation* from *to starve*).

In medical terminology, *-osis* denotes a 'diseased condition' of something, as in *neurosis* (see NEURO-) and *halitosis* 'bad breath' (Latin *halitus* 'breath'), or caused by something, as in *asbestosis*, a serious disorder caused by inhaling fibres of asbestos.

In a more general sense, in some words, *-osis* simply denotes a process of some sort: *metamorphosis* (= 'the process of changing shape' — Greek *morphe* 'shape'), *osmosis* (= a gradual process of absorption or assimilation — Greek *osmos* 'impulse').

> ⚠ Do not confuse *-osis* and *-itis* (see -ITIS).

## -otomy see -TOMY.

## paedo-, paed-

*Paidos* means 'of a boy' in Greek, and this is the root of the modern English word-building element **paedo-** (now sometimes spelt **pedo-** in British English, and usually so in American English). Words containing this word-building element relate to children in some way or another, eg *paediatrics* 'the treatment of childhood diseases' (see IATRO-), and *paedophilia* 'sexual desire directed towards children' (see PHILO-).

In some words, the connection with 'children' is not obvious: *orthopaedics* 'the correction of deformities arising from disease of or injury to the bones' has the **paed-** element in it because it originally meant 'the correction of deformities arising from disease of or injury to the bones in childhood'.

In some words containing this word-building element, the spelling **ped-** is now more common than **paed-**. One such word is *pedagogical* 'relating to teaching, ie teaching children'. In ancient Greece, the *paidagogos* was a slave whose job it was to take boys to school.

## pater-, patri-

From the Latin word for 'father', *pater*. *Paternal* means 'relating to a father' or 'fatherly', and *paternity* is 'fatherhood'. *Patricide* is 'the murder, or murderer, of one's own father' (see -CIDE).

See also FRATER- and MATER-.

## -path, -pathy, patho-

Derived from Greek *patheia* 'suffering', and words related to it, **-path** in English denotes either a person who is suffering from a particular disorder (eg a *psychopath* who suffers from a severe disorder of the mind — see PSYCHO-), or a person who provides therapy for a disorder (eg an *osteopath*, who provides therapy by massage and manipulation of the bones of the body

— Greek *osteon* 'bone'). Related names of disorders and therapies often end in **-pathy**, eg *osteopathy*.

Also connected with the notion of 'disease' is *pathology*, the study of diseases and the changes in body tissues and organs caused by diseases, etc (see -LOGY).

## ped(o)- see PAEDO-.

## penta-

A *pentagon* is a five-sided geometrical shape (Greek *pente* 'five' — see also -GON). The Pentagon, the headquarters of the American armed forces in Washington, is so called because it consists of five concentric pentagonal buildings. In poetry, a *pentameter* is a line which can be divided into five feet (Greek *metron* 'measure'). The *Pentateuch* is the name given to the first five books in the Bible (*teuchos* in Greek is a 'tool' or a 'book'). In sport, the *modern pentathlon* is a five-event contest (Greek *athlon* 'contest') involving running, riding, swimming, shooting and fencing.

## philo-, phil-, -phile

From Greek *philos* 'friend' and *phileein* 'to love'.

*Philosophers* were originally so called because they were considered, or they considered themselves, to be 'friends or lovers of wisdom' (see SOPH-). *Philharmonic* means 'fond of music'. And people who are, for example, *Francophiles* are keen on France and all things French. Some people who are '-philes' are not just lovers, but collectors also: *arctophiles* collect teddy bears, for example (Greek *arktos* 'bear').

There are related nouns ending in **-philia**, eg *Francophilia, arctophilia*; some '-philias' are, however, rather less pleasant than these: *necrophilia*, for example, is a morbid attraction to dead bodies (Greek *nekros* 'dead body').

## -phobia, -phobe

*Phobos* is Greek for 'fear'. There are a great many phobias that have special names in English; among these are, for example, *triskaidekaphobia* which is a fear of the number 13 (Greek *triskaideka* 'thirteen'), *ailurophobia*, a fear of cats (Greek *ailouros* 'cat'), and *arachnophobia*, a fear of spiders (Greek *arachne* 'spider').

Some '-phobias' involve 'hatred' or 'dislike' rather than fear: *Francophobia*, for example, is an intense dislike of the French.

Those who suffer from particular phobias have corresponding names ending in **-phobe**: *ailurophobe, arachnophobe*, etc.

## -phone, phon-

From Greek *phone* 'sound' or 'voice', these word-building elements have to do with sound or speech in modern English. A *telephone* is a device that allows you to hear the sound of someone's voice at a distance (see TELE-), *microphones* and *megaphones* are devices for making sounds louder (see MICRO- and MEGA-), and a *saxophone* was invented by a man whose name was Sax (who also invented another musical instrument, the saxhorn).

In the adjectives *Anglophone* and *Francophone*, the *-phone* means 'speaking (English or French) in everyday life'.

As a word-root at the beginnings of words, we can see *phon-* in, for example, *phonetics* 'the study of speech sounds and speech production'.

## photo-

The original sense of *photo-* has to do with light (Greek *photos* 'of light'), as in *photosensitive* 'affected by light' and *photograph* (see -GRAPH).

However, with the advent of photography, a second sense of *photo-* developed, denoting something to do with photography itself, as in *photocopy* and *photogenic*.

## physio-

*Physio-*, from Greek *physis* 'nature', has two basic meanings in modern English. Firstly, it relates to the natural processes of life, as in *physiology* (see -LOGY), and secondly it may denote the treatment of disease by physical rather than medicinal means, as in *physiotherapy*.

The same Greek word underlies the English word *physics*.

## poly-

*Poly-*, from Greek *polys*, means 'many' or 'several'. *Polynesia* is a part of the world where there are many islands (Greek *nesos* 'island'); a *polyglot* is a person who can speak several languages (Greek *glotta* 'tongue'); and a *polygon* is a geometrical figure with several sides, especially one with more than four sides (see -GON). *Polygamy* is the fact or custom of having more than one wife or husband at one time (see -GAM(Y)).

As a prefixed element in chemistry, *poly-* means 'a polymer of —': *polystyrene* is a polymer of styrene, *polythene* (or *polyethylene*) is the name of a number of polymers of ethylene. The word *polymer* itself contains the *poly-* element: a polymer is a substance whose molecules are a repetitive series of simpler units (Greek *meros* 'a part').

• The Latin-based equivalent of *poly-* is *multi-* (from Latin *multus* 'many'): for example, a *polyglot* could be described as being *multilingual* (Latin *lingua* 'tongue, language').

## pseudo-, pseud-

From Greek *pseudes*, meaning 'false'. As a word-building element added to the beginning of other words, *pseudo-* means 'false', 'sham', 'deceptively

like' or 'imitating', as in *pseudo-science* or *pseudo-Gothic* architecture. A *pseudonym* (see -ONYM) is a false name assumed by a person, especially a writer, in order to conceal his or her identity.

See also QUASI-.

## psycho-, psych-

As is suggested by words such as *psychology* (see -LOGY) and *psychiatry* (see IATRO-), words with the word-building element **psych(o)-** have to do with the 'mind' (Greek *psyche* 'soul'). Other common words with this word-building element are *psychic*, *psychoanalysis* (= a means of treating mental disorders by tracing them to memories or feelings stored forgotten deep in the patient's mind) and *psychotherapy* (= therapy by means of hypnosis, psychoanalysis, etc).

## quadri-, quadru-

**Quadri-** is the Latin-based equivalent of **tetra-**. From a Latin word-building element derived from *quattuor* 'four'. A *quadrilateral* is a four-sided geometrical figure (Latin *lateris* 'of a side'), a *quadruped* is a four-footed animal (Latin *pedis* 'of a foot'), especially a horse, and four babies born together are called *quadruplets*.

## quasi-

From Latin *quasi*, meaning 'as if', this word-building element is used in modern English to indicate that something is only what it claims to be 'to a certain extent' or 'in appearance only', as in a *quasi-historical* novel or the *quasi-judicial* functions of parliament. *Quangos* are 'quasi-autonomous non-governmental organizations' (ie, public bodies not part of the Civil Service but set up and funded by the government, therefore autonomous but only 'to a certain extent').

---

 **Quasi-** is added freely to nouns and adjectives, less commonly to verbs and adverbs.

---

## -rrh-, rh-

In ancient Greek, *rheein* means 'to flow'. Most of the words that contain this **-rrh-** element are medical words that relate to disorders which involve, or were once thought to involve, a 'flow' of something. Most end in **-rrhoea** (**-rrhea** in American English), eg *diarrhoea*, *gonorrhoea* (a sexually-transmitted disease) and *seborrhoea* 'excessive discharge from the sebaceous glands' (which produce a substance that lubricates the hair and skin); *catarrh* (Greek *kata* 'downwards') is the only contrary example.

Two disorders involving a flow of blood are *haemorrhoids* and *haemorrhage* (see HAEMO-). Although the *-rrhage* element comes from a different Greek word, the **-rrh-** can still be remembered as involving a 'flow'.

At the beginning of a word, there is only a single *r*. The *rhythm* of a poem, for example, has much to do with how the poem flows, and to a lesser extent so does its *rhyme*. But many of the words in this category have no longer any apparent connection with the notion of 'flowing', eg *rheumatism* and *rheumatics*.

**-sc-** see -ESC-.

## schizo-

From Greek *schizein*, 'to split'. Spelling points to note are the *ch*, pronounced /k/, and the *z*, pronounced /ts/. Common words in which this element occurs are *schizophrenia* (Greek *phren* 'mind') and *schizophrenic*.

## sci-

In Latin, the word for 'to know' is *scire*, and *scientia* means 'knowledge'. From *scientia* itself are derived English words such as *science*, *scientist* and *scientific*, but the same root is to be found in several other common words such as *omniscient* 'knowing everything' (see OMNI-), *prescience* 'foreknowledge' or 'foresight', *conscience*, *conscientious* and *conscious*.

---

Science was described by the philosopher Herbert Spencer as 'organized knowledge'.

---

## -scope

Words ending in **-scope** usually denote devices that allow you to look at things (*telescope*, *microscope* — see TELE- and MICRO-), or which make things visible (*oscilloscope*, an instrument which makes changes in, for example, electrical waves visible on a screen), or else which allow examination of something that cannot be seen (such as a doctor's *stethoscope* for listening to the sounds of the heart, lungs, etc through the chest-wall — Greek *stethos* 'chest').

## semi-

**Semi-**, which in Latin means 'half-' may in English words mean either literally 'half-' (as in *semicircle* and *semiquaver* or, in a rather broader sense, 'nearly, partly, incompletely' or 'partial' as in *semiconscious*, *semi-skilled*, *semiconductor* (= 'a substance which conducts electricity at high temperatures or when slightly impure, but not at lower temperatures or when pure'), etc.

● The Greek-derived equivalent of **semi-** is **hemi-** (as in *hemisphere*) and the French equivalent (also used in English) is **demi-**. All three of these word-building elements are used together in the name of the musical note *hemidemisemiquaver*, which is one-eighth of a quaver in length (ie 'half of a half of a half quaver').

## simil-, simul-

From Latin *similis* 'like'. Note that there is only one *l* and one *m*.

English words with the *simil-* element are *similar*, *simile* 'a figure of speech which describes something by likening it to something else', *facsimile* 'an exact copy of something' (Latin *fac* 'make') and *verisimilitude* (Latin *verus* 'true').

Note the double *s* in *dissimilar* ('not similar') and *assimilate*.

In some related words, the word-building element has a *u* in the second syllable, eg *simulate* and *simultaneous*.

## soph-

Derived from the Greek words *sophos* 'wise' and *sophia* 'wisdom'. A *philosopher* is, or was originally considered to be, 'a person who loves knowledge' (see PHILO-). Other English words containing this root are *sophisticated*, *sophistry* and *sophomore*, a mainly US word for a second-year university student.

## syn-, sym-, syl-

Note the *y* in this word-building element. In Greek, *syn* means 'with', and this meaning is still apparent in some of the words in which this word-building element appears: if you *sympathize* with someone, you feel for them (see -PATH); a *symphony* is a form of music in which sounds (see -PHONE) harmonize with each other; if you *synchronize* watches, you set them to the same time (see CHRON-); and a *synthesis* is a 'putting things together' (Greek *thesis* 'putting').

In some other words, the meaning is more 'together' than 'with'. In medicine, a *syndrome* (Greek *drome* 'running') is a set of *symptoms* (Greek *piptein* 'to fall') which occur together, and the same *syn-* element forms the beginning of words such as *syllable* 'sounds which are pronounced together' and *synagogue* 'a place where people come together to worship'.

## techno-, techn-

From Greek *techne*, meaning 'skill', this word-building element occurs in words such as *technology*, *technical* and *technique*, and in many new coinages such as *technophobia* (see -PHOBE) or *technofear* 'a fear or dislike of technology' and *technocracy* 'management or government by technical experts' (see -CRACY).

## tele-

From Greek *tele* 'far'. A *television* is a device that lets you see what is happening at a distance (see VIS-), a *telephone* allows you to speak to someone at a distance (see -PHONE), and a *telegram* is a message sent by *telegraph* over a long distance (see -GRAM and -GRAPH).

## terr-

Many people have difficulty remembering how many *t*'s and *r*'s there are in *Mediterranean*. As an aid to correct spelling, it may be helpful to note that the

*-terr-* part of this word comes from the Latin word *terra*, which means 'the earth' or 'land' (the *medi-* part means 'middle' — the Mediterranean Sea is in the middle of, or surrounded by, land). The same root is at the heart of the words *subterranean* 'underground' (Latin *sub* 'under') and *terrestrial* 'living, growing, etc on the ground or on land', and possibly also of *territory*.

## tetra-, tetr-

*Tetra-* is derived from a Greek word and denotes 'four'. It most commonly occurs in English in technical and scientific words, such as *tetrahedron* 'a geometrical figure with four sides' (Greek *hedra* 'a seat'), *tetrachloride* 'a chemical compound containing four chlorine atoms in each molecule', *tetroxide* 'an oxide with four atoms of oxygen in its molecule', and *tetrameter* 'a line of poetry consisting of four feet' (Greek *metron* 'measure').

## theo-, the-

The Greek word *theos* means 'God' or 'a god'. This is found as a root in such English words as *theology* 'the study of God and religion' (see -LOGY), *theocracy* 'a country ruled by God or by a god rather than by a human sovereign' (see -CRACY), and *atheist* 'a person who does not believe in God' (see A-).

## thermo-, therm-

*Thermo-* comes from the Greek words *therme* 'heat' and *thermos* 'hot', and in English denotes 'heat' or 'temperature'. A *thermometer* is a device for measuring temperatures (see -METER), a *thermostat* is a device for keeping temperatures steady (Greek *statos* 'standing'), and *thermonuclear* reactions are nuclear reactions occurring at extremely high temperatures. The same root is also to be seen in *thermal* 'relating to or producing heat' or (of clothing) 'designed to prevent the loss of the body's heat'.

## -tomy

Derived from the Greek word *tome*, meaning a 'cutting'. The cutting comes in two types. It may be an *-ectomy*, which is a 'cutting out' or 'cutting away' (as in *tonsillectomy* 'surgical removal of the tonsils', and *vasectomy*, the contraceptive operation which removes part of the tube (the *vas deferens*) which carries sperm from the testicles). Or it may be an *-otomy*, which is a surgical 'cutting into', as in *lobotomy*, a surgical operation involving cutting into a lobe of an organ of the body, especially the brain.

## tri-

The word-building element *tri-* is derived from Latin *tres* and Greek *treis*, both meaning 'three'. This is a fairly common word-building element in English. A *triangle* is, of course, a geometrical figure with three angles and three sides; a *triathlon* is a sporting three-event contest (Greek *athlon* 'contest') usually comprising swimming, cycling and running; a *tricycle* has three wheels (Greek *kyklos* 'wheel'); a *tripod* has three legs or feet (Greek *podos* 'of a foot');

and a *trident* is a type of spear with three prongs (Latin *dentis* 'of a tooth'). With a different pronunciation of the word-building element, we have *trilogy* 'a group of three related novels, plays or poems' (see -LOGY), and *triplets*.

**Tri-** is a common prefix in scientific and technical language: in chemistry, a *trioxide* is a compound containing three atoms of oxygen, and in botany *trifoliate* means 'having three leaves, or with leaves that are split into three parts' (Latin *folium* 'leaf').

In some words the meaning of **tri-** is ambiguous: *tri-weekly*, for example, can mean either 'once every three weeks' or 'three times a week'.

## uni-

From Latin *unus*, meaning 'one'. A *unicycle* is a one-wheeled cycle (Greek *kyklos* 'wheel'), as opposed to the more usual two-wheeled variety of *bicycle* (see BI-) and the three-wheeled *tricycle* (see TRI-). *Unilateral* action is action taken by one side only (Latin *lateris* 'of a side').

The same Latin word is the root of *unit*, *union* and *unify*.

See also MONO-.

## vis-

The word-building element **vis-** comes from the Latin word *videre*, meaning 'to see'. It is found in many English words, such as *television* 'a device which allows you to see things that are far away' (see TELE-), *visible* 'able to be seen', *vision* and *visual* (and *audiovisual* — see AUDIO-). *Videre* is also the root of the word *video*.

## -vore, -vorous

Words with this word-building element in them are usually technical terms which describe the eating habits of an animal or a person: a *carnivore* eats meat (see CARNI-), a *herbivore* eats plants (see HERBI-), and an *omnivore* eats both (see OMNI-).

The related adjectives end in **-vorous**: *carnivorous*, *herbivorous*, *omnivorous*, *insectivorous*, etc. The Latin word *vorare*, 'to devour', from which this word-building element is derived is also the root of *voracious* 'eating greedily or in large quantities'.

 Do not confuse **-vorous** with **-ferous**, meaning 'carrying' or 'containing' (see -FEROUS).

## zoo-

From Greek *zoion* 'animal'. The commonest word with this word-building element in it is *zoology* 'the scientific study of animals' (see -LOGY). *Zoo* is a shortened form of 'zoological gardens', originally referring specifically to the Zoological Gardens in London.

 The Zoological Gardens in London were established in 1828, but there are records of animal collections far back in history, eg in ancient Egypt about the 15th century BC and in China in the 12th century BC.

Other words formed with *zoo-* are relatively uncommon and fairly technical, eg *zoogeography* 'the study of animal distribution over the earth' (see GEO- and -GRAPH).

# 6

# 1000 Difficult Words

---

## ✧ *How to find a word you cannot spell*

One problem that poor spellers are faced with is how to find a word in a dictionary or in a list such as the one that follows in this chapter, when they do not know how to spell it in the first place.

For example, someone who does not know that there is a 'silent' *p* at the beginning of *pneumonia* or *psychology* would have a fruitless search if they hunted for the correct spelling of these words under *n* and *s* respectively. And even where there are no silent letters to complicate matters, the rules of English spelling will often allow several conceivable spellings of a word, not all of which will necessarily occur to someone who is searching for the correct one: it would, for example, be pointless to search for *physical* under *f*, *xylophone* under *z*, or *ewe* under *y*.

To help overcome this difficulty, this section comprises a list of alternative spellings for various English sounds. If you have searched in the word list below, or in another dictionary, for a word, and failed to find it where you expected it to be, consult the list of possible spellings given here and then try looking for the word you want under some of the other spellings suggested in it. The following table is particularly helpful in that it indicates the 'silent' letters which cause so many problems for those who find spelling difficult.

| Sound | Possible Spelling | Examples |
|-------|-------------------|----------|
| /b/ | b | *book, rub* |
| | bb | *babble, flabby* |
| | bu | *buoy, buy* |
| /p/ | p | *pin, sip* |
| | pp | *apple, nipped* |
| | ph | *shepherd* |
| /d/ | d | *dry, body, cold* |
| | dd | *cuddle, add* |
| | ed | *called* |
| | ld | *could, would, should* |

| Sound | Possible Spelling | Examples |
|-------|-------------------|----------|
| /t/ | t | *tin, not, spilt* |
| | tt | *better, kettle* |
| | th | *Thomas, thyme* |
| | ed | *walked* |
| | pt | *pterodactyl, receipt* |
| | bt | *doubt, debt, redoubtable* |
| | ct | *indict, victuals* |
| | ght | *taught* |
| /g/ | g | *big, get* |
| | gg | *bigger, begging, egg, aggravate* |
| | gh | *ghost, aghast* |
| | gu | *guard, guarantee, vague* |
| | x | *example (x = /gz/)* |
| /k/ | k | *key, break* |
| | c | *can, panic, sceptic* |
| | ck | *back, cackle, panicky* |
| | cc | *tobacco, account* |
| | q(u) | *quite, cheque, liquor* |
| | ch | *character, school* |
| | cq(u) | *acquire, lacquer* |
| | cch | *saccharine* |
| | lk | *folk, talk* |
| | kh | *khaki* |
| | x | *extra, luxury (x = /ks/)* |
| /m/ | m | *me, mime, lump* |
| | mm | *common* |
| | mn | *solemn* |
| | mb | *bomb* |
| | lm | *calm* |
| | gm | *paradigm* |
| | chm | *drachm* |
| | nm | *government* |
| /n/ | n | *not, sun* |
| | nn | *sunny* |
| | kn | *knot, knit* |
| | gn | *gnat* |
| | pn | *pneumonia* |
| | mn | *mnemonic* |
| /ng/ | ng | *sing, longing* |
| | ngue | *tongue* |
| | n | *pink, hankie, finger* |
| | nd | *handkerchief* |

| Sound | Possible Spelling | Examples |
|-------|-------------------|----------|
| /f/ | f | *finger, if, soft* |
| | ff | *off, sniff, coffee* |
| | ph | *physical, photograph* |
| | gh | *cough, enough* |
| | lf | *half, calf* |
| | ft | *often, soften* |
| /v/ | v | *van, sieve, shiver* |
| | vv | *navvy* |
| | f | *of* |
| | ph | *Stephen* |
| | lv | *calves* |
| /s/ | s | *sit, books* |
| | ss | *mess* |
| | c | *city, cynic, mice* |
| | sc | *scent, scene, fascinate* |
| | ps | *psychology* |
| | st | *fasten, castle* |
| | sc | *muscle* |
| | sw | *sword* |
| | sch | *schism* |
| | sth | *asthma* |
| /z/ | z | *zero, fez* |
| | zz | *puzzle, fizzy* |
| | ss | *scissors* |
| | s | *frogs, churches, was, cheese* |
| | x | *xylophone* |
| /ch/ | ch | *church, cheese* |
| | tch | *match, watch* |
| | t | *question, future, righteous* |
| | c | *cello* |
| | cz | *Czech* |
| /j/ | j | *judge* |
| | dg(e) | *judge, judg(e)ment* |
| | g(e) | *age, gem* |
| | gg | *exaggerate* |
| | dj | *adjust* |
| | d | *soldier, graduate* |
| /sh/ | sh | *sheep, fish, fashion* |
| | ch | *chivalry, machine* |
| | s | *sure, tension* |
| | ss | *mission* |
| | sc | *fascist, conscience* |

| Sound | Possible Spelling | Examples |
|---|---|---|
| | c | ocean, special |
| | sch | schist |
| | chs | fuchsia |
| | t | attention |
| /zh/ | s | pleasure, vision, unusual |
| | z | seizure, azure |
| | ge | rouge |
| /th/ | th | thin, ether, tooth |
| /dh/ | th | then, smooth, rhythm |
| /w/ | w | wet, worn |
| | u | quiet |
| | o | choir, one |
| | wh | when, whether |
| /y/ | y | yet, youth |
| | j | hallelujah |
| | i | opinion |
| (/yuu/) | ew | ewe, few, view |
| | u(e) | use, queue, cue |
| | eu | feud, pseudo |
| | eau | beauty |
| /r/ | r | red, fur, pretty |
| | rr | furry, purring |
| | wr | wrong, write |
| | rh | rhyme, rhythm |
| | rrh | diarrhoea, haemorrhage |
| /h/ | h | hot |
| | wh | who |
| /l/ | l | lead, pilfer, spilt, bottle, medal |
| | ll | hell, calling, gorilla |
| /a/, /ah/ | a | hat, car, father, black, castle, path, shah |
| | au | laugh |
| | al | half, calf |
| | ea | heart |
| | e | clerk, sergeant |
| | aa | bazaar |
| | ai | plaid |
| | i | meringue |
| /ay/ | ay | pay, say, prayer |
| | ai | paid, hair |
| | aigh | straight |

| Sound | Possible Spelling | Examples |
|---|---|---|
| | a - e | make, take, age, hare |
| | ea | break, pear |
| | ao | gaol |
| | au | gauge |
| | ei | vein, their |
| | eig(h) | weigh, freight, reign |
| | ey | they, prey |
| | e - e | where |
| | é(e) | café, fiancée |
| | ae | Gaelic, aeroplane |
| /e/ | e | bed, better, berry |
| | ea | bread, instead, pleasure, pear |
| | ai | said, hair |
| | ay | says |
| | a | many, any |
| | a - e | hare |
| | eo | leopard |
| | ei | leisure, heifer, their |
| | ie | friend |
| | ae | aesthetic |
| | e - e | where |
| /ee/ | ee | sheep, beer |
| | ea | team, appear, please |
| | e - e | scene, mere |
| | e | equal |
| | ie | field, fierce |
| | ei | weird, ceiling |
| | ey | key |
| | eo | people |
| | oe | amoeba, phoenix |
| | i | police, souvenir |
| | ay | quay |
| | ae | Caesar |
| /i/ | i | hit, build, guilt, infinite |
| | y | hymn, tyranny |
| | a | accurate, marriage |
| | ie | sieve |
| | ei(g) | foreign |
| | ai | mountain |
| | o | women |
| | u | busy, business |
| | e | English |
| /iy/ | ie | pie, fiery |
| | i - e | bite, fire, ice |

| Sound | Possible Spelling | Examples |
|---|---|---|
| | (e)igh | *fight, height* |
| | y(e) | *try, dye, tyrant* |
| | uy | *buy, guy* |
| | is | *isle* |
| | ais | *aisle* |
| /o/, /aw/ | o | *pot, rotten, John, order* |
| | ou(gh) | *cough, brought* |
| | a(ch) | *watch, yacht* |
| | au(gh) | *caught* |
| | aw | *draw* |
| /oh/, /aw/ | o | *sport, open* |
| | o - e | *bore, wrote, owe* |
| | oa | *soap, broad, load* |
| | oe | *toe* |
| | oo | *brooch, floor* |
| | ou(gh) | *soul, four, though* |
| | ow | *grow* |
| | ew | *sew* |
| | ol | *folk* |
| | eau | *eau de Cologne, beau* |
| | au | *mauve* |
| | eo | *yeoman* |
| /uu/, /oo/ | oo | *food, pool, troop, good* |
| | u | *pull, sure, truth, rude* |
| | ou(gh) | *group, troupe, through, tour* |
| | oul | *would, could* |
| | o - e | *move* |
| | oe | *shoe* |
| | o | *wolf* |
| | ui | *fruit* |
| | ue | *blue, true* |
| | ew | *few, flew* |
| | (o)eu | *rheumatism, manoeuvre* |
| | eau | *beauty* |
| /ow/ | ow | *now, power* |
| | ou(gh) | *ounce, our, plough, mouse* |
| | au | *sauerkraut* |
| /oy/ | oy, uoy | *boy, buoy* |
| | oi | *poison* |
| /u/ | u | *cut, button* |
| | oo | *blood* |
| | ou | *trouble, young* |
| | o | *son, come, tongue, does* |

| Sound | Possible Spelling | Examples |
|---|---|---|
| /uh(r)/ | ear | *heard* |
| | er(r) | *her, fertile, err* |
| | ere | *were* |
| | eur | *chauffeur* |
| | ir | *bird* |
| | o(u)r | *word, journey* |
| | ur(r) | *church, purr* |
| | yr | *myrtle* |
| | olo | *colonel* |

Remember also the silent *h* at the beginning of words such as *heir, hour* and *honour* — if you cannot find a word that you think begins with a vowel, it might be worth looking under *h*.

## ✧ *1000 Commonly Misspelt Words*

The following list contains words which poor spellers frequently misspell, with the user's attention being drawn to the particular difficulties or pitfalls in each case. Unless page numbers are given, cross-references in SMALL CAPITALS are to entries in chapter 4, *Spelling and Word-formation*.

Common misspellings are also listed, clearly indicated as wrong by the symbol ✗, and cross-referred to the correct spellings. Common slips of the pen (or slips of the brain!) are indicated with a ⚠ symbol.

**abandoned**
Do not double the final *n* of *abandon* when adding *-ed* (or *-ing*): see DOUBLING OF FINAL CONSONANTS.

✗ *abberration* see **aberration**.

**abbreviate, abbreviation**
Do not 'abbreviate' these words by omitting one of the *b*'s.

**aberration**
One *b*, and two *r*'s as in *err*.

**abhorrent**
Note the double *r* and the *e*: see -ANCE, -ENCE.

✗ *abismal* see **abysmal**.

**abominable**
The *i* in the third syllable is sometimes dropped in speech; it must not be omitted in writing.

✗ *abreviate* see **abbreviate**.

**abscess**
Note the *sc* in the middle of this word.

**abysmal, abysmally**
Note the *y* of the second syllable; also the ending *-ally* of the second word.

**academy**
Note the *e* of the third syllable. As a memory aid, think of *academic* or the poetic word *academe*.

**accede**
Note the ending *-cede*: see -CEDE, -CEED, -SEDE.

**accelerate, accelerator**
Note the single *l* and the *e* of the third syllable. Note also that *accelerator* ends in *-or*: see -ER, -OR, -AR.

**accept**
⚠ Do not confuse this with *except*.

## accessory
The *-ory* spelling is now standard; *-ary* is used only in legal phrases such as *an accessary after the fact.*

## accidentally
Do not omit the *al*; the *-ly* adverb ending is added to the adjective *accidental* to form this word.

## accommodate, accommodation
Note the double *c* and double *m.*

**✗** *accross* see **across**.

## accumulate, accumulation, accumulator
Two *c*'s but only one *m* and one *l* in these words. Note also that *accumulator* ends in *-or*: see -ER, -OR, -AR.

## accuracy, accurate
Two *c*'s and one *r* in these words.

**✗** *acertain* see **ascertain**.

## achieve, achievement
Note the *ie* spelling: see -EI-, -IE-. Note also that the *e* is not dropped before the ending *-ment.*

## acknowledge
The 'core' of this word is *know*, but note the *c* before the *k.*
*Acknowledgement* and *acknowledgment* are both correct; the form with the *e* retained before *-ment* is now commoner.

**✗** *acomodate* see **accommodate**.

## acquaint, acquaintance
Do not forget the *c* before the *q.*

**✗** *acquarium* see **aquarium**.

## acquiescence
Note the *c* before the *q* and the *sc* in the middle (see -ESC-, page 305), and the ending *-ence* (see -ANCE, -ENCE).

## acquire
Note the *c* before the *q.*

## acquisitive
Like *acquire*, this word has a *c* before the *q.* Note also the spelling *sit*; as a memory aid, think of the related word *acquisitions.*

## acquit, acquittal
Note the *c* before the *q.* Notice also the double *t* in *acquittal*: see DOUBLING OF FINAL CONSONANTS.

## across
There is only one *c* in this word: to go *across* the street means the same as to *cross* the street.

**✗** *acumulate* see **accumulate**.

**✗** *acurate* see **accurate**.

**✗** *acuracy* see **accuracy**.

## address
Note the two *d*'s.

## adequacy, adequate
Points to note in these words are the single *d*, the following *e* and the endings *-acy* (see -ACY, -ASY) and *-ate.*

## adolescence, adolescent
Note the *sc* in these words (see -ESC-, page 305), and the *en* (see -ANCE, -ENCE).

**✗** *adress* see **address**.

## advertise, advertisement
These words must always be spelt *-ise*, never *-ize*: see -ISE, -IZE.

## advise
Must always be spelt *-ise*, never *-ize*: see -ISE, -IZE.
⚠ Do not confuse the verb *advise* with the noun *advice.*

## aerial
Note the *ae.*

## aeroplane
Note the *ae*; *airplane* is correct in American English, but not in British English.

## aerosol
Note the *ae.*

## affect
⚠ Do not confuse this word with *effect* (see AFFECT, EFFECT, page 125).

## affiliate, affiliation
Note the double *f* and single *l* in these words.

**✗** *agast* see **aghast**.

## aggravate, aggravating
Note the double *g* in these words.

## aggression, aggressive
Note the two *g*'s and two *s*'s.

## aghast
This word is related to *ghastly* and *ghost*, and like them has an *h* after the *g*.

✗ *agravate* see **aggravate**.

✗ *agravating* see **aggravating**.

✗ *agression* see **aggression**.

✗ *agressive* see **aggressive**.

✗ *airial* see **aerial**.

✗ *airoplane* see **aeroplane**.

✗ *airosol* see **aerosol**.

## align, alignment
Take care with these words. They are connected in meaning with *line*, but being derived from French follow the French spelling, *ligne*.

## allege, allegation
Note the double *l*. If in doubt about the *g* of *allege*, think of *allegation*; if in doubt about the *e* of *allegation*, think of *allege*.

## almond
Note the *l*.

## a lot
⚠ Two words, not one.

## amateur
Note the single *m* and the *eur*.

✗ *amond* see **almond**.

## anaesthetic
Note the *ae*.

## analyse, analysis, analyst
Note the *y* in these words. Note also that *analyse* must be spelt with an *s* in British English, never *z*: see -ISE, -IZE.

## angle
⚠ Do not confuse this word with *angel*.

## annihilate, annihilation
Note the double *n*, the *h* and the single *l*.

## anoint
Note the single *n* after the *a*.

## anomalous
Note the single *n*, *m* and *l*.

## anonymous
Note the *y*.

## answer
Take care not to omit the *w*. Knowing that *answer* is related to the word *swear* may serve as a memory aid.

## Antarctic
A common error is to omit the *c* between the *r* and the *t*.

## antibiotic
*Anti-* has the meaning 'against' here, therefore *anti-* is correct: see ANTI- (page 298).

## anticlimax
This means 'the opposite of climax', so *anti-* is correct: see ANTI- (page 298).

✗ *apalling* see **appalling**.

✗ *aparatus* see **apparatus**.

✗ *aparent* see **apparent**.

## apartheid
Note the *h* and the *ei*.

✗ *apearance* see **appearance**.

## apologise, apology
Points to note are the single *p* and the *log*. *Apologise* may also correctly be spelt *apologize*: see -ISE, -IZE.

## appalling
Note the double *p* and the double *l*. For the doubling of the *l* of *appal* before *-ing*, see DOUBLING OF FINAL CONSONANTS.

## apparatus
Note the double *p* and the single *r* and *t*.

## apparent, apparently
Note the double *p* and the *e* (see -ANCE, -ENCE).

## appearance
Double *p* and single *r*, and *-ance* for the final syllable (see -ANCE, -ENCE).

✗ *appologise* see **apologise**.

✗ *appology* see **apology**.

## appreciate, appreciation
Note the double *p*.

✗ *aquaint* see **acquaint**.

## aquarium
Note that there is no *c* in this word.

✗ *aquiescent* see **acquiescent**.

✗ *aquire* see **acquire**.

✗ *aquisitive* see **acquisitive**.

✗ *aquit* see **acquit**.

## arbitrary
The third syllable of this word is sometimes dropped in speech. Note the *ra* after the *t*.

## architect, architecture
Note the *ch* in these words.

## Arctic
As with *Antarctic*, the *c* between the *r* and the *t* is often omitted in speech.

## argument
Note that the *e* of *argue* is dropped before -*ment*.

## arthritis
Note the *r* after *a*, sometimes omitted in speech.

✗ *Artic* see **Arctic**.

✗ *asassin* see **assassin**.

## ascertain
Note the *sc*. Memory aid: you try to *ascertain* something because you want to be *as certain* as possible about it.

## asphyxiate, asphyxiation
Note the *ph* and the *y*.

## aspirin
The *i* of the second syllable is often omitted in speech; take care not to do so in writing.

✗ *asma* see **asthma**.

## assassin, assassinate
Note the double *s*'s and the single *n*.

## assistance, assistant
These words have an *a* in the ending: see -ANCE, -ENCE. Note also the double *s*.

## asthma
Note the *th* in this word.

## atheist
Take care with the *ei*, and make sure you do not write 'athiest'.

✗ *athritis* see **arthritis**.

## attach
No *t* before the *ch*: see -CH, -TCH.

## autumn
Note the final *n*, silent in *autumn*, but

pronounced in *autumnal*. No capital needed for the names of seasons.

## auxiliary
Note the *ia*.

## awful, awfully
Note that there is no *e* in these words.

## bachelor
There is no *t* in this word.

## baggage
Note the two *g*'s in the middle of this word.

## baptise, baptize
Both correct: see -ISE, -IZE.

## basically
Do not omit the *al* from this word.

✗ *batchelor* see **bachelor**.

## battalion
Two *t*'s and one *l*, as in *battle*.

## beautiful
Take care with the spelling *eau*.

## beggar
This is one of the few 'doer' words which end in *ar*: see -ER, -OR, -AR.

## beginner, beginning
Note the double *n*'s: see DOUBLING OF FINAL CONSONANTS.

## beguile
Note the *u*.

## behaviour
Note the *iour* ending: see -OR, -OUR.

## believe
Note the *ie*: see -EI-, -IE-.

## besiege
Note the *ie*: see -EI-, -IE-.

✗ *beutiful* see **beautiful**.

✗ *Bhudda* see **Buddha**.

## bigoted
Note the single *g* and single *t*: see DOUBLING OF FINAL CONSONANTS.

## biscuit
Do not forget the *u*. Memory aid: *cuit* in this word means 'cooked', and comes from the same root as French *cuisine* (= cooking).

**bizarre**
Note the single *z* and double *r*.

✗ *bizness* see **business**.

**blancmange**
The French origins of this word (*blanc* = 'white', *manger* = 'to eat') are reflected in its spelling.

**blasphemous, blasphemy**
Note the *ph*.

**boulder**
A *u* is needed in this word if it means 'a rock or stone'; *bolder* means 'more bold'.

**boundary**
Note the ending -*ary*.

**bouquet**
Note the *ou*, *qu* and *et*.

**bourgeois**
Note the *ou*, *ge* and *ois*.

**boutique**
Note the *ou*, the *i* and the *que*.

**boycott**
Ends in two *t*'s.

**breadth**
Note the *a* in this word.

**brief**
Note the ending *ie*: see -EI-, -IE-.

**brigadier**
Note the ending *ier*.

**Britain, British, Briton**
There is only a single *t* in these words but *Brittany* (in France) has a double *t*. Do not confuse the country *Britain* with *Briton*, an inhabitant of the country, and take care to avoid the incorrect spelling *Britian*.

**broccoli**
Double *c*, single *l*.

**brochure**
Watch the *ch* spelling.

**bronchitis**
Note the *ch*.

**bruise**
Note the *ui* and the *s*.

**brusque**
Note the *que*.

**Buddha, Buddhism, Buddhist**
Note the double *d*, and in particular notice the position of the *h* in these words.

**bulletin**
Double *l*, single *t*.

**buoyancy, buoyant**
Like the *buoy* that floats in the sea, these words have a *u* before the *o*.

**bureau**
Note the *eau*. Plural *bureaux* or *bureaus*: see -X, -S.

**bureaucracy, bureaucratic**
Note the *eau*, as in *bureau*, and the -*acy* ending of *bureaucracy*: see -ACY, -ASY.

**burglar, burglary**
*Burglar* is one of the few 'doer' words which end in -*ar*: see -ER, -OR, -AR.

**business**
Do not forget the *i*, although it is not pronounced. Memory aid: this word is spelt as if it was formed from the adjective *busy*, which historically it is (see -Y); in present-day English, the '-ness' noun formed from *busy* is spelt *busyness*. Note that *bizness* is acceptable only as a deliberate misspelling in very informal writing or certain forms of journalism.

**caffeine**
Note the *ei*: see -EI-, -IE-.

**calendar**
*e* in the second syllable, *a* in the third, not the other way round. Memory aid: a *calendar* (a..e..ar) shows the days of *a year*.

**campaign**
Note the *ai* and the *g*.

**cancelled, cancellation**
Note that the *l* of *cancel* is doubled before -*ed* (and -*ing*), and -*ation*: see DOUBLING OF FINAL CONSONANTS.

**canoe**
Present participle *canoeing*: see -E.

**capsize**
Always spelt with a *z*: see -ISE, -IZE.

✗ *caracter* see **character**.

**carburettor**
Note the single *r* and double *t*; *carburetter*

is also correct, but the form ending in *-or* is the more common.

**career**
One *r* only in the middle of this word.

**caress**
One *r* only in the middle of this word.

**Caribbean**
Note the single *r* and double *b*.

✗ *carreer* see **career**.

✗ *carress* see **caress**.

**carriage**
Two *r*'s.

✗ *Carribean* see **Caribbean**.

**cashier**
Note the ending *ier*.

**casual, casually, casualty**
Note the *ua*.

**catalogue**
One *t*, and note also the ending *gue*.

**catarrh**
One *t*, and note also the ending *rrh* (signifying 'running, flowing': see -RRH-, page 321).

**ceiling**
Note the *ei*: see -EI-, -IE-.

**cemetery**
Do not omit the *e* of the third syllable, usually not pronounced in speech.

**changeable**
Note that the *e* of *change* is not dropped before *-able*: see -ABLE, -IBLE.

**character**
Note the initial *ch*.

**characteristically**
Note the ending *-ally*. Do not omit the *al*: see -LY.

**chasm**
Note the initial *ch*.

**chauffeur**
Note the *ch*, *au*, double *f* and *eur*.

✗ *Chech* see **Czech**.

**chief, chiefly**
Note the *ie*: see -EI-, -IE-.

**chilblain**
Notice that one *l* of *chill* is dropped in this compound noun.

**chimney**
Plural *chimneys*: see -Y.

**chocolate**
Do not forget the second *o* of this word, often not pronounced in speech.

**chronically**
Note the initial *ch*. Note also the *al* before the *-ly* ending: see -LY.

**chrysanthemum**
Note the initial *ch* and the *y*.

✗ *cilinder* see **cylinder**.

**clientele**
Note the *ele*.

**cocoa**
Note the final *oa*.

**coconut**
Not *cocoanut*; *cocoa* and *coconuts* come from quite different plants.

**collaborate, collaborator**
Two *l*'s, one *b*. Memory aid: to *collaborate* is to 'work with someone', the core of the word being the same as in *laborious* and *laboratory*, and the *col-* being a form of the Latin word for 'with'. Note also that *collaborator* ends in *-or*: see -ER, -OR, -AR.

**collapsible**
Note the double *l*, and also the ending *-ible*: see -ABLE, -IBLE.

**college**
Note the ending *ege*. If in doubt, think of the related word *collegiate*.

**colossal**
Single *l*, followed by a double *s*. Memory aid: a firm that makes *colossal losses* may go bankrupt.

**commemorate**
Two *m*'s, then a single *m*. The core of this word is the same as that of *memory* and *memorial*, to which *com-* (a form of the Latin word for 'with') is added.

**commitment**
Do not double the *t* of *commit* when it is followed by a suffix (or 'word-ending')

beginning with a consonant. In *committed* and *committing*, the *t* is doubled: see DOUBLING OF FINAL CONSONANTS.

### committee
Two *m*'s, two *t*'s, and two *e*'s.

This word derives the verb *commit*, and as with *committed* and *committing*, the *t* is doubled before the suffix is added: see DOUBLING OF FINAL CONSONANTS.

### comparative
Note the *a* of the third syllable. Memory aid: if you think something is *comparatively* good, you *rate* it more highly than something else.

### comparison
Note the *i* of the third syllable: there is a difference in spelling between *comparison* and *comparative*.

### compatible
-*ible*, not -*able*: see -ABLE, -IBLE.

### competitive, competitor
If in doubt about the *i* of the third syllable, think of the related word *competition*, in which the *i* is clearly pronounced. Note also that *competitor* is one of the 'doer' words which end in -*or*: see -ER, -OR, -AR.

### complexion
Note the *x*: see -CTION, -XION.

### concede
Note the spelling of *cede*: see -CEDE, -CEED, -SEDE.

### conceit, conceited
*ei*, not *ie*: see -EI-, -IE-.

### conceive
*ei*, not *ie*: see -EI-, -IE-.

### conference
Note the *e* of the second syllable, often slurred in speech. Note also the single *r* (see DOUBLING OF FINAL CONSONANTS) and the ending -*ence* (see -ANCE, -ENCE).

### connection
This is the usual spelling of this word, although *connexion* is also correct: see -CTION, -XION.

### connoisseur
This word is full of potential pitfalls!

Note the double *n*, *oi*, double *s* and *eur*.

### conscience
As an aid to spelling, notice that the core of this word is *science*, although the pronunciation is different.

### conscientious
This word is related to *conscience*, but note that *c* of *conscience* changes to *t* in *conscientious*.

### conscious
Note the *sci* in this word, as in *conscience* and *conscientious*.

### contemporary
The end of this word is often slurred in speech; note the spelling *orary*.

### controversial
Note *contro*, not *contra*: as a memory aid, think of *controversy*.

### convalescence, convalescent
Note the *val*, the *sc* (see -ESC-, page 305) and the *en* (see -ANCE, -ENCE).

### convertible
-*ible*, not -*able*: see -ABLE, -IBLE.

### coolly
The ending -*ly* is added to the adjective *cool*, therefore there is a double *l*.

### ✗ *corespondence* see **correspondence**.

### ✗ *coroborate* see **corroborate**.

### coronary
Some people tend to write this word with three *o*'s; note that the third syllable has an *a* in it. Memory aid: *coronary* and *heart* both have *ar* in them.

### correspondence, correspondent
Note the double *r*, and the *en* (see -ANCE, -ENCE).

### corroborate, corroboration
Note the first double *r*, and the following single *b* and *r*.

### counterfeit
*ei*, not *ie*: see -EI-, -IE-.

### courageous
The *e* of *courage* is retained in order to keep the *g* 'soft' (ie pronounced /ʝ/).

### courteous
Note the *e* in this word, as also in

**courtesy**. Note also the *ou* in both these words.

✗ *criptic* see **cryptic**.

✗ *crisanthemum* see **chrysanthemum**.

**critically**
The suffix *-ly* is added to the adjective *critical*, hence the ending *-ally*.

**crochet, crocheted**
The word *crochet* is taken from French, hence the *ch* spelling of a /sh/ sound, and the unpronounced final *t* which remains single when the *-ed* ending is added: see DOUBLING OF FINAL CONSONANTS.

✗ *cronicly* see **chronically**.

**cruelly**
The suffix *-ly* is added to the adjective *cruel*, hence the double *l*.

**cryptic**
Note the *y*.

**currency**
Note the double *r* and the *en*.

**curriculum**
Only the *r* is doubled; the other consonants are all single letters.

✗ *curtesy* see **courtesy**.

**cylinder**
Note the *cy* and the *er*.

**cygnet**
(= a young swan). Note the *cy*.

**cynical**
Note the *cy*. Note also the *-ally* spelling of *cynically*.

**Czech, Czechoslovakia**
The *-slovakia* part presents few problems, but *Czech* and *Czecho-* are sometimes misspelt: note the *cz*.

**daffodil**
Double *f*, single *d* and *l*.

**dairy**
⚠ Do not confuse this with *diary*.

**deceit, deceitful, deceive**
*e* before *i* in these words, because following the letter *c*: see -EI-, -IE-.

**December**
The first syllable of this word is sometimes misspelt. As a memory aid, remember that <u>*December*</u> was once the *tenth* month of the year, and the root of the word is the same as that in <u>*decade*</u> (= ten years) and <u>*decimate*</u>.

**decide, decision, decisive**
Note the *de* and the *c* of these words.

**defence, defensive**
Note the *c* in the noun, and the *s* in the adjective. *Defense* is correct in American English, but not in British English.

**defendant**
Note the ending *-ant*: see -ANCE, -ENCE.

**definite, definitely**
Note the two *i*'s. As a memory aid, remember *defi<u>ni</u>tion* and *defi<u>ni</u>tive*.

**deign**
Note the *ei* (see -EI-, -IE-) and the *g*.

**deliberate**
Note the *de* and the *be*. If in doubt about the <u>*ate*</u>, remember *deliber<u>a</u>tion*.

**delicatessen**
Note the *t* and the *ss*.

**delirious**
Note the *del* and the *ious*.

**demeanour**
Note the *-our* ending: see -OR, -OUR.

**deodorant**
Notice that the *u* of *odour* drops before the *ant*: see -OR, -OUR.

**dependant, dependent**
*-ant* is the correct ending for the noun, *-ent* for the adjective: see -ANCE, -ENCE. Note also the spelling of the noun **de<u>pende</u>nce**.

**derelict**
Note the spelling *rel*.

**descent, descendant**
Note the *sc*.
Like *dependant*, the noun *descendant* ends in *ant*: see -ANCE, -ENCE.

**describe, description**
Note the *de*.

**desiccated**
One *s* and two *c*'s; not the other way

round as some people think: remember *desiccated coconut*.

## despair
Note the *des*: if in doubt, remember *desperation*.

✗ *desparate* see **desperate**.

## despatch see dispatch.

## desperate
Note the *per*, often slurred in speech. If in doubt about the spelling *ate*, think of *desperation*.

## despise
Note the spelling *des*. *Despise* must always be spelt *-ise*, never *-ize*: see -ISE, -IZE.

✗ *dessicated* see **desiccated**.

## detach, detached
There is no *t* before the *ch* in these words: see -CH, -TCH.

## deterrent
Note the double *r*: see DOUBLING OF FINAL CONSONANTS.

## develop
There is no *e* at the end of this word.
Do not double the *p* of *develop* before adding *-ed* and *-ing* in **developed** and **developing**: see DOUBLING OF FINAL CONSONANTS.
As there is no *e* at the end of *develop*, there is no *e* between the *p* and *m* in **development**.

✗ *devide* see **divide**.

✗ *devision* see **division**.

## diamond
Do not forget the *a* in this word.

## diaphragm
Note the *ph* and the silent *g*.

## diarrhoea
Note the *rrh* (which has its origins in a Greek word meaning 'to run, flow': see -RRH-, page 321), and the *oe*.

## diary
⚠ Do not confuse this with *dairy*.

## difference, different
Do not forget the *e* of the second syllable, often slurred in speech; note also the double *f*.

## dilapidated
One *l*, one *p*, one *d*.

## dilemma
One *l*, two *m*'s.

## dilettante
One *l*, two *t*'s.

## diligence, diligent
Note the spelling *lig*.

✗ *dilirious* see **delirious**.

✗ *dimond* see **diamond**.

## diphtheria
Note the *ph*.

## disappear, disappearance
One *s* and two *p*'s, as formed from *dis-* plus *appear(ance)*.

## disappoint
One *s* and two *p*'s, as formed from *dis-* plus *appoint*.

## disapprove, disapproval
One *s* and two *p*'s, as formed from *dis-* plus *approve*.

## disastrous
One *s* in *dis*, and notice that the *e* of *disaster* is dropped before the ending *-ous*.

✗ *disatisfaction* see **dissatisfaction**.

✗ *disatisfied* see **dissatisfied**.

## disc, disk
Both spellings are correct; *disc* is the more common spelling, except in the field of computer science where *disk* is the normal word.

## discipline, disciplinary
Note the *sc*, and the ending *-ary*.

## discourteous
Note the *ou* and the *eous*.

## discrepancy
Note the *an*.

✗ *discribe* see **describe**.

✗ *discription* see **description**.

✗ *disect* see **dissect**.

✗ *disent* see **dissent**.

**dishevelled**
Note the double *l*.

✗ *disimilar* see **dissimilar**.

✗ *disipline* see **discipline**.

**disk** see **disc**.

✗ *disolve* see **dissolve**.

✗ *dispair* see **despair**.

**dispatch, despatch**
Both correct; *dis-* is the commoner.

✗ *dissapear* see **disappear**.

✗ *dissapoint* see **disappoint**.

✗ *dissaprove* see **disapprove**.

**dissatisfaction**
Double *s*, as formed from *dis-* plus *satisfaction*. Similarly with **dissatisfied**.

**dissect**
Contrary to what the pronunciation might lead you to expect, there is a double *s* in this word.

**dissent**
Note the double *s* in this word.

**dissimilar**
Formed from *dis-* plus *similar*, therefore double *s*.

**dissolve**
Note the double *s*, contrary to what the pronunciation might lead you to expect.

**divide, division**
Note the *div*.

**donkey**
Plural *donkeys*: see -Y.

**don'ts**
Note the position of the apostrophe.

**doubt, doubtful**
Note the silent *b*.

**drunkenness**
Formed from *drunken* plus the suffix -*ness*, therefore a double *n*.

**duly**
Notice that the *e* of *due* is dropped in *duly*: see -E.

**dutiful**
The *y* of *duty* changes to *i* before the suffix

-*ful*: see -Y.

**earnest**
Note the *ear* for the word meaning 'serious'. *Ernest* is a man's name.

**earring**
Formed from *ear* plus *ring*, therefore double *r*.

**eccentric**
Note the double *c*.

**ecstasy**
Note the *cs* and the ending -*asy*: see -ACY, -ASY.

**eczema**
Note the *cz*.

**eerily, eeriness**
Contrary to the general rule (see -E), the *e* of *eerie* drops before the -*ly* and -*ness*.

**effect**
⚠ Do not confuse this with **affect**: see AFFECT, EFFECT, page 125).

**effervescence**
Note the double *f*, the *sc* (see -ESC-, page 305), and the *en* (see -ANCE, -ENCE).

**eighth**
Notice that there is only one *t* in this word, although the pronunciation would lead you to expect two.

**elegance, elegant**
Note the *leg* and the *an*: see -ANCE, -ENCE.

**eligible, eligibility**
Note the *lig*; also the -*ible*/-*ibility*: see -ABLE, -IBLE.

**embarrass, embarrassment**
Note the double *r* and double *s*. Note the difference in spelling between *embarrass* and *harass*. Memory aid: you might go *really red* with *embarrassment*.

**encyclopaedia, encyclopedia**
Both correct, but *ae* still the commoner in British English: see -AE-, -E-.

**endeavour**
Note the *ea*, and the *ou*: see -OR, -OUR.

**enquire** see **inquire**.

**enrol, enrolment**
Note that there is only one *l* in these

words. The *l* of *enrol* is doubled in **enrolled** and **enrolling**: see DOUBLING OF FINAL CONSONANTS.

### enthusiastically
Note the ending *-ally*: see -LY.

### envelope
There is an *e* at the end of the word for the folder into which you put a letter.

### equalise, equalize
Notice that the final *l* of a base word (in this case, *equal*) does not double before *-ise/-ize*: see the section on *l* in DOUBLING OF FINAL CONSONANTS.

✗ *ernest* see **earnest**.

### erroneous
Double *r* as in *err* and *error*. Note also the *-eous*.

### etc
⚠ Take care. A common error is to write *ect*.

### etiquette
One *t* at the beginning, two *t*'s at the end.

### exaggerate, exaggeration
Note the double *g*.

### exasperate, exasperation
Note the *per*.

✗ *exaust* see **exhaust**.

### exceed, exceedingly
Note the *ceed*: see -CEDE, -CEED, -SEDE.

### excellent
Note the *c* after the *x*, the double *l* and the *en* (see -ANCE, -ENCE).

### except
⚠ Do not confuse this with **accept**.

### excerpt
Note the *c* after the *x*, and the *p* before the *t*, sometimes slurred in speech.

### excise
Can never be written with a *z*: see -ISE, -IZE.

### exciting
Take care. A common mistake is to omit the *c*.

✗ *exellent* see **excellent**.

### exercise
Cannot be written with a *z*: see -ISE, -IZE.

✗ *exerpt* see **excerpt**.

### exhaust, exhaustion
Do not forget the *h* in these words.

### exhibit, exhibition
Do not forget the *h* in these words.

### exhilarate, exhilaration
Do not forget the *h* in these words. Note also the spelling *lar*. Memory aid — the base of these words is the same as that in *hilarious* and *hilarity*, where the *h* and the *a* are more clearly pronounced.

### exhort, exhortation
Do not forget the silent *h* in these words.

✗ *exibit* see **exhibit**.

✗ *exibition* see **exhibition**.

✗ *exilarate* see **exhilarate**.

✗ *exiting* see **exciting**.

✗ *exort* see **exhort**.

### expense
Note that this word ends in *se*. *s* also in *expensive*

✗ *exstasy* see **ecstasy**.

### extension
Note the *s* in this word: if in doubt, remember *extensive*.

### extraordinary
Do not forget the *a* of *extra* in this word, usually slurred in speech.

### extravagance, extravagant
Note the *a*'s in *-vagance* and *-vagant*: see -ANCE, -ENCE.

### extravert, extrovert
Both correct; the form with *a* is the commoner of the two.

✗ *extrordinary* see **extraordinary**.

### façade
Notice that this word, borrowed from French, should have a small hook-like mark, called a cedilla, under the *c*.

### facetious
Note the spelling of the ending, *ious*.

**fallible**
-*ible*, not -*able*: see -ABLE, -IBLE.

**family**
Do not omit the *i*, often slurred in speech.

**fascinate, fascination**
Note the *sc*.

**favourite**
Note the *ou*, often slurred in speech.

**feasible**
-*ible*, not -*able*: see -ABLE, -IBLE.

**February**
Take care with the spelling of -*ruary*, usually slurred in speech.

**field**
*i* before *e*: see -EI-, -IE-.

**fiend**
*i* before *e*: see -EI-, -IE-.

**fierce**
*i* before *e*: see -EI-, -IE-.

**fiery**
*i* before *e*: see -EI-, -IE-.

✗ *Filipines* see **Philippines**.

**fledgling**
Note that the *e* of *fledge* is dropped before the suffix -*ling*: see -DGE.

**fluorescent**
Note the *u* and *sc* (see -ESC-, page 305).

**fluoride**
Note the *u*.

**foliage**
Note the single *l*.

**foreboding**
*Fore*-, not *for*-: see FORE-, FOR- (page 306).

**foreign, foreigner**
Note the *ei* (see -EI-, -IE-) and the silent *g*.

**forfeit**
Note the *ei*: see -EI-, -IE-.

**forgiveness**
Only one *n*, exactly as the pronunciation would suggest.

**forgo**
*For*-, not *fore*-, as the meaning 'do without' suggests: see FORE-, FOR- (page 306).

**frantically**
Note the ending -*ally*: see -LY.

**friend**
*i* before *e* (see -EI-, -IE-); if in doubt, remember that *friend* ends in *end*.

**frolic**
Note the *k* in *frolicked* and *frolicking*: see -C.

**fulfil, fulfilment**
Note the single *l*'s in these words.
The final *l* of *fulfil* is doubled before -*ed* and -*ing* in **fulfilled** and **fulfilling**: see DOUBLING OF FINAL CONSONANTS.

**fulsome**
Note the single *l* in this word.

**fundamental**
Note the *a* in the second syllable.

**fuselage**
Note the *e* of the second syllable.

**gaiety, gaily**
Note that the *y* of *gay* becomes *i* in these words.

**galloped, galloping**
The *p* is not doubled when -*ed* and -*ing* are added: see DOUBLING OF FINAL CONSONANTS.

**Gandhi**
Watch the position of the *h*.

**gaol**
⚠ Do not confuse this with *goal*.

✗ *garantee* see **guarantee**.

✗ *gastly* see **ghastly**.

**gâteau**
Note the accent over the *a*, and the *eau*. Plural usually *gâteaux*, but *gâteaus* also correct.

**gauge**
Take care to put the *u* in the correct place.

✗ *getto* see **ghetto**.

✗ *Ghandi* see **Gandhi**.

**ghastly**
Watch the *h*.

**ghetto**
Watch the *h*. Plural *ghettos*: see -OS, -OES.

**ghost, ghostly**
Watch the *h*.

## ghoul, ghoulish
Watch the *h*.

✗ *gilt* (= 'blame') see **guilt**.

✗ *gimkana* see **gymkhana**.

✗ *gimnastics* see **gymnastics**.

## gipsy see **gypsy**.

## giraffe
One *r*, two *f*'s.

## glamorise, glamorous
Note that the *u* of *glamour* is dropped before *-ise* and *-ous*: see -OR, -OUR. *Glamorise* may also be spelt with a *z*: see -ISE, -IZE.

## gluttonous, gluttony
Two *t*'s, one *n*.

## glycerine
Note the *y*, the *c* and the *e*.

## gorgeous
Note the *e*.

## gorilla
One *r*, two *l*'s.

## gossiping, gossipy
The *p* of *gossip* does not double before a suffix: see DOUBLING OF FINAL CONSONANTS.

✗ *gost* see **ghost**.

✗ *goul* see **ghoul**.

## government
The *n* of *govern* is not pronounced when *-ment* is added, but must not be omitted in writing.

## governor
Note that this ends in *or*: see -ER, -OR, -AR.

## graffiti
Two *f*'s, one *t*.

## grammar
A common error is *er* for *ar*. As a memory aid, think of *grammatical*.

## grandeur
Note the spelling *eur*.

## grateful
Note the *ate*. This word is connected with *gratitude*.

## gray, grey
The preferred spelling in British English is *grey*; *gray* is also correct, and is standard in American English.

## grief, grieve, grievance
Note the *ie*: see -EI-, -IE-; also the *-ance*: see -ANCE, -ENCE.

## grievous
*i* before *e*, as in *grief* and *grieve*. Note that there is no *i* after the *v*.

## gruesome
Do not forget the *e* of *grue*

## guarantee
Note the *u* and the single *r*.

## guard, guardian
Note the *u*.

## guerrilla
Note the *u*, the double *r*, and the double *l*. A single *r* is also correct, but is less common.

## guess
Note the *u*.

## guest
Note the *u*.

## guide, guidance
Note the *u* in these words. Note also the ending *-ance* in *guidance*: see -ANCE, -ENCE.

## guilt, guilty
Note the *u*.

## gullible
*-ible*, not *-able*: see -ABLE, -IBLE.

## gymkhana
Note the *y* and the *kh*.

## gypsy, gipsy
Both correct, but the *y* spelling is the commoner.

## haemorrhage
Care should be taken with the *ae*, the single *m* and the *rrh* (the same *rrh* as is found in *catarrh* and *diarrhoea* – see -RRH-, page 321).

## handicapped
Notice that the *p* of *handicap* is doubled before a suffix such as *-ed*: see DOUBLING OF FINAL CONSONANTS.

## handkerchief

Notice that this word begins with *hand*, although the *d* is usually slurred in speech. Notice also that the word ends in *chief.*

## happened, happening

Note the double *p*. The *n* is not doubled before *-ed* and *-ing*: see DOUBLING OF FINAL CONSONANTS.

## harangue

Note the single *r* and the final *ue*.

## harass, harassment

Single *r* and double *s*. Note the difference in spelling between *harass* and *embarrass*. Memory aid: you may be *harassed harshly*.

## hazard, hazardous

Notice the single *z*.

## height

Although related to *high*, this word has an *e* in it: see -EI-, -IE-.

## heinous

Note the *ei*: see -EI-, -IE-.

## heir, heiress

Note the silent *h* and the *ei*: see -EI-, -IE-.

## hemorrhage

In British English, usually *haemorrhage*. *Hemo-* is standard in American English.

## herbaceous

Note the ending *eous*.

## hereditary

Note the *a* of *ary*, often slurred in speech.

## hero

Plural *heroes*: see -OS, -OES.

## hiccup, hiccough

Both correct but the first form is preferred. Notice that the *p* is not doubled before *-ed* and *-ing* in **hiccuped** and **hiccuping**: see DOUBLING OF FINAL CONSONANTS.

## hideous

Note the *e*.

✗ *hieght* see **height**.

✗ *hienous* see **heinous**.

## hierarchy

Note the *ie*: see -EI-, -IE-.

## hieroglyphics

Note the *ie* (see -EI-, -IE-), the *y* and the *ph*.

## hindrance

Notice that the *e* of *hinder* is dropped in this word, as its pronunciation indicates. Note also the *-ance*: see -ANCE, -ENCE.

## honorary

Note the ending *ary*, often slurred in speech.

## honourable

Notice that the *u* of *honour* is not dropped before the suffix *-able*: see -OR, -OUR.

## horrible

Note the double *r*, and the ending *-ible* — if in doubt over choosing between *-ible* or *-able*, think of *horrid* (see -ABLE, -IBLE).

## humorous

Notice that the second *u* of *humour* is dropped before the suffix *-ous*: see -OR, -OUR.

## Hungary

Note the *a* in this word; remember the related word *Hungarian*.

## hygiene, hygienic

*ie*, not *ei* (see -EI-, -IE-); note also the *y*.

## hypochondria, hypochondriac

Note the *y* of *hypo*, and the *ch*.

## hypocrisy, hypocrite

Note the *y* of *hypo*, and particularly the *i* and the *s* of the ending of *hypocrisy*. Memory aid: if in doubt about the *i*, think of *hypocritical*.
For *hypocrite*, note also the *e*.

## hysterically

Note the *y* of the first syllable.
Notice also the *-ally* – the suffix *-ly* is added to the adjective *hysterical*.

## idiosyncrasy

Note the *y*, and particularly the ending *asy* (see -ACY, -ASY). If in doubt about the *a*, think of *idiosyncratic*.

## illegal

This word is formed from *il-* (= 'not') and *legal*, hence the double *l*.

## illegible

⚠ Do not confuse this with *eligible*.

This word is formed from *il-* (= 'not') and *legible*, hence the double *l*. Note also *-ible*, not *-able*: see -ABLE, -IBLE.

### illiterate
This word is formed from *il-* (= 'not') and *literate*, hence the double *l*. Note also the single *t* in *lit*.

### imaginary
Note the *a* of the ending *ary*.

### immediate, immediately
Note the double *m*.

### immense
Note the double *m*.

### immigrant, immigration
This means 'a migrant, or migration, *into* a country', hence the double *m*.
⚠ Do not confuse these with *emigrant* and *emigration*, '*out* of a country'.

### immoral
This word is formed from *im-* (= 'not') and *moral*, hence the double *m*.

### immortal
This word is formed from *im-* (= 'not') and *mortal*, hence the double *m*.

### impasse
Note the final *e*.

### impostor
Note the *-or* ending: see -ER, -OR, -AR.

### improvise
Always *-ise*, never *-ize*: see -ISE, -IZE.

### inaccurate
This word is formed from *in-* (= 'not') and *accurate*, therefore only one *n*; note also the double *c*, and the *ate* ending.

### incidentally
Note the *-ally*: the suffix *-ly* is added to the adjective *incidental* to form this word.

### incredible
*-ible*, not *-able*: see -ABLE, -IBLE.

### indefinitely
Note the *fin* and the *ite*. As a memory aid, think of the word *finite*, where the *i*'s are clearly pronounced.

### independent
Note the *-ent* ending, for the noun and

the adjective. Notice that this is different from the spelling rule for *dependent/dependant* (see -ANCE, -ENCE).

### indestructible
Note the ending *-ible*: see -ABLE, -IBLE.

### indict, indictment
Note the *c*'s in these words.

### indifference, indifferent
Note the syllable *fer*, often slurred in speech.

✗ *inditement* see **indictment**.

### inexhaustible
Note the silent *h*, and also the *-ible* ending: see -ABLE, -IBLE.

### in fact
⚠ Always written as two words.

### infallible
*-ible*, not *-able*: see -ABLE, -IBLE.

### inflammable
Note the double *m*; *-able*, not *-ible*: see -ABLE, -IBLE (if in doubt, remember *inflammation*).

### in front
Always written as two words.

### innocent
Note the double *n*.

### innocuous
Note the double *n*.

### innumerable
This word means 'so great as to be *not* (= *in-*) *numberable*', hence the double *n*.

### inoculate, inoculation
Note that there is only <u>one</u> *n* in these words. Note also the single *c* and *l*.

### inquire, enquire, inquiry, enquiry
Spellings with *in* and *en* are equally correct, although some people prefer to use *enquire/enquiry* when all that is meant is a simple asking, and *inquire/inquiry* when a more detailed investigation is meant.

### inseparable
Note the *par*. Memory aid: if people are *inseparable*, they are rarely *apart*.

### in spite of
⚠ Always written as three words.

**install, instal**
Both correct, but the first form is the commoner: see -L, -LL.
Only one *l* in *instalment*.

**instil**
Ends in a single *l*: see -L, -LL.

**interested, interesting**
Note the *e* of the second syllable, often slurred in speech.

**interrogate, interrogation**
Note the double *r*.

**interrupt, interruption**
Note the double *r*.

**intrigue**
Note the final *gue*.

**introduce, introduction**
Note the *o* of *intro-*.

**irascible**
Note the single *r*, as in *ire* and *irate*, the *sc* (see -ESC-, page 305) and the *-ible* (see -ABLE, -IBLE).

**irregular**
This word is formed from *ir-* (= 'not') and *regular*, hence the double *r*.

**irrelevant**
Formed from *ir-* (= 'not') and *relevant*, hence the double *r*.

**irresistible**
Formed from *ir-* (= 'not') and *resistible*, hence the double *r*. Note also the ending *-ible*: see -ABLE, -IBLE.

**irresponsible**
Formed from *ir-* (= 'not') and *responsible*, hence the double *r*. Note also the ending *-ible*: see -ABLE, -IBLE.

**irritable, irritate, irritation**
Note the double *r*. If in doubt about the spelling of the ending in *irritable*, remember *irritate*: see -ABLE, -IBLE.

**itinerary**
Note the spelling of the end of this word, *erary*, often slurred in speech.

**its, it's**
⚠ Do not confuse these two words: *its* = 'of it', *it's* = 'it is' or 'it has'.

**jeopardise, jeopardy**
Note the *o*. *Jeopardise* may also be spelt

*-ize*: see -ISE, -IZE.

**jersey**
Plural *jerseys*: see -Y.

**jeweller**
Note that the *l* of *jewel* is doubled before the ending *-er*: see DOUBLING OF FINAL CONSONANTS.
Both *jewellery* and *jewelry* are correct, but the first form is much the commoner in British English.

✗ *jimkana* see **gymkhana**.

✗ *jimnastics* see **gymnastics**.

**jockey**
Plural *jockeys*: see -Y.

**jodhpurs**
The *h* is often incorrectly placed — note that it stands <u>between</u> the *d* and the *p*.

**journey**
Plural *journeys*: see -Y.

**judgement, judgment**
Both correct, but the former is now the commoner.

**keenness**
Formed from *keen* plus *-ness*, hence the double *n*.

**kidnapped, kidnapping, kidnapper**
Notice that the *p* of *kidnap* is doubled before a suffix: see DOUBLING OF FINAL CONSONANTS.

**kidney**
Plural *kidneys*: see -Y.

**knowledgeable**
The final *e* of *knowledge* is retained before *-able*: see -DGE.

**laboratory**
Note the spelling of the ending *atory*, often slurred in speech.

**laborious**
Notice that the *u* of *labour* is dropped before the suffix *-ious*: see -OR, -OUR.

**labyrinth**
Note the *y*, often slurred in speech.

**lacquer**
Note the *c*, the *qu* and the *e*.

**laid**
Note the spelling: see -Y.

## language
Note the position of the *u*, often incorrectly placed after the *a*. (The pronunciation of the word gives a clear indication of where the *u* should be).

## languor, languorous
Note the *u* after the *g* in these words. Memory aid: remember that these words are related to *languid*, in which the *u* is clearly pronounced.

## laryngitis
Note the *y*.

## lascivious
Note the *sc*.

## leisure
*e* before *i* in this word: see -EI-, -IE-.

## leopard
Note the *o*.

## liaise, liaison
One or other of the *i*'s is sometimes omitted in error; take particular care with the *iai*.

## library
The middle syllable of this word is sometimes slurred in speech — note the *-rary* ending. Memory aid: remember *librarian*, in which the *r* and the *a* are clearly pronounced.

## licence, license
*-ce* for the noun in British English, *-se* for the verb; in American English, *-se* for both: see -CE, -SE.

## lieutenant
Note the spelling of the first syllable of this word.

## liquefy
Note the *e* in this word, one of the few words which end in *-efy*.

## liqueur
Note the *ueu*.
⚠ Do not confuse this with **liquor**.

## literate, literature
There is only a single *t* after the *i*.

## longitude
⚠ By analogy with *latitude*, some people wrongly insert a *t* after the *long*, in speech

and writing.

## loose
⚠ Do not confuse this word, meaning 'not tight', with the verb *to* **lose**.

## luggage
Like *baggage*, *luggage* has two *g*'s in the middle.

## Madeira
This is spelt *ei*: see -EI-, -IE-.

## magnanimous
Notice the *i* of *-animous*: if in doubt, remember *magnanimity* in which the *i* is clearly pronounced.

## maintenance
Note the *e* of *ten*, and the ending *-ance*.

## manageable
The *e* of *manage* is retained before *-able* in order to keep the 'soft' /ǰ/ sound of the letter *g*: see -ABLE, -IBLE.

## manoeuvre
Note the *oeu*. Usually *maneuver* in American English.

## margarine
Note that in spite of the 'soft' /ǰ/ sound of the letter *g*, the *g* is followed by an *a*.

## marmalade
Note the *a* of the second syllable.

## marriage
Do not forget the *i*: remember that this word is derived from *marry*, the *y* changing to an *i* before the suffix *-age*.

## martyr
Note the *y*.

## marvellous
The *l* of *marvel* is doubled before the suffix *-ous*: see DOUBLING OF FINAL CONSONANTS.

## marzipan
Note the *i*.

## massacre
Note the double *s*.

## mayonnaise
Note the double *n*.

## medicine
Note the *i* of the second syllable. If in

doubt, remember *medicinal*, in which the *i* is clearly pronounced.

## medieval, mediaeval
Both correct, but the form with *e* alone is now commoner in British English than that with *ae*, and is standard in American English.

## Mediterranean
Note the single *d* and *t*, and the double *r*. Memory aid: this word means 'in the middle of the land' — *Medi* is connected with *medium*, *terra* with *terrain* and *terrestrial*.

## meringue
The pronunciation of this word reflects its French origins, and so does its spelling — note the *i* and the final *ue*.

## messenger
Note the *eng*.

## meteorology, meteorologist, meteorological
Notice that the core of these words is *meteor*, although the *e* is often slurred in speech.

## milage, mileage
Both correct.

## millennium
Two *l*'s and two *n*'s. Memory aid: this word is based on root-words meaning 'a thousand' and 'years'; the same roots are found in *millimetre* and *annual*.

## millionaire
Two *l*'s, but only one *n*.

## miniature
Note the *a*.

## miniscule see minuscule.

## ministry
The *e* of *minister* is dropped in this word.

## minuscule
Note the *u* of the second syllable: if in doubt, remember *minute* (= 'tiny'). Spelling the word *mini-* was formerly incorrect, but is now widely accepted.

## miraculous
Note the single *l*.

## miscellaneous
Note the *sc*, the double *l* and the ending *eous*.

## mischief, mischievous
*ie*, not *ei*: see -EI-, -IE-.
⚠ Note that there is no *i* before the *ous* in *mischievous*.

## misshapen
This word is formed from *mis-* (= 'badly') and *shape*, hence the double *s*.

## Mississippi
The *s*'s and *p*'s come in pairs.

## misspell, misspelt
These words are formed from *mis-* (= 'badly') and *spell* and *spelt*, hence the double *s*.

## misspent
This word is formed from *mis-* (= 'badly') and *spent*, hence the double *s*.

## moccasin
Double *c*, single *s*.

## monkey
Plural *monkeys*: see -Y.

## mortgage
Note the *t*.

## murderous
Notice that the *e* of *murder* is retained in this word, although often slurred in speech.

## naïve, naive
It is equally correct to write this word with or without a diaeresis over the *i*.
Related nouns are **naivety** (with or without the diaeresis) and **naïveté** (the French form of the word preferred by some, from which the diaeresis should not be omitted.)

## necessary, necessarily, necessity
One *c*, two *s*'s.

## negligence, negligent
Points to take care over are the *i*, and the *-ence* (see -ANCE, -ENCE).

## negligible
Note the *-ible* ending: see -ABLE, -IBLE.

## ✗ *neice* see niece.

## neighbour
*ei*, not *ie*: see -EI-, -IE-.

## neither
*ei*, not *ie*: see -EI-, -IE-.

## niece
*i* before *e* in this word: see -EI-, -IE-.

## ninth
Note that the *e* of *nine* is dropped in this word.

## noticeable
The *e* of *notice* is retained in order to preserve the 'soft' /s/ sound of the letter *c* before the suffix *-able*: see -ABLE, -IBLE.

## nuisance
Note the *ui* and the *-ance*: see -ANCE, -ENCE.

## nutritious
Note the *ious*.

## obscene, obscenity
Note the *sc*.

## obstreperous
Note the *per*.

## occasion, occasional, occasionally
Two *c*'s, one *s*. Note also the *-ally* ending of the third word.

## occupation, occupy
Two *c*'s, one *p*.

## occur
Two *c*'s, and two *r*'s in the derived forms *occurred*, *occurring* and *occurrence*: see DOUBLING OF FINAL CONSONANTS. Note also the *-ence* ending: see -ANCE, -ENCE.

## of
⚠ Often wrongly substituted for *have*:
✗ *He must of done it.*

## offence, offensive
*c* in the noun, but *s* in the adjective in British English. In American English, *offense*.

## offered, offering
The *r* of *offer* is not doubled before a suffix: see DOUBLING OF FINAL CONSONANTS.

## omit, omission
Only one *m* in these words.
The *t* of *omit* is doubled in *omitted* and *omitting*: see DOUBLING OF FINAL CONSONANTS.

## opponent
Two *p*'s, one *n*.

## opportunity
Two *p*'s.

## opposite, opposition
Two *p*'s, one *s*.

## ordinary
Note the *a*, often slurred in speech.

## outrageous
The *e* of *outrage* is retained in order to preserve the 'soft' /j/ sound of the *g* before the suffix *-ous*.

## overrule
This word is formed from *over* and *rule*, therefore two *r*'s are necessary.

## paid
Note the spelling: see -Y.

✗ *pajamas* see **pyjamas**.

## panicked, panicking, panicky
A word ending in *c* usually adds a *k* before *-ed*, *-ing* or *-y*: see -C.

## paraffin
One *r*, two *f*'s — remember that the discoverer of *paraffin* called it that because it has little chemical *affinity* for other substances.

## parallel, paralleled, paralleling
Note the single *r*, the double *l* and the single *l*. Memory aid: a *pair* of *long lines* which *lie parallel*. The final *l* of *parallel* does not double before *-ed* and *-ing*, contrary to the general rule: see DOUBLING OF FINAL CONSONANTS.

## paralyse, paralysis, paralytic
One *r*, one *l*, and note also the *y*. *Paralyse* must not be written with a *z*: see -ISE, -IZE.

## paraphernalia
Note the *ph*, and do not omit the *r* of *pher*.

## parliament, parliamentary
Remember the *i* in these words.

✗ *parrafin* see **paraffin**.

✗ *parralel* see **parallel**.

## passed
⚠ Do not confuse this with *past*.

**passenger**
Note the spelling *eng*.

**past**
⚠ Do not confuse this with *passed*.

**peaceable**
The *e* of *peace* is retained to preserve the 'soft' /s/ sound of the *c* before the suffix -*able*: see -ABLE, -IBLE.

**pendant**
This noun ends in *ant*, just like *dependant*: see -ANCE, -ENCE.

**perennial**
One *r*, two *n*'s, just as in the Latin phrase *per annum*.

**perilous**
One *l* only in this word: see DOUBLING OF FINAL CONSONANTS.

**permissible**
Note the double *s*, and the ending -*ible* (see -ABLE, -IBLE).

**permitted, permitting**
The *t* of *permit* is doubled before a suffix such as -*ed* and -*ing*: see DOUBLING OF FINAL CONSONANTS.

**persistence, persistent**
Note the endings -*ence* and -*ent*: see -ANCE, -ENCE.

**personnel**
There are two *n*'s in the word meaning 'staff, employees'.
⚠ Do not confuse this word with *personal*.

**Pharaoh**
Note the *aoh* at the end of this word.

**Philippines**
One *l* and two *p*'s.

**phobia**
Note the initial *ph*.

**physically**
Note the *ph* and the *y*, especially the -*ally*.

**physique**
The pronunciation of the *i* and the final *que* reflect this word's French origins.

**picnicked, picnicker, picnicking**
*k* is generally added to a word ending in *c* before a suffix beginning with *e*, *i* or *y*: see -C.

**picturesque**
Note the *que*.

**piece**
*i* before *e* in this word: see -EI-, -IE-.

**pigmy** see **pygmy**.

**pillar**
Note the final *ar*.

✗ *piramid* see **pyramid**.

**plateau**
Plural *plateaux* or *plateaus*: see -X, -S.

**plausible**
-*ible*, not -*able*: see -ABLE, -IBLE.

**playwright**
*Wright* here means 'a maker', as in *shipwright*. Do not be misled by the notion of 'writing'.

**pneumonia**
Do not forget the initial silent *p*.

**Portuguese**
Remember the *u* after the *g*.

**possess, possession, possessive**
Two *s*'s twice over in these words.

**possible, possibility**
Note the double *s*, and the *i* before the *b*: see -ABLE, -IBLE.

**posthumous**
Note the silent *h*.

**practice, practise**
In British English, the noun is written with a *c*, the verb with an *s*.

**precede**
Note the ending -*cede*: see -CEDE, -CEED, -SEDE.

**predecessor**
One *c*, two *s*'s, and -*or* at the end (see -ER, -OR, -AR).

**preferable**
One *r*, and -*able*: see -ABLE, -IBLE.

**preference**
One *r* and -*ence* (see -ANCE, -ENCE); if in doubt, remember *preferential*.

**preferred, preferring**
The final *r* of *prefer* is doubled before -*ed* and -*ing*: see DOUBLING OF FINAL

CONSONANTS.

✗ *preist* see **priest**.

## preparation
Note the *par*: remember the related verb *prepare* and adjective *preparatory*.

## priest
*i* before *e* in this word: see -EI-, -IE-.

## principle
⚠ Do not confuse this word (meaning 'rule', 'theory') with *principal* (meaning 'main').

## prisoner
Do not forget the *o* of the second syllable.

## privilege
Notice that this word does <u>not</u> end in -*dge*; note also the *i* of the second syllable.

## probably
Take care over the second syllable *bab*, often slurred in speech.

## procedure
Note the single *e* of the second syllable. This is different from the spelling of *proceed*.

## proceed
Note the spelling of -*ceed*: see -CEDE, -CEED, -SEDE.

## profession, professional
One *f*, two *s*'s.

## professor
One *f*, two *s*'s, and *or* at the end.

## proffer
This word is the only common /prof/ word with a double *f*. It comes from the same Latin word as *offer*.

## profitable, profited, profiting
There is only one *f* in *profit*; the final *t* does not double before a suffix: see DOUBLING OF FINAL CONSONANTS.

## program, programme
*Programme* is the normal spelling in British English, *program* in American English. However, *program* is the spelling generally adopted in computer science. Note that whichever base form is used, the participles are *programming* and *programmed* in British English, while American English allows both *mm* and *m* forms (*programmed/programed*): see DOUBLING OF FINAL CONSONANTS.

## pronunciation
Watch this word. It is related to the verb *pronounce*, but the spelling of *pronunciation* follows its pronunciation.

## propeller
The *l* of *propel* is doubled before a suffix beginning with a vowel and the suffix in this case is *er*: see DOUBLING OF FINAL CONSONANTS and -ER, -OR, -AR.

## prophecy, prophesy
-*cy* for the noun, -*sy* for the verb.

## protein
*ei*, not *ie* — an exception to the general '*i* before *e*' rule: see -EI-, -IE-.

## psychiatry, psychiatrist, psychiatric
These words have as their core *psych-* (= 'mind': see PSYCHO-, page 321), as do *psychic*, *psychology*, *psychologist* and *psychological*. Note the *ps*, the *y* and the *ch* of all these words.

## publicly
This word is an exception to the general rule for forming adverbs from adjectives ending in -*ic* (see -LY); note that -*ly* is added directly to *public*.

## pursue, pursuit
Note the spelling *pur*.

## pygmy, pigmy
Both correct, but *pyg* is preferred.

## pyjamas
Note the *y*: *pajamas* is correct only in American English.

## pyramid
Note the *y*.

## quarrel
Two *r*'s and only one *l*. Note the doubled *l* in *quarrelled* and *quarrelling*: see DOUBLING OF FINAL CONSONANTS.

## querulous
Only one *r* and one *l*.

## questionnaire
All derivatives of *question* have a single *n* (eg *questioned*, *questionable*) except

*questionnaire*, which has two.

### quite
⚠ Do not confuse this word with *quiet*.

### really
This word is formed from *real* plus *-ly*, therefore two *l*'s are needed.

### rebelled, rebelling, rebellion, rebellious
The *l* of *rebel* is doubled before a suffix: see DOUBLING OF FINAL CONSONANTS.

### recede
Note the spelling of *-cede*: see -CEDE, -CEED, -SEDE.

### receipt
*e* before *i* after the *c* (see -EI-, -IE-), and do not forget the silent *p*.

### receive
*ei* after the *c*: see -EI-, -IE-.

### recognise
Do not omit the *g*, often slurred in speech. This word may also be spelt *-ize*: see -ISE, -IZE.

### recommend, recommendation
One *c*, two *m*'s.

### reconnaissance
Two *n*'s, two *s*'s, and *-ance*: see -ANCE, -ENCE.

### reconnoitre
Two *n*'s, as in *reconnaissance*.

### recurrence, recurrent
The final *r* of *recur* is doubled before a suffix beginning with a vowel: see DOUBLING OF FINAL CONSONANTS. Note also the *-ence*: see -ANCE, -ENCE.

### redundant, redundancy
Note the *an*: see -ANCE, -ENCE.

### referral, referred, referring
The final *r* of *refer* is doubled before *-al*, *-ed* and *-ing* in these words, but not in *referee* and *reference*: see DOUBLING OF FINAL CONSONANTS.

### reflection, reflexion
Both correct, but the *ct* form is commoner.

### refrigerator
Notice that although there is a *d* in *fridge*,

there is <u>no</u> *d* in *refrigerator*. Note also the *or*.

### regretted, regretting, regrettable
The *t* of *regret* is doubled before a suffix beginning with a vowel: see DOUBLING OF FINAL CONSONANTS.

### reign
Note the silent *g* in a king or queen's *reign*.

### relevance, relevant
Note the *lev* and the *an*: see -ANCE, -ENCE.

### relief, relieve
*i* before *e*: see -EI-, -IE-.

### reminiscent
Note the *min* and the *sc* (see -ESC-, page 305).

### remittance
Note the double *t* (see DOUBLING OF FINAL CONSONANTS) and the *-ance* (see -ANCE, -ENCE).

### repetition, repetitive
Pitfalls here are the *pet* and *it*. Notice that these two words act as spelling aids to each other: the *it* is clearly pronounced in *repetition*, and the *pet* in *repetitive*.

### reprieve
*i* before *e* in this word: see -EI-, -IE-.

### require
Note the spelling *req*.

### resemble, resemblance
Note the single *s*, and the *-ance* (see -ANCE, -ENCE).

### reservoir
This word is related to *reserve*, which serves as a reminder that there is an *r* before the *v*.

### resign, resigned
Note the silent *g*, which is pronounced in *resignation*.

### resistance, resistant
Note the *an*: see -ANCE, -ENCE.

### responsible, responsibility
Note the *i* before the *b*: see -ABLE, -IBLE.

### restaurant
The second syllable is often slurred in speech, but the *au* must not be omitted in writing.

✗ *retorical* see **rhetorical**.

**retrieve**
*i* before *e* in this word: see -EI-, -IE-.

**reversible**
*-ible*, not *-able*: see -ABLE, -IBLE.

**rhetorical**
Note the *h*.

**rheumatism**
Note the *h* and the *e*.

**rhinoceros**
Note the *h* and the *c*.

**rhubarb**
Note the *h*.

**rhyme, rhythm**
Note the *h* after the *r*, and also the *y*. In the sense of 'poetry', *rime* is archaic.

**ridiculous**
Note the *i* of the first syllable; if in doubt, remember *ridicule* where it is clearly pronounced.

**righteous**
Note the *-eous*.

**rigorous**
The *u* if *rigour* is dropped before the suffix *-ous*: see -OR, -OUR.

**✗ *rime* see rhyme.**

**sabotage**
Note the *bot*.

**saccharine**
Note the double *c* and the *h*. The final *e* is optional when *saccharine* is used as a noun, obligatory in the adjective.

**sacrilege, sacrilegious**
Note the *i* and especially the *eg*. As a memory aid, consider that *sacrilegious* is the opposite of *religious*, and the vowels *e* and *i* are the opposite way round too.

**sapphire**
Note the double *p*.

**✗ *sargeant* see sergeant.**

**satellite**
One *t*, two *l*'s.

**satisfactory**
Note the *-ory* ending: see -ARY, -ERY, -ORY.

**scandalise, scandalous**
The *l* of *scandal* is not doubled before the suffixes *-ise* or *-ous*: see DOUBLING OF FINAL CONSONANTS. *Scandalise* may also correctly be written *-ize*: see -ISE, -IZE.

**scenery**
Note the *sc* (as also in *scene*), and the ending *-ery*: see -ARY, -ERY, -ORY.

**sceptic, sceptical**
Note the *sc*. ⚠ Do not confuse *sceptic* with *septic*. *Skeptic(al)* is correct only in American English.

**sceptre**
Note the *sc* and the *re*.

**schedule**
Note the *sch*.

**scheme**
Note the *sch*.

**science, scientific**
Note the *sc*.

**scissors**
Note the *sc* and double *s*, and also the *or*.

**scrupulous**
One *p* and one *l*.

**scurrilous**
Two *r*'s, one *l*.

**scythe**
Note the *sc*.

**secondary**
Note the *ary* ending, often slurred in speech.

**secretary**
Note the *ary* ending. If in doubt, remember the related adjective *secretarial*, where the *a* is clearly pronounced.

**✗ *seige* see siege.**

**seize, seizure**
These are exceptions to the general 'i before e' rule (see -EI-, -IE-), so need particular care.

**✗ *semitery* see cemetery.**

**sensible**
*-ible*, not *-able*: see -ABLE, -IBLE.

**sentence**
Note the *ence*.

**separable, separate, separation**
Note the *par*: if in doubt, remember that

people that are *separated* are *apart*.

## sergeant
Everything between the *s* and the *t* is a potential source of error: note the *er*, *ge*, and *ant*.

## series
Note the *ie*.

## several
Note the *ver*, often slurred in speech.

## shepherd
A *shepherd* is, of course, a 'sheep-herd': do not forget the *h*.

## sheriff
One *r*, two *f*'s.

## shield
Note the *ie*: see -EI-, -IE-.

## siege
*i* before *e* in this word, as expected from the general rule: see -EI-, -IE-.

## sieve
*i* before *e*: see -EI-, -IE-.

**✗** *sieze* see **seize**.

## silhouette
Note the *h* and the double *t*.

**✗** *silinder* see **cylinder**.

**✗** *simbol* see **symbol**.

## similar, similarity, similarly
One *m*, one *l*.

**✗** *simpathy* see **sympathy**.

## simultaneous
Note the *eous*.

## sincerely
Note the *cere*.

**✗** *sinical* see **cynical**.

**✗** *sinthetic* see **synthetic**.

**✗** *sirup* see **syrup**.

**✗** *sithe* see **scythe**.

## skeptic
This spelling is correct only in American English. In British English, *sceptic*.

## skilful, skilfully
One *l* of *skill* is dropped in *skilful*: see

-L, -LL.

## slanderous
The *e* of *slander* is retained in *slanderous* as the pronunciation indicates.

## soldier
Note the *ie*.

## solemn
Do not forget the final *n*: remember the pronunciation of *solemnize* and *solemnity*.

## solicitor
Note the single *l*, and the -*or* ending (see -ER, -OR, -AR).

## somersault
Note the spelling: this word is not related to *summer*. (**Summersault** is, however, accepted by some people as correct.)

## sovereign, sovereignty
*ei*, not *ie* (see -EI-, -IE-), and note also the *ver* and silent *g*.

## spaghetti
Note the *gh* and the double *t*.

## species
Note the *ie*.

## specifically
An adjective ending in -*ic* adds -*ally* to form an adverb: see -LY.

## spectacles
Note the *ac*.

## speech
Take care. The vowel in this word is not spelt the same way as that of *speak*.

## spelt
Notice that one *l* of *spell* is dropped before the -*t* suffix.

## spilt
One *l* of *spill* is dropped before the -*t* suffix.

## spontaneous
Note the *eous*.

## spring
Seasons are not normally written with an initial capital letter, but *spring* may be written *Spring* for the sake of clarity.

**✗** *sringe* see **syringe**.

## steadfast
Note the *ea*; *stedfast* is an obsolete spelling, but retained, for example, in the motto

of the Boys' Brigade.

**stealth, stealthy**
Note the *ea*.

**stomach**
Note the *o* and the *ch*.

**stupefy**
Note the *e*.

**subtle, subtlety, subtly**
Note the silent *b* in these words, and also the form of the adverb (see -LY).

**succeed**
Double *c*, as the pronunciation indicates, and note also the *-ceed* ending (see -CEDE, -CEED, -SEDE).

**success, succession, successive, successor**
Double *c* and double *s*. Notice also the *-or* ending of *successor* (see -ER, -OR, -AR).

**succinct**
Double *c*, as the pronunciation indicates.

**succulent**
Note the double *c* and the *en*.

**succumb**
Note the double *c* and the final *b*.

**suddenness**
This word is formed from *sudden* plus *-ness*, therefore two *n*'s are needed.

**suffered, suffering, sufferance**
Do not double the *r*: see DOUBLING OF FINAL CONSONANTS. Note also the *fer* and the *-ance* ending in *sufferance*: see -ANCE, -ENCE.

**suggest, suggestion**
Note the double *g*.

**summersault** see **somersault**.

**supercilious**
Note the *c*.

**superintendent**
Take particular care to write *e* in the last syllable.

**supersede**
Note the *ede* ending — this is the only word in English that ends in *-sede*.

**supervise, supervisor**
These words may not be written with a *z*

(see -ISE, -IZE). Note also the *-or* ending of *supervisor*: see -ER, -OR, -AR.

**suppose, supposing**
Not the double *p*.

**surprise, surprised, surprising**
There are <u>two</u> *r*'s in these words. Note that they can never be written with a *z*: see -ISE, -IZE.

**susceptible**
Note the *sc* and the ending *-ible*: see -ABLE, -IBLE.

✗ *sylinder* see **cylinder**.

**symbol**
Note the *y*.

**sympathy, sympathetic**
Note the *y*.

**synthesis, synthesise, synthetic**
Note the *y*. *Synthesise* may also be written with a *z*: see -ISE, -IZE.

**syringe**
Note the *y* and the *i*, sometimes reversed in error.

**syrup**
Note the *y*.

**system**
Note the *y*.
Note the *-ally* ending of ***systematically***. Adjectives ending in *-ic* add *-ally* to form adverbs: see -LY.

✗ *sythe* see **scythe**.

**tariff**
One *r*, two *f*'s, like *sheriff*.

**technically**
Note the *-ally*: the *-ly* adverb ending is added to the adjective *technical*.

**technique**
Note the final *que*.

**televise**
This may not be written with a *z*: see -ISE, -IZE.

**temperamental**
Note the *per*, slurred in speech.

**temperature**
Note the *per*.

## tendency
Note the *-ency*: see -ANCE, -ENCE.

## terrible, terrify, terror
Note the double *r*'s, and the correct spellings of the endings (see -ER, -OR, -AR and -ABLE, -IBLE).

## territory
Note the double *r* and the *-ory* ending, as indicated by the related word *territorial*.

## thief
*i* before *e*, as would be expected from the general '*i* before *e*' rule: see -EI-, -IE-.

## thorough
⚠ Watch the spelling of this word, and do not confuse it with *through*.

## threshold
Although many people pronounce this word /thresh-hohld/, notice that there is in fact only one *h* in the middle, not two.

## tobacco, tobacconist
One *b*, two *c*'s — if in doubt, remember the slang form *baccy*.

## tragically
An adjective ending in *ic* adds *-ally* to form an adverb: see -LY.

## tranquilliser, tranquillity
Note that the *l* of *tranquil* is doubled before *-ise* and *-ity*: see DOUBLING OF FINAL CONSONANTS. *Tranquillizer* is also correct: see -ISE, -IZE.

## transferred, transferring, transferable
The final *r* of *transfer* is doubled before the suffixes *-ed* and *-ing* because the stress is on the syllable *fer*, but note the spelling of *transferable*: see DOUBLING OF FINAL CONSONANTS.

## transmitted, transmitting, transmitter
The final *t* of *transmit* is doubled before a suffix beginning with a vowel: see DOUBLING OF FINAL CONSONANTS.

## transparent
Note the *-ent* ending.

## travelled, travelling, traveller
Note that the *l* of *travel* is doubled before a suffix beginning with a vowel: see DOUBLING OF FINAL CONSONANTS.

## treacherous, treachery
Note the *ea*.

## truly
Unpredictably the *e* of *true* is dropped before *-ly*: see -E.

## Tuesday
Note the *ue* spelling.

## turquoise
Note the *qu*.

## twelfth
Do not omit the *f*, often slurred in speech.

## tyranny
Note the *y* (easier to remember in **tyrant**) and the double *n*.

## tyre
A car's *tyre* is always spelt with a *y* in British English; *tire* is correct in American English.

## unconscious
Note the *sci*.

## underprivileged
Watch the spelling of *-vileged*.

## underrate
This word is formed from *under* plus *rate*, hence the double *r*.

## unduly
The *e* of *due* is dropped before *-ly*, in *duly* and *unduly*: see -E.

## unforgettable
The *t* of *forget* is doubled before a suffix beginning with a vowel: see DOUBLING OF FINAL CONSONANTS.

## unnatural
This word is formed from *un*- plus *natural*, so two *n*'s are needed.

## unnecessary
This word is formed from *un*- plus *necessary*, so two *n*'s are needed.

## usually
This word is formed from *usual* plus *-ly*, hence the double *l*. Note also the *ua*.

## vaccinate, vaccination
Two *c*'s, one *n*.

## vacuum
One *c*, two *u*'s.

**valley**
Plural *valleys*: see -Y.

**valuable**
Note the *-able* ending: see -IBLE, -IBLE.

**vanilla**
One *n*, two *l*'s.

**vegetable**
Remember the *e* of the second syllable: if in doubt, remember *vegetation*.

**vehicle**
Remember the *h*, pronounced in the related adjective *vehicular*.

**vigorous**
The *u* of *vigour* drops before the suffix *-ous*: see -OR, -OUR.

**villain**
⚠ Take care not to write *villian*.

**visitor**
Note the *-or* ending: see -ER, -OR, -AR.

**voluntary**
The *a* is often slurred in speech. Remember it in writing.

**Wednesday**
Note the *dn*.

**weigh, weight**
*ei*, not *ie*: see -EI-, -IE-. If in doubt, remember the spelling of *eight*.

**weird**
*ei* in this word, contrary to what would be expected from the general '*i* before *e*' rule: see -EI-, -IE-.

**where**
⚠ Often accidentally written as, or instead of, *were* and *we're*.

**whisky, whiskey**
Both forms are correct, depending on the origin of the drink: Scotch *whisky* but Irish or American *whiskey*; plurals respectively *whiskies* and *whiskeys*: see -Y.

**wholly**
Note that the *e* of *whole* is dropped before *-ly* is added: see -E.

**withhold**
Note the double *h* in this word.

**wondrous**
Note that there is no *e* in this word.

**woollen, woolly**
Note the double *l*'s: see DOUBLING OF FINAL CONSONANTS.

**yield**
*i* before *e*: see -EI-, -IE-.

**yoghurt, yogurt**
Both correct, and equally common. The spelling *yoghourt* is also correct, but is rarely used now.

**your**
⚠ Do not confuse this word (= 'of you') with *you're* (= 'you are').

# 7

# The Marks of Good Punctuation

In the history of writing, punctuation is a relatively recent invention. Writing developed from drawing during the second half of the 4th century BC, but even the simplest forms of punctuation did not come into use until much later. The system of symbols we use today developed only very gradually, and was not fully established until the 16th century.

But why did punctuation develop? What is it for?

> **Punctuation makes writing or printing easier to read**
>
> (a) **by showing which words belong together in a sentence, and**
>
> (b) **by indicating features of spoken language that cannot be conveyed by the letters of the alphabet.**

Speech consists of much more than just the sounds represented in writing by vowels and consonants. There are rhythms and pauses and variations in pitch and loudness, all of which help to gather words together into groups and to convey certain aspects of meaning. None of these are represented by the letters of the alphabet. Punctuation marks in a written or printed text provide some of the information conveyed by intonation, rhythm, etc in speech, thus distinguishing, for example, a statement (*He's not coming.*) from a question (*He's not coming?*) or an exclamation (*He's not coming!*), or again a single sentence (*I'm afraid I don't like dogs.*) from two sentences (*I'm afraid. I don't like dogs.*). Thus punctuation marks help to make clearer the meaning of what is written or printed.

---

### The effect of omitting punctuation

When the playwright and politician Richard Sheridan was asked to apologize for calling a fellow MP a liar, he gave the following reply:

*Mr Speaker, I said the honourable member was a liar it is true and I am sorry for it. The honourable member may place the punctuation where he pleases.*

---

**apostrophe** see page 219.

## brackets

There are two main types of brackets: ***round brackets*** or ***parentheses*** (see below) and ***square brackets*** (see page 363). Round brackets are the ones most commonly used; square brackets have a more limited and specialized use.

### ✦ Round brackets

> **Round brackets are used to separate off comments and asides from the rest of the sentence.**

Examples:

> *Applications for the vacant post (six copies) should be lodged with the Vice-Chancellor by 1 October.*
> *The result of the election (a 40% swing to the Labour Party) was a crucial factor in his decision to resign.*
> *The novels of Neil Gunn (1891–1973) have enjoyed a recent revival of critical interest.*

Round brackets indicate a greater separation between the comment and its surroundings than do a pair of commas, and dashes a yet greater separation than that created by round brackets. Dashes are also slightly more informal than brackets.

---

 Remember that brackets come in pairs. ***An inserted comment must be both preceded and followed by a bracket.***

An opening bracket should never stand on its own at the end of a line, nor a closing bracket at the beginning of a line. There must always be at least one word following an opening bracket before the text goes over to the next line, and similarly at least one word preceding a closing bracket at the start of a new line.

***Punctuation that belongs to material enclosed within brackets should itself be included within the brackets, whereas punctuation that belongs to the sentence as a whole should be outside the brackets:***

✔   *This has been the cause of a great deal of pain (both mental and physical ).*
✘   *This has been the cause of a great deal of pain (both mental and physical.)*
✔   *(This has been the cause of a great deal of pain, both mental and physical.)*

---

> **In general, do not use brackets to insert one sentence within another.**

Example:

✗    *The new fire-drill regulations (six copies of the regulations are enclosed for members of the Board) have been issued to all departmental heads.*

A long-sentence comment should follow the sentence it is commenting on rather than being inserted into it:

✓    *The new fire-drill regulations have been issued to all departmental heads. (Six copies of the regulations are enclosed for members of the Board.)*

or alternatively, the comment should be reworded to integrate it more fully into the surrounding sentence:

✓    *The new fire-drill regulations (six copies of which are enclosed for members of the Board) have been issued to all departmental heads.*

● **Inserted short sentence exclamations and remarks that serve to designate, define or comment on something immediately preceding <u>are</u> allowable, however:**

> *Joe Black (he's the one who punched the Managing Director at the last office party) was already propping up the bar.*

---

   Notice that a sentence incorporated as a comment into another sentence begins with a <u>small</u> letter rather than a capital, and does not require a full stop at the end, as in the example above. But a parenthetical sentence may end with a question mark or exclamation mark:

> *Jean Jones (have you ever seen her in action?) is the new club champion.*

---

**Round brackets are used as an economical way of indicating alternatives or options.**

Example:

> *Any candidate(s) for the offices of Chairman and Secretary must be formally proposed and seconded by two paid-up members of the Association.*

**When points in a sentence are highlighted by marking them off by numbers or letters, the numbers or letters are often enclosed in round brackets.**

Example:

> *This project needs to be (1) carefully researched and (2) adequately funded.*

## ✦ Square brackets

Square brackets are used to enclose letters, words or phrases which are not in the original text but which have been inserted as comments, corrections, explanations, etc, for example by an editor. Such insertions are frequently necessary when quoted text contains one or more pronouns, the reference of which might not be clear to a reader:

> *He [St Stephen] was the earliest Christian martyr.*

An alternative style is simply to replace the pronoun with the clarifying comment:

> *[St Stephen] was the earliest Christian martyr.*

## colon

> **A colon is used to introduce a part of a sentence that explains or expands on a preceding part of the sentence.**

Examples:

> *I have something important to tell you: John is coming back tomorrow.*
> *This is an excellent play: the characters are believable, the action is gripping and the ending is totally unexpected.*
> *There is one thing I would really like: namely, a much larger house.*

---

 Where there is an introductory word such as *namely*, a comma is acceptable in place of a colon:

> *There is one thing I would really like, namely a much larger house.*

---

What follows the colon may be a *list* of items:

> *We'll need the following things: string, paper, glue, scissors and a pencil.*

If the list begins on a new line, and each of the items on the list is entered on a separate line, the colon preceding the list is sometimes followed by a **dash**:

> *To make the model aeroplane, you will need the following things:—*
> *a sheet of thin cardboard*
> *string*
> *four sheets of A4 paper*
> *glue*
> *scissors*
> *a ruler*
> *a pencil.*

Although not incorrect, the dash here is unnecessary, and is generally best omitted.

A colon should <u>not</u> normally be inserted immediately after the verb *to be*:

**✗**    *The one thing we need is: patience.*
**✓**    *The one thing we need is patience.*
**✓**    *There is one thing we need: patience.*

The only exception to this rule is when the words which complete the sentence are set off in list form on separate lines, in which case a colon is permissible:

**✓**    *The matters that need to be decided on urgently are:*
   (*a*)    *publication date*
   (*b*)    *price*
   (*c*)    *jacket.*

---

**When two parts of a sentence are balanced one against the other, with the second part not so much expanding on or completing what has been said in the first part but rather contrasting with it, they may be separated by a colon.**

Examples:

> *Knowledge is one thing: the opportunity to use it is quite another.*
> *To err is human: to forgive, divine.*

However, ***the semicolon is generally preferred in this position*** nowadays:

> *You may be sorry; I am delighted.*

Note that ***if there is a conjunction linking the two parts of the sentence, a comma should usually be used rather than a colon or semicolon***:

> *You may be sorry, but I am delighted.*

---

**A colon is often used to introduce direct speech or quoted material.**

- ***Direct speech*** may be preceded either by a colon or by a comma:

> *John suddenly shouted: 'Look out! He's coming back!'*

or, equally correctly,

> *John suddenly shouted, 'Look out! He's coming back!'*

A comma is used especially in recording informal conversation, a colon in more solemn or formal contexts. A colon is frequently used in introducing speech in plays, etc:

> *John: Look out! He's coming back!*
> *Peter: Where can we hide?*

364

- With **quoted material**, the punctuation to use depends on the length of the quotation. A short quotation (anything which consists of no more than one sentence and is no more than, say, four lines long) should be incorporated directly into the surrounding sentence, within quotation marks and without preceding punctuation:

> *Shakespeare once said that 'all the world's a stage'.*

A longer quotation, however, should generally be separated off from the rest of the text by being preceded by a colon and a one-line space and followed by a one-line space, and by being indented slightly from the left-hand margin :

> *This point is clearly illustrated by Daniel's assertion that:*
>
> > *all the facts with which a grammar deals are to be found in the language to which the grammar belongs; and it is in the language itself, not in books, that these facts are to be primarily sought. Grammarians do not impose rules on a language; they merely collect from the language rules already in existence, and set them forth in an orderly way.*
>
> *If only this had been the case, much pain (both mental and physical) would have been avoided in the past. ...*

Note that **quotation marks are <u>not</u> needed in this case**.

---

**Colons are used between numbers to indicate ratios.**

Example: *18 : 12 = 3 : 2.*

---

**Colons are used after headings in certain types of business correspondence, such as memoranda.**

Example:

> *To: ...*
> *From: ...*
> *Date: ...*
> *Re: ...*

---

 In American practice, a colon is used between the hours and the minutes in writing the time (eg *3 : 45*) where in British usage a point would be used (*3.45*).

Again in American practice, a colon is used after the initial salutation in a business letter:

> *Dear Mr Jones:*
> *Thank you for ...*

---

**A colon is often used to separate a book title and its subtitle.**

Example:

*Classics and Commercials: A Literary Chronicle of the Forties*

## comma

This entry is divided into sections covering the use of the comma in ***general writing*** (see immediately below), the use of the comma in addresses, dates, etc in ***letter-writing*** (see page 374), and the use of commas in ***numbers*** (see page 375).

### ✦ The comma in general writing

**A comma is used to indicate a pause or slight break in a sentence.**

Examples:

*I'd give anything not to go, but I'm afraid I must.*
*Whatever you have to say, make it brief.*
*In the same way, he had grown to like his little room, which, like his jacket pockets, was filled with possessions he had gathered over the years.*

- *A comma is <u>obligatory</u>*

    **i)   *between a main clause and a preceding dependent clause (eg one that begins with* when, where, how, since, although, *etc):***

    ✓   *When he arrived home, the children ran to hug him.*
    ✗   *When he arrived home the children ran to hug him.*

But when the dependent clause follows the main clause, the conjunction linking the two clauses comes between them, so indicating the point of division, and no comma is needed:

    ✓   *The children ran to hug him when he arrived home.*
    ✓   *I said that I might be late.*

---

 Sentences without *that* after a verb of saying, eg *I said I might be late*, are an exception to the above rule. No comma is needed, even though the conjunction indicating the junction between the two clauses has been omitted.

---

***ii) when there is a balance or contrast between the parts of a sentence:***

✓    *He was a clever boy, yet he failed the exam.*

✗    *He was a clever boy yet he failed the exam.*

*The bigger they are, the harder they fall.*

*From each according to his abilities, to each according to his needs.*

— Karl Marx

 An even stronger balance or contrast may be punctuated by a **semicolon**:

> *He was a clever boy; nevertheless, he failed all his exams.*

On the other hand, ***when two very short phrases are contrasted or balanced, no comma is required***, though it is not incorrect to insert one:

✓    *the more the merrier*

✓    *the more, the merrier*

***iii) when the second part of the sentence expresses a consequence or result of what is said in the first part:***

✓    *She works in the evenings, so her husband looks after the children.*

✗    *She works in the evenings so her husband looks after the children.*

 The above rule does not apply when the two parts are linked by *and*:

✓    *Do that again and I'll smack you.*

***iv) whenever it is necessary to clarify the structure or meaning of a sentence by inserting a break:***

*She felt sick and tired of looking at modern 'art'.*
*She felt sick, and tired of looking at modern 'art'.*

*For this week only, coats will be half-price.*
*For this week, only coats will be half-price.*

As a general rule, a comma should be considered wherever there is a possibility of a reader being uncertain of the structure and meaning of a sentence, or where there is a danger of them being misled by the juxtaposition of words that do not actually belong together:

✗    *Where appropriate compensation will be paid by the insurance company.*

✓    *Where appropriate, compensation will be paid by the insurance company.*

✗    *Inside the hall was packed with a capacity audience.*

✓    *Inside, the hall was packed with a capacity audience.*

367

However, when commas are being inserted to clarify the structure of a sentence, care must be taken not to separate subjects from verbs or verbs from their objects by inserting a comma between them. This is often done when the subject is long and complex, but is not correct:

✗   *The mouse that John's clever little cat killed, had eaten the cheese.*
✓   *The mouse that John's clever little cat killed had eaten the cheese.*

✗   *The hat that she wore to the wedding, is the one she bought in Harrods.*
✓   *The hat that she wore to the wedding is the one she bought in Harrods.*

The only exception to this rule is when two identical words are juxtaposed, in which case a comma may optionally be inserted to avoid confusion:

✓   *What her name is, is of absolutely no interest to me at all.*

- **A comma may <u>optionally</u> be inserted between two parts of a sentence in order to indicate a slight pause in what is being said:**

✓   *They're down at the pub celebrating their win on the Lottery.*
✓   *They're down at the pub, celebrating their win on the Lottery.*

The pause may be required in order to cast greater emphasis on what follows or to emphasize the separateness of the actions being described:

✓   *I was late on Monday and so was John.*
✓   *I was late on Monday, and so was John.*

✓   *Fred was reading, Joan was watching television and the girls were playing Scrabble.*
✓   *Fred was reading, Joan was watching television, and the girls were playing Scrabble.*

**The best rule to follow when deciding whether or not to insert an optional comma is to punctuate the sentence according to how you would want it to be spoken: if you would want there to be a slight pause, put in the comma; if you would not want a pause, leave the comma out.**

See also the notes on necessary and optional commas on page 371 below.

- **No comma is required if the parts of a sentence are closely connected to each other in sense or theme and are joined by a linking word such as** and, **because** or **that:**

*I was late on Monday because the car wouldn't start.*
*She hurriedly packed a suitcase and phoned for a taxi to go to the station.*
*I did tell you that I might be late.*

American practice differs slightly from British usage. In American English, it is normal to insert a comma between clauses even where there

<u>is</u> a close connection of sense or topic between them. Compare British English

> *She works in the evenings in order to save some money for her holidays.*
> *She packed an overnight bag and left by the 10 o'clock train.*

and the American equivalents

> *She works in the evenings, in order to save some money for her holidays.*
> *She packed an overnight bag, and left by the 10 o'clock train.*

---

**Introductory words, words which form an inserted comment or an additional piece of information, or the name of the person being spoken to, should be separated from the rest of the sentence by commas.**

**There should be a comma after *yes* and *no*, and before *please*.**

---

Examples:

> *I don't much like the idea. However, you can go if you want to.*
> *Yes, you're quite right.*
> *There's only one thing I really need at the moment: namely, a long hot bath.*
> *I put it to you, ladies and gentlemen, that the Government has earned your support.*
> *He stopped the car and, leaving the engine running, ran back to the scene of the accident.*
> *Her second play, <u>Storm in a Teacup</u>, was an even greater success.*
> *One theory, not previously made public, was that the bomb had gone off prematurely, killing the bombers themselves.*
> *See who that is at the door, will you, dear.*
> *You'll have to come back tomorrow, I'm afraid.*
> *Put the books down over there, please.*

---

⚠ **Common errors to avoid**

1.   Care must be taken to check that there is a comma **both before and after** words inserted into the middle of a sentence. It is a common error to omit one or other comma, or indeed both:

✓   *This was a wicked and, as far as I can see, a pointless act of vandalism.*
✗   *This was a wicked and as far as I can see, a pointless act of vandalism.*
✗   *This was a wicked and, as far as I can see a pointless act of vandalism.*

✗   *A lot of what he said was of course nonsense.*
✓   *A lot of what he said was, of course, nonsense.*

2.   Care should also be taken to ensure that the commas are in their <u>correct positions</u>, that is immediately before and after the inserted words, neither excluding part of the insertion nor including any of the

369

surrounding sentence. Wrong positioning of one or other comma is a common error:

✗    *He found his spectacles, and picking up the newspaper again, sat down to read.*

✓    *He found his spectacles and, picking up the newspaper again, sat down to read.*

That the first comma is misplaced in the first example can be seen by removing the inserted clause between the two commas and seeing what is left:

✗    *He found his spectacles sat down to read.*

Clearly the *and* does not belong to the inserted clause but to the surrounding sentence:

✓    *He found his spectacles and sat down to read.*

- **'Defining' and 'non-defining' relative clauses**

A relative clause is one that begins with a word such as *who, which* or *that*:

*He's not the sort of person <u>who'd do a thing like that</u>.*
*The thing <u>that annoys me most</u> is that he doesn't seem to care.*

In some cases there is no relative pronoun linking the clauses at all:

*The book <u>you're looking for</u> is over there.*

It is important to be aware of the difference between a relative clause that makes a comment or gives additional information about the noun it refers to and one which serves to identify or pick out the noun it refers to. 'Commenting', or 'non-defining', relative clauses are separated off by commas, whereas 'identifying', or 'defining', relative clauses are not. Compare

*The boy, who was here last night, is her brother.*
(Here it is assumed that it is already clear which boy is being spoken about, and the clause '*who was here last night*' merely gives additional information about him.)

*The boy who was here last night is her brother.*
(Here the words '*who was here last night*' identify which boy is being talked about, to restrict the application of the word *boy* to one particular boy.)

Similarly:

*The students, who attend classes every day, are making good progress.*
(ie, all students are making good progress)
*The students who attend classes every day are making good progress.*
(ie, only the students who attend classes every day are making good progress)

> **Adjectives, nouns, adverbs, phrases, etc occurring together in a sentence in the form of a list of parallel items are usually separated from one another by commas.**
>
> **When the last two items of such a list are linked by *and*, a comma before the *and* is optional.**
>
> **When all the items are linked by *and*, no commas are required.**

Examples of *necessary commas*:

> *a cold, wet, windy day*
> *I came for a holiday, I liked what I saw, I decided to stay — it's as simple as*
>    *that.*

Examples of *optional commas*:

> *a great, wise(,) and just king*
> *I like swimming, tennis(,) and football.*
> *She sings, dances(,) and paints.*
> *We need to deal with this quickly, quietly(,) and efficiently.*
> *She took out her keys, opened the door(,) and went in.*

(In the case of phrases and clauses as opposed to single words, the longer the phrases or clauses are, the better it is to insert the optional comma, but there is no hard-and-fast rule.)

Examples *with* **and** *and without commas*:

> *a great and wise king*
> *Our king is great and wise and just.*
> *She sings and dances and paints.*

---

⚠ American practice differs slightly from British: whereas British practice now favours *x, y and z*, the American preference is for *x, y, and z*.

---

The same options apply with *or*:

> *Which do you do best — sing, dance(,) or paint?*

- **Further points**

    i) *When only two adjectives precede a noun, they are nowadays often not separated by a comma:*

> ✓ *a large, furry animal*
> ✓ *a large furry animal*

However, the comma is still preferable, as its presence or absence can sometimes alter the implied meaning of what has been written — see the boxed note following point (iii) below.

ii) *When two adjectives together convey a single idea, they should not be separated by a comma:*

*a great big dog*

(*Great* modifies *big* and serves to emphasize the size of the dog.)

*Good old Sam!*

(*Good* and *old* together form a single expression denoting approval or praise.)

iii) *If the last of two or more adjectives is more closely linked to the following noun than the other adjective(s), or if it forms a single unit of meaning, then it should not be preceded by a comma:*

*a foolish old man* (= an old man who is foolish)

*a pretty little girl* (= a little girl who is pretty)

*a cold, wet, windy Autumn day* (= an Autumn day that is cold, wet and windy)

If two adjectives linked by *and* form a single unit of meaning, there should be no comma before the *and*:

✓  *a big, noisy, yellow and green bus*
✗  *a big, noisy, yellow, and green bus*

---

⚠  Depending on the meaning to be conveyed, a comma may be appropriate in one sentence but wrong in an otherwise identical sentence. For example, *He bought a new, red car* implies that he bought a new car which also happened to be red, whereas *He bought a new red car* (with no comma) implies that he already had a red car which he replaced with another red car.

**A useful test for commas**

A useful test to help you decide whether or not to insert a comma between two adjectives is to substitute an *and* for the proposed comma. *If you can put an* **and** *in, then you can put in a comma; if you cannot put an* **and** *in, do not put a comma in.*

For example, you could not correctly say *a great and big dog* or *Good and old Sam!*, which confirms that it is correct to omit commas in *a great big dog* and *Good old Sam!*; but you could say *a cold and wet and windy day*, which confirms that it is correct to write *a cold, wet, windy day*.

---

iv) *A semicolon should be used instead of a comma to make clear the structure of a sentence where commas alone are not sufficient to*

***do this***, eg to show that certain items in a list are more closely connected to each other than they are to other items in the list, or where a sentence consists of a number of long clauses or phrases which are themselves punctuated with several commas:

✗    *Among the area's chief industries are shipbuilding, automobile engineering and steel manufacturing, textiles and clothing, coal-mining, and brewing.*

✓    *Among the area's chief industries are shipbuilding, automobile engineering and steel manufacturing; textiles and clothing; coal-mining; and brewing.*

✗    *Copies of the report have been faxed to our offices in Lagos, Nigeria, Nairobi, Kenya, and Harare, Zimbabwe.*

✓    *Copies of the report have been faxed to our offices in Lagos, Nigeria; Nairobi, Kenya; and Harare, Zimbabwe.*

✓    *The meal was a great success, with a starter of prawn cocktail garnished with tomato, lemon, and mint and other herbs; followed by a fish pie containing smoked cod, bacon, peppers and creamed potatoes; and to finish, a chocolate gâteau decorated with pears, strawberries, icecream and whipped cream.*

**A comma is used to separate direct speech from the rest of the sentence.**

Examples:

*Peter at once said, 'I want to come too.'*
*'I wouldn't stay now,' she said, 'even if you begged me to.'*
*'I want to come too,' said Peter.*

**When the verb of saying, asking, etc precedes the whole of what is said, a colon may be used instead of a comma:**

*Peter at once said: 'I want to come too.'*

The comma is more frequently used than the colon in informal writing. The colon is more formal.

 ***When the whole statement (verb of saying and the words spoken) is itself something that is said, it is permissible to omit the comma, but not wrong to insert it:***

✓    *'What did he say?' 'He said "I want to come too".'*
✓    *'What did he say?' 'He said, "I want to come too".'*

**A comma may be used to show that a word or words have been omitted from a sentence.**

373

This use of the comma is subject to two main constraints:

Firstly, the omitted word or words must have already been used earlier in the sentence:

> *Some people like to invest their money in property; others, in the stock market.*
(ie, 'others like to invest their money in the stock market'.)

Secondly, there must be some punctuation mark in the sentence which creates a stronger break than a comma does, such as the semicolon in the above example. If there is no other punctuation mark, or only a comma, no comma should be used to mark an omission:

✗    *She was in love with him and he, with her.*
✗    *She was in love with him, and he, with her.*
✓    *She was in love with him, and he with her.*

## ✦ Commons in letter-writing

**Commas are <u>not</u> normally used in writing addresses nowadays.**

Formerly, it was normal practice to insert commas at the end of each line and between the building number and the street name:

> *Mr J Smith,*
> *16, Cavendish Place,*
> *EDINBURGH,*
> *EH11 5JT*

Nowadays, in line with the current tendency in British English to use as little punctuation as possible, the commas are generally omitted:

> *Mr J Smith*
> *16 Cavendish Place*
> *EDINBURGH*
> *EH11 5JT*

 Although commas are now almost always omitted in typewritten addresses, some people still prefer them in handwritten addresses. They are not necessary in such cases, but not incorrect.

**A comma is not required between the month and year in dates.**

Examples:

*25th June 1995*
*25 June 1995*

 A comma <u>should</u>, however, be inserted between the day of the month and the year if they are juxtaposed:

*June 25, 1995*

**A comma is normally placed after *Dear Sir*, etc at the beginning of an informal, handwritten letter and after *Yours sincerely*, etc at the end of the letter, but is now usually omitted in a typewritten, business letter.**

(See, for example, the specimen business letter on page 455.)

### ✦ Commas in numbers

**In five-figure numbers and above, either a comma or a thin space should be inserted before every three figures counting from the right. Four-figure numbers may be written with a comma or a thin space, or else with no break between the numerals at all.**

*35 000* or *35,000*
*2 335 000* or *2,335,000*
*4500* or *4 500* or *4,500*

Commas are nowadays generally found only in handwritten work. In typewritten and printed material, numbers are usually punctuated with thin spaces.

 American preferred usage is for commas rather than thin spaces in numbers over 1000.

### dash

In handwritten texts, it is usual to make all dashes the same length, but in printing there are two lengths of dash, — and –, the longer dash being known as an ***em-dash*** and the shorter one as an ***en-dash***. ('Ems' and 'ens' are printers' measures, corresponding to the widths of the letters *m* and *n* respectively.) The longer dash is used to ***separate off*** parts of a sentence (see below), while the shorter dash is, on the other hand, used as a ***linking element***, similar in many ways to a hyphen (see page 378).

## ✦ Long dashes

> **A long dash may be used to introduce an explanation or expansion of something that has just been said.**

Examples:

> *These are the characteristics of a good play — the characters should be believable, the action gripping, and the ending unexpected.*

In this use, the dash is similar to the colon, but there are important differences between these two punctuation marks:

i) **When introducing a single item that refers back to something already mentioned, a dash is preferred to a colon:**

> *A spectre is haunting Europe — the spectre of Communism.*
>
> *— Karl Marx*

> *The Common Law of England has been laboriously built about a mythical figure — the figure of the 'Reasonable Man'.*
>
> *— A P Herbert*

ii) **When introducing a number of points or items, as in the first example above, the dash is considered more informal than the colon.**

---

⚠️ A dash is sometimes used along with a colon to introduce a list. A dash is acceptable, but not necessary, if the list begins on a new line:

✔ *Things to do before holiday:—*
   *stop milk*
   *cancel papers*
   *post Mum's birthday card*
   *leave keys and hotel address with Mrs B*

A dash should <u>not</u> be used when the list immediately follows the colon on the same line:

✗ *First gather together all the ingredients for the cake:— eggs, butter, flour, sugar, milk, cherries and sultanas.*

✔ *First gather together all the ingredients for the cake: eggs, butter, flour, sugar, milk, cherries and sultanas.*

---

iii) **While a colon is used to introduce words which expand on or complete what has gone before, a dash should be used to introduce words which sum up what has gone before:**

> *There are three things we need: more time, more money and more help.*
> *More time, more money and more help — these are the three things we need.*

iv) **A dash often indicates a slightly stronger separation between the parts of a sentence than a colon does**, with the second part being added as an afterthought, a punchline or an unexpected humorous or paradoxical comment rather than simply as an expansion or explanation of what has been said in the first part:

> *She's the sort of woman who lives for others — you can tell the others by their*
> *hunted expression.*
>
> — C S Lewis

**A dash may be inserted in a sentence in order to emphasize what follows.**

Examples:

> *He can do it — and he will!*
> *The one thing we need is — patience.*
>
> *Frank Harris is invited to all the great houses in England — once.*
>
> — (attributed to) Oscar Wilde

If the highlighted word or phrase occurs in the middle of a sentence, it is separated from the rest of the sentence by two dashes:

> *There is nothing — absolutely nothing — half so much worth doing as simply*
> *messing about in boats.*
>
> — Kenneth Grahame

**Two dashes may be used to mark off a parenthesis or an aside.**

Examples:

> *I'm told his new car — some fancy foreign job, I believe — cost over £18 000.*
>
> *We know, Mr Weller — we who are men of the world — that a good uniform*
> *must work its way with the women, sooner or later.*
>
> — Charles Dickens

In such cases, dashes give a more informal tone to what is written than commas or brackets do, and so should not be used in writing of a more formal nature.

 An inserted comment must be ***both preceded and followed*** by a dash, unless it comes at the end of a sentence, in which case only the introductory dash is needed.

**If a sentence breaks off in the middle, a dash is used to mark the break.**

Examples:

> *What really annoys me is that he actually thought — oh, but what's the use of going on about it now?*
> *'Well, I'll be —,' he muttered.*

> **A dash may be used to indicate that something has been omitted from a word or sentence.**

Examples:

> *Her affair with Lord — was the talk of the town.*
> *We visited the little village of M— in the course of our journey.*

This is often the case when the intention is to avoid spelling out an expletive:

> *What the — is she on about?*
> *Quite honestly, I think he's just a f—g nuisance.*

An alternative way of avoiding spelling out an expletive in full is to use asterisks:

> *I went to see him about it, but he just told me to f\*\*\* off.*

This use of dashes and asterisks to avoid spelling out expletives has led to the formation of new, milder swear-words. *Damn it!* was often printed as *D— it!*, so creating *Dash it!*, and more recently *f—g* and *f\*\*\* off* have given rise to *effing* and *eff off*.

## ◆ Short dashes

The short linking dash is used specifically in the following contexts:

i) *to indicate ranges:*

> *the 1914 – 1918 War*
> *pages 467 – 481*
> *volumes I – IV*
> *An A – Z Guide to the Birds of Britain*

A common error is to use an en-dash to link items in a phrase beginning with *between* or *from*, especially dates:

**✗**   *between 1987 – 95*
**✗**   *from 1918 – 1939*

This is not good usage. The correct forms are:

**✓**   *between 1987 and 1995*
**✓**   *from 1918 to 1939*

ii) **to link two or more words that together modify a following word, where the words do not themselves form a compound:**

> the space – time continuum
> the Sapir – Whorf hypothesis
> a 3 – 0 win for Arsenal
> the Paris – Lyon autoroute

Nowadays, a hyphen is frequently used in this position, especially in handwriting, where it is hard to make a clear distinction between two lengths of dash and a hyphen. This use of the hyphen rather than an en-dash is not incorrect, but a dash is still considered better by many people.

A hyphen should, in any case, always be used when the words do together form a compound word. Compare:

> the *Sino-Japanese War* ('Sino-Japanese' is a compound adjective, as shown by the *o* ending of the first part, therefore hyphenated)
> the *US–Japan Security Treaty* ('US' and 'Japan' are two separate items of equal weight in this construction, therefore linked by a dash)
> *After the war, Alsace became part of the imperial territory of Alsace-Lorraine.* ('Alsace-Lorraine' is a single territory, therefore hyphenated)
> *in the Alsace–Lorraine–Luxembourg region of Europe* ('Alsace', 'Lorraine' and 'Luxembourg' are three separate units, therefore linked by dashes)

Notice that these linking en-dashes should have no spaces or only thin spaces before and after them, whereas the separating em-dashes usually have larger spaces before and after them.

## exclamation mark

> **An exclamation mark is used in place of a full stop to indicate emphasis or strong emotion such as anger, surprise or desperation, or after an exclamation.**

Example:

> *'I can't stand working here any longer!' she screamed, throwing the contents of her in-tray on the floor.*
> *Good heavens! What are you doing here?*
> *What a lovely garden!*
> *Don't you dare you say that to me again!*
> *Help!*

 **Meaning or structure — which governs the choice of punctuation mark?**

It occasionally happens that there is a clash between the <u>form</u> of a sentence and its intended <u>meaning</u>. For example, some sentences in the form of questions are really exclamations (*Wasn't that just great*), and this can cause uncertainty over which punctuation mark to use.

*In general, the correct punctuation mark to use is the one which matches the <u>underlying meaning</u> (eg, question or exclamation) of the sentence rather than its form:*

> *Wasn't that a marvellous film!*

(This is expressing an opinion, not asking for one. If it is <u>intended</u> as a question, it should end with a question mark.)

> *What on earth are you doing!*

(An exclamation of surprise or anger. Here again, if it is <u>intended</u> as a question, it must be punctuated with a question mark.)

- An exclamation mark often stands at the end of a command, but *a command need not end with an exclamation mark* unless to indicate that it is being said with particularly strong emphasis:

> *'Sit down, all of you.'*
> *No one moved.*
> *'Sit down when I tell you!', he shouted.*

- An exclamation mark is often used as a means of emphasizing the feeling expressed in the sentence it is attached to, especially in informal writing such as personal letters:

> *It was really lovely to see you all last week!*
> *Your hospitality was much appreciated!*

This use of the exclamation mark is deprecated by some authorities, but it seems unexceptionable if not overdone.

 Sometimes more than one exclamation mark is used at the end of a sentence, in order to emphasize the strength of the emotion expressed:

> *He didn't come!!!*

or else an exclamation mark is added to a question mark:

> *Really?!*

This is acceptable only in informal contexts such as personal letters or light fiction, although in general a single punctuation mark should be sufficient to indicate any emotion implied in any context.

*Exclamation marks should, in any case, be used sparingly* in any writing (insert too many and their effect becomes weakened), and *not at all in formal writing such as reports and minutes of meetings* in which a dispassionate and objective style of writing is required.

**Communication without words**

When the French writer Victor Hugo contacted his publishers to inquire how well his new book *Les Misérables* was selling, the entire content of the telegram he sent was '*?*'.

The publishers' reply was '*!*'.

---

> **An exclamation mark may be used to indicate that what has just been said is not meant to be taken seriously.**

Example:

> *A lot of very odd things have been happening round here lately. Perhaps we'll be seeing little green men next!*

---

The exclamation mark is the literary equivalent of a man holding up a card reading LAUGHTER to a studio audience.

— Miles Kington

---

> **An exclamation mark in parentheses is sometimes used to draw attention to something the writer finds surprising in a statement.**

The exclamation mark should be placed immediately after the word or words the reader's attention is being drawn to:

> *Although he said he enjoyed(!) being ill, he was clearly depressed that morning.*

## full stop

A *full stop* is also known as a *period*.

The main uses of the full stop are *to mark the end of a sentence* (see immediately below), *to close an abbreviation* (see page 384), and, in groups of three, *to indicate an omission* (see page 384).

### ✦ Full stops as sentence markers

> **The main use of the full stop is to mark the end of a sentence.**

Examples:

> *John is coming.*
> *Two and two makes four.*

---

 In punctuating direct speech, a full stop is replaced by a comma if the quoted speech precedes the verbs of saying, wondering, etc:

> *'I have no complaints,' she said with a smile.*
> *'Let's just forget it,' replied the girl.*

---

**If there is no good reason to use a question mark or an exclamation mark, then use a full stop.**

The full stop is in a sense the 'neutral' indicator of the end of a sentence. Only questions should end with a question mark, and only exclamations or sentences expressing strong emotion should be followed by an exclamation mark. See the entries for QUESTION MARK and EXCLAMATION MARK (pages 386 and 379 respectively) for fuller details.

---

 **Meaning or structure — which governs the choice of punctuation mark?**

Some sentences in the form of statements are really questions (*I was wondering if you would care to join us*), and this can cause uncertainty over which is the correct punctuation mark to use.

**In general, the correct punctuation mark to use is the one which matches the <u>underlying meaning</u> (statement, question or exclamation) of the sentence rather than its grammatical form:**

> *Can you pass me the butter, please.*

(This is a request, not a question, so mark the end with a full stop. However, a question mark is also correct in this case, as indicative of the intonation pattern used.)

With longer requests of this type, a more statement-like intonation pattern is normal, and therefore a full stop is the correct punctuation mark to use:

> *Would the parent or guardian of a little boy aged about four and answering to the name of Jeremy please come to the manager's office to collect him.*

> *I was wondering if you'd like to come too?*

(An implied question in the form of a statement. The intention is to ask a question, not to tell someone what you were thinking.)

### • Full stops or commas?

When two pieces of information are separate statements, not closely connected grammatically (eg by a conjunction) or logically, they should stand as two separate sentences, and therefore be separated by a full stop, not a comma. A common error is to run what ought to be separate sentences together into a sort of 'super-sentence', punctuated only by commas:

> ✗   *The train at platform 10 is the London train, it leaves in five minutes.*

The two statements about the train have no logical or grammatical connection with each other, and should therefore form two separate sentences:

> ✓   *The train at platform 10 is the London train. It leaves in five minutes.*

A longer example of the same phenomenon can be seen in this extract from a fictional diary:

> *Leo and I just walked and walked, we came to a square with the Cathedral de Santa Cecilia at one end, in the square were tables and chairs with people sitting reading newspapers and chatting, we sat at a table and decided to try coffee this time, in England we never drink it, but it smelt so good, the man wanted to know if we wanted it black or white, we said black with some milk in, he gave us a strange look.*
>
> — Spike Milligan

Correctly punctuated, the passage consists of eight separate sentences:

> *Leo and I just walked and walked. We came to a square with the Cathedral de Santa Cecilia at one end. In the square were tables and chairs, with people sitting reading newspapers and chatting. We sat at a table and decided to try coffee this time. In England we never drink it, but it smelt so good. The man wanted to know if we wanted it black or white. We said black with some milk in. He gave us a strange look.*

The opposite error to that discussed above is to separate information that should form a single sentence into two or more 'pseudo-sentences', ie inserting a full stop when only a comma is necessary, or even no punctuation at all:

> ✗   *People can join insurance schemes for private health care. Of which BUPA and AMI are the best known.*
> ✓   *People can join insurance schemes for private health care, of which BUPA and AMI are the best known.*
>
> ✗   *There were no clues. As to what had happened.*
> ✓   *There were no clues as to what had happened.*

> ⚠   Note that what has been said here about 'pseudo-sentences' which contain information that ought to be included in a single sentence does not apply to the punctuation of the other types of partial sentence which are entirely natural and correct in conversation. Such elliptical sentences are correctly punctuated with full stops:

> ✓    *I don't disagree with you. Far from it.*
> ✓    *I love you. Honestly. Believe me. I do.*

## ✦ Full stops after abbreviations

For a discussion of the use of full stops with abbreviations, see ABBREVIA-
TIONS, page 204.

> ⚠    If the last word in a sentence is an abbreviation that itself ends in a full
> stop (eg *Co.* for 'Company'), do not add a second full stop to mark the
> end of the sentence:
>
> ✗    *I used to work for William Brown and Co..*
> ✓    *I used to work for William Brown and Co.*
>
> It is, however, quite correct to follow the full stop of an abbreviation by
> any other punctuation mark:
>
> ✓    *Didn't he once work for William Brown and Co.?*

## ✦ Full stops indicating an omission

> **Three full stops separated by thin spaces are used to indicate
> that a sentence is uncompleted or that something has been
> omitted from it.**

Examples:

> *There was a long, eerie silence. We waited and waited …*
> *Her mother was inconsolable; she lay in her cabin, weeping, weeping …*

Omission marks are particularly useful in quoted material to show that what
is being quoted is not the complete text of the original but has some words
omitted. Consider, for example, the following passage from a grammar book
by Evan Daniel:

> *All the facts with which a grammar deals are to be found in the language to
> which the grammar belongs; and it is in the language itself, not in books, that
> these facts are primarily to be sought. Grammarians do not impose rules on a
> language; they merely collect from the language rules already in existence,
> and set them forth in an orderly way.*

This passage could be shortened in quotation in various ways, with the
omissions indicated by omission dots:

> *As Evan Daniel has said, 'all the facts with which a grammar deals are to be
> found in the language to which the grammar belongs; …'.*

*As Evan Daniel has said, '. . . it is in the language itself, not in books, that these facts are primarily to be sought'.*

*As Evan Daniel has said, 'All the facts with which a grammar deals are to be found in the language to which the grammar belongs; and it is in the language itself . . . that these facts are primarily to be sought'.*

⚠ When a sentence ends in omission dots, **it is not necessary to add a further full stop**. Some authorities do recommend the addition of a fourth dot (so making three omission marks and one full stop), but this seems unnecessary and the majority opinion seems to be slightly in favour of having only three.

## hyphen see page 252.

## interrogation mark see QUESTION MARK.

## inverted commas see QUOTATION MARKS.

## oblique

The **oblique**, also called the **slash** or the **solidus**, has five main uses:

i) **to present alternatives:**

*Bring your swimming costume and/or a tennis racquet.*
*Tea/coffee will be served.*
*Dear Sir/Madam*
*When the new lodger arrives, he/she will be need to be introduced to his/her flatmates.*
*A writer nowadays is supposed to avoid sexist assumptions. S/he tries to avoid gender references in his/her writing.*

ii) **to indicate a period of time**, especially in a financial or academic context:

*I was at university in the years 1960/64.*
*I've just received my 1994/5 tax form.*

(This could also be done with short 'en-dashes':

*I was at university in the years 1960 – 64.*

See page 378.)

iii) **to link items, eg on a route or itinerary:**

> *The London/Oxford/Birmingham express was derailed at Reading.*
> *The Edinburgh/Amsterdam/Frankfurt flight is now half an hour late.*

(This could also be done with short 'en-dashes': see page 378.)

iv) **in certain specific contexts, to indicate an abbreviation:**

> *His mail should be re-addressed c/o Brown, 16 Caven Place.* (= 'care of')
> *Charge it to his a/c.* (= 'account')
> *Major Bateman is the officer i/c provisions.* (= 'in charge of')

v) **in measurements, to express rates or ratios:**

> *100 km/hr* (= 'kilometres per hour')

## parentheses see BRACKETS.

## period see FULL STOP.

## question mark

The *question mark* is also known as an *interrogation mark*.

> **The main use of the question mark is to indicate direct questions.**

Examples:

> *Is John coming?*
> *Which is your car?*

Questions may differ from statements with regard to their word-order (compare *Is John coming?* and *John is coming*) or they may contain a special question word such as *how, why, what, who,* etc. But in some cases a question mark will be the only indication that a sentence is a question rather than a statement:

> *John's coming with us too.*
> *John's coming with us too?*

> **Meaning or structure — which governs the choice of punctuation mark?**
>
> *In general, the correct punctuation mark to use is the one which matches the <u>underlying meaning</u> (statement, question or exclamation) of the sentence rather than its grammatical form:*
>
> > *Can you pass me the butter, please.*
> >
> > (This is a request, not a question, so should end with a full stop. However, a question mark is also correct in this case, as indicative of the intonation pattern used.)

With longer requests of this type, a more statement-like intonation pattern is normal, and therefore a full stop is the correct punctuation mark to use:

> *Would the parent or guardian of a little boy aged about four and answering to the name of Jeremy please come to the manager's office to collect him.*

> *What on earth are you doing?*
> *What on earth are you doing!*

(If intended as a question, the sentence must be punctuated with a question mark. However, if it is an exclamation of surprise, anger, or whatever, it should be punctuated as such.)

> *'I suppose she did work much too hard at the Settlement?' 'Incurably so.'*

(The first sentence is intended as a question, not a statement of opinion, and therefore must be punctuated as a question.)

See also the remarks on indirect questions below.

---

**Question marks should as a rule only be used to close <u>direct</u> questions, ie questions in direct speech.**

**There should be no question mark at the end of indirect questions, ie questions in reported speech.**

---

Compare the following:

> *'Is that your car?' she asked.*
> *She asked whether that was his car.*

> *'Where are you going?'*
> *He asked where they were going.*

---

 There are, however, two cases in which it is correct to punctuate an indirect question with a question mark:

    i)   *if the indirect question is expressing a polite request:*

> *I wonder if you could help me? I'm looking for Princes Street.*

    ii)   *if the indirect question is in reality expressing a tentative direct question:*

> *I was wondering if you'd like to come too?*

Notice also the punctuation of the following:

> *Where is she, I wonder?*
> *'Where is she?', I wondered.*
> *'Where is she, I wonder?', he said.*

Sometimes more than one punctuation mark is used at the end of a sentence, in order to emphasize the strength of emotion expressed:

> *Really??* (or even *Really?!*)

This is perfectly acceptable in informal contexts such as personal letters or light fiction, so long as it is not overdone, but it is quite out of place in more formal writing. In general, a single punctuation mark should be sufficient.

- **The critical question mark**

A question mark in parentheses may be used to draw attention to something suspicious or uncertain in a statement:

> *He gave his name as Ellis(?) and said that he was looking for work.*
> *In this regard, we could consider the poetry of Geoffrey Chaucer (?1340–1400) and the paintings of Hieronymus Bosch (?1450–1516).*

## quotation marks

**Quotation marks** are also known as *inverted commas* or *quotes*. They are use *to mark off direct speech* (see below), *to mark off quoted speech or quotations* (see page 390), and *to highlight words or phrases* (see page 390).

There are two types of quotation mark: *single* '...' and *double* "...". Both are correct, but British English tends to favour single quotes, while American English generally prefers double quotes: see page 391.

✦ **Quotation marks and direct speech**

> **Quotation marks are used to enclose direct speech.**

Examples:

> *'Do come in,' he said.*
> *'Why not?' said Florence.*
> *'Help!' he shouted.*

> ⚠ Quotation marks should enclose the speaker's actual words and not a reported version of those words. It is a common error to put quotes round reported speech:
>
> ✓ *She asked him timidly, 'Do you still plan to go home tomorrow?'*
> ✓ *She asked him timidly if he still planned to go home the following day.*
> ✗ *She asked him timidly 'if he still planned to go home the following day'.*

- As a general rule, *punctuation marks that belong to, or are part of, the quoted material should be kept within the quotation marks, while punctuation marks that belong to the surrounding sentence are kept outside the quotes*, as in the above examples and the following ones:

> *He said to her firmly: 'You must help him.'*
> *'You must help her,' he said.*
> *'You', he said, 'must help her.'*

(The commas do not belong to the sentence *You must help her*, therefore are placed outside the quotation marks.)

> *'You, John,' he said, 'must help her.'*

(The first two commas belong to the sentence *You, John, must help her*, therefore are placed inside the quotation marks.)

> *His mother called to him, 'Are you ready yet?'*

(The question mark belongs with the words *Are you ready yet*, therefore is placed inside the quotation marks.)

> *Did he say 'I'm ready now'?*

(The question mark belongs with the words *Did he say*, therefore is placed outside the quotation marks.)

---

 American practice places commas and full stops (but not other punctuation marks) before quotation marks rather than after them regardless of textual logic.

---

• When the end of a passage of quoted direct speech coincides with the end of the whole sentence, and there ought logically to be <u>two</u> punctuation marks — one belonging to the quoted words and one belonging to the whole sentence — it is often correct to insert only <u>one</u> punctuation mark and simply to take the other one for granted. The following rules apply:

i) *full stop + quotation mark + full stop is reduced to full stop + quotation mark:*

> ✗ *I think he said, 'I'll be there soon.'.*
> ✓ *I think he said, 'I'll be there soon.'*

ii) *question mark + quotation mark + full stop is reduced to question mark + quotation mark:*

> ✗ *I said to her, 'I beg your pardon?'.*
> ✓ *I said to her, 'I beg your pardon?'*

The same holds for an *exclamation mark:*

> ✗ *Hugh shouted to her, 'Look out for that car!'.*
> ✓ *Hugh shouted to her, 'Look out for that car!'*

iii) *question/exclamation mark + quotation mark + question/exclamation mark <u>may be</u> reduced.*

(a) If the two marks are not identical, both should be retained:

> ✓ *Why did he shout 'Look out for that car!'?*

389

(b) If the two marks are identical, it would be logical to keep both, and it is not wrong to do so:

✔  *Why did you say 'Who goes there?'?*

but it is considered preferable by many people to omit one or other of the marks, even though it is not strictly logical to do so since each of them is attached to a different part of the sentence:

✔  *Why did you say 'Who goes there?'*
✔  *Why did you say 'Who goes there'?*

## ✦  Quotations

A short quotation (anything which consists of no more than one sentence and is no more than about four lines long) should be incorporated directly into the surrounding sentence, within quotation marks:

>   *Shakespeare once said that 'all the world's a stage'.*

A longer quotation should generally be separated off from the rest of the text by being preceded and followed by a one-line space, indented slightly from the left-hand margin, preceded by a colon, and without quotation marks:

>   *This point is clearly made by Daniel (1890), who asserts that:*
>
>>   *grammarians do not impose rules on a language; they merely collect from the language rules already in existence, and set them forth in an orderly way.*
>
>   *If this had been the case ...*

Notice that in the case of short quotations incorporated into the text, the final full stop is placed <u>outside</u> the quotation marks, which is the opposite to what is done with direct speech. Compare:

>   *Shakespeare once said that 'all the world's a stage'.*

and

>   *I think he said, 'I'll be there soon.'*

## ✦  Highlighting with quotation marks

Quotation marks are a convenient way of highlighting words or phrases:

>   *They spoke a very archaic kind of English, full of 'thous' and 'thees'.*
>   *We had a delightful meal at the new French restaurant followed by several 'wee drams' back at the house.*
>   *The table was what we in Scotland call 'shoogly'.*
>   *What does 'an accessary after the fact' mean?*

Quotation marks may also indicate disagreement with the use of a word:

>   *What he calls a 'dialect' is actually a language with a large grammar and vocabulary of its own.*

Both single and double quotes are correct, but modern British usage prefers single quotes (see the section below). However, if there is a quotation or highlighted passage within another quotation, both single and double quotes must be used:

> *'What do you mean by "an accessary after the fact"?' he asked.*

• Single quotes are often used to highlight the titles of books, periodicals, plays, films, etc:

> *We're going to 'West Side Story' at the Lyceum tonight.*
> *Her life is too hectic for her to tackle long novels like 'War and Peace'.*

---

⚠ Sometimes single quotes are in danger of being confused with apostrophes:

> *Check your references in 'Whitaker's Almanac' and the 'Writers' and Artists' Yearbook'.*

For this reason, underlining or italic type is often preferred. But the traditional method of indicating titles of books, articles, poems, etc by putting them within quotation marks is still correct.

Note that in ***academic writing***, the requirements are more precise, when compiling a ***bibliography***, for example:

i)  Enclose in quotation marks (do <u>not</u> italicize or underline) titles of articles and essays, chapters and sections of books, and unpublished works such as dissertations:

> Bewley, Marius. 'Scott Fitzgerald and the Collapse of the American Dream', in *The Eccentric Design: Form in the Classic American Novel.* New York: Columbia University Press, 1959

ii)  Italicize (or underline) titles of published books, plays, pamphlets, periodicals, and classical works (except books of the Bible or other scriptures):

> Mizener, Arthur. *The Far Side of Paradise.* Boston: Houghton Mifflin, 1951

iii)  Italicize (or underline) titles of poems only if they have been separately published under that title, otherwise enclose titles of poems in quotations.

(Note that the above bibliographical references are examples of a slightly different style of entry to that described in Appendix F, page 494. Both styles are correct.)

---

## ✦ Single quotes and double quotes

One advantage that double quotation marks have over single is that double quotes are clearly different from apostrophes. Nevertheless, single quotes are preferred in British usage, while Americans prefer double quotation marks.

If a word or phrase enclosed within quotation marks is itself incorporated within a longer stretch of speech also enclosed within quotation marks, single quotes should be used for the main quotation and double quotes for the incorporated quotation:

> *'Next week we shall examine the "stream of consciousness" technique in greater detail,' the tutor announced.*

Since American preference is for double quotation marks rather than single, thier practice is the opposite to the above, being single quotation marks within double quotation marks:

> *"Next week we shall examine the 'stream of consciousness' technique in greater detail," the tutor announced.*

## semicolon

The *semicolon* is used both to create a break in a sentence (see below) and to group elements of a sentence together (see page 393).

### ✦ Semicolons as markers of sentence breaks

> **A semicolon is used to mark a stronger and more definite break in a sentence than the break made by a comma, but less of a break than that between two separate sentences, which is indicated by a full stop.**

Examples:

> *He may have seemed a competent prime minister, yet he totally failed to appreciate the changing circumstances of the country.*

(There could have been a comma after *minister*, but a semicolon has been used instead in order **to make a greater break** between the two clauses and so to emphasize the contrast between what is said in the first clause and what is said in the second.)

> *I will say no more about your behaviour; the subject is closed.*

(To use a full stop instead of a semicolon, so making two separate sentences, would have been to create too strong a break between two statements that are obviously closely connected. The semicolon has therefore been used **to lessen the break**.)

> **A semicolon is frequently used when there is a balance or antithesis between what is said in one clause and what is said in a following clause.**

Examples:

> *As a neighbour, he deserved our courtesy and consideration; as a politician, he provoked our silent scorn.*

*You may be sorry; I am delighted.*
*To err is human; to forgive, divine.*

---

 In proverbs and pithy sayings, a ***colon*** is often used instead of a semicolon:

> *To err is human: to forgive, divine.*

Either punctuation mark is correct, but in general the semicolon is preferred nowadays.

---

In cases such as those above, the semicolon is used where a connecting word could have been used instead:

*We liked John; we disliked his politics.*
*Although we liked John, we disliked his politics.*

*You may be sorry; I am delighted.*
*You may be sorry, but I am delighted.*

Notice that when the clauses are linked by a conjunction, the punctuation mark to use between the clauses is a comma rather than a semicolon. In a sense, a semicolon functions as a sort of connector between clauses that are not joined by a conjunction. (Indeed, sometimes a semicolon is desirable simply to avoid the overuse of conjunctions.).

---

 Some connecting words are themselves often preceded by a semicolon rather than being an alternative to one. Among these are *also, consequently, furthermore, moreover, nevertheless, hence* and *however.*

> *The Egyptians were masters of practical geometry; hence the pyramids.*
> *Churchill was a great man; moreover, he had a sense of history.*

Some writers might prefer to use full stops instead of semicolons in these sentences. This would not be incorrect, but stylistically the effect of full stops would be to separate the clauses from each other more than the semicolons do.

---

### ✦ Grouping parts of a sentence by semicolons

**Semicolons should be used to indicate grouping within a series of items otherwise separated by commas, or to clarify the structure of a sentence which consists of a number of long clauses or phrases which are themselves punctuated with several commas.**

Examples:

*Among the area's chief industries are shipbuilding, automobile engineering and steel manufacturing; textiles and clothing; coal-mining; and brewing.*

*Copies of the report have been faxed to our offices in Lagos, Nigeria; Nairobi, Kenya; and Harare, Zimbabwe.*

*There was an alpine garden with sea-pinks, saxifrages, thyme and candytuft; a herbaceous border full of hosta, geum, aquilegia, astilbe, phlox, delphinium and potentilla; and at the far end there was a splendid wall of fuchsia, broom, rhododendrons and other flowering shrubs.*

**slash, solidus** see OBLIQUE.

# 8

# Questions of Pronunciation

In the first section of this chapter (see below), a number of general aspects of English pronunciation are dealt with.

The second section (beginning on page 405) provides guidance on many individual words and names about whose pronunciation there are often doubts (and sometimes intense arguments).

## ✧ *Among the General Rules of English Pronunciation*

### abbreviations

Abbreviations are shortened forms of words, phrases, titles, etc. For a full description of the different types, see page 1.

The rules of pronunciation vary from one category of abbreviation to another.

> **Abbreviations that are shortened forms of single words are usually pronounced as the full form of the word.**
>
> **The same holds for contractions that include the last letter of the shortened word.**

Examples:

*approx.* is said as 'approximately'
*esp.* is said as 'especially'
*MS* is said as 'manuscript'

*Rd* is said as 'road'
*St* is said as 'saint' or
'street'

---

⚠ A few ***abbreviations of British county names*** are, however, often pronounced as they look rather than as the equivalent full forms:

*Berks* (= /bahrks/)
*Bucks* (= /buks/)
*Hants* (= /hants/)
*Herts* (= /hahrts/)
*Lancs* (= /langks/)
*Lincs* (= /lingks/)

*Notts* (= /nots/)
*Northants* (= /nawr-**thants**/)
*Staffs* (= /stafs/)
*Wilts* (= /wilts/)
*Yorks* (= /jawrks/)

---

but on the other hand, *Beds* is said as 'Bedfordshire' and *Leics* as 'Leicestershire'.

***viz.***
***Viz.*** is the usual abbreviation of the Latin word *videlicet* (= 'namely'). It is sometimes pronounced /viz/, but this pronunciation is considered facetious by some people and is therefore not appropriate in formal situations. It may be said in full (/vi-**de**-li-sit/), but normally it is replaced in speech by 'namely'.

---

**Abbreviations consisting of initial letters of words should be pronounced as strings of individual letters.**

Examples:

$MA$ (= /em **ay**/)      $USA$ (= /yuu es **ay**/)      $GCSE$ (= /jee see es **ee**/)

 There is sometimes a free choice between pronouncing the individual letters of an abbreviation or saying the words in full: *SF*, for example, may be said as /es **ef**/ or in full as 'science fiction'.

● Where more than the initial letter of an abbreviated word is incorporated into the abbreviation, the spoken form depends on the structure of the abbreviation. If the letters do not form a pronounceable syllable, the abbreviation is pronounced as a string of letters:

$BSc$ (= /bee es **see**/)      $PhD$ (= /pee aych **dee**/)

but if a cluster of letters taken from the beginning of a word is pronounceable as a syllable, then it is so pronounced in the abbreviation:

$BEd$ (= /bee **ed**/)      $BMus$ (= /bee **mus**/)      $DPhil$ (= /dee **fil**/)

 Notice that in all abbreviations of the above types, the main stress is always on the last letter or syllable.

---

**Abbreviated forms of units of measurement are generally pronounced as the full forms.**

Examples:

$10\,km$ (= 'ten kilometres')      $10\,lb$ (= 'ten pounds')
(but $10\,cc$ may be said as /ten see **seez**/)

> **Acronyms (words formed from the initial letters or initial syllables of other words) are always pronounced as words.**

Examples:

> *Aids*, from *Acquired Immunodeficiency Syndrome*, (= /aydz/)
> *APEX*, from *advance purchase excursion*, (= /ay-peks/)
> *Nato*, from *North Atlantic Treaty Organization*, (= /nay-toh/)

> **Chemical symbols are replaced by the names of the chemicals or elements in speech except when used in chemical equations, when they are generally spoken as letters.**

Example: *NaCl* (= 'sodium chloride'; but in a chemical equation = /en ay see el/)

## double consonants

Most double consonants of written English are pronounced as single sounds: eg a<u>nn</u>ounce, ba<u>ff</u>le, bi<u>gg</u>er, i<u>mm</u>ortal, pu<u>zz</u>le, etc. Some, however, are not.

> **When the negative prefix *un-* is attached to a word which begins with an /n/ sound, the juxtaposed *n*'s are pronounced as a double consonant.**

Examples: *unknown* (= /un-nohn/), *unnatural*, *unneighbourly*.

When *-ly* is added to an adjective ending in *-al*, the juxtaposed *l*'s are sounded as a single consonant: *politically*, *historically*, etc. However, if *-ly* is added to some other word ending in an /l/ sound, the two *l*'s are normally pronounced as a double consonant: *futilely*, *genteelly*.

*Wholly* may be correctly pronounced with either a single or a double /l/.

> **In compound words, any juxtaposed identical consonants are sounded as double consonants.**

Examples: *midday*, *eel-like*, *table lamp*, etc.

# foreign words in English

English has, over the centuries, absorbed many words from other languages. Most of these are not now treated as foreign words at all, and their pronunciation is entirely anglicized. However, there are many words and phrases of foreign origin in regular use in English which retain their original pronunciation (or something close to it), and there is often uncertainty about how such words and phrases should be pronounced. Those that occur most frequently are dealt with individually in the second section of this chapter (beginning on page 405), but some general pronunciation guidelines are given here.

- **French**

In general, borrowings from French should be pronounced in a way that matches French pronunciation as closely as possible. This is particularly true of the French nasalized vowels, as in *vin blanc* and *aide-de-camp* but these may be, and other vowels certainly usually are, anglicized to a greater or lesser extent, substituting, for example, /ong/ for /oᵑ/, and so on.

Note that *ch* in French is pronounced /sh/, not /ch/. This is true also in many words brought into English from French, such as *brochure, champagne, chic, crèche, echelon,* etc. The letter *g* is pronounced /zh/, as in English *beige*: /bayzh/.

Final consonants are usually not pronounced in French, except before a following vowel. Compare the *x* and *s* of *faux pas* (pronounced /foh **pah**/) with the *x* of *faux ami* (pronounced /fohz-a-**mee**/).

*gn* = /ny/, as in the French pronunciation of *Boulogne* (= /buu-**lony**/).

*ll* after an *i* may be either /y/, as in *ratatouille*, or /l/, as in *mille*. The name of the cream-and-pastry cake *millefeuille* is pronounced /meel-**fuhy**/.

*eu* is pronounced something like /uh/, and *u* something like an /ee/ with the lips rounded as for /uu/.

- **German**

The consonants of German are pronounced as follows:

*ch* = /kh/ (the same as for Scots *ch* in *loch*), as in the name of the composer *Bach*; after *i* and *e*, the *ch* is pronounced with a sound between /kh/ and /sh/;

*sch* = /sh/, as in *Anschluss*;

*j* = /y/, not /j/ as in English *jam*;

*w* = /v/, as in *Auf Wiedersehen*;

*z* = /ts/, as in *Nazi*.

German vowel sounds are as follows:

*ie* = /ee/ and *ei* = /iy/ (so *Riesling* is pronounced /**reez**-ling/, not /**riyz**-ling/);

*au* is pronounced /ow/, but *äu* and *eu* are pronounced /oy/ (so *Fräulein* is /froy-liyn/, not /frow-liyn/);

*ö*, sometimes written *oe*, is pronounced something like /uh/;

*ü* is like a French *u*, something like an /ee/ with the lips rounded as for /uu/.


● **Italian**

The main points to note in the pronunciation of Italian are:

*gl* = /ly/ (as in *tagliatelle* and *zabaglione*);

*gh* = /g/ (as in *spaghetti*);

*gn* = /ny/ (as in *gnocchi*);

*g* before *e* or *i* = /j/ (as in *arpeggio*);

*ch* = /k/ (as in *Chianti*);

*c* before *e* or *i* = /ch/ (as in *ciao*).

In initial position, Italian *z* is usually pronounced /z/ in English, but within a word it is often pronounced /ts/ or /dz/, as it is in words such as *scherzo* and *intermezzo*.


● **Latin**

Latin words and phrases used in English are generally said with a strongly anglicized pronunciation, which is quite different from the way they were pronounced in ancient Rome. It is not always easy to predict the exact anglicized pronunciation of such words and phrases, however, without a knowledge of Latin, but the following rules generally apply:

unstressed *i*'s are pronounced /i/; stressed *i*'s are usually pronounced /iy/, as in *ad infinitum* (/ad in-fi-**niy**-*tum*/) and *bona fide* (/**boh**-*na* **fiy**-di/), but may be a short /i/, as in *ab initio* (/ab i-**nish**-i-oh/);

at the end of a word, Latin *i* is pronounced /iy/, as in the plurals of borrowings from Latin ending in -*i*, such as *stimuli*, *cacti* and *fungi*, and in many biological names, such as *Musci* (/mu-siy/, the technical name for the mosses);

the letters *ae* are pronounced /ee/, as in *amicus curiae* (/**kyuu**-ri-ee/), and in many biological names such as *Muscidae* (/**mus**-i-dee/, the technical name for the house-flies).

Occasionally, and unpredictably, some Latin words and phrases are not normally anglicized in pronunciation. In *curriculum vitae*, for example, *vitae* is generally pronounced /vee-tiy/ as in Roman Latin rather than /viy-tee/ as might be expected from the rules given above.

As examples of the pronunciation of other vowels, note the following (an *r* is pronounced in exactly the same positions as it is when you are speaking English, depending on your accent):

> *inter alia* (/in-*ter* ay-li-*a*/)
> *quod erat demonstrandum* (/kwod e-**rat** de-mon-**stran**-*dum*/)
> *pro bono publico* (/proh **boh**-noh **pub**-li-koh/)
> *modus operandi* (/**moh**-*dus* o-*pe*-**ran**-diy/)
> *fons et origo* (/**fonz** et o-**riy**-goh/)

Before *e* and *i*, *c* is generally pronounced /s/, as in *circa* (/**sir**-*ka*/) and *g* is pronounced /j/. However, before *i*, *t* and *c* may be pronounced /sh/, as in *prima facie* (/**priy**-*ma* **fay**-shi/) and *ab initio* (/*ab* i-**nish**-i-oh/).

- ### Spanish

The words that have been borrowed into English from Spanish give some indication of how Spanish words are to be pronounced:

*ñ*, as in *mañana*, is pronounced /ny/;

*ch* is pronounced /ch/, as in *macho*;

> ⚠  Not /k/ as in a common English pronunciation of *machismo*.

*j* = /kh/, the sound of the *ch* in Scots *loch*, as in the name of the Spanish wine *Rioja*;

*z* is pronounced /th/ in European Spanish, as is *c* when followed by *i* or *e*; in American Spanish, both are pronounced /s/.

- ### Welsh

Welsh sounds are most commonly met with in Welsh place-names, although there are a few words that have been brought into everyday English from Welsh, such as *eisteddfod* and *cwm*. Some of these (eg *eisteddfod*) are generally pronounced in a fully or fairly anglicized form, others in a manner closer to Welsh pronunciation.

The key points of the pronunciation of Welsh are as follows:

*ll* is pronounced with a sound which is rather like a combination of /h/ and /l/ (English-speakers who find this sound difficult to produce often substitute /l/ or /thl/);

*dd* = /dh/;

*f* = /v/ and *ff* = /f/;

*ch* is pronounced /kh/ as it is in Scottish English.

As for the vowels:

*w* = /oo/;

*y* = /u/ or /ee/;

*u* = /i/;

*ai, ei* and *au* are all pronounced /iy/.

## intrusive *r* and linking *r*

In some accents of English, a written *r* is not pronounced before another consonant or at the end of a word: *bar* = /bah/, *cord* = /kawd/, and so on. In other accents, such as Scottish English, such *r*'s are pronounced: *bar* = /bar/, *cord* = /kord/, etc. Accents of English can thus be divided between those that are 'r-pronouncing' and those that are 'non-r-pronouncing'.

In the 'non-r-pronouncing' accents, an *r* at the end of a word <u>is</u>, however, pronounced when it is followed by a vowel at the beginning of the next word ( *far away* = /fahr a-way/) or by a word-ending beginning with a vowel (*barring* = /bahr-ing/). This is known as a '*linking* r'.

In some accents, however, speakers go further than this and pronounce an *r* between vowels in similar positions to where they insert linking *r*'s even where there is no *r* in the written word: eg *law and order* is pronounced as if it was *lore and order*, and *gnawing* rhymes with *ignoring*. These *r*'s are known as '*intrusive* r's'.

These so-called 'intrusive *r*'s', inserted between vowels in speech where there are no *r*'s in the written form of the words, are often condemned, but without justification. Such pronunciations are simply one characteristic of the speech habits of one section of the English-speaking community, and are no more to be condemned than any other feature of pronunciation in any other accent.

## stress

A vowel or a syllable in a word is said to be ***stressed*** when it is said with more force, loudness or emphasis than the other vowels or syllables in that word. For example, in *photograph*, the stress is on the first syllable *pho-*, whereas in *photography* it is on the second syllable, *-tog-*.

In this book, the stressed vowel or stressed syllable is indicated by the symbol ' preceding it: '*photograph, pho'tography*.

### ✦ Changes in stress position

Some words which were formerly regularly pronounced with the stress on the initial syllable (eg '*applicable*, '*controversy*, '*despicable*, '*formidable*, '*hospitable*, '*metallurgy*, and so on) now have alternative pronunciations with the stress on

401

the second syllable: *con'troversy*, *me'tallurgy*, etc. Although disapproved of by some people, who consider only the older pronunciations to be correct, such modern pronunciations are well established and should now be fully accepted.

### ✦ Stress in compounds and phrases

Most speakers of English are aware that there is a difference between a *blackbird* and a *black bird*. In grammatical terms, the difference is that *blackbird* is a compound noun (denoting a particular species of bird), whereas *black bird* is a phrase consisting of an adjective and a noun (denoting any bird that is black).

This grammatical difference is reflected, or indicated, in speech by a difference in stress pattern: the compound noun *blackbird* is stressed on the first element, and the phrase *black bird* on the second element. This difference in stress pattern holds good for almost all compounds and phrases: compare a *'silversmith* and a *silver 'spoon*, and a *'singing teacher* (a teacher who teaches singing) and a *singing 'teacher* (a teacher who happens to be singing).

 Most street names have the stress pattern of phrases (*London 'Road*, *London 'Crescent*, *London 'Avenue*), but 'streets' have the compound-noun stress pattern (*'London Street*).

### ✦ Stress differences between adjectives, nouns and verbs

Some words, mostly two-syllable words of Latin origin, are stressed on the first syllable when they are nouns or adjectives and on the second syllable when they are verbs:

*'frequent accidents at work*
*They all swore that they would never again fre'quent that evil place*

*De Montfort was a 'rebel against the King.*
*To seize the throne, he had to re'bel against his father and murder his older brothers.*

There are many words in English that behave in this way, among which are:

| | | | |
|---|---|---|---|
| absent | discard | insult | rebel |
| accent | discharge | object | record |
| conduct | exploit | perfect | refund |
| conflict | export | permit | reject |
| contest | extract | pervert | subject |
| contrast | frequent | present | suspect |
| convert | import | produce | torment |
| convict | incline | protest | upset |

Some words of more than two syllables also show a similar differentiation, eg *alternate, attribute* and *overflow*:

> *Stretch up 30 times with al'ternate hands.*
> *Her expression seemed to 'alternate so swiftly and appealingly between gaiety*
> *and despair.*

From small beginnings in only a few words some centuries ago, these stress patterns have spread steadily through English vocabulary, and still exert influence today. There is a continuing tendency — but no more than a tendency (it is not an absolute rule) — to make two-syllable words conform to the above pattern. Recent 'converts' to the pattern are, for example, *ally*, *dispute, recess* and *research*, originally stressed on the second syllable but now, as nouns, frequently stressed on the first. Similarly, certain words originally stressed on the first syllable for both noun and verb have developed optional second-syllable stress for the verb: for example, both as a noun and a verb, *contact* is usually stressed on the first syllable, but second-syllable stress is now also possible for the verb.

There is no reason to consider such innovations in stress patterns incorrect. Once the new stress patterns are well established in the language, they should be considered fully acceptable (although there is no hard-and-fast criterion for deciding exactly when a new form has become sufficiently well established to be considered acceptable, or indeed when an older form can no longer be considered acceptable). However, an understanding of the analogical processes and forces involved in such changes may at least lead to fewer pointless arguments about the rights and wrongs of the new stress patterns.

 Interestingly, there is a counter-trend developing in some words (eg *contrast, export*), in that although there are separate stress patterns for noun and verb, the noun stress pattern is coming to be used for the verb also.

## word-endings

The pronunciation of some common word-endings:

### -ade

Usually pronounced /-ayd/ (eg *lemonade, barricade*).

In a few words of French origin, **-ade** is pronounced /-ahd/, eg *façade, charade* (but /*sha*-rayd/ is also accepted), *promenade* (but in dancing /pro-*me*-nayd/).

### -ado

Generally pronounced with an /ah/, as in *bravado* and *incommunicado*, but usually /-ay-doh/ in *bastinado*, and always in *tornado*.

### -atus, -ata, -atum

Words with these endings are mostly derived from Latin. The **-a-** of the ending is generally pronounced /ay/, as in *hiatus* and *ultimatum*, but in some words (eg *apparatus* and *data*) an /ah/ pronunciation is also possible, and in a few (eg *stratum, desideratum, erratum*, and their plurals *strata, desiderata, errata*) it is the much commoner pronunciation.

In borrowings from Italian, only /-ah-ta/ is correct: *cantata, chipolata, sonata, toccata*.

## -age
The usual pronunciation of this suffix is /-ij/, as in *average, cabbage, luggage, peerage, tonnage*, etc.

In some words of French origin, the ending is generally pronounced /-ahzh/ or /-ahj/:

| | | | |
|---|---|---|---|
| arbitrage | collage | espionage | mirage |
| badinage | corsage | fuselage | montage |
| barrage | dressage | garage | sabotage |
| camouflage | entourage | massage | |

*Arbitrage* and *garage* may also be pronounced /-ij/.

## -ed
In verbs, the past-tense and past-participle ending **-ed** is generally not pronounced as a separate syllable except after a /t/ or /d/: *walked, formed, reached*, etc, but *knitted, wounded*, etc.

The **-ed** is, however, pronounced as a separate syllable when it occurs in adjectives such as *naked, wicked* and *wretched*. Some of these adjectives have the same form as past participles of verbs, but are pronounced differently, the verb forms being pronounced as one or two syllables in accordance with the rule given above, and the adjective forms always being pronounced as two syllables: *blessed* (sometimes said as one syllable even as an adjective), *cursed, dogged, jagged, learned, ragged*, etc.

In addition, note the differences in meaning and pronunciation of the following:

**aged**: two syllables in the sense of 'very old' (*Help the Aged*), one syllable in the sense 'of the age of' (*a man aged between 25 and 30*);

**beloved**: three syllables as a noun, or as an adjective preceding a noun, otherwise two syllables;

**crooked**: in the sense of 'dishonest', two syllables; describing the bent handle of a stick, one syllable.

- **-ed + -ly/-ness**
When **-ly** and **-ness** are added to a word ending in **-ed** which is not sounded as a separate syllable (eg *deserved, good-natured*), sometimes the **-ed** becomes a full syllable (as in *deservedly* = /de-**zerv**-id-li/) and sometimes it does not (as in *good-naturedly* = /good-**nay**-*churd*-li/).

The rule is that ***the -ed only becomes a full syllable when it immediately follows a stressed syllable***, as in, for example:

| | | | |
|---|---|---|---|
| *advisedly* | *dazedly* | *markedly* | *pronouncedly* |
| *allegedly* | *deservedly* | *perplexedly* | *resignedly* |
| *assuredly* | *designedly* | *preparedly* | *surprisedly* |
| *avowedly* | *fixedly* | *professedly* | *unreservedly* |

Some words of this type allow both pronunciations, with a full syllable and with a non-syllabic ***-ed-***: *strainedly* may be /straynd-li/ or /strayn-id-li/, and similarly *depravedly*, *depressedly*, *relievedly*, *subduedly*, *barefacedly* and *shamefacedly*. *Boredly* and *tiredly* admit only the non-syllabic pronunciation.

With ***-ness***, there is a much greater tendency to the non-syllabic pronunciation than with ***-ly***. Although a few words tend to have the full syllabic /-id-/ pronunciation (eg *fixedness* /fiks-id-nis/, *markedness*, *unpreparedness*), most do not. It is in fact never wrong to pronounce words of this type with a non-syllabic ***-ed-***.

# ✧ *A Guide to Correct Pronunciations*

Should *controversy* be stressed on *con-* or *-tro-*? Does it matter whether you rhyme *apartheid* with *hide* or *height* or *hate*? Is *machismo* pronounced with a /k/ sound or with /ch/? Is there in all cases only one correct pronunciation for a word, or is some variation in pronunciation permitted — and if so, how much variation? We can say three things about this:

i)   Firstly, there are some words which may correctly be pronounced in more than one way. *Either* and *neither*, for example, may both be pronounced with an /ee/ vowel or an /iy/ vowel in the first syllable. Some people may prefer /ee/ and others /iy/, but both forms are correct.

ii)   Secondly, people from different parts of the country, or the world, speak with different accents, that is, with differences in pronunciation that identify their social background and/or the place they were brought up in. Most people can, for example, recognize regional accents such as a Welsh accent, a Scottish accent or an American accent, and can often also guess people's social backgrounds (or 'class') from their pronunciation.

iii)   Thirdly, and this is something many people forget, a language is not something that is fixed in one form for all time. No one in the 20th century speaks English the way that Chaucer spoke it in the 14th century or as Shakespeare spoke it around the beginning of the 16th century. To take one example, what speakers of English today pronounce as /nay-*chur*/ (ie, the word *nature*), Chaucer would have pronounced as something like /nah-**tioor**/ and Shakespeare as /ne-*tur*/, both correct pronunciations at the time but neither correct now. So even if there is only one correct pronunciation of a given word at a particular time, a different pronunciation may be correct at a later time, and there will often be a period of overlap when both pronunciations are current, with the older pronunciation slowly going out of fashion while the newer one becomes increasingly established. This is a natural process in language, and not one that can be discussed in simple terms of 'right' and 'wrong' pronunciations.

- **Are some accents better than others?**

An accent is simply one particular way of pronouncing a language, which a child learns from his or her parents, relatives and friends. All accents are to this extent equally correct: they are simply reflections of the pronunciation habits of particular speech communities.

But it is not surprising that, just as certain social backgrounds carry more prestige than others, so also the accents associated with certain social backgrounds are generally considered more prestigious than others, though perhaps less so than in the past. In this sense, some accents may be considered, by some people at least, to be 'better' than others.

---

I'd always had a terrible fight to get work in Britain on account of my Edinburgh accent.

— Sean Connery

---

In the United Kingdom there is one accent that has, at least until quite recently, enjoyed particular prestige. It is that accent associated with, for example, the BBC, the Queen and other members of the Royal Family, and certain famous English public schools. It is the accent that is normally taught to foreign learners of British (as opposed to American) English throughout the world, and is the accent that is generally taken as the standard for pronunciations in most English dictionaries and other reference books. It is most often referred to as *Received Pronunciation*, or *RP* for short.

Nowadays, however, RP is not the only accent to be heard among BBC announcers, and regional accents are much more generally accepted than formerly. Nevertheless, the regional accents which are considered acceptable are still for the most part those that are often considered 'educated' accents. Research has shown that many regional accents, particularly those associated with what has traditionally been called the 'working class' of large cities such as Glasgow, Liverpool and Birmingham, do still carry a certain undesirable stigma, and that even among those who themselves speak with such accents, RP and other 'educated' accents are considered more desirable or more pleasant to listen to. (It should, of course, not be forgotten that some people may consider RP and similar accents *un*desirable and *un*pleasant precisely because of their association with the upper classes: in some places, RP speakers may be thought of as too 'posh' or 'lah-di-dah'.)

- **Are some pronunciations of words right and others wrong?**

Although we have noted above that there are certain acceptable ways in which pronunciation may vary, clearly there are limits to what can be considered correct pronunciations (although it may not be clear exactly what the limits are). For example, while there may be room for disagreement about whether *controversy* should be stressed on the first syllable or on the second, no native speaker of English in the 1990s would pronounce the word with stress on the -*y*. Such a pronunciation would therefore quite simply be 'wrong'.

There is, unfortunately, no clear criterion for deciding exactly when a pronunciation that was once considered incorrect is to be considered correct. Opinions will always differ. Perhaps the best that can be said is that while, in language as in ethics, two wrongs do not make a right, in language at least, two million 'wrongs' probably do: that is, 'if enough people say it and accept it, it must be considered correct'. This will not please many purists, but there simply is no other criterion that is valid for language, and appeals to, for example, logic or tradition are vain. All that writers on language can do is describe what valid options and alternatives exist at a particular time, comment on areas of doubt and disagreement (and a comparison of any two usage books will quickly show that even the authorities often disagree with one another), and make recommendations or proffer warnings (eg that certain pronunciations may in certain situations render the speaker liable to criticism).

- **Recommended pronunciations**

The comments and recommendations in the list that follows should be considered in the light of the remarks made above. We are rarely dealing with simple matters of 'right' and 'wrong'. Pronunciations that are marked ✗ are generally to be taken as 'incorrect' only in the sense that they are pronunciations that have not (at least, not yet) found general acceptance or else are pronunciations that have now gone out of fashion, while those that are marked ✓ are for the most part ones which were formerly incorrect but which should now be considered fully acceptable even though they are still sometimes the subject of criticism. In entries where neither symbol is used, the comments and recommendations are self-explanatory.

A key to the phonetic symbols used is to be found on pages x and xi.

**abdomen**
Generally stressed on the first syllable: /**ab**-*doh*-*men*/.

Stress on the second syllable is also correct: /ab-**doh**-*men*/.

**ab initio**
*Initio* may be pronounced /i-nish-i-oh/, /i-nis-i-oh/ or /i-nit-i-oh/.

**abseil**
Generally /ab-sayl/.
/ap-sayl/ and /ap-siyl/ are also correct.

**absolute**
Generally pronounced rhyming with *loot*.
/-lyuut/ is also correct.

*Absolutely* is usually stressed on the first syllable when standing in front of the word it modifies: *Keep 'absolutely still*.
Stressed on the third syllable when standing on its own: *'Are you sure about that?' 'Oh, abso'lutely.'*

**abyss**
Generally stressed on the second syllable.
Stress on the first syllable is also correct.

**academician**
Main stress on the fourth syllable; lesser stress on either the first or, less commonly, the second syllable.

**accolade**
Generally pronounced with stress on the first syllable and rhyming with *paid*: /a-*ko*-layd/.
Less common, but correct, pronunciations are /a-*ko*-lahd/, /a-*ko*-layd/ and /a-*ko*-lahd/.

**accomplice, accomplish**
The second syllable is generally pronounced as in *come*: /a-kum-plis/, /a-kum-plish/.
Pronunciation as in *comma* is also correct: /a-kom-plis/, /a-kom-plish/.

**acetic**
The second syllable is generally pronounced rhyming with *seat*.
A pronunciation rhyming with *set* is also correct.

**acoustic**
Pronounced /a-kuu-stik/.
✗ /a-kow-stik/ is old-fashioned.

**acumen**
Generally stressed on the first syllable: /a-*kyoo*-men/.

Stress on the second syllable is now not common, but still correct: /a-kyuu-*men*/.

**adept**
When used as a noun, generally stressed on the first syllable, but stress on the second syllable is also correct.
When used as an adjective, generally stressed on the second syllable, but stress on the first syllable is also correct.

**ad hoc**
*Hoc* rhymes equally correctly with *sock* or with *soak*.

**ad infinitum**
Pronounced /ad in-fi-niy-*tum*/.

**ad nauseam**
Pronounced /ad naw-zi-*am*/.

**adult**
In British English, both as a noun and as an adjective, generally stressed on the first syllable: /a-dult/.
Stress on the second syllable is less common but correct in British English, and standard in American English.

**adversary**
Generally stressed on the first syllable: /ad-*ver*-sa-ri/.
Stress on the second syllable is less common but correct: /ad-ver-*sa*-ri/.

**aegis**
Pronounced /ee-jis/.

**aeon**
Pronounced /ee-*on*/ or, with a stronger vowel in the second syllable, /ee-on/.
✗ Not /iy-*on*/ or /ay-*on*/.

**aerie** see EYRIE.

**aesthete**
In British English, generally pronounced /ees-theet/.
/es-theet/ is less common but correct in British English, standard in American English.

**aesthetic**
Pronounced /is-thet-ik/ or /es-thet-ik/.

**aficionado**
Pronounced /a-fish-i-*oh*-nah-doh/, /a-fis-i-*oh*-nah-doh/, or /a-fish-*oh*-nah-doh/.
✗ Not /-nay-doh/.

**again, against**
The second syllable is generally pronounced with the vowel-sound of *get*. Pronunciation with the vowel sound of *gate* is also correct but less common.

**aged**
In the sense of 'having a certain age' (eg *a man aged about 30*), pronounced as one syllable: /ayjd/. Also in less common, technical senses applied to eg horses and wine.
In the sense of 'old and infirm' (as in *an aged man* and *Help the Aged*), pronounced as two syllables: /ay-*jed*/.

**aggrandize**
Generally stressed on the second syllable: /*a*-gran-diyz/.
Stress on the first syllable is not common, but is correct.
***Aggrandizement*** is stressed on the second syllable. The third syllable may be either /-diz/ or /-diyz-/: /*a*-gran-diz-*ment*/ or /*a*-gran-diyz-*ment*/.

**ague**
Pronounced /ay-gyuu/.

**aide-de-camp**
Generally pronounced /ayd *duh* ko^{ng}/ (more or less as in French).
A more anglicized pronunciation is acceptable: /ayd *duh* kahmp/.

**à la mode**
Pronounced /a la mohd/.

**albumen, albumin**
Stress on the first syllable.
✗ Second-syllable stress is now considered old-fashioned.

**allied**
Follows whichever stress pattern is preferred for the verb ***ally*** (see below), except where the following word is stressed on the initial syllable, in which case ***allied*** is stressed on the first syllable also.

**ally**
As a noun, generally stressed on the first syllable; second-syllable stress is not common but correct.

As a verb, generally stressed on the second syllable; first-syllable stress is not common but correct.

**almanac**
The first syllable is generally pronounced /awl-/.
/ol-/ and /al-/ less common but also correct.

**almond**
The *l* in this word is silent. Say /ah-mond/.

**almoner**
Generally /ah-*mo*-ner/.
/al-*mo*-ner/ is also correct.

**alms**
The *l* is silent: say /ahmz/.

**alter ego**
The preferred pronunciation is /al-*ter* ee-goh/.
***Ego*** may equally correctly be /e-goh/.
✓ Pronouncing ***alter*** like the verb *to alter* is also correct, but disapproved of by some people.

**alternate**
As a verb, stressed on the first syllable: /awl-*ter*-nayt/.
As an adjective and noun, stressed on the second syllable: /awl-ter-nit/.

**altogether**
Stressed on the first syllable when preceding the word it modifies: *That's not 'altogether true.*
Stressed on the third syllable when following the word it modifies: *That's a different matter alto'gether.*

**amateur**
Generally pronounced /a-*ma*-tur/.
/a-*ma*-chur/ and /a-*ma*-choor/ are also correct.

**ambiance**
Generally pronounced /am-bi-*ans*/.
A more French-sounding pronunciation, /o^{ng}-bi-o^{ng}s/, is also correct.

**amen**
Equally correctly /ah-men/ or /ay-men/.

**amenity**
The second syllable may equally correctly rhyme with *mean* or *men*.

## amicable
Stress on the first syllable.

## amok
May be pronounced /*a*-mok/ or /*a*-muk/. *Amuck* is always pronounced /*a*-muk/.

## amontillado
Pronounced /*a*-mon-ti-lah-doh/ or /ah-mon-ti-lyah-doh/.

## amuck see AMOK.

## analogous
The word ends in /-*gus*/, not /-*jus*/.

## anno Domini
The final syllable of *Domini* may equally correctly rhyme with *nigh* or *knee*.

## anti-
In British English, pronounced /an-ti-/; in American English usually /an-tiy-/.

## antiquary
Stressed on the first syllable.

## apartheid
Generally pronounced /*a*-pahrt-hayt/. An *h*-less pronunciation, /*a*-pahr-tayt/, is also considered correct by most authorities, as are both /*a*-pahrt-hiyt/ and /*a*-pahr-tiyt/.
✗ /*a*-pahrt-hiyd/ or /*a*-pahr-tiyd/ are not generally accepted as correct.

## a posteriori
May be pronounced /ay pos-teer-i-aw-riy/ or /ah pos-te-ri-oh-ree/.
A mixture of the two, /ay pos-te-ri-aw-riy/, is also correct.

## apparatus
Generally pronounced /*a*-*pa*-ray-tus/. /*a*-*pa*-rah-*tus*/ and /*a*-*pa*-ra-*tus*/ are also correct.

## applicable
Generally stressed on the second syllable; stress on the first syllable is much less common but not incorrect.

## apposite
Generally rhymes with *opposite*, but the final syllable may also correctly be pronounced /-ziyt/.

## appreciate
The *c* may be pronounced /sh/ or /s/.

## apricot
Generally pronounced /ay-pri-kot/. /*a*-pri-kot/ is less common but equally correct.

## a priori
May be pronounced /ay priy-aw-riy/ or /ah pree-ri-oh-ree/,
A mixture of the two, /ay priy-aw-ree/, is also correct.

## aquatic
Pronounced /*a*-kwa-tik/ or, less commonly, /*a*-kwaw-*tik*/.

## arbitrarily
Best stressed on the first syllable, and pronounced with 5 syllables: /ahr-bi-*tra*-ri-li/.
Stress on the third syllable is acceptable only in informal speech.

## arbitrary
This word has 4 syllables. Be careful not to lose the *-ra-*: /ahr-bi-*tra*-ri/.

## arctic
Always pronounce the first *c*:
✓ /ahrk-tik/.
✗ Not /ahr-tik/.

## aristocrat
Generally stressed on the first syllable. Second-syllable stress is less common in British English, but not incorrect, and is standard in American English.

## armada
Pronounced /ahr-mah-*da*/.
✗ /ahr-may-*da*/ is now considered old-fashioned.

## art deco, art nouveau
The former is generally /ahrt/, the latter /ahr/.

## artisan
Generally stressed on the final syllable in British English: /ahr-ti-zan/.
A pronunciation with stress on the first syllable, originally only American, is increasingly common in British English, and is now considered correct.

## ascetic
Pronounced /*a*-set-ik/.

**asphalt**
Generally /as-falt/ or /as-fawlt/.
/ash-falt/ and /ash-fawlt/ are also correct.
✗ Never /ash-felt/.

**aspirant**
Generally /as-pi-rant/.
The former standard pronunciation /as-piyr-ant/ is now not common.

**asthma**
In British English, usually pronounced /as-ma/; less commonly /asth-ma/.
In American English, /az-ma/.

**ate**
/et/ is slightly commoner than /ayt/, but both are correct.

**attribute**
Stressed on the first syllable as a noun, on the second syllable when a verb.

**audacious**
Pronounced /aw-day-shus/.
✗ Not /ow-day-shus/.

**au fait**
Pronounced /oh fay/ or /oh fe/.

**auld lang syne**
Pronounced /old lang siyn/ (/o/ as in *pot*), or /awld lang siyn/.
✗ Non-Scots should note that the last word is not /ziyn/.

**aural, oral**
*Aural* means 'relating to hearing and the ears', *oral* 'relating to speaking and the

mouth'. Unfortunately, in many accents of English, these two words are identical in sound: /aw-ral/.
Since this may at times cause confusion, some speakers pronounce *aural* as /ow-ral/, and *oral* as /oh-ral/ or /o-ral/ (with /o/ as in *pot*). Although deprecated by many authorities, this is a sensible and acceptable way of making the words distinct. (Note that /oh-ral/ is preferable to /o-ral/, as in some accents of English it is *aural* that is pronounced /o-ral/.)

**automaton**
Stress on the second syllable: /aw-tom-a-ton/.

**auxiliary**
The *x* is generally pronounced /gz/, but /ks/ is also correct.
Take care not to lose the *y* sound after the *l*.

**avoirdupois**
Both /av-wahr-dyoo-pwah/ and /av-er-duh-poiz/ are correct.

**awry**
Pronounced /a-riy/.

**azure**
Generally pronounced /a-zhur/, but /a-zyoor/ and /a-zyur/ are increasingly common.
Also correct are /ay-zhur/, /ay-zyoor/ and /ay-zyur/.

**Achilles**
Pronounced /a-kil-eez/.

**Adidas®**
Pronounced /a-di-das/ or /a-dee-das/.

**Aeneas**
Pronounced /ee-nee-as/.

**Aeschylus**
Pronounced /ees-kil-us/.

**Aesop**
Pronounced /ee-sop/.

**Alnwick**
The *l* and the *w* are silent. Pronounced /a-nik/.

**Antarctic**
Always pronounce the first *c*: /an-tahrk-tik/.
Similarly in *Antarctica*.

**Antigone**
Pronounced /an-tig-o-ni/.

**Antigua**
Pronounced /an-tee-ga/.

**Aphrodite**
Four syllables: say /a-fro-diy-ti/.

**Arctic**
Always pronounce the first *c*: /ahrk-tik/.

411

**Argentine**
As the name of the country, generally ends in /-tiyn/.
As the name of an inhabitant of the country, generally ends in /-teen/.
But both forms are possible for either meaning.

**Aristophanes**
Pronounced /a-ri-stof-*a*-neez/.

**Arkansas**
Pronounced /ahr-*kan*-saw/.

**Asia**
Pronounced /ay-*sha*/ or /ay-*zha*/.

**Augustine**
In British English, generally stressed on the second syllable: /aw-**gus**-tin/.
First-syllable stress is also acceptable: /aw-*gus*-teen/.

**Azerbaijan**
Pronounced /a-*zer*-biy-jahn/.

**bade**
Pronounced /bad/.
/bayd/ is generally reserved for poetry.

**balcony**
The first syllable is pronounced /bal-/.
✗ Not /bawl-*ko*-ni/.

**banal**
Best pronounced /*ba*-nahl/.
✗ /bay-*nal*/ is not yet fully accepted.

**baroque**
Usually pronounced /*ba*-rok/.
/*ba*-rohk/ is also correct.

**basalt**
Begins with /ba-/ and rhymes with *salt*.
✗ /bay-/.
The stress may be on either syllable.

**bas-relief**
Pronounced /bah-ri-leef/ or /bas-/.

**bathos**
Pronounced /bay-thos/.

**baton**
First syllable pronounced as in *bat*.
Second syllable may be /-ton/ or, with a weak vowel, /*-ton*/.

**baulk**
The *l* may be equally correctly pronounced or omitted.

**behove**
Rhymes with *rove* and *wove*.
The American English form of the word is **behoove**, rhyming with *move*.

**beloved**
As an adjective preceding a noun (*my beloved child*) or when used as a noun (*This is my beloved*), pronounced as three syllables: /bi-luv-id/.
After a verb (*The house was much beloved by her father*) or in a verbless clause (*Much beloved by her father, the house unfortunately burned down some years ago*), pronounced as two syllables: /bi-luvd/.

**berserk**
Equally correctly stressed on the first or the second syllable.
The *s* may be pronounced /s/ or /z/, /z/ being the commoner.
Even when unstressed, the first syllable may be pronounced with a long vowel, as in *berth*, but a short unstressed vowel, as in the second syllable of *camber* is also correct.

**bestial**
The first syllable is pronounced as *best*;
✗ not *beast*.

**blackguard**
The *ck* is not pronounced.
**-guard** may be pronounced with a full /ah/, as in *guard*, or with a weaker unstressed vowel, as in the second syllable of *haggard*.

**blancmange**
The *nc* is silent; the initial syllable is pronounced /bla-/.
The second syllable is pronounced /-mo$^{ng}$zh/, more or less as in French, or with a more anglicized pronunciation /-monj/.

**blessed**
As the past tense and past participle of the verb *to bless*, pronounced /blest/.

As an adjective, pronounced /bles-id/ (as in *Take that blessed dog away, will you!*).

**boatswain**
Usually written *bosun* or *bo'sun*. Even when written in full, this word should be pronounced /boh-sun/.

**bolero**
As the name of a Spanish dance, this word is pronounced with the stress on the second syllable.
As the name of an item of clothing, usually stressed on the first syllable, but second-syllable stress is not incorrect.

**bona fide**
Usually /boh-na fiy-dee/, but a more Latin-like pronunciation, /boh-na fee-day/, is also correct.
✗ Do not rhyme *fide* with *tide*.

**booth**
The *th* may be sounded /dh/ as in *breathe* or /th/ as in *breath*.

**bouquet**
Most commonly pronounced /buu-kay/. Stress on the first syllable not incorrect, but less common.

The pronunciation /boh-kay/ also still correct, but very uncommon.

**bourbon**
Pronounced /boor-bon/ if it is a biscuit, /buhr-bon/ or /boor-bon/ if it is a type of whiskey.
/boor-bon/ also for the family name of the Bourbons.

**breeches**
In the sense of 'trousers', pronounced /brich-iz/.

**brochure**
Almost always stressed on the first syllable, but stress on the second syllable is not incorrect.

**brusque**
Pronounced /broosk/ or /brusk/.

**buffet**
In the sense of a 'self-service meal' or a 'refreshment counter in a train, etc', pronounced /boo-fay/ or /bu-fay/.
✗ Not /bu-fit/.

---

**Beauchamp**
Pronounced /bee-cham/.

**Beaufort**
Pronounced /boh-fort/.

**Beaujolais**
Pronounced /boh-zho-lay/.

**Beaulieu**
Pronounced /byuu-li/.

**Beaumont**
Pronounced /boh-mont/.

**Beijing**
Pronounced /bay-jing/.

**Belorussia**
Pronounced /be-loh-ru-sha/ or /bye-loh-ru-sha/.
The second form alone applies if the name of the country is spelt *Byelorussia*.

**Berkeley**
Pronounced /bahr-kli/ in British English, /buhr-kli/ in American English.

**Berkshire**
Pronounced /bahrk-shir/.

**Berwick**
Pronounced /be-rik/; the *w* is silent.

**Bewick**
Pronounced /byuu-ik/.

**Bicester**
Pronounced /bis-ter/.

**Boulogne**
In English, pronounced /boo-loyn/, in French /buu-lony/.

**Breughel** see BRUEGHEL.

**Bromwich**
The *w* is always silent.
The *ch* is usually pronounced /ch/, sometimes /j/.

**Brueghel**
/broy-*gel*/ or /bruh-*gel*/.

**Buccleuch**
Pronounced /*bu*-kluu/.

**Buchanan**
Generally pronounced /byoo-ka-*nan*/; but in Scotland usually pronounced /*bu*-ka-*nan*/.

**Buenos Aires**
Pronounced /*bway*-nos iyr-eez/ or /*bwe*-nos/.

**Bunsen burner**
/bun-*sen*/ or /boon-*sen*/.

**Burkina Faso**
Pronounced /bur-kee-*na* fa-soh/.

**Byelorussia** see BELORUSSIA.

**Byzantine**
/bi-*zan*-tiyn/ seems to be the commonest pronunciation, but /biy-/ is also correct for the first syllable and /-teen/ and /-tin/ for the last syllable.
Stress on the first syllable is also correct, in which case the word may be /*biz*-*an*-tiyn/ or /-teen/.

**cacao**
Pronounced /*ka*-kah-oh/ or /*ka*-kay-oh/.

**cadaver**
Now usually /*ka*-da-*ver*/ or /*ka*-dah-*ver*/. /*ka*-day-*ver*/ is still correct but going out of fashion.
*Cadaverous*, however, is always pronounced /-da-/.

**cadre**
Pronounced /kah-*der*/ or, less commonly, /kah-*druh*/.

**café**
Usually stressed on the first syllable.

**caliph**
/kay-lif/ and /ka-lif/ are both correct.

**camellia**
The second syllable *-me-* should be pronounced to rhyme with the pronoun *me*.

**canine**
/kay-niyn/ is commoner than /ka-niyn/, but both are correct.

**capercailzie**
The *z* is silent: /ka-*per*-kay-li/ or /kay-*per*-/.
(On the pronunciation of the *z*, see the note at MENZIES.)

**capitalist**
Stress on the first syllable.

**carillon**
In British English, usually stressed on the second syllable and rhyming with *million*;

stress on the first syllable is less common but correct.
In American English pronounced /ka-ri-lon/.

**carousel**
Pronounced /ka-*ru*-sel/.

**caryatid**
Stressed on the second-last syllable: /ka-ri-a-tid/.

**catacombs**
Pronounced /-kuumz/ or /-kohmz/. The former is the commoner.

**catechism**
The *ch* is pronounced /k/.

**catechumen**
Pronounced /ka-*te*-kyuu-*men*/.

**cause célèbre**
Pronounced /kohz say-leb-*ruh*/.
⚠ Do not drop the final syllable of *célèbre*.

**caviare**
Stress on the first or last syllable; first-syllable stress is now much the more common.

**ceilidh**
The *dh* is silent: say /kay-li/.

**centenary**
/sen-tee-*na*-ri/ is the most common pronunciation.
/-te-*na*-ri/ is also correct.

**centrifugal**
Usually /sen-tri-**fyuu**-*gal*/.
Stress on the second syllable is rather old-fashioned, but still correct.

**centripetal**
Usually /sen-tri-pi-*tal*/, but /sen-tri-**pee**-*tal*/ now becoming commoner.
✗ Not /-pe-*tal*/.

**certification**
Stress on *cer-*, not on *-ti-*.

**cervical**
Pronounced /ser-**viy**-*kal*/ or /ser-vi-*kal*/.

**ceteris paribus**
Pronounced /ket-*e*-rees pa-ri-*bus*/, or /set-/.
For those who prefer a more Latinized pronunciation, /**kay**-*te*-rees pa-ri-boos/.

**chagrin**
Pronounced /**shag**-rin/.
✗ There is no need to pronounce this word as if it was French, with /a$^{ng}$/ in the second syllable.

**chamois**
The name of the animal should be pronounced /**sham**-wah/.
Chamois leather is pronounced /**sha**-mi/.

**chancre**
Pronounced /**shang**-ker/.

**charade**
Pronounced /*sha*-**rahd**/ or, less commonly, /*sha*-**rayd**/.

**chassis**
The final *s* is not pronounced in the singular noun, but is pronounced in the plural.
The initial *ch* is pronounced /sh/.

**chastisement**
Now usually /cha-**stiyz**-*ment*/.
The older pronunciation, /cha-**stiz**-*ment*/, is now rare, but still correct.

**chauffeur**
Pronounced /shoh-*fer*/ or /shoh-fuhr/.

**chemotherapy**
Pronounced /**kee**-moh-/ or /**ke**-moh-/.

**chic**
/sheek/ is preferable to /shik/.
✗ Never /chik/.

**chicanery**
Pronounced /shi-**kay**-*ne*-ri/.

**chimera**
Pronounced /kiy-**mee**-*ra*/ or /ki-**mee**-*ra*/.
✗ Not /shi-/.

**chiropodist**
Usually pronounced with an initial /k/, but /shi-ro-*po*-dist/ is also correct.

**choleric**
Pronounced /ko-*le*-rik/.

**chutzpa**
Best pronounced /khoot-*spa*/; if you cannot manage the initial /kh/ sound (the same sound as the *ch* in *loch*), /h/ is acceptable.
✗ Not with initial /k/.

**cicatrice**
Stress on the first syllable.
The final syllable is pronounced /-tris/;
✗ never /-triys/.

**cigarette**
Usually pronounced with stress on the last syllable.
Stress on the initial syllable also correct.

**circa**
Nowadays pronounced /sir-*ka*/.
✗ Not /kir-*ka*/.

**cirrus**
Pronounced /si-*rus*/.

**clandestine**
/klan-**des**-tin/ and /klan-**des**-tiyn/ are the most common pronunciations, but stress on the first syllable is also correct.

**clangour**
Rhymes with *anger*, not with *banger*.

**claustrophobia**
The first syllable may be pronounced /klaw-/ or /klo-/.
✗ /klow-/ is incorrect.

**cliché**
Stress this word on the first syllable.

## clientele
Preferred pronunciations are /klee-on-tel/, /klee-*en*-tel/ or, with a more French-sounding vowel, /klee-o$^{ng}$-tel/.
/kliy-*en*-tel/ is normal in American English, and heard in British English also, but not all authorities on British English accept it as correct.

## clique
Pronounced /kleek/.

## clothes
Take care to pronounce the *th* in formal speech.
✗ /klohz/ is acceptable only in very informal English.

## coccyx
Pronounced /kok-siks/.

## codify
Preferably /kohd-i-fiy/ (the word is connected with *code*).
/kod-i-fiy/ is less common, but not incorrect.

## cognizance
The *g* is generally sounded, but it is not wrong to pronounce the word /kon-i-zans/.

## cognoscenti
This word is of Italian origin.
The usual pronunciation is half-Italian and half-English: /kog-*no*-shen-tee/.
A more Italianized form, /ko-*nyoh*-shen-tee/ is also correct.

## coiffeur
Preferred pronunciation is /kwah-fuhr/.
/kwa-/ and /kwo-/ also correct.
Be careful to distinguish this word from *coiffure*, pronounced /kwah-fyoor/.

## colander
Usually pronounced /kul-*an-der*/.
/kol-/ also acceptable.

## collect
As the name of a prayer, this is stressed on the first syllable.

## combat
As a noun and an adjective, always stressed on the first syllable.
As a verb, usually stressed on the first syllable, but stress on the second syllable also correct.

First syllable usually pronounced /kom-/; /kum-/ also correct.

## combatant, combative
Both stressed on the initial syllable.
First syllable usually pronounced /kom-/; /kum-/ also correct.

## commandant
Usually stressed on the initial syllable.
Stress on the final syllable also correct.

## communal
Stressed on the first syllable.

## commune
As a noun, stressed on the first syllable.
As a verb, usually stressed on the second syllable; stress on the initial syllable also correct.

## comparable
Stress on the first or the second syllable.
If the second syllable is stressed, it should be pronounced /-par-/.
✗ Not /kom-payr-/.

## compensatory
Usually stressed on the third syllable.
Stress on the second syllable also correct.

## compilation
Rhyming the second syllable with *pill* is correct.
✓ Rhyming the second syllable with *pile* is also correct, although not all authorities accept it.

## complaisant
Pronounced /kom-play-*zant*/.
Do not confuse this word with *complacent*, pronounced /kom-play-*sent*/.

## complex
As an adjective, this may be stressed on either syllable.
As a noun, stressed on the first syllable.

## composite
As an adjective or as a noun, this word is stressed on the first syllable, and rhymes with *opposite*.
Rhyming the final syllable with *site* is also acceptable, and is the normal pronunciation when the word is used as a verb.

## comptroller
This is an obsolete spelling of *controller*, still used in some official titles.

It is pronounced as *controller*.

### conch
Both /kongk/ and /konch/ are correct.

### conduit
Usually pronounced /kon-dyoo-it/ or /kun-/.
/kon-dit/ and /kun-dit/ are older and now less popular pronunciations, but are still correct.

### confidant, confidante
Stress on the final syllable or the first syllable.
With first-syllable stress, the final syllable should be /-dant/, with a full vowel rather than the weak vowel heard in *confident*.

### congener
Pronounced /kon-*je-ner*/.

### congeries
Pronounced /kon-jeer-eez/ or /kon-je-ri-eez/.

### congratulatory
Usually stressed on *-lat-*, pronounced /-layt-/.
Stress on *-grat-* also correct, in which case *-lat-* is pronounced with a weak vowel, /-lat-/.

### conjugal
Stress on the first syllable.

### constable
Pronounced /kun-/ or /kon-/.

### consummate
As a verb, stressed on the first syllable, and ends in /-mayt/.
As an adjective, may be stressed on either the first or the second syllable, with the final syllable pronounced /-mat/.
The second syllable generally pronounced /-su-/; /-syoo-/ also correct when the stress is on the first syllable.

### contact
As a noun, stressed on the first syllable.
As a verb, stressed on either the first or the second syllable.

### contemplative
As an adjective, usually stressed on the second syllable, but may be stressed on the first syllable.

Best stressed on the second syllable when used as a noun meaning 'a person leading a life of religious contemplation'.

### contrary
In the sense of 'opposite', pronounced /kon-*tra-ri*/.
In the sense of 'perverse', /*kon*-tray-ri/, as in the nursery rhyme *Mary, Mary, quite contrary, ...*
The adverb **contrarily** follows the stress patterns and pronunciation of **contrary**, according to the sense intended.
✗ Not /*kon*-tra-ri-li/.

### contrast
Stressed on the first syllable as a noun.
As a verb, stressed on the second syllable.

### contribute
Pronounced /*kon*-tri-byuut/.
Stress on the first syllable is now much less common, but is still considered correct by most, though not all, authorities.

### controversy
The older /kon-*tro-ver*-si/ is steadily being replaced by the more recent arrival /*kon*-tro-*ver*-si/.

### contumacy
Stress on the first syllable: /kon-tyoo-*ma*-si/.

### contumely
Best pronounced with three syllables: /kon-tyoom-li/.
A four-syllable pronunciation, ending with /-i-li/, is also correct.
Stress generally on the first syllable, but second-syllable stress also correct.

### conversant
Stress on the second syllable in British English, on the first syllable in the USA.

### converse
Usually stressed on the first syllable.

### conversely
Usually stressed on *-verse-*.

### corps
Pronounced /kawr/ in the singular, /kawrz/ in the plural.

### corpuscle
The *c* before the *l* is silent: /kawr-pu-*sel*/.
Stress also correct on the second syllable.

## courteous

The first syllable rhymes with *curt*.

## courtesan

The first syllable rhymes with *court*.
Stress may be on either the first or the last syllable.

## courtesy

The first syllable rhymes with *curt*.

## covenanter

Generally stressed on the first syllable, as is *covenant*.
In Scotland always, and elsewhere sometimes, stressed on *-nant-* when referring to a Scottish adherent of the National Covenant or the Solemn League and Covenant (17th-century documents written in support of Presbyterianism).

## covert

Pronounced /ku-*vert*/ or, less commonly, /koh-*vert*/.

## coxswain

Like *boatswain*, this is generally said in a contracted form, /kok-*sn*/, but /kok-swayn/ is also correct.

## coyote

Best pronounced as three syllables, /koy-oh-ti/ or /kiy-oh-ti/.
/koy-oht/ and /kiy-oht/ are also correct.

## crèche

Pronounced /kresh/ or /kraysh/

## crème de menthe

Pronounced /krem *de* month/.

## crèpe

Pronounced /krayp/ or /krep/.

## cross

Pronounced /kros/.
/kraws/ is old-fashioned, but still correct.

## cui bono

Pronounced /kwee boh-noh/ or /kuu-ee bo-noh/.

## cul-de-sac

*Cul-* may rhyme with *cull* or *full*.

## culinary

The preferred pronunciation nowadays is /ku-li-*na*-ri/.
/kyuu-li-*na*-ri/ is also accepted as correct.

## cumulus

Pronounced /kyuu-*myoo-lus*/.

## cupola

The first syllable is stressed, and is pronounced as in *Cupid*.
✗ Not as in *cup*.

## curriculum vitae

Usually /*ku*-rik-*yoo-lum* vee-tiy/.
A more anglicized form /viy-tee/ is also correct.

## cyclical

Pronounced /sik-li-*kal*/ or /siyk-li-*kal*/.

## czar

Pronounced /zahr/ or /tsahr/.

---

### Caius

In the name of the Cambridge University college, this is pronounced /keez/.

### Caribbean

Usually stressed on the third syllable.
Stress on *-rib-* is also acceptable.

### Cassiopeia

Pronounced /ka-si-*oh*-pee-*a*/.

### Celtic

Pronounced with an initial /k/ except when referring to the Glasgow or Belfast football teams, whose names are pronounced /sel-tik/.

### Chablis

Pronounced /sha-blee/.

### Charybdis

Pronounced /*ka*-rib-dis/.

### Cherwell

The first syllable is pronounced /chahr-/.

### Cheviot

May be pronounced /chee-vi-*ot*/ or /che-vi-*ot*/.

**Cheyenne**
Usually pronounced /shy-**an**/.
/shy-**en**/ also correct.

**Chianti**
Pronounced /ki-**an**-ti/.

**Chicago**
Pronounced /shi-**kah**-goh/.
/shi-**kaw**-goh/ is also correct in
American English, but not in British
English.

**Chiswick**
The *w* is silent: say /**chiz**-ik/.

**Cholmondeley**
Pronounced /**chum**-li/.

**Chopin**
Pronounced /sho-pa$^{ng}$/ or /shoh-
pa$^{ng}$/.

**Cinque Ports**
The first word is pronounced
/**singk**/.

**Cinzano®**
Pronounced /chin-**zah**-noh/ or /chin-
**tsah**-noh/.

**Citroen®**
Pronounced /**sit**-roh-*en*/ or /**sit**-*ren*/.

**Clarenceux**
Pronounced /kla-*ren*-suu/ or
/-*syuu*/.

**Clwyd**
Pronounced /**kluu**-id/.

**Cockburn**
The *ck* is silent: say /**koh**-burn/.

**Cointreau®**
Pronounced /**kwon**-troh/ or /kwahn-
troh/.

**Connecticut**
The middle *c* is silent: say /*ko*-ne-ti-
*kut*/.

**Constable**
As the name of the painter,
pronounced /kun-**sta**-bel/.

**Copenhagen**
Pronounced /koh-*pen*-hay-gen/ or
/-hah-*gen*/.

**Covent Garden**
The first word may be /ko-*vent*/ or
/ku-*vent*/.

**Coventry**
Pronounced /ko-*ven*-tri/ or /ku-*ven*-
tri/.

**Crichton**
Pronounced /**kriy**-*ton*/.

**Cro-magnon**
Pronounced /kroh-**man**-*yon*/ or
/-**mag**-*non*/.

**Culzean**
Pronounced /*ku*-layn/.
(See MENZIES for a comment on
the *z*.)

---

**dachshund**
Pronounced /dak-*sund*/, /**daks**-hoond/
or /**dash**-*und*/.

**daemon**
Usually pronounced /**dee**-*mon*/.
/**diy**-*mon*/ and /**day**-*mon*/ also correct
and avoid possible confusion with *demon*.

**Dáil**
Pronounced /**doyl**/.
In full, the Irish parliament is the *Dáil
Eireann*, /doyl **ayr**-*en*/.

**dais**
Formerly always /**days**/.
Now usually /**day**-is/, but /**days**/ is still
correct.

**data**
Usually /**day**-ta/.
Also /**dah**-ta/ and /**da**-ta/, especially in
technical contexts.

**dauphin**
Pronounced /**doh**-fa$^{ng}$/ or /**daw**-fin/.

**debacle**
Pronounced /di-**bah**-*kel*/ or /**day**-bah-
*kel*/.
If spelt *débâcle*, preferably /**day**-bah-
*kel*/.

**debris**
Pronounced /**deb**-ree/, /**day**-bree/ or
/**de**-bree/.
If spelt *débris*, preferably /**day**-bree/.

419

## debut

Pronounced /day-byuu/ or /de-byuu/.
If spelt *début*, preferably /day-byuu/.

## débutante

Whether written with or without an accent, may be pronounced in several ways: /de-byoo-tahnt/ or /-tant/ or /-tont/.
Also with the first syllable pronounced /day-/.
Also, closer to the French pronunciation of the word, /day-byoo-to$^{ng}$t/.

## decade

Stressed on the first syllable.

## decorous

Stressed on the first syllable.

## defect

As a verb, stressed on the second syllable. As a noun, may be stressed on either syllable when the word is used as a noun, first-syllable stress is now much commoner than stress on the second syllable.

## deficit

Put the stress on the first syllable.

## deify, deity

Both /day-/ and /dee-/ are correct in both these words, the former being the commoner.

## deleterious

The stress in this word is on the third syllable, which is pronounced like *tea*.
The first syllable is pronounced as *dell*.

## delirious

Second syllable usually pronounced /-lir-/.
/-leer-/ also accepted as correct.

## demise

Pronounce this word to rhyme with *rise* rather than *trees*.

## demonstrable

Usually stressed on the second syllable. Stress on the first syllable also correct.

## denouement

With or without an accent on the first *e*, this word is pronounced /day-nuu-mo$^{ng}$/.

## depilatory

Stress on the second syllable, which rhymes with *pill*.

## depot

In British English, always /de-poh/.
/dee-poh/ only in American English.

## deprivation

Pronounced /de-pri-/ or, less commonly, /dee-priy-/.

## desideratum

Pronounced /di-zid-*e*-rah-*tum*/ or, less commonly, /-ray-*tum*/.
The *s* may also be /s/.

## desperado

Ends in /-rah-doh/.

## despicable

May be stressed on either the first or the second syllable.

## desuetude

Stress on either the first syllable (/**des**-wi-tyuud/) or, less commonly, on the second (/di-**syuu**-i-tyuud/).

## desultory

Stress on the first syllable.
The *s* usually pronounced /s/, but /z/ also correct.

## detente

Pronounced /day-to$^{ng}$t/ or /day-tont/.

## deteriorate

Take care to pronounce all five syllables of this word: *de-te-ri-o-rate*.

## detour

Stress on the first syllable.

## detritus

Pronounced /di-triy-*tus*/.

## deus ex machina

Pronounced /**dee**-*us* eks *ma*-**shee**-*na*/ or /**day**-*us* eks ma-ki-*na*/.

## devolution

The first syllable is pronounced /dee-/ or, less commonly, /de-/.

## diagnose

May be stressed on the first or the last syllable.

## dichotomy

The first syllable may be pronounced /diy-/ or /di-/.

## dilatory

Pronounced /di-*la-to*-ri/.

**dilemma**
Pronounced /di-le-*ma*/ or /diy-le-*ma*/.

**dinghy**
Pronounced /**ding**-i/ or /**ding**-gi/.

**diphtheria, diphthong**
Pronounce the *ph* as /f/.
✗ Pronouncing the *ph* as /p/ is not correct.

**direct**
The first vowel may equally correctly be pronounced as in *die* or as in *did*.

**disastrous**
This word has only three syllables: *di-sas-trous*.
✗ Do not pronounce it as if it was spelt *disasterous*.

**disciplinary**
May be stressed on the first or the third syllable.

**disparate**
Stress on the first syllable.

**disputable**
Stress on the second syllable.

**dispute**
As a verb, stressed on the second syllable. As a noun, stressed on the first or the second syllable.

**dissect**
Pronounced /di-**sekt**/ or /diy-**sekt**/.

**distribute**
Usually stressed on the second syllable. Stress on the first syllable is less common, and deprecated by some authorities.

**divers**
Stressed on the first syllable: /**diy**-*verz*/.

**diverse**
Usually stressed on the second syllable: /diy-**vers**/.
Stress on the first syllable is also correct.

**doctrinal**
Stress on the second syllable: /dok-**triy**-*nal*/.

**dogged**
As an adjective, this word has two syllables.

**dolce far niente**
Pronounced /dol-chi fahr nee-en-ti/.
Similarly, **la dolce vita** is pronounced /lah **dol**-chi vee-*ta*/.

**doldrums**
The *o* may be pronounced /o/ or /oh/.

**dolour**
Pronounced the same as *dollar*.

**domicile**
The final syllable may rhyme with *tile* or *till*.

**double entendre**
Pronounced /duu-*bel* o<sup>ng</sup>-to<sup>ng</sup>-*druh*/ or /duu-*bel* on-ton-*druh*/.
✗ Do not pronounce **double** as /du-*bel*/ as if it was the English word *double*.

**dour**
Originally from Scots, this word rhymes with *poor*.
✗ Do not rhyme it with *dower*.

**doyen**
Pronounced /**doy**-*en*/ or /dwa-ya<sup>ng</sup>/.

**drachm**
The *ch* is silent: say /dram/.

**dreamed**
Pronounced /dreemd/ or /dremt/. /drempt/ is also correct.

**droll**
This word rhymes with *roll*.

**drought**
Pronounced /drowt/.
✗ Not /drowth/.

**dynasty**
In British English, pronounced with a short /i/ in the first syllable. /diy-*nas*-ti/ is correct only in American English.
Similarly with **dynastic**.

**Dynast** may be either /di-*nast*/ or /diy-nast/ in British English, the latter being the only acceptable pronunciation in American English.

**Dalyell**
Also *Dalzell* and *Dalziel*.
In Scotland, pronounced /di-el/ (for the pronunciation of the *z*, see the note at MENZIES).
Elsewhere, may be pronounced /dal-/.

**Darius**
As the name of the ancient Persian king, pronounced /*da*-riy-*us*/.

**Derby**
Pronounced /dahr-bi/.

**Des Moines**
Pronounced /*de* moyn/.

**Dionysus**
Pronounced /diy-*o*-niy-*sus*/.

**Domesday**
Pronounced like, and sometimes written as, *Doomsday*.

**Don Juan**
Pronounced /don juu-*an*/ or /don hwahn/.

**Don Quixote**
Pronounced /don kwik-*sot*/ or /don ki-hoh-ti/.

**Dordogne**
In English, pronounced /dawr-doyn/.
In French /dor-dony/.

**Dulwich**
Pronounced /dul-ij/.

**Dunfermline**
Stressed in the second syllable, and rhymes with *bin*.

**Dyfed**
Pronounced /duv-id/.

---

**ebullient**
The second syllable may rhyme with *dull* or *full*.

**echelon**
Pronounced /e-*she*-lon/.

**economic**
Either /ee/ or /e/ in the first syllable.

**ecumenical**
Either /ee/ or /e/ in the first syllable.

**efficacy**
Stressed on the first syllable.

**ego**
The first syllable may equally correctly be pronounced as in *eagle* or as in *egg*.
The same is true for *egocentric*, *egoism* and *egotism*.

**egregious**
Pronounced /i-gree-*jus*/.

**eisteddfod**
Pronounced /iy-sted-*fod*/ or, a little closer to the Welsh pronunciation, /iy-stedh-vod/.

**elegiac**
Pronounced /e-*le*-jiy-ak/.

**elicit**
Usually pronounced /i-li-sit/.
/ee-li-sit/ and /e-li-sit/ are also correct.

**elite**
The first syllable may be /i/, /ay/ or /e/.

**elixir**
Stress on the middle syllable.
The final syllable may be pronounced /-*seer*/ or /-*sir*/.

**emend**
Pronounced /i-mend/ or /ee-mend/.
✗ Not /e-mend/ which would lead to possible confusion with *amend*.

**encephalitis**
The *c* may be pronounced /s/ or /k/.
Similarly in most other medical words beginning with *enceph-*.

**enclave**
Pronounced /en-klayv/.
✗ Not /o$^{ng}$-klayv/.

**encyclical**
The syllable -*cyc*- rhymes with *sick*.
✗ Not as in *cycle*.

**enervate**
Pronounced /e-*ner*-vayt/.

## ennui

Pronounced /o^ng-nwee/ or /on-wee/.

## enquire

Usually pronounced /in-kwiyr/.
Those who make a distinction in meaning between **enquiring** and **inquiring** would be better to make a distinction in pronunciation also, and pronounce this word as /en-kwiyr/.
Similarly with **enquiry**.

## entirety

Pronounced as four syllables.

## entourage

Stress on the first syllable, pronounced /on-/ or /o^ng-/.
The final syllable is pronounced /-rahzh/.

## envelope

/en-*ve*-lohp/ is the best pronunciation.
/on-*ve*-lohp/ and /o^ng-*ve*-lohp/ are also correct.

## epee

Pronounced /ay-pay/ or /e-pay/.

## ephemeral

Second syllable pronounced /-fee-/ or /-fe-/.

## epicurean

The preferred pronunciation is /e-pi-kyoo-ree-*an*/.
Stress on the third syllable is also common although deprecated by some authorities.

## epitome

This word has four syllables and is stressed on the second: /i-pi-*to*-mi/.

## epoch

Usually pronounced /ee-pok/.
Those who pronounce the *ch* of *loch* as /kh/ may say /ee-pokh/.

## equerry

The older pronunciation of this word, still preferred by many people, is with the stress on the second syllable.
Stress on the first syllable is now probably more common.

## equitable

Stress on the first syllable.

## ersatz

Usually /er-zats/ or /uhr-zats/.
Stress on the second syllable also correct, as is the pronunciation of *s* as /s/.

## esoteric

The first syllable is pronounced /e/ or /ee/.

## espionage

Usually pronounced /es-pi-*on*-ahzh/.

## et alii

Pronounced /et ay-li-iy/ or /et a-li-ee/.
Often abbreviated **et al**, pronounced /et al/.

## et cetera

✗ Be careful not to pronounce the *t* of **et** as if it was a *k*.

## evocation

Pronounced /ee-voh-**kay**-*shon*/ or /e-voh-**kay**-*shon*/.

## evolution

Pronounced /ee-voh-**luu**-*shon*/ or /e-voh-**luu**-*shon*/.
Also /-**lyuu**-*shon*/.

## exacerbate

Stress is on the second syllable.
The *x* may be pronounced /gz/ or /ks/.

## execrable

Stress on the first syllable.

## ex gratia

Usually /eks **gray**-*sha*/.
/eks **grah**-ti-*a*/ is also correct.

## exigency

Stress on the first or second syllable.

## ex officio

Usually /eks *oh*-fish-i-oh/ or /-fik-i-oh/.

## expatiate

The second vowel is pronounced as in *pay*.

## expiatory

Stress on the first syllable, with the vowel in the third syllable pronounced /ay/ or /a/, or stress on the third syllable, pronounced /ay/.

**explicable**

Usually stressed on the second syllable. Stress on the first syllable is also correct.

**exquisite**

Usually stressed on the second syllable. Stress on the first syllable is also correct.

**extraordinary**

It is quite correct not to pronounce the first *a*.

**eyrie**

Pronounced /eer-i/, /ayr-i/ or /iyr-i/.

---

**Ecce Homo**

Pronounced /e-ki hoh-moh/. Also /ek-si/ or /e-chi/, and /ho-moh/.

**Edwardian**

/ed-**wawr**-di-*an*/ or, less commonly, /ed-**wahr**-di-*an*/.

**Evelyn**

As a man's name, pronounced /**eev**-lin/; as a woman's name, /**eev**-lin/, /**ev**-lin/ or /**ev**-*e*-lin/.

---

**fait accompli**

Usually /fayt *a*-kom-plee/.

Stress on *-pli* is also correct, as is the use of vowels closer to the original French pronunciation, /fet a-ko$^{ng}$-plee/.

✗ Do not pronounce the *o* as /u/, as in *accomplish*.

***Faits accomplis*** is usually pronounced the same as the singular. It is also correct to pronounce the final *s* of ***accomplis*** as in a normal English plural, and to pronounce the *s* of *faits*.

Acceptable pronunciations closer to the original French are /fayz a-kom-plee/ and /fez a-kom-**plee**/.

**fakir**

Pronounced /**fay**-keer/, /**fah**-keer/ or /*fa*-**keer**/.

**falcon**

/**fawl**-*kon*/, /**fol**-*kon*/ and /**faw**-*kon*/ are all correct.

/**fal**-*kon*/ is also correct in some British accents.

**farrago**

The second syllable may be /-rah-/ or, less commonly, /-ray-/.

**fascia**

In most senses, this word is pronounced /**fay**-shi-*a*/.

As a term in biology and medicine, /**fa**-shi-*a*/.

**faute de mieux**

Pronounced /foht *de* myuh/.

**faux pas**

Pronounced /foh pah/.

The final *s* is pronounced in the plural.

**febrile**

Pronounced /**fee**-briyl/ or /fe-/.

**fecund**

The vowel of the first syllable may equally correctly be pronounced as in *seek* and in *second*.

**femme fatale**

Pronounce this (more or less) as in French: /fam *fa*-**tahl**/.

**femur**

Pronounced /**fee**-*mur*/.

The plural ***femora*** is pronounced /**fe**-mo-ra/.

**fetid, foetid**

The first vowel in this word may be pronounced /ee/ or /e/.

For the *oe* spelling, /ee/ is commoner.

**fiat**

Pronounced /**fee**-at/ or /**fiy**-at/.

**fifth**

Be sure to pronounce the second *f*.

**figurative**

Pronounced /**fig**-*u*-ra-tiv/ or /**fig**-*yoo*-ra-tiv/.

**figure**

Pronounced /**fig**-*ur*/ or /**fig**-*yoor*/.

**figurine**

Pronounced /**fig**-*u*-reen/ or /**fig**-*yoo*-reen/.

Stress also correct on the final syllable.

**filet mignon**

Pronounced /**fee**-lay meen-**yon**/ or /meen-**yo**$^{ng}$/.

**finance**
Pronounced /fiy-nans/, /fiy-nans/ or /fi-nans/.

**flaccid**
Pronounced /fla-sid/ or /flak-sid/.

**foetid** see FETID.

**forbade**
The second syllable may be pronounced /-bad/ or /-bayd/.

**forecastle**
Say /fohk-*sl*/.
✗ Do not give this word a 'spelling pronunciation' /fawr-kas-l/.

**forehead**
Pronounced /fo-rid/ or /fawr-hed/.

**formidable**
Stressed on the first or second syllable.

**forte**
Usually /fawr-ti/ in British English.
/fawrt/ is the normal pronunciation in American English.

**forthwith**
Usually /-with/.
/-widh/ is also correct.

**foyer**
Pronounced /foy-ay/ or /fwa-yay/.
✗ Not /foy-*er*/.

**fracas**
The *s* is silent in the singular: /fra-kah/.
The plural is /fra-kahz/.
The usual American English pronunciation is /fray-*kas*/ in the singular, with a plural *fracases* /fray-*ka-siz*/.

**fraulein**
Whether written **Fräulein**, the correct German form, or without the capital letter and the accent, as often in English, this is pronounced /froy-liyn/.
✗ Not /frow-liyn/.

**frequent**
As a verb, stressed on the second syllable.

**frontier**
Stressed on the first or, less frequently, on the second.
The **front-** part is usually pronounced like *front*, but /front-/ is also correct.

**fructose**
The *u* is usually pronounced as in *pluck*, but pronouncing it as in *fruition* is also correct.

**fuchsia**
Pronounced /fyuu-*sha*/.

**fulminate**
Pronounced /fool-mi-nayt/ or /ful-mi-nayt/.

**fulsome**
**Ful-** rhymes with *full*.

**fungi**
The *g* is a hard /g/ in **fungus**.
It may be either hard or soft (/j/) in **fungi** and **fungicide**.
**Fungi** may correctly rhyme with *eye* or *me*.

**furore**
This word has three syllables, and is stressed on the second: /fyoo-raw-ri/.

---

**Farquhar**
The *h* is silent.
The *qu* is usually pronounced /k/, but some pronounce it /kw/.

**February**
Pronunciations that omit the first *r* and the *a* are now correct, but the most accepted pronunciation pronounces both.

---

**gala**
Pronounced /gah-*la*/ or, less commonly, /gay-*la*/.

**gallant**
Usually stressed on the first syllable.
Stress on the second syllable is correct for the (now relatively rare) adjectival sense 'amorous' and noun sense 'lover'.

**garage**
/ga-rahzh/ , /ga-rahj/ or /ga-rij/ are the most common forms.

/*ga*-rahzh/ and /*ga*-rahj/ are also correct, but some people consider them rather affected.

**gaseous**
Pronounced /gas-i-*us*/, /gay-si-*us*/ and /gay-zi-*us*/.
✗ Not /gay-*shus*/.

**genera** see GENUS.

**genre**
Pronounced /zho<sup>ng</sup>-*ruh*/ or /zhon-*ruh*/.

**genuine**
Rhymes with *pin* in British English.
✗ Does not rhyme with *pine*.

**genus**
Pronounced /jee-*nus*/ or /je-*nus*/.
Plural /je-*ne-ra*/.

**geography, geometry**
✗ Do not slur the first part of these words: pronounce the **geo-** as two syllables.

**geyser**
As the name of a type of water heater, pronounced /gee-*zer*/.
In the sense of a gushing hot spring, /gee-*zer*/ or /giy-*zer*/.

**gibber, gibberish**
Pronounce the *g* with a soft /j/, not a hard /g/.

**glacial**
The first vowel has the sound of the *a* in *ace*.
The *c* is /sh/ or /s/.

**glacier**
Pronounced /glas-i-*er*/ or /glay-si-*er*/.

**glazier**
The first vowel must always be pronounced as the *a* in *ace*.
The *z* is equally correctly /zh/ or /z/.

**glycerine**
The last syllable rhymes with *seen* or *sin*.
If spelt without the final *e*, rhyme with *sin*.

**golf**
The only correct pronunciation nowadays is /golf/.
✗ /gof/, /gawlf/ and /gowf/ are all old-fashioned.

**gone**
This rhymes with *on*, not *pawn* (in accents in which these vowels are different).

**gooseberry**
In RP, the *s* is pronounced /z/.
In other accents of English, **goose-** may be pronounced like *goose*.

**gourmand**
Pronounced /goor-*mand*/ or /gawr-*mand*/.

**gourmandise**
Rhymes with *tease*.

**gourmet**
As with **gourmand**, the first syllable of this word is /goor-/ or /gawr-/.

**government**
It is quite acceptable to drop the *n* before the *m*.

**graph**
/ah/ is now commoner than /a/ in accents in which there is a choice between two *a* sounds.

**gratis**
Pronounced /grah-tis/, /gra-tis/ or, less commonly, /gray-tis/.

**greasy**
Equally correctly /grees-i/ or /greez-i/.

**grievous**
✗ This word does <u>not</u> rhyme with *devious* and *previous*. There is no *i* after the *v*.

**grimace**
Pronounced /gri-*mas*/ or /gri-mays/.

**grovel**
Pronounced /grov-*el*/ or /gruv-*el*/.

**guerrilla**
✗ Do not pronounce the *u*.

**gunwale**
This word rhymes with *funnel* and *tunnel*.
✗ Do not pronounce the *w*.

**gyro**
In this word, and all words beginning with **gyro-**, the *g* is a soft /j/.

**Gaelic**
Pronounced /gay-lik/ or /ga-lik/.
The second pronunciation is preferred by some because it is closer to the Gaelic pronunciation of *Gaidhlig*, but the first pronunciation is commoner in English.

**Giovanni**
Pronounced /joh-vah-ni/, or /jee-oh-/, or /-va-ni/.

**Glasgow**
Pronounced /glahz-goh/ or /glahs-goh/.

**Glenrothes**
Pronounced with three syllables: /glen-roth-is/.

**Gloucester**
Pronounced /glo-*ster*/.

**Golgotha**
Stress on the first syllable.

**Gollancz**
Pronounced /go-lants/, /gol-ants/ or /gol-angks/.

**Granada**
Pronounced /gra-nah-*da*/.

**Graves**
As the name of a French wine, pronounced /grahv/.

**Greenwich**
Pronounced /gren-ich/ or /gren-ij/.

**Grenada**
Pronounced /gre-nay-*da*/.

**Grosvenor**
The s is silent: say /grohv-*nor*/.

**Gruyere**
Pronounced /gruu-yer/.

**Gwynedd**
Pronounced /gwin-*edh*/.

---

**hagiography**
Usually pronounced /hag-i-/, but /haj-i-/ and /hayj-i-/ also correct.

**halcyon**
The first syllable rhymes with *pal*.
✗ Do not rhyme **hal-** with *hall*.

**hara-kiri**
Take care to say this as it is written: /ha-*ra*-keer-i/.
✗ Not /ha-ri-ka-ri/.

**harass, harassment**
In most accents, stressed always on the first syllable.
In some accents, a distinction in stress is made depending on the sense of the word. Compare *The soldiers 'harassed the enemy as they retreated* and *There are so many demands on my time at the moment, I feel completely ha'rassed*.

**harem**
Equally correct are /hah-reem/, /hah-reem/ and /hayr-*em*/.

**hectare**
Rhymes with *fair* or with *far*.

**hedonism**
The first syllable rhymes with *heed* or *head*.

**hegemony**
Best stressed on the second syllable, with either a hard or a soft *g*.
/he-ji-*mo*-ni/ is also correct.

**heinous**
The first syllable rhymes with either *hay* or *he*, but ✗ not with *high*.
✗ Note that there is no *i* between the *n* and the **-ous** ending.

**herculean**
May be stressed on either the second or the third syllable.

**heroin**
Three syllables. Rhymes with *heroine*, ✗ not with *join*.

**hiatus**
Pronounced /hiy-ay-*tus*/.

**homo-**
If stressed on the first syllable, /hoh-moh-/ is commoner than /ho-moh-/ but both are correct.
Similarly /hoh-mi-oh-/ and /ho-mi-oh-/ for **homoeo-**.

**homogenize**
Stress on the second syllable.

**honorarium**
The initial *h* is silent.
The word rhymes with *aquarium*.

**honorary**
The *h* is silent.

**hors d'oeuvre**
Pronounced /awr duhvr/.
⚠ Always pronounce the final *r*.

**hospitable**
Stress on the second syllable or, less commonly, on the first.

**hovel**
Pronounced /hov-*el*/ or, less commonly, /huv-*el*/.

**hover**
Pronounced /hov-*er*/ or, less commonly, /huv-*er*/.

---

**Harwich**
Pronounced /ha-rij/ or /-rich/.

**Hegira**
Pronounced /he-ji-*ra*/ or /hi-jiy-*ra*/.

**Herstmonceux**
Pronounced /herst-*mon*-syuu/ or /-suu/.

**Hertford**
Pronounced /hahrt-*ford*/
✗ /hahr-*ford*/ is old-fashioned.

**Himalayas**
Stressed on either the third syllable (/hi-*ma*-lay-*az*/) or the second (/hi-mah-li-*az*/).

**Hiroshima**
Usually stressed on the second syllable; may be stressed on the third.

**Holborn**
In the name of a part of London, the *l* is usually silent (/hoh-*burn*/), but may be pronounced (/hohl-*burn*/).

**Houston**
As the name of a city in Texas, pronounced /hyuu-*ston*/.
As a family name, /huu-*ston*/.

**Huguenot**
Rhymes with *know* or, less commonly, with *not*: say /hyuu-*ge*-noh/ or /hyuu-*ge*-not/.

---

**ideology**
Pronounced /iy-di-o-*lo*-ji/ or /i-di-o-*lo*-ji/.

**idyll**
Pronounced /i-dil/ or /iy-dil/.
Similarly with **idyllic**, stressed on the second syllable.

**ignominy**
Stress on the first syllable.

**illustrative**
Stress on the first syllable.
Third syllable pronounced /-stray-/ or, with a weak vowel, /-*stra*-/.

**imbroglio**
The *g* is silent: say /im-broh-li-oh/.

**impasse**
Pronounced /im-pas/, /am-pas/, /om-pas/, or, closer to the original French, /a$^{ng}$-pas/.

**impious**
Usually /im-pi-*us*/.

✓ Also /im-piy-*us*/, sometimes criticized, but correct.

**importune**
Stress on the second or the final syllable.

**impotent**
Stress on the first syllable.

**imprimatur**
Pronounced /im-pri-**may**-*tur*/ or /im-pri-mah-*tur*/.

**improvisation**
The third syllable may be pronounced /-viy-/ or, less commonly, /-vi-/.

**impugn**
The *g* is silent: say /im-pyuun/.

**inchoate**
The *ch* is pronounced /k/.
Stress usually on the second syllable, but first-syllable stress also correct.

Final syllable may be pronounced /-ayt/ or /-at/.

**incommunicado**
Ends in /-kah-doh/.

**incomparable**
Stress on the second syllable.

**indefatigable**
Stress on the third syllable.

**indict**
Pronounced as if spelt *indite*.

**indisputable**
Stress on the third syllable.

**inexorable**
Stress on the second syllable.

**inexplicable**
Usually stressed on the third syllable; second-syllable stress is also correct.

**infamous**
Stress on the first syllable.

**infinite**
The final syllable always rhymes with *it* in normal speech.
Only in singing, eg hymns, should it be pronounced rhyming with *white*.

**inherent**
Stress on the second syllable.
Second syllable usually pronounced like *here*; also correctly pronounced /-he-/.

**inhospitable**
Stress usually on the third syllable.
Stress on the second syllable is also correct.

**innovative**
Pronounced /in-*oh*-vay-tiv/ or /in-oh-vay-tiv/, or /-*va*-tiv/.

**inquiry**
Make the second syllable the same as in *inquire*.
/ing-kwi-ri/ is an American pronunciation.

**insouciance**
Pronounced /in-suu-si-*ans*/ or a more French-sounding /a$^{ng}$-suu-si-o$^{ng}$s/.

**intaglio**
Pronounced /in-tah-li-oh/ or /in-ta-li-oh/.

**integer**
Stress on the first syllable.
The *g* is a soft /j/, not a hard /g/.

**integral**
Stress usually on the first syllable; second-syllable stress also correct.
✗ Not / in-tri-*gal*/.

**interdict**
Pronounced as it is spelt: /in-*ter*-dikt/ (Compare INDICT.)

**internecine**
Pronounced /in-*ter*-nee-siyn/.

**interpolate**
Stress on the second syllable.

**interstice**
Stress on the second syllable.
Ends in /-is/, not /-iys/

**intestinal**
Usually /in-tes-ti-*nal*/.
/in-tes-tiy-*nal*/ is also correct.

**in toto**
Pronounced /in toh-toh/.

**intricacy**
Stress on the first syllable.

**inveigh**
Rhymes with *way*.

**inveigle**
The *ei* may be pronounced to rhyme with the vowel of *bee* or *bay*.

**inventory**
Stress on the first syllable.

**involve**
Pronounced /in-volv/ or, mainly in the south of England, /in-vohlv/.

**iodine**
The last syllable may correctly be pronounced like *dean*, *dine* or *din*.

**irascible**
Pronounce the *i* as in *it*, not as in *ire*.

**irrefragable**
Stress on the second syllable.

**irrefutable**
Stress on the third syllable or, less commonly, on the second.

**irreparable**
Stress on the second syllable.
✗ Not as in *repair*.

**irrevocable**
Stress on the second syllable.
✗ Not as in *revoke*.

**issue**
Pronounced /i-shuu/ or /i-syuu/.

**isthmus**
The *th* is usually silent, but may correctly be pronounced.

---

**Ibiza**
Pronounced /i-bee-*tha*/.

**Iran**
In British English, /i-rahn/ or /i-ran/.

/iy-ran/ acceptable only in American English.

**Islay**
/iy-*la*/ is preferable to /iy-lay/.

---

**jejune**
Pronounced /ji-juun/.

**jewellery**
Pronounced with only three syllables. Usually the third *e* is not sounded (/juu-*el*-ri/).
A pronunciation in which the second *e* is dropped (/juu-*le*-ri/) is also widely accepted.

**jojoba**
Pronounced /hoh-hoh-*ba*/.

**jubilee**
Stress on the first syllable.

**junta**
Pronounced exactly as it looks: say /jun-ta/.
✗ There is no need to try to make the word sound Spanish.

---

**Jain**
Pronounced /jiyn/.

**January**
Equally correctly pronounced /jan-yoo-*a*-ri/ or /jan-yoo-ri/.

---

**karaoke**
Although the spelling suggests otherwise, pronounced /ka-ri-oh-ki/.

**kilometre**
Pronounced /kil-*o*-mee-*ter*/ or /ki-lom-i-ter/.

**kinetic**
First syllable pronounced as in *kin* or as in *kind*.

**knoll**
This has the same vowel-sound as *know*.

**kudos**
Pronounced /kyuu-dos/.

---

**Kabul**
Usually /kah-bool/.
/kaw-bool/ and /*ka*-bool/ are also correct.

**Kenya**
Formerly /keen-*ya*/; now usually /ken-*ya*/.

**Keswick**
The *w* is silent.
Pronounced /kez-ik/.

**Keynes**
As the name of the economist, /kaynz/.
In *Milton Keynes*, pronounced /keenz/.

**Kirkcaldy**
The *l* is silent: say /*kir*-kaw-di/

**Kirkcudbright**
Pronounced /*kir*-kuu-bri/.

---

## laboratory
Stress on the second syllable.
Correctly pronounced with five syllables or with four (dropping the second *o*).

## lamentable
Stress on the first syllable

## languor
Pronounced /lang-*gor*/.

## largesse
Stress on either the first or the second syllable.
The *g* may be pronounced /j/ or /zh/.

## larynx
First syllable is /la-/.
✗ Not /lay-ringks/.

## lasso
Pronounced /*la*-suu/.

## lather
Usually /lah-*dher*/ in the south of England.
/la-*dher*/ is also acceptable.

## leaned
Usually /leend/; /lent/ is also correct.

## leaped
Usually /leept/; /lept/ also correct.

## learned
As an adjective (*a learned professor*), pronounced as two syllables.
As the past tense or past participle of *learn*, one syllable, /lernd/ or /lernt/.

## leeward
Generally /lee-*ward*/.
In nautical circles usually /loo-*ard*/ or /lyoo-*ard*/.

## leisure
Rhymes with *pleasure* in British English.
The first syllable has an /ee/ sound in American English.

## length
Usually /length/ or /lengkth/.
In some educated British accents, /lenth/ is also correct.

## liaison
Stress on the second syllable.
The final syllable is equally correctly /-*zon*/ or /-*zo*ng/.

✗ Do not pronounce the first vowel as in *lie*.

## library
✓ It is not wrong to drop the first *r*, but you may be criticized for doing so.

## lichen
Pronounced /liy-*ken*/ or /lich-*en*/.

## lien
Pronounced /lee-*en*/ or /leen/.

## lieu
Pronounced /luu/ or /lyuu/.

## liqueur
Pronounced with stress on the second syllable: /li-*kyoor*/.
✗ Do not confuse with **liquor**, pronounced /lik-*or*/.

## liquorice
Usually ends in /-ris/, but /-rish/ also correct.

**litchi** see LYCHEE.

## long-lived
*-lived* pronounced as in *to give*, not as in *alive*.

## longevity
Pronounce the *ng* as in *sponge*: say /lon-je-vi-ti/.

## longitude
Pronounce the *ng* as in *longer* or as in *sponge*.
⚠ Note that there is no *t* after the *g*.

## lough
This is the Irish equivalent of Scottish *loch*; pronounced as *loch*.

## lugubrious
Stress on the second syllable, which may be /-guu-/ or /-gyuu-/.

## luxury
The *x* is pronounced /ks/.
Pronounced /gz/ in **luxuriant** and **luxurious**.

## lychee
Pronounced /liy-chee/ or /liy-chee/ or, the usual pronunciation for the spelling **litchi**, /li-chee/.

---

**Lesotho**
Pronounced /*le*-suu-tuu/.

**Liebfraumilch**
Pronounced /leeb-frow-milk/ or /leeb-frow-milkh/.

**Llan-**
Acceptable pronunciations of the

Welsh *ll* in English are /l/ and /thl/, as in **Llandudno** (/lan-did-noh/ or /thlan-did-noh/), **Llanelli** (/(th)la-neth-li/), and **Llangollen** (/(th)lan-goth-*len*/).

**Lympne**
Pronounced /lim/.

---

**macabre**
The *r* may be pronounced or omitted.

**machete**
The *ch* is pronounced /sh/.
Rhymes with *petty*.

**machination**
The *ch* may be pronounced as in *machine* or as in *technical*.

**macho, machismo**
Pronounced /mach-oh/ and /*ma*-chiz-moh/.
✓ *Machismo* may also correctly be pronounced /*ma*-kiz-moh/.

**macrame**
Stress on the second syllable.

**madame**
May be pronounced the same as *madam* or with the stress on the second syllable, /*ma*-dahm/.
See also MESDAMES.

**magazine**
Usually stressed on the third syllable; first-syllable stress is also correct.

**maladroit**
The final syllable is pronounced /-droyt/.
✗ Not /-drwah/.

**malinger**
Rhymes with *finger*.

**mall**
Rhymes with *ball*, except in the names of certain London streets (see PALL MALL).

**mamma, mama**
With two *m*'s in the middle, stressed on the second syllable.
With one *m* in the middle, stressed on either syllable.

**mandatory**
Stress usually on the first syllable.
✓ Second-syllable stress (-**day**-) is now becoming accepted.

**maniacal**
Pronounced /*ma*-niy-*a*-kal/.

**manifold**
Although derived from *many*, the first part of this word is pronounced /**ma**-ni-/.

**margarine**
The *g* may be either a hard /g/ or soft /j/. Stress is usually on the last syllable; first-syllable stress is also correct.

**marinade**
Rhymes with *lemonade*.

**massage**
Stress on the first syllable.
The *g* is pronounced /j/ or /zh/.

**matriarch**
Pronounced /may-tri-ahrk/.

**matrix**
Pronounced /may-triks/

**mausoleum**
Stress on the third syllable.
The *s* is pronounced /s/ or /z/.

**mauve**
Rhymes with *rove*.

**maybe**
Pronounced /may-bee/.
✗ /mi-bi/ acceptable only in informal speech.

**medicament**
Stress on either the first or the second syllable.

**medicine**
Correct with either two or three syllables.

**mélange**
Pronounced /may-lo^{ng}zh/ or /may-lahnzh/.

**mêlée**
Pronounced /me-lay/ or /me-lay/.
✗ Never rhyming with *lea*.

**mesdames**
Stress on the second syllable: /may-dahm/.

**metallurgy**
In British English, usually stressed on the second syllable.
Stress on the first syllable, the usual American pronunciation, also correct.

**metamorphosis**
Equally correctly stressed on **-mor-** or **-pho-**.

**metastasis**
Stress on the second syllable.

**métier**
Pronounced /may-ti-ay/ or /me-ti-ay/.

**mezzanine**
Rhymes with *keen*.
✗ Never rhymes with *nine*.
The *zz* is pronounced /z/ or /ts/.

**midwifery**
Stress on **mid-** or on **-wif-**.
**-wif-** rhymes with *cliff*, ✗ not with *wife*.

**mien**
Pronounced as *mean*.

**migraine**
Pronounced /mee-grayn/ or, less commonly, /miy-grayn/.

**migratory**
Stress on the first syllable (/miy-*gra-to*-ri/), or less commonly, on the second (/miy-**gray**-*to*-ri/).

**milieu**
*Mi-* rhymes with *sea*.

Stress usually on the first syllable, but also correctly on the second.

**minutiae**
Pronounced /miy-nyuu-shi-ee/ or /mi-nyuu-shi-ee/.
/-shi-iy/ is also correct.

**miscellany**
Stress on the second syllable.

**mischievous**
✗ Note that there is no *i* after the *v*. This word does not rhyme with *devious*.

**mnemonic**
The first *m* is silent.

**mocha**
The *ch* is pronounced /k/.
The *o* may be as in *no* or as in *not*.

**momentary**
Stress on the first syllable, as also usually in **momentarily**.
✓ **Momentarily** also correctly stressed on **-tar-**, although this pronunciation is often criticized.

**monetary**
**mon-** pronounced /mun-/, as in *money*, or /mon-/.

**moussaka**
Pronounced /moo-sah-*ka*/.

**mullah**
The first syllable rhymes with either *dull* or *full*.

**municipal**
Stress on the second syllable.

**mutatis mutandis**
Usually /myoo-tah-tees myoo-tahn-dees/.
First syllable of each word also /moo-/; final syllable also /-dis/.
✗ Not /myoo-tay-tees/.

---

**Magdalen, Magdalene**
As the names of, respectively, an Oxford and a Cambridge college, pronounced /mawd-lin/.

**Mainwaring**
Pronounced /man-*e*-ring/ or /mayn-wayr-ing/.

**Majorca**
The *j* is pronounced /y/ or/j/.

**Marseilles**
Pronounced (more or less) as in French: /mahr-say/.

**Marylebone**
Pronounced /ma-ri-li-*bon*/ or /mar-li-*bon*/.

**Menzies**
In Scotland, the traditional pronunciation /ming-iz/ is still used for the family name.
The English pronunciation /men-ziz/ is now generally used throughout Britain for the name of the chain of bookshops and stationers.
(In this and some other words and names of Scottish origin, the letter now written *z* was not originally a *z* at all but a different letter altogether used in older Scots to represent a /y/ sound, hence the pronunciation — see, for example, CAPERCAILZIE and CULZEAN. Scots who object to the non-Scottish pronunciation of *Menzies* should note that the same change in pronunciation under the influence of the spelling has already

taken place in the clan name *Mac-Kenzie* and in place-names such as *Cockenzie* and *Lenzie*.)

**Michigan**
The *ch* is pronounced /sh/; ✗ not /ch/.

**Milngavie**
Pronounced /mil-giy/ or /mul-giy/.

**Mobile**
As the name of the US town, pronounced /moh-**beel**/.

**Mojave**
Pronounced /*moh*-hah-vi/.

**Moscow**
In British English, /mos-koh/. /-kow/ only in American English.

**Mozzarella**
Pronounced /mo-*tsa*-re-*la*/.

**Munich**
Pronounced /**myuu**-nik/ or /-nikh/.

**Muscadet**
Pronounced /mus-*ka*-day/.

**Muslim**
Pronounced /**mooz**-lim/ or /muz-lim/.

---

**nadir**
Pronounced /nay-deer/ or /na-deer/.
✗ Not /-der/.

**naive**
Pronounced /niy-eev/ or /nah-eev/.
*Naivety* is pronounced with three syllables (*na-ive-ty*) or four (*na-iv-e-ty*).

**naphtha**
Pronounced /naf-*tha*/ or /nap-*tha*/.

**necessarily**
In formal speech, best pronounced with the main stress on the first syllable.
✓ Also correctly stressed on *-sar-*, although this pronunciation is often criticized.

**nephew**
The *ph* may be pronounced /f/ or /v/.

**nicety**
Pronounce with three syllables.

**niche**
Usually pronounced /neesh/.
/nich/ is also correct.

**nihil obstat**
Pronounced /niy-hil ob-stat/ or /ni-hil/.

**nisi**
As in *decree nisi*, pronounced /niy-siy/.

**noblesse oblige**
Pronounced /noh-**bles** oh-bleezh/.

**nom de plume**
Pronounced /nom *de* pluum/.
Also /noh$^{ng}$/ as in French.
Also correctly with stress on *plume*.
Plural *noms de plume* pronounced as the singular. ✗ 'Nom de plumes' is acceptable only in informal English.

**nomenclature**
Stress on the second syllable.

**nonchalance**
The *ch* is pronounced /sh/ as in French. The vowels are fully anglicized: /non-*sha-lans*/.

**nougat**
Pronounced /nuu-gah/ or /nug-*et*/.

**nuance**
Pronounced /nyuu-ons/, /nyuu-ahns/, /nyuu-o^{ng}s/ or /nyuu-*ons*/.

**nuclear**
Pronounced /nyuu-*kli-ar*/.
✗ Not /nyuu-*kyoo-lar*/.

---

**Neanderthal**
Pronounced /ni-an-*der*-tahl/.

**Nestlé**
Pronounced /ne-*sel*/ or /nes-lay/.

**Newcastle**
Stress on the first syllable is standard.
Often stressed on the second syllable by speakers from the area around Newcastle.

**Newfoundland**
As the name of a Canadian province, pronounced /nyuu-*fun*-land/ or /nyoo-**fownd**-*land*/. Usually /nyoo-**fownd**-*land*/ for the breed of dog.

**Norwich**
Pronounced /no-rij/ or /no-rich/.

---

**obdurate**
Stressed on the first syllable.

**obeisance**
Pronounce as three syllables: **o-bei-sance**.
**o-bei-** is pronounced like *obey*.

**obligatory**
Stress on the second syllable.
✗ Do not stress on the third syllable.

**obscenity**
The second syllable rhymes with *men*.

**occult**
Stressed on either the first or the second syllable.

**octavo**
Pronounced /ok-*tay*-voh/.

**off**
Pronounced /of/.
✗ /awf/ is old-fashioned.

**often**
Pronounced /of-/.
✗ /awf-/ is old-fashioned.

The *t* is usually silent, but it is not wrong to pronounce it.

**ominous**
*o* as in *dominate*; ✗ not as in *omen*.

**onerous**
The first vowel is pronounced as in *own* or *on*.

**ophthalmic**
Pronounced /of-thal-mik/ or /op-thal-mik/.

**opus**
Pronounced /oh-*pus*/.

**oral** see AURAL.

**oregano**
Stress on the third syllable.

**otiose**
The *t* may be pronounced /t/ or /sh/: /oh-ti-ohs/ or /oh-shi-ohs/, or /-ohz/.

**overt**
Stress on the first or the second syllable.

---

**Odysseus**
Pronounced /oh-**dis**-yoos/ or /oh-dis-i-*us*/.

**Oedipus**
Pronounced /ee-di-*pus*/.

---

## p

In formal contexts say *penny* or *pence*.
/pee/ is informal.

## pace

Pronounced /pah-chay/ or /pay-see/.

## paella

Pronounce the *ll* as /*l*/.
✗ Not /-el-*ya*/.

## pampas

Strictly speaking, this is the plural of
*pampa*, therefore /pam-*paz*/.
Often treated as a singular, and
pronounced /pam-*pas*/.

## panegyric

Stressed on the third syllable: /pa-*ne*-ji-
rik/.
✗ Not /-jiy-rik/.

## papa

Usually stressed on the second syllable.

## paprika

Stress on the first or the second syllable.

## paracetamol

The third syllable rhymes with *seat* or *set*.

## paradigm

The *g* is silent: say /pa-*ra*-diym/.
In *paradigmatic*, the *g* is pronounced:
say /pa-*ra*-dig-ma-tik/.

## par excellence

Pronounced /pahr ek-*se*-lo$^{ng}$s/, approximately as in French.

## pariah

Pronounced /*pa*-riy-a/ or, less commonly, /pa-ri-*a*/.

## parliament

Generally pronounced /pahr-*la*-ment/,
but /pahr-li-*a*-ment/ is also correct.

## parsimony

Stress on the first syllable.

## participle

Usually stressed on the first syllable, and
pronounced with four syllables (*par-ti-
ci-ple*).
✓ Stress on the second syllable is also
acceptable.

## particularly

This word should be pronounced with
five syllables: *par-ti-cu-lar-ly*.

✗ Do not lose the *-cu-* or the *-lar-* in
speech.

## partisan

Stress on the first or third syllable.

## pasty

As a noun (eg *a Cornish pasty*),
pronounced /pas-ti/ or /pahs-ti/.
As an adjective, pronounced /pay-sti/.

## pâté

Stressed on the first syllable.

## patent

Usually /pay-tent/.
In some technical senses (eg the patent
on a new product) sometimes /pa-*tent*/.

## pathos

Pronounced /pay-thos/.

## patrial

Pronounced /pay-tri-*al*/ or /pa-tri-*al*/.

## patriarch

Pronounced /pay-tri-ahrk/.

## patriot, patriotic

Either /pay-/ or /pa-/.

## patron

Begins with /pay-/, as does *patroness*.
*Patronage* begins with /pa-/. *Patro-
nize* may be pronounced with /pa-/ or
/pay-/.

## pejorative

Stress is usually on the second syllable
nowadays: /pi-jo-*ra*-tiv/.
✓ First-syllable stress, although now
rare, is still correct: /pee-*jo*-ra-tiv/.

## penchant

Pronounced /po$^{ng}$-sho$^{ng}$/, more or less as
in French.

## peremptory

Stress on the second or, less commonly,
the first syllable.

## perhaps

In formal speech, always two syllables.
/praps/ is acceptable only in informal
speech.

## periphrasis

Stress on the second syllable.

**per se**
Usually /per say/.
/per see/ is also correct.

**pharmaceutical**
Stress on the third syllable, which is
pronounced /-syuu-/ or /-suu-/.

**pharynx**
Pronounced /fa-ringks/.

**philharmonic**
The *h* after the *l* may be pronounced or
omitted.

**phlegm**
The *g* is silent in **phlegm**, but pronounced in **phlegmatic**.

**phthisis**
Pronounced /thiy-sis/, /fthiy-sis/ or /tiy-
sis/.

**physiognomy**
Stress on the third syllable.
The *g* is usually silent /fi-zi-o-*no*-mi/), but
it is not incorrect to pronounce it (/fi-zi-
og-*no*-mi/).

**piano**
Pronounce the *a* as /a/.
✗ /ah/ is old-fashioned.
*Pianist* is best said as three syllables
(**pi-an-ist**) and stressed on the first syllable.

**piazza**
The double *z* may be pronounced /ts/ or
/dz/.
✗ Not /z/ in British English, although
this is correct in American English.

**picture**
The *c* should be clearly pronounced.
✗ Not *pitcher*.

**pièce de résistance**
Pronounce /pee-es *de* ray-**zee**-sto^ng s/ or
/ray-zee-sto^ng s/.
✗ Not /ri-**zis**-*tans*/.

**piña colada**
Pronounced /pee-*na ko*-lah-*da*/ or, more
like Spanish, /pee-*nya*/.

**piquant**
Pronounced /pee-*kant*/ or /-kahnt/.
✗ Not /-ko^ng /.

**piracy**
First vowel usually as in *pirate*.
/pi-*ra*-si/ also correct.

**pistachio**
The *ch* is pronounced /sh/.

**placebo**
Stress on the second syllable, which
rhymes with *sea*.

**plaid**
In most British and American accents,
pronounced /plad/.
In Scotland, /playd/.

**plait**
Usually pronounced /plat/.
In some accents, /playt/.

**plastic**
/pla-stik/ or, much less commonly, /plah-
stik/.
Some people find the latter pronunciation rather affected.

**plebeian**
Stress on the second syllable, which
rhymes with *sea*.

**plebiscite**
Rhymes with *bite* or *bit*.

**plethora**
Stress on the first syllable.

**pogrom**
Stress on the first syllable.

**poignant**
Pronounced /**poy**-*nyant*/ or /**poy**-*nant*/.

**polemic**
Pronounced /*poh*-lem-ik/.
✗ Not /-leem-/.

**poltergeist**
The *o* is pronounced /oh/ or /o/.
The *g* is a hard /g/.

**pomegranate**
Usually pronounced with four syllables,
but the older pronunciation with three
syllables (/pom-gra-nit/) is still correct.

**pommel**
Pronounced /pum-*el*/ or /pom-*el*/.

**porpoise**
Pronounced /pawr-*pus*/ in most accents
of British English.

Scots pronounce the second syllable /-poyz/.
Compare TORTOISE.

## portentous
Ends in /-tus/.
✗ Not -tious.

## poste restante
Pronounced /pohst re-sto<sup>ng</sup>t/ or /re-stont/.

## posthumous
The *h* is silent.
The first *o* is pronounced as in *not*;
✗ not as in *no*.

## postpone
It is equally correct to pronounce the *t* or to drop it.

## pot-pourri
Pronounced /poh-**poor**-i/ or /poh-poo-ree/.

## precedence
Stress usually on the first syllable rather than on the second, but both are correct. When stressed, the first vowel may be pronounced as in *press* or as in *priest*.

## precedent
As a noun, stressed on the first syllable, with the same options for the first vowel as ***precedence***.
As an adjective, usually stressed on the second syllable.
***Unprecedented*** has the <u>noun</u> *precedent* as its core, and is therefore stressed on ***-pre-***.

## predilection
Pronounced /pree-di-lek-*shon*/
✗ Not /-lik-/.

## preferable
Stressed on the first syllable.

## premature
Stress on either the first or the last syllable.
The first syllable is pronounced /prem-/ or, less commonly, /preem-/.
The final syllable is pronounced /-tyoor/ or /-choor/.

## premier
Usually /prem-i-*er*/.
✓ /preem-i-*er*/ is also correct, although deprecated by some.

## presage
As a noun, pronounced /pre-sij/.
As a verb, /pre-sij/ or /pree-**sayj**/.

## prescience
✗ Does not rhyme with *science*.
Stressed on the first syllable; pronounced /pre-si-*ens*/ or /pre-shi-*ens*/.

## prestige
Pronounced /pre-**steezh**/.

## prestigious
Pronounced /pre-stij-*us*/.

## prima donna
Pronounced /**pree**-*ma* do-na/.

## prima facie
Pronounced /**priy**-*ma* fay-shi/.
or /**fay**-shi-ee/.

## primarily
Stress on the first syllable or, less commonly, the second.
With second-syllable stress, pronounced /priy-**me**-ri-li/ or /priy-**ma**-ri-li/.

## pristine
Pronounced /**pri**-steen/.

## privacy
Pronounced /**pri**-*va*-si/ or /**priy**-*va*-si/.

## privation
Pronounced /priy-**vay**-*shon*/.

## privy
Pronounced /**pri**-vi/.

## probity
The *o* is pronounced /oh/.

## proboscis
Pronounced /*proh*-**bo**-sis/ or /*proh*-**boh**-sis/.

## process
As a noun, pronounced /**proh**-ses/ or, less commonly, /**pro**-ses/.
As a verb, has the same pronunciation options, except in the sense of 'to move in a procession', in which case stress on the second syllable: /proh-**ses**/.

## progress
As a noun, pronounced /proh-gres/ or, less commonly, /pro-gres/.
As a verb, /proh-**gres**/ or /proh-gres/.

## prohibition
The *h* is usually silent.

## project
As a verb, stressed on the second syllable.
As a noun, usually /pro-jekt/, though /proh-jekt/ is also acceptable.

## promenade
In most senses, pronounced /pro-*me*-nahd/.
In square dancing, /pro-*me*-nayd/.

## promissory
Stress on the first syllable.

## pronunciation
Second syllable pronounced /-nun-/.
✗ Not /-nown-/. (Note that the word is spelt -*nun*-, not -*noun*-.)

## pro rata
Usually /proh rah-*ta*/; /ray-*ta*/ is also correct.

## protean
Usually stressed on the second syllable; first-syllable stress also correct.

## protégé
Stressed on the first syllable.
The *o* may be pronounced as in *not* or as in *no*.

## proven
Pronounced /pruu-*ven*/.
/proh-*ven*/ only for the Scottish legal term *not proven*.

## proviso
The *i* is pronounced /iy/.

## puissance
As a term in show-jumping, pronounced /pwee-so$^{ng}$s/ or /pwee-sons/.

## pulverize
*Pul*- rhymes with *dull*.

## pursuivant
Pronounced /pur-si-*vant*/ or /pur-swi-*vant*/.

## pyramidal
Stress on the second syllable: /pi-ra-mi-*dal*/.

---

### Pall Mall
Pronounced /pal **mal**/ (see note at MALL).
### Peugeot®
Pronounced /puh-zhoh/.
✗ Not /pyuu-zhoh/.
### Plaid Cymru
Pronounced /pliyd kum-ri/.

### Punjab
Pronounced /pun-jahb/ or /pun-jahb/.
✓ /poon-/ also acceptable now although originally an error.
### Pwllheli
The usual English pronunciation of this Welsh place-name is /pu-thel-i/.

---

## quaff
Pronounced /kwof/ or /kwahf/.

## quagmire
Stress on the first syllable, which is pronounced /kwag-/ or /kwog-/.

## qualm
Pronounced /kwahm/.

## quantum
Pronounced /kwon-*tum*/.

## quasi
Usually /kway-ziy/ or /kway-siy/.
/kwah-zi/ and /kwa-ziy/ are also acceptable.

## quatercentenary
First syllable pronounced /kwa-/ or, less commonly, /kwo-/.
✗ Not /kwaw-/ as in *quarter*.

**questionnaire**
Pronounce the first two syllables as in *question*.
✗ /kes-/ is old-fashioned.

**quiescent**
Usually /kwi-**es**-*ent*/.
/kwiy-**es**-*ent*/ is also correct.

---

**Quasimodo**
Pronounced /kwah-zi-**moh**-doh/ or, less commonly, /kwaw-/

**Quixote**
Usually /kwik-**sot**/, also /ki-**hoh**-ti/.
(*Quixotic* always /kwik-**sot**-ik/).

---

**rabid**
Pronounced /**ra**-bid/ or, less commonly, /**ray**-bid/.

**raison d'être**
Pronounced /ray-zoh$^{ng}$ de-*truh*/.

**rapport**
The *t* is silent: say /ra-**pawr**/.

**rapprochement**
Pronounced /ra-**prosh**-mo$^{ng}$/.

**rationale**
Pronounced /rah-*sho*-**nahl**/.

**recess**
Both as a noun or a verb, may be stressed on the first or the second syllable.
Some people stress the noun on the first syllable and the latter on the second, in line with the typical noun and verb stress patterns (see STRESS DIFFERENCES BE-TWEEN ADJECTIVES, NOUNS AND VERBS, page 402).

**recognize**
⚠ Always pronounce the *g*.

**recondite**
Stress on the first or, less commonly, the second syllable.

**recuperate**
Stress on the second syllable, which is pronounced /-**kuu**-/ or /-**kyuu**-/.

**reductio ad absurdum**
Pronounced /ri-**duk**-ti-oh ad ab-**surd**-*um*/ or /ri-**duk**-shi-oh/, or /ri-**dook**-ti-oh/.

**referable**
Stressed on the second syllable.

**regime**
Pronounced /ray-**zheem**/.

**regimen**
Pronounced /**re**-ji-*men*/.

**remedial**
Stress on the second syllable, which has the same vowel sound as *me*.
The same applies to *remediable*.

**remembrance**
Three syllables, not four.
⚠ There is no vowel between the *b* and the *r*.

**remonstrate**
Usually stressed on the first syllable.
Stress on the second syllable is not now common, but still correct.

**Renaissance**
Pronounced fully anglicized (/ri-**nay**-sans/), or more like French (/*ruh*-nay-so$^{ng}$s/), or something in between (/ri-**nay**-so$^{ng}$s/).
Distinguish this from *renascence*, pronounced /ri-**na**-*sens*/ or /ri-**nay**-*sens*/.

**renege**
In spite of the following *e*, the *g* is pronounced as a hard /g/.
The vowel in the second syllable may be /ee/ or /ay/.

**reportage**
Either /re-pawr-**tahzh**/ or /ri-**pawr**-tij/.

**reputable**
Stressed on the first syllable.

**research**
Both as a noun and as a verb, usually stressed on the second syllable.
First-syllable stress is also correct.
Some people distinguish noun from verb by stressing the former on the first syllable and the latter on the second, in line with the typical noun and verb stress patterns (see STRESS DIFFERENCES BE-TWEEN ADJECTIVES, NOUNS AND VERBS, page 402).

**respite**
Rhymes with either *spit* or *spite*.

**restaurant**
Pronounced /res-*toh*-ront/, /res-*toh*-rong/, /res-*toh*-ront/ or /res-*toh*-ro$^{ng}$/.
⚠ Note that there is no *n* in **restaurateur**, pronounced /res-*toh*-ra-tuhr/.

**reveille**
Usually /ri-*va*-li/.
/ri-*ve*-li/ is also correct.

**revolve**
Pronounced /ri-*volv*/ or, mainly in the south of England, /ri-*vohlv*/.

**ribald**
Pronounced /ri-*bald*/ or /riy-*bald*/, or, less commonly, /-bawld/.

**ricochet**
Stress on the first or last syllable.
✗ Do not pronounce the *t*. The word rhymes with *may*. The pronunciation /-shet/ is now very old-fashioned, if not actually obsolete.

**risible**
Rhymes with *visible*.

**risqué**
Stress on the first or the last syllable.
✗ Do not pronounce this like *risky*; the final syllable rhymes with *may*.
The first syllable is generally pronounced as in *risk*. A more French-sounding /ree-/ is correct, but not necessary.

**romance**
Stress on the second syllable.

**rotatory**
Stress on the second syllable (/roh-*tay*-*to*-ri/) or, less commonly, on the first (/roh-*ta*-to-ri/).

**rotund**
Stress on the second syllable.

**rowan**
Pronounced /roh-*an*/ except in Scotland, where it is /row-*an*/.

**rowlock**
Best pronounced /ro-*lok*/ or /ru-*lok*/.
✗ /roh-*lok*/ is becoming more common, but is not used by those who regularly use rowlocks.

---

**Raleigh**
As the name of the Elizabethan seaman, now usually /rah-li/, although he himself probably pronounced his name /raw-li/.
In other cases, /ra-li/.

**Ralph**
The older form /rayf/ has generally been replaced by the spelling pronunciation /ralf/, but is still correct.

**Rheims**
Pronounced /reemz/.

**Riesling**
Pronounced /reez-ling/ or /rees-ling/.
✗ Not /riyz-ling/.

**Rievaulx**
Pronounced /ree-voh/.

**Rioja**
Pronounced /ree-oh-*ka*/ or /ree-oh-*kha*/.

---

**sacrilegious**
Rhymes with *religious*.

**salivary**
Stress on the first syllable (/*sa*-li-*va*-ri/) or the second (/*sa*-liy-*va*-ri/).

**salmonella**
The first *l* is pronounced in this word, although not in *salmon*.

**salve**
Usually /salv/.
In the sense of 'to soothe' or 'a soothing ointment', also pronounced /sahv/.

**sandwich**
Ends in /-wij/ or /-wich/.
The *d* may equally correctly be pronounced or dropped.

## sangfroid

Best more or less as in French: /so^ng-frwah/.
/song-/, /sahng-/ and /sang-/ are also acceptable.

## sanguine

The *ng* is pronounced as in *finger*.
The word rhymes with *pin*.

## satiety

Pronounced /sa-tiy-e-ti/.

## satyr

Pronounced /sa-tur/.
✗ Does not rhyme with *satire*.
/say-tur/ only in American English.

## sauna

Pronounced /saw-na/.
✓ /sow-na/ is correct but has never really caught on.

## scabrous

Pronounced /skayb-rus/.

## scallop

Pronounced /sko-lop/.
✗ Rhyming *scallop* with *gallop* is not yet generally accepted.

## scarify

Pronounce the first syllable to rhyme with *scar*; ✗ not as in *scare*.

## scenario

Pronounced /si-nah-ri-oh/ or, less commonly, /si-nay-ri-oh/.

## schedule

Begins with /sh/ in British English, /sk/ in American English.

## schemata

Strictly speaking, this word should be stressed on the first syllable.
✓ Second-syllable stress is increasingly common, although still deprecated by many people. Compare STIGMATA.

## schism

Usually /skiz-im/, but /siz-im/ is still correct.

## schist

Pronounced /shist/.

## schizophrenic

*Schizo-* is pronounced /skit-soh-/.
The second part is usually pronounced /-fre-nik/, but /-free-nik/ is also correct.

## scone

Pronounced /skon/ or /skohn/.
(Compare the pronunciation of the place-name *Scone* in the boxed section below.)

## second

In the sense 'to transfer elsewhere', stressed on the second syllable.
In the sense of 'to support (a suggestion, etc)', stressed on the first syllable.

## secretary

Pronounced with four syllables, *se-cre-ta-ry*, or three, *se-cre-tri*.
✗ Do not, however, drop the *r* of the second syllable.

## secretive

Stress on the first syllable.

## segue

Pronounced /say-gway/ or /seg-way/.

## shaman

Pronounced /sha-man/, /shay-man/ or /shah-man/.

## sheikh

Usually /shayk/.
✓ /sheek/ is often criticized but is correct.

## short-lived

*-lived* as in *to live*, not as in *alive*.

## simultaneous

In British English, the first syllable is pronounced /sim-/.
/siym-/ is correct only in American English.

## sinecure

This word has three syllables: *si-ne-cure*.
The first syllable may rhyme with *sin* or *sign*.

## sine die

Pronounced /siy-ni diy-ee/ or /sin-ay dee-ay/.
✗ Never like English *sign* and *dye*.

**sine qua non**
Pronounced /sin-ay kwah non/ or /nohn/ or, less commonly, /siy-ni kway non/.

**sixth**
✗ Do not drop the /s/ sound from the final consonant cluster /-ksth/. Particular care is needed with *sixths*, which ends in /-ksths/.

**slaver**
In the sense of 'to dribble', usually /sla-*ver*/, but /slay-*ver*/ is also correct.

**sleight**
Pronounce *sleight* like *slight.*

**sloth**
Pronounced /slohth/ or /sloth/.

**slough**
In the sense of 'bog', this word rhymes with *cow.*
In the sense of 'to shed skin', it is pronounced /sluf/.

**sojourn**
Usually /soj-*urn*/ or /suj-*urn*/.
Also with a full /u/ sound in the second syllable: /soj-urn/.
/soh-/ in the first syllable is a common and acceptable variant.

**solder**
Pronounce the *l.*
The *o* is pronounced /o/ or /oh/.

**solecism**
The *o* is pronounced /o/ or /oh/.

**solenoid**
The *o* is usually pronounced /oh/, but /o/ is also acceptable.

**solve**
Pronounced /solv/ or, mainly in the south of England, /sohlv/.

**sonorous**
Usually stressed on the first syllable.
Second-syllable stress is also correct.

**sophomore**
Three syllables in British English (often only two in American English, with the middle *o* being dropped).
The first *o* is pronounced /o/.

**sotto voce**
Pronounced /sot-oh voh-chi/.

**species**
The *-ci-* is pronounced /sh/ or /s/.
In *specious*, it is always /sh/.

**spinach**
Ends in /j/ or /ch/.

**spontaneity**
The syllable *-ne-* rhymes equally correctly with *nay* or with *knee.*

**stanch**
Pronounced /stahnch/ or /stawnch/.

**stasis**
Pronounced /stay-sis/.

**status**
Usually pronounced /stay-*tus*/.
/sta-*tus*/ is American, except in the pronunciation of the Latin phrase *status quo*.

**stereo**
Pronounced /ste-ri-oh/ or, less commonly, /steer-i-oh/.
The same applies to all words beginning with *stereo-*.

**stigmata**
Strictly speaking, should be stressed on the first syllable.
✓ Second-syllable stress is increasingly common, although deprecated by many people. (Compare SCHEMATA.)

**strafe**
Originally pronounced /strahf/, which is still correct.
Under the influence of the spelling, /strayf/ has become the more common pronunciation and is now accepted as correct also.

**stratosphere**
Begins with /strah-*to*-/.

**stratum**
Pronounced /strah-*tum*/ or /stray-*tum*/.

**stratus**
Pronounced /stray-*tus*/ or /strah-*tus*/.

**strength**
The standard pronunciations are /strength/ and /strengkth/
/strenth/ also acceptable in some educated British accents.

443

**strychnine**
The *ch* is pronounced /k/
The final syllable *-nine* rhymes with *seen*.

**suave**
Pronounced /swahv/.
✗ Although formerly correct, /swayv/ is nowadays considered incorrect or at best facetious.

**subpeona**
Pronunciations with and without the *b* are equally correct.

**subsidence**
Stress on the first syllable (/sub-si-*dens*/) or the second (/sub-siy-*dens*/).

**succinct**
The *cc* is pronounced /ks/.
✗ Not /*su*-singkt/.

**suffragan**
The *g* is a hard /g/.

**suit**
Pronounced /suut/ or, less commonly, /syuut/.

**summa cum laude**
Pronounced /soo-*ma* koom low-day/.

**supine**
Stress on either the first or the second syllable.

**supply**
As the adverb formed from the adjective *supple*, pronounced as two or three syllables: /sup-li/, /sup-*el*-li/, /sup-*e*-li/.
The spelling *supplely* should be pronounced as three syllables.

**surety**
Pronounce as three syllables.

**surveillance**
Pronounce the *ll* as /l/.
Only in American English is it correct to omit the /l/ sound.

**swathe**
Pronounced /swaydh/.

**sycophant**
The *y* is pronounced /i/ or, less commonly, /iy/.

**synod**
The *y* is pronounced /i/.

**syringe**
Pronounced as two syllables.
Usually stressed on the second syllable, but first-syllable stress is also correct.

---

**Salisbury**
Pronounced /sawlz-*bu*-ri/ or /solz-*bu*-ri/.

**Sandwich**
Ends in /-wij/ or /-wich/.
The *d* may equally correctly be pronounced or dropped.

**Sarawak**
Stress on the second syllable.

**Saudi**
Usually pronounced /sow-di/.
/saw-di/ is also correct.

**Sauternes**
Pronounced /soh-tern/.

**Schofield**
Pronounced /skoh-feeld/.

**Scone**
Pronounced /skuun/.

**Scylla**
Pronounced /si-*la*/.

**Shrewsbury**
Usually /shrohz-*bu*-ri/.
/shruuz-*bu*-ri/ is also acceptable.

**Singhalese**
Pronounced /sing-*a*-leez/ or /sing-*ga*-leez/.
The spelling *Sinhalese* is pronounced /sin-*ha*-leez/.

**Sioux**
Pronounced /suu/.

**Sophocles**
Pronounced /so-*fo*-kleez/.

**Southwark**
The *w* is silent: say /sudh-*ark*/.

**Soviet**
Pronounced /soh-vi-*et*/ or, less commonly, /so-vi-*et*/.

**Strathaven**
The *th* is silent: say /stray-*ven*/.

**table d'hôte**
Pronounced /tah-*bel*-doht/.

**tagliatelle**
Pronounced /tal-*ya*-te-li/.
✗ Not /tag-/.

**t'ai chi**
Pronounced /tiy jee/ or /tiy chee/.
In full, ***t'ai chi ch'uan*** (/chwahn/).

**taoiseach**
Pronounced /tee-*shakh*/ or /tee-*shak*/.

**taxidermist**
Stress on the first syllable.

**temporarily**
Stress on the first syllable or, informally, on the third.

**tenable**
Pronounce ***ten-*** as the number *ten*.
/teen-/ is rare and rather old-fashioned.

**terminus ad quem**
Pronounced /ter-mi-*nus* ad kwem/.
Similarly, ***terminus a quo*** is pronounced /ter-mi-*nus* ah kwoh/.

**tête-à-tête**
Pronounced /tay-*ta*-tayt/ or /te-*ta*-tet/.

**timbre**
Pronounced /ta^{ng}-*bruh*/ or /tam-*ber*/.
✗ Does not rhyme with *timber*.

**timeous**
(Mostly Scottish and South African; = 'timely')
Pronounced as *time* + *-ous*: /tiym-*us*/.
✗ Not /tim-i-*us*/.

**tirade**
Pronounced /tiy-**rayd**/ or, less commonly, /ti-**rayd**/.

**tissue**
Pronounced /ti-shuu/ or /ti-syuu/.

**tonne**
This word has the same pronunciation as *ton*.

**torte**
May be pronounced as one syllable or two.

**tortilla**
Pronounced /tawr-**tee**-*ya*/ or /tawr-til-*a*/.

**tortoise**
Pronounced /tawr-*tus*/ in most accents of English.
✓ Scots pronounce the second syllable /-toyz/. (Compare PORPOISE.)

**tournedos**
The *s* is silent.

**tourniquet**
The final *t* is silent: say /tuur-ni-kay/.

**trait**
The final *t* may be pronounced or silent.

**trajectory**
Stress on the second syllable or, less commonly, the first.

**transferable**
Stress on the second syllable or, less commonly, the first.

**transparent**
The syllable ***-par-*** may be pronounced as in *parent* or as in *parity*.

**trauma**
Pronounced /traw-*ma*/ or, less commonly, /trow-*ma*/.
Similarly for ***traumatic***.

**travail**
Stress on the first syllable or, less commonly, the second.

**traverse**
✓ Stressable on either syllable, both as a noun and as a verb, but usually stressed on the first syllable as a noun and on the second as a verb (compare STRESS DIFFERENCES BETWEEN ADJECTIVES, NOUNS AND VERBS, page 402).

**trefoil**
Usually pronounced /tre-foyl/.
/tree-foyl/ is also correct.

**tribunal**
Usually stressed on the second syllable: /triy-**byuu**-*nal*/ or /tri-**byuu**-*nal*/.
Stress on the first syllable (/**tri**-byoo-*nal*/) is also correct.

**troll**
Rhymes with *roll* or with *doll*.

**troth**
Rhymes with *both* or with *cloth*.

**turbine**
The final syllable *-bine* may be pronounced as in *combined* or to rhyme with *bin*.

**tureen**
Stress on the second syllable.
The first syllable is correctly pronounced with or without a /y/ sound after the /t/.

**turquoise**
Usually /tur-kwoyz/.
Other correct pronunciations are /tur-kwahz/, /tur-koyz/ and, less commonly, /tur-kwawz/.

**tutu**
Pronounced /tuu-tuu/.
✗ Do not insert a /y/ after the /t/.

**twelfth**
✗ Do not omit the /f/.

**Taoism**
Pronounced /ta-oh-iz-*em*/ or /tow-iz-*em*/, or /dow-iz-*em*/.
✗ Not /tay-oh-/.

**Tucson**
Pronounced /tuu-son/.

**Tutankhamen**
/tuu-*tan*-kah-*men*/.
If spelt ***Tutankhamun***, pronounced /tuu-*tan*-kah-*moon*/ or /tuu-*tan*-kah-**moon**/.

**ultra vires**
Usually /ul-*tra* viyr-eez/.
A more Latinized /ool-trah **vee**-rayz/ is also correct.

**umbilical**
Both /um-**bil**-i-*kal*/ and /um-bi-liy-*kal*/ are correct.

**unprecedented** see PRECEDENT.

**untoward**
Usually stressed on the third syllable, but stress on the second syllable (/un-**toh**-*ard*/) is also correct.

**urinal**
Pronounced /**yuu**-ri-*nal*/ or /yoo-riy-*nal*/.

**urine**
Rhymes with *bin*.

**usage**
The *s* may be pronounced /s/ or /z/.

**usual**
Equally correctly pronounced as three syllables (/**yuu**-zhoo-*al*/) or two (/**yuu**-*zhal*/).

**Upanishad**
Strictly, /uu-**pun**-i-*shad*/.
✓ Anglicized forms such as /yuu-pan-i-shad/ are also correct.

**Uranus**
Pronounced /**yoor**-a-*nus*/ or /yoo-ray-*nus*/.

**Urdu**
Pronounced /**oor**-duu/ or /ur-duu/.

**Urquhart**
Pronounced /ur-*kart*/.

**Utah**
Usually /**yuu**-tah/ in British English, /**yuu**-taw/ in American English.

**vacuum**
Equally correctly three syllables (/**vak**-yoo-*um*/) or two (/vak-yuum/).

**vade-mecum**
/vah-di-**may**-koom/ is now commoner than /vay-di-**mee**-*kum*/, but both are correct.

**valance**
Rhymes with *balance*.

**valence**
The first part of this word rhymes with *vale*.
The same is true for ***valency***.

**valet**
Pronounced /va-lit/ or /va-lay/.

**vapid**
Rhymes with *rapid*.
✗ Not /vay-pid/.

**vase**
Pronounced /vahz/ in British English, more usually /vayz/ or /vays/ in American English.

**vehement**
Stress on the first syllable.
The *h* may be pronounced or silent.
✗ Not /vi-**hee**-*ment*/.

**vehicle**
Stress on the first syllable.
The *h* is silent — compare VEHICULAR.

**vehicular**
Stress on the second syllable.
The *h* is pronounced — compare VEHICLE.

**veldt**
Whether written *veldt* or *veld*, pronounced /felt/ or /velt/.

**venison**
Pronounce as three syllables.
The *s* is pronounced /s/ or /z/.
✗ Dropping the *i* is now considered old-fashioned.

**verbatim**
Pronounced /ver-**bay**-tim/ or, less commonly, /ver-**bah**-tim/.

**Very light**
Pronounced /veer-i liyt/ or /ve-ri/.

**veterinary**
Stress on the first syllable.
May be pronounced as five syllables: *ve-te-ri-na-ri*.
One or other of the unstressed syllables

are usually elided in normal speech. Opinions vary as to which elided forms are acceptable, but /vet-rin-ri/ and /vet-na-ri/ are certainly acceptable.

**via**
Pronounced /viy-a/ or /vee-a/.

**vicarious**
Pronounced /vi-**kayr**-ri-*us*/ or, less commonly, /viy-**kayr**-ri-*us*/.

**vice versa**
*Vice* may be pronounced as two syllables (/viy-si/) or as one (/viys/).

**victuals**
The *c* is silent: say /vit-*alz*/.
Similarly with *victualler*: /vit-*ler*/.

**viola**
As the name of a flower, usually /viy-*o*-la/.
/vee-o-la/ and /viy-oh-la/ are also correct.
As the name of the musical instrument, usually /vi-**oh**-la/ or /viy-**oh**-la/.

**vis-à-vis**
Pronounced /vee-za-vee/.

**viscid**
Pronounced /vis-id/.

**vitamin**
In British English, usually /vi-*ta*-min/.
/viy-*ta*-min/ is also correct, and is standard in American English.

**volte-face**
Pronounced /volt-fahs/.

**voluntarily**
Stress on the first syllable or, in informal speech, on the third.

**vouchsafe**
Stressed on either the first or the second syllable.

---

**van Gogh**
In British English, usually /van gokh/.
/van gof/ is also correct.
In American English, /van goh/ or /van gokh/.

**Velasquez**
The *qu* is pronounced /kw/ in British English, /k/ in American English.

The *z* is pronounced /z/ or /th/ in British English, /s/ in American English.
Stress always on the second syllable.

**Volkswagen®**
Usually pronounced /volks-wa-gen/.
/folks-/ and /-vah-gen/ are also correct.

**waistcoat**
Usually pronounced as if *waist* + *coat*.
✓ /wes-*kot*/ is old-fashioned but still
correct.
The *t* of *waist* may be pronounced or
silent.

**werewolf**
Pronounced /wer-woolf/ or, less commonly, /weer-woolf/.

**wholly**
The *ll* may be pronounced as a double
/l-l/ sound or as a single /l/.

**whooping cough**
*Whoop-* is in this case pronounced

/huup-/.

**wizened**
Pronounced /wiz-*end*/.
✗ Not /wiyz-*end*/.

**wont**
Usually pronounced as *won't*.
Rhyming with *want* is also correct.

**wrath**
Usually pronounced /roth/ or /rohth/.
In some accents, also /rath/ or /rahth/.

**wroth**
Pronounced /rohth/ or /roth/.

---

**Warwick**
The second *w* is silent.

**Wednesday**
The first *d* may equally correctly be
pronounced or silent.

**Wellesley**
Pronounced /wels-li/.

**Wodehouse**
Pronounced /wood-hows/.

**Woolwich**
The second *w* is silent: say /wool-ij/
or /wool-ich/.

**Worcester**
Pronounced /woo-*ster*/.

**Xerox®**
Pronounced /zeer-oks/.
✗ Not /ze-roks/.

**Xerxes**
Pronounced /zerk-seez/.

**Xhosa**
Pronounced /kaw-*sa*/ or /koh-*sa*/,
or /-*za*/.

---

**yoghurt**
Pronounced /yo-*gurt*/ or, less commonly,
/yoh-*gurt*/.

**zabaglione**
The *g* is silent: say /za-ba-**lyoh**-ni/.

**zoology**
Pronounced /zoh-o-*lo*-ji/ or /zoo-o-*lo*-ji/.
In words beginning with **zoo-** that are
not directly related to **zoology**, the
initial syllable **zo-** is always pronounced
/zoh-/.

---

**Yom Kippur**
Pronounced /yom ki-**poor**/ or /ki-**pur**/.

**Yosemite**
Pronounced /yoh-se-mi-ti/.

# Appendix A:
## Writing Effective English: Planning and Presentation

A good essay, report or other piece of writing is one in which the **relevant information** is set out **in an appropriate order** to form **a clear argument**, **explanation or exposition**.

> **The three keys to producing effective writing are:**
>
> (a) planning
>
> (b) selection, and
>
> (c) presentation.

## ✦ Planning and selection

> **The purpose of planning is to help you**
>
> (a) focus on what you want or need to say,
>
> (b) avoid digression and repetition, and
>
> (c) structure your argument properly.
>
> **This involves making a draft of what you intend to say.**

> **Step 1:** Make a skeleton or rough outline of what you want to say.

Jot down, in a few words, what you think might be the key points in what you are going to say, then organize them into a logical order that presents an effective argument. It may help to number them in order of importance, to give you an idea of the relative amount of time and/or space you might want to devote to each of them.

> **Step 2:** Decide on your sources of information, and gather from them the information you need.

If you are looking for information in books, make use of the contents pages and the index to select the parts of the book you need to read. Keep clear in your mind the type, level and amount of information you require. Take written notes — do not trust to your memory. If there are useful quotations you might want, note them carefully when you see them.

If you are gathering material from several sources, note which source you are taking any point from: you may want to refer to it again, and you may also need a note of the sources you have used in order to make a bibliography.

> ⚠ Be realistic about how much time is available for this part of your work. There is no point in spending so much time gathering information that the final writing stage has to be rushed.

**Step 3: Write down the facts in note form under the various headings in your skeleton outline.**

All that is needed is short notes, perhaps a few sentences in length, that will allow you to see how the information you now have can be put together into a coherent argument.

**Step 4: Arrange your information and opinions into a planned argument.**

Read through your skeleton and notes again, and decide what the key points now are. It may be useful to highlight these in some way, so that you do not lose sight of them. Re-assess their relative importance, and decide in what order you now want to introduce them.

Gather your information into paragraphs, with each paragraph having one key point as its 'core'. All the sentences in a paragraph should contribute or relate to this central key point. If you move on to a new point, begin a new paragraph.

Try to keep each paragraph short. If a paragraph is very long, check to see if there is more than one 'key point' in it, each of which could be made the core of a separate paragraph. On the other hand, check that there is at least one key point in every paragraph: any paragraph that does not include a separate point should be amalgamated with the preceding or following one.

Make sure that your sentences are not so long or complicated that they obscure the meaning of what you are saying. If a sentence is so long and complex that a reader might lose track of what is being said, split the sentence into smaller parts.

> **Step 5: When you have finished your draft, check it over thoroughly.**

Check that all the points have been covered, and in a logical order. Check that all the information you have included is really needed.

Write a good opening paragraph (to introduce the topic you are discussing) and a good closing paragraph (to sum up what you have said). Try to ensure that there is a smooth transition from one paragraph to the next throughout.

In more formal writing, if you have quoted from your sources or borrowed significant ideas from them, make sure that you acknowledge these by giving the name of the author and the title of the book or article the information was found in. (For more details on how to do this, see QUOTATIONS and BIBLIOGRAPHIES in Appendix F, pages 496 and 494.)

## ✦ Presentation

When you have ordered your material appropriately and set it out in paragraphs, you should check it for details of style, and make sure that you are using the right words, with correct spelling, grammar and punctuation.

---

**Good style**

The 18th-century writer Jonathan Swift summed up good style as *'proper words in proper places'*.

---

## • Vocabulary

Check that all the words you have used mean what you intend them to mean. Think carefully whether they will be understood by the reader, and whether they are suitable for the type of work you are writing (not too informal or slangy, nor on the other hand too formal and pretentious). Avoid clichés (see Appendix D, page 474) and repetitions of the same expression.

It is not necessary in formal writing to search out especially formal words to replace every 'ordinary' word. Most everyday words (like *buy*, *go* and *stop*) are as appropriate in formal contexts as in informal ones, and there is no need to replace them with more formal-sounding ones (like *purchase*, *proceed* or *cease*). Contractions such as *I'll*, *he'd*, *don't* and *couldn't* are, however, too colloquial to be used in formal writing, and all such shortened forms should be replaced by their fully-spelt-out equivalents: *I will*, *he would*, *do not*, etc.

Avoid vague and woolly words (*nice* is the classic example). Make sure also that all the words are contributing to the meaning of the text. Two things to watch out for in particular are ***tautologies*** (in which two or more words or phrases say the same thing):

✗   *<u>Finally</u>, I would like to say <u>in conclusion</u> that ...*
✗   *<u>Returning back</u> to my original point, ...*
✗   *<u>Everyone</u> was <u>unanimous</u> in their praise.*
✗   *to <u>continue on</u>*

and unnecessary **padding** (in which words are used that contribute nothing at all to the message):

✗   *in the present crisis <u>situation</u>* (= 'in the present crisis')
✗   *a confrontation of a most distressing <u>nature</u>* (= 'a most distressing confrontation')
✗   *Many people complain on a daily <u>basis</u> about housing.* (= 'daily')

If you need to use a technical term that your reader might not understand, give a brief explanation of its meaning in parentheses immediately after the first instance of using it, within the sentence or in a following sentence.

If you want, eg for stylistic reasons, to deliberately introduce a colloquialism or slang expression into writing of a more formal nature, you should place it within quotation marks.

- **Grammar**

Check your work for grammatical correctness, eg that you have written in complete sentences, with a subject and verb, and if necessary an object, in every sentence. You should also check that you have not run sentences together. Check that the verb in every sentence agrees with its subject.

You should check particularly carefully for any errors that you know you yourself are especially liable to make. Have a checklist of these in mind.

- **Spelling**

Check the spelling of any words you are not absolutely sure about. As with grammar, you should have a checklist in your mind of any words you know you are prone to misspell. Check carefully for words that are easily confused and misspelt, eg *their* and *there*, *goal* and *gaol*, *were* and *where* (see pages 333 – 359).

- **Punctuation**

Choice of punctuation (commas, full stops, etc) should for the most part be made during step 4. At this present stage, check in particular the use of paired punctuation marks: a common error is to put parentheses, commas or dashes at the beginning of an inserted comment and then to forget to close them again or else to close them in the wrong place — if you have a punctuation mark indicating the beginning of a comment or insertion, you must have a second one indicating the end of it, when the main part of the sentence resumes (see examples in the entries for COMMA, DASH and PARENTHESES in the *Punctuation* chapter).

# Appendix B:
## Types of Written English

## agendas

An *agenda* (Latin *agenda* 'things to be done') is a list of items of business to be discussed at a meeting, set out in the order in which the matters are to be dealt with. An agenda is generally circulated to potential participants some time before the meeting so that they can make any necessary preparations for it, such as obtaining facts and figures relevant to the matters to be discussed.

> **An agenda should**
>
> **i) define the purpose of the meeting (eg whether it is a committee meeting, an annual general meeting, an extraordinary general meeting, etc) and state what organization it is a meeting of; and**
>
> **ii) outline the business to be dealt with at the meeting.**

The usual order for items on an agenda is:

appointment of chairman or chairwoman (if not already appointed before the meeting);

apologies for absence;

reading and approval of the minutes of the previous meeting;

matters arising from these minutes;

correspondence received;

reports of officials of the organization (eg the secretary and the treasurer);

reports of committees, sub-committees or working parties;

named items of business;

any other business (ie, matters participants want to raise at the meeting but which have not been listed on the agenda);

date of next meeting.

If a formal motion is to be discussed at the meeting, the full wording of that motion should be included in the agenda. If new officials (eg chairman/ chairwoman, secretary, treasurer) have to be elected at the meeting, the election should immediately follow 'reports of officials of the organization' on the agenda, before any other items of business.

## applications for positions of employment

>  Great care should be taken when writing a letter of application. A well-written letter could lead to an interview, whereas a badly written letter will probably lead to your application being rejected.

Unless your handwriting is difficult to read, your application should be handwritten, in blue or black ink. You should state clearly in your application (eg in the heading to the letter) what post you are applying for, and where you heard about the position or saw the advertisement for it. Further information you should include is:

> your age, education and training;
>
> your present job (if you have one) and any previous employment;
>
> any other experience, qualifications or interests relevant to the post.

Along with the application, you should provide the names and addresses of two or three referees, or refer to any testimonials you are enclosing. (If you are enclosing testimonials, send photocopies rather than the originals.) Say why you are applying for the post, and describe what you think makes you particularly suitable for it. If you are in employment, say why you wish to leave your current job. Finally, state your willingness to keep any appointment for an interview.

• An alternative approach is to send a short letter of application explaining where you read or heard about the vacancy and why you are interested in the post. With the letter, enclose a copy of your ***curriculum vitae*** (or *cv*), which is a summary of your personal details (such as your age, sex and marital status), your qualifications and your career experience. Many job advertisements specifically ask for this nowadays. For details of how to write a curriculum vitae, see the entry for CV's on page 459.

## business letters

Effective formal and business correspondence requires careful attention to certain conventions. Business letters are just one type, but probably the commonest type, of formal letter, and many of the points that follow are equally applicable to the more general kind of formal letter discussed on page 462. Business letters do, however, have certain conventions, for example with regard to layout, that do not apply to other types of formal letter.

> **Business letters should be brief, to the point, accurate and courteous. You should get to the point quickly and say what you have to say briefly, clearly, logically and politely.**

## ✦ Setting out a business letter — the standard format

The appearance of a business letter is very important. A letter should be good to look at as well as easy to read, so the following points should be kept in mind:

i) Get a good balance between the size of the sheet of paper and what you have written on it. If the letter is short, do not squeeze it all up at the top

---

1.                          **LAROUSSE PLC**
                    Address of company office, etc


2.    Ref: GD/cj

3.    1 June 1995

4.    Brown Brothers plc
      3 John Street
      LONDON
      N18 0RH

5.    Attention: Mr M Smith

6.    Dear Sirs

7.    GUIDE TO GRAMMAR AND USAGE

8.1   Thank you for your letter of 26 May asking for two advance copies of
      the *Guide to Grammar and Usage.*

8.2   As requested, I am sending you two copies of the book under
      separate cover so that you can circulate them amongst your staff in
      order that you may gauge their reaction to the book and judge its
      suitability as an office reference manual. I feel confident that you and
      your staff will find this *Guide* the most comprehensive and helpful
      work of its kind. The separate chapters for each topic and the
      detailed indexes, in particular, make it very easy to consult.

8.3   If you have any questions or comments about the book, please do not
      hesitate to get in touch with us again.

9.    Yours faithfully


10.   George Davidson
      Dictionaries & Language Editor

11.   cc JW, MGU

12.   Encs

---

of the page; if necessary, use double spacing to cover more of the page, and allow large margins at the top and bottom of the sheet, and on the right and left sides of the page.

ii)   It looks bad to have your signature squeezed in at the very bottom of a page, or to have a second page with nothing on it but the complimentary close (eg 'Yours faithfully') and the signature, so set out your letter in such a way as to avoid this.

● The most widely used layout for a business letter nowadays is the 'fully blocked' style with 'open' punctuation. This means that all paragraphs, headings, etc in the letter are set against the left-hand margin (with no indents for new paragraphs), and as little punctuation as possible is used, only as much as is needed for the sake of clarity (abbreviations do not require full stops, for example).

● The letter is an example of the typical structure of a business letter:

Note the following points regarding the above specimen:

1.   An official letter or business letter is always written on the firm's or organization's headed notepaper. The name, address, telephone number, etc of the company or organization printed at the top of the page is known as the ***letterhead***. The letterhead may be centred on the page, as in the example given here, or else it may be aligned with the left-hand margin.

2.   There is often an ***internal reference***, comprising the initials of the person signing the letter and of the typist. This is usually at the beginning of the letter but may occasionally be at the end. If replying to a letter with an internal reference, you should quote this as well as your own if you have one:

*Your reference: ...*
*Our reference: ...*

3.   Leave a two-line space before the date of the letter. The date should be set out in full. There is no need to abbreviate it, nor to punctuate it.

4.   After the date, type the name and address of the person or organization the letter is being sent to. Again leave two clear lines before this. No punctuation is needed at the ends of lines in the address.

5.   If the letter is for the attention of a particular person in the company or organization, follow the address with 'For the attention of' (sometimes shortened to 'Attention' or abbreviated 'FAO').

6.   This part of the letter is known as the ***salutation***. It requires capital letters. *Sir* or *Madam* is required if you do not know the addressee personally. If you are replying to a letter signed 'pp' (see point 10 below),

reply to the author of the letter, not the person who signed it. If the letter is being sent to a firm and is marked 'for the attention of' a particular person, most authorities say that the letter should be addressed to the firm (ie 'Dear Sirs'), though some say that it is equally correct to address the salutation to the person named in the 'attention' line. Follow the salutation by a one-line space.

7.  A subject heading helps to ensure that the letter is passed to the right person once it reaches its destination, and it quickly indicates to the reader what the letter is about. The subject heading also usually indicates the subject under which a copy of the letter should be filed in your own files.

8.  The text of the letter. A good business letter should generally consist of three parts:

   8.1 **Introduction** (one paragraph). The introductory paragraph states the subject of your letter, and acknowledges your correspondent's previous letter (if there has been one), quoting its date.

   8.2 **Development** (one or more paragraphs). The main body of the letter deals in a methodical way with the subject referred to in the introduction (eg, it lists facts, puts forward arguments, gives detailed explanations, outlines a proposed course of action). Splitting up this section of the letter by means of subject or topic headings or numbered paragraphs is helpful when the matter under discussion is long or complicated.

   8.3 **Conclusion** (one paragraph). The final paragraph of a business letter is usually kept for general expressions of goodwill.

---

⚠  It is nowadays considered preferable to close with a simple statement including a subject-and-verb construction rather than opening the final sentence with a present participle like *trusting, hoping, wishing*, etc:

✓ *I look forward to hearing from you.*
✗ *Looking forward to hearing from you.*

---

9.  This part of the letter is known as the **complimentary close**. There are nowadays only two forms of formal complimentary close used in business letters: *Yours faithfully* if the letter begins with *Dear Sir* or *Dear Madam*, and *Yours sincerely* if the salutation contains a personal name (eg *Dear Mr Smith*). There should be no capital letter at the beginning of *faithfully* or *sincerely*, and no comma at the end of this line. This may be, but need not be, followed on the next line by the name of the firm, followed by a 5- or 6-line space for the signature, which is immediately followed by. . .

10.   A typed version of the signatory's name and their designation (ie, their position in the firm or organization). If the letter has been signed on behalf of the sender by someone else, eg a secretary or personal assistant, the person signing the letter should sign their own name, not the name of the person who dictated the letter, but the name typed below should be that of the sender, not the signer. The sender's name should be prefaced 'pp', which means *per pro*, Latin for 'for and on behalf of':

---

Yours sincerely


*Jane Nicol*


*pp*   George Davidson
Dictionaries & Language Editor

---

12.   The last line indicates whether or not the letter is accompanied by enclosures. It may be preceded by a line (marked 11 in the specimen letter) indicating people to whom copies of your letter have been sent for information. (The abbreviation 'cc' stands for 'carbon copies', but of course in these days of modern technology the copies are rarely if ever *carbon* copies.)

If the references have not been put at the beginning of the letter (see 2, page 455), they should be inserted below part 10.

- **Continuation sheets**

If the length of the letter requires a second sheet of paper, this second sheet (and any subsequent sheet) should be on plain, not letterheaded, paper. The page number, the date, and the addressee's name should all be at the head of the page against the left-hand margin:

---

2/

1 June 1995

Brown Brothers Ltd


(Continuation of text of letter)

---

- **Further points to note**

1.  Always check that all the correspondent's questions have been answered in your reply. Be as brief as possible, but also be specific and give full details, eg relevant dates, prices, descriptions of articles, specifications, components. Consider your letter from the reader's point of view: what you take for granted might not always be obvious to the person receiving the letter.

2.  Keep your sentences short and to the point. Remember also that long paragraphs are harder to follow than short paragraphs.

3.  Be courteous and tactful. Always keep in mind the reader's possible response to what you have said. Look especially for diplomatic ways of pointing out other people's mistakes (eg *'We do not appear to have received ...'* rather than *'You forgot to send us ...'*).

4.  If you are writing on behalf of a firm, use 'we', 'us', etc. If you are writing as an individual, use 'I', 'me', etc.

5.  In the past, writers of business letters frequently used a special jargon, such as *'ult.'* for 'of last month' or *'inst.'* for 'of this month'. Nowadays this is not considered good style, and business letters should always be written in normal, everyday, Standard English.

## complaints

To ensure that your complaint is dealt with the minimum of fuss, you must state the facts coolly and clearly. ***Be firm, but always be tactful and polite.***

Make sure you have your facts correct, and set them out clearly and logically. If possible, make clear what action you want the organization or person to take in order to satisfy your complaint. As with any other formal or business letter, make the subject clear at the outset by giving the letter a heading (see item 7 of the specimen business letter on page 455); if there is some clear means of identifying a faulty product, such as a product number or order number, put this in the title of the letter.

If you are writing with a complaint to a business firm and you do not know the name of the person responsible for dealing with complaints, address your letter to the *Customer Complaints Department*. (There may not be a 'customer complaints department', but by addressing your letter in this way, you make the nature of the letter clear and so ensure that your letter will quickly reach the person whose job it is to deal with complaints.)

## cv's (curricula vitae)

Many job advertisements ask applicants to send a brief letter of application along with a ***curriculum vitae***. This should be set out neatly, preferably on one sheet of paper (though more may be necessary), and typed rather than handwritten. On the cv you should list your full name, address, telephone number, date of birth, sex, marital status and nationality; the schools and colleges you attended, your educational qualifications and training; your previous jobs (if any), and the salaries for these jobs (if this information is asked for); any hobbies and outside interests, positions of responsibility you hold or have held (eg in a club or association), etc; and the names and addresses of two or three (whichever you are asked for) referees (ie, people who know you and have agreed to give their opinions of your character and your suitability for the post advertised). When submittimg a letter of application and a cv, it is a good idea to mention one or two of your relevant skills or qualifications in the letter as well as listing them in the cv, in order to draw attention to them.

## essays

The main points on how to prepare and write an essay are covered in Appendix A, *Writing Effective English: Planning and Presentation* (see pages 449 – 452).

---

 Remember that an examiner is looking for a well-planned and neatly presented piece of writing; freshness and originality of approach; well-constructed and varied sentences and paragraphs; and correct grammar, punctuation and spelling.

---

• Before anything else, think carefully about the topic or question that has been set — are you sure about what you are being asked to do? There will usually be some key word or phrase that tells you exactly what you are expected to do: *compare, contrast, describe, summarize, explain, demonstrate, illustrate, show*, and so on. Take care that the essay you write does what it has been asked to do: when asked to contrast two things, for example, it is not enough for you simply to describe them — you must also explicitly draw attention to the ways in which they differ from one another; when asked to show or demonstrate something, you must use the data at your disposal in such a way as to prove what you have been asked to prove — it is not enough simply to list the data without showing what conclusions are to be drawn from it.

• A *general essay* or *composition* is not quite the same as an *academic essay*. An academic essay, such as might be required in science, history or geography, should be as objective as possible, setting out data and drawing conclusions from it. But a general essay is usually looking for not just facts but your own personal input, a lively and individual approach, and personal impressions, feelings, thoughts, opinions and memories. There are four main types of general essay:

a *narrative*, which tells a story;

a *descriptive essay*, a word-picture of a person or place;

a *discursive essay*, presenting facts, opinions or arguments; and

a *reflective essay*, which is much like a discursive essay but more personal or speculative.

When selecting a topic for an essay, decide which of these styles is going to be most appropriate for the subject you will be writing about. Some essays may require a combination of these styles.

If you are writing a narrative that involves dialogue, what is said by each character must begin in a separate paragraph.

## forms

When filling in a form:

    i)   first read the whole form, including the instructions and footnotes, carefully through from beginning to end before you start to fill it in;

    ii)   reread the instructions telling you how to fill in the form;

    iii)   then fill in the form a section at a time, following the instructions carefully, eg with regard to deleting or circling words or phrases, marking boxes with a cross or a tick, or filling in with an appropriate word or phrase.

Make any marks or deletions clear and definite. If written answers are asked for, print them rather than write them. You may type your answers unless the instructions state otherwise. If using a pen rather than a typewriter, always use black or blue ink.

## invitations

There are two types of formal invitation: a printed card and a formal letter. There are slight differences in style between the two.

• An invitation on a printed card is always written in the third person: *Mr John Brown requests the pleasure of the company of* ...'. There should be no date, nor a salutation (*Dear* ...) or complimentary close (*Yours sincerely* ...).

The invitation should include the name(s) of the person or people making the invitation, the name(s) of the person or people being invited, the reason for the invitation (wedding, party, dinner, etc), the date and time of the function or event (and the time it finishes, if there is a set time), and the place of the function or event.

Following the invitation, there are often the letters *RSVP*, an abbreviation of the French words for 'Please Reply'.

• An invitation in the form of a letter should have a salutation and a complimentary close. It may be written in either the third person (*X invites Y* ...) or, slightly less formally, in the first and second persons (*I am writing to invite you* ...). The invitation should otherwise include the same information as in the printed-card form.

- **Replying to an invitation**

Write in the same style as is used in the invitation (*'X thanks Y for their kind invitation to ...'* or *'Dear X, Thank you for your kind invitation to ...'*). You should repeat the main details of the invitation (ie, date and place of the function or event), and state that you have pleasure in accepting the invitation or, alternatively, that you regret you are unable to attend (in which case you should state the reason).

## letters

There are three main types of letter that you may find yourself having to write at some time or another:

*informal letters* (eg letters to friends and relatives),

*formal letters* (eg letters to your local councillor or Member of Parliament), and

*business letters*.

The conventions and rules for formal letters and business letters are, not surprisingly, stricter than those governing informal letter-writing. You should always remember, however, that no matter what sort of letter you are writing, it is easier for someone to misunderstand the written word than the spoken word. In speech, you can modify or clarify what you have said if you see that it has been misunderstood or has unintentionally caused offence, but this is not possible in writing, since you will normally not be present when what you have written is being read. You must, therefore, carefully check what you have written to ensure that what has been said conveys your intended message clearly and correctly, and you should always try to imagine your reader's possible reactions to what they will be reading.

- **Informal letters**

There is little need for guidance on writing informal, personal letters. When you are writing to friends and relatives, you are free to write as you think fit, in a relaxed, colloquial style.

Informal, personal letters may be handwritten, typed or written on a word-processor. However, letters expressing personal feelings such as condolences, apologies or thanks should if at all possible be handwritten.

- **Formal letters**

A formal letter is very similar in layout to a business letter (see BUSINESS LETTERS, page 454). However, a formal letter will normally be less heavily structured than a business letter: there are fewer conventions of form to be adhered to. You must of course put your address, the date, and the name and address of the person or organization you are writing to, and begin your letter with an appropriate salutation. It is useful to give your letter a heading, as this helps the recipient to see at once what the letter is about.

The body of a formal letter should be structured much as that of a business letter, but instead of using the conventional abbreviations found at the beginning and end of business letters, such as 'Encs' (= 'enclosures') and 'cc' (= 'copied to ...'), it is better to write out such points in full within the letter itself, ie '*I enclose ...* ', and '*I am sending a copy of this letter to ...*'.

Obviously, the conventions of courtesy, accuracy, clarity, brevity and relevance that apply to business letters apply equally to all types of formal letter.

### • Business letters
See the separate entry for BUSINESS LETTERS, page 454.

### • Envelopes
The name and address of the recipient should be so positioned on the envelope that the overall appearance of the envelope is pleasantly balanced. Write addresses slightly to the lower left-hand side of the envelope, generally starting about halfway down the envelope in order to leave room for the stamp and to avoid the top line of the address being obscured by the postmark.

In modern business correspondence, the address is usually typed in 'block' form, with each line starting at the same distance from the left-hand side of the envelope, and without commas at the ends of lines:

Mr J Morrison
4 Cranston Drive
LONDON
NW20 3HS

However, the 'sloped' form of address, with each new line beginning slightly further to the right than the line above it, is still preferred by many people, especially in handwritten addresses.

Mr J Morrison
4 Cranston Drive
LONDON
NW20 3HS

The post code should always be included, as the last item in the address, and preferably on a separate line. In all addresses, pay particular attention to street numbers, post codes and the name of the road. (Is it 'Street', 'Drive', 'Avenue', etc?) If the address is handwritten, make sure your writing is clear.

---

◪ **Addressing mail to the USA**

The United States postal authorities have issued guidelines on addressing mail in order to ensure that addresses on mail are compatible with the US Postal Service's automated equipment.

Addresses should be clearly legible (typewritten if possible), entirely in capital letters, and without punctuation marks. The recommended layout is:

First line:   ADDRESSEE'S NAME
Second line:  NUMBER, STREET, APARTMENT NUMBER or
              POST OFFICE BOX NUMBER
Third line:   CITY, STATE, POSTAL CODE
Fourth line:  UNITED STATES OF AMERICA

---

If the letter is private and to be opened only by a particular person rather than, say, by their secretary, write *Personal* or *Confidential* to the left of the envelope above the name of the addressee. If you are writing to someone in a large organization, add the name of their department or office if possible, or the person's title.

## memoranda (memos)

Memos are used for sending messages to employees or colleagues within an organization (though not necessarily in the same building). A business organization usually has its own standard printed memo form specifying, for example,

*To:* —
*From:* —
*Date:* —
*Reference:* —
*Subject:* —

Although a memo is a sort of letter, there should be no formal salutation ( '*Dear* —') at the beginning nor a complimentary close ( '*Yours sincerely*') at the end. As with letters, if enclosures are sent with the memo, *Enc(s)* should be added at the foot of the memo, aligned with the text against the left-hand margin.

## minutes

Minutes are a formal record of a meeting. They summarize the proceedings of the meeting, in the order in which the items on the agenda were dealt with. They include:

i)    a title, stating the type of meeting (eg committee meeting, annual general meeting), the name of the organization, and the date, time and place of the meeting;

ii)    a note on attendance, stating who was present (with the chairperson's name first), and noting apologies for absence;

(For a meeting with a large attendance, such as an annual general meeting, it is sufficient to note only the names of the committee members present, along with the <u>number</u> of ordinary members attending.)

iii)    corrections (if any) to the minutes of the last meeting, and a note that the minutes were read, approved and signed by the chairperson as a correct record of the meeting;

iv)    a summary of the business discussed at the meeting, including correspondence received and action taken (eg replies to be sent), summaries of reports, other business, the vote of thanks (if there is one), the date, time, and place of the next meeting, and when the meeting closed.

Minutes should be written in the past tense and in the third person (see REPORTED SPEECH, page 106). Great care should be taken to avoid ambiguities in wording that could later give rise to uncertainty about the meaning of matters recorded (see, for example, the note on REFUTE on page 191).

Since they are intended to <u>summarize</u> the business of a meeting, minutes need not go into great detail, but must be sufficiently clear and include sufficient information to enable those who were not at the meeting to follow the course of the discussions and to understand the reasons for decisions that were taken. Minutes may, where appropriate, include records of suggestions that were not accepted by the meeting. The full wording of all motions and amendments put to the meeting should be recorded, along with a note of their proposers and seconders and the result of any votes taken.

**précis** see SUMMARIES.

## reports

Reports provide information or state findings, and may also put forward suggestions and make recommendations.

> **The hallmarks of a good report are clarity, simplicity and objectivity. It must be carefully structured, and the information given in it must be arranged logically, so that the reader can grasp the meaning and implication quickly and easily.**

The tone of a report should be impersonal, and the views presented should be balanced and free from bias. As far as possible, the facts should speak for themselves, though you may of course want to draw particular attention to the implications of certain data in your conclusions and recommendations. You must ensure that all the facts, figures and calculations are accurate, and that abbreviations and symbols have been used consistently and will be easily understood by the person reading the report.

The main aspects of the preparation and writing of a report are covered in Appendix A, *Writing Effective English: Planning and Presention* (see page 449). Particular points to note on report-writing are the following:

i) The first essential is to have in your mind a clear idea of the purpose of the report. Is it mainly intended to state facts, to persuade, to set out the pros and cons of a problem, or to make and justify certain recommendations? Who is the report for, and how much do they already know about the subject under discussion? Is technical terminology appropriate, or should the report aim to be as non-technical as possible? The answers to such questions as these will obviously affect the style and presentation of the report you produce.

ii) When you have gathered your facts and ideas and filed them in a logical order under appropriate headings as outlined in Appendix A, decide on your conclusions and/or recommendations. Select sufficient facts to support the conclusions and recommendations. (Do not labour a point — once you have made it and justified it, pass on to the next point.)

iii) Once drafted, reports should be accurately written or, if possible, typed, and attractively presented in a neat cover. If the report is to be duplicated or printed, check the typescript <u>before</u> it is copied. Check that the numbering of pages and paragraphs is uniform.

The following arrangement of material is helpful:

***Title page***: This normally includes the title of the report (you should choose a suitable title unless the title has been given to you), the name(s) of the writer(s) of the report, and the date of completion or submission of the report. (Alternatively, the name(s) and date may come at the end of the report.)

***Contents page***: If the report is fairly long and comprises several sections and subsections, it may be useful for the reader to get an overview of its structure in a contents page.

***Terms of reference***: This should consist of an initial paragraph or paragraphs (the initial section, if your report has several sections) comprising a statement of the instructions given; the purpose and scope of the report; a statement of the problem to be addressed, etc.

*Presentation of facts*: This is the main body of the report, containing a presentation and analysis of the data. A system of numbering paragraphs or sections is often used in reports. A single number denotes the chapter (or section), a second number a section (or subsection), a third number a further subdivision of that, and so on:

6   Traffic management schemes in some European cities

6.1   In France

6.1.1   Paris

6.1.2   Lyon

6.1.3   Marseille

6.2   In Germany

The numbers are generally kept aligned with the left-hand margin (as above), but indenting is also acceptable:

6   Traffic management schemes in some European cities

   6.1   In France

      6.1.1   Paris

      6.1.2   Lyon

      6.1.3   Marseille

   6.2   In Germany

It is also acceptable to use bracketed letters of the alphabet to indicate subdivisions:

6   Traffic management schemes in European cities

   6.1   In France

      6.1.1   Paris

   (a) ...

   (b) ...

      6.1.2   Lyon

Headings should be underlined or in a different typeface to make them stand out from the rest of the text. Whatever layout you use, make sure that it is clear and easy to follow.

If the main issue in any section is obscured by small details, consider moving the minor pieces of information to footnotes or an appendix. (See the notes on FOOTNOTES on page 496.)

*Conclusions*: Make sure that the conclusions follow logically from the stated facts.

*Recommendations*: Make sure that your recommendations follow logically from your conclusions. You may, if appropriate, anticipate possible objections, by stating them and answering them in this section.

***Bibliography***: Make sure that the sources of the data you put forward are clearly acknowledged. It may be necessary, or at least useful, to include a note of your sources in a bibliography (see BIBLIOGRAPHIES in Appendix F, page 494).

***Appendices***: The appendices may include material which supports the case being made but which is too bulky or cumbersome to be placed in the body of the text, eg statistical tables, graphs or long extracts quoted from other documents.

## summaries or précis

A summary is a condensed version of a longer text (or perhaps several texts). Brevity is obtained by identifying and selecting what is essential to the text and stating this succinctly. A summary must remain faithful to the original, and must contain all its key points (but nothing more than the key points).

To write a summary:

i)   Read the original text carefully several times so that the main theme or central argument becomes clear; then study each section of the document in turn, picking out the main points and underlining or highlighting them. (Not all paragraphs may be of equal importance: the introductory and closing paragraphs, for example, may have little worth noting, whereas the central paragraphs may contain many important points.) It may help you to organize the summary if you number the points you have highlighted.

ii)   Eliminate any repetitions, lists, examples and detailed descriptions.

iii)   Using your own rewording where necessary, note in short sentences the points you have highlighted. Be as brief as possible without changing the facts or the sense. Points made in direct speech in the original version should be written in the form of reported speech (see the entry on REPORTED SPEECH, page 106).

iv)   Check each point you highlighted in the original passage against your summary to ensure that you have not omitted any, and make any necessary modifications to what you have written if either the facts or the sense of the original text have not been adequately conveyed by your shortened version. You may have to retain technical terms from the original text, so take care that the meaning of these terms remains clear in the summary.

v)   Combine the notes into a continuous text, paragraphing the sentences appropriately. Avoid disconnected statements and aim for a logical flow of sentences to provide continuity of thought.

vi)   After writing the summary, read it over again at least twice, once to make sure that it gives a clear and fair impression of the original document and that it will make sense to the reader, and a second time to check for misspellings, poor grammar or bad punctuation.

When summarizing a number of documents, such as a series of letters, it is useful to begin by writing an index of them in chronological order, with brief notes on their contents. However, when you are writing the précis itself, it is not necessary that you cover every individual item in the series, and any document not material to the overall argument may be ignored.

# Appendix C:
## Political Correctness

---

'Political correctness' is the avoidance of any expression that could be understood to denigrate, discriminate against or exclude people on the grounds of their age, race, religion, sex, sexual orientation, etc.

Rightly or wrongly, many expressions that were generally considered inoffensive in the past are now deemed unacceptable by many people. You should be careful to avoid in your writing anything that could be regarded as in any way 'sexist', 'racist', 'ageist' or otherwise biased against or offensive to any person or group on any of the above-mentioned or similar grounds.

### ✦ Sexism

Of all the 'isms' to avoid, sexism is probably the most difficult to deal with, because it is well entrenched in our language, both in vocabulary and in grammar. For example, there is no third-person singular pronoun in English that can refer neutrally to people of either sex, and traditionally *he, him* and *his* have been taken to refer (where the sense demanded or allowed it) to human beings of both sexes, eg

*A solicitor's first responsibility is to his client.*
*A great writer creates a world of his own.*

Similarly, *man* has been used to refer to men and women collectively or to human beings as a species:

*Man is a gregarious animal.*

Although still current, such usages are no longer acceptable to many people, and are best avoided in order not to cause needless offence. Ways of getting round these and other potentially offensive locutions are discussed below.

#### • *-ess*

Words ending in the suffix *-ess* should be used with caution nowadays. Many of them are going, or have already gone, out of fashion, and a few (eg *Jewess* and *Negress*) are now usually considered downright insulting.

Still acceptable are the explicitly female forms of titles of nobility, such as *princess, duchess, countess* and *baroness*, and of animal names, such as *lioness* and *tigress*.

The acceptability level of specifically feminine forms of job titles and professions varies but as a general rule is steadily decreasing:

i)   *actress* is still acceptable, although some actresses prefer to be considered actors, but *authoress, poetess* and *sculptress* are definitely out of date now.

---

I'm an <u>actor</u>. An <u>actress</u> is someone who wears boa feathers.
— Sigourney Weaver

---

ii)   *Seamstress* and *songstress* are obsolete, but *seamstress* may be appropriate in historical contexts. A number of other **-ess** words are acceptable in historical or literary contexts only: *adultress, murderess, shepherdess*. In other contexts, use the non- **ess** forms.

iii)   *Waitress* is deprecated by some people, but no acceptable alternative has caught on yet (although both *waitperson* and *waitron* have been suggested). *Waiter* is still taken by most people to denote a male person.

iv)   In Christian religious bodies, women may be *abbesses* or *prioresses*, but it is not correct to refer to female Christian priests as *priestesses*, although it was considered not incorrect to do so as recently as 30 or 40 years ago; *priestess* now always denotes a female priest in a religion other than Christianity.

v)   Some people now recommend the use of *flight attendant* rather than *air hostess* or *stewardess*.

vi)   Use *instructor, patron* and *proprietor* rather than the corresponding **-ess** forms.

Note also that some of the **-ess** forms still in use have more restricted meanings than the equivalent masculine/neutral forms: a small shop or laundrette may have a *manageress*, but in larger businesses women are usually called *managers* like their male counterparts. A *mayoress* is not a female *mayor* but the wife or female partner of a mayor. An *ambassador* may be male or female, the feminine form *ambassadress*, if used at all, denoting the ambassador's wife or female partner. And although in technical legal senses an *heiress* is simply a female heir, in general usage the word more often denotes specifically a woman or girl who has inherited, or expects to inherit, great wealth.

- **man, men**

To refer to both men and women, or to human beings in general, replace **man/men** by words or phrases such as *humans, human beings, men and women* (or *women and men*) or *people*. Compound words which include *man* in the general sense of 'people' should be replaced by neutral terms: say *artificial, synthetic, manufactured* rather than *man-made, working hours* instead of *manhours, human beings* or *humankind* rather than *mankind*, and so on. Other uses of **man** to watch out for and avoid are those that occur in idioms such as *the best man* *for the job, the man in the street, man to man, no man's land, a one-man show* and *every man for himself.*

Similarly, compound words with **man** as the final element should be replaced if **-man** actually means 'man or woman':

i)   On the one hand, it is often possible to use a sex-neutral term:

*firefighter* rather than *fireman*
*intermediary* rather than *middleman*
*non-specialist* rather than *layman*
*police officer* rather than *policeman*
*representative* rather than *spokesman*

(Note that care should be taken also to avoid sexual bias in related derived words. Say, for example, *fair play* rather than *sportsmanship*, and find suitable neutral ways of expressing *brinkmanship, craftsmanship, draughtsmanship, horsemanship, marksmanship, seamanship, showmanship, swordsmanship, yachtsmanship,* etc. For many of these, *skill* is a possible alternative.)

ii)   Where the sex of the person concerned is known, it is usually acceptable to use sex-specific terms, so long as this is done consistently for both sexes: *policeman/policewoman, spokesman/spokeswoman, sportsman/sportswoman.*

iii)   The use of **-person** (eg *chairperson, postperson*) is probably disliked by as many people as approve of it, and is therefore best avoided if possible. *Chair* is similarly preferred by some and disliked intensely by others.

In the plural, compound nouns ending in **-men** should be replaced by other forms, eg *businessmen* by *business people, Frenchmen* by *the French, policemen* by *the police* or *police officers*, etc.

As a verb, **man** should be replaced by, eg, *operate, staff, attend*, etc.

- **he, him,** etc

There are several ways of avoiding using **he, him,** etc when referring to both males and females:

i)   One is to use *he or she, him or her*, etc. This can be cumbersome, however, if it needs to be repeated several times in a sentence, and in such cases is therefore best avoided. The shorter forms *he/she, him/her*, etc are acceptable on forms or in instruction manuals, and are probably acceptable in reports, but have no place in essays or formal letters. The same goes for *s/he* (which only works in the subjective case anyway, as there is no accepted equivalent shortening for *him/her* or *his/her*).

ii)   Another way of getting round the problem is to use *they, them*, etc:

*Has somebody here parked their car on the double yellow lines outside?*
*If anyone else does that, they'll be in serious trouble.*

Some people object to this as ungrammatical, but it is a sensible solution to the problem, one which has been adopted by some of the best writers of

English over the past centuries and which is increasingly accepted.

iii)   A third way of avoiding the problem is to rephrase what you have written in such a way as to avoid using a third-person singular pronoun at all, eg by making the subject plural rather than singular:

> *A person is considered neurotic if he suffers from his problems in living, and psychotic if he makes others suffer*

could be rewritten

> *People are considered neurotic if they suffer from their problems in living, and psychotic if they make others suffer.*

### • Needless reference to a person's sex

In general, there is no need to refer to *lady doctors, women judges, female reporters,* etc, nor to *male nurses,* etc.

### ✦ Racism

There is less racism in English vocabulary than there is sexism. Words to avoid are:

i)   slang terms such as *Chink, Paki, spade, wog,* etc;

ii)   traditional terms for racial groups that the members of these groups now find unacceptable, eg *Red Indian* (prefer *Native American*), *Eskimo* (prefer *Inuit*);

iii)   terms such as *Irish* and *Jew* used in derogatory senses that are offensive to members of these national or racial groups.

### ✦ Religion

i)   slang terms such as *Prod, Pape,* etc;

ii)   traditional terms that the members of the groups concerned now find unacceptable, eg *Mohammedan* (say *Muslim* or *Moslem*).

### ✦ Physical and mental capability

The term *handicapped* is considered unacceptable by some people nowadays. One preferred term, especially in the USA, is *challenged,* as in *visually challenged* as a substitute for *blind, physically challenged* for *physically handicapped, mentally challenged* for *mentally handicapped.*

# Appendix D:
## Idioms, Figures of Speech and Clichés

An *idiom* is an expression with a meaning that cannot be guessed at or derived from the meanings of the individual words which together form it. Examples of English idioms are *put up with*, *face the music*, *go the whole hog* and *in the soup*.

A *figure of speech* is an expression in which words are used in a striking or unusual way for special effect. There are a number of different types of figure of speech, among which are:

i) **similes**, in which one thing is compared to something else, usually by means of the words *as* or *like*: *smoking a pipe as big as a factory chimney* □ *His words were like a slap across her face.*

ii) **metaphors**, in which attention is drawn to the similarity between two things by saying that one thing <u>is</u> the other rather than simply like it as in a simile: *Last night's vote was a slap in the face for the Government.*

iii) **metonymy**, in which a word or phrase denoting one thing is used to refer to or imply some related thing, such as *the bottle* (= 'alcoholic drink') in *He's been fine for a while, but now the pressure is on, I think he's starting to hit the bottle again.*

iv) **synecdoche** (pronounced /si-nek-*do*-ki/), in which a word denoting a part of something is used to denote the whole thing, such as *heads* (= 'people') in *Older and wiser heads might have been more cautious in their approach.*

v) **litotes**, in which something is affirmed by denying its opposite. A well-known example is St Paul's assertion that he was a citizen *of no mean city* (ie, of an important city).

A *cliché* is a phrase or combination of words which was striking and effective when it was first used but which has become stale and feeble through repetition.

- *Idioms* are a normal and natural part of any language, and there is no reason to avoid them, although care must be taken to use only idioms

474

appropriate to the sort of English you are writing (eg avoiding slang expressions in formal or technical writing).

• *Figures of speech*, if not overused, are also appropriate to most forms of writing, as they enliven and add interest to what you are writing. They are, however, best avoided in very technical writing.

---

 One figure of speech to avoid, or at least to handle very carefully, is the so-called *mixed metaphor*, in which two or more metaphors used together create a rather incongruous or perhaps completely ludicrous image:

> *They're always biting the hand that lays the golden egg.*
> — (Attributed to) Samuel Goldwyn

> *Our backs are against the wall, so we need to sit on the fence and keep both ears to the ground.*

---

• *Clichés* pose more of a problem. The advice generally, and wisely, given is that clichés should be avoided in careful writing, as they are boring and unimaginative images (that being the definition of a cliché) rather than striking and effective ones. Cliché-filled writing may give your reader the impression that, since you have not taken the trouble to find an interesting and original way of expressing your thoughts, you have perhaps no interesting and original thoughts to express.

---

**A politician's cliché-ridden speech**

It was clitch after clitch after clitch.

— (Attributed to) Ernest Bevin

---

One part of the problem lies in deciding what is or is not a cliché. There is, unfortunately, no clear line separating worn-out clichés from well-established idioms. Idioms, figures of speech and clichés are not separate and distinct categories, but to a great extent overlap. For example, *to get on like a house on fire* is both an idiom and a figure of speech (a simile), and also in many people's opinion a cliché. Similarly, *That's not my cup of tea* is to some people simply an established English idiom, but to others a cliché. The same can be said for, eg, *a bone of contention*.

A second part of the problem lies in the fact that, even if you recognize that something is a cliché, it may still express exactly what you are trying to say. Is it nevertheless to be avoided on every occasion? Perhaps not, but you should always remember that a cliché that you find acceptable may still irritate someone reading your work and therefore create a bad impression. Caution is required, and if you can find another way of expressing your thought, it would generally be safer to do so.

> **As a general guideline, it is best to look very carefully at and consider replacing any phrase or saying involving a figure of speech, such as a simile or a metaphor, that you yourself are very familiar with. It may be an idiom, but it is likely to be a cliché.**

The following lists provide examples of the sort of expressions that are best considered clichéed, and therefore to be used with caution or avoided altogether:

i) **Common similes**:

as bright as a button
as bold as brass
as cool as a cucumber
as clear as crystal/mud
as cunning as a fox
as flat as a pancake

as like as two peas in a pod
as nutty as a fruitcake
as poor as a church mouse
as sick as a parrot
as weak as a kitten

like a bat out of hell
like a bear with a sore head
(to grin) like a Cheshire cat
like a duck to water

(to drink) like a fish
(to eat) like a horse
like a knife through butter
(to stick out) like a sore thumb

ii) **Common metaphors**:

a baptism of fire
to coin a phrase
to explore every avenue
flavour of the month
the long arm of the law

the march of time
over the moon
to take the bull by the horns
to throw out the baby with the bathwater

iii) **Common sayings, quotations and catchphrases**:

All good things must come to
    an end
A stitch in time (saves nine)
Beggars can't be choosers

the blind leading the blind
Blood is thicker than water
If you can't beat them, join them
Slow and steady wins the race

iv) **Common idioms and set phrases**:

to add insult to injury
as they say/as the saying goes
at the end of the day
last but not least
not for love or money

hell for leather
in no uncertain terms
in this day and age
when all is said and done

v) **Predictable and overused collocations**:

alive and kicking
cool, calm and collected

fast and furious
hale and hearty

*home and dry*
*hook, line and sinker*
*lock, stock and barrel*

*sadder but wiser*
*short and sweet*

*active consideration*
*blissful ignorance*
*a burning question*

*a categorical denial*
*a gaping hole*
*graphic details*

vi) **Vogue words and buzz words:**

| | | | |
|---|---|---|---|
| *acid test* | *dynamic* | *interface* | *situation* |
| *challenging* | *facility* | *meaningful* | *syndrome* |
| *constructive* | *in-depth* | *ongoing* | *track record* |
| *dimension* | *interactive* | *parameter* | *viable* |

# Appendix E:
## Correct Forms of Address

At some time you may need to write to or address in a formal speech a peer of the realm, a member of the clergy or some other person holding an official title or position. You may be aware that etiquette requires the use of certain phrases such as 'Your Grace', 'Your Worship' or 'My Lord', but may be uncertain about which form to use in a particular situation. This appendix provides information on the correct way to begin and end a letter and on what to write in the address at the head of the letter and on the envelope. It also gives the correct spoken forms of address. (Where no specific spoken form of address is given, you may assume that no special style exists.)

---

**◪  Some general notes**

**1.  *Opening a letter***
The simplest way of beginning a formal letter is 'Dear Sir/Madam'. For a less formal letter, 'Dear Mr/Dr/Mrs/Miss'. If you are writing to a knight or a peer, it is usual to address them as 'Dear Sir F—', 'Dear Lady S—', etc, as appropriate.

**2.  *Closing a letter***
The simplest way of closing a formal letter is 'Yours faithfully'. The longer, very formal ceremonial styles are now seldom used, but they have been noted in the following entries where they are still appropriate, even if not now necessary.

If at the beginning of the letter you have addressed the person by their name (eg 'Dear Lord S—') or their specific title (eg 'Dear Lord Mayor'), close with 'Yours sincerely'.

**3.  *Courtesy titles***
Children of peers hold titles of nobility 'by courtesy', that is by common consent and tradition rather than by legal right. Holders of such courtesy titles are addressed according to their rank of their title, but without 'The', 'The Right Hon.' or 'The Most Hon.'.

**4.  *Ranks***
Ranks in the armed forces and ecclesiastical and ambassadorial ranks precede titles in the peerage, eg 'Colonel the Earl of —' or 'the Rev. the Marquess of —'. Similarly with academic ranks such as 'Professor'.

5. *The Royal Family*
Although the correct forms of address for use in letters to members of the Royal Family are given below, it is in fact normal practice for letters to be addressed to a private secretary, equerry or lady-in-waiting rather than to members of the Royal Family directly.

Note: *In the forms of address given below, 'F—' stands for 'forename' and 'S—' for 'surname'.*

### Air Force Officers see OFFICERS.

### Ambassador, British
*Address on letter/envelope*: 'His/Her Excellency' (which may be shortened to 'HE'), followed by the ambassador's name (or title if they have one), followed optionally by 'HM Ambassador'.
('His/Her Excellency' or 'HE' should not be used within the United Kingdom. The wife/husband of an ambassador is not entitled to 'Her/His Excellency'.)

*Begin letter*: 'Sir' or 'Madam' (or whatever is appropriate to the person's rank according to the rules in the other entries in this appendix). 'Dear Ambassador' is also correct, but less formal.

*Close*: 'I have the honour to be, Sir/Madam (or whatever is appropriate to the person's rank), Your Excellency's obedient servant'. Less formally: 'Believe me, my dear Ambassador, Yours sincerely'.

*Spoken address*: 'Your Excellency' at least once, thereafter 'Sir' or 'Madam', or by name.

### Ambassador, Foreign
*Address on letter/envelope*: 'His/Her Excellency the Ambassador of —' or 'His/Her Excellency the — Ambassador'.
(The wife/husband of an ambassador is not entitled to the style 'Her/His Excellency'.)

*Begin letter*: 'Your Excellency'. (In the letter, refer to the person as 'Your Excellency' once, thereafter as 'you'.) Less formally: 'Dear Ambassador'.

*Close*: 'I have the honour to be, Sir/Madam (or whatever is appropriate to the person's rank), Your Excellency's obedient servant'. Less formally: 'Believe me, my dear Ambassador, Yours sincerely'.

*Spoken address*: 'Your Excellency' at least once, thereafter 'Sir' or 'Madam', or by name.

### Archbishop (Church of England and other Anglican churches)
*Address on letter/envelope*: 'The Most Reverend the Lord Archbishop of —'.
The Archbishops of Canterbury and York are Privy Counsellors and should be addressed as 'The Most Reverend and Right Hon. the Lord Archbishop of —'.

*Begin letter*: 'My Lord Archbishop' or, less formally, 'Dear Archbishop'.

*Spoken address*: 'Your Grace'; begin an official speech 'My Lord Archbishop'.

**Retired archbishops** revert to the status of bishop: see RETIRED BISHOP under BISHOP (CHURCH OF ENGLAND, ETC).

## Archbishop (Roman Catholic)

*Address on letter/envelope*: 'His Grace the Archbishop of —'.

*Begin letter*: 'My Lord Archbishop' or, less formally, 'Dear Archbishop'.

*Close*: 'I remain, Your Grace, Yours faithfully', or simply 'Yours faithfully'.

*Spoken address*: 'Your Grace' or, less formally, 'Archbishop'.

For a ***retired archbishop***:

*Address on letter/envelope*: 'The Most Reverend Archbishop S—'.

Otherwise as above.

## Archdeacon

*Address on letter/envelope*: 'The Venerable the Archdeacon of —'.

*Begin letter*: 'Dear Archdeacon' or 'Dear Sir', more formally, 'Venerable Sir' .

*Spoken address*: 'Archdeacon'; begin an official speech 'Venerable Sir'.

## Army Officers see OFFICERS.

## Attorney-General

As for a SECRETARY OF STATE.

## Baron

*Address on letter/envelope*: 'The Right Hon. Lord S—'.

*Begin letter*: 'My Lord' or, less formally, 'Dear Lord S—'.

*Spoken address*: 'My Lord' or, less formally, 'Lord S—'.

## Baroness

For a ***baron's wife***:

*Address on letter/envelope*: 'The Right Hon. Lady S—'.

*Begin letter*: 'Dear Madam' or, less formally, 'Dear Lady S—'.

*Spoken address*: 'Madam' or, less formally, 'Lady S—'.

For a ***baroness in her own right***:

*Address on letter/envelope*: either as for a BARON'S WIFE, or, if she prefers, as 'The Right Hon. the Baroness S—'.

Otherwise as for a BARON'S WIFE.

## Baron's daughter

*Address on letter/envelope*: If she is unmarried, 'The Hon. F— S—'.

If married to a commoner, 'The Hon. Mrs S—'.

If married to a baron or a knight, 'The Hon. Lady S—'.

If the wife of a peer or courtesy peer, address as appropriate to that rank.

*Begin letter*: 'Dear Madam', or according to rank.

*Spoken address*: 'Miss/Mrs S—', or according to rank.

## Baron's son

*Address on letter/envelope*: 'The Hon. F— S—'.

The eldest sons of barons in the Scottish peerage are usually addressed 'The Master of [peerage title]'.

*Begin letter*: 'Dear Sir'.

*Spoken address*: 'Mr S—' or 'Sir'.

A Master may also be addressed as 'Master'.

## Baron's son's wife

*Address on letter/envelope*: 'The Hon. Mrs [husband's forename and surname]'.

If the daughter of a viscount or baron, 'The Hon. Mrs S—.

If the daughter of a duke, marquess or earl, address as such.

*Begin letter*: 'Dear Madam', or according to rank.

*Spoken address*: according to rank.

## Baronet

*Address on letter/envelope*: 'Sir F— S—, Bt'.

*Begin letter*: 'Dear Sir' or, less formally, 'Dear Sir F—'.

*Spoken address*: 'Sir F—'.

## Baronet's wife

*Address on letter/envelope*: 'Lady S—'.

If she has the title 'Lady' by courtesy, 'Lady F— S—'.

If she has the courtesy style 'The Hon.', this precedes 'Lady'.

*Begin letter*: 'Dear Madam' or, less formally, 'Dear Lady S—'.

*Spoken address*: 'Madam' or, less formally, 'Lady S—'.

## Bishop (Church of England and other Anglican churches)

For a *diocesan bishop*:

*Address on letter/envelope*: 'The Right Reverend the Lord Bishop of —'.

The Bishop of London is a Privy Counsellor, so is addressed as 'The Right Rev. and Right Hon. the Lord Bishop of London'.

The Bishop of Meath is by tradition styled 'The Most Reverend', not 'The Right Reverend'.

*Begin letter*: 'My Lord' or, less formally, 'Dear Bishop'.

*Spoken address*: 'Bishop'; begin an official speech 'My Lord'.

For a *suffragan bishop*:

*Address on letter/envelope*: 'The Right Reverend the Bishop of —'.

*Begin letter*: 'Dear Bishop', 'My Lord' or 'Right Reverend Sir';

*Spoken address*: 'Bishop'; begin an official speech 'My Lord' or 'Right Reverend Sir'.

For a *retired bishop*:

*Address on letter/envelope*: 'The Right Reverend F— S—'.

If a privy Counsellor, 'The Right Rev. and Right Hon. F— S—'.

*Begin letter*: 'Dear Bishop', 'My Lord' or 'Right Reverend Sir'.

*Spoken address*: 'Bishop'; begin an official speech 'My Lord' or 'Right Reverend Sir'.

For a *bishop in the Episcopal Church in Scotland*:

*Address on letter/envelope*: 'The Right Reverend F— S—', Bishop of —'.

Otherwise as for a bishop of the Church of England.

(The bishop who holds the position of *Primus* is addressed in writing as 'The Most Reverend the Primus'. *Begin letter*: 'Dear Primus'. *Spoken address*: 'Primus'.)

## Bishop (Roman Catholic)

*Address on letter/envelope*: 'His Lordship the Bishop of —' or 'The Right Reverend F— S—, Bishop of —'.
In Ireland, 'the Most Reverend' is used instead of 'The Right Reverend'.
If an ***auxiliary bishop***, address as 'The Right Reverend F— S—, Auxiliary Bishop of —'.

*Begin letter*: 'My Lord' or, less formally, 'Dear Bishop' or 'Dear Bishop S—'.

*Close*: 'I remain, My Lord (or, now more rarely, 'My Lord Bishop'), Yours faithfully'; or simply 'Yours faithfully'.

*Spoken address*: 'My Lord' or, less formally, 'Bishop'.


## Business firms

*Address on letter/envelope*: The term 'Messrs' is now old-fashioned. It cannot in any case be used with the name of a limited company, nor in addressing a firm (a) which does not trade under a surname, (b) whose name includes a rank or title, or (c) which bears the name of a woman.

*Begin letter*: 'Dear Sirs'.

For further details, see BUSINESS LETTERS in Appendix B, page 454.


## Cabinet Minister see SECRETARY OF STATE.


## Canon (Church of England and other Anglican churches)

*Address on letter/envelope*: 'the Reverend Canon F— S—'.

*Begin letter*: 'Dear Canon' or 'Dear Canon S—'.

*Spoken address*: 'Canon' or 'Canon S—'.


## Canon (Roman Catholic)

*Address on letter/envelope*: 'The Very Reverend Canon F— S—'.

*Begin letter*: 'Very Reverend Sir'. or 'Dear Sir'; less formally, 'Dear Canon' or 'Dear Canon S—'.

*Spoken address*: 'Canon S—'.


## Cardinal

*Address on letter/envelope*: 'His Eminence Cardinal S—'.
If an archbishop, 'His Eminence the Cardinal Archbishop of —'.

*Begin letter*: 'Your Eminence' or, now more rarely, 'My Lord Cardinal'.

*Close*: 'I remain, Your Eminence (or 'My Lord Cardinal'), Yours faithfully'.
A Roman Catholic may close more ceremonially with 'I have the honour to be, My Lord Cardinal, Your Eminence's devoted and obedient child'.

*Spoken address*: 'Your Eminence' or, less formally, 'Cardinal S—'.


## Chairman of County Council, Regional Council, etc

*Address on letter/envelope*: 'the Chairman of the — Council' or, less formally, by name.

*Begin letter*: 'Dear Mr Chairman', ***even if the holder of the office is a woman***. Less formally, by name.

*Spoken address*: 'Mr Chairman', ***even to a woman***, or by name.

## Chief Constable

*Address on letter/envelope*: 'F— S— (adding 'Esq.' in the case of a man), Chief Constable, — Constabulary (or '— Police')'.

*Begin letter*: 'Dear Sir/Madam' or, less formally 'Dear Chief Constable' or 'Dear Mr/Mrs (etc) S—'.

## Chief Rabbi

*Address on letter/envelope*: 'The Very Reverend the Chief Rabbi' or 'The Chief Rabbi (Dr) F— S—'.

*Begin letter*: 'Dear Chief Rabbi' or 'Dear Sir'.

*Spoken address*: 'Chief Rabbi', or by name.

## Christian Clergy

### *Church of England and other Anglican churches*:

*Address on letter/envelope*: 'The Reverend F— S—'.

*Begin letter*: 'Dear Sir/Madam' or 'Dear Mr/Mrs (etc) S—'.

### *Church of Scotland and other Protestant churches*:

*Address on letter/envelope*: 'The Reverend F— S—.

*Begin letter*: 'Dear Sir/Madam' or 'Dear Mr/Mrs (etc) S—'.

### *Roman Catholic*:

*Address on letter/envelope*: 'The Reverend F— S—'.

If he is a member of a religious order, the initials of the order should be added after the name.

*Begin letter*: 'Dear Reverend Father'.

 In American English, it is considered correct to refer to a member of the clergy as, for example, 'Reverend Smith'. Although now common in British English also, it is not correct. Say 'Mr/Mrs/Miss Smith'.

## Companion of an order of knighthood

The initials 'CB', 'CMG' or 'CH' (as it may be) follow the ordinary form of address.

## Consul, British

*Address on letter/envelope*: 'F— S— (adding 'Esq.' in the case of a man), British Consul-General/Consul/Vice-Consul'.

If a Consul-General, Consul or Vice-Consul holds Her Majesty's Commission, they are addressed as 'HM Consul', etc, rather than as 'British Consul', etc.

## Councillor

*Address on letter/envelope*: 'Councillor F— S—' (if a man); 'Councillor Mrs/Miss F— S—' if a woman.

*Begin letter*: 'Dear Councillor S—', 'Dear Councillor Mrs/Miss S—' or, less formally 'Dear Mr/Mrs/Miss S—'.

## Countess

*Address on letter/envelope*: 'The Right Hon. the Countess of —'.

*Begin letter*: 'Madam' or, less formally 'Dear Lady S—'.

*Spoken address*: 'Madam' or, less formally 'Lady S—'.

## Dame

*Address on letter/envelope*: 'Dame F— S—', followed by the letters of the order concerned (eg *DCB* for the Order of the Bath, *DCVO* for the Royal Victorian Order, etc).

If a peeress or the daughter of a duke, marquess or earl, 'Lady F— S—' followed by the letters of the order.

If entitled to be styled 'The Hon.' then this precedes 'Dame'.

*Begin letter*: 'Dear Madam' or, less formally 'Dear Dame F—'.

*Spoken address*: 'Madam' or, less formally 'Dame F—'.

## Dean (Anglican)

*Address on letter/envelope*: 'The Very Reverend the Dean of —'.

*Begin letter*: 'Very Reverend Sir' or, less formally 'Dear Dean'.

*Spoken address*: 'Dean'; begin an official speech 'Very Reverend Sir'.

## Doctor

### Medical doctors:

Physicians, anaesthetists, pathologists and radiologists are addressed as 'Doctor'. Surgeons, whether they hold the degree of Doctor of Medicine or not, are known as 'Mr/Mrs/Miss'. In England and Wales, obstetricians and gynaecologists are addressed as 'Mr/Mrs/Miss', but in Scotland, Ireland and elsewhere as 'Doctor'.

### Holders of doctorates:

In addressing a letter to the holder of a doctorate, the initials DD, LLD, MD, MusD, etc may be placed after the ordinary form of address, as 'The Rev. John Smith, DD', 'John Brown, Esq., LLD'. Alternatively, address to 'The Rev. Dr Smith', 'Dr John Brown', etc.

*Begin letter*: 'Dear Sir/Madam' or, less formally 'Dear Dr S—'.

## Dowager

On the marriage of a peer or baronet, the widow of the previous holder of the title becomes 'Dowager'.

*Address on letter/envelope*: 'The Right Hon. the Dowager Countess of —', 'The Right Hon. the Dowager Lady —', etc.

(If there already is a Dowager still living, she retains this title, the later widow being addressed 'The Most Hon. F—, Marchioness of—', 'The Right Hon. F—, Lady —', etc. It should be noted, however, that many dowagers prefer the style which includes their first names to that including the title dowager.)

Otherwise as for the wife of a peer.

## Duchess

*Address on letter/envelope*: 'Her Grace the Duchess of —'.

*Begin letter*: 'Dear Madam' or, less formally 'Dear Duchess'.

*Spoken address*: 'Your Grace' or, less formally 'Duchess'.

(For a royal duchess, see PRINCESS.)

## Duke

*Address on letter/envelope*: 'His Grace the Duke of —'.
*Begin letter*: 'My Lord Duke' or, less formally 'Dear Duke'.
*Spoken address*: 'Your Grace' or, less formally 'Duke'.
(For a royal duke, see PRINCE.)

## Duke's daughter

*Address on letter/envelope*: 'Lady F— S—.
> If married to a peer, she is addressed according to her husband's rank only; this, however, does not necessarily hold in the case of peers by courtesy.
> If married to a person with the style 'The Hon.', she does not adopt this but retains the title 'Lady'.

*Begin letter*: 'Dear Madam'.
*Spoken address*: 'Madam'.

## Duke's eldest son and son's heir

*Address on letter/envelope*: A duke's eldest son takes his father's second-highest title. This courtesy title is treated as if it were an actual peerage (but see the notes on courtesy titles in the General Notes above, page 478).
> The son's eldest son takes his grandfather's third title, also being addressed as if a peer.

(*Begin letter*, etc according to rank).

## Duke's eldest son's wife

*Address on letter/envelope*: Address as if her husband's courtesy title were an actual peerage (but see the notes on courtesy titles in the General Notes at the beginning of the appendix, page 478).

## Duke's younger son

*Address on letter/envelope*: 'Lord F— S—'.
*Begin letter*: 'My Lord'.
*Spoken address*: 'My Lord' or, less formally 'Lord F—'.

## Duke's younger son's wife

*Address on letter/envelope*: 'Lady [husband's forename and surname]'.
*Begin letter*: 'Dear Madam'.
*Spoken address*: 'Madam' or, less formally 'Lady [husband's forename].

## Earl

*Address on letter/envelope*: 'The Right Hon. the Earl of—'.
*Begin letter*: 'My Lord' or, less formally 'Dear Lord —'.
*Spoken address*: 'My Lord' or, less formally 'Lord —'.
(For an earl's wife, see COUNTESS.)

## Earl's daughter

As for a DUKE'S DAUGHTER.

## Earl's eldest son and son's wife

As for a DUKE'S ELDEST SON AND SON'S WIFE.

## Earl's younger son and son's wife

As for a BARON'S SON AND SON'S WIFE.

## Governor of a colony or Governor-General

*Address on letter/envelope* 'His Excellency [name and/or title], Governor (-General) of —'. The Governor-General of Canada has the rank of 'Right Honourable' which he retains for life. The wife of a Governor-General is styled 'Her Excellency' only within the country her husband administers.

*Begin letter*: 'Sir', or according to the person's rank (eg 'My Lord'); or, less formally 'Dear Mr S—', 'Dear Sir F—', etc.

*Close*: 'I have the honour to be, Sir (or 'My Lord', if a peer), Your Excellency's obedient servant'.

*Spoken address*: 'Your Excellency'.

## Judge, High Court

*Address on letter/envelope*: 'The Hon. Mr/Mrs Justice S—' (NB: 'Mrs' *even to an unmarried woman*); less formally 'Sir/Dame F— S—'.

*Begin letter*: 'Dear Sir/Madam' or, less formally 'Dear Judge' or 'Dear Sir/Dame F—'. If you are writing on judicial matters, 'My Lord/Lady'.

*Spoken address*: 'Sir/Madam'.

A High Court judge may be addressed as 'My Lord/Lady' or referred to as 'Your Lordship/Ladyship' only when sitting on the bench or when dealing with judicial matters.

## Judge, Circuit

*Address on letter/envelope*: 'His/Her Honour Judge S—' If a knight, 'His Honour Judge Sir F— S—'.

*Begin letter*: 'Dear Sir/Madam' or, less formally 'Dear Judge'.

*Spoken address*: 'Sir/Madam'.

Address a circuit judge as 'Your Honour' only when he/she is on the bench or dealing with judicial matters.

## Judge, Irish

As for an English CIRCUIT JUDGE.

## Judge, Scottish see LORD OF SESSION.

## Justice of the Peace (England and Wales)

*Address on letter/envelope*: Address according to the person's rank. The letters 'JP' may optionally be added after the person's name in addressing a letter.

*Spoken address*: Refer to and address as 'Your Worship' when he/she is on the bench. Otherwise according to the person's rank.

## Knight Bachelor

As for a BARONET, except that 'Bt' is omitted.

## Knight of the Bath, of St Michael and St George, etc

*Address on letter/envelope*: 'Sir F— S—', followed by the letters of the order concerned (eg *KCB* for the Order of the Bath, *KCMG* for the Order of St Michael and St George, etc).

*Begin letter*: 'Dear Sir'.

## Knight of the Garter or of the Thistle
*Address on letter/envelope*: The initials 'KG' or 'KT' follow the name.
*Begin letter*, etc according to the person's rank.

## Knight's wife
As for a BARONET'S WIFE or according to her own rank.

## Lady Mayoress
*Address on letter/envelope*: 'The Lady Mayoress of —'.
*Begin letter*: 'My Lady Mayoress' or, less formally 'Dear Lady Mayoress'.
*Spoken address*: 'Lady Mayoress'; formally, eg to begin a speech,'My Lady Mayoress'.

## Lady Provost
*Address on letter/envelope*: 'The Lady Provost of —',
*Begin letter*: 'My Lady Provost' or, less formally 'Dear Lady Provost'.
*Spoken address*: 'Lady Provost'; formally, eg to begin a speech,'My Lady Provost'.

## Lord Advocate of Scotland
*Address on letter/envelope*: 'The Right Hon. the Lord Advocate, QC' or 'The Right Hon. F— S—, QC'.
*Begin letter*: 'Dear Sir', or 'My Lord' if a peer; less formally 'Dear Lord Advocate'.
Otherwise according to the person's rank.

## Lord Chancellor
*Address on letter/envelope*: 'the Right Hon. the Lord Chancellor'.
*Begin letter*: 'My Lord' or, less formally 'Dear Lord Chancellor'.
Otherwise according to the person's rank.

## Lord Chief Justice
*Address on letter/envelope*: 'The Right Hon. the Lord Chief Justice of England'.
The Lord Chief Justice of Northern Ireland is addressed in the same manner unless he is a knight, in which case he is addressed as 'The Right Hon. Sir F— S—, Lord Chief Justice of Northern Ireland'.
*Begin letter*: 'My Lord' or, less formally 'Dear Lord Chief Justice'.
Otherwise according to his rank as a peer.

## Lord High Commissioner to the General Assembly
*Address on letter/envelope*: 'His/Her Grace the Lord High Commissioner'.
*Begin letter*: 'Your Grace'.
*Close*: 'I have the honour to remain, Your Grace's most devoted and obedient servant'.
*Spoken address*: 'Your Grace'.

## Lord Justice-Clerk
*Address on letter/envelope*: 'The Hon. the Lord Justice-Clerk'.
If a Privy Counsellor, 'The Right Hon.'.

*Begin letter*: 'My Lord' or, less formally 'Dear Lord Justice-Clerk'.

*Spoken address*: 'My Lord'; refer to as 'Your Lordship'.

(The wife of the Lord Justice-Clerk is styled and addressed in the same manner as the wife of a Lord of Session.)

### Lord Justice-General of Scotland

*Address on letter/envelope*: 'The Right Hon. the Lord Justice-General'.

*Begin letter*: 'My Lord' or, less formally 'Dear Lord Justice-General'.

*Spoken address*: 'My Lord'; refer to as 'Your Lordship'.

(The wife of a Lord Justice-General is styled and addressed in the same manner as the wife of a Lord of Session.)

### Lord Justice of the Court of Appeal

*Address on letter/envelope*: 'The Right Hon. Lord Justice S—'.

*Begin letter*: 'My Lord' or, less formally 'Dear Lord Justice'.

*Spoken address*: 'My Lord'; refer to as 'Your Lordship'.

### Lord Mayor

*Address on letter/envelope*: The Lord Mayors of London, York, Belfast, Cardiff and Dublin are styled 'the Right Hon. the Lord Mayor of —'; other Lord Mayors are styled 'The Right Worshipful the Lord Mayor of —'.

*Begin letter*: 'My Lord Mayor', ***even if the holder of the office is a woman***; less formally 'Dear Lord Mayor'.

*Spoken address*: 'Lord Mayor'; formally, eg to begin a speech, 'My Lord Mayor'.

### Lord Mayor's wife see LADY MAYORESS.

### Lord of Appeal in Ordinary and his wife

As for a BARON and BARONESS.

(Their children are styled in the same way as a BARON'S DAUGHTER and BARON'S SON.)

### Lord of Session in Scotland

*Address on letter/envelope*: 'the Hon. Lord S—.

If a Privy Counsellor, 'The Right Hon.'.

*Begin letter*: 'My Lord' or, less formally 'Dear Lord S—'.

*Spoken address*: 'My Lord'; refer to as 'Your Lordship'.

(The wife of a Lord of Session is styled 'Lady' and is addressed in the same way as a BARON'S WIFE, but without the prefix 'The Right Hon.'.)

### Lord Provost

*Address on letter/envelope*: 'The Right Hon. the Lord Provost of Edinburgh/Glasgow', but 'The Lord Provost of Aberdeen/Dundee'.

*Begin letter*: 'My Lord Provost' or, less formally 'Dear Lord Provost'.

*Spoken address*: 'Lord Provost'; formally, eg to begin a speech, 'My Lord Provost'.

### Lord Provost's wife see LADY PROVOST.

## Marchioness
*Address on letter/envelope*: 'The Most Hon. the Marchioness of —'.
*Begin letter*: 'Madam' or, less formally 'Dear Lady —'.
*Spoken address*: 'Madam'.

## Marquess
*Address on letter/envelope*: 'The Most Hon. the Marquess of —'.
*Begin letter*: 'My Lord' or, less formally 'Dear Lord —'.
*Spoken address*: 'My Lord'.

## Marquess's daughter
As for a DUKE'S DAUGHTER.

## Marquess's sons and sons' wives
As for a DUKE'S SONS and DUKE'S SONS' WIVES.

## Master
(a title borne by the eldest son of a baron or viscount in the peerage of Scotland) see
BARON'S SON.

## Mayor
*Address on letter/envelope* 'The Worshipful the Mayor of —'; in the case of cities and
certain towns, 'The Right Worshipful'.
*Begin letter*: 'Mr Mayor', ***even if the mayor is a woman***, although some women
prefer 'Madam Mayor'; less formally 'Dear Mr Mayor'.
*Spoken address*: 'Mr Mayor'.

## Mayoress
*Address on letter/envelope*: 'The Mayoress of —'.
*Begin letter*: 'Madam Mayoress' or, less formally 'Dear Mayoress'.
*Spoken address*: 'Mayoress'.

## Member of Parliament
*Address on letter/envelope*: Add 'MP' to the usual form of address.
*Begin letter*, etc according to the person's rank.

## Moderator of the General Assembly of the Church of Scotland
*Address on letter/envelope*: 'The Right Reverend the Moderator of the General Assembly
of the Church of Scotland' or 'The Right Reverend F— S—'.
*Begin letter*: 'Dear Sir' or 'Dear Moderator'.
*Spoken address*: 'Moderator'.
(***Former moderators*** are styled 'The Very Reverend'.)

## Moderator of the General Assembly of the United Reformed Church
*Address on letter/envelope*: 'The Right Reverend F— S—'.
*Begin letter*: 'Dear Moderator'.
*Spoken address*: 'Moderator' or 'Mr Moderator'.
(***Former moderators*** are styled 'The Reverend'.)

## Monsignor

*Address on letter/envelope*: 'The Reverend Monsignor F— S—'.

*Begin letter*: 'Reverend Sir' or, less formally 'Dear Monsignor S—'.

Spoken address: 'Monsignor S—'.

## Officers in the Army, Navy and Air Force

*Address on letter/envelope*: The professional rank precedes any other rank or title, eg
'Admiral the Right Hon. the Earl of —', 'Lieut.-Col. Sir F— S—, KCB'.
Officers below the rank of Rear-Admiral and Marshal of the Royal Air Force are
entitled to 'RN' (or 'Royal Navy') and 'RAF' respectively after their name. Army
officers of the rank of Colonel or below may follow their name with the name of
their regiment or corps (or an accepted abbreviation of the name).

*Begin letter*: according to the person's civil rank.

### *Retired officers*:

*Address on letter/envelope*: Officers above the rank of Lieutenant (in the Royal Navy),
Captain (in the army) and Flight Lieutenant (in the Royal Air Force) may
continue to use and be addressed by their armed forces rank after being placed
on the retired list.
The word 'retired', or any abbreviation of it, should not normally be placed after
the person's name.

## Pope

*Address on letter/envelope*: 'His Holiness the Pope'.

*Begin letter*: 'Your Holiness' or 'Most Holy Father'.

*Close*: If you are a Roman Catholic, 'I have the honour to be, your Holiness's most
devoted and obedient child' (or 'most humble child').
If you are not Roman Catholic, 'I have the honour to be (or 'remain'), Your
Holiness's obedient servant'.

*Spoken address*: 'Your Holiness'.

## Prebendary

As for a CHURCH OF ENGLAND CANON.

## Prime Minister

*Address on letter/envelope*: According to the person's rank.
The Prime Minister is a Privy Counsellor (see separate entry) and the letter
should be addressed accordingly, eg 'The Right Hon. F— S—, MP'.

*Begin letter*: according to rank (eg 'Dear Sir/Madam'), or, less formally 'Dear Prime
Minister'.

Otherwise according to rank.

## Prince

*Address on letter/envelope*: If a duke, 'His Royal Highness the Duke of—'.
If not a duke, but a child of the sovereign, 'His Royal Highness the Prince F—'.
Otherwise 'His Royal Highness Prince F— of [Kent or Gloucester]'.
(But see the General Notes at the beginning of the appendix, page 478.)

*Begin letter*: 'Sir'. Refer to as 'Your Royal Highness'.

*Close*: 'I have the honour to remain (or be), Sir, Your Royal Highness's most humble and obedient servant'.

*Spoken address*: 'Your Royal Highness' once, thereafter 'Sir'.

## Princess

*Address on letter/envelope*: If a duchess, 'Her Royal Highness the Duchess of —'.

If not a duchess, the daughter of a sovereign is addressed as 'Her Royal Highness the Princess F—' followed by any title she holds in marriage.

'The' is omitted in addressing a princess who is not the daughter of a sovereign. A princess by marriage is addressed 'HRH Princess [husband's forename] of —'.

(But see the General Notes at the beginning of the appendix, page 478.)

*Begin letter*: 'Madam'. Refer to as 'Your Royal Highness'.

*Close*: as for a prince, substituting 'Madam' for 'Sir'.

*Spoken address*: 'Your Royal Highness' once, thereafter 'Ma'am'.

## Privy Counsellor

*Address on letter/envelope*: If a peer, 'the Right Hon. the Earl of —, PC'.

If not a peer, 'The Right Hon. F— S—', without the 'PC'.

*Begin letter*, etc according to the person's rank.

## Professor

*Address on letter/envelope*: 'Professor F— S—'

(The styles 'Professor Lord S—', 'Professor Sir F— S—', etc are frequently used but are deprecated by some people.)

If the professor is in holy orders, 'The Reverend Professor'.

*Begin letter*: 'Dear Sir/Madam', or according to the person's rank (eg 'Dear Sir F—', etc).

*Spoken address*: 'Professor S—' or according to the person's rank (eg 'Sir F—').

## Provost, Roman Catholic

As for a ROMAN CATHOLIC CANON.

## Provost, Town

*Address on letter/envelope*: 'The Provost of —'.

*Begin letter*: 'Dear Provost'.

*Spoken address*: 'Provost'.

## Queen

*Address on letter/envelope*: 'Her Majesty the Queen'.

*Begin letter*: 'Madam, with my humble duty' (but see the General Notes at the beginning of the appendix, page 478). Refer to as 'Your Majesty'.

*Close*: 'I have the honour to remain (or be), Madam, Your Majesty's most humble and obedient servant'.

*Spoken address*: 'Your Majesty' once, thereafter 'Ma'am'; begin an official speech 'May it please Your Majesty'.

## Queen Mother

As for the QUEEN, substituting 'Queen Elizabeth The Queen Mother' for 'The Queen'.

491

## Queen's Counsel

Add 'QC' to the ordinary form of address, but not if addressing a letter to a person holding one of the higher legal appointments such as a High Court Judge or Lord of Appeal in Ordinary.

## Rabbi

*Address on letter/envelope*: 'Rabbi [initial and surname]' or, if a doctor, 'Rabbi Doctor [initial and surname]'.

*Begin letter*: 'Dear Sir/Madam' or, less formally 'Dear Rabbi S—'.

*Spoken address*: 'Rabbi S—' or 'Doctor S—'.

## Secretary of State

*Address on letter/envelope*: 'The Right Hon. F— S—, MP, Secretary of State for —', or, if on official business, 'The Secretary of State for —'.

Otherwise according to the person's rank.

## Viscount

*Address on letter/envelope*: 'The Right Hon. the Viscount —'.

*Begin letter*: 'My Lord' or, less formally 'Dear Lord —'.

*Spoken address*: 'My Lord' or, less formally 'Lord —'.

## Viscountess

*Address on letter/envelope*: 'The Right Hon. the Viscountess —'.

*Begin letter*: 'Madam' or, less formally 'Dear Lady —'.

*Spoken address*: 'Madam' or, less formally 'Lady —'.

## Viscount's daughter, son and son's wife

As for a BARON'S DAUGHTER, BARON'S SON and BARON'S SON'S WIFE.

- ## Orders, decorations and academic degrees

When letters representing awards and qualifications are written after a person's name, they should be added in the following order:

i) ***Bt*** (for 'Baronet') must precede all other sets of letters.

ii) Decorations and honours, such as ***VC*** (= 'Victoria Cross'), ***CBE*** (= 'Commander of the Order of the British Empire'), ***OBE*** (= 'Order of the British Empire'), ***DSC*** (= 'Distinguished Service Cross'), ***GM*** (= 'George Medal'), etc.

iii) Royal appointments such as ***PC*** (= 'Privy Counsellor'), ***QC*** (= 'Queen's Counsel'), ***JP*** (= 'Justice of the Peace'), etc. Of these, ***QC*** is the only one that must be used in addresses. ***PC*** is rarely used, and ***JP*** is only required if the letter concerns matters directly connected with that office.

iv) University degrees.

v) Medical qualifications.

vi) Fellowships and memberships of professional bodies, societies, etc. Election to certain distinguished bodies should always be recognized by appending the appropriate initials to the person's name, eg **FRS** (= 'Fellow of the Royal Society'), **RA** (= 'Royal Academician'), **FBA** (= 'Fellow of the British Academy').

vii) Other appointments or offices, eg **MP** and **WS** (= 'Writer to the Signet', a member of a Scottish solicitor's society).

# Appendix F:
## Bibliographies, References, Quotations and Footnotes

*Note that in examples in this appendix, underlining indicates places where you should use either italics or underlining in your writing.*

## bibliographies

When you are writing an essay or a report, you may need to provide a list of the sources you have consulted. Such a list is known as a *bibliography*.

There are a number of conventions that should be observed when you are writing a bibliography:

i)   A bibliography should always begin on a fresh page. Do not run it on from the end of the essay or report.

ii)   A bibliography should include the sources of information that you have actually used, ie those which have contributed in some way to what you have written. You should not simply list all the books or articles you have read.

iii)   The information you give in an entry in a bibliography should include the name of the author (or authors), the title of the work consulted, and details about when, where and by whom it was published.

- **Layout**

There are a number of ways of setting out the information in a bibliography. The following is one which is commonly used and generally accepted.

i)   The name(s) of the author(s) should be given in the order *surname* then *first name*: *Landon, Leonard*. The author's first name may be indicated simply by its initial letter, and any other names should normally be indicated solely by initials: *Landon, L.J.* □ *Landon, Leonard J.*

If there are two authors, link the names by *and*: *Landon, L. and Landon, W*. If there are three authors, link the names of the second and third with *and*: *Landon, L., Landon, W. and Mackenzie, J*. If there are four or more authors, it is common practice to name only the first author, and indicate the others by 'et al' (= *et alii*, Latin for 'and others'): *Landon, L et al*.

⚠ In some books, for example dictionaries or encyclopaedias, there may be no named author, in which case you should list the book in your bibliography under the name of the editor, followed by '(ed)', or, in the case of larger works such as multi-volume encyclopaedias, under the name of the work itself, which should be underlined or (if you have access to a word-processor) printed in italic type.

ii)    Immediately after the name(s) of the author(s) should come the year in which the book or article was published, in parentheses if you prefer: *Landon, L. 1979* or *Landon, L. (1979)*. (A note of the year of publication of a book can generally be found on the page after the title page.) If you are listing two or more books or articles by the same author(s), all of which have been published in the same year, refer to them as eg *(1979a)*, *(1979b)*, *(1979c)*, etc.

For an alternative position for the year of publication, see (vii) below.

iii)    Works should be listed in the bibliography in alphabetical order according to the surname of the author (or of the first author if there is more than one), and then by the year of publication. All publications written by a single author should be listed before any publications by that author in collaboration with others:

*Landon, L. (1979)* ...
*Landon, L. (1983a)* ...
*Landon. L. (1983b)* ...
*Landon, L. and Landon, W. (1981)* ...

iv)    Next should come the title of the publication. If it is the title of a book, then it should be underlined or printed in italics. If it is the title of an article in a book or journal, the title should not be underlined or in italics, but the name of the book or journal it is published in should be:

[article]    *Landon, L. (1979) On word structure. Linguistic Investigations.*
[book]    *Landon, L. (1983) Arabic Words in English.*

If you are listing the title of an article in a periodical, you must add the volume number and the numbers of the pages the article appears on. These should not be underlined or in italic type:

*Landon, L. (1979) On word structure. Linguistic Investigations 3, 58–9.*

If the book you are referring to is one volume of a set, you should state the volume number, and if there is more than one edition of the book, you should state what edition you are referring to. Both of these pieces of information immediately follow the title of the book, in parentheses. (Information about which edition of the book you have can usually be found on the page following the title page, along with the year of publication.)

v)    Lastly, if the publication is a book, you should state the place of publication and the name of the publisher:

> Landon, L. (1983) <u>Arabic Words in English</u>. Edinburgh: Belmont Press.

(If, as is the case with many books, there is more than one town listed as the place of publication, give only the first-named town in your bibliography.)

vi)   If you are referring to an article, poem, etc in a book, you must give a complete reference for the book, and indicate the pages on which the item you are referring to stands:

> Landon, L. (1982) Danish word-structure, in M. Smith (ed.) <u>Words and their Structure</u>, 33–37. Edinburgh: Belmont Press.

vii)   An alternative position for the date of publication is shown in the following examples:

> [article]   Landon, L. On word structure. <u>Linguistic Investigations</u> 3 (1979), 58–9.
> [book]   Landon, L. <u>Arabic Words in English</u>. Edinburgh: Belmont Press, 1983.

## footnotes

You may use footnotes to provide additional information or comments that you do not want to include in the run of the text, or else to give details of the source of the information you have just given. Footnotes should be indicated by an arabic numeral after the word or at the end of the passage to which they refer, the number being raised slightly above the level of the line of writing:

> As Shakespeare once said[1], 'all the world's a stage'.

the relevant footnote in this case perhaps having the form:

> [1] <u>As You Like It</u> (II.vii.139).

The numbering of footnotes may begin at '1' on each new page or at the start of each section or chapter, or else the numbering may run consecutively through the whole document.

Footnotes, being at the foot of the page, are easier for the reader, as the information is immediately visible, but they can pose problems of layout. An alternative is to put all such notes in an appendix at the end of the chapter or of the whole book or document (in which case they are known as **endnotes**). Endnotes are easier to lay out than footnotes, but have the disadvantage that the information they contain is not immediately to hand on the relevant pages of the document.

## quotations

Short prose quotations of not more than four lines should be incorporated directly into the run of your own text, and identified as quotations by means of quotation marks:

*Shakespeare once said that 'all the world's a stage'.*

Longer quotations should be separated off from the rest of the text: they begin on a new line (usually after a one-line space), are indented from the left-hand margin, and are not marked off by quotations marks. The end of the text the quotation runs on from is punctuated with a colon:

> *This point is clearly illustrated by Daniel's assertion that:*
> *all the facts with which a grammar deals are to be found in the language to which the grammar belongs; and it is in the language itself, not in books, that these facts are primarily to be sought. Grammarians do not impose rules on a language; they merely collect them from the language rules already in existence, and set them forth in an orderly way.*

- If you are quoting poetry, the same rules apply, but, in addition, if the quotation is short and incorporated into your writing, ends of lines should be indicated by slashes, and beginnings of lines by capital letters (if they begin with capitals in the original):

> *As Byron has said, 'All tragedies are finish'd by a death, / All comedies are ended by a marriage'.*

In longer quotations separated off from the run of your text, the lines of verse should be set out on separate lines as in the original poem or play:

> *As Byron has said:*
>
> *Knowledge is not happiness, and science*
> *But an exchange of ignorance for that*
> *Which is another kind of ignorance.*

- Make sure that if you quote something you quote it accurately. In general, words quoted should be exactly as they are in the original text.

---

 The word ***sic*** (= Latin 'thus') is used in quotations to confirm that a misspelling or ungrammatical structure (a) was in the original passage, (b) has been left in the quotation deliberately, and (c) is therefore not an error on the part of the person quoting the passage. It is usually enclosed in square brackets:

> *As James Joyce put it: 'My patience are [sic] exhausted'.*

but some authorities recommend round brackets:

> *As James Joyce put it: 'My patience are (sic) exhausted'.*

---

However, minor changes are permissible for the sake of correct grammar, good punctuation and clarity. It may, for example, sometimes be necessary to substitute a noun or phrase in your text for a pronoun in the original in order to make the meaning of the quotation clear. This is quite acceptable, but any such alteration should be clearly indicated by putting the word or words you have substituted within square brackets. For example, a quotation from an article on the Huns which read in the original text:

> *They were primitive pastoralists who knew nothing of agriculture*

might for the sake of clarity be altered to:

> *[The Huns] were primitive pastoralists who knew nothing of agriculture.*

Alternatively, the clarifying words may be added <u>after</u> the words to be clarified rather than substituted for them:

> *They [the Huns] were primitive pastoralists who knew nothing of agriculture.*

The only alteration you need not indicate in this way is the change of a capital letter at the beginning of a sentence in the original text to a lower-case letter where the quotation is not the beginning of a sentence in your written text:

> *Irwin states that 'they [the Huns] were primitive pastoralists who knew nothing of agriculture'.*

It is quite acceptable to omit part of a passage you are quoting if it is not relevant to the point you are making. In this case, the fact that something has been omitted should be shown by three full stops or 'ellipsis points':

> *... Daniel's assertion that:*
> > *all the facts with which a grammar deals are to be found in the language to which the grammar belongs; and it is in the language itself ... that these facts are primarily to be sought.*

If the omitted part comes at the end of a sentence, the sentence may end with four points, ie three ellipsis points plus the final full stop, or simply with the three ellipsis points.

## references

There are a number of ways of indicating the source of a piece of information or a quotation you have included in your work:

i)  One way is to use footnotes:

> *... Daniel's assertion[2] that:*
> > *all the facts with which a grammar deals are to be found in the language to which the grammar belongs; and it is in the language itself ... that these facts are primarily to be sought.*

The footnote in this case would be in the form:

> [2] *Evan Daniel (1898)* <u>*The Grammar, History and Derivation of the English Language,*</u> *p. 1. London: National Society's Depository.*

This method is best if you are not attaching a separate bibliography to your work, and therefore need to give full details of the sources referred to as you go along.

**◪ Shortened forms of references**

Only the first footnote reference need be written out in full. Thereafter it is possible to use shortened forms of references.

One acceptable shortened form of reference to the above-named book would be:

⁴ *Daniel, <u>English Language</u>, p. 5.*

If reference is made to the same work in two or more <u>consecutive</u> footnotes, it is possible to use the abbreviation *ibid.* (short for Latin *ibidem* 'in the same place') in the second and subsequent footnotes:

⁴ *Daniel, <u>English Language</u>, p. 5.*
⁵ *ibid. p. 6.* ⁶ *ibid. p. 10.*

Two other Latin abbreviations that are sometimes used in footnote references are *op. cit.* (Latin *opere citato* 'in the work cited') and *loc. cit.* (Latin *loco citato* 'in the place cited', ie on the same page or in the same paragraph). These refer to works or parts of works already mentioned but not necessarily in an immediately preceding footnote. They are for this reason best avoided, as their use obliges readers to hunt back to find what the 'work cited' or 'place cited' is. It is always better to use the shortened form of reference given above, which clearly names the work you are referring to, or, where appropriate, *ibid.* which always refers to the last-mentioned work in a nearby footnote.

ii)     Another way of referring to a book, poem, etc is simply to give the source in brackets immediately before or after the information or quotation:

*As Byron has said, 'All tragedies are finish'd by a death, / All comedies are ended by a marriage'. (<u>Don Juan</u>, stanza 9)*

This is not to be recommended if there are many such references in your work, as they would tend to disrupt the flow of what you have written.

iii)     A third way, usually used only in technical writing, is to refer to sources of information by the author's surname and the year of publication, in the run of text itself:

*More information on this point can be found in Landon (1985).*
*Landon (1985:24) provides further details of this process.*

# Appendix G:
## Figures and Dates

---

## dates

The most frequently used style for writing dates nowadays is *6 November 1994*. It is certainly the one to use in formal and business letters. Other styles, such as *November 6th 1994* or *6th November 1994* are not incorrect, but now usually found only in informal letters. Note that the forms with *-st, -nd, -rd* and *-th* are obligatory if the day is not followed by the month: *I saw him on the 6th.*

Commas are not required in dates. Some people do prefer to insert one after the day in the second style above — thus *November 6th, 1994* — but, while not wrong, it is unnecessary to do so. If, however, the day of the week precedes a date, it should be followed by a comma: *Tuesday, 6 November 1994.*

The whole date may be written in numbers (eg *6/11/94* or *6.11.94*), but this is best avoided in business contexts as it can lead to confusion: in British English *6.11.94* means '6 November 1994', but in American English it would be understood as '11 June 1994'.

---

 Odd as it may look, in the year 2000 the correct abbreviated form of a date will be, for example, *4.3.00.*

---

- **Years**

When pairs of years are linked by a dash, it is normal to give only as much of the second year as is required for clarity:

> *'1975 to 1983'* can be written *1975–83*

> *'1992 to 1994'* can be written *1992–4*

The numbers from 10 to 19 are written out in full whether clarity requires it or not:

> *'1914 to 1918'* is written ✓ *1914–18*, not ✗ *1914–8*

If the linked dates are in different centuries, write out the second date in full:

> *'1892 to 1905'* is written ✓ *1892–1905*, not ✗ *1892–905*

No shortening of years is possible with dates BC because of the ambiguities that that could cause: for example, if *251–224 BC* was abbreviated to *251–24 BC*, it would be indistingushable from *251 BC–24 BC*.

⚠ It is not correct to combine prepositions and dashes in dates:

✗    *between 1914–1918*
✗    *from 1914–1918*

If the first date is preceded by a preposition, the second should be preceded by a preposition or a conjunction:

✓    *between 1914 and 1918*
✓    *from 1914 to 1918*

📕 The abbreviation *AD* should, strictly speaking, precede the year number ('*AD 1995*' means 'in the year of our Lord 1995'), but '*1995 AD*' is now also acceptable. Although '*A*' (for Latin *anno*) means 'in the year', precede *AD* dates by *in*: *in AD 1995*. To avoid specifically Christian connotations in dates, some people now prefer to use *CE* (= 'Common Era') instead of *AD*: *in 1994 CE*.

*BC* should follow the year number: *in 753 BC*. Again, to avoid specifically Christian connotations in dates, some people now prefer to use *BCE* (= 'before the Common Era'): *in 753 BCE*.

- **Centuries**

Many people are expecting the 20th century to end on 31 December 1999. It doesn't. Since there was, obviously, no year 0, the first century AD began with year 1 and ended with year 100, and the second century began with year 101. The 20th century therefore began on 1 January 1901 (not 1900) and will end on 31 December 2000 (<u>not</u> 1999). The 21st century will begin on 1 January 2001. (Note, however, that the 'nineteen-hundreds' began on 1 January 1900 and will end on 31 December 1999. The 'nineteen-hundreds' are therefore not quite the same as the '20th century'.)

## figures in written work

- **Figures or words?**

Opinions vary as to when to use figures for numbers and when to use words. As a general rule, however:

> **figures are preferred in technical writing, words in writing of a less technical and more literary nature.**

To this general rule, it is necessary to add a few additional do's and don'ts:

i) Even *in non-technical writing*, it is correct to use figures for numbers above a certain point. Unfortunately, authorities differ on where the changeover point should be: some advocate using words for numbers lower than 100 and figures for numbers from 100 upwards, but there are some who prefer to use words only for numbers up to and including 9, or 10,

501

or 12. It does not really matter which number you choose as the changeover point, so long as you are consistent in what you write after you make the choice.

*In technical writing*, you should use words only for numbers lower than 10, except in the cases indicated in the following rules.

ii)    Regardless of the general rule, if for some reason you want numbers to stand out from the text, it is better to use figures than words. Here again, be consistent once you have made the choice.

iii)    If a number that you would write in figures stands at the beginning of a sentence, write it in words.

iv)    Do not use a mixture of styles for numbers that are related to each other, eg because they refer to the same noun. Make the smaller number match the style of the larger number. For example, if you have chosen 9 as your changeover point from words to figures, do not nevertheless write ✗ *eight or 10 books*, but rather ✓ *8 or 10 books*.

v)    Use *words to express vague amounts* (eg *hundreds of people*), but *figures to express exact quantities*, as in measurements, prices, percentages, scores, etc:

> *£100*
> *32° F*
> *won by an innings and 3 runs*
> *elected with a majority of only 11 votes*

vi)    With *ages*, both figures and letters are correct, but there is a general tendency to use figures. Even if your chosen changeover point from words to figures is 100, use figures rather than words when the number is followed by '-year-old':

> ✓    *76-year-old*
> ✗    *seventy-six-year-old*

vii)    Simple *fractions* (eg ¼, ⅔, ¾) standing alone should be written out as words: *At least one-third of the population didn't vote in the election.* More complex fractions and fractions in combination with a whole number should be in figures (eg ¹⁄₃₂ or 5¾), as should fractions in combination with a following noun denoting a unit of measurement (eg ¾-*inch nails*).

- ● **Commas in numbers**

Formerly, numbers above 999 required commas to be inserted between every group of three digits counting from the right: *4,999* □ *444,999* □ *2,444,999.*

This style is still correct and common, but it is now also correct to write numbers without commas. If there are no commas, four-figure numbers may be written closed up (*4500*) or with a thin space where a comma could be inserted (*4 500*), and five-figure numbers and above are written with a thin space before every three figures counting from the right (ie, where commas could have been inserted): *35 056 □ 2 335 000.*

- **Measurements**

Contrary to the practice with dates, numbers should not be abbreviated in measurements:

   ✓   *263–265 mm*
   ✗   *263–5 mm*

- **Money**

When writing out sums of money comprisng both pound and pence, only the symbol £ should be used, not both £ and *p*:

   ✓   *£5.76*
   ✗   *£5.76p.*

- **Time**

There is sometimes confusion over the use of ***a.m.*** and ***p.m.*** The following points should be noted:

i)   It is equally correct to write ***a.m.*** and ***p.m.*** with or without full stops.

ii)   When referring to times that are an exact number of hours, it is correct to write only the number for the hour, but not wrong to add '00' for the minutes:

   ✓   *5 p.m.*
   ✓   *5.00 p.m.*

iii)   The question whether '12 p.m.' is midday or midnight (and therefore '12 a.m.' midnight or midday) is rather confused. Since ***a.m.*** means 'before midday' (Latin *ante meridiem*) and ***p.m.*** means 'after midday' (Latin *post meridiem*), both would seem equally appropriate for '12 o'clock at night' (which is both twelve hours before and twelve hours after midday) and neither appropriate for '12 noon' (which is neither 'before midday' nor 'after midday'). Traditionally, however, ***midday is considered to be 12 p.m. and midnight 12 a.m.*** Five minutes past midday is *12.05 p.m.*, and five minutes past midnight *12.05 a.m.*, and so on for other times.

# Appendix H:
## American English and British English

The form of English described in this book is for the most part Standard British English. Standard American English differs from British English in various ways — in pronunciation, in grammar, in vocabulary, in spelling, even in punctuation. Throughout this book, mention is made of many of these differences in the relevant chapters and entries. This appendix provides an overview of the most important or noticeable of the differences between the two standard languages.

### ✦ Pronunciation

#### • General differences in pronunciation

**British English** /ah/
In many words that have an /ah/ sound in British English followed by a fricative sound (/f/, /s/ or /th/) or a nasal (/n/ or /m/), American English has an /a/, as in *after, ask, banana, can't, dance, half, laugh, pass, path* and *rather*.

**British English** /i/
Where British English has /i/ in final position in words such as *city* and *happy*, American English has /ee/.

**British English** /o/
In American English, words such as *block, got, pond, probable* and *top* are pronounced with an /ah/ sound. In words in which the vowel is followed by /f/, /s/, /th/, /r/, /g/ or /ng/ (eg in *coffee, dog, cross, forest* and *long*), a longer vowel similar to /aw/ is also common.

**British English** /yoo/, /yuu/
After /t/, /d/, /n/, /l/, /s/ and /th/, American English generally has /oo/ rather than /yoo/ if the vowel is stressed, eg in *duty, lurid, new, suit* and *tune*; but the /y/ sound is retained in unstressed syllables (eg in *menu* and *value*).

**British English** /iyl/
In most words ending in *-ile*, American English generally pronounces the final syllable as /il/ rather than /iyl/ as in British English, eg in *futile* and *fragile*. In some words, /iyl/ is possible or required, eg in *juvenile* and *prehensile*. In general, the longer or more technical a word is, the more likely it is to be pronounced /iyl/.

504

## British English /t/
In words such as *latter*, *metal* and *writing*, the *-tt-/-t-* is pronounced in American English with the same sound as that of the *-dd-/-d-* of *ladder*, *medal* and *riding*.

## /r/
In most accents of American English (but not, for example, in New York and the southern states), /r/ is pronounced at the ends of words and before consonants. However, even in *r*-pronouncing accents, the *r* is often not pronounced when it follows an unstressed vowel and is itself followed by another *r*, eg in *governor*.

## British English /ahr/ spelt *-er-*
In words such as *clerk* and *Derby*, where British English preserves an older pronunciation with /ahr/, American speech has /uhr/.

## British English /-a-ri/
American English tends to give greater prominence than British English does to the suffixes *-ary*, *-ory* and often also *-ery*; as for example in *monetary* (BrE /-ta-ri/ or /-tri/, AmE /-te-ri/), *confectionary* (BrE /-na-ri/, AmE /-ne-ri/), *obligatory* (BrE /-to-ri/, AmE /-taw-ri/).

## British English /nt/
In American English, /t/ is often not pronounced after /n/ when what follows is an unstressed vowel, as for example in *Atlantic*, *gentleman*, *international*, *plenty* and *winter*.

- **Pronunciation differences in individual words**

In addition to the general differences listed above, there are many differences between British English and American English in the pronunciation of individual words. A selection of such words follows:

| | | | |
|---|---|---|---|
| *anti-* | BrE | /an-ti-/ | AmE often /an-tiy-/ |
| *depot* | BrE | /de-poh/ | AmE /dee-poh/ |
| *epoch* | BrE | /ee-pok/ | AmE /e-pok/ |
| *lever* | BrE | /lee-ver/ | AmE usually /le-ver/ |
| *leisure* | BrE | /le-zhur/ | AmE usually /lee-zhur/ |
| *lieutenant* | BrE | /lef-te-nant/ | AmE /luu-te-nant/ |
| *moustache* | BrE | /mus-tahsh/ | AmE /mus-tash/ |
| *schedule* | BrE | /she-dyool/ | AmE /ske-jool/ |
| *shone* | BrE | /shon/ | AmE /shohn/ |
| *simultaneous* | BrE | /si-mul-/ | AmE usually /siy-mul-/ |
| *suggest* | BrE | /su-jest/ | AmE usually /sug-jest/ |
| *tomato* | BrE | /to-mah-toh/ | AmE /to-may-toh// |
| *vase* | BrE | /vahz/ | AmE usually /vays/ |
| *vitamin* | BrE | /vi-ta-min/ | AmE /viy-ta-min/ |
| *z* | BrE | /zed/ | AmE /zee/ |
| *zenith* | BrE | /ze-nith/ | AmE /zee-nith/ |

## ✦ Grammar

### collective nouns

A singular verb is normally used with collective nouns in American English, where British English allows either a singular or a plural verb: *Our staff monitors the latest developments in language daily.*

### do

American English does not use *do* as British English does in the following examples:

> *We don't have to go but we can do if you want* (AmE *we can if you want*)
> *'Will you fix that for me?' 'I have done.'* (AmE *I have*)

### gotten

**Gotten** now exists in British English only in expressions such as in *ill-gotten gains*. In other cases, the past participle is *got*. In American English, *gotten* is used when a process is involved (*He's gotten a new car*), but *got* when a state of possession is implied (*He's got a car*). As in British English, *He's got to go* means 'he must go', whereas *He's gotten to go* means 'he has received permission to go'.

### have

The question form *Has she enough money?* is not used in American English, which uses the forms, also possible in British English, *Does she have enough money?* and *Has she got enough money?* Similarly with the negative statement form *She hasn't enough money*, as opposed to *She doesn't have enough money* and *She hasn't got enough money.*

### past tense

The simple past-tense form of a verb is often used in American English where British English would use a perfect tense: *Did she leave yet?*

### subjunctive verbs

After verbs, nouns and adjectives which denote requiring, demanding, ordering, urging, etc, the subjunctive is more extensively used in American English than in British English: *We demand that she be dismissed at once* □ *his demand that she leave immediately* □ *It is vital that she leave tomorrow.*

### will/shall

**Will** is used rather than **shall** to form the simple future tense with first-person pronouns: *We will come back again soon.*

## ✦ Vocabulary

There are many differences in vocabulary between British English and American English, of which the following is a selection:

| | | | |
|---|---|---|---|
| BrE | *aubergine* | AmE | *eggplant* |
| BrE | *autumn* | AmE | *fall* |
| BrE | *biscuit* | AmE | *cookie* |
| BrE | *bonnet (of car)* | AmE | *hood* |

| BrE | | AmE | |
|-----|-----|-----|-----|
| BrE | *boot (of car)* | AmE | *trunk* |
| BrE | *camp bed* | AmE | *cot* |
| BrE | *candy floss* | AmE | *cotton candy* |
| BrE | *caravan* | AmE | *trailer* |
| BrE | *car park* | AmE | *parking lot* |
| BrE | *chips* | AmE | *French fries* |
| BrE | *condom* | AmE | *rubber* |
| BrE | *cot* | AmE | *crib* |
| BrE | *courgettes* | AmE | *zucchini* |
| BrE | *crisps* | AmE | *chips* |
| BrE | *cupboard* | AmE | *closet* |
| BrE | *drawing-pin* | AmE | *thumb tack* |
| BrE | *first floor* | AmE | *second floor* |
| BrE | *garden* | AmE | *yard* |
| BrE | *ground floor* | AmE | *first floor* |
| BrE | *guard (on train)* | AmE | *conductor* |
| BrE | *handbag* | AmE | *purse* |
| BrE | *holiday* | AmE | *vacation* |
| BrE | *lift* | AmE | *elevator* |
| BrE | *paraffin* | AmE | *kerosene* |
| BrE | *pavement* | AmE | *sidewalk* |
| BrE | *petrol* | AmE | *gas* |
| BrE | *suppose* | AmE | *guess* |
| BrE | *sweets* | AmE | *candy* |
| BrE | *tap* | AmE | *faucet* |
| BrE | *tights* | AmE | *pantyhose* |
| BrE | *trousers* | AmE | *pants* |
| BrE | *ugly* | AmE | *homely* |
| BrE | *vest* | AmE | *undershirt* |
| BrE | *waistcoat* | AmE | *vest* |

## ✦ Spelling

### • General differences between British and American spelling

i)  British English *-our*
    American English *-or*

American English has *-or* in words such as *armor*, *color*, *flavor* and *humor*. (*Glamour* and *saviour* may be spelt as in British English, however.)

ii)  British English *-re*
     American English *-er*

American English has *-er* in words such as *center*, *fiber*, *meter*, *specter* and *theater*. But to show the hard /g/ and /k/ sounds, *acre*, *massacre*, *ogre*, etc. (Note, however, *meager*, not *meagre*.)

iii)   British English *-ll-*, *-pp-*, *-tt-*
       American English *-l-*, *-p-*, *-t-*

In inflections and derivatives of words ending in *l*, *p*, *t* not immediately preceded by a single stressed vowel (see *Spelling and Word-formation*, page 203), American English generally does not double the final letter as British English does:

British English: *cancelled, counsellor, dishevelled, equalled, kidnapped, traveller, worshipping*
American English: *canceled, counselor, disheveled, equaled, kidnaped, traveler, worshiping*
(but American English *formatting* as in British English)

Note also British English *carburettor* and *woollen*, American English *carburetor* and *woolen*.

iv)   British English *-l*
      American English *-ll*

At the ends of certain two-syllable words, American English generally has a double *l* where British English has a single *l*:

British English: *appal, distil, enrol, fulfil, instil, skilful, wilful*
American English: *appall, distill, enroll, fulfill, install, instill, skillful, willful*

v)   British English **ae/oe** or **e**
     American English **e**

The tendency to replace *ae* and *oe* by *e* in words derived form Latin and Greek is more strongly developed in American English than in British English:

British English: *aesthetic, amoeba, diarrhoea, foetus, haemoglobin, oesophagus*
American English (more often): *esthetic, ameba, diarrhea, fetus, hemoglobin, esophagus*
(but *aerobics* and *aerosol* in American English also)

vi)   British English *-ize* or *-ise*
      American English *-ize*

In verbs that can be spelt either *-ise* or *-ize*, the use of *-ize* is now standard in American English. Note also the spellings *analyze, paralyze*, etc as opposed to the British English *paralyse, analyse*, etc.

vii)   As a rule, hyphens are used less frequently in American English than in British English, eg *dining room* rather than *dining-room*.

- **Spelling differences in individual words**

British English: *axe, catalogue, cheque, cigarette, cosy, defence, draught, good-bye, grey, jewellery, licence, manoeuvre, moustache, offence, pyjamas, practice/practise, pretence, programme, sceptic, sulphur, storey, tyre*

American English: *ax, catalog, check,* (also) *cigaret, cozy, defense, draft,* (also) *good-by, gray, jewelry, license, maneuver, mustache, offense, pajamas, practise, pretense, program, skeptic, sulfur, story, tire*

## ✦ Punctuation

The main differences between American and British practice are as follows:

### i) Commas between clauses:

American English prefers some punctuation (usually a comma) between clauses in compound sentences where there is none in British English:

British English *I was late home on Monday because I couldn't start the car.*
American English *I was late home on Monday, because I couldn't start the car.*

### ii) Commas in lists:

In American English, a comma is inserted before *and* in lists:

British English *x, y and z*
American English *x, y, and z.*

### iii) Quotation marks:

The American preference is for double quotation marks rather than single (and therefore for single quotation marks within double quotation marks for quotes within quotes). American practice also places commas and full stops (but not other punctuation marks) before quotation marks rather than after them, regardless of textual logic (see *Punctuation*, page 360).

British punctuation: *By an 'abstract object', McArthur means something which is 'neither spatial nor temporal'.*
American punctuation: *By an "abstract object," McArthur means "neither spatial nor temporal."*

## ✦ Dates

An important difference between American and British English is in the way of writing dates.
In Britsh English, '6/11/95' would mean '6 November 1995', whereas in American practice, it denotes '11 June 1995'.

# Index of Words and Phrases

In the following index, general topics are listed in roman typeface, specific words in italics.

Two categories of word are not listed in the index:

   i)   Words listed in the *Pronunciation* chapter (pages 407 to 448) and the *1000 Commonly Misspelt Words* (pages 333 to 359). To find these, consult the chapters directly.

   ii)   Words given as examples of the rules explained in the *Spelling and Word-formation* chapter. To find these, look up the appropriate section of that chapter. (For example, to check whether *competitor* ends in *-er* or *-or*, you should consult the entry *-er, -or, -ar*. This is listed in the index at *-ar*, at *-er* and at *-or*. But the word *competitor* itself is not listed in the index.) The same applies to words exemplifying the general pronunciation rules explained in the *Pronunciation* chapter (pages 395 to 405).

# Index of Words and Phrases

# Index of Words and Phrases